CATALOGUE OF THE PAMPHLETS, BOOKS, NEWSPAPERS, AND MANUSCRIPTS RELATING TO THE CIVIL WAR, THE COMMONWEALTH, AND RESTORATION, COLLECTED BY GEORGE THOMASON, 1640-1661

VOL. II.

CATALOGUE OF THE COLLECTION, 1653-1661 NEWSPAPERS. INDEX.

LONDON:
PRINTED BY WILLIAM CLOWES AND SONS, LIMITED,
DUKE STREET, STAMFORD STREET, S.E., AND GREAT WINDMILL STREET, W.

THE THOMASON TRACTS.

1653.

Jan. 1.—An Act for continuing John Bradshaw Chancellor, and Bartholomew Hall Attorney-General, of the Dutchy of Lancaster. *s. sh. Printed by John Field.* **669. f. 16. (79.)**

Jan. 1.—An Act impowring the Commissioners for Inspecting the Treasuries to issue Warrants for payment of the Monies appointed for the use of the Navy. *s. sh. Printed by John Field.*
669. f. 16. (78.)

[Jan. 1.]—A New-yeers Gift for England and all her Cities, Ports and Corporations, and all such therein who are fit for the same and desire it. *To be sold by Will. Larnar.* (1 Jan.) **E. 684. (19.)**

[Jan. 3.]—A Holy Life here, the only Way to Eternal Life hereafter. By R. S. [i.e. Richard Stanwix.] 2 pt. *Printed for John Martin and James Allestrye.* (3 Jan.) **E. 1276.**

[Jan. 3.]—Merlinus Anonymus. An Ephemeris for 1653. By Raphael Desmus. *Printed by F. M.* (3 Jan.) **E. 1348. (1.)**

[Jan. 3.]—Westrow Revived. A Funerall Poem without Fiction. Composed by Geo. Wither. pp. 70. *Printed by F. Neile.* (3 Jan.)
E. 1479. (4.)

Jan. 5.—By the Parliament. A Proclamation commanding all Romish Priests to depart out of this Commonwealth. *s. sh. Printed by John Field.*
669. f. 16. (80.)

[Jan. 6.]—Spirituall Experiences of sundry Beleevers, held forth by them at severall solemne meetings and conferences to that end. By Vavasor Powel. The second impression. pp. 431. *Printed for Robert Ibbitson.* (6 Jan.) **E. 1389.**

[Jan. 7.]—Zion's sad Tears, for Nineveh's Just Fears. Being some few directed Observations of Divine Mercy & Sinful Returns. (7 Jan.)
E. 684. (25.)

[Jan. 8.]—The Bishop of London, the Welsh Curate and Common Prayers, with Apocrypha in the End. By Will. Erbery. 4 pt. (8 Jan.) **E. 684. (26.)**

II.

B

1653.

[**Jan. 8.**]—The Dutch-mens Pedigree. [A satire, with an engraving caricaturing Tromp and De Witt.] *s. sh.* (8 Jan.)

669. f. 16. (81.)

[**Jan. 10.**]—A Cat may look upon a King. [By Sir Anthony Weldon. A satirical account of the life of James I.; with an engraved portrait of him as frontispiece, faced by a woodcut of a cat on the titlepage.] pp. 105. *Printed for William Roybould.* (10 Jan.) **E. 1408. (2.)**

[**Jan. 10.**]—The Naturall and Experimentall History of Winds, &c. Written in Latine by Francis, Viscount St. Alban. Translated by R. G., Gent. pp. 384. *Printed for Humphrey Moseley.* (10 Jan.) **E. 1278.**

[**Jan. 11.**]—A View of the Threats and Punishments recorded in the Scriptures. By Zachary Bogan. pp. 641. *Printed by H. Hall for R. Davis: Oxford.* (11 Jan.) **E. 1271.**

Jan. 12.—[An Order of the Lord Mayor and Aldermen fixing the price of Sea-Coal in the City of London at twelve pence the bushel.] *s. sh. Printed by James Flesher.* **669. f. 16. (82.)**

[**Jan. 12.**]—An Humble Vindication of a Free Admission unto the Lords-Supper. Two sermons by John Humfrey. pp. 87. [See also below: 4 Feb., E. 1314. (2.) and 3 June, 1654, E. 1496. (2.)] *Printed for E. Blackmore.* (12 Jan.) **E. 1314. (1.)**

[**Jan. 14.**]—The Card of Courtship: or the Language of Love. pp. 168. *Printed by J. C. for Humphrey Moseley.* (14 Jan.) **E. 1308. (2.)**

[**Jan. 18.**]—Cases Considered and Resolved, wherein all the tender godly conscientious Ministers in England are concerned, or Pills to Purge Malignants. By Thomas Brooks. *Printed by M. Simmons for John Hancock.* (18 Jan.) **E. 684. (28.)**

[**Jan. 23.**]—The Anatomical Exercises of Dr. William Harvey concerning the motion of the Heart and Blood, with the preface of Zachariah Wood. 3 pt. *Printed by Francis Leach.* (23 Jan.) **E. 1477. (2.)**

[**Jan. 25.**]—The Salvation of the Saints by the Appearances of Christ. By John Durant. pp. 304. *Printed by R. J. for Livewell Chapman.* (25 Jan.) **E. 1248. (1.)**

[**Jan. 26.**]—Leviathan drawn out with a Hook; or, animadversions upon Mr. Hobbs his Leviathan. By Alex. Rosse. pp. 102. *Printed by Tho. Newcomb, for Richard Royston.* (26 Jan.) **E. 1324. (2.)**

[**Jan. 26.**]—Some Animadversions and Observations upon Sr. Walter Raleigh's Historie of the World. By Alexander Ross. pp. 72. *Printed by William Du-gard for Richard Royston.* (26 Jan.) **E. 1324. (3.)**

[**Jan. 27.**]—A Lamentacion over the Ruines of this oppressed Nacion, by James Nayler. And a Warning to the Rulers of England not to usurp dominion over the Conscience, by George Fox. *Printed for Tho. Wayt: York.* (27 Jan.) **E. 727. (9.)**

1653.

[**Jan. 27.**]—Perfection and Peace : a sermon preached in the Chappel of Sir Robert Cook at Dyrdans. By Tho. Fuller. *Printed by Roger Norton for John Williams.* (27 Jan.) **E. 1244. (3.)**

Jan. 28.—A Letter from the General Meeting of the Officers of the Army [undertaking "by all lawful means to endeavour the procuring" of the reforms promised by Parliament]. *s. sh. Printed by Henry Hills and Thomas Brewster.* **669. f. 16. (83.)**

[**Jan. 28.**]—An Abstract of the several Letters and choice Occurrences brought by the last Post from Denmark, France, Sweden and Holland. *Printed for George Horton.* (28 Jan.) **E. 684. (32.)**

Jan. 28.—The Onely Right Rule for Regulating the Lawes and Liberties of the People of England. Presented to the L. Generall Cromwell. *Printed for the Subscribers and are to be sold by W. L.* **E. 684. (33.)**

[**Jan. 28.**]—Petrus Cunæus, of the Common-Wealth of the Hebrews. Translated by C. B. pp. 166. *Printed by T. W. for William Lee.* (28 Jan.) **E. 1311. (2.)**

[**Jan. 28.**]—A Treatise tending to shew that the Just and Holy God may have a Hand in the unjust actions of Sinfull Men. By Thomas Whitfield. *Printed for John Wright.* (28 Jan.) **E. 684. (34.)**

[**Jan. 28.**]—The True Advancement of the French Tongue, or, A new Method for the attaining of it. By Claudius Mauger. pp. 257. *Printed by Tho. Roycroft for G. Martin.* (28 Jan.) **E. 1246. (1.)**

[**Jan. 29.**]—Vindiciæ Foederis ; or, A Treatise of the Covenant of God entered with Man-Kinde. By Thomas Blake. pp. 488. [See also below : 12 June, 1654, E. 740. (10.)] *Printed for Abel Roper.* (29 Jan.) **E. 685.**

[**Jan. 31.**]—Scripture Rules to be observed in Buying and Selling. *s. sh. Printed for John Rothwell.* (31 Jan.) **669. f. 16. (84.)**

[**Jan. 31.**]—Writs Judiciall, shewing the nature of all manner of Executions, as they are now used in the Court of Common Pleas. Collected out of the presidents of Richard Brownlow. pp. 80. *Printed by Tho: Roycroft for Henry Twyford.* (31 Jan.) **E. 803.**

[**Feb. 1.**]—A Relation of a Disputation between Dr. Griffith and Mr. Vavasor Powell. *Printed by M. S. and are to be sold by Livewell Chapman.* (1 Feb.) **E. 686. (1.)**

[**Feb. 2.**]—An humble Apologie for Learning and Learned Men. By Edward Waterhous. pp. 263. *Printed by T. M. for M. M., G. Bedell and T. Collins.* (2 Feb.) **E. 1237. (1.)**

[**Feb. 3.**]—Miscellanea Magna. The second Century. [A list of satirical misinterpretations of Latin legal phrases.] *s. sh. Printed for G. T.* (3 Feb.) **669. f. 16. (85.)**

1653.

[Feb. 4.]—A Boundary to the Holy Mount. In answer to An Humble Vindication of Free Admission to the Lords Supper published by Mr. Humphrey. By Roger Drake. pp. 208. [See above : 12 Jan., E. 1314. (1.) and also below : 1 Dec. 1654, E. 1466. (2.)] *Printed by A. M. for Stephen Bowtell.* (4 Feb.) **E. 1314. (2.)**

[Feb. 4.]—A Faithfull Friend true to the Soul : or, the Soules Self-examination. By Timothy Rogers. pp. 347. *Printed for E. Brewster and G. Sawbridge.* (4 Feb.) **E. 1390.**

Feb. 5.—[An Order of the Commissioners of Sewers for the " scouring and cleansing " of the Fleet Ditch and River Wells.] *s. sh. Printed by Henry Hills for John Bellinger.* **669. f. 16. (88.)**

[Feb. 5.]—A Brief Explication of the first fifty Psalms. By David Dickson. pp. 351. *Printed by T. M. for Ralph Smith.* (5 Feb.) **E. 1249. (2.)**

[Feb. 8.]—Reports of J. Gouldsborough, one of the Protonotaries of the Court of Common Pleas ; or, his Collection of choice Cases agitated in the Courts at Westminster in the latter yeares of Queen Elizabeth. With notes by W. S. [i.e. William Sheppard.] *Printed by W. W. for Charles Adams.* (8 Feb.) **E. 209.**

[Feb. 8.]—Six new Playes, viz. The Brothers, The Sisters, The Doubtfull Heir, The Imposture, The Cardinall, The Court Secret. By James Shirley. [With an engraved portrait of the author.] pp. 429. *Printed for Humphrey Robinson and Humphrey Moseley.* (8 Feb.) **E. 1226.**

Feb. 9.—Votes of Parliament for setting apart a Day of Publique Fasting. *s. sh. Printed by John Field.* **669. f. 16. (89.)**

[Feb. 10.]—A Discovery of Subterraneal Treasure : viz. of all manner of Mines and Minerals, with plain Directions for the finding of them. [By Gabriel Plattes.] pp. 60. *Printed for J. E. and are to be sold by Humphrey Moseley.* (10 Feb.) **E. 686. (11.)**

[Feb. 10.]—Gerardo, the unfortunate Spaniard. Or, a pattern for lascivious lovers. Written by Don Goncalo de Cespides and Meneces, made English by L. D. [i.e. Leonard Digges.] pp. 421. *Printed by William Bentley, and are to be sold by William Shears.* (10 Feb.) **E. 1234. (1.)**

[Feb. 10.]—Poems : by Francis Beaumont. The Hermaphrodite, the Remedy of Love, Elegies, Sonnets, with other poems. pp. 205. *Printed for Laurence Blaiklock.* (10 Feb.) **E. 1236. (3.)**

[Feb. 11.]—Catholike History collected out of Scripture, Councels, Ancient Fathers and Modern Authentick Writers. Occasioned by a Book written by Dr. Thomas Vane, intituled The Lost sheep returned home. By Edward Chisenhale. pp. 539. *Printed by J. C. for Nath. Brooks.* **E. 1273.**

1653.

[Feb. 11.]—The Heart Opened to Christ Jesus. Translated out of High Dutch. pp. 110. *Printed by John Macock.* (11 Feb.)
E. 1287. (1.)

[Feb. 11.]—The Doubting Beleever : a treatise. By Obadiah Sedgwick. pp. 316. *Printed by R. I. for S. Bowtell.* (11 Feb.) **E. 1310. (1.)**

[Feb. 12.]—The Sinner's Tears, in meditations and prayers. By Tho. Fettiplace. pp. 169. *Printed for Humphrey Moseley.* (12 Feb.)
E. 1328. (1.)

[Feb. 12.]—Tabulæ Fœneratoriæ, or, Tables for the Forbearance and Discompt of Money. By Roger Clavell. *Printed by J. Flesher for Nicholas Bourn.* (12 Feb.) **E. 1272. (2.)**

[Feb. 12.]—The Way of Reformation of the Church of England declared and justified. *Printed for Henry Seile.* (12 Feb.) **E. 686. (13.)**

[Feb. 14.]—A Christian Family builded by God, directing all governours of families how to act. By Robert Abbott. pp. 106. *Printed by J. L. for Philemon Stephens.* (14 Feb.) **E. 1233. (2.)**

[Feb. 14.]—The Life of Tamerlane the Great. pp. 61. *Printed by T. R. & E. M. for Tho. Underhill.* (14 Feb.) **E. 686. (14.)**

[Feb. 15.]—The Civil Magistrates Power in matters of Religion Modestly Debated, together with a Brief Answer to a certain Slanderous Pamphlet called Ill News from New-England, by John Clark. By Thomas Cobbet. pp. 158. [See above : 13 May, 1652, E. 664.] *Printed by W. Wilson for Philemon Stephens.* (15 Feb.) **E. 687. (2.)**

[Feb. 15.]—Responsoria ad Erratica Piscatoris, or, A Caveat for Old and New Prophanenesse, by way of reply to two Pamphlets ; the one called a Caveat for Old and New Sabbatarians, by Edward Fisher ; the other called Festorum Metropolis, by an unknowne Author. By John Collinges. pp. 144. [See above : 7 Jan. 1650, E. 589. (2.)] *Printed for Richard Tomlins.* (15 Feb.) **E. 687. (1.)**

[Feb. 16.]—The Downfal of Dagon : or certain signes of the sudden ruine of the Parliament and Army. (16 Feb.) **E. 804. (20.)**

[Feb. 17.]—Animadversions on Mr. William Dell's Book intituled The Crucified and Quickned Christian. By Humfry Chambers. pp. 84. *Printed by R. N. for Sa. Gellibrand.* (17 Feb.) **E. 686. (4.)**

Feb. 18.—A Perfect Relation of the great Fight between the English and Dutch, 18 Feb., neer the coast of Portsmouth. *Printed for George Horton.* **E. 688. (4.)**

[Feb. 18.]—A Relation of the Engagement of the Fleet under Gen. Blake, Gen. Deane and Gen. Munke with the Dutch Fleet under Van Trump. Abstracted out of severall Letters to the Councell of State. *Printed for Robert Ibbitson.* **E. 688. (8.)**

1653.

Feb. 18.—A Letter from Admiral Vantrump to the Lords and Burga-masters of Amsterdam, touching his Engagement with the English. *Printed by E. Alsop.* **E. 689. (22.)**

Feb. 18.—Concordia rara sonorum, or A Poem upon the late Fight at Sea. By I. D., Esq. *Printed for J. Ridley.* **E. 689. (31.)**

[Feb. 18.]—For the Right Honourable Captaine General Cromwel, Major General Harrison and the rest of the Souldiery. A few humble Proposals of several faithful friends. (18 Feb.) **E. 687. (8.)**

[Feb. 18.]—De usu & authoritate Juris Civilis Romanorum in dominiis principum Christianorum libri duo. Authore Arthuro Duck. pp. 362. *Typis Richardi Hodgkinsonne.* (18 Feb.) **E. 1221. (2.)**

[Feb. 18.]—Glory sometimes afar off, now stepping in; or, The great Gospel-Mysterie of the Divine Nature in Saints. [By Thomas Higgenson.] *Printed for Giles Calvert.* (18 Feb.) **E. 687. (9.)**

[Feb. 18.]—The Soul's Cordiall. By Christopher Love. The third volume [of Love's Sermons, etc. Edited by James Cranford. With an engraved portrait of the author]. *Printed for Nathaniel Brooke.* (18 Feb.) **E. 1230.**

[Feb. 19.]—A Call to the Churches; or, A Packet of Letters to the Pastors of Wales presented to the Baptized Teachers there. By Will. Erbery. pp. 51. (19 Feb.) **E. 688. (1.)**

[Feb. 19.]—Thunder from the Throne of God against the Temples of Idols. [By Samuel Chidley.] *Published by M. P.* (19 Feb.) **E. 688. (2.)**

[Feb. 20.]—Speedy Help for Rich and Poor. Or certain physicall discourses touching the vertue of Whey, Cold Water, Wine-Vineger. Written in Latine by Hermannus van der Heyden. *Printed by James Young for O. P., and are to be sold by John Saywell.* (20 Feb.) **E. 1305. (1.)**

[Feb. 24.]—A New Modell humbly proposed, seriously to be considered of, concerning a new Representative. *Printed by Francis Leach.* (24 Feb.) **E. 688. (9.)**

Feb. 26.—Another great Victorie obtained by Vice-Admiral Pen against the Hollanders, with the full particulars thereof, together with a list of the ships taken, 26 Feb. *Printed for G. Horton.* **E. 689. (1.)**

Feb. 27.—A Declaration of the present Proceedings of the French, Danes and Hollanders, touching the King of Scots. And a Letter sent to the Parliament of England from the Generals at Sea, concerning the Engagement of the Enemy, 27 Feb. *Printed by E. Alsop.* **E. 689. (10.)**

[Feb. 27.]—Ezekiel's Wheels: a treatise concerning Divine Providence. By Tho: Duresme [i.e. Thomas Morton, Bishop of Durham]. pp. 242. *Printed by J. G. for Richard Royston.* (27 Feb.) **E. 1251. (2.)**

1653.

[**Feb. 27.**]—Pelecanicidium: or the Christian Adviser against Self Murder. By Sir William Denny. [In verse. With a frontispiece representing a pelican feeding its young upon its own blood.] pp. 318. *Printed for Thomas Hucklescott.* (27 Feb.) **E. 1233. (1.)**

[**Feb. 28.**]—An Exact Collection of choice Declarations, with the Entries of Judgments thereupon affirmed, in the reignes of Queene Elizabeth, King James and the late King Charles. Collected by W. S. [i.e. William Sheppard.] pp. 271. *Printed by T. W. and T. R., for John Place.* (28 Feb.) **E. 210. (1.)**

[**Feb.**]—The Declaration & Agreement of the Ministers of the County of Sussex concerning the associating & right regulating of the Churches of Christ. [In MS. throughout.] **E. 804. (15.)**

[**Feb.**]—The Nullity of the Pretended-Assembly at Saint Andrews & Dundee : wherein are contained the Representation for Adjournment, the Protestation & Reasons thereof, together with a Review and Examination of the Vindication of the said P. Assembly. pp. 339.

E. 688. (13.)

[**Feb.**]—A Designe for Plentie, by an Universall Planting of Fruit-Trees : tendred by some Wel-wishers to the Publick. *Printed for Richard Wodenothe.* **E. 686. (5.)**

[**Feb.**]—A Warning to the World, being sundry strange Prophesies revealed to Nic. Smith, living at Tillington in Sussex. **E. 688. (11.)**

[**Feb.**]—A Brief Description of an edition of the Bible in the original Hebrew, Samaritan and Greek, with the most ancient translations. [A prospectus of Bishop Walton's Polyglott Bible.] *s. sh.*

669. f. 16. (86.)

[**Feb.**]—Propositions concerning the printing of the Bible in the Original and other learned Languages. [A second prospectus of Bishop Walton's Polyglott Bible.] *s. sh.* **669. f. 16. (87.)**

[**March 1.**]—Quaestiones tres in Novissimorum Comitiorum Vesperiis Oxon. discussæ. An Pædobaptismus sit licitus? Aff. An Christus, in quem baptizamur, sit Deus? Aff. An Hæretici, qua Hæretici, sint ultimo supplicio damnandi? Neg. Resp. H. Savage. *Typis L. Lichfield : Oxoniæ.* (1 March.) **E. 689. (3.)**

[**March 1.**]—Thirty Queries modestly propounded in order to a Discovery of the Truth in that Question ; Whether the Civil Magistrate stands bound to interpose his Authority in matters of Religion. By John Goodwin. [See also below : 28 March, E. 690. (3.) and (5.), and 19 April, E. 691. (16.)] *Printed by J. M. for Henry Cripps and Lodowick Lloyd.* (1 March.) **E. 689. (4.)**

March 2.—The Speeches and Confession of Arthur Knight and Thomas Laret at the places of Execution in Russel Street near Covent Garden and at Islington. *Imprinted for G. Horton.* **E. 689. (8.)**

1653.

March 2.—The Speech of Mr. Arthur Knight, who was executed in the Covent Garden. *Printed for Tho. Heath.*　　**E. 689. (7.)**

[**March 8.**]—Miscellania, or, Poems of all sorts, with divers other Pieces. By Richard Fleckno. pp. 146. *Printed by T. R. for the Author.* (8 March.)　　**E. 1295. (1.)**

[**March 9.**]—The Declaration and Speech of the Lord Admiral Vantrump, and his setting up the great Standard of Broom for the States of Holland, for the cleering of the Narrow seas of all English-men. *Printed for G. Horton.* (9 March.)　　**E. 689. (13.)**

[**March 12.**]—Some Returns to a Letter which came from a General Meeting of Officers of the Army of England, Scotland and Ireland, sitting at Westminster. Also A blast from the Lord, or a Warning to England. By Ben. Nicholson. *Printed for Giles Calvert.* (12 March.)　　**E. 689. (18.)**

[**March 12.**]—Saul's Errand to Damascus with his Packet of Letters from the High-Priests, against the disciples of the Lord. Or, a Transcript of a Petition contrived by some persons in Lancashire against a peaceable & godly people there, by them nick-named Quakers. [By George Fox.] *Printed for Giles Calvert.* (12 March.)

E. 689. (17.)

[**March 15.**]—The Down-Fall of the Unjust Lawyers, with the monopolizing Officers, and the Rising of the Just. By Edmund Leach. *Printed by E. Cotes.* (15 March.)　　**E. 689. (21.)**

[**March 18.**]—Singing of Psalmes the Duty of Christians. Sermons, by T. F., Minister in Exon. pp. 175. *Printed by A. M. for Christopher Meredith.* (18 March.)　　**E. 1482. (3.)**

[**March 20.**]—Ale ale-vated into the ale-titude. Or, a learned oration before a civill assembly of ale-drinkers. By John Taylor. (20 March.)

E. 1432. (1.)

March 22.—Regii Sanguinis Clamor ad Coelum adversus Paricidas Anglicanos. pp. 189. *Ex Typographiâ Adriani Ulac: Hagæ-Comitum* [*London*].　　**E. 1396.**

March 22.—An Act for continuance of the Customs until 26 March 1654. *s. sh. Printed by John Field.*　　**669. f. 16. (90.)**

[**March 22.**]—The Antiquity and Excellency of Globes. [With an engraved plate.] *Printed by M. S. and are to be sold by Tho. Jenner.* (22 March.)　　**E. 689. (27.)**

[**March 25.**]—Syzygiasticon Instauratum, or, An Ephemeris of the Places and Aspects of the Planets calculated for the Yeare 1653. By Joshua Childrey. *Printed by T. Mabb.* (25 March.)　　**E. 1471. (1.)**

March 26.—Cupid and Death. A Masque. As it was presented before his Excellencie, the Embassadour of Portugal, 26 March. Written by J. S. [i.e. James Shirley.] *Printed by T. W. for J. Crook & J. Baker.*

E. 690. (4.)

1653.

[**March 26.**]—A short Relation of a long Journey, encompassing the principalitie of Wales, from London. Whereunto is annexed an epitome of the history of Wales. Performed by the riding, going, crawling, running, and writing of John Taylor. (26 March.) **E. 1432. (2.)**

[**March 27.**]—L. Colonel John Lilburne revived. Shewing the cause of his late long silence and cessation from Hostility against alchemy St. Oliver and his rotten Secretary. [See also below: 1 April, E. 211. (6.)] (27 March.) **E. 689. (32.)**

[**March 28.**]—An Advertisement to the Jury-Men of England touching Witches. Together with a difference between an English and Hebrew Witch. *Printed by I. G. for Richard Royston.* (28 March.) **E. 690. (6.)**

[**March 28.**]—An Apologie for Mr. Iohn Goodwin, who makes 30 Queries whether it be the Magistrates Duty to interpose his Authoritie in matters of Religion. [See above: 1 March, E. 689. (4.), and also below: 19 April, E. 691. (16.)] *Printed for John Wright.* (28 March.) **E. 690. (5.)**

[**March 28.**]—Master John Goodwins Quere's questioned, concerning the Power of the Civil Magistrate in matters of Religion. [See above: 1 March, E. 689. (4.), and also below: 19 April, E. 691. (16.)] *Printed for T. Underhill.* (28 March.) **E. 690. (3.)**

[**March 29.**]—An Account of the Church Catholick. In answer to II. Letters sent to Edward Boughen. pp. 64. *Printed by E. Cotes for Richard Royston.* (29 March.) **E. 690. (7.)**

[**March 29.**]—Brevis Disquisitio: or a brief enquiry touching a better way then is commonly made use of, to refute Papists, and reduce Protestants to certainty and unity in religion. *Printed for Richard Moone.* (29 March.) **E. 1306. (2.)**

March 30.—To the Councel of State. The Petition of the Post-Masters of the several Roads of England. [With an Order of Council continuing them in their employment.] *s. sh.* **669. f. 16. (91.)**

[**March 31.**]—A Glympse of that Jewel, Judicial, Just, Preserving Libertie. By Jo. Streater. *Printed for Giles Calvert.* (31 March.) **E. 690. (11.)**

[**April 1.**]—The Wiltshire Petition for Tythes explained. By E. C. and R. E. *Printed for William Larnar.* (1 April.) **E. 690. (12.)**

April 1.—Vincit qui patitur or Liutenant Colonel John Lylborne decyphered in a short answer of Captaine Wendy Oxford to a false pamphlet of the said Lylborns intituled Iohn Lylborne Revived. [See above: 27 March, E. 689. (32.)] **E. 211. (6.)**

[**April 1.**]—A Warning to the World, being sundry strange Prophesies revealed to Nicholas Smith. (1 April.) **E. 211. (7.)**

1653.

[**April 2.**]—A Book of Fruits & Flowers, shewing the Nature and Use of them, either for Meat or Medicine. [With engravings.] *Printed by M. S. for Tho: Jenner.* (2 April.) **E. 690. (13.)**

[**April 2.**]—The Manuall of the Anatomy of the Body of Man. By Alexander Read. Fourth edition. [With engraved titlepage and plates.] *Printed by T. Newcomb for Richard Thrale.* (2 April.)
E. 1522.

April 2.—[A notice requesting patronage for the " Old Post " and not the " New Undertakers," for the carrying of letters, etc. MS. note by Thomason : " The same 2 of Aprill, this was cast about upon the Exchange."] *s. sh.* [See also below : 20 April, 669. f. 16. (95.)]
669. f. 16. (92.)

[**April 4.**]—A Mission of Consolation, usefull for all afflicted persons. By W. S. [i.e. William Slingsby.] pp. 150. *Printed by W. B. for John Williams.* (4 April.) **E. 1552.**

[**April 5.**]—A Treatise touching Falling from Grace. By John Griffith. pp. 66. *Printed by H. Hills & are to be sold by Richard Moon.* (5 April.)
E. 690. (17.)

April 8.—A Collection of the several Acts of Parliament from the 16 of January 1649 to the 8 of April 1653. pp. 1942. *Printed for Edward Husband.* **E. 1060, 1061.**

April 11.—A True Report of the Charges of the five Hospitalls in London [i.e. Christ's Hospital, St. Bartholomew's, St. Thomas's, Bridewell and Bethlehem] the yeare past. *s. sh.* **669. f. 16. (94.)**

April 11.—Wisdome's Judgment of Folly. Delivered in a sermon at the Spital in the Solemn Assembly of the City, by Thomas Horton. pp. 71. *Printed by T. Maxey for Samuel Gellibrand.* **E. 691. (4.)**

[**April 11.**]—[An appeal, in verse, to the Lord Mayor and Common Council to carry on the scheme of Employment of the Poor at Bridewell.] *s. sh. Printed by James Flesher.* (11 April.)
669. f. 16. (93.)

[**April 13.**]—A Word of Reproof to the Priests or Ministers who boast of their Ministery and yet live in Pride, &c. By William Tomlinson. *Printed for Thomas Wayte.* (13 April.) **E. 691. (9.)**

[**April 15.**]—Causes of the Lords Wrath against Scotland. [By James Guthrie. With a " Postscript which could not be gotten printed " in MS. in Thomason's hand.] pp. 97. **E. 691. (11.)**

[**April 18.**]—Vox Plebis ; or, the Voice of the oppressed Commons of England against their Oppressors. (18 April.) **E. 691. (13.)**

[**April 19.**]—The Apologist Condemned ; or, A Vindication of the Thirty Queries concerning the Power of the Civil Magistrate in matters of Religion. By way of answer to An Apologie for Mr. John Goodwin, and Mr. J. Goodwin's Queries Questioned. By the author of the said

1653.

Thirty Queries. [See above : 1 March, E. 689. (4.) and 28 March, E. 690. (3.) and (5.)] *Printed by J. M. for Henry Cripps and Lodowick Lloyd.* (19 April.)   **E. 691. (16.)**

[April 19.]—Heavens Glory, Hells Terror. Two treatises by Christopher Love. [With an engraved portrait of the author as frontispiece, and a woodcut printer's device on the titlepage.] 2 pt. *Printed for John Rothwell.* (19 April.)   **E. 692. (2.)**

[April 20.]—God's Anger and Man's Comfort. Two sermons, by Thomas Adams. pp. 88. *Printed by Thomas Maxey for Samuel Man.* (20 April.)   **E. 691. (18.)**

April 20.—Mercurius Alethes ; or, A Petition of the Corrupt Party dissolved at Westminster 20 April. [A satire.] *Printed neer Pauls Stable.*   **E. 725. (11.)**

[April 20.]—The Stumbling-Stone. Wherein the University is reproved by the Word of God. Delivered partly to the University-Congregation in Cambridge, partly to another in the same town. By William Dell. [See also below : 1 May, E. 699. (2.)] *Printed by R. W. for Giles Calvert.* (20 April.)   **E. 692. (1.)**

[April 20.]—To all Ingenuous People. A second intimation from the New Undertakers for conveyance of letters at half the rates to severall parts of England and Scotland. [See above : 16 April, 669. f. 16. (92.)] *s. sh.* (20 April.)   **669. f. 16. (95.)**

[April 21.]—To His Excellency the Lord General Cromwel. The Humble Remonstrance of many thousands in and about the City of London, on behalf of all the Free-Commoners of England. (21 April.)   **E. 692. (4.)**

April 22.—A Declaration of the Lord Generall and his Councel, shewing the grounds for the Dissolution of the late Parliament. *Printed by Henry Hills and Thomas Brewster.*   **E. 692. (6.)**

—— [Another edition.]   **E. 693. (3.)**

April 22.—A Declaration of the Generals at Sea concerning the late Dissolution of the Parliament. [Expressing their determination to continue in the duties entrusted to them by the Parliament.] *s. sh. Printed by Thomas Newcomb.*   **669. f. 16. (96.)**

[April 23.]—A Remonstrance to the Valiant Souldier and the rest of the Creditors of the Common-Wealth, concerning the Publique-Faith Souldiers Arrears and other Publique Debts of the Nation. By Samuel Chidley. *Printed for the Author.* (23 April.)   **E. 692. (5.)**

[April 24.]—The Army Vindicated in their late Dissolution of the Parliament. By John Spittlehouse. *Printed for Richard Moone.* (24 April.)   **E. 693. (1.)**

[April 24.]—A Platform of Church-Discipline, agreed upon by the Elders of the Churches assembled in Synod at Cambridge in New-

1653.

England. *Printed in New-England, and reprinted in London for Peter Cole.* (24 April.)   **E. 692. (7.)**

[April 24.]—The Dark Lantern. Containing a dim discoverie in riddles, parables and semi-riddles, intermixt with cautions, remembrances and predictions, as they were represented to their author in his solitary musings. By Geo. Wither. pp. 74. *Printed by R. Austin, and are to be sold by Richard Lowndes.* (24 April.)   **E. 1432. (3.)**

[April 25.]—Ten Queries. By a Friend of the now dissolved Parliament. [In MS. throughout, in Thomason's hand.]   **E. 693. (5.)**

[April 25.]—The Apostolical and True Opinion concerning the Holy Trinity revived and asserted. By John Biddle. pp. 95. [See also below 8 Sept. 1654, E. 809. (25.)] (25 April.)   **E. 1479. (1.)**

[April 25.]—A Discovery of the First Wisdom from Beneath, and the Second Wisdom from Above. Written by a Quaker, who is prisoner for the testimony of the Truth at Applebie, whose name is James Nayler. *Printed for Giles Calvert.* (25 April.)   **E. 693. (4.)**

[April 25.]—The Principles of Christian Religion. With a briefe method of the doctrine thereof. Now fully corrected and enlarged by the author, James Ussher. [With an engraved portrait of the author.] pp. 123. *Printed for George Badger.* (25 April.)   **E. 1535. (1.)**

[April 27.]—To the Lord General Cromwell. A few Proposals relating to Civil Government. By John Rogers. *s. sh. Printed for Robert Ibbitson.* (27 April.)   **669. f. 16. (97.)**

[April 27.]—A Supply to a Draught of an Act or System proposed, as is reported, by the Committee for Regulations concerning the Law. *Printed for Thomas Brewster.* (27 April.)   **E. 693. (7.)**

[April 27.]—The Cryes of England to the Parliament for the continuance of good entertainment to the Lord Jesus his Embassadors, collected as they came up from the severall counties [of Wilts and Southampton]. *Printed for Thomas Underhill.* (27 April.)   **E. 693. (10.)**

April 28.—A briefe representation of the sad Condition of that once flourishing town of Marleborough, as it hath been represented by severall letters. [Describing the great fire at Marlborough, 28 April.] *s. sh.*   **667. f. 17. (5.)**

[April 28.]—The Life of the Apostle St. Paul written in French by the famous Bishop of Grasse [Antoine Godeau] and now Englished by a Person of Honour [Edward, Lord Vaux]. pp. 358. *Printed by James Young for Henry Twyford.* (28 April.)   **E. 1546.**

[April 28.]—Renatus Des-cartes excellent Compendium of Musick ; with Animadversions thereupon [by William, Viscount Brouncker]. pp. 94. *Printed by Thomas Harper, for Humphrey Moseley and Thomas Heath.* (28 April.)   **E. 693. (11.)**

1653.

April 30.—A Declaration of Oliver Cromwell, Captain General of all the Forces of the Commonwealth. [Constituting a Council of State. The names of the members are supplied in MS. in Thomason's hand.] *s. sh. Printed by William Du-Gard.* **669. f. 17. (6.)**

[April 30.]—A brief Vindication of William Jervis against the scandalous aspersions of John Hodder, gent. By way of a narrative. *s. sh.* (30 April.) **669. f. 17. (1.)**

[April 30.]—Certain Verses written by severall of the authors friends [Sir John Denham and others], to be reprinted with the second edition of Gondibert [by Sir William Davenant]. (30 April.) **E. 1484. (2.)**

[May 1.]—The Holy History. Written in French by Nicolas Talon, S. J. and translated into English by the Marquess of Winchester. [With an engraved title-page.] pp. 418. *Printed by T. W. for J. Crook & J. Baker.* (1 May.) **E. 212.**

May 1.—Saul smitten for not smiting Amalek according to the severity of the Command. Delivered in a sermon at Somerset House. By Richard Coppin. *Printed and are to be sold by William Larnar and Richard Moon.* **E. 711. (8.)**

May 1.—A Sermon preached at St. Maries, Cambridge, or, An Essay to the Discovery of the Spirit of pretended Inspiration that disturbes and strikes at the Universities. By Joseph Sedgwick. Together with an Appendix, wherein Mr. Dell's Stumbling-Stone is replied unto. [See above: 20 April, E. 692. (1.)] *Printed by R. D. for Edward Story, Bookseller at Cambridge.* **E. 699. (2.)**

[May 2.]—The Infants Advocate. Of Circumcision on Jewish, and Baptism on Christian children. By Thomas Fuller. pp. 215. *Printed by R. Norton for J. Williams.* (2 May.) **E. 1431. (1.)**

[May 2.]—A Philologicall Commentary; or, An Illustration of the most obvious and usefull Words in the Law. By E. L. [i.e. Edward Leigh.] pp. 237. *Printed by T. Mabb for Charles Adams.* (2 May.) **E. 1481. (2.)**

[May 3.]—Another Declaration wherein is rendered a further account of the Reasons for Dissolving the Parliament. By the Lord Generall and his Council. *Printed for T. Brewer at the Royal Exchange.* (3 May.) **E. 693. (17.)**

May 3.—A Letter written to a Gentleman in the Country touching the Dissolution of the late Parliament. [Signed: N. LL. Dated 3 May. MS. note by Thomason: "by Mr. John Milton." Attributed also to John Hall of Durham. See letter of Professor C. H. Firth in the "Athenaeum," 6 Feb. 1897.] *Printed by F. Leach, for Richard Baddeley.* **E. 697. (2.)**

1653.

May 3.—Arcula Gemmea; or, A Cabinet of Jewels, discovering the nature of Pretious Stones. By Thomas Nicols. [Originally printed by Thomas Buck at Cambridge, under the title of "A Lapidary," 4 Sept. 1652.] pp. 239. *Printed for Nathaniel Brooke.* **E. 694. (1.)**

[**May 3.**]—Bibliotheca Parliamenti, libri theologi, politici, historici, qui prostant venales in vico vulgo vocato Little-Britain. [A satire.] (3 May.) **E. 693. (19.)**

[**May 3.**]—Βλασφημοκτονία : The Blasphemer slaine with the Sword of the Spirit. [By Philopsychus Philalethes, i.e. Matthew Poole.] pp. 80. *Printed by T. M. for Joh. Rothwell.* (3 May.) **E. 1550. (1.)**

[**May 3.**]—Diatriba de Justitia Divina. Authore Johanne Owen. pp. 296. *Impensis Tho. Robinson : Oxoniæ.* (3 May.) **E. 1482. (2.)**

May 3.—A List of all the Prisoners in the Upper Bench Prison remaining in Custody. *Printed for Livewell Chapman.* **E. 213. (8.)**

[**May 3.**]—The Worcestershire Petition to the Parliament for the Ministry of England, defended [by Richard Baxter]. In answer to book [by George Fox?] called A Brief Discovery of the threefold Estate of Antichrist. [See also below : 18 June, 1655, E. 843. (1.)] *Printed for Thomas Underhill and Francis Tyton.* (3 May.) **E. 693. (18.)**

[**May 4.**]—The Beauty of Holiness ; or, A Description of the Excellency and Content which is to be found in Wayes of Purity. By Tho. Hall. pp. 197. *Printed by A. M. for John Browne.* (4 May.) **E. 1471. (2.)**

May 5.—The Humble Remonstrance of the General Councel of Officers met at Dalkeith in behalf of the Forces of Scotland, shewing the hearty concurrence with his Excellency dissolving the late Parliament. *Printed for Giles Calvert.* **E. 697. (1.)**

[**May 5.**]—A Mite to the Treasury, of consideration in the Common-Wealth. By J. W., a Well-wisher to the Publique. *Printed by T. Newcomb in Thames Street.* (5 May.) **E. 694. (5.)**

[**May 9.**]—A great and terrible Fight at Sea neer the Coast of Holland, between the English Fleet and the Dutch Fleet. Together with a humble Representation to the Lord Gen. Cromwell and the Officers of the Army. *Printed for Robert Eeles.* (9 May.) **E. 694. (8.)**

[**May 9.**]—Newgates Remonstrance to the Lord. Gen. Cromwell ; or, the Petitions of the poor distressed Debtors and Convicts. *Printed for G. Horton.* (9 May.) **E. 694. (9.)**

[**May 9.**]—A Christian Sober & Plain Exercitation on the two grand practicall Controversies of these Times : Infant Baptism and Singing of Psalms. By Cuthbert Sidenham. pp. 210. *Printed for Robert White.* (9 May.) **E. 1443. (1.)**

1653.

[May 9.]—A Considerable Question about Government. By Isaac Pennington, Junr. *Printed for Giles Calvert.* (9 May.)

E. 694. (6.)

[May 9.]—Ψυχοσοφία: or, Natural & Divine Contemplations of the passions & faculties of the soul of man. In three books. By Nicholas Mosley. pp. 270. *Printed for Humphrey Mosley.* (9 May). E. 1431. (3.)

[May 10.]—Lenthall's Lamentation. [In verse. In MS. throughout, in Thomason's hand.] (10 May.) E. 694. (11.)

[May 10.]—Precious Remedies against Satans Devices, or Salve for Believers and Unbelievers Sores. By Thomas Brookes. The second edition. pp. 378. *Printed by M. Simmons for John Hancock.* (10 May.)

E. 1426.

[May 12.]—A List of the Prisoners of the Upper Bench Prison, who have taken the Benefit of the Act of Parliament for the Relief of Poor Prisoners. *Printed by T. Mabb for Livewell Chapman.* (12 May.)

E. 213. (9.)

[May 13.]—An Exposition of the Epistle of Jude. By William Jenkyn. The first part. pp. 640. *Printed by Th. Maxey for Samuel Gellibrand.* (13 May.) E. 695.

[May 13.]—Moses and Aaron; or The Types and Shadows of our Saviour in the Old Testament opened and explained. By T. Taylor. pp. 309. *Printed for John Williams.* (13 May.) E. 696. (2.)

[May 13.]—A Treatise of Effectual Calling and Election. By Christopher Love. [With an engraved portrait of the author as frontispiece.] pp. 259. *Printed for John Rothwell and John Clark.* (13 May.)

E. 696. (1.)

May 16.—To the Lord General Cromwell and his Councel. The Petition of Arise Evans. [Praying for the restoration of Charles II.] *s. sh.*

669. f. 17. (7.)

[May 16.]—To His Excellency the Lord General Cromwell. The Petition of Arise Evans. [A MS. abridgment, in Thomason's hand, from the printed copies.] E. 697. (3.)

May 16.—Divinity in Mortality, or the Gospel's excellency and the preacher's frailty. A sermon preached at the funerals of Mr. Richard Goddard. By Nath. Hardy. *Printed by A. M. for Nathanael Webb and William Grantham.* E. 708. (1.)

[May 17.]—Αὐτάρκεια, or the Art of Divine Contentment. By Thomas Watson. pp. 280. *Printed by T. R. & E. M. for Ralph Smith.* (17 May.) E. 1510. (1.)

[May 17.]—Comfort and Counsel for dejected Souls. By John Durant. pp. 259. *Printed for R. I. and are to be sold by Tho. Newberry.* (17 May.) E. 1434. (2.)

1653.

[**May 18.**]—A Warning seriously offered to the Officers of the Army
and others in Power. *Printed by Henry Hills, to be sold by Thomas
Brewster.* (18 May.)   **E. 697. (8.)**

[**May 19.**]—[A MS. copy, in Thomason's hand of a set of laudatory
verses begging Cromwell to ascend the throne. Note by Thomason:
"Written under his picture and hunge upon the Exchange."]
(19 May.)   **E. 697. (17.)**

[**May 19.**]—A Warning-Piece Discharged; or, Certain Intelligence
communicated to the Lord General Cromwel, in relation to the election
of a New Representative. By John Spittlehouse. *Printed for Richard
Moone.* (19 May.)   **E. 697. (11.)**

[**May 19.**]—An Apologie for our Publick Ministerie and Infant-Baptism.
By William Lyford. *Printed by William Du-Gard, for Joseph Crauford.*
(19 May.)   **E. 697. (9.)**

May 20.—To His Excellency Oliver Cromwell, Captain General, and to
the Councel of the Army. The humble Representation of severall
Aldermen and other Citizens of London, etc. [Praying for the
summoning of a Parliament. With the order of the Council of State,
upon the reading of this Representation, that all who signed it, "and
have any place of publick Trust, be forthwith dismissed"; and with "a
copy of verses, in relation to the Lord General Cromwel as they were
set up on the Exchange."] *s. sh.*   **669. f. 17. (8.)**

[**May 20.**]—The Army no Usurpers; shewing that the present Army
in their late dissolving of the Parliament have done nothing contrary to
law. *Printed for Giles Calvert.* (20 May.)   **E. 697. (13.)**

[**May 20.**]—The Compleat Angler, or, the Contemplative Man's
Recreation. pp. 246. [The Dedication signed: Iz. Wa. This is the
first edition of Izaak Walton's Compleat Angler.] *Printed by T. Maxey
for Rich. Marriot.* (20 May.)   **C. 31. a. 41. (1.)**

[**May 20.**]—Five New Playes, viz. The Madd Couple well macht, The
Novella, The Court Begger, The City Witt, The Damoiselle. By
Richard Brome. *Printed for Humphrey Moseley, Richard Marriot and
Thomas Dring.* (20 May.)   **E. 1423.**

[**May 20.**]—Paradoxes or Encomions in the Praise of being lowsey,
Treachery, Nothing, Beggery, etc. By S. S. *Printed for W. N.*
(20 May.)   **E. 1477. (1.)**

[**May 20.**]—The Querers and Quakers Cause at second hearing; or, the
Quaking faction discovered to be a new branch of an old root, revived
by Satan. pp. 58. *Printed by I. G. for Nathaniel Brooke.* (20 May.)
                                                              E. 697. (14.)

[**May 21.**]—Tears of Repentance; or, A further narrative of the
progress of the Gospel amongst the Indians in New-England. Related
by Mr. Eliot and Mr. Mayhew. *Printed by Peter Cole.* (21 May.)
                                                              E. 697. (16.)

1653.

[**May 21.**]—Philosophical Fancies. Written by the Right Honourable, the Lady Newcastle. pp. 94. *Printed by Tho. Rycroft for J. Martin & J. Allestrye.* (21 May.) **E. 1474. (1.)**

[**May 21.**]—A Treatise of Tithes. Written by a wel-wisher to Religion, and Proprietie. *Printed by J. F., for W. Lee.* (21 May.)
E. 697. (15.)

[**May 23.**]—A Remonstrance manifesting the lamentable Miseries of the Creditors and Servants of the late King, Queen and Prince. (23 May.) **E. 693. (13.)**

[**May 23.**]—The King of Denmark his Declaration concerning the English Merchants Ships lying in Copenhagen. Translated by Edward Smith. *Printed at Copenhagen, and reprinted at London for Henry Cripps and Lodowick Lloyd.* (23 May.) **E. 693. (14.)**

[**May 23.**]—The Anabaptist washt and washt, and shrunk in the washing ; or, A Scholasticall Discussion of the much-agitated controversie concerning Infant-Baptism. Occasioned by a publike disputation in the Church of Newport-Pagnell betwixt Mr. Gibs, Minister there, and the author Richard Carpenter, Independent. [With an engraved frontispiece bearing a portrait of the author.] pp. 469. *Printed by William Hunt.* (23 May.) **E. 1484. (1.)**

[**May 23.**]—Some Gospel Treasures Opened. Sermons by John Everard. pp. 830. *Printed by R. W. for Rapha Harford.* (23 May.)
E. 1424 and 1425.

[**May 24.**]—An Appeal from Chancery to the Lord General and his Councel. [By Nathanael Burt. A protest against the condition of the administration of the Law.] *Printed for William Larnar.* (24 May.) **E. 697. (21.)**

[**May 24.**]—The Profession of the Church of ——, in cheerfull conjunction with many other neighbour Churches, who in order to further Reformation and the exercise of Christ's Discipline, have all agreed in the same Profession. [A form in blank.] (24 May.) **669. f. 17. (10.)**

[**May 24.**]—A Little Starre, giving some light into the counsels and purposes of God. By William Mason. pp. 186. *Printed by G. D. for Giles Calvert.* (24 May.) **E. 1505. (1.)**

[**May 24.**]—The Scarlet Gown, or the history of all the present Cardinals of Rome. Written originally in Italian and translated into English by H. C. [i.e. Henry Cogan.] [With an engraved frontispiece, representing a Cardinal in his robes.] pp. 162. *Printed for Humphrey Moseley.* (24 May.) **E. 1433. (1.)**

[**May 24.**]—A Treatise containing three things. 1. A Discovery of the insupportable Burthen of Sinne. 2. The restlesse Resolution of a Soule to returne to God. 3. A Discovery of the Entertainment that wandring hearts meet with in their returnes to God. By Lieutenant

1653.

Collonel Paul Hobson. pp. 144. *Printed by M. S. for Thomas Brewster.* (24 May.) **E. 1479. (3.)**

May 25.—A Schedule or List of the Prisoners in the Fleet remaining in custody. *Printed by S. G., for Livewell Chapman.* **E. 698. (13.)**

May 26.—The Petition and Representation of several Aldermen and other Citizens of London concerning the Re-sitting of the late Parliament. Together with the Representors' names and an Order of the Councel of State for the discharging them from all places of publike trust in the Common-Wealth. *Printed for George Horton.*
E. 698. (16.)

[**May 27.**]—An Answer to Monseiur de la Militiere his impertinent dedication of his Imaginary Triumph to the King of Great Britain, to invite him to embrace the Roman Catholic Religion. By John Bramhall. pp. 226. *Printed at the Hague.* (27 May.) **E. 1542. (1.)**

[**May 27.**]—The French Cook, prescribing the way of making ready of all sorts of Meats. Written in French by Monsieur De La Varenne, and now Englished by I. D. G. [With an engraving of a cook at work.] pp. 276. *Printed for Charls Adams.* (27 May.)
E. 1541. (1.)

[**May 27.**]—A True Breviate of the Great Oppressions and Injuries done to Evan Vaughan, Post-Master of Ireland, by Edmond Prideaux, Post-Master of England. (27 May.) **E. 698. (7.)**

[**May 30.**]—To the Lord General Cromwel and the Councel of State: the Remonstrance of divers well-affected inhabitants of the town of Colchester. [Praying for "the performance of many vows and engagements."] *s. sh.* (30 May.) **669. f. 17. (11.)**

[**May.**]—[A Copy of Verses in praise of Charles I. In MS., in Thomason's hand.] *s. sh.* **669. f. 17. (4.)**

[**May.**]—Reasons why the Supreme Authority of the Three Nations, for the time, is not in the Parliament but in the new-established Councel of State. *Printed for Richard Moore.* **E. 697. (19.)**

May.—A List of the Common-wealth of England's Navie at Sea, in the expedition in, under the command of Col: Richard Deane, and Col: George Monke, Generals and Admirals. *s. sh. Printed by M. Simmons, and to be sold by Tho. Jenner.* **669. f. 17. (34.)**

[**May.**]—Some Proposals by a well-wisher to His Highnes and the Parliament. [Signed: M. J.] *s. sh.* **669. f. 17. (2.)**

May.—The Crying Sin of England of not caring for the Poor. Sermons preached at Lutterworth in May 1653. By John Moore. *Printed by T. M. for Antony Williamson.* **E. 713. (7.)**

[**June 1.**]—Refreshing Drops and Scorching Vials severally distributed to their proper subjects. By Christopher Goad. pp. 254. *Printed by R. W. for Giles Calvert.* (1 June.) **E. 698. (12.)**

1653.

June 1.—[An Ordinance of the Council of State, appointing a Committee to enquire into the claims of the "Adventurers" in Ireland.] *Printed for Giles Calvert.* **E. 1062. (1.)**

June 2.—An Elegie upon the death of the thrice noble Generall, Richard Dean, who departed this life the 2ᵈ of June. By J. R., Merchant. [With a woodcut.] *s. sh. Printed by Tho: Rycroft, and are to be sold by Tho: Jenner.* **669. f. 17. (21.)**

June 2.—A Declaration from the General and Council of State, to incite all the good people of these Nations to thankfullness for the late great Victory at Sea obtained by the Fleet of this Commonwealth against the Dutch, upon the second and third of June. *s. sh. Printed for Giles Calvert, Henry Hills and Thomas Brewster.* **669. f. 17. (13.)**

June 2.—The Particulars of all the late Bloody Fight at Sea. *Printed for R. Ibbitson.* **E. 699. (4.)**

June 2.—A True Relation of the late great Sea Fight. *Printed by Henry Hills, to be sold at his house and by Thomas Brewster.* **E. 699. (5.)**

[June 3.]—The Parliament routed : or, Here's a House to let. [A satirical ballad.] *s. sh.* (3 June.) **669. f. 17. (12.)**

June 3.—A Declaration of the further proceedings of the English Fleet upon the Coast of Holland, 3 to 8 June. *Printed for George Horton.* **E. 699. (11.)**

June 3.—A Letter from the Fleet, with a diurnal account of the affairs between the English and the Dutch, 3 to 9 June. *Printed by J. C.* **E. 699. (14.)**

[June 6.]—Thomas Gataker his Vindication of the Annotations [on Jer. x. 2] by him published, against the scurrilous aspersions of William Lillie, as also against the Expositions of John Swan and another. pp. 192. *Printed by J. L. for Philemon Stephens.* (6 June.) **E. 699. (1.)**

[June 7.]—More Hearts and Hands appearing for the Work. Being two letters, the one sent from Col. Robert Overton, Governour of Hull, to the Lord Generall Cromwel, the other to the Councel of Officers sitting at White-Hall, wherein their reall affection is declared towards the Armies happy procceding. *Printed by Matthew Simmons.* (7 June.) **E. 699. (7.)**

[June 7.]—A Copy of Verses upon the late Fight at sea. [In MS., in Thomason's hand.] **E. 699. (9.)**

[June 7.]—Πανσεβεία : or, A View of all Religions in the World. By Alexander Ross. [With an engraved portrait.] pp. 578. *Printed by James Young for John Saywell.* (7 June.) **E. 1513.**

June 9.—A Declaration and Order of the Lord Generall Cromwell and his Councill, for the continuance of the Assessment from 24 June to

1653.

25 Dec., at the rate of £120,000 by the moneth, towards the maintenance of the Armies and Navies of this Commonwealth. *Printed by and for H. Hills, G. Calvert and T. Brewster.* **E. 1062. (2.)**

[June 9.]—The Sure Foundation: or, Certain Principles of Christian Religion. By Paul Salomeau. pp. 73. *Printed by A. M. and are to be sold by Henry Seile.* (9 June.) **E. 1544. (1.)**

[June 10.]—Fides Apostolica. Or, a discourse asserting the received authors and authority of the Apostles' Creed. By Geo. Ashwell. pp. 308. *Printed by Leon. Lichfield for Jo. Godwin and Ric. Davis: Oxford.* (10 June.) **E. 1433. (2.)**

[June 11.]—A Confutation of the Assertions of Mr. Samuel Oates, in relation to his not practising the laying on of hands on all baptized Believers. By John Spittlehouse. *Printed for Richard Moone.* (11 June.) **E. 699. (12.)**

[June 12.]—A Faithful Discovery of a treacherous design of Mystical Antichrist displaying Christ's Banners. Containing an examination of many doctrines of the Quakers in Yorkshire. [By Joseph Kellet, John Pomroy, Paul Glisson & others.] pp. 59. [See also below: 30 Jan., 1654, E. 727. (12.), 14 Feb., 1654, E. 729. (5.) and 14 Aug., 1654, E. 808. (10.)] *Printed by H. Hills for Thomas Brewster.* (12 June.) **E. 699. (13.)**

[June 13.]—A Voice from the Temple to the Higher Powers, wherein is shewed that it is the duty of Saints to search the Prophecies of Holy Scripture which concern the Later Times. By John Canne. *Printed by Matthew Simmons.* (13 June.) **E. 699. (16.)**

June 14.—Propositions for Peace presented to the States of Holland by the subjects of the Netherlands. With a diurnal of the affaires now on foot in Denmark, Sweden and the United Provinces concerning the Soveraignty of the Commonwealth of England. Translated out of Dutch. [A letter, dated 14 June.] *Printed for G. Horton.* **E. 701. (4.)**

June 14.—The Banished man's suit for Protection to the Lord Generall Cromwell. Being the humble address of Lieutenant Colonel John Lilburn. *s. sh. Printed by Thomas Newcomb.* **669. f. 17. (16.)**

[June 14.]—Anthropometamorphosis. Man Transform'd ; or, the Artificial Changling historically presented. By J. B. [i.e. John Bulwer. A treatise on the practices of various peoples in adorning or deforming the body. With an engraved frontispiece, and an engraved portrait of Bulwer ; also illustrated with woodcuts throughout the text.] pp. 559. *Printed by William Hunt.* (14 June.) **E. 700.**

[June 14.]—The Judiciall Arraignment, Condemnation, Execution & Interment of the late pernicious endenized Dutch Devil Excize and its infernal Imps Excize-Men. (14 June.) **E. 699. (17.)**

1653.

[June 15.]—The first Book of the Works of Mr. Francis Rabelais, Doctor in Physick. The Second Book of the Works of Mr. Francis Rabelais. [Translated by Sir Thomas Urquhart.] 2 vol. *Printed for Richard Baddeley.* (15 June.) **E. 1429.**

June 16.—An Order and Declaration of the Council of State, concerning the Determination of severall claims now depending before the Commissioners for removing Obstructions. *s. sh. Printed for Giles Calvert, Henry Hills and Thomas Brewster.* **669. f. 17. (19.)**

June 16.—At the Councill of State. [An Order respecting the Manors and Estates directed to be sold by the Commissioners for Sequestrations.] *s. sh. Printed for Giles Calvert, Hen. Hills and Tho. Brewster.* **669. f. 17. (17.)**

June 16.—An Instruction unto Josias Bervers, Francis Massenden, Sir William Roberts, John Packer, Henry Pit, Mathias Valentine and Robert Aldsworth. [Authorising them to hear and determine certain claims to Estates forfeited for Treason.] *s. sh. Printed for Giles Calvert, Henry Hills and Thomas Brewster.* **669. f. 17. (18.)**

June 16.—A Second Address directed to the Lord Generall Cromwell, and the Councell of State : being the Petition of Lieutenant Colonell John Lilburne. [Praying for " protection, and suspension of any proceedings against him under the Act for his banishment."] *s. sh. Printed by Tho. Newcomb.* **669. f. 17. (20.)**

[June 16.]—The Declaration of the States of Holland concerning the King of Scots. With the resolution of Van Trump, together with his orders to all Court of Admiralties. Also a diurnal of the Dutch Occurrences. [Two letters.] *Printed for Geo. Horton.* (16 June.) **E. 701. (7.)**

[June 17.]—A Christian's Duty and Safety in evil times. Sermons. By Christopher Love. [With an engraved portrait of the author.] pp. 184. *Printed for E. Brewster and George Sawbridge.* (17 June.) **E. 1434. (3.)**

[June 19.]—Meditations of the Mirth of a Christian Life and the Vaine Mirth of a Wicked Life, with the Sorrows of it. By Zach. Bogan. pp. 560. *Printed by H. Hall for R. Davis: Oxford.* (19 June.) **E. 1486. (1.)**

June 20.—A Third Address directed to the Lord Generall Cromwell, and the Councell of State : being the Petition of Lieutenant Colonell John Lilburne, prisoner in Newgate. [Praying for release, and promising submission to the Government.] *s. sh. Printed by Tho. Newcomb.* **669. f. 17. (22.)**

[June 20.]—Hieraspistes : A Defence by way of Apology for the Ministry and Ministers of the Church of England. By John Gauden. pp. 594. *Printed for Andrew Crooke.* (20 June.) **E. 214.**

1653.

[June 21.]—'Η 'Αποστασία ὁ 'Αντίχριστος : or, a Scriptural discourse of the Apostasie and the Antichrist by way of comment on the twelve first verses of 2 Thess. 2. By E. H. pp. 164. (21 June.)
E. 701. (12.

June 22.—A Defensive Declaration of Lieut. Col. John Lilburn, against the unjust sentence of his banishment by the late Parliament. Unto which is annexed an appendix directed from the said Lieut.-Col. John Lilburn to his Excellency, dated from his captivity in Newgate.
E. 702. (2.)

[June 22.]—A Jury-man's Judgement upon the case of Lieut.-Col. John Lilburne : proving by well-grounded arguments that they ought not to finde him guilty upon the Act of Parliament made for his banishment. (22 June.)
E. 702. (6.)

June 22.—An Additional Remonstrance to the valiant and wel-deserving Souldier and the rest of the Creditors of the Common-wealth concerning the Publick Faith, Souldiers Arrears, &c. With a little friendly touch to L. Coll. John Lilburne. By Samuel Chidley. *Printed for the Author.*
E. 711. (7.)

[June 22.]—Milk for Babes in Christ. By Martin Fynch. pp. 168. *Printed for Thomas Brewster.* (22 June.)
E. 1481. (1.)

[June 22.]—Philadelphia ; or, xl. queries propounded for the discovery of truth in this case of conscience : Whether persons baptized, as themselves call Baptism, after a profession of Faith, may or may not lawfully hold communion with such Churches, who judg themselves truly baptized, though in infancy, and before such a profession ? By J. G., a Minister of the Gospel of Jesus Christ. [See also below : 23 Sept., E. 713. (17.)] *Printed by J. M. for Henry Cripps and Lodowick Lloyd.* (22 June.)
E. 702. (7.)

[June 22.]—Sal Scylla : or, a letter written from Scilly to Mr. John Goodwin. [With reference to his book entitled "Redemption redeemed." The letter is signed : Christopher Salter.] *Printed by J. M. for Henry Cripps and Lodowick Lloyd.* (22 June.)
E. 702. (5.)

[June 23.]—Bibliotheca Parliamenti. Libri theologici, politici, historici, qui prostant venales in vico vulgo vocato Little Britain. Classis secunda. Done into English for the Assembly of Divines. [A satire.] (23 June.)
E. 702. (8.)

[June 23.]—A High and Heavenly Eccho. By a faithful Minister of the Gospel. [In verse.] *s. sh. Printed for John Rothwell.* (23 June.)
669. f. 17. (23.)

[June 23.]—Some Baptismal abuses briefly discovered ; or a cordial endeavour to reduce the administration and use of Baptism to its primitive purity. By William Allen. pp. 119. [See also below :

1653.

21 July, 1655, E. 849.] *Printed by J. M. for Henry Cripps and Lodowick Lloyd.* (23 June.) **E. 702. (12.)**

[**June 24.**]—No Age like unto this Age : or, Times Unparallel'd Oppression, Oppression, Oppression. Being the cries in Kent against the great oppression of Tythes, Unjust Justices and Corrupt Magistrates. Presented to the Consideration of the Rt. Hon. Captain General Cromwel. *Printed by J. C.* (24 June.) **E. 702. (13.)**

[**June 24.**]—The Petition rejected by the Parliament, being tendered to them in behalf of Lieut. Col. John Lilburn, and in behalf of the liberties of all the people of England, highly violated by their unjust Act made for his banishment, *etc. s. sh.* (24 June.)
669. f. 17. (24.)

[**June 24.**]—An Elegiack Memoriall of General Deane. [Signed : Th. Tw.] *s. sh. Printed by M. S. for Tho: Jenner.* (24 June.)
669. f. 17. (25.)

[**June 25.**]—To Parliament. The Petition of divers afflicted Women, in behalf of M: John Lilburn, prisoner in Newgate, *s. sh.* (25 June.)
669. f. 17. (26.)

June 25.—The Condemned Man's Reprieve : or, God's Love Token, flowing in upon the heart of William Blake, a penitent sinner. [Dated from Exeter Gaol.] **E. 705. (18.)**

[**June 25.**]—The Two Great Mysteries of Christian Religion, the Ineffable Trinity ⎱ explicated. By Godfree Goodman, Bishop Wonderfull Incarnation ⎰ late of Gloucester. pp. 109. *Printed by J. Flesher.* (25 June.)
E. 216. (1.)

[**June 27.**]—The Law's Discovery : or, a brief detection of sundry notorious Errors and Abuses contained in our English Laws. By a well-wisher to his countrey. *Printed by R. I. for G. B.* (27 June.)
E. 702. (18.)

[**June 27.**]—A Pathway unto England's perfect settlement. By Capt. Robert Norwood. pp. 61. [See also below : 2 Aug., E. 708. (19.)] *Printed for Rich. Moone.* (27 June.) **E. 702. (16.)**

[**June 29.**]—By the Lord General and the Council of State. [A Declaration respecting those " who do assemble together in a riotous manner, and by violence dispossess the Adventurers for draining the great Level of the Fenns."] *s. sh. Printed for Giles Calvert, Thomas Brewster, and by and for Henry Hills.* **669. f. 17. (27.)**

[**June 29.**]—An Antidote against the Poyson of the Times, wherein the many points of Christian Religion denied in these back-sliding dayes are proved by the Testimony of the Scriptures. [The preface signed : Adam Martindale.] *Printed for Luke Fawn.* (29 June.) **E. 1478. (1.)**

1653.

[June 29.]—A Call out of Egypt and Babylon. Briefe hints concerning Marriage, Baptism, &c. [By Richard Farnworth.] *Printed for Giles Calvert.* (29 June.)   **E. 703. (5*.)**

[June 29.]—A Discovery of Faith ; shewing the way that leadeth to Salvation. [By Richard Farnworth.] Also a letter of James Nayler to severall friends about Wakefield. *Printed for Giles Calvert.* (29 June.)   **E. 703. (6**.)**

[June 29.]—A Discovery of Truth and Falshood. [By Richard Farnworth.] *Printed for Giles Calvert.* (29 June.)   **E. 703. (5**.)**

[June 29.]—An Easter-reckoning, or, a Free-will offering Shewing the difference of the Ministery of Christ and the Ministery of the World or of Antichrist. [By Richard Farnworth.] (29 June.)   **E. 703. (5.)**

[June 29.]—The Generall-Good to all people : or, the Lord's free love running forth freely to his own people in these latter days. With something in answer to the Petition put up to the Parliament by many of the City and County of York. By Richard Farnworth. *Printed for Giles Calvert.* (29 June.)   **E. 703. (6.)**

[June 29.]—God's Covenanting with his People : wherewith they are reconciled, and at peace with their Maker. By Richard Farnworth. pp. 51. *Printed for Giles Calvert.* (29 June.)   **E. 703. (6*.)**

[June 29.]—The Life of Faustus Socinus, described by a Polonian Knight [Samuel Przypkowski, translated by John Biddle. With a colophon bearing a woodcut printer's device of Richard Moone]. pp. 61. *Printed for Richard Moone.* (29 June.)   **E. 1489. (1.)**

[June 29.]—Several Petitions answered, that were put up by the priests of Westmorland against James Nayler and Geo. Fox. Also an exhortation to the people. [With the text of the petitions, and a prefatory epistle by Richard Farnworth.] pp. 60. *Printed for Giles Calvert.* (29 June.)   **E. 703. (4.)**

June 29.—A Commission and Instructions to Charles Fleetwood, Lieutenant General of the Army in Ireland, Edmund Ludlow, Miles Corbet and John Jones, impowering them to cause all the Lands to be forthwith surveyed, in order to the satisfying of Adventurers for Ireland. 29 June and 2 July. *Printed for Giles Calvert, Thomas Brewster, and by and for Henry Hills.*   **E. 1062. (3.)**

[June 30.]—The Cause of the Poor pleaded. By Samuel Richardson. *Printed by M. Simmons for Livewell Chapman.* (30 June.)

                                                  E. 703. (9.)

[June 30.]—Eight Reasons categoricall : wherein is examined and proved, that it's probable the Law-Common will stand. By Albertus Warren. *Printed by E. Cotes for John Place.* (30 June.)

                                                  E. 703. (11.)

1653.

[June 30.]—Multum in parvo : or a summary narrative on behalfe of prisoners captived for debt, and of all concerned natives. Presented to the consideration of the Lord General Cromwell, his Counsell of State. *Printed for J. H.* (30 June.) **E. 703. (7.)**

June.—The Anagram of John Lilburne. O I burn in hell. [With an acrostic on the name "John Lilburne." MS. in Thomason's hand. For a printed copy of this, see below : July, E. 703. (21.)]
E. 702. (9.)

June.—A Treatise of Fruit-trees. With the alimentall and physicall use of fruits. By Ra: Austen. 2 pt. [With an engraved titlepage to pt. I.) *Printed for Tho. Robinson : Oxford.* **E. 701. (5.) and (6.)**

July 1.—An Order of the Lord General Cromwell, and the Council of State, for continuing the powers of the Commissioners for Indempnity. *s. sh. Printed for Giles Calvert, Thomas Brewster, and by and for Henry Hills.* **669. f. 17. (29.)**

[July 1.]—To the Lord Generall Cromwell and the Councel of State. The Petition of many thousands of Prisoners for Debt, remonstrating the illegality of arrests, *etc. s. sh.* (1 July.) **669. f. 17. (28.)**

July 1.—The Prisoner's most mournful Cry : or, an epistle written by John Lilburne, prisoner in Newgate, unto the Rt. Hon. John Fowke, Lord Maior of London. **E. 703. (12.)**

[July 2.]—A Memento for Holland : or, A True History of the barbarous Cruelties used on the English Merchants residing at Amboyna in the East Indies by the Netherland Government Councel there. [With a wood-cut.] *Printed by James Moxon.* (2 July.) **E. 1475. (1.)**

July 2.—Lieu. Col. John Lilburn's Plea in Law, against an Act of Parliament of the 30 of January 1651, entitled, An Act for the execution of a judgment against John Lilburn. Penned by a faithful lover of the fundamental laws and liberties of the free people of England. The second edition, much inlarged, *etc.* **E. 703. (12*.)**

[July 2.]—England's Warning-Peece gone forth. Written upon an occasion of the coming forth of a book [" England's Gentle Admonition "] of one Thomas Robbins. By Richard Farneworth. *Printed for Tho. Wayte : York.* (2 July.) **E. 703. (14.)**

July 4.—The Lord General Cromwel's Speech delivered in the Council-Chamber. **E. 813. (13.)**

July 4.—[A List of Names in MS., in Thomason's hand, with the heading : "These are the Members of Barbones Parliament, as they were pleased to call themselves. 4 July."] **E. 698. (19.)**

[July 4.]—The Quakers shaken : or, A Fire-brand snach'd out of the Fire. Being a briefe Relation of Gods wonderfull Mercie extended to John Gilpin. [See also below : 21 Oct., E. 715. (7.)] *Printed for Simon Waterson.* (4 July.) **E. 216. (2.)**

1653.

[July 5.]—A Description & Plat of the sea-coasts of England, from
London, up all the river of Thames, all along the coasts to Newcastle,
all along Scotland, the Orchades and Hitland, where the Dutch begin
their fishing.   As also all those parts over against us, as Norway,
Denmarke, the Sound, Holland and Zealand.   Unto which is added a
list containing the monethly wages of all officers, seamen and others
serving in the States ships.   *Printed by M. S. for Tho. Jenner.*   (5 July.)
E. 703. (17.)

[**July 5.**]—The first Addresses to the Lord General with the Assembly
of Elders elected by him and his Council for the management of this
Commonwealth.   Containing certain rules how to advance to Kingdom
of Jesus Christ over the face of the whole Earth.   By John Spittlehouse.   [See also below : 2 Aug., E. 708. (9.)]   *Printed by J. C. for*
himself and Richard Moone.   (5 July.)   **E. 703. (19.)**

[July 5.]—Rules of Civil Government.   In a short Dialogue between
a Country man and a Scholar.   By Robert Sprye.   pp. 60.   *Printed*
for John Hancock.   (5 July.)   **E. 1484. (3.)**

[July 5.]—A Vindication of a Short Treatise of Tythes, lately written
and excepted against by a pamphlet, stilled The Funeral of Tythes, &c.
Printed by T. Newcomb for Thomas Heath.   **E. 705. (3.)**

July 6.—An Additional Instruction unto Josias Berners, Francis
Mussenden, Sir William Roberts, John Parker, Henry Pit, Mathias
Valentine and Robert Aldworth.   [Concerning "An Additional Act
for sale of several Lands and Estates forfeited for Treason."   See
above : 16 June, 669. f. 17. (18.)]   *s. sh.   Printed for Giles Calvert,*
Thomas Brewster, and by and for Henry Hills.   **669. f. 17. (30.)**

July 6.—To Parliament.   The Petition of divers well-affected persons.
[Praying that the "unjust oppression of Tithes and forced Maintenance
may be abolished."]   With the favourable answer from the Parliament.
s. sh.   Printed by F. Neile.   **669. f. 17. (33.)**

[July 6.]—A brief Remembrance when the report concerning the
pretended Ryot in the Isle of Axholm shall be read.   Humbly tendred
to Parliament by the Freeholders and Commoners within the Mannor
of Epworth in the said Isle, against certain Undertakers who call
themselves participants in the drayning of the Level of Hatfield Chase.
(6 July.)   **669. f. 17. (31.)**

[July 7.]—The Saints Everlasting Rest : or, a treatise of the blessed
state of the Saints in their enjoyment of God in Glory.   By Richard
Baxter.   The fourth edition.   4 pt.   *Printed for Thomas Underhill and*
Francis Tyton.   (7 July.)   **E. 704.**

[July 7.]—Seasonable Observations on a late book intituled A System of
the Law : so far as it relates to the High Court of Chancery and the
fees and proceedings thereof.   By Philostratus Philodemius.   pp. 62.
Printed by R. W. for Edw. Dod and Nath. Ekins.   (7 July.)   **E. 705. (4.)**

1653.

July 9.—The fundamental Lawes and Liberties of England claimed, asserted, and agreed unto by several peaceable persons of the city of London, Westminster, Southwark, Hamblets and places adjacent; commonly called Levellers. Presented to the consideration of all the free people of this Commonwealth.   **E. 705. (5.)**

[**July 10.**]—Christian Concord : or the Agreement of the Associated Pastors and Churches of Worcestershire. *Printed by A. M. for Thomas Underhill and Francis Tyton.* (10 July.)   **E. 216. (3.)**

[**July 10.**]—Mercurius Rusticus : the downfall of Tythes. The Countryman discovering the pride, lewdness, covetousness, and ambition of the fat beneficed Priests, incroaching Tythe-mongers, and oppressing Impropriators. (10 July.)   **E. 705. (6.)**

[**July 10.**]—A Message from God by a Dumb Woman to the Lord Protector. By Elinor Channel. Published according to her desire by Arise Evans. (10 July.)   **E. 1471. (3.)**

July 10.—The second Letter from John Lilburn, prisoner in Newgate, to the Lord Major. [Concerning his trial, etc.]   **E. 706. (5.)**

July 12.—A Declaration of the Parliament of the Commonwealth. [Declaring themselves to be the Parliament, and stating their aims.] *Printed by John Field.*   **E. 1062. (4.)**

July 13.—Severall Informations and Examinations taken concerning Lieutenant Colonell John Lilburn, concerning his apostacy to the party of Charles Stuart and his intentions in coming over into England out of Flanders. *Printed by H. Hills, and for G. Calvert and T. Brewster.* (13 July.)   **E. 705. (14.)**

[**July 13.**]—Malice detected, in printing certain Informations and Examinations concerning Lieut. Col. John Lilburn.   **E. 705. (19.)**

July 13.—The Triall of Mr. John Lilburn, 13 to 16 July.   **E. 708. (3.)**

July 13.—The Tryall of Leiutenant Colonell John Lilburn at the Sessions in the Old Bayly. With the new exceptions brought by the said John Lilburn. Also the order for the said John Lilburne to appeare again to receive sentence on Tuesday next. *Printed by J. C.*   **E. 710. (22.)**

July 13.—The Tryall of Mr. John Lilburn at the Sessions House in the Old Baily. Together with a diurnal of each days proceedings, in order to his tryal, 13 July to 13 Aug. Taken in short-hand. *Printed for G. Horton.*   **E. 710. (21.)**

[**July 13.**]—A new Ballad to the tune of Coc-lorrell. [In MS. in Thomason's hand.] (13 July.)   **E. 705. (10.)**

[**July 14.**]—A Catalogue of the Names of the New Representatives. [With numerous corrections in Thomason's MS.] *s. sh.* (14 July.)
                    669. f. 17. (14.)

July 14.—To Parliament. The Petition of many grieved People of the Cities of London and Westminster, and places adjacent ; in behalf of

1653.

John Lilburne, prisoner in Newgate.   [With the copy of a letter from Lilburne to Lord Chief Baron Wilde, dated 14 July, demanding a copy of his indictment.]   *s. sh.*   **669. f. 17. (35.)**

[July 14.]—The Christian Moderator.   Third part.   Or, the Oath of Abjuration arraign'd.   [Signed: William Birchley, i.e. John Austin.]   *Printed by J. G. for Richard Lowndes.*   (14 July.)   **E. 705. (15.)**

[July 14.]—Love and Fear the inseperable Twins of a Blest Matrimony. A sermon occasioned by the late nuptialls between Mr. William Christmas and Mrs. Elizabeth Adams.   Preached in St. Dionis Back-Church by Nathanael Hardy.   *Printed by A. M. for Nathanael Webb and William Grantham.*   (14 July.)   **E. 705. (16.)**

[July 15.]—To every Member of Parliament, Charles Hotham of Peter House in Cambridge presents this account of the proceedings of the Committee for Reformation of the Universities, in their depriving him of his Fellowship, together with his exceptions against those proceedings. *s. sh.*   (15 July.)   **669. f. 17. (32.)**

[July 16.]—The Exceptions of John Lilburne to a Bill of Indictment preferred against him, grounded upon a pretended Act [of 30 Jan., 1651], intituled, An Act in Parliament against John Lilburn.   *Printed for Richard Moon.*   (16 July.)   **E. 705. (20.)**

July 16.—A Conference with the Souldiers.   Or, a parley with the party of horse, which with drawn sword entred the Sessions at Mr. John Lilburn's trial, 16 July.   **E. 705. (25.)**

July 16.—Oyes, Oyes, Oyes.   At the Quest of Inquirie holden in the Court of common Reason, Law and just Right, it is found that Mr. John Lilburn committed no crime in appealing to the people on 16 July.

                                                E. 708. (7.)

[July 16.]—A Caveat to those that shall resolve, whether right or wrong, to destroy J. L. [i.e. John Lilburne.]   (16 July.)   **E. 705. (21.)**

[July 18.]—Doctor Lamb revived ; or Witchcraft condemn'd in Anne Bodenham, a servant of his, who was executed the Lent Assizes last at Salisbury.   By Edmond Bower.   *Printed by T. W. for Richard Best and John Place.*   (18 July.)   **E. 705. (24.)**

July 20.—An Account of the late Violence committed, 20 July, by some Souldiers upon the Generall Assembly of the Kirke of Scotland.

                                                E. 708. (23.)

[July 20.]—The Way to Heaven discovered.   By Robert Purnell. pp. 204.   *Printed for William Ballard of Bristol, and are to be sold by J. Grismond: London.*   (20 July.)   **E. 1489. (2.)**

[July 22.]—An Application of some passages in the foregoing Proposi-tions and Profession.   With an answer to some objections.   Written by Richard Baxter, to prevent the causeless separation of any sincere Christians from our Churches, especially for the satisfaction of the

1653.

inhabitants of Kederminster. pp. 119. *Printed by A. M. for Thomas Underhill and Francis Tyton.* (22 July.)   **E. 706. (6.)**

[July 21.]—Calamus Mensurans : The Measuring Reed. Or, the Standard of Time. Containing an exact computation of the Yeares of the World, from the Creation thereof to the Destruction of Jerusalem by the Romans. In two parts. By John Swan. *Printed for John Williams.* (21 July.)   **E. 706. (4.)**

July 25.—To the Right Honorable, his Excellency Oliver Cromwell and to the whole Councell J. F. wisheth health and increase of true honor. [A petition.]   **E. 216. (4.)**

[July 25.]—Doctor Lamb's Darling : or strange news from Salisbury. Being a relation of the contract and engagement made between the Devil and Mistris Anne Bodenham. *Printed for G. Horton.* (25 July.)   **E. 707. (2.)**

[July 26.]—The deep Sighes and sad Complaints of the souldiers of Captain Needham's troop in Colonel Hackers regiment, for wanting of justice and judgment. Articles exhibited by Thomas Fothergil against Capt. Needham. A word to the Army. [See also below : 5 Aug., E. 710. (1.)] (26 July.)   **E. 707. (8.)**

July 27.—An Act appointing a Committee for the Army and Treasurers at War. *Printed by John Field.*   **E. 1062. (5.)**

July 28.—An Act for Constituting Commissioners for Ordering and Managing the Affairs of the Admiralty and Navy. *Printed by John Field.*   **E. 1062. (6.)**

July 28.—An Act touching the several Receipts of the Revenue and Treasuries of the Commonwealth. *Printed by John Field.*   **E. 1062. (7.)**

[July 29.]—Unto every individual Member of Parliament : the humble Representation of divers afflicted Women-Petitioners, on the behalf of Mr. John Lilburn. *s. sh.* (29 July.)   **669. f. 17. (36.)**

[July 29.]—A brief Relation of the beginning and ending of the troubles of the Barbadoes, with the true causes thereof. Set forth by A. B., a diligent Observer of the Times. *Printed by Peter Cole.* (29 July.)   **E. 708. (5.)**

July 29.—A true Relation of the last great Fight at Sea, 29 and 31 July, between the English and the Dutch, as it was presented to the Councill of State in two letters from General Monck. *Printed for Giles Calvert, Henry Hills and Thomas Brewster.*   **E. 710. (6.)**

July 29.—The full Particulars of the last Sea-fight between the fleets of England and Holland. *Printed for G. Horton.*   **E. 708. (18.)**

July 29.—A true Relation of the last great fight between the English fleet and the Dutch fleet. *Printed for Thomas Hewer, and sold in the Old Baily.*   **E. 708. (19.)**

1653.

July 30.—An Act for setling the Jurisdiction of the Court of Admiralty. *Printed by John Field.* **E. 1062. (8.)**

[**July 30.**]—A Work for none but Angels & Men. A book shewing what the Soule is. [In verse. By Sir John Davies. Illustrated with engraved plates.] pp. 54. *Printed by M. S. for Tho. Jenner.* (30 July.) **E. 708. (6.)**

[**July.**]—John Lilburne. Anagram. O! I burn in hell. [With an acrostic on the name " John Lilburne."] *s. sh.* **E. 703. (21.)**

July.—A Remonstrance of the Case of the late Farmers of the Customes, with their Petition to the Parliament. [Signed by John Jacob, Job Harby, Nicholas Crisp and John Harrison.] *s. sh.* **669. f. 17. (55.)**

July.—A New Letany. [Satirical verses. In MS., in Thomason's hand.] **E. 703. (13.)**

[**Aug. 1.**]—The true manner of the sitting of the Parliament of the Commonwealth. Together with a perfect catalogue of their names, and for what places they serve. [With an engraving representing the interior of the House of Parliament during a sitting.] *s. sh.* *Printed by R. I. for Peter Stent.* (1 Aug.) **669. f. 17. (37.)**

Aug. 1.—Proposals [signed : J. R.] in behalfe of the poore of this nation. With some briefe considerations propounded to Parliament. **E. 708. (12.)**

Aug. 1.—The Upright Man's Vindication : or, an Epistle writ by John Lilburn, prisoner in Newgate, unto his friends at Theobalds in Hartfordshire. Occasioned by Major William Packer's calumniating the said Mr. John Lilburn. **E. 708. (22.)**

Aug. 1.—A True Discovery of the Ignorance, Blindness and Darkness of those who are called Magistrates about Carlile in Cumberland. [An account of the examination of George Fox, 1 Aug.] *Printed for G. Calvert.* **E. 740. (8.)**

[**Aug. 1.**]—A Brief Description of the Fifth Monarchy, or Kingdome, that shortly is to come into the World. And a prognostick of the time when this fifth Kingdome shall begin. By William Aspinwall. [See also below : 10 Dec., E. 1498. (1.)] *Printed by M. Simmons, and sold by Livewell Chapman.* (1 Aug.) **E. 708. (8.)**

Aug. 2.—An Act for taking away Fines upon Bills, Declarations and Original Writs. *s. sh.* *Printed by John Field.* **669. f. 17. (39.)**

Aug. 2.—To every individual Member of Parliament, the representation of divers apprentices of London on behalf of Mr. Lilburn, now prisoner in Newgate. **E. 710. (5.)**

—— [Another edition.] **669. f. 17. (38.)**

[**Aug. 2.**]—An Additional Discourse relating unto a treatise lately published by Capt. Robert Norwood, intituled, A Pathway unto England's perfect Settlement. With something concerning the Jewish

1653.

Civil Constitutions. With a brief answer to Mr. John Spittlehouse, in his book bearing the title, The first Addresses to his Excellencie, &c. [By Robert Norwood.] pp. 66. [See above : 27 June, E. 702. (16.) and 5 July, E. 703. (19.)] *Printed for Richard Moon.* (2 Aug.) **E. 708. (9.)**

[**Aug. 2.**]—The Trap-Pannians, alias Trap-Pallians, alias Trap-Tonians. A detection of some unparall'd plots, attempts and perpetrations practised by a Knot a Knaves, in and about the city of London. [A satire, in prose and verse. Signed : S. H.] (2 Aug.) **E. 708. (10.)**

[**Aug. 2.**]—A new Proclamation : or a warning peece against Blasphemers, Ranters, Quakers and Shakers, both men and women. [In verse, signed : J. F.] *Printed for M. S.* (2 Aug.) **E. 708. (11.)**

[**Aug. 3.**]—Reasons against the Bill entituled An Act for County Registers, Wills and Administration. With tables of fees and forms of declarations. *Printed for Robert White.* (3 Aug.) **E. 708. (15.)**

Aug. 4.—To Parliament. The Petition of many of the well-affected of the County of Kent. [Praying for the abolition of Tithes and Forced Maintenance. With the answer of Parliament.] *s. sh.* [See also below : 9 Sept., E. 712. (17.)] *Printed by Henry Hills.*

669. f. 17. (40.)

[**Aug. 4.**]—A second Vindication of a short Treatise of Tythes lately written and excepted against by a second printed paper, styled, Tythes totally routed by Magna Charta. *Printed for Thomas Heath.* (4 Aug.)

E. 708. (20.)

[**Aug. 4.**]—Capsula Aurea, continens methodicam disputationem scientiæ de Cœlo. Autore Gulielmo Whiting. pp. 253. *Impensis autoris : prostat autem venalis apud Joannem Williams.* (4 Aug.) **E. 1432. (4.)**

[**Aug. 4.**]—Three Treatises, being the substance of sundry discourses : viz. I. The Fixed Eye, or the Mindful Heart, on Psal. xxv. 15. II. The Principal Interest, or the Propriety of the Saints in God, on Micah vii. 7. III. God's Interest in Man, natural and acquired, on Psal. cxix. 4. By Mr. Joseph Symonds. [With an engraved portrait of the author.] pp. 351. *Printed by J. Macock for Luke Fawn.* (4 Aug.)

E. 1440. (1.)

[**Aug. 5.**]—A brief Narration of the Tryall of Captain Nedham at a court-marshall at Whitehall, in way of reply to a pamphlet by one Tho. Fothergill entituled The deep Sighs and sad complaints of some late Souldiers in Capt. Nedham's troop. [See above : 26 July, E. 707. (8.)] *Printed by H. Hills and sold at his house and at Mrs. Michels shop.* (5 Aug.) **E. 710. (1.)**

[**Aug. 5.**]—An Exposition of the Nineth Chapter of the Epistle to the Romans : wherein is proved that the Apostle's scope therein is to main-main his great doctrine of justification by faith. By John Goodwin. pp. 408. *Printed by John Macock for Henry Cripps and Lodowick Lloyd.* (5 Aug.) **E. 709.**

1653.

Aug. 6.—[A Notice by the Lord Mayor of London to the Ministers and Churchwardens of the several parishes, desiring them to collect old linen, " to be sent to the sea-coast, for the dressing of the wounds of the souldiers who were wounded in the late Ingagement at sea."] *s. sh.*

669. f. 17. (41.)

[**Aug. 6.**]—A Treatise of Prayer and Divine Providence as relating to it. By Edward Gee. pp. 499. *Printed by J. M. for Luke Fawn.* (6 Aug.)

E. 1430.

Aug. 6.—A Plea at large for John Lilburn. Penned for his use and benefit by a Well-Wisher to the fundamental laws, liberties and freedoms of the free people of England, and exposed to publick view.

E. 710. (3.)

Aug. 8.—An Additional Act for Stating and Determining the Accompts of the Officers and Soldiers of the Army in Ireland. *Printed by John Field.* **E. 1062. (9.)**

[**Aug. 8.**]—The Second Part of the Tragedy of Amboyna : or, a relation of a most cruel design of the Dutch in the New Netherlands in America, for the mining and murthering of the English Colonies in New England. *Printed for Thomas Matthews.* (8 Aug.)

E. 710. (7.)

[**Aug. 9.**]—The Complaint of many Free-holders, Farmers and others, of the Commonwealth of England, against the unlawfull planting of English Tobacco. [Signed : Robert Read.] With an Act of Parliament prohibiting the same. *s. sh.* (9 Aug.)

669. f. 17. (42.)

Aug. 10.—A Voyce from the Heavenly Word of God ; as a Representation to every Member of Parliament, in the behalf of Mr. John Lilburne, close prisoner in Newgate. *s. sh.* *Printed at London.*

669. f. 17. (43.)

[**Aug. 11.**]—A Word to the Jury in the behalfe of John Lilburn. *s. sh.* (11 Aug.) **669. f. 17. (44.)**

[**Aug. 11.**]—A Discussion of that Great Point in Divinity, the Sufferings of Christ. By John Norton. pp. 270. *Printed by A. M. for Geo. Calvert.* (11 Aug.) **E. 1441. (1.)**

[**Aug. 11.**]—Mr. Feake's Hymne. Christ Church. [In MS., in Thomason's hand.] (11 Aug.) **E. 710. (13.)**

[**Aug. 11.**]—The Manner of the Proceedings in the Courts of the Great Sessions in the counties of Mountgomery, Denbigh and Flint, within North Wales, as it now is. Published by R. V. [i.e. Rice Vaughan ?] (11 Aug.) **E. 710. (14.)**

Aug. 12.—A Declaration of the Parliament for a time of Publique Thanksgiving upon the five and twentieth of this instant August, for the Great Victory at Sea. *s. sh.* *Printed by John Field.* **669. f. 17.**

1653.

Aug. 13.—The humble and further Demand of John Lilburn, prisoner at the Bar, in order to the inabling of him to plead to the Bill of Indictment preferred against him ; whereunto he is required to plead.
E. 710. (16*.)

[Aug. 13.]—The Companions of Good Consciences : or an appeal of moderation, justice and equity, of righteousnesse, peace and love, unfolded in the law of God and Nature, to the consciences of all. *Printed for Giles Calvert.* (13 Aug.) **E. 710. (17.)**

[Aug. 13.]—The Queen, or the Excellency of her Sex. An excellent old play, found out by a Person of Honour and given to the publisher, Alexander Goughe. *Printed by T. N. for Thomas Heath.* (13 Aug.)
E. 216. (5.)

Aug. 14.—A Charge of High Treason exhibited against Oliver Cromwell. See below : 14 Sept. **669. f. 17. (52.)**

Aug. 14.—Thankfulness in Grain ; or, A Good Life the best Return. A sermon preached in St. Dionis Back-Church. By Nath. Hardy. pp. 52. *Printed by T. W., for Nath. Webb and Will. Grantham.* **E. 723. (6.)**

[Aug. 15.]—A List of the Names of all the Members of this present Parliament, with the respective Counties and Places for which they serve. With the Names of the Members of the severall Committees. *s. sh. Printed by R. Ibbitson.* (15 Aug.) **669. f. 17. (45.)**

[Aug. 15.]—The Sea's Magazine opened : or, the Hollander dispossest of his usurped trade of fishing upon the English seas : also his intended universality of ingrossment of trade. *Printed for William Ley.* (15 Aug.) **E. 710. (20.)**

[Aug. 15.]—A second Voyce from the Temple to the Higher Powers : wherein is proved that the Decrees and Institutions of Popes and Popish Counsels ought by the present supream authority of this nation to be taken away. By John Canne. *Printed by M. Simmons.* (15 Aug.)
E. 710. (19.)

[Aug. 15.]—The Shield Single against the Sword Doubled. To defend the Righteous against the Wicked. Whereby are waved those cuts and blows which Mr. Erbury deals to the Righteous ; and wherein also is shewed that his now New-Light is No-Light, but Blackness of Darkness. By Henry Nicols. pp. 77. [See above : 21 July, 1652, E. 671. (13.)] *Printed by J. M. for H. Cripps and L. Lloyd.* (15 Aug.) **E. 710. (18.)**

[Aug. 16.]—Milke and Honey, or, A Miscellaneous Collation of many Christian Experiences, Sayings, Sentences, &c. With a second part of Orthodox Paradoxes. By Ralph Venning. 2 pt. *Printed by T. R. & E. M. for John Rothwell.* (16 Aug.) **E. 1508. (1.)**

Aug. 16.—More Light to Mr. John Lilburnes Jury. [In the form of a letter. By John Lilburne.] **E. 710. (23.)**

II.   D

1653.

[**Aug. 17.**]—The Saints Guide, or Christ the Rule, and Ruler of Saints. By John Webster. *Printed for Giles Calvert.* (17 Aug.)
E. 710. (26.)

[**Aug. 17.**]—The Foundation of the Font discovered to the view of all that desire to behold it. And, The baptizing of Men and Women in rivers and fountains proved to be a standing Ordinance in the Church of Christ. By Henry Haggar. pp. 132. [See also below: 25 Nov. 1658, E. 961.] *Printed for Giles Calvert.* (17 Aug.)   E. 711. (1.)

[**Aug. 17.**]—The Power and Glory of the Lord shining out of the North. With a Warning to the People of England of all sorts not to oppose Christ in his Kingdom. By James Nayler. *Printed for Giles Calvert.* (17 Aug.)
E. 711. (2.)

Aug. 19.—The Afflicted Mans Out-Cry; or, An Epistle of John Lilburn, Prisoner in Newgate, to Mr. Feak.   E. 711. (7*.)

Aug. 19.—The Tryall of L. Col. John Lilburn at the Session House in the Old Baily. *Printed for D. B.*   E. 711. (9.)

Aug. 24.—An Act touching Marriages and the Registring thereof; and also touching Births and Burials. *Printed by John Field.*
E. 1062. (10.)

Aug. 25.—Ad Populum: or, A Low-Country Lecture to the People of England after a Thanksgiving Dinner, 25 Aug. *Printed for G. B.*
E. 711. (16.)

[**Aug. 25.**]—The Just Defence of John Lilburn against such as charge him with Turbulency of Spirit. (25 Aug.)   E. 711. (10.)

[**Aug. 27.**]—Sionis Certamina et Triumphus. Per Robertum Horsmannum. [In Latin verse.] pp. 126. (27 Aug.)   E. 1490. (1.)

[**Aug. 29.**]—The English Physitian, enlarged. By Nicholas Culpeper. pp. 398. *Printed by Peter Cole.* (29 Aug.)   E. 1455. (1.)

[**Aug. 30.**]—An Act for the more speedy and effectual bringing in of the Arrears of the Excize. *Printed by John Field.*   E. 1062. (11.)

Aug. 30.—An Exact and True Relation of a great Engagement between the English and Dutch Fleets upon the Coast of Holland. [With a wood-cut.] *Printed for G. H.*   E. 712. (8.)

[**Aug. 31.**]—Two Letters: The one to a subtile Papist: The other to a zealous Presbyterian. By T. Swadling. *Printed for Charles Adams.* (31 Aug.)   E. 712. (1.)

[**Aug.**]—The Ghost: or, the Woman wears the Breeches. A comedy written in the year MDCXL. [In verse.] *Printed by William Bentley for Thomas Heath.*   E. 710. (8.)

[**Aug.**]—[Verses by various writers upon "the Hollow Tree of Hampstead." With an engraving of it by W. Hollar.] *s. sh. Printed by E. Cotes for M. S.*   669. f. 17. (46.)

1653.

[**Sept. 1.**]—An Item against Sacriledge : or, Sundry Queries concerning Tithes. *Printed by Abraham Miller for Thos. Underhill.* (1 Sept.)

E. 712. (3.)

Sept. 2.—To the Supreme Authority of the Nation, the Parliament of England. The Petition of the Lord Mayor, Aldermen and Commons of the City of London, in Common Councell assembled. [In favour of a Presbyterian settlement.] *Printed by James Flesher.* E. 712. (11.)

[**Sept. 2.**]—A Caution to the Parliament, Councel of State, and Army ; that the Commonwealth be no longer deceived in their Accounts. [By John Ufflet.] *Printed by J. C.* (2 Sept.) E. 712. (6.)

[**Sept. 2.**]—A brief Apologie for the pious and painfull Ministers of the Church of England. By a Friend to Purity and Unity, etc. *Printed for John Wright.* (2 Sept.) E. 712. (4.)

Sept. 3.—An Act concerning the Planters of Tobacco. *Printed by John Field.* E. 1062. (13.)

[**Sept. 3.**]—Enchiridium Epigrammatum Latino-Anglicum. An Epitome of Essais, Englished out of Latin by Rob. Vilvain. ff. 191. *Printed by R. Hodgkinsonne for the Author.* (3 Sept.) E. 1619. (1.)

[**Sept. 3.**]—A Learned Discourse of Ceremonies retained and used in Christian Churches. Written by Lancelot Andrews, late Bishop of Winchester. [Edited by Edward Leigh. With an engraved portrait of the author.] pp. 77. *Printed for Charles Adams.* (3 Sept.)

E. 1535. (2.)

Sept. 5.—A Brief Dialogue between Creditor & Prisoner, clearly setting forth how both have been abused for many years. *Printed by Tho. Newcomb.* (5 Sept.) E. 713. (5.)

Sept. 6.—An Act for continuance of the Receipts of Excize until Dec. 29. *Printed by John Field.* E. 1062. (14.)

[**Sept. 6.**]—The Right of Tithes asserted : by our old Saxon Lawes. A Discourse proving them to be neither Popish nor Antichristian. (6 Sept.) E. 712. (9.)

Sept. 7.—The Keepers of the Liberties of England by Authority of Parliament, to all Parsons, Justices of the Peace, and other officers greeting. [Letters Patent, directing collections to be made for the relief of the sufferers by the fire which occurred in the parish of St. Sepulchre, London, 22 July, 1650.] *s. sh.* 669. f. 17. (50.)

Sept. 7.—The Keepers of the Liberties of England by Authority of Parliament to all Parsons, Justices of the Peace and other Officers, Greeting. [Letters Patent, ordering collections to be made for the relief of sufferers by the fire at Newmarket, 11 Aug. 1651.] *s. sh.*

669. f. 17. (51.)

Sept. 8.—An Explanatory Additional Act for the sale of the remaining Fee-Farm Rents. *Printed by John Field.* E. 1062. (15.)

1653.

[Sept. 8.]—The Army Armed, and their just Powers stated. By S. H., Senior [i.e. Samuel Hunton.] *Printed for William Ley.* (8 Sept.)

E. 712. (15.)

[Sept. 8.]—A Letter to Leiutenant Collonel John Lilburn, now Prisoner in the Tower. *Printed by Henry Hills.* (8 Sept.)   **E. 712. (14.)**

[Sept. 8.]—A Briefe Treatise concerning the chiefe dispute of this time about Tithes. By Bevill Turmiger. *Printed for R. Lowndes.* (8 Sept.)   **E. 712. (13.)**

[Sept. 9.]—The Arrow of the Almighty shot out of the Creatures Bowe, against the uncalled Ministers in England. By Geo. Baitman. pp. 122. *Printed by R. I. for William Hutcheson.* (9 Sept.)

E. 712. (16.)

[Sept. 9.]—Exceptions many and just against two Injurious Petitions exhibited to the Parliament, the one 16 July, the other 4 Aug. 1653. Both of them not only against Tithes, but against all constrained Maintenance of Ministers. By Theophilus Philadelphus. [See above : 4 Aug., 669. f. 17. (40.)] *Printed by L. Lichfield : Oxford, for Tho. Robinson.* (9 Sept.)   **E. 712. (17.)**

Sept. 10.—The Answer of the Emperour of Germany to the letter sent from the King of Scots for the supply of Men and Monies against England. Also the putting forth of the Dutch Fleet to Sea. (10 Sept.) *Printed for George Horton.*   **E. 713. (2.)**

[Sept. 10.]—A Bundle of Myrrhe, or, Several sweet Truths spiritually unfolded. By H. P., Minister of the Gospel [i.e. H. Prime.] pp. 60. *Printed by R. I. for Livewell Chapman.* (10 Sept.)   **E. 1476. (1.)**

[Sept. 10.]—Twelve Queries, humbly presented to the consideration of Parliament, about the two soule-oppressing yokes of a Forced Maintenance and Ministry. *s. sh. Printed for Samuel Howes.* (10 Sept.)

669. f. 17. (49.)

[Sept. 12.]—The Saints Guide, or, Christ the Rule and Ruler of Saints. Manifested by way of Positions, Consectaries and Queries. By John Webster. *Printed for Giles Calvert.* (12 Sept.)   **E. 712. (5.)**

[Sept. 13.]—The Way to Thrive : or, The Heavenly Thrift teaching a man so to thrive heere, that he may thrive for ever hereafter. By Alexander Mingzeis. (13 Sept.)   **E. 1475. (2.)**

[Sept. 13.]—A Wife, not ready made but bespoken. In four pastorall Eglogues. [By Robert Aylett.] Second edition : wherein are some things added, etc. *Printed for A. R.* (13 Sept.)   **E. 1455. (2.)**

Sept. 14.—A Charge of High Treason exhibited against Oliver Cromwell Esq. [MS. note by Thomason : " This Libell was scatred about the streets upon Wednesday night the 14 of Aug : " or rather 14 Sept. See Gardiner : History of the Commonweath, vol. 2, p. 303. See also below : 20 Oct., E. 715. (5.)]   **669. f. 17. (52.)**

1653.

Sept. 14.—An Argument in Defence of the Right of Patrons to Advousons, as it was delivered to the Committee for Tythes, 14 Sept. [MS. note: By "Counsellor Nortclife."] *Printed for Edward Blackmore.* **E. 713. (14.)**

[Sept. 14.]—The Case of Ministers Maintenance by Tithes, as in England, plainly discussed in Conscience and Prudence. By John Gauden. *Printed by Thomas Maxey for Andrew Cook.* **E. 220. (1.)**

Sept. 14.—A further Continuance of the Grand Politick Informer, discovering the wickednesse and mysteries of the present State iniquities on foot about 14 Sept. **E. 221. (4.)**

Sept. 17.—An Act for continuing the Priviledges and Jurisdictions of the County of Lancaster. *s. sh. Printed by John Field.*
669. f. 17. (53.)

Sept. 17.—Sad and serious thoughts, or the sense and meaning of the late Act concerning Marriages; explained in a letter. [Signed: C. C.]
E. 713. (8.)

[Sept. 19.]—A Letter from the North. [Complaining of the alleged misconduct and oppression of the Parliament, etc.] *s. sh.* (19 Sept.)
669. f. 17. (54.)

[Sept. 19.]—A Remonstrance of the fight in Legorn-Road between the English and the Dutch. By Henry Appleton. *Printed by John Field.* (19 Sept.) **E. 1068. (5.)**

[Sept. 21.]—Certain Considerations of present Concernment: touching this Reformed Church of England. With a particular Examination of An: Champny, his exceptions against the Ordination of the Protestant Bishops and Pastors of this Church. By H. Ferne. pp. 356. *Printed by J. G. for R. Royston.* (21 Sept.) **E. 1520.**

[Sept. 22.]—An Explanation of the Commission of Jesus Christ in relation to the Gifts, Work and Maintenance of his Ministers. By John Spittlehouse. *Printed by J. C. and are to be sold by Richard Moone.* (22 Sept.) **E. 713. (15.)**

[Sept. 23.]—A Second Word to the Army, putting them in mind of all the Breaches of Promises, which the Author hereof, with many thousands more, have taken notice of. (23 Sept.) **E. 713. (16.)**

[Sept. 23.]—An Answer to Mr. J. G. his XL. Queries, touching the Lawfulness or unlawfulness of holding Church-Communion between such who have been Baptized after their Beleeving, and others who have not otherwise been Baptized then in their Infancie. By W. A. pp. 96. [See above: 22 June, E. 702. (7.)] *Printed for the Author.* (23 Sept.) **E. 713. (17.)**

[Sept. 23.]—A Letter from Mr. Crashaw to the Countess of Denbigh against Irresolution and Delay in matters of Religion. [A poem.] (23 Sept.) **E. 220. (2.)**

1653.

[**Sept. 24.**]—A Gospel Plea, interwoven with a Rational and Legal, for the Lawfulnes & Continuance of the ancient settled Maintenance and Tenthes of the Ministers of the Gospel. By William Prynne. [With a separate leaf containing a portrait of Prynne and a list of his various imprisonments.] *Printed by E. Cotes for Michael Sparke.* (24 Sept.) **E. 713. (12.)**

Sept. 25.—The Crowne of Righteousnes, or, the glorious Reward of Fidelity in the discharge of our duty. In a sermon preached in S. Botolphs, Aldersgate, at the funeral of Mr. Abrah: Wheelock. Whereunto is added an encomium of him. By William Sclater. *Printed by J. G. for John Clarke.* **E. 221. (6.)**

Sept. 26.—An Act for the Satisfaction of the Adventurers for Lands in Ireland, and of the Arrears due to the Soldiery there, and for the encouragement of Protestants to Plant and Inhabit Ireland. pp. 66. *Printed by John Field.* **E. 1062. (16.)**

[**Sept. 26.**]—The Grand Conspiracy of the Members against the Minde, of Jewes against their King. Foure sermons by John Allington, a sequestred Divine. pp. 220. *Printed by J. G. for R. Royston.* (26 Sept.) **E. 1524.**

[**Sept. 26.**]—A Total Rout, or a brief discovery of a Pack of Knaves and Drabs, intituled Pimps, Panders, Hectors, Trapans, Nappers, Mobs, and Spanners. [A satire, in verse.] *s. sh. Printed for R. E.* (26 Sept.) **669. f. 17. (56.)**

[**Sept. 26.**]—An Hue and Cry after the Fundamental Lawes and Liberties of England. Occasionally written upon the stealing of one of the grand Assertors of them out of Newgate. [Signed : Anonimus, i.e. John Lilburne.] *Europe : Printed in a year of Melodius Discord.* (26 Sept.) **E. 714. (1.)**

[**Sept. 27.**]—The good Old Way ; or, Perkins improved, in a plain exposition of those depths of Divinity briefly comprized in his Six Principles. By Charles Broxolme. pp. 428. *Printed for John Rothwel and Thomas Maxey.* (27 Sept.) **E. 1483. (1.)**

Sept. 28.—The Petition of the well-affected of the County of South-Hampton in behalf of the Ministers of the Gospel. *Printed for R. Ibbitson.* **E. 714. (8.)**

[**Sept. 29.**]—Paradoxes. By J. De la Salle. pp. 165. *Printed for Francis Eaglesfield.* (29 Sept.) **E. 1550. (2.)**

Sept. 29.—A Sermon preached at the election of Sir Christopher Pack, as Lord Mayor of London. By Richard Vines. *Printed for Abel Roper.* **E. 858. (4.)**

[**Sept.**]—[An engraved portrait of Charles II. MS. note by Thomason : "At Paris, Sept."] *s. sh.* **669. f. 17. (48.)**

1653.

[Sept.]—To the Parliament of the Commonwealth, the Petition of Sir John Stawell. [Concerning the sequestration of his estates, etc.]

E. 1072. (1.)

Sept.—[A Proclamation by the Supreame Lord the free borne People of England. In MS. throughout, in Thomason's hand. Note at end: "This Libell was printed and scattered by and down the Streete about the latter end of Sept."]

E. 714. (7.)

[Sept.]—Mens divinitus inspirata Sanctissimo Patri Innocentio Papæ X, super quinque propositiones Cornelij Jansenij, et Mens Divi Augustini illvstrata de duplice adjutorio gratiæ Authore P. Fr. Francisco à Sancto Augustino Macedo. 2 pt. *Excudebat R. Nortonus.* E. 218.

[Oct. 2.]—Anatomical Exercitations concerning the Generation of living animals. To which are added particular discourses of births, and of conceptions, &c. By William Harvey. [With an engraved portrait of the author.] pp. 556. *Printed by James Young for Octavian Pulleyn.* (2 Oct.) E. 1435.

[Oct. 3.]—The New Earth, or, The True Magna Charta of the past Ages and of the Ages or World to come. By John Brayne. pp. 100. *Printed for Richard Moon.* (3 Oct.) E. 714. (9.)

Oct. 3.—To the Parliament of the Common-wealth of England. [A narrative of the persecution of the Quakers in the North of England, by Anthony Pearson.] E. 714. (10.)

[Oct. 4.]—Two Treatises: I. The Saints Communion with Jesus Christ. II. Acquaintance with God. As it was lately delivered to the Church of God at Great Yarmouth, by John Brinsley. pp. 207. *Printed for Tho. Newberry.* (4 Oct.) E. 1547. (1.)

Oct. 5.—An Act for the Relief of Creditors and Poor Prisoners. *Printed by John Field.* E. 1062. (17.)

[Oct. 5.]—The Anatomical History of Thomas Bartholinus, concerning the Lacteal Veins of the Thorax. *Printed by Francis Leach for Octavian Pulleyn.* (5 Oct.) E. 1521. (2.)

[Oct. 5.]—New Anatomical Experiments of John Pecquet. pp. 177. *Printed by T. W. for Octavian Pulleyn.* (5 Oct.) E. 1521. (1.)

[Oct. 6.]—A New List of all the Members of this present Parliament, etc. *s. sh. Printed by Robert Ibbitson.* (6 Oct.) 669. f. 17. (57.)

[Oct. 6.]—The Afflictions of the Afflicted presented to Consideration. Or, The unjust Actions of Tythe-Mongers discovered. [By Abel Wescot and others.] *Printed for the good of the Commonwealth.* (6 Oct.) E. 714. (14.)

Oct. 7.—An Act for Accompts and clearing of Publique Debts. *Printed by John Field.* E. 1062. (18.)

1653.

[**Oct. 8.**]—The Due Right of Tithes examined. By way of answer to some passages in Mr. Fishers Baby-Baptism. By an Aged Gentleman. *Printed for Thomas Pierrepont.* (8 Oct.) **E. 714. (16.)**

[**Oct. 9.**]—An Apologie for the Reformed Churches. By John Daille. Translated out of French [by Thomas Smith, Fellow of Magdalen College, Oxford], and a preface added, containing the Judgement of an University-man concerning Mr. Knot's last book against Mr. Chillingworth ["Infidelity unmasked"]. *Printed by Th. Buck: Cambridge.* (9 Oct.) **E. 1471. (4.)**

[**Oct. 10.**]—Caesar and Pompey: A Roman Tragedy, declaring their Warres. By George Chapman. (10 Oct.) **E. 714. (17.)**

[**Oct. 11.**]—Downfal of Tythes no Sacriledge; or Certain earnest and important Queries, with their Reasons or Grounds. By Ellis Bradshaw. *Printed for H. Cripps and L. Lloyd.* (11 Oct.) **E. 714. (18.)**

[**Oct. 11.**]—Englands Anathomy, or The Generall Crie of the People for a speedy redress of their persuing grievances, presented unto the Lord Generall Cromwell. By T. D., Minister of Jesus Christ. *Printed for R. E.* (11 Oct.) **E. 714. (21.)**

Oct. 12.—The Picture of Mercurius Politicus: or, Some of his Falsities and Mistakes, mentioned in his Intelligence of 12 Oct., concerning the Dispute in Lumbard Street, detected and disproved. By John Webster. *Printed for T. Webster & R. Hammond.* **E. 715. (15.)**

Oct. 12.—A Monstrous Dispute: or, The Language of the Beast, in Two Men professing themselves Ministers of the Gospel, at a Publike Dispute in Lumber-street, 12 Oct. By William Erbery. *Printed by J. C. for Giles Calvert.* **E. 714. (25.)**

Oct. 13.—An Act for Confirmation of the Sale of the Lands and Estate of Sir John Stowel, Knight of the Bath. *s. sh. Printed by John Field.* **669. f. 17. (62.)**

[**Oct. 13.**]—An Act touching Idiots and Lunatiques. *s. sh. Printed by John Field.* **669. f. 17. (58.)**

[**Oct. 17.**]—The Right Method for a settled Peace of Conscience and Spiritual Comfort. In 32 Directions. By Richard Baxter. The second edition corrected, and augmented. pp. 538. [See also below: 20 April, 1658, E. 939. (1.)] *Printed for T. Underhil.* (17 Oct.) **E. 1514.**

[**Oct. 18.**]—Ministers for Tythes, being a manifest proof that these men are no Ministers of the Gospel, who follow the Magistrate for a worldly maintenance. By William Erbery. *Printed by J. C. for Giles Calvert.* (18 Oct.) **E. 714. (26.)**

Oct. 19.—An Act impowring the Committee for the Army to state and determine the Accompts of all Officers and Soldiers, for Moneys by them received from 26 March 1647 until 25 July 1653. *Printed by John Field.* **E. 1062. (19.)**

1653.

[**Oct. 20.**]—Sedition Scourg'd, or A View of that Rascally & Vene-
mous Paper entituled, A Charge of High-Treason exhibited against
Oliver Cromwell. [See above : 14 Sept., 669. f. 17. (52.)] *Printed by
Hen. Hills for Rich. Baddeley.* (20 Oct.) **E. 715. (5.)**

Oct. 21.—An Act enabling the Commissioners of Parliament for Com-
pounding with Delinquents to dispose of two parts of the Estates of
Recusants for the benefit of the Commonwealth. *Printed by John Field.*
E. 1062. (20.)

Oct. 21.—An Act for the better Discovery and Prosecution of Thieves
and High-way Men. *Printed by John Field.* **E. 1062. (21.)**

[**Oct. 21.**]—The Standard of the Lord lifted up against the kingdom of
Satan, or an Answer to a book entituled The Quakers Shaken, written
by John Gilpin. By Christopher Atkinson. [See above : 4 July,
E. 216. (2.)] *Printed for Giles Calvert.* (21 Oct.) **E. 715. (7.)**

[**Oct. 24.**]—A Catechisme to be learned for the Training up of Youth
and others, in the grounds of the Christian Religion. *Printed by
Rober Ibbitson.* (24 Oct.) **E. 1473. (1.)**

Oct. 27.—By the Council of State. [An order with respect to certain
mutinous meetings of sailors, threatening extreme penalties, and
promising the speedy payment of prize-money.] *s. sh. Printed by
Henry Hills for him, Giles Calvert, and Thomas Brewster.*
669. f. 17. (59.)

[**Oct. 27.**]—The Misticall Marriage ; or, Experimental Discoveries of
the heavenly Marriage betweene a Soule and her Saviour. By F.
Rous. [With an engraved titlepage.] pp. 351. *Printed by J. C. for
John Wright.* (27 Oct.) **E. 1525.**

[**Oct. 27.**]—The Rules of Dispute, practised by Christ and his Apostles,
for deciding the controversies of that Age, and our Rule for the determining of our own. By John Brayne. *Printed for Richard Moon.*
(27 Oct.) **E. 715. (12.)**

Oct. 28.—An Additional Article to the Laws of War and Ordinances
of the Sea. [Making death the penalty for any mutinous act committed
or abetted by discharged sailors.] *s. sh. Printed by John Field.*
669. f. 17. (60.)

[**Oct. 28.**]—The strange Wonder of the World, or the Great Gyant
described. [With a wood-cut.] *Printed by J. C. and T. W.* (28 Oct.)
E. 715. (16.)

[**Oct. 28.**]—The Mad Mans Plea : or, A Sober Defence of Captaine
Chillintons Church. By W. E. [i.e. William Erbery.] (28 Oct.)
E. 715. (17.)

Oct. 29.—An Act for continuing the Powers of Commissioners for
Compounding, &c., Advance of Money, and for Indemnity. *s. sh.
Printed by John Field.* **669. f. 17. (61.)**

1653.

Oct. 30.—The Magistrates Dignity and Duty. A sermon preached at Pauls Church, before the Lord Maior and Aldermen. By William Spurstowe. *Printed by T. C. for J. Rothwell.* **E. 727. (3.)**

[**Oct. 31.**]—Wast Land's Improvement, or certain Proposals made to the Committee appointed by Parliament. [Signed: E. G.] (31 Oct.) **E. 715. (18.)**

[**Oct. 31.**]—Miscellanea Spiritualia : or Devout Essayes : the second part, composed by the Honorable Walter Montagu Esq., Abbot of Nanteul. pp. 264. *Printed for John Crook, Gabriel Bedell and Partners.* (31 Oct.) **E. 220. (3.)**

[**Oct. 31.**]—Cabala, Mysteries of State, in letters of the great Ministers of K. James and K. Charles. *Printed for M. M. G. Bedell and T. Collins.* (31 Oct.) **E. 221. (3.)**

[**Oct. 31.**]—The Bloody Almanack or, Monethly Observations and Predictions for the year of our Lord 1654. *Imprinted for G. Horton.* (31 Oct.) **E. 221. (1.)**

[**Oct. 31.**]—[News from Newcastle. In verse.] (31 Oct.) **E. 221. (2.)**

[**Oct.**]—To the Supreme Authority the Parliament of the Commonwealth, the Lord General Cromwell, and his Councell, the humble Remonstrance of Sir John Stawell. Concerning the sequestration of his estates, etc.] [See also below : 15 Feb., 1655, E. 1072. (3.) & 18 May, 1655, E. 1072. (4.)] *Printed by T. R. for Henry Twyford.* **E. 1072. (2.)**

[**Nov. 1.**]—The Plots of Jesuites : viz. of Robert Parsons, Adam Contzen, Tho. Campanella, &c. How to bring England to the Romane Religion without tumult. Translated out of the original copies. [With an engraved frontispiece.] *Printed for Mich. Spark.* (1 Nov.) **E. 715. (19.)**

[**Nov. 1.**]—The Shepherds Calendar. By Edmund Spencer. [Translated into Latin verse by Theodore Bathurst. With the English text.] pp. 147. *Printed for M. M. T. C. & G. Bedell.* (1 Nov.) **E. 1437. (1.)**

[**Nov. 2.**]—The Combat of Love and Friendship. A comedy. [In verse and prose.] By Robert Mead. pp. 75. *Printed for M. M. G. Bedell and T. Collins.* (2 Nov.) **E. 715. (23.)**

[**Nov. 3.**]—The Holy Lives of God's Prophets. By J. H. [With an engraved frontispiece representing Job.] pp. 123. *Printed for Wil. Hope.* (3 Nov.) **E. 1493. (1.)**

Nov. 4.—An Act for Redress of Delays and Mischiefs arising by Writs of Error, etc. *Printed by John Field.* **E. 1062. (22.)**

Nov. 4.—An Act concerning the Determination of several Claims now depending before the Commissioners for Removing Obstructions. *Printed by John Field.* **E. 1062. (24.)**

Nov. 4.—An Act for repealing of a branch of a certain Act of the late Parliament entituled : An Act subscribing the Engagement. *Printed by John Field.* **E. 1062. (23.)**

1653.

[**Nov. 4.**]—Πανθεολογία, or the Summe of Practical Divinity practiz'd in the Wilderness, and delivered by our Saviour in his Sermon on the Mount. Being observations upon the fourth, fifth, sixth and seventh chapters of St. Matthew. By Tho. White. pp. 182. *Printed by A. M. for Jos. Cranford.* (4 Nov.) **E. 1466. (1.)**

[**Nov. 6.**]—Illustrissimo Domino Israeli la Gherfelt Sacræ Regiæ Majestatis Sueciæ in Angliam Legato Propempticon. [In Latin hexameters. By F. Macedo.] (6 Nov.) **E. 1069. (2.)**

Nov. 7.—The Life of Jacob Behmen. Written by Durand Hotham, 7 Nov. *Printed for H. Blunden.* **E. 1068. (6.)**

[**Nov. 7.**]—Sagrir. Or Doomes-day drawing nigh, with Thunder and Lightening to Lawyers. By John Rogers. pp. 150. *Printed by R. J. for Giles Calvert.* (7 Nov.) **E. 716. (1.)**

[**Nov. 7.**]—Dod, or Chathan. The Beloved ; or, the Bridegroom going forth for his Bride. By John Rogers. pp. 106. *Printed for R. Ibbitson.* (7 Nov.) **E. 716. (2.)**

[**Nov. 7.**]—Ohel or Beth-shemesh. A Tabernacle for the Sun : or Irenicum Evangelicum. An Idea of Church-Discipline. By John Rogers. pp. 564. [See also below : 1 Dec., E. 722. (3.)] *Printed for R. I. & G. & H. Eversden.* (7 Nov.) **E. 717.**

[**Nov. 9.**]—The Art of Logick ; or the entire body of Logick in English. By Zachary Coke. pp. 222. *Printed by Robert White for George Calvert.* (9 Nov.) **E. 1436. (2.)**

[**Nov. 10.**]—Vindiciæ Justificationis Gratuitæ. Justification without Conditions ; or the Free Justification of a Sinner explained. By W. Eyre. pp. 210. [See also below : 18 Jan., 1654, E. 736. (14.), 20 April, 1654, E. 733. (10.), 13 June, 1654, E. 741. (3.), 3 Oct., 1654, E. 234. (2.), 13 Nov., 1654, E. 817. (1.) and 10 June, 1656, E. 881. (4.)] *Printed for R. I. and are to be sold by Tho. Brewster.* (10 Nov.) **E. 718. (5.)**

[**Nov. 11.**]—The Babe of Glory breaking forth in the broken Flesh of the Saints. By William Erbery. [See also below : 29 Jan., 1654, E. 727. (11.)] *Printed by J. C. for Giles Calvert.* (11 Nov.) **E. 718. (7.)**

[**Nov. 11.**]—The North Star : or, Some Night-Light shining in North-Wales with some Darke Discoveries of the day of God approaching. By William Erbery. pp. 142. (11 Nov.) **E. 718. (8.)**

Nov. 12.—An Act for regulating the Making of Stuffs in Norfolk and Norwich. *Printed by John Field.* **E. 1062. (25.)**

Nov. 12.—[A Declaration of the Council of State, in accordance with an Act of Parliament, for the protection of all persons peaceably assembled for public worship, except Papists.] *s. sh. Printed by Henry Hil's.* **669. f. 17. (63.)**

1653.

[**Nov. 12.**]—The Secretary in Fashion. Or, an elegant and compendious way of writing all manner of Letters. Composed in French by Sr de la Serre. Newly revised and very much augmented with a collection of many choice Epistles, written by the most refined wits of France. Translated by J. M. [i.e. John Massinger. With an additional titlepage, engraved.] pp. 280. *Printed for Humphrey Moseley.* (12 Nov.) **E. 1438. (1.)**

[**Nov. 14.**]—Joannis Seldeni Vindiciae secundum integritatem existimationis suæ, per convitium de Scriptione Maris Clausi insolentius laesæ in vindiciis Maris Liberi adversus Petrum Baptistam Burgum Hagae Comitum jam nunc emissis. pp. 64. *Apud Cornelium Bee.* (14 Nov.) **E. 719. (1.)**

[**Nov. 14.**]—The Grand Prerogative of Humane Nature. Namely, the Soul's naturall or native immortality shewed by many arguments, and also defended against the rash and rude conceptions of a late presumptuous author, who hath adventured to impugne it. By G. H. [i.e. Guy Holland.] pp. 134. *Printed by Roger Daniel, and are to be sold by Anthony Williamson.* (14 Nov.) **E. 1438. (2.)**

[**Nov. 14.**]—Baptism without Bason, or, Plain Scripture-proof against Infant-Baptism. By William Kaye. *Printed by Ja. Cottrel for Rich. Moon.* (14 Nov.) **E. 715. (13.)**

[**Nov. 14.**]—The Resurrection of the Witnesses and Englands Fall from (the mystical Babylon) Rome, clearly demonstrated to be accomplished. By M. Cary, alias Rande. The second edition, much enlarged. pp. 148. [See above : 13 April, 1649, E. 550. (21.), for an answer to the first edition, which is not in the Thomason collection.] *Printed by H. Hills for R. C.* (14 Nov.) **E. 719. (2.)**

[**Nov. 14.**]—שער או פתח אל לשון הקדש. A Gate or Door to the Holy Tongue. [A Hebrew Grammar.] By William Robertson. pp. 132. *Printed by J. Flesher for Joseph Cranford.* (14 Nov.) **E. 1486. (2.)**

[**Nov. 14.**]—England's Remonstrance, or, A Word in the Ear to the scattered Members of the late Parliament. By Robert Purnel. *Printed by E. Alsop.* (14 Nov.) **E. 719. (3.)**

[**Nov. 16.**]—The Sinner's Tears, in Meditations and Prayers. By Tho. Fettiplace. [With an engraved allegorical frontispiece.] pp. 169. *Printed for Humphrey Moseley.* (16 Nov.) **E. 1529. (1.)**

Nov. 16.—Death's Alarum ; or, Security's Warning-Piece. A sermon preached in S. Dionis Back-Church at the Funerall of Mrs. Mary Smith. By Nathaniel Hardy. *Printed by J. G. for Nath. Web and Will. Grantham.* **E. 725. (4.)**

[**Nov. 17.**]—The Deputation of Angels, or, the Angell-Guardian. By Robert Dingley. *Printed by T. R. for Edw. Dod.* (17 Nov.)
E. 1505. (2.)

1653.

[**Nov. 18.**]—The Modern States-man. By G. W. [i.e. George Wither?]
pp. 263. *Printed by Henry Hills.* (18 Nov.) **E. 1542. (2.)**

[**Nov. 18.**]—Cloria and Narcissus. A delightful and new romance.
Written by an honourable person. pp. 327. *Printed by S. G. and are
to be sold by Anth. Williamson.* (18 Nov.) **E. 1437. (2.)**

[**Nov. 18.**]—The Ladies Companion, with many excellent receipts.
pp. 82. *Printed by W. Bentley for W. Shears.* (18 Nov.)
E. 1528. (2.)

[**Nov. 18.**]—Merlinus Anonymus. An Ephemeris for the year 1654.
By Raphael Desmus. *Printed by F. Neile.* (18 Nov.) **E. 1487. (1.)**

[**Nov. 18.**]—The Quakers confuted, being an Answer unto nineteen
Queries propounded by them to the Elders of the Church of Ducken-
field in Cheshire. By Samuel Eaton. pp. 79. [See also below :
13 May, 1654, E. 735. (9.)] *Printed by R. White for Thomas Brewster.*
(18 Nov.) **E. 719. (8.)**

[**Nov. 18.**]—Considerations concerning Common Fields and Inclosures,
dialoguewise digested into a Discourse between two supposed Friends,
Philopeustus and Parrhesiastes. *Printed for Abel Roper.* (18 Nov.)
E. 719. (9.)

[**Nov. 20.**]—Στερέωμα : The Establishment, or, A Discourse tending to
the setling of the minds of men about some of the chiefe Controversies
of the present times. pp. 180. *Printed by J. G. and are to be sold by
John Bartlet.* (20 Nov.) **E. 720. (1.)**

Nov. 21.—An Act for the Establishing an High Court of Justice.
Printed by John Field. **E. 1062. (26.)**

Nov. 21.—Clavis ad aperiendum Carceris Ostia, or, The High Point of
the Writ of Habeas Corpus discussed. It being the Case of Mr. John
Streater, he being committed by an Order of Parliament, 21 Nov.
Printed by James Cottrel. **E. 731. (18.)**

Nov. 21.—A Narration of the late accident in the New-Exchange,
21 and 22 Nov. Written by Don Pantaleon Sa from Newgates
Prison. [See also below : 10 Dec., 669. f. 17. (66.)] **E. 723. (14.)**

Nov. 21.—A Briefe Reply to the Narration of Don Pantaleon Sa, by
one of the sisters of the gentleman murthered on the New-Exchange.
E. 724. (9.)

[**Nov. 21.**]—The Real Presence and Spirituall of Christ in the Blessed
Sacrament proved, against the Doctrine of Transubstantiation. By Jer.
Taylor. pp. 347. *Printed by James Flesher for Richard Royston.*
(21 Nov.) **E. 1462. (1.)**

[**Nov. 22.**]—A Contemplation of Heaven : with an exercise of Love, and
a descant on the Prayer in the garden. By a Catholique Gent. [i.e.
Thomas White.] pp. 182. *Printed at Paris.* (22 Nov.) **E. 1533. (1.)**

1653.

[**Nov. 22.**]—The Discipline of Gathered Churches. Together with Spirituall Hymnes by way of Paraphrase upon the book of Canticles. [Apparently imperfect, wanting all but the hymns.] *Printed for R. Ibbitson.* (22 Nov.) **E. 1545. (1.)**

Nov. 22.—An Act for the Deafforestation, Sale and Improvement of the Forests, Lands and Hereditaments heretofore belonging to the late King, Queen and Prince. pp. 58. *Printed by John Field.*

E. 1062. (31.)

[**Nov. 22.**]—Lieut. Colonel John Lilb. tryed and cast : or, His Case and Craft discovered. pp. 164. *Printed by M. Simmons.* (22 Nov.)

E. 720. (2.)

[**Nov. 22.**]—Poems, by Francis Beaumont. pp. 208. *Printed for William Hope.* (22 Nov.) **E. 1455. (3.)**

Nov. 24.—An Act for an Assessment at the rate of £120,000 by the moneth for six moneths, from 24 Dec. to 24 June next, towards the maintenance of the Armies and Navies of this Commonwealth. pp. 77. *Printed by John Field.* **E. 1062. (32.)**

[**Nov. 24.**]—The Want of Church-Government no warrant for a total omission of the Lord's Supper. Or, a debate of this question, whether or no the Sacrament of the Lord's Supper may, according to Presbyteriall principles, be lawfully administered in an un-presbyterated Church. Whereunto is now added a reply unto Mr. Fullwood his pretended examination of the aforesaid discourse. By Henry Jeanes. pp. 336. *Printed by H. Hall for Th. Robinson : Oxford.* (24 Nov.) **E. 1494. (1.)**

[**Nov. 26.**]—Severall Papers : some of them given forth by George Fox, others by James Nayler, Ministers of the Eternall Word of God, of whom the world is not worthy and therefore doth persecute under the name of Quakers. Gathered together by A. P. [i.e. Anthony Pearson.] (26 Nov.) **E. 720. (5.)**

[**Nov. 27.**]—The Voice of Michael the Archangel to the Lord Protector for the Salvation of himself and the three Nations. Presented by Arise Evans. (27 Nov.) **E. 1480. (2.)**

[**Nov. 28.**]—Hymen's Præludia ; or, Love's Master-piece. Being the second part of that romance Cleopatra [by Gauthier de Costes]. Rendered into English by Robert Loveday. [With an engraved frontispiece.] pp. 256. *Printed by J. G. for R. Lowndes.* (28 Nov.)

E. 1459. (1.)

[**Nov. 28.**]—A Character of a Diurnal-Maker. By J. C. [i.e. John Cleveland.] (28 Nov.) **E. 720. (6.)**

[**Nov. 29.**]—[An Order of the Council of State, "that Doctor Homes have the Sole Impressions of the book lately published by him, entituled, 'The Resurrection Revealed, or The Dawning of the Day-Starre, &c.'"] *s. sh.* **669. f. 17. (64.)**

1653.

[**Nov. 29.**]—The Black and Terrible Warning Piece ; or, A Scourge to Englands Rebellion. Truly representing the horrible iniquity of the times, the dangerous proceedings of the Ranters and the holding of no Resurrection by the Shakers. *Printed for George Horton.* (29 Nov.)
E. 721. (7.)

[**Nov. 29.**]—Clavis Apocalyptica ad incudem revocata; vel, Clavis Recusa; Apocalypsis, quoad temporis supputationem, reclusa. [By William Strong. With a diagram.] (29 Nov.) **E. 1463. (2.)**

[**Nov. 29.**]—Conjectura Cabbalistica. Or, a conjectural essay of interpreting the minde of Moses, according to a Threefold Cabbala : viz. literal, philosophical, mystical, or divinely moral. By Henry More. pp. 251. *Printed by James Flesher, and are to be sold by William Morden, Bookseller in Cambridge.* (29 Nov.) **E. 1462. (2.)**

[**Nov. 29.**]—De Morbis Puerorum ; or, A Treatise of the Diseases of Children. By Robert Pemell. pp. 58. *Printed by J. Legatt for Philemon Stephens.* (29 Nov.) **E. 721. (3.)**

[**Nov. 29.**]—A Discourse touching the Spanish Monarchy. By Thomas Campanella. Translated into English [by Edmund Chilmead]. pp. 232. *Printed for Philemon Stephens.* (29 Nov.) **E. 722. (1.)**

[**Nov. 29.**]—Divinity no Enemy to Astrology. By T. S. [i.e. Thomas Swadlin.] *Printed by J. G. for Nathaniel Brooke.* (29 Nov.) **E. 721. (1.)**

[**Nov. 29.**]—A History of New-England, from the English planting in 1628 untill 1652. [By Edward Johnson.] pp. 236. *Printed for Nath. Brooke.* (29 Nov.) **E. 721. (4.)**

[**Nov. 29.**]—Lux in Tenebris. Or, A Clavis to the Treasury in Broad Street. [By Thomas Fauntleroy. An attack on the Commissioners of Excise.] *Printed for Francis Tyton.* (29 Nov.) **E. 721. (5.)**

[**Nov. 29.**]—Tractatus de facultatibus Simplicium. The second part of the Treatise of the nature and qualitie of such Physical Simples as are most frequently used in Medicines. By Robert Pemell. *Printed by J. Legatt for Philemon Stephens.* (29 Nov.) **E. 721. (2.)**

[**Nov. 29.**]—A Treatise of Spirituall Infatuation, being the present visible Disease of the English Nation. Delivered in several Sermons at the Hague, by W. Stampe. pp. 215. *Printed by Sam. Brown : Haguæ.* (29 Nov.) **E. 1545. (2.)**

[**Nov. 30.**]—A Brief Anatomie of Women, being an invective against, and apologie for, the Bad and Good of that sexe. *Printed by E. Alsop.* (30 Nov.) **E. 722. (2.)**

Nov.—Mercies for Men : prepared in, and by, Christ even for such as neither know them nor him. A discourse delivered at the Munday meetings at Black Friers. By Thomas Moor, junior. pp. 144. *Printed by R. I.* **E. 744. (1.)**

1653.

[**Dec. 1.**]—Bethshemesh Clouded; or, Some Animadversions on the Rabbinical Talmud of Rabbi John Rogers, called his Tabernacle for the Sunne. By Zach. Crofton. pp. 231. [See above: 7 Nov., E. 717.] *Printed by A. M. for Joseph Crauford.* (1 Dec.) **E. 722. (3.)**

[**Dec. 2.**]—A Letter or Word of Advice to the Saints, known or unknown. By Thomas Hickes the elder. [A pamphlet upon Infant Baptism and the Lord's Supper.] (2 Dec.) **E. 723. (1.)**

Dec. 3.—An Act for constituting Commissioners for ordering and managing the Affairs of the Admiralty and Navy. *s. sh. Printed by John Field.* **669. f. 17. (65.)**

[**Dec. 3.**]—Nathans Parable. Sins Discovery, with its Filthy Secret lurking in the brest of Men. By Edmund Chillenden. (3 Dec.) **E. 723. (3.)**

[**Dec. 4.**]—The Tryal of Spirits both in Teachers & Hearers. Wherein is held forth the certain downfal of the Antichristian Clergie of these nations. By William Dell. Whereunto is added, a Confutation of divers errors delivered by Mr. Sydrach Simpson in a sermon preached the last commencement there. 3 pt. *Printed for Giles Calvert.* (4 Dec.) **E. 723. (4.)**

[**Dec. 5.**]—Two brief Meditations. I. Of Magnanimitie under Crosses. II. Of Acquaintance with God. By E. W. [i.e. Edward Waterhouse.] 2 pt. *Printed by Thomas Maxey.* (5 Dec.) **E. 1461. (1.)**

[**Dec. 7.**]—Dissertatio de Pace, &c. Or, a discourse touching the Peace & Concord of the Church. Wherein is argued that not so much a bad Opinion, as a bad Life, excludes a Christian out of the kingdom of heaven. pp. 68. *Printed by Ja: Cottrel for Rich. Moone.* (7 Dec.) **E. 1495. (1.)**

[**Dec. 8.**]—A Discovery of Charity Mistaken; or, Some Reasons against Committees forcing the Parliaments plundered Ministers to pay fifth parts to Sequestred Ministers Wives and Children. [Signed: R. Williamson.] *Printed at the desire of a Friend.* (8 Dec.) **E. 723. (10.)**

[**Dec. 9.**]—A Treatise of Adhering to God, written by Albert the Great, Bishop of Ratisbon; put into English by Sir Kenelme Digby. pp. 139. *Printed for Henry Herringman.* (9 Dec.) **E. 1529. (2.)**

[**Dec. 9.**]—To Sir Kenelme Digby, upon his two incomparable Treatises of Philosophy. [Verses, by John Sergeant.] (9 Dec.) **E. 723. (11.)**

Dec. 10.—A Declaration of the Council of State with reference to " the tumultuous and barbarous actings at the New Exchange upon the 21 and 22 of November last." [See above: 21 Nov., E. 723. (14.)] *s. sh. Printed by Henry Hills.* **669. f. 17. (66.)**

[**Dec. 10.**]—The Bloudy Vision of John Farley, interpreted by Arise Evans. With another vision signifying peace and happiness. Also a

1653.

refutation of a pamphlet lately published by one Aspinwall, called, A brief Description of the fifth Monarchy. pp. 72. [See above : 1 Aug. E. 708. (8.)] (10 Dec.) **E. 1498. (1.)**

[Dec. 11.]—A Banquet of Essayes, fetcht out of Famous Owens Confectionary, disht out and serv'd up at the Table of Mecœnas. By Henry Harflete. pp. 86. *Printed by T. R. & E. M. and are to be sold by Joseph Barber.* (11 Dec.) **E. 1504. (1.)**

Dec. 12.—An Exact Relation of the Proceedings and Transactions of the late Parliament, dissolved 12 Dec. By L. D. *Printed for Livewell Chapman.* **E. 729. (6.)**

Dec. 12.—A True Narrative of the Cause and Manner of the Dissolution of the late Parliament. By a Member of the House then present.

E. 724. (11.)

Dec. 12.—An Answer to a Paper entituled A True Narrative of the cause and manner of the Dissolution of the late Parliament. *Printed by T. N. for G. Calvert.* **E. 725. (20.)**

[Dec. 12.]—Water-Dipping no Firm Footing for Church-Communion. Proving it necessary for persons baptized after the new mode of Dipping to continue Communion with those Churches of which they were Members before the said Dipping. By John Goodwin. pp. 90. *Printed by J. M. for Henry Cripps and Lodowick Lloyd.* (12 Dec.) **E. 723. (15.)**

[Dec. 12.]—A New Plea for the Old Law [i.e. the Common Law of England]. By Albertus Warren. *Printed by T. R., for Henry Twyford.* (12 Dec.) **E. 724. (1.)**

[Dec. 13.]—Some Modest and Sober Considerations about Tythes. *Printed by Peter Cole.* (13 Dec.) **E. 1456. (1.)**

[Dec. 13.]—The Copy-Holders Plea against the Excess of Fines. *Printed by Peter Cole.* (13 Dec.) **E. 724. (4.)**

[Dec. 15.]—A False Jew ; or, A wonderfull discovery of a Scot [Thomas Ramsey], baptized at London for a Christian, circumcised at Rome to act a Jew, re-baptized at Hexham for a Believer, but found out at Newcastle to be a Cheat. [See also below : 16 Jan. 1654, E. 726. (8.)] *Printed for Richard Tomlins.* (15 Dec.) **E. 724. (6.)**

Dec. 16.—By the Council. [A Proclamation, declaring the Government by a Lord Protector and successive triennial Parliaments to be established, and Oliver Cromwell to be Lord Protector.] *s. sh. Printed by Henry Hills.* **669. f. 17. (67.)**

Dec. 16.—The Government of the Common-wealth as it was publickly declared at Westminster. *Printed by William Du-Gard and Henry Hills.* **E. 1063. (37.)**

Dec. 16.—The Articles signed by His Highness Oliver Cromwel, Lord Protector of the Commonwealth of England, Scotland and Ireland. *s. sh. Printed for G. Horton.* **669. f. 17. (72.)**

II.   E

1653.

Dec. 16.—The Articles. [A MS. copy, in Thomason's hand of the preceding.] *s. sh.* **669. f. 17. (73.)**

Dec. 16.—A Declaration concerning the Government of the Three Nations by the Lord Protector Cromwell. And his speech to the Lord Commissioners of the Broad Seal of England ; with the Oath taken by his Highness. *Printed by R. Wood.* **E. 725. (2.)**

[**Dec. 16.**]—The Peace-Maker. Being a letter from J. W. in London to N. C. in Holland, wherein is set forth the state of the last Treatie. *Printed by M. Simmons.* (16 Dec.) **E. 724. (7.)**

Dec. 16.—A Shock of Corn coming in its Season. A sermon preached at the Funeral of William Gouge. By William Jenkyn. [With an engraved frontispiece.] *Printed for Samuel Gellibrand.* **E. 735. (22.)**

Dec. 19.—A Remonstrance to the Creditors of the Commonwealth of England, concerning the Publique Debts of the Nation. [By Samuel Chidley.] *s. sh.* **669. f. 17. (68.)**

[**Dec. 19.**]—Truth's Defence against the Refined Subtilty of the Serpent. By George Fox and Richard Hubberthorn. pp. 107. *Printed for Tho. Ways.* (19 Dec.) **E. 724. (12.)**

[**Dec. 19.**]—Bartholomæi Wegelini de Obedientia Christi perfecta disputatio theologica. Una cum Theologi Angli cujusdam [i.e. Thomas Gataker] stricturis. *Excudebat J. C. & prostant venales apud Gulielmum Ley.* (19 Dec.) **E. 1486. (3.)**

[**Dec. 19.**]—The Temples Foundation laid ; or, A Way for Setlement of Religion. By M. T. *Printed by G. D. for Giles Calvert.* (19 Dec.) **E. 724. (13.)**

[**Dec. 19.**]—Academiarum Examen ; or, The Examination of Academies ; wherein is examined the matter, method and customes of Academick and Scholastick Learning. By Jo. Webster. pp. 110. [See also below : 26 May, 1654, E. 738. (5.)] *Printed for Giles Calvert.* (19 Dec.) **E. 724. (14.)**

[**Dec. 20.**]—Lillies Banquet : or, the Star-Gazers Feast, with the manner and order how every dish is to be placed upon his great table at Christmas, for all sects and sorts of persons. [A satire, in verse, With a woodcut representing an owl, dressed as a doctor, writing in a book.] *s. sh. Printed for R. Eels.* (20 Dec.) **669. f. 17. (69.)**

Dec. 21.—By the Lord Protector. A Proclamation of his Highnes, for continuing all persons being in office for the execution of publike justice at the time of the late change of Government, until his Highnes further direction. *s. sh. Printed by Henry Hills.* **669. f. 17. (70.)**

[**Dec. 21.**]—The Mad-Merry Merlin ; or, The Black Almanack. [A satire.] *Printed for G. H.* (21 Dec.) **E. 725. (1.)**

[**Dec. 21.**]—Newes coming up out of the North sounding towards the South. A warning to England the Nations elsewhere the terrible Day

1653.

of the Lord is appearing. [By George Fox.] *Printed for Giles Calvert.* (21 Dec.) **E. 725. (5.)**

[**Dec. 22.**]—Algebra: or, The Doctrine of Composing, Inferring and Resolving an Equation. By Rich: Balam. pp. 160. *Printed by J. G. for R. Boydell.* (22 Dec.) **E. 1543. (1.)**

Dec. 22.—Θανατοκτασία, or Death Disarmed. A sermon preached at St. Maries in Cambridge, at the publich Funerale of Dr. Hill, late Master of Trinity Colledge. By Anthony Tuckney. pp. 175. *Printed for J. Rothwell.* **E. 1508. (2.)**

—— [Another edition.] *Printed for J. Rothwel and S. Gellibrand.*
E. 1523. (2.)

[**Dec. 22.**]—Σνγκρητισμός. Or, Dis-satisfaction Satisfied. In seventeen Queries tending to satisfie the scruples of persons dis-satisfied about the late Revolution of Government in the Common-Wealth. By J. G. [i.e. John Goodwin.] *Printed by J. Macock for H. Cripps and L. Lloyd.* (22 Dec.) **E. 725. (7.)**

Dec. 23.—The First New Persecution; or, A true narrative of the cruel usage of two Christians [Quakers] by the Mayor of Cambridge [William Pickering]. *Printed for G. Calvert.* **E. 725. (19.)**

[**Dec. 23.**]—The two grand Ingrossers of Coles, viz. the Wood-monger and the Chandler. In a dialogue expressing their cruell raising the price of Coales. *Printed for John Harrison.* (23 Dec.) **E. 725. (8.)**

[**Dec. 23.**]—A Cryer in the Wildernesse of England, declaring the Baptisme of the eternal Spirit to be the onely Baptisme in Christ's Kingdome. By Edward Punch. pp. 85. *Printed by T. M. for Richard Moone.* (Dec. 23.) **E. 725. (7*.)**

Dec. 24.—An Ordinance for Continuing the Excise. *Printed by Henry Hills.* **E. 1063. (33.)**

Dec. 24.—An Ordinance for Continuation of one Act of Parliament entituled, An Act for Redemption of Captives. *Printed by Henry Hills.* **E. 1063. (34.)**

Dec. 24.—An Ordinance for the Reviving of an Act of Parliament entituled, An Act for Probate of Wills and Granting Administrations. *Printed by Henry Hills.* **E. 1063. (35.)**

Dec. 25.—A Man-Child born, or God manifested in the Flesh. Delivered in a sermon at Giles Cripplegate, London. By Richard Coppin. *Printed and are to be sold by William Larner and Richard Moon.* **E. 745. (1.)**

Dec. 26.—An Ordinance for alteration of several Names and Forms heretofore used in Courts, &c. *Printed by Henry Hills.* **E. 1063. (36.)**

Dec. 29.—An Ordinance appointing Commissioners for the better ordering and bringing in the Duty of Excize. *Printed by William Du-Gard and Henry Hills.* **E. 1063. (38.)**

1653.

[**Dec. 30.**]—A Christian and Brotherly Exhortation to Peace, directed unto the Soverain States of England and the Netherlands. *Printed for Richard Wodenothe.* **E. 725. (14.)**

Dec. 31.—An Ordinance for Continuing the Powers of Commissioners for Compounding, &c. *Printed by William Du-Gard and Henry Hills.* **E. 1063. (39.)**

[**Dec.**]—To His Highnesse Lord General Cromwell, Lord Protector, &c. The humble Cautionary Proposals of John Rogers, Minister of the Gospel. *s. sh.* **669. f. 17. (71.)**

[**Dec.**]—[An Advertisement of a Professor of "Astrology and Physick," in Eagle and Childe Alley, Shoe Lane.] *s. sh.* **E. 723. (5.)**

To the following no date, except that of the year, can be assigned.

1653.—A true and perfect Narrative of the several proceedings in the case concerning the Lord Craven, before the Commissioners for Sequestrations and Compositions, the Council of State, the Parliament (6 March, 1650): and upon the indictment of perjury preferred and found (20 May, 1653) against Major Richard Faulconer, the single and material witness against the Lord Craven, concerning the petition to the King of Scots. [The preface is signed: "Anth. Craven."] *Printed by R. White.* **E. 1071. (1.)**

1653.—The Lord Craven's Case as to the confiscation and sale of his estate by judgment of Parliament, related and argued and objections answered, on the behalf of the Commonwealth. Together with a short examination of a certain pamphlet, intituled, A true and perfect Narrative of the several proceedings in the case concerning the Lord Craven, &c. *Printed by William DuGard.* **E. 1071. (2.)**

1653.—A Reply to a certain Pamphlet written by an unknowing and unknown author, who take upon him to answer the True and perfect narrative of the Several proceedings concerning the Lord Craven. *Printed by R. White.* **E. 1071. (3.)**

1653.—The Answer of the Corporation of Moniers in the Mint to two false Libells [by Peter Blondeau] printed at London. **E. 1070. (2.)**

1653.—A True Narrative of some Remarkable Proceedings concerning the Ships Samson, Salvador and George, and several other Prize-ships, depending in the High Court of Admiraltie. By Thomas Violet. pp. 114. *Printed by William Du-Gard.* **E. 1070. (3.)**

1653.—Lyra Prophetica Davidis Regis; sive, Analysis critico-practica Psalmorum. Studio Victorini Bythneri. *Typis Jacobi Flesher, prostat apud Cornelium Bee.* **E. 478.**

1654.

[**Jan. 2.**]—A Confutation of the Assertions of Mr. Samuel Oates, in relation to his not practising the laying on of hands on all baptized Believers. By John Spittlehouse. *Printed for Richard Moone.* (2 Jan.)
E. 725. (15.)

[**Jan. 4.**]—The Authority of God over Men in the Law, cleared. Shewing that its no persecution for the Magistrate as Jehovah's deputy to enforce it on the people. By John Brayne. *Printed for Rich. Moone.* (4 Jan.)
E. 725. (17.)

[**Jan. 4.**]—A Woe against the Magistrates, Priests and People of Kendall in Westmerland. Also the Stumbling-block removed from weak mindes who are offended at the Quakers. [By Francis Howgill.] (4 Jan.)
E. 725. (18.)

[**Jan. 5.**]—Divine and moral Speculations, in metrical numbers, upon various subjects. By Dr. R. Aylet. 4 pt. *Printed for Abel Roper.* (5 Jan.)
E. 1439.

[**Jan. 5.**]—A Treatise of the High Rebellion of Man against God in Blasphemy. With an examination of an Ordinance made by the Lords, and an Act made by the late Parliament, against the same. By John Brayne. *Printed for Richard Moon.* (5 Jan.)
E. 725. (22.)

Jan. 7.—The Cry of a Stone; or, A Relation of something spoken in Whitehall by Anna Trapnel, being in the Visions of God, 7 to 19 Jan. pp. 76.
E. 730. (3.)

Jan. 9.—An Olive-Leaf; or, Some peaceable considerations to the Christian Meeting at Christs-Church in London, 9 Jan. By William Erbery. *Printed by J. Cottrel.*
E. 726. (5.)

[**Jan. 12.**]—Festorum Metropolis. The Metropolitane Feast, or the Birthday of our Saviour Jesus Christ, annually to be kept holy by them that call upon him, proved by Scriptures. By Allan Blayney. The second edition, refined. pp. 119. *Printed by T. M. for Steven Chatfield.* (12 Jan.)
E. 1493. (2.)

[**Jan. 14.**]—The perfect Pharise under Monkish Holines, opposing the fundamental principles of the Doctrine of the Gospel manifesting himself in the generation of men called Quakers. Published by Thomas Weld, Rich. Prideaux [and others], Ministers in Newcastle. pp. 51. [See also below: 9 May, E. 735. (2.), & 3 June, E. 738. (16.)] *Printed for Richard Tomlins.* (14 Jan.)
E. 726. (7.)

[**Jan 15.**]—The Blessed Birth-Day celebrated in some Meditations. [In verse.] By Charles Fitz-Geffry. *Printed by T. M. for Stephen Chatfield.* (15 Jan.)
E. 1481. (3.)

Jan. 16.—An Order by the Commissioners of the Admiralty and Navy, concerning the payment of the Prize-money due to Seamen and Souldiers,

1654.

and their Widows, that have served at sea in this last years expedition. *s. sh. Printed for Laurence Blaiklock and T. Hewer.* **669. f. 17. (74.)**

[**Jan. 16.**]—Banners of Love displaied over the Church of Christ, walking in the Order of the Gospel at Hexham, against the Jesuitical Design lately attempted by the false Jew [Joseph Ben Israel]. An Answer, [by Thomas Tillam], to a Narrative stuff'd with Untruths, by four Newcastle Gentlemen. [See above: 15 Dec., 1653, E. 724. (6.)] *Printed by Henry Hills.* (16 Jan.) **E. 726. (8.)**

[**Jan. 18.**]—Confusion Confounded. Wherein is considered the Reasons of the Resignation of the late Parliament and the establishment of a Lord Protector. *Printed by Henry Hills.* (18 Jan.) **E. 726. (11.)**

[**Jan. 18.**]—The Grand Catastrophe; or, the Change of Government. By Johannes Cornubiensis. *Printed by R. I.* (18 Jan.) **E. 726. (12.)**

[**Jan. 18.**]—Richard Baxter's Admonition to Mr. William Eyre of Salisbury concerning his miscarriages in a book lately written for the Justification of Infidals against Benjamin Woodbridge, James Cranford and the Author. [See above: 10 Nov., 1653, E. 718. (5.)] *Printed by A. M. for Thomas Underhill.* (18 Jan.) **E. 726. (14.)**

[**Jan. 18.**]—A True Prophecy of the Mighty Day of the Lord which is appeared in the North of England. By William Deusbery, Quaker. *Printed for Giles Calvert.* (18 Jan.) **E. 726. (15.)**

[**Jan. 18.**]—A Woman forbidden to speak in the Church. The Truth cleared and the ignorance both of Priests and Peeple discovered. By Richard Farneworth [a Quaker]. *Printed for Giles Calvert.* (18 Jan.) **E. 726. (16.)**

Jan. 19.—An Ordinance for Repealing of several Acts touching the subscribing or taking the Engagement. *Printed by William Du-Gard and Henry Hills.* **E. 1063. (40.)**

[**Jan. 19.**]—An Ordinance declaring that the Offences herein mentioned, and no other, shall be adjudged High Treason within the Common-Wealth. *Printed by William Du-Gard and Henry Hills.* **E. 1063. (41.)**

[**Jan. 24.**]—Dianea: an excellent new romance. Written in Italian by Gio. Francisco Loredano. Translated by Sir Aston Cokaine. pp. 367. *Printed for Humphrey Moseley.* (24 Jan.) **E. 1452. (1.)**

[**Jan. 24.**]—A Lost Ordinance Restored; or, Eight Questions in reference to the Laying On of Hands answered, by John More. *Printed for Richard Moone.* (24 Jan.) **E. 727. (1.)**

[**Jan. 24.**]—The Wise Virgin, or, A wonderfull Narration of a Childe of eleven years of age, when stricken dumb deaf and blinde, yet was heard to utter glorious Truths concerning Christ, Faith and other subjects. Her name is Martha Hatfield. By James Fisher. pp. 150. *Printed for John Rothwell.* (24 Jan.) **E. 1510. (2.)**

1654.

[**Jan. 24.**]—Ζωοτομία ; or, Observations on the present Manners of the English, briefly anatomizing the Living by the Dead. By Richard Whitlock. pp. 568. *Printed by Tho. Roycroft & are to be sold by Humphrey Moseley.* (24 Jan.)   **E. 1478. (2.)**

[**Jan. 25.**]—De baptismatis infantilis vi & efficacia disceptatio, privatim habita inter Samuelem Ward et Thomam Gatakerum. pp. 271. *Typis Rogeri Danielis.* (25 Jan.)   **E. 1436. (1.)**

[**Jan. 26.**]—The Names of all the Dukes, Marquesses, Earls, Viscounts & Barons in England Scotland & Ireland, in and since the raign of Queen Elizabeth, to this year 1653. By John Taylor. (26 Jan.)   **E. 1463. (1.)**

Jan. 28.—An Ordinance appointing a Committee for the Army, and Treasurers at War. *Printed by William Du-Gard and Henry Hills.*   **E. 1063. (42.)**

Jan. 28.—[An Ordinance concerning certain details of the Monthly Assessment.] *Printed by William Du-Gard and Henry Hills.*   **E. 1063. (43.)**

[**Jan. 28.**]—Churches gathered against Christ and his Kingdom. By James Nayler. *Printed for Giles Calvert.* (28 Jan.) **E. 727. (10.)**

[**Jan. 29.**]—The Academie of Eloquence. Containing a compleat English Rhetorique. By Tho. Blount. [With an engraved frontispiece, bearing portraits of Lord Bacon and Sir Philip Sidney.] pp. 232. *Printed by T. N. for Humphrey Moseley.* (29 Jan.)   **E. 1526.**

Jan. 29.—Proh Tempora ! Proh Mores ! or, An unfained Caveat to all True Protestants not in any case to touch any of these three Serpents ; viz. Mr. Erbery's Babe of Glory, The Mad-mans Plea, Mr. Christopher Feakes Exhortations. By J. N., a Mechanick. [See above : 11 Nov., 1653, E. 718. (7.)] *Printed by T. N.* (29 Jan.) **E. 727. (11.)**

[**Jan. 30.**]—A Return to the Priests about Beverley for their Advisement. [An answer to "A Faithful Discovery of a treacherous Design of Mystical Antichrist," by J. Kellet and others. See above : 12 June, 1653, E. 699. (13.)] (30 Jan.)   **E. 727. (12.)**

[**Jan. 30.**]—Strena Vavasoriensis. A New-Years-Gift for the Welch Itinerants ; or, A Hue and Cry after Mr. Vavasor Powell. [By Alexander Griffith.] *Printed by F. L.* (30 Jan.) **E. 727. (14.)**

[**Jan. 30.**]—The Lady Pecunia's Journey unto Hell, with her speech to Pluto, maintaining that she sends more Soules to Hell than all his Fiends. With Pluto's answer and applause. [A satire, in verse, by Humphrey Crouch. With two woodcuts.] *s. sh. Printed for John Clarke.* (30 Jan.)   **669. f. 17. (75.)**

[**Feb. 1.**]—The Lord's Prayer unclasped : with a vindication of it against all Hereticks cal'd Enthusiasts. By James Harwood. pp. 328.

1654.

Printed for the Author, and are to be sold by G. and H. Eversden.
(1 Feb.)   **E. 1497. (1.)**

[**Feb. 2.**]—The Survey of Policy ; or, A Free Vindication of the Commonwealth of England against Salmasius and other Royallists.   By Peter
English.   pp. 191.   *Printed at Leith.*   (2 Feb.)   **E. 727. (17.)**

[**Feb. 7.**]—Jus Divinum Ministerii Evangelici ; or, The Divine Right
of the Gospel-Ministry.   Published by the Provincial Assembly of
London.   2 pt.   *Printed for G. Latham, J. Rothwell, S. Gellibrand,
T. Underhill, and J. Cranford.*   (7 Feb.)   **E. 728 (1.)**

[**Feb. 8.**]—Mr. Recorders Speech to the Lord Protector, 8 Feb., being
the day of His Highnesse Entertainment in London.   *Printed by R. I.
for Mathew Walbancke.*   **E. 729. (2.)**

[**Feb. 8.**]—A True State of the Case of the Commonwealth, in reference
to the late established Government by a Lord Protector and a Parliament.   pp. 52.   *Printed by Tho. Newcomb.*   (8 Feb.)   **E. 728. (5.)**

[**Feb. 9.**]—The Declaration of Arise Evans, from his study in the Black
Fryars, concerning his Highness the Lord Protector, and the Government of the three nations of England, Scotland and Ireland.   With his
prophetick proposals touching Mr. Feak and Mr. Simpson and the rest
of the Independent party.   *Printed for G. Convert.*   (9 Feb.)
                                                           E. 224. (1.)

Feb. 10.—An Ordinance for the better ordering and disposing the
Estates under Sequestration.   *Printed by William Du-Gard and Henry
Hills.*   **E. 1063. (44.)**

[**Feb. 10.**]—The Essence, Quintessence, Insence, Innocence, Lye-sence, &
Magnifisence of Nonsence upon Sence : or Sence upon Nonsence.   By
John Taylor.   [In verse.]   (10 Feb.)   **E. 1465. (1.)**

[**Feb. 13.**]—Protection perswading Subjection.   Proving His Highness
to be the aptest person for place of Lord Protector.   By E. M., Esq.
Printed by Henry Hills.   (13 Feb.)   **E. 729. (4.)**

[**Feb. 13.**]—Animal Cornutum, or the Horn'd Beast.   Wherein is contained a brief method of the grounds of Astrology ; whereunto is
annexed an examination of a spurious pamphlet [by J. Brayne], intituled
Astrology proved to be the Doctrine of Dæmons.   By J. Gadbury.
12 pt.   *Printed for William Larnar.*   (13 Feb.)   **E. 1495. (2.)**

[**Feb. 13.**]—Διατριβὴ περὶ Παιδο-βαπτισμοῦ.   Or, A Consideration of Infant
Baptism, wherein are many things of Mr. Tombes about it answered.
Together with a digression in answer to Mr. Kendall.   By J. H.
[i.e. John Horne.]   pp. 160.   [See above : 28 Nov., 1652, E. 682. (3.)]
Printed by J. M. for H. Cripps and L. Lloyd.   (13 Feb.)   **E. 729. (3.)**

Feb. 14.—A full and perfect Relation of the Great Plot [of Thomas
Dutton and others] against the Lord Protector [discovered 14 Feb.].
Printed for G. Horton.   **E. 730. (1.)**

1654.

[Feb. 14.]—A Treasonable Plot discovered. The names of those that are taken and sent prisoners to the Tower. [Thomas Dutton, and eleven others.] (14 Feb.) *Printed by Robert Ibbitson.* **E. 730. (2.)**

[Feb. 14.]—The Discovery of Mans Returne to his First Estate by the operation of the Power of God in the great work of Regeneration. By William Densbury [Dewsbury]. *Printed for Giles Calvert.* (14 Feb.)
E. 729. (7.)

[Feb. 14.]—Light Risen out of Darkness. Wherein something is written in reply to a book set forth by the dry and night Vines in and about Beverley, who nicknameth the People of God and calleth them Quakers [i.e. "A Faithful Discovery," by Joseph Kellet and others]. By Richard Farnworth. pp. 59. [See above : 12 June, 1653, E. 699. (13.)] *Printed for Giles Calvert.* (14 Feb.) **E. 729. (5.)**

[Feb. 14.]—The Man of Peace ; or, The Glorious appearance of the great God in his People, rising as a Man of War, to waste the Assyrian ; that is, the Mighty Oppressor. By William Erbery. *Printed by James Cottrel.* (14 Feb.) **E. 729. (11.)**

[Feb. 14.]—A Twofold Catechism : the one simply called, A Scripture-Catechism, the other, A Brief Scripture-Catechism for Children. By John Biddle. pp. 175. *Printed by J. Cottrel for R. Moone.* (14 Feb.)
E. 1473. (2.)

[Feb. 14.]—White Salt : or, A Sober Correction of a Mad World in some Wel-wishes to Goodness. By John Sherman. pp. 242. *Printed by E. Cotes for R. Royston.* (14 Feb.) **E. 1517.**

[Feb. 15.]—The great and bloody Visions interpreted by Arise Evans. Foretelling the establishing of a glorious government under His Highness the Protector, likewise the restoring of the Churches. *Printed for G. Convert.* (15 Feb.) **E. 224. (2.)**

[Feb. 16.]—Look about you : or a Groatsworth of good Councel for a Peny : being a variety of Councels, Cautions and Directions. *s. sh. Printed for G. Horton.* (16 Feb.) **669. f. 17. (76.)**

Feb. 17.—An Ordinance touching the Levying of the latter Three Months Assessment appointed by an Act of the late Parliament. *Printed by William Du-Gard and Henry Hills.* **E. 1063. (45.)**

Feb. 17.—An Ordinance of Explanation touching Treasons. *s. sh. Printed by William Du-Gard and Henry Hills.* **669. f. 17. (77.)**

[Feb. 17.]—The certain Travailes of an uncertain Journey, begun on Tuesday, 9 Aug. and ended on Saturday, 3 Sept. following, 1653. By John Taylor. [In verse.] (17 Feb.) **E. 1434. (1.)**

[Feb. 20.]—King Charls his Starre ; or, Astrologie defined, and defended by Scripture. By $\odot$ 4 $\underline{1000}$ IS A' $\underline{10}$ 2 [i.e. Arise Evans]. (20 Feb.)
E. 1482. (3.)

1654.

[Feb. 21.]—A New Catechism, short and plain. Published for the benefit of Shaffham School, Norfolk. By Geo. Dochant. (21 Feb.)

E. 1470. (2.)

[Feb. 23.]—Elliptical or Azimuthal Horologiography, comprehending severall wayes of describing Dials. By Samuel Foster. [Illustrated with woodcuts.] pp. 204. *Printed by R. & W. Leybourn, for Nicholas Bourn.* (23 Feb.)   E. 730. (7.)

[Feb. 23.]—Mrs. Shaws Innocency restored and Mr. Clendon's Calumny retorted. *Printed by T. M. for G. A.* (23 Feb.)   E. 730. (8.)

[Feb. 23.] The Song of Solomon. In meeter, as Psalm 25. *Printed by T. R. & E. M. for Ralph Smith.* (23 Feb.)   E. 1468. (1.)

Feb. 25.--Σῶμα πτῶμα, αὐτὸς ἐνιαυτός. The year running into his first Principles. A sermon intended to be preached at the funeral of Edmund Whitwell. By Philip Perrey. *Printed by W. B., for John Saywell.*   E. 729. (8.)

Feb. 27.—Collonel Morgans Letter concerning his taking the Garrison of Kildrummie from the Highlanders in Scotland. *Printed by F. Neile.*

E. 731. (6.)

[Feb. 27.]—A Discours Apologetical; wherein Lilies lewd and lowd Lies in his Merlin or Pasqil for the Yeer 1654 are cleerly laid open. By Tho. Gataker. pp. 104. *Printed for R. Ibbitson for Thomas Newberry.* (27 Feb.)   E. 731. (1.)

[Feb. 27.]—A true Representation of the state of the Bordering Customary Tenants in the North under an Oppressing Landlord. (27 Feb.)   E. 730. (12.)

Feb. 28.—An Ordinance for Reviving the Jurisdiction of the County Palatine of Lancaster. *Printed by William Du-Gard and Henry Hills.*

E. 1063. (46.)

[March 6.]—Shinkin ap Shone, her Prognostication for the ensuing Yeer, 1654. *Printed for the Author.* (6 March.)   E. 731. (5.)

March 7.—The whole manner of the Treaty, with the several Speeches that passed in the Banqueting-house at White-hall, between His highness the Lord Protector and the Embassadors of the United provinces of Holland. *Printed by T. L.*   E. 731. (14.)

[March 7.]—Generation-Work : the second part. Being an exposition of the Seven Vials, and other Apocalyptical mysteries. By J. Tillinghast. pp. 266. *Printed by R. I. for Livewell Chapman.* (7 March.)   E. 1491. (1.)

[March 8.]—A Cry of Bloud of an innocent Abel against two bloudy Cains, being a Discovery of two Cavalier Brothers Conspiracy ageinst another Brother of the Parliament Party. [By John Musgrave.] (8 March.)   E. 731. (8.)

1654.

[March 8.]—The Independants Catechism. The second edition, corrected by J. C., Gentleman. (8 March.) **E. 731. (9.)**

March 10.—Christ the Riches of the Gospel and the Hope of Christians. A sermon preached at the funerall of Mr. William Spurstow. By Simeon Ashe. *Printed by A. M. for G. Sawbridge.* **E. 744. (11.)**

[March 10.]—The New Brawle, or Turnmill-street against Rosemary Lane, being a Mock Comedy by two Actors, John Hold-my-staff and Doll Doe-little. *Printed by Nan Quiet.* (10 March.) **E. 1477. (4.)**

[March 10.]—A True Testimony of Obedience to the Heavenly Call. [By Richard Hubberthorn.] (10 March.) **E. 731. (13.)**

[March 11.]—Strange and wonderful Newes from Whitehall, or, the mighty visions proceeding from Mistris Anna Trapnel. *Printed for Robert Sele.* (11 March.) **E. 224. (3.)**

[March 14.]—The Quakers wilde Questions objected against the Ministers of the Gospel, and many sacred acts and offices of Religion. With brief answers thereunto. By R. Sherlock. pp. 156. *Printed by E. Cotes for R. Royston.* (14 March.) **E. 1495. (3.)**

[March 16.]—A Paper sent forth into the world from them that are scornfully called Quakers, declaring why they deny the Teachers of the world. [By George Fox.] *Printed by Giles Calvert.* (16 March.) **E. 731. (20.)**

March 17.—An Ordinance for Continuing the Excise. *Printed by William Du-Gard and Henry Hills.* **E. 1063. (47.)**

[March 17.]—A Few Words occasioned by a Paper lately printed, stiled A Discourse concerning the Quakers. By James Nayler. (17 March.) **E. 731. (23.)**

[March 17.]—Several Letters written to the Saints of the Most High, to build them up in the Truth. By William Deusbury, James Nayler, George Fox, John Whitehead. (17 March.) **E. 731. (22.)**

[March 17.]—Jack Pudding: or, A Minister made a Black-Pudding. Presented to Mr. R. Farmer, Parson of Nicholas Church in Bristol: by W. E. [i.e. William Erbery.] (17 March.) **E. 731. (24.)**

[March 17.]—Wit and Folly in a-maze. [In verse.] *s. sh.* *Printed for I. Moxon.* (17 March.) **669. f. 17. (78.)**

[March 18.]—Severall Circumstances to prove that Mris. Jane Berkeley and Sr. William Killigrew have combined together to defraud me of an estate. [By Richard Lygon.] (March 18.) **E. 732. (1.)**

March 20.—A Declaration of His Highness the Lord Protector, inviting the People of England and Wales to a Day of Solemn Fasting and Humiliation. Given at Whitehall. *s. sh.* *Printed by Henry Hills and William Du-Gard.* **669. f. 17. (79.)**

March 20.—An Ordinance for settling and confirming of the Mannors of Framlingham and Saxtead, and the Lands, Tenements, and Here-

1654.

ditaments thereunto belonging, devised by Sir Robert Hitcham to certain charitable uses. *Printed by Henry Hills and William Du-Gard.*

E. 1063. (54.)

March 20.—An Ordinance declaring that the proceedings in case of Murther in Ireland shall bee as formerly. *Printed by William Du-Gard and Henry Hills.* E. 1063. (52.)

March 20.—An Ordinance for Passing Custodies of Idiots and Lunaticks. *Printed by William Du-Gard and Henry Hills.* E. 1063. (51.)

March 20.—An Ordinance for Continuation of an Act intituled, An Act for laying an Imposition upon Coles towards the Building and Maintaining Ships for Guarding the Seas. *Printed by William Du-Gard and Henry Hills.* E. 1063. (50.)

March 20.—An Ordinance appointing Commissioners for Approbation of Publique Preachers. *Printed by William Du-Gard and Henry Hills.*

E. 1063. (49.)

March 20.—An Ordinance for Continuation of an Act of Parliament intituled An Act for the Continuation of the Customs. *Printed by William Du-Gard and Henry Hills.* E. 1063. (48.)

[March 20.]—An Explication and Application of the seventh Chapter of Daniel, wherein is briefly shewed the Downfall of the four Monarchies, and in particular the Beheading of Charles Stuart, who is proved to be the Little Horn. By William Aspinwall. *Printed by R. I. for Livewell Chapman.* (20 March.) E. 732. (2.)

March 23.—An Ordinance for continuing an Act for Impressing of Seamen. *Printed by William Du-Gard and Henry Hills.* E. 1063. (53.)

March 23.—An Ordinance for Relief of Persons that have acted in the service of the Parliament. *Printed by William Du-Gard and Henry Hills.* E. 1063. (55.)

[March 23.]—A List of some of the Grand Blasphemers and Blasphemies, which was given in to the Committee for Religion. *s. sh.* *Printed by Robert Ibbitson.* (23 March.) 669. f. 17. (80.)

[March 24.]—Look about you now or never ; or, Two Groatsworth of good Councel for a penny. [With a woodcut.] *s. sh.* *Imprinted for G. Horton.* (24 March.) 669. f. 17. (81.)

[March 25.]—To all that would know the Way to the Kingdome. A Direction to turne your minds within. By Geo. Fox. (25 March.)

E. 732. (8.)

March 26.—A Treatise of Humilitie. Published by E. D., Parson sequestred. pp. 241. *Printed for Thomas Johnson.* 26 March.

E. 1544. (2.)

[March 28.]—Declarations, Counts and Pleadings in English. The second part ; being the authentique forme of Presidents in the Court of Common Pleas. Collected by Richard Brownlow. [With an

1654.

engraved portrait of the author.] pp. 495. *Printed for Matthew Walbancke and John Place.* (28 March.) **E. 226.**

[**March 30.**]—Vavasoris Examen & Purgamen : or, Mr. Vavasor Powells Impartiall Triall : who hath appealed to God and his Country and is found Not Guilty. Published by Edward Allen, John Griffith, etc. *Printed for Thomas Brewster and Livewell Chapman* (30 March.)
E. 732. (12.)

[**March 30.**]—A Warning to all in this proud City called London to call them to Repentance. [By George Fox.] *s. sh.* (30 March.)
669. f. 17. (82.)

March 31.—An Ordinance for Suspending the proceedings of the Judges named in the Act intituled An Act for the Relief of Creditors and Poor Prisoners. *Printed by William Du-Gard and Henry Hills.*
E. 1063. (56.)

March 31.—An Ordinance prohibiting Cock-Matches. *Printed by William Du-Gard and Henry Hills.* **E. 1063. (57.)**

March 31.—An Ordinance for Better Amending and Keeping in Repair the Common High-Waies within this Nation. *Printed by William Du-Gard and Henry Hills.* **E. 1063. (59.)**

[**March 31.**]—Truth will never shame its Master. [An address to Cromwell, in verse.] By John Paine. (31 March.) **E. 732. (14.)**

[**April 1.**]—The Idol of the Clownes, or Insurrection of Wat the Tyler. [By John Cleveland.] pp. 148. (1 April.) **C. 31. a. 41. (2.)**

April 3.—An Ordinance for continuing one Act of Parliament entituled An Act for Probate of Wills, etc. *Printed by William Du-Gard and Henry Hills.* **E. 1063. (58.)**

April 5.—Articuli Pacis, Unionis & Confoederationis inter Olivarium, Dominum Protectorem Reipub. Angliæ ab una, et Ordines Generales Foederatarum Belgii Provinciarum ab altera parte, conclusæ. *Typis Guil. Du-Gard & Hen. Hills.* **E. 738. (19.)**

April 5.—Articles of Peace agreed between Oliver Lord Protector of the Commonwealth of England, Scotland and Ireland, and the States General of the United Provinces of the Netherlands. *Printed by William Du-Gard and Henry Hills.* **E. 1063. (68.)**

April 5.—The Articles of the Perpetual Peace concluded between the Common-wealth on the one Part and the States-General on the other Part. Translated out of the Dutch copie. **E. 734. (4.)**

April 5.—A Brief Narration of the Examination of George Bateman upon a charge laid against him by Henry Eddan and others. With the sentence of the Bench. **E. 735. (7.)**

April 6.—An Ordinance for adjourning part of Easter Term. *s. sh.* [See also below : 8 April, 669. f. 17. (84.)] *Printed by Henry Hills and William du-Gard.* **669. f. 17. (83.)**

1654.

[April 6.]—A Declaration concerning State-Farthings; or, Certain Remonstrative Reasons for the allowance thereof. By Thomas Dunstervile. *Imprinted for the Author.* (6 April.)   **E. 732. (18.)**

April 7.—Some Queries returned to the Author of the late Declaration, inviting the good people of the Land to humiliation, 7 April. [See above : 20 March, 669. f. 17. (79.)]   **E. 738. (3.)**

April 8.—An Ordinance for adjourning part of Easter Term. [Ordering a further adjournment, and repealing the Ordinance of 6 April.] *s. sh. Printed by William du-Gard and Henry Hills.*   **669. f. 17. (84.)**

[April 8.]—This was the word of the Lord which John Camm and Francis Howgill was moved to declare to Oliver Cromwell. (8 April.)
          E. 732. (22.)

[April 8.]—The Trumpet of the Lord sounded and his Sword drawn, by them who are scornfully called Quakers. [By George Fox.] *Printed for Giles Calvert.* (8 April.)   **E. 732. (23.)**

[April 10.]—The Kings Censure upon Recusants that refuse the Sacrament of the Lords Supper. By Thomas Marshal. *Printed for Francis Cowles.* (10 April.)   **E. 732. (24.)**

April 11.—An Ordinance impowring Commissioners to put in execution an Act of Parliament intituled An Act Prohibiting the Planting of Tobacco in England. *Printed by William Du-Gard and Henry Hills.*
          E. 1063. (60.)

[April 11.]—Peace Protected, and Discontent Dis-armed. Wherein the seventeen Queries lately published to allay the discontents of some about the late Revolution of Government are reinforced. [By the Author of the said seventeen Queries to John Goodwin. See above : 22 Dec., 1653, E. 725. (7.)] pp. 78. *Printed by I. Macock for H. Cripps & L. Lloyd.* (11 April.)   **E. 732. (27.)**

April 12.—An Ordinance for settling of the Estates of several Excepted Persons in Scotland in Trustees. *Printed by William Du-Gard and Henry Hills.*   **E. 1063. (65.)**

April 12.—An Ordinance for uniting Scotland into one Common-Wealth with England. *Printed by William Du-Gard and Henry Hills.*
          E. 1063. (63.)

April 12.—An Ordinance for Erecting Courts Baron in Scotland. *Printed by William Du-Gard and Henry Hills.*   **E. 1063. (64.)**

April 12.—An Ordinance touching Surveyors of the High-Waies. *Printed by William Du Gard and Henry Hills.*   **E. 1063. (61.)**

April 12.—An Ordinance of Pardon and Grace to the People of Scotland. *Printed by William Du Gard and Henry Hills.*   **E. 1063. (62.)**

[April 12.]—Letters of Mounsieur de Balzac. Translated out of French into English by Sʳ Richard Baker and others. [With an engraved

1654.

title-page.] 4 pt. *Printed for John Williams & Francis Eaglesfield.*
(12 April.) **E. 1444.**

[**April 12.**]—To all the Faithful Servants of Jesus Christ, especially to such as labour in the Word through England and Wales. [A circular of the Commissioners for Approbation of Publick Preachers.] *Printed by T. R. & E. M. for Ralph Smith.* (12 April.) **E. 733. (2.)**

[**April 12.**]—The Prisoners Remonstrance, or, The Desires and Proposals of such Prisoners as are willing to pay their just Debts. *Printed by R. Wood.* (12 April.) **E. 733. (3.)**

[**April 12.**]—A True Alarm in weakness, unto Babel, from God, by his spi-right mind in the soul. By John Cole-venman. *s. sh.* (12 April.) **669. f. 17. (85.)**

[**April 13.**]—The Spirit of God in Man. By Richard Russel. *Printed by T. Lock.* (13 April.) **C. 31. a. 41. (3.)**

[**April 15.**]—The Glorie of the Lord arising, shaking terribly the Earth, and overturning all. With a word to the Heads of the Nation. By those whom the world calls Quakers. *Printed for Giles Calvert.* (15 April.) **E. 733. (6.)**

[**April 15.**]—A Warning from the Lord to the Inhabitants of Under-barrow. Also a word to my Brethren, who is by the world scornfully called Quakers. By Edward Burrough. *Printed for Giles Calvert.* (15 April.) **E. 733. (5.)**

[**April 16.**]—Cheap Riches: or, A Pocket-Companion made of five hundred Proverbiall Aphorismes. By Nathanael Church. pp. 115. *Printed for John Perry.* (16 April.) **E. 1541. (2.)**

April 18.—An Ordinance for Further Suspending the proceedings of the Judges named in an Act intituled An Act for the Relief of Creditors and Poor Prisoners. *Printed by William Du-Gard and Henry Hills.* **E. 1063. (66.)**

April 20.—A small Mite, in memory of the late deceased Mr. William Erbery, being an Acrostick on the letters of his Name and an Elegie on his death. [Signed: J. L.] **E. 1472. (2.)**

[**April 20.**]—Unbeleevers no subjects of Justification, nor of mystical Union to Christ. A sermon preached at New-Sarum, with a Vindication of it from the calumniations cast upon it by Mr. William Eyre in his Vindiciæ Justificationis. By T. Warren. pp. 255. [See above 10 Nov. 1653, E. 718. (5.)] *Printed by E. T. for John Browne.* (20 April.) **E. 733. (10.)**

April 22.—By the Council. [A notice that peace between the Commonwealth and the States General has been ratified, and will be publicly declared on the 26th April, from which time restitution is to be made of all ships taken on either side.] *s. sh. Printed by Will. du-Gard and Hen. Hills.* **669. f. 17. (86.)**

1654.

[**April 25.**]—A Brief Remonstrance touching the Pre-emption of Tyn, and the Coynages thereof. (25 April.) **E. 733. (13.)**

April 26.—By the Lord Protector. A Proclamation of the Peace made between this Common-Wealth and that of the United Provinces of the Netherlands. *s. sh. Printed by William du-Gard and Henry Hills.*

669. f. 17. (87.)

April 26.—The Speech of Collonel Malcomb Rogers at the place of Execution at Edenborough. *Printed for George Horton.* **E. 735. (6.)**

April 26.—The Bloudy Field, or, The great Engagement of the English and Scottish Forces beyond Sterling. *Imprinted for George Horton.*

E. 733. (16.)

April 27.—Oratio Serenissimi Protectoris Elogium complectens, Oxoniæ habita quinto Kalend. Maii a Joanne Harmaro. *Excudebat Henry Hall: Oxoniæ.* **E. 812. (19.)**

[**April 28.**]—Britania Triumphalis; A brief history of the Warres and other State-Affairs of Great Britain, from the Death of the late King to the Dissolution of the last Parliament. pp. 207. *Printed for Samuel Howes.* (28 April.) **E. 1487. (2.)**

[**April 29.**]—Of the Internal and Eternal Nature of Man in Christ. [MS. note by Thomason : "Written by the Earle of Pembrok."] *Printed by John Macock.* (29 April.) **E. 734. (1.)**

May 1.—By the Lord Protector. A Proclamation of His Highness concerning a Cessation of all Acts of Hostility between the Commonwealth of England and that of the United Provinces. *Printed by William Du-Gard and Henry Hills.* **E. 1063. (67.)**

[**May 3.**]—The Mystery of the two Witnesses unvailed. Together with the seaventh Trumpet, and the Kingdome of Christ explained. By John Robotham. pp. 370. *Printed by M. S. for G. and H. Eversden.* (3 May.) **E. 1469. (3.)**

May 4.—An Ordinance for Further Doubling upon and Finishing the Sale of Deans & Chapters Lands, Mannors of Rectories, Gleablands, etc. *Printed by William Du-Gard and Henry Hills.* **E. 1064. (1.)**

May 4.—An Additional Ordinance for the Excise. *Printed by William Du-Gard and Henry Hills.* **E. 1064. (2.)**

[**May 5.**]—Jus Patronatus, or, A Briefe Legal and Rational Plea for Advowsons. By William Prynne. *Printed for Edward Thomas.* (5 May.)

E. 735. (1.)

[**May 8.**]—The Greatnes of the Mystery of Godlines. Opened in severall sermons by Cuthbert Sydenham. pp. 266. *Printed by W. Hunt for Richard Tomlins.* (8 May.) **E. 1499. (1.)**

May 8.—Hear, O Earth, ye earthern men and women, etc. [A rhapsodical address "for the building the Lords Tent," signed "by me

1654.

Thean Ram Taniah, Leader of the people, named Theauraujohn. 8 May."]
s. sh. **669. f. 17. (88.)**

May 9.—By the Lord Protector. A Declaration setting apart Tuesday, 22 May, for a publique day of Thanksgiving for the Peace concluded between this Commonwealth and that of the United Provinces, and for the late seasonable Rain. *s. sh. Printed by William du-Gard and Henry Hills.* **669. f. 17. (89.)**

[**May 9.**]—The Orthodox Evangelist, or, A Treatise wherein many great Evangelical Truths are discussed and confirmed. By John Norton. pp. 355. *Printed by John Macock for Henry Cripps & Lodowick Lloyd.* (9 May.) **E. 734. (9.)**

[**May 9.**]—An Answer to the Booke [by Thomas Welde and others] called The perfect Pharisee under Monkish Holinesse. By James Nayler. [See above : 14 Jan., E. 726. (7.), and also below : 3 June, E. 738. (16.)] (9 May.) **E. 735. (2.)**

[**May 9.**]—A Discourse between Cap. Kiffin and Dr. Chamberlain about Imposition of Hands. (9 May.) **E. 735. (4.)**

[**May 12.**]—Scrinia Sacra ; Secrets of Empire, in letters of illustrious persons. A supplement of the Cabala. With many famous passages of the reigns of K. Henry VIII, Q. Elizabeth, K. James and K. Charles. pp. 355. *Printed for G. Bedel and T. Collins.* (12 May.) **E. 228. (2.)**

[**May 12.**]—The Right Constitution and true Subjects of the Visible Church of Christ ; with its order, ordinances, ministery and government. By Thomas Collier. pp. 86. *Printed by Henry Hills.* (12 May.) **E. 1495. (4.)**

[**May 12.**]—Ah, Ha. Tumulus, Thalamus : two counter-poems. The first, an Elegy upon Edward late Earl of Dorset [by James Howell] ; the second an Epithalamium to the Lord M[arquess] of Dorchester. *Printed for Humphrey Moseley.* (12 May.) **E. 228. (1.)**

[**May 13.**]—Rome's Conviction : or, A Discoverie of the unsoundness of the main Grounds of Rome's Religion, in answer to a book called the right Religion, evinced by L. B. By William Brownsword. pp. 383. *Printed by J. M. for Luke Fawn.* (13 May.) **E. 1474. (2.)**

[**May 13.**]—An Answer to a Book which Samuel Eaton put up to the Parliament, called Quakers Confuted. pp. 55. [See above : 18 Nov., E. 719. (8.)] *Printed for Giles Calvert.* (13 May.) **E. 735. (9.)**

May 16.—An Ordinance of Explanation of a former Ordinance entituled An Ordinance for better Amending the Common High-Waies. *Printed by William Du-Gard and Henry Hills.* **E. 1064. (5.)**

May 16.—An Ordinance for holding the Countie-Court for the Countie of Chester at the town of Northwich during the continuance of the Plague in Chester. *Printed by William Du-Gard and Henry Hills.* **E. 1064. (4.)**

1654.

May 16.—An Ordinance for Continuing an Ordinance entituled An Ordinance for further suspending the proceedings of the Judges named in an Act entituled An Act for Relief of Creditors and Poor Prisoners. *Printed by William Dugard and Henry Hills.* **E. 1064. (3.)**

[**May 17.**]—A Practical Discourse of Prayer. By Thomas Cobbet. pp. 551. *Printed by T. M. for Ralph Smith.* (17 May.) **E. 1457.**

[**May 18.**]—All vain janglers, imitatours and licentious persons shut out of the Scriptures. The old Serpents voice or Antichrist discovered opposing Christ in his kingdome. By James Nayler. (18 May.) **E. 735. (13.)**

[**May 19.**]—The Complaint of Mary Blaithwaite, setting forth her sad condition, occasioned by the late dissolution of Parliament. (19 May.) **E. 735. (15.)**

May 20.—A True Relation of the great Plot discovered against his Highness the Lord Protector, 20 May. *Printed for G. Horton.* **E. 738. (2.)**

May 20.—A great Fight in Scotland between the English Forces commanded by General Monk and the King of Scots Forces under Lieut. Gen. Middleton. *Printed for G. Horton.* **E. 738. (9.)**

May 23.—By the Lord Protector. [A Proclamation ordering a return, from the house-keepers of London, Westminster and Southwark, of the names of all persons lodging with them on 19th May, and since.] *s. sh.* *Printed by William du-Gard and Henry Hills.* **669. f. 17. (90.)**

[**May 23.**]—A Declaration to the Free-born People of England concerning the Government of the Commonwealth. [By John Lilburn.] *Printed for George Horton.* (23 May.) **E. 735. (18.)**

[**May 23.**]—A Politick Commentary on the Life of Caius July Cæsar. Written by Caius Suetonius Tranquillus. Chap. I. [Continued in "Perfect & Impartial Intelligence," of which this is actually No. 1.] *Printed by R. Moon.* (23 May.) **E. 735. (17.)**

May 24.—By the Lord Protector. [A Proclamation deferring the meeting of the Commissioners of the Peace between the Commonwealth and the States General.] *s. sh. Printed by William du-Gard and Henry Hills.* **669. f. 17. (91.)**

[**May 24.**]—The Order of Causes of Gods Fore-knowledge, Election and Predestination. By Henry Haggar. *Printed by James Cottrel for Richard Moone.* (24 May.) **E. 735. (20.)**

[**May 24.**]—An Exposition of the Epistle of Jude, formerly delivered in sundry lectures in Christ-Church, London. By William Jenkin. The second part. pp. 686. *Printed by Tho. Maxey for Samuel Gellibrand.* (24 May.) **E. 736.**

[**May 24.**]—The New Non-conformist; who having obtained help of God, doth persist unto this very day; witnessing some of those Glorious Things which the Apostles, the Prophets, & Moses, did say should come

1654.

to pass. [By Christopher Feake.] *Printed for Livewel Chapman.* (24 May.) **E. 737. (1.)**

[**May 24.**]—A Little Stone, pretended to be out of the Mountain, tried and found to be a Counterfeit. Or, an Examination & Refutation of Mr. Lockyers Lecture preached at Edinburgh, anno 1651, concerning the Mater of the Visible Church. By James Wood. pp. 386. *Printed by Andro Anderson for George Swintoun & Robert Broun: Edinburgh.* (24 May.) **E. 737. (2.)**

[**May 25.**]—The Nuptialls of Peleus and Thetis, consisting of a Mask and a Comedy [each in three acts and in verse. By James Howell]. 2 pt. *Printed for Henry Herringman.* (25 May.) **E. 228. (3.)**

May 26.—An Ordinance for the Preservation of the Works of the Great Level of the Fenns. *Printed by William Du-Gard and Henry Hills.* **E. 1064. (6.)**

[**May 26.**]—An Alarm to the present men in Power, the Officers of the Army, and all Oppressors. From some oppressed People of England, on behalf of themselves and others. [MS. note by Thomason: "This Libell scattred abroad in the streets in the night tyme."] *s. sh.* (26 May.) **669. f. 19. (1.)**

[**May 26.**]—The Court of Rome; wherein is sett forth the whole government thereof. And a Direction for such as shall travell to Rome how they may with most ease view all those rarities which are to be seene there. Translated out of Italian by H. C. [i.e. Henry Cogan]. pp. 275. *Printed for Henry Herringman.* (26 May.) **E. 1456. (2.)**

[**May 26.**]—A Plea for Anti-Pædobaptists against the Vanity and Falshood of scribled Papers entituled, The Anabaptists anatomiz'd and silenc'd. By John Tombes. *Printed by Henry Hills.* (26 May.) **E. 738. (7.)**

[**May 26.**]—Vindiciæ Academiarum, containing some briefe Animadversions upon Mr. Webster's Book, stiled, The Examination of Academies. [By Seth Ward, Bishop of Salisbury.] pp. 65. [See above: 19 Dec., 1653, E. 724. (14.)] *Printed by Leonard Lichfield: Oxford.* (26 May.) **E. 738. (5.)**

[**May 27.**]—The Last Will & Testament of Lieutenant Col. John Lilburn: with his Speech to some Friends in Jersey a little before his Death. [Fictitious.] (27 May.) **E. 738. (8.)**

[**May 29.**]—The Path-Way to Health, wherein are to be found most excellent Medicines of great vertue. First gathered by Peter Levens and now newly corrected and augmented. pp. 331. *Printed for J. W.* (29 May.) **E. 1472. (1.)**

May 29.—An Anniversary Ode upon the King's Birthday. Written for this yeare 1654, being his 24 yeare. *Printed for Samuel Browne: Hague.* **E. 745. (24.)**

1654.

[May 30.]—Joannis Miltoni Angli pro Populo Anglicano Defensio secunda. Contra infamem libellum anonymum [by Pierre Du Moulin] cui titulus, Regii sanguinis clamor ad coelum adversus parricidas Anglicanos. pp. 173. *Typis Neucomianis.* (30 May.) E. 1487. (3.)

[May 30.]—Directions to Sub-Commissioners about their Accompts. *Printed by John Macock and Gartrude Dawson.* (30 May.)
E. 1064. (7.)

[May 30.]—A second part of the Prisoners Remonstrance, shewing their sad and heavy Pressures, with a speedy Remedy and a way for the Inlargement of all Prisoners for Debt. (30 May.) E. 738. (11.)

May 31.—The Tryal of Col. Ashburnham before the Lord Protectors Council at White-Hall. *Imprinted for George Horton.* E. 738. (17.)

May.—The Heart opened by Christ ; or the conditions of a troubled Soul that could find no rest nor satisfaction in anything below the Divine Power and Glory of God. By Richard Farnworth. 745. (7.)

[May.]—A Prophetical Revelation given from God himself unto Matthew Coker. *Printed by James Cottrel.* E. 734. (7.)

[May.]—A Short and Plain Narrative of Matthew Coker in reference to his Gift of Healing. *Printed by James Cottrel.* E. 734. (8.)

[May.]—Panegyrici Cromwello scripti. [*Printed at Leyden.*]
E. 231. (1.)

June 2.—An Ordinance of Explanation touching the Jurisdiction of the Court of Admiralty. *Printed by William Du-Gard and Henry Hills.*
E. 1064. (8.)

[June 2.]—The Melancholy Cavalier : or, Fancy's Master-piece. A poem, by J. C. [With a woodcut on the titlepage, representing a cavalier, smoking a pipe, seated at a table on which lies a broken sword.] *Printed for C. R.* (2 June.) E. 1493. (3.)

[June 2.]—Sighs for Righteousness : or the Reformation this day calls for stated in some sad and serious Queries proposed to our Rulers. (2 June.) E. 738. (14.)

[June 3.]—A Discovery of the Man of Sin acting in a Mystery of Iniquitie, or, An Answer to a Book set forth by way of reply to an Answer of James Nayler's to The Perfect Pharisee [by Thomas Welde and others]. By James Nayler. pp. 51. [See above : 14 Jan. E. 726. (7.) and 9 May, E. 735. (2.)] *Printed for Giles Calvert.* (3 June.)
E. 738. (16.)

[June 3.]—A Scripture-Rule to the Lord's Table. Or, observations upon M. Humphrey's his treatise intituled, An Humble Vindication of Free Admission to the Lord's Supper. Being the result of the discourses of some preachers in the County of Gloucester. Digested by Anthony Palmer. [See above : 12 Jan. 1653, E. 1314. (1.)] pp. 182. *Printed by A. M. for E. Brewster and G. Sawbridge.* (3 June.) E. 1496. (2.)

1654.

[**June 4.**]—The Comfort of the Soul laid down by way of Meditation upon some heads of Christian Religion. By John Anthony. pp. 364. *Printed for G. Dawson and are to be sold by John Mountague.* (4 June.)
E. 739. (1.)

[**June 5.**]—Tyrants and Protectors set forth in their Colours. Or, the Difference between good and bad Magistrates. By J. P. pp. 52. *Printed for H. Cripps and S. Lloyd.* (5 June.) **E. 738. (18.)**

[**June 6.**]—Annotationes in Vetus Testamentum, et in Epistolam ad Ephesios incerto autore e bibliotheca Joannis Archiep. Eboracensis in lucem erutæ. [Edited by A. Scattergood.] pp. 476. *Per Thomam Buck: Cantabrigiæ.* (6 June.) **E. 1428.**

June 6.—The Saints longings after their Heavenly Country. A sermon preached at St. Pauls Church by Ralph Robinson. *Printed by R. I. for Stephen Bowtel.* **E. 848. (3.)**

June 6.—Living Loves betwixt Christ and Dying Christians. A sermon preached at M. Magdalene Bermondsey at the funeral of Jeremiah Whitaker. By Simeon Ashe. pp. 82. *Printed by T. M. for Ralph Smith.* **E. 482. (3.)**

[**June 6.**]—The Antipathy betwixt Flesh and Spirit. In answer to several accusations against the people called Quakers. By Richard Hubberthorne. *Printed for Giles Calvert.* (6 June.) **E. 739. (2.)**

[**June 7.**]—The Tempestuous Soul calmed by Jesus Christ. Being an extract of severall sermons preached by Anthony Palmer. pp. 107. *Printed by A. M. for E. Brewster and G. Sawbridge.* (7 June.) **E. 1496. (3.)**

June 8.—An Ordinance for Relief of Creditors and Poor Prisoners. *Printed by William Du-Gard and Henry Hills.* **E. 1064. (13.)**

June 8.—An Ordinance for an Assessment for Six Moneths for maintenance of the Armies and Navies of this Common-wealth. *Printed by William Du-Gard and Henry Hills.* **E. 1064. (10.)**

June 8.—The Form of an Indenture between the Sheriff and the Electors of Persons to serve in Parlament for Counties. **E. 1064. (9.)**

June 9.—An Ordinance for enabling the Judges of the Northern Circuit to hold Assizes and Gaol-Deliveries at Durham. **E. 1064. (11.)**

June 8. - Thau Ram Tanjah his Speech in his Claim, verbatim. [Claiming the crowns of France and Rome.] *s. sh.* **669. f. 19. (2.)**

[**June 8.**]—Of the Internal and Eternal Nature of Man in Christ. [By William Herbert, Earl of Pembroke.] pp. 64. *Printed by John Macock.* (8 June.) **E. 740. (6.)**

June 9. —An Ordinance for the further doubling of two thousand pounds upon Deans and Chapters Lands, Manors of Rectories, Gleab-lands, &c.
E. 1064. (12.)

[**June 9.**]—Some Particulars concerning the Law, sent to Oliver Cromwell. [By John Camm.] (9 June.) **E. 740. (9.)**

1654.

[June 10.]—Mene, Tekel, Perez ; or, A Little Appearance of the Hand-Writing against the Powers and Apostates of the Times. A letter to Oliver Lord Cromwel. By John Rogers. (10 June.) **E. 231. (2.)**

[June 11.]—A Plea for a Reproached Ministry, or, One good word for the Godly Ministers of England. By Robert Walwyn. pp. 141. *Printed for Edward Brewster.* (11 June.) **E. 1548. (1.)**

[June 12.]—The Reduction of a Digressor : or Rich. Baxter's reply to Mr. George Kendall's Digression in his book against Mr. Goodwin. pp. 144. *Printed by A. M. for Thomas Underhill and Francis Tyton.* (12 June.) **E. 741. (1.)**

[June 12.]—Rich. Baxters Apology against the Modest Exceptions of Mr. T. Blake [in " Vindiciae Foederis "], and the Digression of Mr. G. Kendall. pp. 155. [See above : 29 Jan., 1653, E. 685.] *Printed for T. Underhill and F. Tyton.* (12 June.) **E. 740. (10.)**

[June 12.]—Richard Baxter's Confutation of a Dissertation for the justification of Infidels ; written by Ludiomæus Colvinus, alias Ludovicus Molinæus [i.e. Louis Du Moulin], against his brother Cyrus Molinæus. pp. 182. *Printed by R. W.* (12 June.) **E. 741. (2.)**

June 13.—An Ordinance for Establishing an High Court of Justice. *Printed by William Du-Gard and Henry Hills.* **E. 1064. (14.)**

[June 13.]—Rich : Baxter's Admonition to Mr. William Eyre of Salisbury, concerning his miscarriages in a book lately written for the Justification of Infidels, against M. Benj. Woodbridge, M. James Cranford and the author. [See above : 10 Nov., 1653, E. 718. (5.)] *Printed by A. M. for Thomas Underhill and Francis Tyton.* (13 June.)

E. 741. (3.)

[June 13.]—An Unsavoury Volume of Mr. Jo. Crandon's anatomized : or a Nosegay of the choicest flowers in that Garden, presented to Mr. Joseph Caryl by Rich. Baxter. pp. 84. *Printed by A. M. for Thomas Underhill and Francis Tyton.* (13 June.) **E. 741. (4.)**

[June 14.]—A Comment on Ruth, together with two Sermons. By Thomas Fuller. pp. 300. *Printed for G. & H. Eversden.* (14 June.)

E. 1456. (3.)

[June 14.]—The Combate between the Flesh and the Spirit. Being the substance of xxvii. sermons preached by Mr. Christopher Love. To which is added The Christian's Directory : in xv. sermons. [Edited by William Taylor.] 2 pt. *Printed by T. R. & E. M. for John Rothwell.* (14 June.) **E. 742. (2.)**

[June 17.]—Alimony Arraign'd ; or, The Remonstrance and Appeal of Thomas Ivie from the High Court of Chancery to the Lord Protector. pp. 52. (17 June.) **E. 231. (3.)**

[June 17.]—Dies Dominicus Redivivus : or, the Lord's Day Enlivened. Or, a treatise as to discover the practical part of the Evangelical Sabbath :

1654.

so to recover the spiritual part of that pious practice. By Philip Goodwin. pp. 476. *Printed by J. L. for Andrew Kembe.* (17 June.)

E. 1470. (3.)

[**June 19.**]—The Dividing of the Hooff: or the seeming-contradictions throughout Sacred Scriptures distinguish'd, resolv'd and apply'd. By William Streat. pp. 496. *Printed by T. H. for the Author, and sold by W. Sheers.* (19 June.) **E. 743. (1.)**

[**June 20.**]—Τραγήματα, Sweet-Meats. Or, Resolves in all Cases who are Beleevers. In which many Divine Delicates are unvailed. By H. Walker. pp. 147. *Printed for R. Ibbitson.* (20 June.) **E. 1707. (2.)**

[**June 20.**]—Opus Astrologicum, or, An Astrological Work left to Posterity. By Nich. Culpeper. *Printed by J. Cottrel for Ri. Moone and Steph. Chatfield.* (June 20.) **E. 1503. (1.)**

June 21.—An Ordinance for bringing the Publique Revenues of this Common-Wealth into one Treasurie. *Printed by William Du-Gard and Henry Hills.* **E. 1064. (15.)**

June 21.—An Ordinance appointing who shall bee Justices of Assize for the County Palatine of Lancaster. *Printed by William Du-Gard and Henry Hills.* **E. 1064. (16.)**

[**June 21.**]—Comarum ἀκοσμία. The Loathsomnesse of Long Haire. By Thomas Hall. pp. 125. *Printed by J. G. for Nathanael Webb and William Grantham.* (21 June.) **E. 1489. (3.)**

[**June 22.**]—A Catalogue of the Names of the Members of the last Parliament, whereof those marked with a Starre were for the Godly Learned Ministry and Universities. *s. sh. Printed by A. M.* (22 June.)

669. f. 19. (3.)

[**June 22.**]—The Scotch Occurrences, impartially relating the present state of both armies, with their several actions. Likewise the orders of General Monk to all the English forces to march up against the Highlanders in one intire body ; and the speech of Gen. Middleton to his souldiers. *Imprinted for George Horton.* (22 June.) **E. 744. (6.)**

June 23.—An Ordinance for giving further time for Approbation of Publique Preachers. *Printed by William Du-Gard and Henry Hills.*

E. 1064. (17.)

June 23.—An Ordinance for the Regulation of Hackney Coachmen in London. *Printed by William Du-Gard and Henry Hills.*

E. 1064. (18.)

June 23.—An Ordinance for the further Encouragement of the Adventurers for Lands in Ireland. *Printed by William Du-Gard and Henry Hills.* **E. 1654. (20.)**

[**June 23.**]—The Parson's Guide ; or, the Law of Tithes. By W. S., Esq. [i.e. William Sheppard.] *Printed for W. Lee, D. Pakeman and G. Bedell.* (23 June.) **E. 744. (9.)**

1654.

[June 23.]—Principles of Christian Doctrine illustrated with Questions and Scripture Answers. By John Warren. *Printed for Nath. Webb & Will. Grantham.* (23 June.) **E. 1480. (1.)**

[June 24.]—A Remonstrance and Declaration of England and Wales, touching the late writs of the Lord Protector for the chusing of a new Parliament. *Imprinted by Robert Wood.* (24 June.) **E. 744. (10.)**

June 27.—An Ordinance for Distribution of the Elections in Scotland. *Printed by William Du-Gard and Henry Hills.* **E. 1064. (21.)**

June 27.—An Ordinance for Distribution of the Elections in Ireland. *Printed by William Du-Gard and Henry Hills.* **E. 1064. (22.)**

[June 27.]—To all that would know the Way to the Kingdom, whether they be in forms, without forms, or got above all forms. Given forth by Geo. Fox. (27 June.) **E. 745. (2.)**

June 28.—An admirable Speech by the Maior of Reading [Henry Frewen], upon the occasion of the late choice of a Burgess for that town, 28 June. With a narrative of the whole proceedings. Published by a well-wisher to the present Government. **E. 745. (17.)**

[June 28.]—Divine Poems. Written by Thomas Washbourne. pp. 141. *Printed for Humphrey Moseley.* (28 June.) **E. 1534. (1.)**

June 29.—An Ordinance against Challenges, Duells, and all provocations thereunto. *Printed by William Du-Gard and Henry Hills.* **E. 1064. (23.)**

June 29.—An Ordinance for continuing the Committee for the Army and Treasurers at Warr. *Printed by William Du-Gard and Henry Hills.* **E. 1064. (24.)**

[June 29.]—A Memento for the People, about their Elections of Members for the approaching Parliament. *s. sh. Printed for Rich. Moone.* (29 June.) **669. f. 19. (4.)**

[June 29.]—A Whip of small cords to scourge Antichrist out of the Temple of God. Whereunto is added, The Sheerer sheer'd and casheered, the Shaver shav'd & the Grinder ground. By Matthew Coker. *Printed by James Cottrel.* (29 June.) **E. 745. (5.)**

June 30.—An Ordinance impowring the Commissioners of the Customes for the better suppressing of Drunkennes and prophane Cursing and Swearing in persons imployed under them. **E. 1064. (25.)**

June 30.—The Triall of Mr. John Gerhard, Mr. Peter Vowell and Sommerset Fox by the High Court of Justice, 30 June. With a declaration of the plot to have murthered the Lord Protector and the Councill and proclaimed Charles Steuart King. *Printed by Robert Ibbitson.* **E. 231. (4.)**

June 30.—The Tryal of Colonel John Gerard, Mr. Peter Vowel, and Mr. Somerset Fox, before the High Court of Justice in Westminster Hall. With the charge of high treason against them, and their speeches in answer thereunto. *Imprinted by Robert Wood.* **E. 745. (9.)**

1654.

[June 30.]—Heaven on Earth; or, A Serious Discourse touching a wel-grounded Assurance of Mens everlasting Happiness. By Thomas Brooks. pp. 607. *Printed by R. I. for John Hancock.* (30 June.)
E. 1446.

[June.]—Musarum Oxoniensium ᾿Ελαιοφορία, sive, Ob Fædera, auspiciis Oliveri Reipub. Ang. Domini Protectoris inter Rempub. Britannicam & Ordines Fæderatos Belgii fæliciter stabilita, Gentis Togatæ ad vada Isidis Celeusma Metricum. pp. 104. *Excudebat Leonardus Lichfield: Oxoniæ.*
E. 740. (1.)

[June.]—Oliva Pacis. Ad Illustrissimum Oliverum Reipub. Angliæ Dominum Protectorem de Pace cum Fæderatis Belgis feliciter sancita Carmen Cantabrigiense. *Ex celeberrimæ Academiæ Typographeo: Cantabrigiæ.*
E. 740. (2.)

June.—The Character of a Protector. [Satirical Verses. In MS., in Thomason's hand.] June. *s. sh.*
E. 743. (2.)

[July 1.]—Good-Ale monopolized, and the Tapsters persecuted : or Justice right or wrong. [By Raphael Desmos. A satire on Robert Tichborne.] *Printed by Robert Goodfellow.* (1 July.)
E. 745. (8.)

[July 2.]—A New Dialogue between Dick of Kent and Wat the Welchman. By Laurence Price. [With two woodcuts representing the interlocutors.] *Printed for John Andrews.* (2 July.)
E. 1487. (4.)

[July 3.]—Soule-Reviving Influences of the Sun of Righteousnesse. By John Smith. pp. 205. *Printed for Giles Calvert.* (3 July.)
E. 1485. (1.)

July 4.—An Ordinance prohibiting Horse-Races for Six Moneths. *Printed by William Du-Gard and Henry Hills.*
E. 1064. (26.)

July 4.—Elisha his Lamentation upon the suddain translation of Elijah. Opened in a sermon at the funeral of Mr. William Strong. By Obadiah Sedgwick. *Printed by R. W. for Francis Tyton.*
E. 745. (14.)

[July 5.]—Revenge for Honour. A tragedie. By George Chapman. pp. 63. *Printed for Richard Marriot.* (5 July.)
E. 231. (5.)

[July 8.]—The Paynims Songs. 1 Canton. (8 July.)
E. 745. (15.)

Juillet 8.—Homelie sur l'Evangile selon Saint Jean, Chap. 20 ver. 17 prononcée dans l'Eglise Françoise de Westminster. Par Gabriel le Roi dit des Brosses. *Imprimé par Thomas Newcomb.*
E. 1483. (2.)

[July 8.]—Some Pious Treatises. Being, 1. A Bridle for the Tongue ; 2. The Present Sweetness and future Bitterness of a delicious sin. 3. A Christians Groans under the body of sin. 4. Proving the Resurrection of the same body committed to the dust. 5. Tractatus de Clavibus Ecclesiæ. By Christoph. Blackwood. pp. 103. *Printed for Giles Calvert.* (8 July.)
E. 745. (16.)

July 10.—The true and perfect Speeches of Colonel Gerhard upon the scaffold at Tower Hill, and Mr. Peter Vowel at Charing Cross, 10 July.

1654.

Likewise the speech of the Portugal Ambassador's brother upon the scaffold. *Imprinted for G. Horton.* **E. 745. (19.)**

July 10.—The Last Speech of M. Peter Vowell, which he intended to have delivered, had he been permitted, upon the tenth of July, being the day of his suffering death. Written by himself. **E. 805. (4.)**

July 10.—A true and impartial Relation of the death of M. John Gerhard, who was beheaded on Tower-hill. **E. 805. (10.)**

July 10.—A Vindication of Thomas Henshaw, concerning a pretended Plott for which John Gerharde and Peter Vowell were murthered on 10 Aug. [or rather, July]. *Printed at the Spaw.* **E. 812. (17.)**

July 12.—A List of Knights & Burgesses for several counties elected 12 July, to serve in the next Parliament to be held at Westminster, 3 Sept. *Printed by Francis Leach.* **E. 805. (6.)**

July 13.—The Copy of a Letter sent out of Wiltshire to a gentleman in London; wherein is laid open the dangerous designes of the Clergy in reference to the approaching Parliament. By a true friend to the publique interest. *Printed for Livewell Chapman.* **E. 809. (18.)**

[July 15.]—The Marrow of Complements; or, A forme of Instructions for all variety of Love-letters. [The preface signed : Philomusus.] pp. 188. *Printed for Humphrey Moseley.* (15 July.) **E. 1530. (1.)**

[July 16.]—A Few Words to all Judges, Justices and Ministers of the Law in England. From Anthony Pearson. *Printed for Giles Calvert.* (16 July.) **E. 231. (6.)**

July 19.—A true Relation of the Rowting of Middleton's Army in Scotland. As it was presented to the Lord Protector in two letters, one from General Monck, and the other from Col. Morgan. *Printed by William Du-Gard and Henry Hills.* **E. 806. (9.)**

July 20.— A true and Sad Relation of the burning, sinking and blowing up of the English ships in the river of Thames. Likewise the discovery of a conspiracie upon the river. *Imprinted for G. Horton.*

E. 805. (9.)

[July 20.]—Heptameron, or the History of the Fortunate Lovers. Written by Margaret de Valoys, Queen of Navarre. Now made English by Robert Codrington. pp. 528. *Printed by F. L. for Nath. Ekins.* (20 July.) **E. 1468. (2.)**

[July 24.]—A New Lesson for the Indoctus Doctor. Containing a vindication of a book called Indoctus Doctor Edoctus from the impertinent bablings of Theophilus Brabourn. By J. Collinges. [See also below : 17 Nov., E. 817. (9.)] *Printed by J. G. for Joseph Cranford.* (24 July.) **E. 805. (12.)**

[July 24.]—The Judgement set, and the Bookes opened. In severall sermons at Alhallows Lumbard-street, by John Webster. pp. 312. *Printed for R. Hartford and N. Brooks.* (24 July.) **E. 805. (13.)**

1654.

[July 24.]—A Legacy for Saints; being several experiences of the dealings of God with Anna Trapnel. Written with her own hand. [Edited by John Proud and Caleb Ingold.] pp. 64. *Printed for T. Brewster.* (24 July.) **E. 806. (1.)**

[July 25.]—The Euroclydon Winde commanded to cease. Being a moderate vindication of the Lord Protector. Also something in behalf of the desolate Church and King Charles. With an Apology of the Author concerning the year 1653. By Arise Evans. pp. 88. *Printed for the Author.* (25 July.) **E. 1491. (2.)**

[July 29.]—A Rule for Ministers and People, whereby they may see how they are engaged, one towards another, by God's Word. By N. C., a servant of Christ, and of his Church assembled at Orpington. *Printed for Giles Calvert.* (29 July.) **E. 806. (5.)**

[July 29.]—A Message sent from Charles King of Sweden to Oliver, Lord Protector of the Commonwealth. With the letters of credence sent from his Majesty to Monsieur Bonnel, concerning the articles of peace and union. [Two news-letters.] *Printed for G. Wharton.* (29 July.) **E. 806. (6.)**

[July 30.]—The Great Earthquake, Revel. 16. 18, or Fall of all the Churches. Discovering the Apostasie of purest Churches. By William Erbery. [With a preface, containing a character of the author, signed : J. W.] pp. 52. *Printed for Giles Calvert.* (30 July.) **E. 806. (7.)**

[July 31.]—A True Testimony of the zeal of Oxford-Professors and University-men, who persecute the servants of the living God, following the example of their brethren of Cambridge. By Richard Hubberthorne. *Printed for Giles Calvert.* (31 July.) **E. 806. (8.)**

Aug. 1.—An Ordinance for Indempnity to the English Protestants of the Province of Munster in Ireland. *Printed by William Du-gard and Henry Hills.* **E. 1064. (27.)**

Aug. 1.—An Ordinance appointing a Committee of the Adventurers for Lands in Ireland, for determining differences among the said Adventurers. **E. 1064. (28.)**

Aug. 1.—Gray Hayres crowned with Grace. A sermon preached at Redriff at the funerall of Thomas Gataker. [By Simeon Ashe.] pp. 80. *Printed by A. M. for George Sawbridge.* **E. 818. (3.)**

Aug. 2.—The Ranters last Sermon. With the manner of their meetings, ceremonies and actions, also their blasphemous tenents; delivered in an Exercise, 2 Aug. Also God's Judgements shewed upon Ranters, Quakers and Shakers, and other wicked persons. By J. M., a deluded Brother, lately escaped out of their Snare. *Printed by J. C.*

E. 808. (1.)

1654.

[**Aug. 2.**]—The Illustrious Hugo Grotius of the Law of Warre and Peace, with annotations and memorials of the Author's life. [Translated by Clement Barksdale.] pp. 660. *Printed by T. Warren for William Lee.* (Aug. 2.) **E. 1445.**

[**Aug. 2.**]—A Trial of Faith, wherein is discovered the ground of the faith of the hypocrite, which perisheth, and the faith of the Saints, which is founded upon the everlasting Rock. By James Parnell. (2 Aug.) **E. 706. (11.)**

[**Aug. 3.**]—Church-Incense; or, Divine Ejaculations. Composed by Hen. Church, published since his death by his son N. C. [i.e. Nathaniel Church.] pp. 62. *Printed for J. Rothwell.* (3 Aug.) **E. 1535. (3.)**

[**Aug. 5.**]—The Country-mans Recreation, or the art of Planting, Graffing and Gardening, in three books. With rules for the preparation of the Hop Garden. Whereunto is added the art of Angling. [By Thomas Barker. Illustrated with wood-cuts.] 4 pt. *Printed by T. Mabb for William Shears.* (5 Aug.) **E. 806. (16.)**

[**Aug. 5.**]—Physicall and Chymicall Works, composed by Geor : Phædro, sirnamed the Great, of Gelleinen. Selected out of the Germane and Latine language, by the industry of John Andreas Schenckins of Graffenberg. pp. 133. *Printed for William Sheares.* (5 Aug.) **E. 1497. (2.)**

[**Aug. 7.**]—Another great and admirable Victory obtained by the Lord Gen. Monk against the Scottish forces : with the routing of General Glencairn's brigade. With several other remarkable occurrences touching State affairs. *Printed by R. Wood.* (7 Aug.) **E. 808. (2.)**

[**Aug. 7.**]—Mr. Baxter's Aphorisms exorised and authorized. Or an examination of and answer to a book by Mr. Ri: Baxter entituled Aphorisms of Justification. Together with a vindication of Justification by meer Grace, from Popish and Arminian sophisms. By John Crandon. 2 pt. *Printed by M. S., and sold by T. Brewster and L. Chapman.* (7 Aug.) **E. 807.**

[**Aug. 8.**]—Truth Defended : or, certain accusations answered, cast upon us who are called Quakers. By Edward Burrough. [With a prefatory epistle signed : Francis Howgill.] (8 Aug.) **E. 808. (3.)**

Aug. 9.—Tithes a curse to all Nations but Canaan, and a disturbance and vexation to all people but the Hebrews. Demonstrated in the case of Isaack Graye, now a prisoner for the non-payment of Tithes. [In the form of a petition by Isaack Graye.] *Printed for the Author, and sold by William Larner and Richard Moon.* **E. 809. (20.)**

Aug. 9.—A Christians Delight, or, Morning-Meditations upon XCVII. Choice Texts of Scripture. By Maritius Bohemus. pp. 230. *Printed by Tho. Maxey for John Rothwell.* (9 Aug.) **E. 1473. (3.)**

1654.

Aug. 11.—An Additionall Ordinance for the Relief of Creditors and Poor Prisoners. *Printed by William Du-Gard and Henry Hills.*

E. 1064. (29.)

Aug. 11.—An Ordinance for the better redress of the Abuses committed upon the River of Thames and Waters of Medway. *Printed by William Du-Gard and Henry Hills.* **E. 1064. (30.)**

[**Aug. 11.**]—The Tree of Christian Faith : a true information how a man may be one Spirit with God, and what man must do to perform the works of God. Written in high Dutch by Jacob Behmen. pp. 56. *Printed by John Macock.* (11 Aug.) **E. 808. (8.)**

[**Aug. 12.**]—An Apology for the Ministers of Wilts in their actings at the election of members for the approaching Parliament : in answer to a letter pretending to lay open the dangerous designes of the clergy. By Humphrey Chambers, John Strickland, Adoniram Bifield, Peter Ince. *Printed for Ralph Smith.* (12 Aug.) **E. 808. (9.)**

[**Aug. 14.**]—A short Answer to a book set forth by seven Priests [i.e. " A Faithful Discovery" by J. Kellet and others] who call themselves Ministers of the Gospel of Christ, but are discovered to be lyers and slanderers. [Subscribed : "From them whom the world scornfully calls Quakers." See above : 12 June, 1653, E. 699. (13.)] *Printed for Giles Calvert.* (14 Aug.) **E. 808. (10.)**

[**Aug. 14.**]—An Image of our Reforming Times : or Jehu in his proper colours. Displayed in some exercitations on 2 Kings 9 and 10 chapters. Concluding with a word to Jehu, Jehonadab his counsellor and the despised persecuted people of God. By Col. Edw. Lane. *Printed for L. Chapman.* (14 Aug.) **E. 808. (11.)**

[**Aug. 15.**]—True Judgement, or the Spiritual-Man judging all things, but he himself judged of No Man. [By George Fox.] *Printed for Giles Calvert.* (15 Aug.) **E. 808. (12.)**

Aug. 16.—At the Generall Sessions of the Publike Peace holden for the City of London. [An Order of the Justices, restricting the number of Ale-Houses.] *s. sh.* **669. f. 19. (22.)**

[**Aug. 17.**]—Spirituall wickednesse in Heavenly places, proclayming Freedome to the Forme, but persecuting the Power : or an answer to a booke intituled Freedom of Religious Worship. [By James Nayler.] (17 Aug.) **E. 808. (16.)**

[**Aug. 18.**]—To you that are called by the name of Baptists, or the Baptized people, that do what you do by imitation from John Baptist, Christ, and the Apostles, who had not the form without the power to reform ; but you have only the form. [By Richard Farnworth.] Also several other things given forth from The Spirit of the Lord [signed : J. N. and G. F., i.e. James Nayler and George Fox]. (18 Aug.)

E. 808. (18.)

1654.

[**Aug. 21.**]—Daily Observations or Meditations, divine, morall. Written by a person of Honour and Piety [Arthur Capel, Lord Capel]. pp. 114. (21 Aug.)   **E. 808. (19.)**

Aug. 21.—An Ordinance appointing Commissioners to Survey the Forests and Lands heretofore belonging to the late King, Queen and Prince. *Printed by William Du-Gard and Henry Hills.*   **E. 1064. (45.)**

Aug. 21.—The Confession of Mr. Humphrey Marston, and his speech at the place of execution. *Printed for G. Horton.*   **E. 809. (1.)**

[**Aug. 21.**]—Certain Letters written to severall persons. [By Arthur Capel, Lord Capel.]   (21 Aug.)   **E. 808. (19*.)**

Aug. 22.—An Ordinance for the better regulating and limiting the jurisdiction of the High Court of Chancery. *Printed by William Du-Gard and Henry Hills.*   **E. 1064. (31.)**

[**Aug. 25.**]—A Word from the Lord to all the World, and all professors in the World, spoken in parables. By them who are redeemed out of the curse, to serve the living, called Quakers. [A series of short pieces by George Fox, James Nayler and others.] *Printed for Giles Calvert.* (25 Aug.)   **E. 809. (6.)**

[**Aug. 26.**]—The continuance of the High Court of Chancery vindicated to be absolute necessary, the abuses and corruptions being removed. By many citizens well knowing of such abuses. *Printed for Lawrence Chapman.* (26 Aug.)   **E. 809. (7.)**

[**Aug. 28.**]—A Declaration against all Profession and Professors that have not the life of what they profess. From the righteous seed of God, whom the World, Priests, and People, scornfully calls Quakers. [Signed : G. F., i.e. George Fox.] *Printed for Giles Calvert.* (28 Aug.)   **E. 809. (8.)**

Aug. 29.—An Ordinance for the ejecting of Scandalous, Ignorant and Insufficient Ministers and School-Masters. *Printed by William Du-Gard and Henry Hills.*   **E. 1064. (32.)**

Aug. 29.—An Ordinance appointing the Excise of Allum and Copperace. *Printed by William Du-Gard and Henry Hills.*   **E. 1064. (33.)**

Aug. 30.—An Ordinance for taking an Accompt of the Moneys received upon the Act for the better propagation of the Gospel in Wales, &c. *Printed by William Du-Gard and Henry Hills.*   **E. 1064. (41.)**

Aug. 30.—An Ordinance for Sale of Four Forrests or Chases reserved for Collateral Securitie to the Souldiers. *Printed by William Du-Gard and Henry Hills.*   **E. 1064. (34.)**

Aug. 30.—A Declaration of several of the Churches of Christ and Godly People in and about the citie of London ; concerning the Kingly Interest of Christ and the present suffrings of his cause and Saints in England. [With the names of 150 of the signatories to the declaration.] *Printed for Livewel Chapman.*   **E. 809. (15.)**

1654.

Aug. 31.—To the Right Honble the Councell. The Petition of Jno. Mews, etc. [Protesting against the election to Parliament of Aldermen Adams and Langham. In MS., in Thomason's hand.] *s. sh.*

669. f. 19. (5.)

[**Aug.**]—Syzygiasticon Instauratum, or an Almanack & Ephemeris for 1654. By Richard Fitzsmith. pp. 92. *Printed for the Author, and are to be sold by Henry Eversden.* **E. 1500. (1.)**

Aug.—Life out of Death. A Sermon preached at Chelsey, on the recovery of an honourable Person [Sir John D'Anvers]. By Thomas Fuller. *Printed for John Williams.* **E. 1441. (3.)**

[**Sept. 1.**]—The Prime Work of the first Tripple Parliament; or the modest motion of Religion's friends, humbly tendered by way of petition to the first Representative of Great Britain and Ireland. *Printed by T. W.* (1 Sept.) **E. 809. (13.)**

[**Sept. 1.**]—The Voice of the Spirit. Or, an essay towards a discoverie of the witnessings of the Spirit. To which is added, Roses from Sharon, or sweet experiences reached out by Christ to some of his beloved ones in this Wildernes. By Samuel Petto. 2 pt. *Printed for Livewell Chapman.* (1 Sept.) **E. 1500. (2.)**

[**Sept. 1.**]—Certaine Queries propounded to the most serious consideration of those persons now in power, or any others whom they doe, or may concerne. By John Spittlehouse. *Printed for Livewell Chapman.* (1 Sept.) **E. 809. (14.)**

Sept. 2.—An Act for admitting Protestants in Ireland to Compound. *Printed by William Du-Gard and Henry Hills.* **E. 1064. (42.)**

Sept. 2.—An Ordinance for the better Maintenance and Encouragement of Preaching Ministers and for uniting of Parishes. *Printed by William Du-Gard and Henry Hills.* **E. 1064. (35.)**

Sept. 2.—An Ordinance to enable such Souldiers as served the Commonwealth in the late Wars, to exercise any Trade. *Printed by William Du Gard and Henry Hills.* **E. 1064. (36.)**

Sept. 2.—An Ordinance touching the Office of Postage of Letters, inland and foreign. *Printed by William Du-Gard and Henry Hills.* **E. 1064. (37.)**

Sept. 2.—An Ordinance for the giving libertie for the Carrying of Millstones, Stone, Timber, &c. *Printed by William Du-Gard and Henry Hills.* **E. 1064. (38.)**

Sept. 2.—An Ordinance for further Doubling upon Deans & Chapters Lands. *Printed for William Du-Gard and Henry Hills.* **E. 1064. (40.)**

Sept. 2.—An Ordinance touching Fines. *Printed by William Du-Gard and Henry Hills.* **E. 1064. (39.)**

Sept. 2.—An Ordinance for reviving and continuing an Act of Parlament for recovery of many thousand Acres of Ground in Norfolk and Suffolk

1654.

surrounded by the rage of the Sea. *Printed by William Du-Gard and Henry Hills.* **E. 1064. (43.)**

Sept. 2.—An Ordinance for bringing several branches of the Revenew under the government of the Commissioners for the Treasury and Court of Exchequer. *Printed by William Du-Gard and Henry Hills.*

E. 1064. (44.)

[Sept. 2.]—A brief View and Defence of the Reformation of the Church of England, by King Edward and Q. Elizabeth. pp. 70. *Printed for Simon Miller.* (2 Sept.) **E. 1476. (2.)**

Sept. 3.—More Warning Yet. Being a true relation of a strange Apparition seen at Hull. *Printed by J. Cottrel for Richard Moore.*

E. 811. (1.)

Sept. 4.—His Highnesse the Lord Protectors Speeches to the Parliament in the Painted Chamber, 4 Sept. and 12 Sept. 2 pt. *Printed by T. R. and E. M. for G. Sawbridge.* **E. 812. (11.)**

Sept. 4.—An Answer to one part of the Lord Protector's Speech; or, A Vindication of the Fifth Monarchy-men, in reference to an accusation of evil charged upon them in his Speech to Parliament, 4 Sept. By John Spittlehouse. *Printed for Livewel Chapman.* **E. 813. (19.)**

[Sept. 4.]—A true Separation between the power of the Spirit, and the imitation of Antichrist. [Signed: Richard Hubberthorne.] (4 Sept.)

E. 809. (16.)

Sept. 5.—[A Resolution of Parliament "that no Petition against any Election of Member already returned for England or Scotland shall be received after three weeks from this day."] *s. sh. Printed by John Field.* **669. f. 19. (13.)**

[Sept. 5.]—A Clear Optick discovering to the Eye of Reason, that Regality is not inconsistent with the ends of Government, and that the Recusants are hugely mistaken in the constitution of their Roman Hierarchy. Roughly set out in an addresse to the Parliament. By Anthony Norwood. *Printed for Richard Moon and Edward Thomas.* (5 Sept.) **E. 809. (21.)**

[Sept. 5.]—A brief Historical Relation of the Empire of Russia. By J. F. *Printed by J. C. for William Larnar.* (5 Sept.) **E. 1485. (2.)**

[Sept. 5.]—Of the Nature of Faith: a sermon. By Barten Holyday. *Printed by S. G. for W. Lee.* (5 Sept.) **E. 809. (17.)**

[Sept. 7.]—The New Birth: in which is brought forth the New Creature. With a description of the true Marks and Characters thereof. [The dedicatory epistle signed: Richard Bartlet.] pp. 73. *Printed by W. H. for L. Blaiklock.* (7 Sept.) **E. 1503. (2.)**

[Sept. 8.]—To Parliament. The Petition of divers Citizens and Inhabitants in and about London. [Various suggestions for ensuring the Liberty of the People.] *s. sh.* (8 Sept.) **669. f. 19. (6.)**

1654.

[**Sept. 8.**]—The Copy of a Petition to the Lord Protector by Bassett Jones of Lammihangel in the county of Glamorgan, against Colonel Philip Jones. With his Highness order thereupon, the said Colonel's answer, and the reply of the said Bassett. (8 Sept.) **E. 809. (26.)**

[**Sept. 8.**]—The Divinity of the Trinity cleared, by wiping off the false glosses put upon several places of Scripture by Mr. John Biddle, in his book intituled The Apostolical and true Opinion touching the Holy Trinity &c. [By John Brayne. See above : 25 April, 1653, E. 1479. (1.)] *Printed by J. C., and sold by Edward Blackmore.* (8 Sept.)
E. 809. (25.)

[**Sept. 10.**]—Hemeroscopeion anni 1654. By Geo. Wharton. pp. 84. *Printed by J. G. for James Crumpe.* (10 Sept.) **E. 1469. (1.)**

Sept. 12.—The Last Speech of the Lord Protector to Parliament. *Printed by R. Wood.* **E. 234. (1.)**

[**Sept. 12.**]—The true Doctrine of Justification asserted & vindicated from the errors of many, and more especially Papists and Socinians. By Anthony Burgesse. pp. 456. *Printed for Thomas Underhill.* (12 Sept.) **E. 810.**

[**Sept. 12.**]—Vindiciæ Veritatis ; or, An Answer [by Nathaniel Fiennes] to a Discourse [by David Buchanan] intituled Truth it's Manifest. Wherein also divers Passages touching the late Transactions are inserted. pp. 246. (12 Sept.) **E. 811. (2.)**

[**Sept. 13.**]—The Covenant of God with Abraham opened. Wherein I. The duty of Infant-baptism is cleared, II. Something added concerning the Sabbath. By William Carter. pp. 176. *Printed by T. C. for John Rothwell.* (13 Sept.) **E. 811. (5.)**

Sept. 14.—[A Declaration of Parliament concerning " the Recognition of the Government by the Members of this Parliament."] *s. sh. Printed by William du-Gard and Henry Hills.* **669. f. 19. (7.)**

[**Sept. 14.**]—A Declaration of the Proceedings of the Lord Protector and his reasons touching the late change in Parliament. With the new Test tendered to each Member. [With a woodcut portrait of Cromwell on the titlepage.] *Printed by R. Wood.* (14 Sept.) **E. 811. (6.)**

[**Sept. 15.**]—A Perfect List of the Members returned, and approved on by the Councill, to Parliament. *s. sh. Printed for R. Ibbitson.* (15 Sept.)
669. f. 19. (8.)

[**Sept. 15.**]—A Message from the Lord to the Parliament of England. By George Fox. (15 Sept.) **E. 812. (2.)**

[**Sept. 15.**]—Conference touchant le Pedobaptesme, tenüe à Paris entre le Sieur Jean Mestrezat et Theodore Naudin. pp. 66. *Imprimé à Londres par Thomas Creake.* (15 Sept.) **E. 812. (3.)**

1654.

[Sept. 16.]—Englands Warning-Piece ; or, the unkenneling of the Old
Foxes with their Cubes.   Wherein is contained the Summary of Romes
late designs against England.   [By Jeffrey Corbet.]   (16 Sept.)
                                                    E. 812. (4.)

[Sept. 17.]—The Spiritual Seaman : or, A Manual for Mariners, comprehending the principal heades of the Christian Religion, handled in
an allusion to the Sea-mans Compass.   By John Durant.   pp. 91.
Printed for I. Chapman.   (17 Sept.)   **E. 1547. (2.)**

Sept. 18.—Dæmonium Meridianum : Satan at Noon, or, Antichristian
Blasphemies punished by the hand of Justice.   Being a Relation of the
Proceedings of the Commissioners of the County of Berks against John
Pordage, late Minister of Bradfield.   By Christopher Fowler.   pp. 178.
Printed for Francis Eglesfield.   **E. 840. (1.)**

Sept. 19.—A Declaration of the Lord Protector and the Parliament for
a Day of Solemn Fasting and Humiliation.   *Printed by William
Du-Gard and Henry Hills.*   **E. 1064. (46.)**

[Sept. 21.]—Something in answer to a Petition to Oliver Cromwel from
the Subscribers in Cumberland which are called Justices and Commissioners.   Also the Examination of some Friends at the Assizes at
York.   (21 Sept.)   **E. 812. (7.)**

[Sept. 22.]—A Sermon of the Fifth Monarchy.   By Tho. Goodwin.
Printed for Livewel Chapman.   (22 Sept.)   **E. 812. (9.)**

[Sept. 24.]—A Dialogue concerning the practicall use of Infant-Baptisme.
By Simon Ford.   2 pt.   *Printed by S. G. for John Rothwell.*   (24 Sept.)
                                                 E. 1440. (2.)

[Sept. 25.]—A Seasonable, Legall and Historicall Vindication and
chronologicall Collection of the old fundamentall Liberties of all English
Freemen.   By William Prynne.   pp. 60.   *Printed for the Authour and
are to be sold by Edward Thomas.*   (25 Sept.)   **E. 812. (10.)**

[Sept. 26.]—The Immediate Call to the Ministery of the Gospel witnessed
by the Spirit.   With a declaration of the persecution of Richard
Hubberthorne, James Parnell, Ann Blayling, by William Pickering,
Mayor of Cambridge.   *Printed for Giles Calvert.*   (26 Sept.)
                                                 E. 812. (13.)

[Sept. 26.]—For the Souldiers and all the Officers of England, Scotland
and Ireland, a warning from the Lord, that they forget not his kindness, but call to mind his mercies and their own promises.   [By
Edward Burrough.]   *s. sh.*   (26 Sept.)   **669. f. 19. (9.)**

Sept. 27.—Truth cleared of Scandals.   Occasioned by the meeting of
Baptists and Quakers at Harliston, 27 Sept.   By Richard Farnworth.
[See also below : 9 June, 1655, E. 842. (10.) and 4 Nov., 1655,
E. 857. (8.)]   **E. 820. (3.)**

1654.

[**Sept. 28.**]—The Spouse rejoycing over Antichrist and triumphing over the Devill. By James Michel. [In verse.] *Printed and are to be sold in Cannons-street.* (28 Sept.) **E. 1603. (1.)**

[**Sept. 29.**]—Four Tables of Divine Revelation. Written by Jacob Behm, and Englished by Henry Blunden. [With an engraved frontispiece of allegorical design.] *Printed for H. Blunden.* (29 Sept.) **E. 1068. (6*.)**

Sept. 29.—A Sermon preached at the election of Sir Thomas Viner as Lord Mayor of London. By Richard Vines. *Printed for Abel Roper.* **E. 858. (4.)**

[**Sept. 30.**]—An Apology for the Present Government and Governour. By Samuel Richardson. *Printed and to be sold by Gyles Calvert.* (30 Sept.) **E. 812. (18.)**

[**Sept.**]—To Parliament. The Petition of Richard Tuttell, Barbican, London. [Protesting against his imprisonment by the Committee for Indemnity.] *s. sh.* **669. f. 19. (10.)**

[**Sept.**]—To Parliament. The Petition of Samuel Vassall. [Claiming payment of money due for the service of his ship the Mayflower, and of compensation for imprisonment and losses under the late King, voted by Parliament but never paid.] *s. sh.* **669. f. 19. (11.)**

[**Sept.**]—To Parliament. The Petition of William Caddy of Taunton, and Nicholas Ward of Chard, in the County of Somerset. [Praying for compensation for persecution suffered at the hands of Sir John Stawell.] *s. sh.* **669. f. 19. (12.)**

[**Sept.**]—To Parliament. The Petition of Humphrey Bagaley. [Protesting against his imprisonment.] *s. sh.* **669. f. 19. (15.)**

[**Sept.**]—To Parliament. The Petition of Nathaniel Jones, of Bridgewater in the County of Sommerset, Clerk. [Protesting against the illegality of the sequestration of his estates.] *s. sh.* **669. f. 19. (16.)**

[**Sept.**]—To Parliament. The Petition of divers persons in the County of Derby. [For the repayment of money advanced for the service of Parliament.] *s. sh.* **669. f. 19. (17.)**

[**Sept.**]—To Parliament. The Petition of poore Prisoners [for debt], in the severall Prisons in and about London. [Praying that they may be speedily brought to trial ; and that, in view of the expense of bringing witnesses to London, either they may be tried "in their own Counties where they reside," or their witnesses may be examined there, and their examination sent up.] *s. sh.* **669. f. 19. (14.)**

[**Sept.**]—To Parliament. The Petition of Tho: Nevill, Prisoner in the Fleet, in the behalfe of himself and many more in and about London. [The substance of this petition is the same as that of the preceding.] *s. sh.* (Sept.) **669. f. 19. (18.)**

1654.

Sept.—A Brief of the Papers touching a Market petitioned for, to be held in Clements Inne Fields, as it stood before the Parliament in the yeare 1652, and of what hath since been offered therein, and done by his Highnesse and the Council. *s. sh.*   **669. f. 19. (19.)**

[**Oct. 1.**]—Apotelesma : or, the Nativity of the World and the Revolution thereof, with astrologicall judgements thereupon.   By George Wharton. *Printed for Tho: Vere and Nath: Brook.*   (1 Oct.)   **E. 1500. (4.)**

[**Oct. 1.**]—Ephemeris.   Or a diary astronomicall, meteorologicall, chronologicall, for 1655.   By George Wharton.   [With an engraved portrait of the author.]   *Printed for Tho: Vere and Nath: Brook.*   (1 Oct.)
E. 1500. (3.)

[**Oct. 1.**]—A Second Beacon Fired.   Humbly presented to the Lord Protector and Parliament.   [By Luke Fawne, Samuel Gellibrand, and others, petitioning for the suppression of blasphemous books.]   [See also below : 24 Nov., 1654, E. 817. (16.), and 5 Jan., 1655, E. 821. (18.)]   *Printed for the Subscribers.*   (1 Oct.)   **E. 813. (1.)**

[**Oct. 2.**]—An Admonition to My Lord Protector and his Council, of their present Danger.   [The preface signed : J. H., i.e. James Howell ?] (2 Oct.)   **E. 813. (2.)**

[**Oct. 2.**]—Theatri Tabidorum Vestibulum ; seu, Exercitiones Dianoeticæ cum historiis et experimentis demonstrativis.   Per Christopherum Bennettum.   pp. 126.   *Typis Tho. Newcomb, impensis Sam. Thomson.*   (2 Oct.)
E. 1601. (1.)

[**Oct. 3.**]—Answers to severall Queries put forth to the Quakers by Philip Bennett ; also Answers to severall other subtil Queries put forth by John Reeve.   By Edward Burrough and Francis Howgill.   *Printed for Giles Calvert.*   (3 Oct.)   **E. 813. (4.)**

[**Oct. 3.**]—A Exercitation concerning the Nature of Forgivenesse of Sin. By Thomas Hotchkis.   pp. 353.   *Printed by T. M. for Tho. Underhill.* (3 Oct.)   **E. 1518.**

[**Oct. 3.**]—The Orthodox Doctrine concerning Justification by Faith asserted and vindicated.   Wherein the book of Mr. William Eyre is examined, and the doctrine of Mr. Baxter concerning Justification is discussed.   By John Eedes.   pp. 62.   [See above : 10 Nov., 1653, E. 718. (5.)] *Printed for Henry Cripps and Lodowick Lloyd.*   (3 Oct.)   **E. 234. (2.)**

[**Oct. 7.**]—Prophecy Maintain'd ; or, A Vindication of the Advertisement to the City of London.   By Fra. Wilde.   pp. 89.   (7 Oct.)
E. 1485. (3.)

[**Oct. 8.**]— Articles of Religion, presented to our late King Charles at the Isle of Wight, and now tendred to the consideration of the Supreme Authority of this Nation.   *Printed for John Tompkins.* (8 Oct.)   **E. 813. (8.)**

1654.

[**Oct. 8.**]—Appius and Virginia. A tragedy. By John Webster. pp. 61. *Printed for Rich. Marriot.* (8 Oct.) **E. 234. (3.)**

Oct. 9.—To his Highnesse the Lord Protector, and to Parliament : a Preparative to the Humiliation-Day, on the eleventh of Oct., 1654. Presented 9 Oct., 1654. [Complaining of the Parliaments neglect in dealing with petitions : signed, " Your Son-in-Law, Thomas Philpot."] *s. sh.* **669. f. 19. (20.)**

[**Oct. 10.**]—A Prospect of Eternity, or, Mans everlasting condition opened and applyed. By John Wells. pp. 409. *Printed by E. C. for Joseph Cranford.* (10 Oct.) **E. 1476. (3.)**

[**Oct. 10.**]—A Commemoration of the great Deliverance from the Powder-Plot. [In verse. By John Turner.] *Printed by J. B., for John Collins.* (10 Oct.) **E. 813. (10.)**

[**Oct. 11.**]—True Christianity : or, Christs absolute Dominion and Mans necessary Self-resignation, in two Assize Sermons preached at Worcester. By Richard Baxter. pp. 216. *Printed for Nevill Simmons.* (11 Oct.) **E. 1543. (2.)**

[**Oct. 12.**]—Divine Opticks, or, A Treatise of the Eye, discovering the Vices and Virtues thereof. Chiefly grounded on Psal. 119, 37. By Robert Dingley. pp. 105. *Printed by J. M. for H. Cripps & L. Lloyd.* (Oct. 12.) **E. 1472. (3.)**

[**Oct. 14.**]—Vaticinium Causuale. A Rapture occasioned by the late miraculous Deliverance of the Lord Protector from a desperate Danger. By Geo. Wither. [In verse.] *Printed for T. Ratcliffe and E. Mottershed.* (14 Oct.) **E. 813. (14.)**

[**Oct. 16.**]—A Warning from the Lord, occasioned by a late Declaration of the Lord Protector inviting the people of England and Wales to a day of solemn Fasting and Humiliation. By G. F. [i.e. George Fox.] *Printed for Giles Calvert.* (16 Oct.) **E. 813. (15.)**

Oct. 17.—Swiftsure. At a Councel of War held aboard. [Resolutions as to " whether it be lawful for sea-men to tender their grievances by way of petition," etc.] *s. sh.* **669. f. 19. (32.)**

[**Oct. 18.**]—To his Highness the Lord Protector, &c., and our General. The Petition of several Colonels of the Army. [Protesting against the establishment of a standing army under the command of a single person. Signed by Thomas Saunders, John Okey, Matthew Allured.] *s. sh.* (18 Oct.) **669. f. 19. (21.)**

[**Oct. 18.**]—A Declaration and Protestation against the new Tax and Extortion of Excise in general and for Hops in particular. By William Prynne. *Printed for the Author.* (18 Oct.) **E. 813. (16.)**

[**Oct. 18.**]—Soul Mercies precious in the eyes of Saints, or the great things the Lord doth for the Souls of his Beloved Ones. By Samuel Heskins. pp. 105. *Printed by J. M. for H. Cripps.* (18 Oct.) **E. 1504. (2.)**

1654.

[**Oct. 19.**]— A True Account of the late Conspiracy against the Lord
Protector. pp. 95. *Printed by Thomas Newcomb.* (19 Oct.)
E. 813. (22.)

[**Oct. 19.**]—Some Mementos for the Officers and Souldiers of the Army.
(19 Oct.) **E. 813. (20.)**

Oct. 19.—The Doctrine of the Bodies Fragility, with a Divine Project
discovering how to make these vile bodies of ours glorious by getting
gracious Souls. A sermon preached at Martins, Ludgate, at the Funeral
of Dr. Samuel Bolton, Master of Christ College, Cambridge. By Edmund
Calamy. *Printed for Joseph Moore.* **E. 814. (8.)**

[**Oct. 23.**]—Inquisitio Anglicana; or, The Disguise discovered. Shewing
the proceedings of the Commissioners at White-hall in the examinations
of Anthony Sadler. [See also below : 25 Nov., E. 818. (2) and 1 Dec.,
E. 818. (10.)] *Printed by J. Grismond for Richard Royston.* (23 Oct.)
E. 813. (23.)

[**Oct. 23.**]—A Triple Reconciler, stating the Controversies, whether
Ministers have an Exclusive power of Communicants from the Sacra-
ment, whether any persons Unordained may lawfully Preach, whether
the Lords Prayer ought not to be used by all Christians. By Thomas
Fuller. pp. 144. *Printed by Will. Bently for John Williams.* (23 Oct.)
E. 1441. (2.)

[**Oct. 24.**]—Bellum Tartaricum, or the Conquest of the Empire of China
by the invasion of the Tartars. Written originally in Latine by Martin
Martinius, and now translated into English. [With an engraved
portrait of "Theinmingus, Emperour of the Western Tartars."] pp. 240.
Printed for John Crook. (24 Oct.) **E. 1499. (2.)**

[**Oct. 26.**]— The true Gospel-Faith witnessed by the Prophets and
Apostles, and collected into thirty Articles. By Tho: Lover. [See also
below : 20 Oct., 1655, E. 855. (1.)] *Printed for Francis Smith.*
(26 Oct.) **E. 1492. (1.)**

[**Oct. 26.**]—A Voice from the Word of the Lord to those grand Impostors
called Quakers. By John Griffith. [See also below : 24 Nov., E. 817.
(16.)] *Printed for Francis Smith.* (26 Oct.) **E. 1492. (2.)**

Oct. 30.—Colonell Shapcott his Speech in Parliament. With the case
of the Secluded Members of this Parliament. **E. 816. (7.)**

Oct. 30.—The Speech of Colonel Shapcott, Knight for Devonshire, in
behalf of K. Charles the second. *s. sh.* **669. f. 19. (34.)**

[**Oct.**]—To Parliament. The Petition of Edward, Earle of Meath. [For
the restitution of estates in Ireland wrested from his father by the Earl
of Strafford.] *s. sh.* **669. f. 19. (23.)**

[**Oct.**]—To Parliament. The Petition of the Prisoners for Debt in the
Upper-Bench Prison. [Praying that their cases may be tried without
pleading of Counsel, *etc.*] *s. sh.* **669. f. 19. (24.)**

1654.

[**Oct.**]—To Parliament. The Petition of the Inhabitants of the severall Parishes of Clement Danes, Savoy, Covent Garden, Martin in the Fields, Giles in the Fields, and the Parishes and Places adjoining in the County of Middlesex. [For the settlement of the market in Clements Inn Fields.] *s. sh.* **669. f. 19. (24.)**

[**Oct.**]—To Parliament. The Petition of Margaret, Countesse of Worcester. [For an allowance out of the confiscated estate.] *s. sh.*
669. f. 19. (27.)

[**Oct.**]—To Parliament. The Remonstrance and Petition of Susanna Bastwick, the distressed widow of John Bastwick, Doctor in Physick, and her children. [Praying for relief and recompense for the sufferings of her husband in the service of the Parliament.] *s. sh.*
669. f. 19. (28.)

[**Oct.**]—A Proclamation to all, of all sorts, high and low, rich and poore, wherein is proclaimed the Law-Royal [i.e. the Rights of the People], which in keeping thereof is true Liberty. Given forth by force and power for every one to observe upon pain of death. By William Covell. [An attack on the Government.] *s. sh.* **669. f. 19. (29.)**

[**Oct.**]—Reasons humbly offered, why the Sale of the Lands and Estates, belonging to the late Bishop of Durham, should not be confirmed. *s. sh.*
669. f. 19. (26.)

Nov. 1.—Katherine Pettus, Plaintiffe, Margaret Bancroft, Defendant, In Chancery. [A representation of part of Plaintiff's case, "to the Committee that is to bring in a Bill for the relief of Creditors and poore Prisoners."] *s. sh.* **669. f. 19. (30.)**

[**Nov. 1.**]—The Ladies Cabinet enlarged and opened, containing many rare secrets of Preserving, Physick, Cookery. By Lord Ruthven. pp. 227. *Printed by T. M. for M. M. G. Bedell and T. Collins.* (1 Nov.) **E. 1528. (1.)**

[**Nov. 1.**]—A Brief Exposition on the XII Smal Prophets. By George Hutcheson. 3 vol. *Printed for Ralph Smith.* (1 Nov.)
E. 1453 and 1454.

[**Nov. 2.**]—The Lord Craven's Case briefly stated. *Printed by Tho. Newcomb.* (2 Nov.) **E. 234. (4.)**

Nov. 2.—Safe Conduct, or the Saints Guidance to Glory. Opened in a sermon preached at Dunstans in the East, London, at the funerall of Mrs. Thomasin Barnardiston. By Ralph Robinson. pp. 93. *Printed by R. I. for Stephen Bowtell.* **E. 823. (7.)**

[**Nov. 2.**]—The Principles of Faith, presented by Mr. Tho. Goodwin, Mr. Nye, Mr. Sydrach Simson and other Ministers to the Committee of Parliament for Religion. [See also below: 28 Nov., E. 818. (4.)] *Printed for Robert Ibbitson.* (2 Nov.) **E. 234. (5.)**

1654.

[**Nov. 3.**]—A Briefe Polemicall Dissertation concerning the true Time of the Inchoation and Determination of the Lords Day Sabbath, wherein is clearly manifested that the Lords Day begins and ends at Evenings. By William Prynne.   pp. 92.   *Printed by T. Mabb for Edward Thomas.* (3 Nov.)   E. 814. (11.)

[**Nov. 3.**]—Merlinus Anonymus. An Ephemeris for the year 1655. By Raphael Desmus.   *Printed by F. Neile.*   (3 Nov.) C. 31. a. 41. (4.)

[**Nov. 3.**]—An Answer to a Paper called, A Petition of Thomas Ellyson. [Signed : Francis Howgill.]   (3 Nov.)   E. 814. (10.)

[**Nov. 4.**]—To His Highness the Lord Protector. The Petition of the Sea-men belonging to the Ships of the Commonwealth of England. [Protesting against pressed service, and the irregularity of payment.] *s. sh.*   (4 Nov.)   669. f. 19. (33.)

[**Nov. 4.**]—A brief Relation of the proceedings before His Highness Councel concerning the Petitioners of the Isle of Ely against George Glapthorne.   (4 Nov.)   E. 814. (12.)

[**Nov. 4.**]—An Answer to the Animadversions [by John Owen] on the Dissertations concerning Ignatius's Epistles and the Episcopacie in them asserted. By Henry Hammond.   pp. 219.   *Printed by J. G. for Richard Royston.*   (4 Nov.)   E. 814. (13.)

[**Nov. 4.**]—The younger Brothers Advocate; or, A line or two for Younger Brothers. With their Petition to Parliament. By Champianus North-tonus.   *Printed by W. W.*   (4 Nov.)   E. 234. (5*.)

Nov. 5.—The Pillar and Pattern of Englands Deliverances. Presented in a Sermon to the Lord Mayor and Aldermen at Pauls. By Thomas Horton.   *Printed by R. I. for Jo. Clark.*   E. 815. (1.)

[**Nov. 6.**]—Refreshing Streams flowing from the Fulnesse of Jesus Christ. Sermons, by William Colvill.   pp. 501.   *Printed by A. M. for Joseph Cranford.*   (6 Nov.)   E. 815. (2.)

[**Nov. 6.**]—Saint Chrysostome his Paraenesis, or Admonition wherein he recalls Theodorus the fallen. Or, generally, an exhortation for desperate sinners. Translated by the Lord Viscount Grandison, prisoner in the Tower.   pp. 126.   *Printed for Thomas Dring.*   (6 Nov.) E. 1531. (2.)

[**Nov. 6.**]—The Bloody Almanack ; or, Astrological Predictions and Monthly Observations setting forth the changes that will happen in 1655.   *Printed for G. Horton.*   (6 Nov.)   E. 816. (1.)

Nov. 7.—By the Mayor. [An Order in blank to the Aldermen of the various Wards, with instructions for keeping a more vigilant Night Watch.] *s. sh.*   669. f. 19. (35.)

[**Nov. 7.**]—Something in answer to a book called Choice Experiences given forth by J[ane] Turner. Also the copy of a Letter sent to the Anabaptists in Newcastle. By Edward Burrough.   (Nov. 7.) E. 816. (2.)

1654.

[**Nov. 7.**]—A Treatise of the Sabbath. By William Pynchon. Whereunto is annexed a Treatise of Holy Time. pp. 263. *Printed for Thomas Newberry.* (7 Nov.)   **E. 816. (5 and 6.)**

[**Nov. 9.**]—Arcana Aulica ; or, Walsingham's Manual of Prudential Maxims for the States-man and the Courtier. pp. 153. *Printed by T. C. for John Wright.* (9 Nov.)   **E. 1527. (1.)**

[**Nov. 9.**]—Refractoria Disputatio : or, The Thwarting Conference, in a Discourse between Thraso, one of the late Kings Colonels, Neutralis, a sojourner in the City, Prelaticus, a chaplain to the late King, Patriotus, a well-willer to the Parliament. [Signed : T. L. W.] pp. 157. *Printed by Robert White.* (9 Nov.)   **E. 1502. (1.)**

[**Nov. 10.**]—A Letter sent from the King att Cologne to Henry Duke of Gloucester att Paris. [In MS. throughout, in Thomason's hand.] (10 Nov.)   **E. 816. (11.)**

[**Nov. 10.**]—The Citie Matrons ; or, The Three Monemental Mobbs. [A satire.] (10 Nov.)   **E. 816. (12.)**

[**Nov. 11.**]—An Acquittance or Discharge from Dr. E. H. [i.e. Edward Hyde] his demand of a fifth part of the Rectory of Br. [i.e. Brightwell] in Barks. By John Ley. (11 Nov.)   **E. 816. (13.)**

[**Nov. 11.**]—A Treatise concerning Enthusiasme. By Meric Casaubon. pp. 228. *Printed by R. D. for Thomas Johnson.* (11 Nov.)   **E. 1452. (2.)**

[**Nov. 13.**]—A Modest Vindication of the Doctrine of Conditions in the Covenant of Grace, and the defenders thereof from the aspersions of Arminianism and Popery which Mr. W. E. [i.e. William Eyre] cast on them. By John Graile. With a Preface wherein is a discovery of the judgment of Dr. Twisse in the point of Justification, clearing him from Antinomianism, by Constant Jessop. Whereunto is added, A Sermon preached at the funeral of John Grail, by Humphrey Chambers. pp. 174. [See above : 10 Nov. 1653, E. 718. (5.)] *Printed for Matthew Keinton.* (13 Nov.)   **E. 817. (1 and 2.)**

[**Nov. 14.**]—A Brief Explication upon Psalm 50 to Psalm 100. By David Dickson. pp. 399. *Printed by T. M. for Thomas Johnson.* (14 Nov.)   **E. 1442. (1.)**

Nov. 16.—An Epitaph on that renowned lady, Elizabeth Cromwel, Mother to his Highness the Lo. Protector, who died Nov. 16, and lieth buried in Westminster Abbey. [Signed : J. L., i.e. J. Long.] *Printed by James Cottrel.*   **669. f. 19. (41.)**

[**Nov. 17.**]—The Birth of a Day : being a treatise theologicall, morall and historicall ; representing the vicissitudes of all humane things. By J. Robinson. pp. 102. *Printed by Roger Daniel ; and are to be sold by Thomas Johnson.* (17 Nov.)   **E. 1493. (4.)**

1654.

[**Nov. 17.**]—A Character whereby the false Christs may be known, in two Letters sent to severall Priests in Liestershire after two severall Meetings betwixt them and those called Quakers. By Richard Farnworth. *Printed by Giles Calvert.* (17 Nov.) **E. 817. (8.)**

[**Nov. 17.**]—The Second Part of the Change of Church-Discipline. Also a Reply to Mr. Collins his Answer to Mr. Brabournes First Part. By Theophilus Brabourne. pp. 104. [See above: 24 July, E. 805. (12.), and also below: 14 April, 1655, E. 832. (2.)] *Printed for the Author.* (17 Nov.) **E. 817. (9 and 10.)**

[**Nov. 24.**]—The Fiery darts of the Divel quenched; or, Something in answer to A Second Beacon fired, by Luke Fawne, John Rothwel and others. By Francis Howgil. [See above: 1 Oct., E. 813. (1.)] Also, something in answer to A Voice from the Word of the Lord, by John Griffith. [See above: 26 Oct., E. 1492. (2.)] *Printed for Giles Calvert.* (24 Nov.) **E. 817. (16.)**

[**Nov. 24.**]—Considerable Considerations to be considered of. [A Presbyterian pamphlet.] By S. L., Minister of the Gospel. (24 Nov.) **E. 817. (17.)**

[**Nov. 25.**]—Merlinus Democritus; or, The Merry-conceited Prognosticator. By W. Liby. [A satire on Lilly's prognostications.] *Printed for G. Horton.* (25 Nov.) **E. 818. (1.)**

[**Nov. 25.**]—An Apologeticall Letter to a Person of Quality, concerning a scandalous and malicious passage, in a conference lately held between an Inquisitor at White-Hall and Mr. Anthony Sadler, published in his Inquisitio Anglicana. By Jo. Hall, Bishop of Norwich. [See above: 23 Oct., E. 813. (23.)] *Printed for N. B.* (25 Nov.) **E. 818. (2.)**

[**Nov. 28.**]—The Foure Wishes of Mr. John Humphrey, in conclusion of his Sermons printed 1653, intituled, An Humble Admission unto the Lord's Supper, etc. *s. sh.* (28 Nov.) **669. f. 19. (42.)**

[**Nov. 28.**]—A New Method of Physick. Written in Latin by Simeon Partlicius. Translated into English by Nicholas Culpeper. pp. 548. *Printed by Peter Cole.* (28 Nov.) **E. 1475. (3.)**

[**Nov. 28.**]—The Sword of the Lord drawn and furbished against the man of sin. In answer to a paper ["The Principles of Faith"] by Thomas Goodwine, one Nye, and Sydrach Sympson. By Christopher Atkinson, a Quaker. [See above: 2 Nov., E. 234. (5.)] *Printed by Giles Calvert.* (28 Nov.) **E. 818. (4.)**

[**Nov. 28.**]—Grati Falisci Cynegeticon. Or, A poem of Hunting, by Gratius the Faliscian. Englished and illustrated [with notes] by Christopher Wase. pp. 178. *Printed for Charles Adams.* (28 Nov.) **E. 1531. (3.)**

[**Nov. 30.**]—Expository Notes with Practical Observations towards the opening of the five first Chapters of Genesis. By Benjamin Needler.

1654.

pp. 288. *Printed by T. R. & E. M. for Nathanael Webb and William Grantham.* (30 Nov.)   **E. 1443. (2.)**

[**Nov. 30.**]—A Premonition of sundry Sad Calamities yet to come. Grounded upon an explication of the twenty fourth chapter of Isaiah. By William Aspinwall. *Printed for Livewell Chapman.* (30 Nov.)

E. 818. (7.)

Nov. 30.—[An Epitaph on John Selden, who died 30 Nov. In Latin and English, signed : J. D.] *Printed by Tho. Newcomb.*

669. f. 19. (46.)

[**Nov.**]—To Parliament. The Petition of Mary Countess of Sterling [and others, heirs of Sir Peter and Lady Powel, challenging their wills, by which, through the alleged fraud of Thomas and Anne Levingston, they have been disinherted]. *s. sh.*   **669. f. 19. (31.)**

[**Nov.**]—To Parliament. The Petition of Katherine Stone, widdow, and Henry Stone, her son. The Answer of Nathanael Snape and Samuel Foxley, to this Petition, which is false and scandalous in divers particulars, as followeth. *s. sh.*   **669. f. 19. (38.)**

[**Nov.**]—To Parliament. The Petition of a great number of Imprisoned Freemen for Debt, of the City of London, who yet lye in Ludgate, [" That their cases may speedily be determined, without pleading of Councel."] *s. sh.*   **669. f. 19. (39.)**

[**Nov.**]—To Parliament. The Petition of divers Citizens of London, on behalfe of themselves and others who have advanced moneys for the use of the Commonwealth, and doubled the same at Weavers Hall. [For repayment.] *s. sh.*   **669. f. 19. (40.)**

[**Nov.**]—To Parliament. The Petition of severall well affected persons, purchasers of the estate of William Lord Craven. [For confirmation of the sale.] *s. sh.*   **669. f. 19. (45.)**

[**Nov.**]—To the Honorable, the Referees of His Highnesse most Honourable Councel, in the Cause between Sir John Stowell and the Purchasers. The Petition of William Lawrence of Edenburgh, Esq. [Praying, as one of the purchasers, " that no proceedings be suffered against him otherwise than is by law allowable against a person not summoned and out of the nation."] *s. sh.*   **669. f. 19. (37.)**

[**Nov.**]—Reasons for Establishment of Publike Sale. Humbly tendered, as well as in behalf of the Commonwealth, as likewise of the Purchasers of the Estate of Sir John Stowel. [With the declaration of Parliament, dated 13 Oct., 1653, confirming the sale of Sir John Stawell's estates.] *s. sh.*   **669. f. 19. (36.)**

[**Nov.**]—The State of the Case in brief, between the Countess of Sterlin, and others, by Petition in Parliament, Plaintiffs ; and M^{ris} Levingston, Defendant. *s. sh.*   **669. f. 19. (43.)**

1654.

[**Nov.**]—A Brief of the Case of the Officers belonging to the Court of Wards and Liveries not yet recompensed for the loss of their Offices, by taking away the said Court. *s. sh.* **669. f. 19. (44.)**

[**Nov.**]—Merlini Anglici Ephemeris. Astrologicall predictions for 1655. By William Lilly. [With an engraved portrait of the author.] pp. 93. *Printed for the Company of Stationers, and H. Blunden.* **E. 1500. (5.)**

[**Dec. 1.**]—Mr. Sadler Re-examined ; or, his Disguise discovered. Shewing the grosse mistakes and falshoods in his Inquisitio Anglicana. [By Philip Nye. See above : 23 Oct., E. 813. (23.)] *Printed for Nathanael Webb and William Grantham.* (1 Dec.) **E. 818. (10.)**

[**Dec. 1.**]—Drops of Myrrhe. Or, Meditations and Prayers, fitted to divers of the preceding arguments. *Printed by R. W. for Rich. Davis : Oxon.* (1 Dec.) **E. 1469. (2.)**

[**Dec. 1.**]—A Rejoynder to Mr. Drake, or a reply unto his book entituled, A Boundary to the holy Mount. By John Humfrey. pp. 270. [See above : 4 Feb., 1653, E. 1314. (2.), and also below : 12 July, 1656, E. 1593.] *Printed by F. L. for E. Blackmore.* (1 Dec.) **E. 1466. (2.)**

[**Dec. 1.**]—Λόγοι Εὔκαιροι. Essayes and Observations, theologicall & morall. Together with some Meditations & Prayers. By a Student in Theologie. pp. 107. *Printed by R. W. for R. Davis : Oxon.* (1 Dec.) **E. 1496. (1.)**

[**Dec. 2.**]—Hypocrisie Discovered in its Nature and Workings. Delivered in several Sermons, by Cuthbert Sidenham. pp. 212. *Printed by W. H. for Rich. Tomlins.* (2 Dec.) **E. 1504. (3.)**

[**Dec. 2.**]—An Old Parliamentary Prognostication made at Westminster for the New-Year. (2 Dec.) **E. 818. (11.)**

[**Dec. 4.**]—The Royall Merlin ; or, Great Brittains Loyal Observator. [Astrological predictions for 1655.] *Printed for George Horton.* (4 Dec.) **E. 818. (12.)**

[**Dec. 5.**]—Politick Maxims and Observations, by Hugo Grotius. Translated by H. C., S. T. B. pp. 142. *Printed for Humphrey Moseley.* (5 Dec.) **E. 1527. (2.)**

[**Dec. 7.**]—A Heavenly Conference between Christ and Mary after his Resurrection, wherein the intimate familiarity between Christ and a Believer is discovered. [Edited by Simeon Ashe, J. Nalton and J. Church.] pp. 237. *Printed for John Rothwel.* (7 Dec.) **E. 1512. (1.)**

[**Dec. 8.**]—A Petition for the Vindication of the Publique use of the Book of Common-Prayer from aspersions lately cast upon it. Occasioned by the late Ordinance for the ejecting of ignorant and insufficient Ministers and Schoolmasters. By Lionel Gatford. pp. 62. *Printed for John Williams.* (8 Dec.) **E. 818. (17.)**

[**Dec. 8.**]—Great Britains Remembrancer, looking in and out. Tending to the Increase of the Monies of the Commonwealth. Presented to

1654.

the Lord Protector and Parliament by Ralphe Maddison, Kt. *Printed by Tho. Newcomb for Humphrey Moseley.* (8 Dec.) **E. 818. (18.)**

[**Dec. 9.**]—A Brief Relation of the strange and unnatural practices of Wessel Goodwin, Mehetabell Jones and Elizabeth Pigeon. (9 Dec.)

E. 818. (19.)

[**Dec. 9.**]—Knowledge of the Times : or the resolution of the question how long it shall be unto the End of Wonders. By John Tillinghast. pp. 346. *Printed by R. I. for L. Chapman.* (9 Dec.) **E. 1467. (1.)**

[**Dec. 11.**]—A Copy of a Letter concerning the election of a Lord Protector. *Printed by Tho. Newcomb.* (11 Dec.) **E. 818. (20.)**

[**Dec. 11.**]—The Eighth Book of Mr. Jeremiah Burroughs. Being a Treatise of the Evil of Evils, or the Exceeding Sinfulness of Sin. pp. 537. *Printed by Peter Cole.* (11 Dec.) **E. 819.**

Dec. 12.—[A new Confession of Faith, or the first principles of the Christian Religion necessary to bee laid as a foundation by all such as desire to build on unto perfection. Represented by a Committee of Divines [F. Cheynell and others] unto the grand Committee for Religion as fitt to be owned by all such Ministers as are or shall be allowed to receive the publique maintenance for their works in the Ministry. Propounded to the Parliament, 12 Dec. Imperfect : wanting the title-page, which is supplied in MS. by Thomason, with a note.]

E. 826. (3.)

[**Dec. 12.**]—The Innocent Lord ; or, The Divine Providence. Being the incomparable History of Joseph. Written originally in French by De Ceriziers, and now rendred into English by Sir William Lowre. pp. 143. *Printed by S. G. for Charles Adams.* (12 Dec.) **E. 1480. (3.)**

[**Dec. 13.**]—The Testimony of the Everlasting Gospel witnessed through Sufferings. [Experiences of Richard Hubberthorn, James Lancaster and Christopher Atkinson, Quakers.] (13 Dec.) **E. 818. (23.)**

[**Dec. 13.**]—The Golden Grove, or a Manuall of Daily Prayers and Letanies, fitted to the dayes of the week. By the author of The Great Exemplar [i.e. Jeremy Taylor. With an engraved allegorical frontispiece]. pp. 161. *Printed by J. F. for R. Royston.* (13 Dec.)

E. 1532. (1.)

[**Dec. 15.**]—Canaans Flowings, or a second part of Milk & Honey ; being another Collation of many Christian Experiences. By Ralph Venning. pp. 229. *Printed for John Rothwel.* (15 Dec.) **E. 1480. (4.)**

[**Dec. 16.**]—An Exact Narrative of the Attempts [at conversion] made upon the Duke of Glocester. Published for the satisfaction of all true Protestants. *Printed for F. Eglesfield.* (16 Dec.) **E. 820. (4.)**

Dec. 16.—A Sermon, preached at the Funerall of Andrew Pern. By Samuel Ainsworth. *Printed for William Gilbertson : London ; and are to be sold by Thomas Collins in Northampton.* **E. 487. (3.)**

1654.

[**Dec. 18.**]—A Message sent from the Lord Protector to the Great
Turk, with his demands and the releasing of the English Captives [at
Algiers]. *Printed for Peter Mitchel.* (18 Dec.) **E. 820. (5.)**

[**Dec. 18.**]—A Petition presented to the Lord Protector and the Parliament by divers Ministers, for the establishment of themselves and
others in the places to which they were admitted to officiate, without
Institution from the Bishops. *Printed for Edw. Brewster.* (18 Dec.)
E. 820. (6.)

[**Dec. 18.**]—A Faithful Discovery of a treacherous design of Mystical
Antichrist, by Joseph Kellet, John Pomroy and Paul Glisson. Con-
taining an examination of many doctrines of the Quakers, by Christopher
Feak, John Simpson and George Cokayn. [Second edition.] pp. 56.
Printed for Thomas Brewster. (18 Dec.) **E. 820. (7.)**

Dec. 19.—Rules, Directions and By-Laws made by the Court of Aldermen of the City of London by vertue of the late Ordinance. *Printed
by James Flesher.* **E. 1064. (19.)**

Dec. 19.—A brief and perfect Journal of the proceedings and successe
of the English Army in the West Indies [from its departure from
Portsmouth, 19 Dec., 1654] until 24 June, 1655. Together with some
quæres inserted and answered. By I. S. **E. 853. (29.)**

[**Dec. 19.**]—The Oppressed Close Prisoner in Windsor-Castle, his Defiance
to the Father of Lyes. Occasioned by some late scandalous Reports
raised to the dishonour of that cause wherein he is engaged. By
Chri. Feake. pp. 119. *Printed for L. Chapman.* (19 Dec.)
E. 820. (10.)

[**Dec. 19.**]—The Second Part of a Seasonable Legal and Historical
Vindication of the Fundamental Liberties of English Freemen. By
William Prynne. pp. 148. *Printed for the Author, and are to be sold
by Edward Thomas.* (19 Dec.) **E. 820. (11.)**

[**Dec. 21.**]—Quaking Principles dashed in pieces by the standing and
unshaken Truth. Being an examination of the tenents held forth by
certain Northern People. By Henoch Howet. [See also below : 5 May,
1655, E. 835. (2.)] *Printed by Henry Hills.* (21 Dec.) **E. 821. (2.)**

[**Dec. 22.**]—Truth appearing through the Clouds of undeserved Scandal
and Aspersion. Or, a brief account of some particulars clearly evincing
the illegality of the sentence of ejectment passed by the Commissioners
of Berks against Dr. John Pordage of Bradfeild. (22 Dec.)
E. 821. (4.)

Dec. 24.—Humble Advice : or the heads of those things which were
offered to many honourable Members of Parliament by Mr. Richard
Baxter, at the end of his sermon, 24 Dec., at the Abby in Westminster.

1654.

With some additions. *Printed for Thomas Underhill and Francis Tyton.* **E. 821. (14.)**

Dec. 25.—Another great and bloody Plot against his Highness the Lord Protector : with the manner how a dreadfull blow should have been given on Christmas Day. Likewise a list of the names of some of the chief conspirators. *Printed for G. Horton.* **E. 823. (1.)**

[Dec. 26.]—Truth cleared from Reproaches and Scandals, laid upon it by those who goes by the name of Judges, and who went the Northern Circuit. Also some examinations of those whom the world called Quakers. [By Cuthbert Hunter.] (26 Dec.) **E. 821. (7.)**

[Dec. 28.]—The Title of Sir Thomas Dawes, Thomas Cromwell, Humfrey Walrond, and Josias Tully, to certain improved Lands in the West and North Fenns in the County of Lincoln ; together with the objections and answers to the same, as it now depends in Parliament. *s. sh.* (28 Dec.) **669. f. 19. (56.)**

[Dec. 31.] Nil Novi. This years fruit from the last years Root. Occasioning a sudden glance upon the true Resurrection, the perfect perfection, and perfect obedience. Written in a letter to a friend, by Henry Pinnel. pp. 50. *Printed by J. C. for Richard Moone.* (31 Dec.) **E. 821. (11.)**

[Dec.]—To Parliament. The Petition of Edward Hanchett, Usher of the late Court of Wards and Liveries. [For compensation for the loss of his office through the abolition of the Court.] *s. sh.* **669. f. 19. (47.)**

[Dec.]—To Parliament. The Petition of Sir John Stawell. [With reference to two pamphlets, entitled, " Reasons for the Establishment of Publike Sales," and " The Petition of William Lawrence of Edenburgh Esq. ; with reasons why the Petitioner's purchase ought not to be questioned by Sir John Stawell." [See above : Nov., 669. f. 19. (36.) and (37.)] **669. f. 19. (51.)**

[Dec.]—To Parliament. The Petition of Edward Dendy [Marshal of the Upper Bench Prison. Disclaiming all responsibility for the escape of prisoners, on the plea of inadequate security]. *s. sh.* **669. f. 19. (53.)**

[Dec.]—To Parliament. The Petition of Richard Ford, Nathaniel Manton, and Thomas Papillon, of London, Merchants. [Respecting the importation of whale oil and bone.] *s. sh.* **669. f. 19. (54.)**

[Dec.]—To Parliament. The Petition of Thomas Brewer, William Pawlin, Elizabeth Quested and Anne Beswick, creditors of Ulick Earl of St. Albans and Clanricard on the behalf of themselves and other the creditors of the said Earl. [MS. note by Thomason : " A Petition against John Bradshaw."] *s. sh.* **669. f. 19. (55.)**

1654.

[**Dec.**]—To Parliament. The Petition of the Subscribers, on the behalf of themselves and other reduced Officers and Souldiers therein concerned. [For payment of arrears. With twenty-two signatures.] *s. sh.*
669. f. 19. (57.)

[**Dec.**]—The poor Prisoners Petition for Charity against Christmas. To Parliament. The Petition of the miserable poor Prisoners in Wood Street Compter, and in behalfe of the rest of the poore Prisoners in and about London. *s. sh.* **669. f. 19. (50.)**

[**Dec.**]—To Parliament. The Petition of Anne Henshaw, late wife and executrix of Benjamin Henshaw, on the behalf of herself and her seven children. [In relation to a claim by assignment upon an annuity granted to the late Earl of Carlyle and charged upon the Customs Duties.] *s. sh.* **669. f. 19. (49.)**

[**Dec.**]—Rules and Orders for the Court of Common Pleas at Westminster. Made and published by the Judges of the said Court, in the term of St. Michael, 1654. pp. 53. *Printed for Richard Marriot.*
E. 821. (5.)

[**Dec.**]—Rules and Orders for the Court of the Upper Bench at Westminster. Made and published by the Judges of the said Court, in the terme of St. Michael, 1654. *Printed for Abel Roper.* **E. 821. (6.)**

[**Dec.**]—[An address, signed in the name of the Corporation for the Poor of the Corporation of the City of London, by Edward Odling, entreating that "the Grand Act for imploying and releiving the Poor of the whole Nation," may be put into force; and calling for "an additionall Act for the Corporation of the Poor of the City of London."] *s. sh.*
669. f. 19. (48.)

[**Dec.**]—The Sad and Lamentable Case of the Tenants of the late Deane and Chapter of Durham. [Praying for relief.] *s. sh.*
669. f. 19. (52.)

[**Dec.**]—Doctor Hill's Funeral-Sermon; or, a New-yeers-Gift to all the Clergie. [A satire. By Henry Hasselwood.] 2 pt. *To be sold by Richard Moon.* **E. 821. (19.)**

To the following no date, except that of the year, can be assigned.

[**1654.**]—Panegyricus Clarissimo Anglorum Imperatori Olivero Cromwello scriptus. [MS. note by Thomason: "This Panegyrick was written by the Chaplain to the Portugall Embassador," i.e. J. R. de Sá e Meneses.]
E. 1069. (4.)

1654.—Chocolate; or, An Indian Drinke. [A treatise in praise of it.] By Antonio Colminero, and rendred in the English by James Wadsworth. *Printed by J. G. for John Dakins dwelling neare the Vine*

1654.

*Taverne in Holborne, where this Tract, together with the Chocolate it selfe,
may be had.* **E. 1671. (1.)**

1654.—A Compend of Chronography, containing four thousand thirty yeer
complet, from Adams Creation to Christs Birth. By Robert Vilvain. Price
at Press, 3d. *Printed by R. Hodgkinsonne for the Author.* **E. 897. (8.)**

[**1654.**]—De Judaicis Erroribus ex Talmuth libellus Hieronymi de Sancta
Fide, medici, quondam Judæi. pp. 62. *Tiguri Anno 1552 primo excusus
apud Andream Gesnerum, jam vero Hamburgi denuo impressus per Jacobum
Rebenlinum.* **E. 1465. (2.)**

1654.—A Legacie left to Protestants, containing eighteen controversies.
[The preface signed : T. B., i.e. Thomas Bayly ?] pp. 200. *Printed at
Dowa.* **E. 1667. (2.)**

1654.—Theoremata Theologica : Theological Treatises. Eight Theses of
Divinity. Compiled or collected by Rob. Vilvain. Price at Press in Sheets,
3s. pp. 522. *Printed by R. Hodgkinsonne for the Author.* **E. 898.**

1655.

[**Jan. 1.**]—Observations concerning the Chancery ; with some proposals for
the redress of the inconveniences in the practise thereof. (1 Jan.)
E. 821. (12.)

[**Jan. 3.**]—The Great Case of Transplantation in Ireland discussed. [By
Vincent Gookin.] [See also below: 9 March, E. 829. (17.) and 12 May,
E. 829. (17.)] *Printed for I. C.* (3 Jan.) **E. 234. (6.)**

[**Jan. 3.**]—A Compleat & Perfect Concordance of the English Bible.
By R. W. [i.e. Robert Wickens.] pp. 880. *Printed by H. Hall for
Th. Robinson: Oxford.* (3 Jan.) **E. 1447.**

[**Jan. 4.**]—The Disswasive from the Errors of the Time vindicated from
the exceptions of Mr. Cotton and Mr. Tombes. By Robert Baily.
pp. 88. [See above : 9 Feb., 1648, E. 426. (8.)] *Printed by Evan
Tyler for Samuel Gellibrand.* (4 Jan.) **E. 234. (7.)**

[**Jan. 4.**]—The Marrow of Alchemy. By Eirenæus Philoponos Philalethes [i.e. George Starkey ? In verse]. The second part. pp. 61.
Printed by R. I. for Edward Brewster. (4 Jan.) **E. 1490. (2.)**

[**Jan. 5.**]—A Fresh Discovery of the High-Presbyterian Spirit. Or the
Quenching of the second Beacon fired. Declaring the un-Christian
dealings of the authors of a pamphlet entituled A Second Beacon fired,
&c. in presenting a falsified passage out of one of Mr. John Goodwins
books. Together with the responsatory epistle of the said Beacon
Firers [Luke Fawne and others], upon which epistle some animadversions are made. By John Goodwin. pp. 84. [See above : 1 Oct.,
1654, E. 813. (1.) and also below : 28 Jan., E. 826. (8.)] *Printed for
the Author, and sold by H. Cripps and L. Ll.* (5 Jan.) **E. 821. (18.)**

1655.

[**Jan. 8.**]—Rich. Baxter's Confession of his Faith, especially concerning the interest of Repentance and sincere Obedience to Christ in our Justification & Salvation. pp. 462. *Printed by R. W. for Tho. Underhill and Fra. Tyton.* (8 Jan.) **E. 822.**

[**Jan. 11.**]—The Holy Order; or Fraternity of the Mourners in Sion. Whereunto is added, Songs in the Night: or, Cheerfulnesse under Affliction. By J. H., B. N. [i.e. Joseph Hall, Bishop of Norwich.] 2 pt. *Printed by J. G. for Nathaniel Brooke.* (11 Jan.) **E. 1530. (2.)**

[**Jan. 12.**]—Mr. Evans and Mr. Pennington's Prophesie concerning seven yeers of Plenty and seven yeers of famine and pestilence. Together with the coming of the Fifth Monarchy. (12 Jan.) **E. 823. (6.)**

[**Jan. 12.**]—The Description and use of the Universall Quadrat. By Thomas Stirrup. [Illustrated with diagrams.] pp. 212. *Printed by R. & W. Leybourne for Tho. Pierrepont.* (12 Jan.) **E. 823. (8.)**

[**Jan. 12.**]—A Publick Disputation sundry dayes at Killingworth in Warwickshire, betwixt John Bryan and John Onley, upon this question, Whether the Parishes of this Nation generally be true Churches. pp. 66. *Printed for W. Larnar.* (12 Jan.) **E. 823. (9.)**

[**Jan. 13.**]—The Christian in Compleat Armour. Or, a treatise of the Saints' War against the Devil. The first part. By William Gurnall. pp. 396. *Printed for Ralph Smith.* (13 Jan.) **E. 824. (1.)**

[**Jan. 13.**]—A Declaration of the Army concerning the apprehending of Major Gen. Overton and the rest of the officers in Scotland who stand in opposition against the Lord Protector and the present government. Likewise a Remonstrance to the people. *Printed for G. Horton.* (13 Jan.) **E. 824. (2.)**

[**Jan. 14.**]—The common Salvation contended for, and the Faith which was once delivered to the Saints: or, an answer to a book called a plain answer to eighteen Queries of John Whitehead, put forth by William Kays [or rather, Kaye]. By Francis Howgill. *Printed for Giles Calvert.* (14 Jan.) **E. 824. (3.)**

[**Jan. 15.**]—God's Unchangeableness: wherein is proved that Oliver Cromwell is by the providence of God Lord Protector of England Scotland and Ireland. By George Smith, Gent. pp. 55. *Printed for Tho. Underhill and Lawrence Chapman.* (15 Jan.) **E. 824. (4.)**

[**Jan. 17.**]—The First Anniversary of the Government under the Lord Protector. [In verse.] *Printed by Thomas Newcomb for Samuel Gellibrand.* (17 Jan.) **E. 480. (1.)**

Jan. 18.—[A Representation to Parliament in favour of the draining of Lindsey Level. Signed: William Killigrew.] *s. sh.* **669. f. 19. (59.)**

[**Jan. 19.**]—Manzinie his most exquisite Academicall Discourses upon several choice subjects. Turned into French by that famous wit

1655.

Monsieur de Scudery, and Englished by an Honourable Lady. pp. 150. *Printed for Humphrey Moseley.* (19 Jan.)　　　**E. 825. (5.)**

[**Jan. 20.**]—Charls Stuart and Oliver Cromwel united; or, Glad tidings of Peace to all Christendom. By Walter Gostelow. pp. 312. [See also below: 22 Jan., 669. f. 19. (66.)] *Printed for the Author.* (20 Jan.)　　　**E. 1503. (3.)**

Jan. 22.—His Highness' Speech to the Parliament at their Dissolution. *Printed by Henry Hills, Printer to His Highness the Lord Protector.*

　　　E. 826. (22.)

Jan. 22.—A Declaration of his Highness the Lord Protector, upon his actual dissolution of Parliament. With the grounds and reasons which moved him thereunto. [With a woodcut portrait of Cromwell.] *Printed by Robert Wood.*　　　**E. 826. (13*.)**

Jan. 22.—The Speech of His Highness the Lord Protector to the Parliament, upon his dissolving of the House. Also a declaration of the manner of the Parliament's proceedings immediately before their breaking up. *Printed for G. Horton.*　　　**E. 826. (4.)**

[**Jan. 22.**]—For the Lord Protector. [A letter from Walter Gostelo, with respect to his book "Charls Stuart and Oliver Cromwel united." *s. sh.* [See above: 20 Jan., E. 1503. (3.)]　　　**669. f. 19. (66.)**

[**Jan. 22.**]—Mans Inbred Malady, or the Doctrine of Original Sin maintained. By George Burches. pp. 129. *Printed by W. Wilson.* (22 Jan.)　　　**E. 1708. (2.)**

[**Jan. 23.**]—The English Hermite, or, Wonder of this Age. Being a relation of the life of Roger Crab, living neer Uxbridg, taken from his own mouth, who counteth it a sin to eate any sort of Flesh, Fish or living Creature, or to drinke any Wine, Ale or Beere, etc. *Printed and sold in Popes Head Alley, and at the Exchange.* (23 Jan.)

　　　E. 826. (1.)

[**Jan. 23.**]—A Figure of the true & Spiritual Tabernacle, according to the inward Temple in the Spirit. By H. N. [i.e. Hendrik Niclas.] pp. 195. *Printed for Giles Calvert.* (23 Jan.)　　　**E. 1507. (1.)**

[**Jan. 23.**]—The Fulness and Freeness of God's Grace in Christ declared. I. In the point of Election, by a middle way between Calvin and Arminius, and different from them both. II. How God orders and appoints men to their final ends. In two parts. By Francis Duke. *Printed by Thomas Newcomb, for John Clark.* (23 Jan.)　**E. 825. (6.)**

[**Jan. 23.**]—The Great Mysteries of Godlinesse and Ungodlinesse. The one opened from Scripture, the other discovered from the writings and speakings of a generation of deceivers called Quakers. By R. Farmer. pp. 95. [See also below: 9 April, E. 831. (11.)] *Printed by S. G. for William Ballard, bookseller in Bristol, and Joshua Kirton in St. Paul's Churchyard.* (23 Jan.)　　　**E. 480. (2.)**

H 2

1655.

[**Jan. 27.**]—A Declaration of the Members of Parliament, lately dissolved by Oliver Cromwell, Esquire. [An attack upon Cromwell.] *s. sh.* (27 Jan.) **669. f. 19. (67.)**

Jan. 28.—The Way to true Happinesse, or the Way to Heaven open'd. In a sermon before the Lord Mayor and Aldermen of London. By Ralph Venning. *Printed by T. R. and E. M. for John Rothwell.* **E. 830. (8.)**

[**Jan. 28.**]—An Apologie for the six Book-sellers, subscribers of the second Beacon fired. Or, a vindication of them from the aspersions cast upon them by M. John Goodwin in a late pamphlet intituled A Fresh Discovery of the High Presbyterian Spirit. By one that subscribes not his name, because he confesseth himself to be Nullius Nominis. [See above : 1 Oct., 1654, E. 813. (1.), and 5 Jan., 1655, E. 821. (18.)] *Printed by S. G. for Matthew Keinton.* (28 Jan.) **E. 826. (8.)**

[**Jan. 30.**]—The Doctrine of our Martyers remembred, concerning the Supper of the Lord. By W. Kaye. *Printed for Martha Harrison.* (30 Jan.) **E. 826. (12.)**

[**Jan. 30.**]—A Free, Plain and Just Way concerning Communion and Excommunication at or from the Lord's Table. With a Christian account concerning the same. With answers to the objections to the contrary. By William Kaye. (30 Jan.) **E. 826. (11.)**

[**Jan. 30.**]—The Gossip's Braule, or, the Women weare the breeches. A mock comedy. (30 Jan.) **E. 826. (10.)**

[**Jan.**]—To Parliament. The Petition of John Wagstaff. [Praying for the exclusion of Sir Richard Temple, Bart., M.P. for the County of Warwick, as unqualified, by reason of his being a minor, to sit in Parliament.] *s. sh.* **669. f. 19. (61.)**

[**Jan.**]—To Parliament. The Petition of Henry Harbotle, on the behalf of himself and above 100 of the poor Tenants within the Barony of Langley in the County of Northumberland. [Praying for the restitution of certain rights.] *s. sh.* **669. f. 19. (65.)**

[**Jan.**]—To Parliament. The Petition of George Wither. [Respecting his purchase of a forfeited estate, formerly belonging to John Denham.] *s. sh.* **669. f. 19. (60.)**

[**Jan.**]—England's Publick Faith ; or, the Poorest Creditors unto the Richest Debtors : their solicitous appeal to men of piety, honour and zeal. *s. sh.* **669. f. 19. (58.)**

[**Feb. 2.**]—Reflections upon Monsieur Des Cartes's Discourse of a method for the well-guiding of Reason, and discovery of Truth in the Sciences. Written in French and translated by J. D. [i.e. John Davies.] pp. 93. *Printed by Tho. Newcomb.* (2 Feb.) **E. 1491. (3.)**

[**Feb. 3.**]—A Brief Survey of the Prophetical and Evangelical Events of the last Times. By Capt. John Browne. *Printed by Gartrude Dawson.* (3 Feb.) **E. 826. (18.)**

1655.

Feb. 4.—A Petitionary Remonstrance presented to O. P. [i.e. Oliver Protector] by J. G. [i.e. John Gauden] in behalf of his distressed brethren, Ministers of the Gospel, who were deprived of all publique imployment by His Declaration, 1 Jan. *Printed by Thomas Milbourn for Andrew Crook.* **E. 765. (7.)**

[**Feb. 6.**]—Ἱεροτελεσία Γαμική. Christ at the Wedding. The pristine Sanctity of Christian Marriages, as they were celebrated by the Church of England. By John Gauden. *Printed by E. Cotes for Andrew Crook.* (6 Feb.) **E. 480. (3.)**

Feb. 8.—An Order and Declaration for an Assessment of threescore thousand pounds by the moneth, for six moneths, for the maintenance of the Armies and Navies of this Commonwealth. *Printed by Henry Hills and John Field.* **E. 1064. (47.)**

[**Feb. 11.**]—The Poores Advocate, shewing what an incomparable favour it is to the Rich that there are the Poor to accept of their Charity. By R. Younge. *Printed by R. & W. Leybourn, and are to be sold by James Crump in Little Bartholomews Well-Yard; and to be lent gratis at the Blue Pales, short of Shoreditch Church, leaving two pence untill they do return them.* (11 Feb.) **E. 1452. (3.)**

Feb. 14.—An Ordinance for reviving the Court of the Dutchy of Lancaster. *Printed by Henry Hills and John Field.* **E. 1064. (48.)**

[**Feb. 14.**]—A Northern Blast, or the Spiritual Quaker converted: being soul-saving advice to the giddy people of England, who are running headlong to destruction. By G. Emmot. [See also below: 25 May, E. 840. (9.)] *Printed for R. Lambert: York.* (14 Feb.) **E. 826. (27.)**

[**Feb. 15.**]—By His Highness: a Proclamation prohibiting the disturbing of Ministers and other Christians in their Assemblies and Meetings. *s. sh. Printed by Henry Hills and John Field.* **669. f. 19. (68.)**

Feb. 15.—An Ordinance for the Continuance and Maintenance of the Alms-Houses and Alms-Men called Poor Knights, whereof the late Dean and Canons of Windsor were Feoffees in Trust. *Printed by Henry Hills and John Field.* **E. 1064. (50.)**

[**Feb. 15.**]—An Answer of the Purchasers of the Lands late of Sir John Stawel, by Act of Parliament exposed to sale for his treason, to a pamphlet intituled, The humble Remonstrance of Sir John Stawel. Together with the answer of John Ashe to divers scandals mentioned in that Remonstrance. As also a Petition and several reasons for establishment of Publick Sales, tendred by Wil. Lawrence, one of the Judges in Scotland. pp. 89. [See above: Oct., 1653, E. 1072. (2.), and also below: 18 May, E. 1072. (4.)] *Printed by Thomas Newcomb.* (15 Feb.) **E. 1072. (3.)**

1655.

[**Feb. 15.**]—The Resurrection of Dead Bones, or, The Conversion of the Jewes. Written by J. J., Philo-Judæus. pp. 124. *Printed for Giles Calvert.* (15 Feb.) **E. 1501. (1.)**

[**Feb. 16.**]—A new and further Discovery of another Plot against the Lord Protector. Together with a list of the names of the chief conspirators. *Printed for George Horton.* (16 Feb.) **E. 826. (29.)**

[**Feb. 17.**]—The Ninth, Tenth and Eleventh Books of Mr. Jeremiah Burroughs : containing three treatises. I. Of Precious Faith. II. Of Hope. III. The Saints Walk by Faith on Earth ; by Sight in Heaven. Being the last sermons that the author preached at Stepney. [With an engraved portrait of the author.] pp. 436. *Printed by Peter Cole.* (17 Feb.) **E. 827. (1.)**

[**Feb. 17.**]—Τριαμβεισις Celsissimi Domini Oliverii Cromwelli. Authore Edmundo Litsfield. [In Latin hexameters.] *Excudebat Jacobus Moxon.* (17 Feb.) **E. 1069. (1.)**

Feb. 17.—Stablishing against Shaking : or, a discovery of the Prince of Darknesse powerfully now working in the deluded people called Quakers. Being the substance of one sermon preached, 17 Feb., at Shalford in Essex. By Giles Firmin. pp. 56. [See also below : 26 July, 1656, E. 884. (4.)] *Printed by J. G. for Nathanael Webb and William Grantham.* **E. 885. (13.)**

[**Feb. 18.**]—Matthiæ de L'Obel Stirpium Illustrationes ; plurimas elaborantes inauditas plantas subreptitiis Joh: Parkinsoni rapsodiis, ex codice MS. insalutato, sparsim gravatæ. Ejusdem adjecta sunt ad calcem Theatri Botanici [of John Parkinson], ἁμαρτήματα. Accurante Guil: How. pp. 170. *Typis Tho: Warren, impensis Jos. Kirton.* (18 Feb.) **E. 827. (2.)**

[**Feb. 19.**]—The Quakers unmasked, and clearly detected to be but the spawn of Romish Frogs, Jesuites and Franciscan Freers, sent from Rome to seduce the intoxicated giddy-headed English nation. By William Prynne. *Printed for Edward Thomas.* (19 Feb.)
                                                        E. 828. (1.)

[**Feb. 20.**]—The Covenant of Life opened : or, a treatise of the Covenant of Grace. By Samuel Rutherfurd. pp. 368. *Printed by Andro Anderson for Robert Brown.* (20 Feb.) **E. 828. (2.)**

[**Feb. 20.**]—Collonel James Hay's Speech to the Parliament upon the Debate concerning Toleration. As it was taken by Anonimus, a Member of the House, and sent to the press. (20 Feb.) **E. 828. (4.)**

[**Feb. 22.**]—Ornitho-logie ; or, The Speech of Birds. [By Thomas Fuller. The dedication signed : J. S., i.e. John Stafford.] pp. 55. *Printed for John Stafford.* (22 Feb.) **E. 1646. (3.)**

[**Feb. 22.**]—[A Speech on toleration in matters of religion made to King James V. of Scotland by one of his Councillors.] *Printed by Henry Hills and John Field.* (22 Feb.) **E. 828. (8.)**

1655.

[**Feb. 23.**]—Monastichon Britanicum : or, a historicall narration of the first founding and flourishing state of the antient monasteries of Great Brittaine in the tymes of the Brittaines and Primitive Church of the Saxons. By R. B. [i.e. Richard Broughton.] *Printed for Henry Herringman.* (23 Feb.) **E. 1461. (2.)**

[**Feb. 24.**]—By His Highness. A Proclamation prohibiting Horse-Races for six moneths. *s.sh. Printed by Henry Hills and John Field.* **669. f. 19. (69.)**

[**Feb. 24.**]—XI Choice Sermons. With a Catechisme, expounding the grounds and principles of Christian Religion. By William Gay. pp. 318. *Printed for Humphrey Moseley.* (24 Feb.) **E. 1458. (1.)**

Feb. 28.—An Order and Declaration of the Lord Protector touching the continuance of the Duty of Excize and New Impost. *Printed by Henry Hills & John Field.* **E. 1064. (49.)**

[**Feb. 28.**]—The World's Wonder, or the Quakers Blazing Starr : with an astronomical judgment given upon the same from 2 Cor. ii., 13, 14, 15. Proving them to be altogether deluded by Satan. By Edmund Skipp. pp. 65. [See also below : 20 June, E. 843. (9.)] *Printed by Henry Hills.* (28 Feb.) **E. 829. (4.)**

[**Feb. 28.**]—[A note respecting Archbishop Langton's division of the Bible, and a list of the compilers of the Book of Common Prayer.] *Printed for Samuel Mearne.* (28 Feb.) *s. sh.* **E. 480. (4.)**

[**Feb.**]—Wisdomes Tripos, or rather its Inscription, Detur Sapienti, in three treatises. I. Of Worldly Policy. II. Of Morall Prudence. III. Of Christian Wisdome. By Charles Herle. pp. 242. *Printed for Samuel Gellibrand.* **E. 1511.**

[**Feb.**]—A Reply to a Paper written by one of the Six Clerks, intituled An Answer to a printed Paper of the Under-clerks in Chancery, intituled Reasons to be offered, &c. **E. 826. (17.)**

[**March 1.**]—The Pure Language of the Spirit of Truth, set forth for the confounding false languages. Or, Thee and Thou in its place is the proper language to any single person whatsoever. [By Richard Farnworth.] *Printed for Giles Calvert.* (1 March.) **E. 829. (5.)**

[**March 2.**]—Precepts for Christian Practice. By Edward Reyner. Eighth edition, inlarged. pp. 453. [See also below : 8 Aug., E. 851. (6.)] *Printed by T. R. & E. M. for Thomas Newberry.* (2 March.) **E. 1451.**

[**March 3.**]—A Collection of Private Devotions : in the Practise of the Antient Church, called the Hours of Praiers. [By John Cosin, Bishop of Durham.] pp. 271. *Printed for Richard Royston.* (3 March.) **E. 1689.**

[**March 3.**]—A true Declaration of the suffering of the innocent, wherein is discovered the zeale of the Magistrates and people of Banbury. Declared in a letter sent to William Allen, called Justice of Peace, by Anne Audland, whom the world scornfully calls Quaker. *Printed and sold by Giles Calvert.* (3 March.) **E. 829. (7.)**

1655.

[March 3.]—Truth's Testimony; and a Testimony of Truths appearing in Power, Life, Light & Glory. With an humble appeal to his Highness, Oliver, Lord Protector, as a general redress for all people. By Richard Coppin. pp. 88. (3 March.) **E. 829. (8.)**

[March 3.]—Turne Over, Behold and Wonder. [A satire, in verse. With a woodcut representing a colloquy between three men mounted on asses.] *Printed at Layghten Buzzard by the Assignes of Tom Ladle.* (3 March.) **E. 480. (5.)**

[March 5.]—The Pearle of Peace & Concord, or, A Treatise of Pacification betwixt the dissenting Churches of Christ. First written in the German language by Johannes Bergius & now translated by Mauritius Bohemus. pp. 188. *Printed by T. C. for John Rothwell.* (5 March.) **E. 1509. (1.)**

[March 5.]—Innocence appearing through the dark Mists of Pretended Guilt; or, A Narration of the illegal proceedings of the Commissioners of Berks against John Pordage, in which he is vindicated from the aspersions of Blasphemy, Necromancie, and Scandal in his life. Written by the said John Pordage. pp. 114. *Printed for Giles Calvert.* (5 March.) **E. 1068. (7.)**

[March 6.]—The Unmasking and Discovering of Anti Christ, with all the false Prophets, by the true light which comes from Christ Jesus. Written forth to convince the Seducers, and for the undeceiving of the Seduced. By George Fox. *Printed for Giles Calvert.* (6 March.) **E. 829. (9.)**

[March 6.]—The Spirituall Man judgeth all things : or the Spirituall Man's True Judgment. [By Richard Farnworth.] *Printed for Giles Calvert.* (6 March.) **E. 829. (10.)**

[March 6.]—A Shield of the Truth, or the Truth of God cleared from scandals and reproaches. Written from the Spirit of God by James Parnel. *Printed for Giles Calvert.* (6 March.) **E. 829. (11.)**

[March 7.]—Witchcraft cast out from the Religious Seed and Israel of God : and the Black Art, or Nicromancery Inchantments, Sorcerers, Wizards and Witchcraft discovered. [The preface signed: R. F., i.e. Richard Farnworth.] *Printed for Giles Calvert.* (7 March.) **E. 829. (12.)**

[March 8.]—Vindiciæ Christi at Obex Errori Arminiano. A Plea for Christ, and Obstruction to the first passage whereat the Errors of Arminius steal into the hearts of Men. Delivered in three sermons, by Richard Lewthwat. *Printed by R. W. for Nath. Webb and William Grantham.* (8 March.) **E. 480. (6.)**

[March 9.]—The Interest of England in the Irish Transplantation, stated. Being chiefly intended as an answer to a scandalous seditious pamphlet, entituled, The great Case of Transplantation in Ireland discussed. By Richard Laurence. [See above: 3 Jan., E. 234. (6.), and also below : 12 May, E 838. (7.)] *Printed by Henry Hills.* (9 March.) **E. 829. (17.)**

1655.

[**March 9.**]—Lawles Tythe-Robbers discovered, who make Tythe-Revenue a mock-mayntenance, being encouraged thereunto by the defect of law and justice about Ministers maintenance. [By Richard Culmer.] *Printed for Thomas Newbery.* (9 March.) **E. 829. (18.)**

[**March 9.**]—'Ευχοδία. Or, a Prayer-Song. Being sacred poems on the Birth and Passion of our Blessed Saviour. In two parts. By Daniel Cudmore. [With an engraved frontispiece.] *Printed by J. C. for William Ley.* (9 March.) **E. 1498. (2.)**

[**March 10.**]—Concordiæ inter Evangelicos quærendæ consilia, quæ ab Ecclesiæ in Transsylvania Evangelicæ Pastoribus & Scholæ Albæ Juliacensis Professoribus in synodo congregatis approbata fuerunt an. MDCXXXIV, et tunc ipsorum nomine Johanni Duræo transmissa ad promovendam Evangelicarum Ecclesiarum unionem cujus tum se præstabat sollicitatorem. (10 March.) **E. 830. (2.)**

[**March 12.**]—The Golden Grove, or a Manuall of Daily Prayers and Letanies. By the author of the Great Exemplar [i.e. Jeremy Taylor.] pp. 169. *Printed by J. F. for R. Royston.* (12 March.) **E. 1532. (2.)**

[**March 12.**]—Ishmael and his Mother cast out into the Wilderness amongst the wild beasts of the same nature : or, a reply to a book entitulled, The Scriptures proved to be the Word of God, put forth by one of Ishmaels children [S. Townsend]. Given forth from the Spirit of the Lord in us Christopher Atkinson, George Whitehead, James Lancaster, Thomas Simonds. *Printed for Giles Calvert.* (12 March.) **E. 830. (3.)**

[**March 12.**]—The Railer rebuked, in a reply to a paper subscribed Ellis Bradshaw, who calls it The Quakers whitest devil unvailed. By James Nailer. (12 March.) **E. 830. (4.)**

[**March 12.**]—The Trumpet of the Lord blowne ; or, a Blast against Pride and Oppression, and the defiled liberty which stands in the flesh. By James Parnel. *Printed for Giles Calvert.* (12 March.) **E. 830. (5.)**

[**March 13.**]—A Discovery of the Latitude of the loss of the Earthly Paradise by Original Sin.—Syons Redemption discovered. By George Hammon. pp. 195. *Printed by Robert Ibbitson for Francis Smith.* (13 March.) **E. 1680. (1.)**

[**March 13.**]—A Rod to drive out the Wilde Bores and Subtill Foxes from amongst the Vines. Or, a gift sent to the Priests, that they may acknowledge their errors. By R. Farneworth. *Printed and sold by Giles Calvert.* (13 March.) **E. 830. (6.)**

[**March 15.**]—A Letter to His Highness the Lord Protector, from Captain Unton Crooke, signifying the totall defeat of the Cavaliers in the West, under Sir Joseph Wagstaffe. *Printed by Henry Hills and John Field.* **E. 830. (15.)**

1655.

[**March 15.**]—David's Enemies discovered. Or a discovery of that custome which the priests of this generation would make an ordinance of, to blind the eyes of the simple, as this priest Clapham in his 6 arguments, which is here answered by Christopher Atkinson, George Whitehead. Also a brief reply unto Frederick Woodall's three Principles and Resolves, from one Richard Hubberthorne. *Printed for Giles Calvert.* (15 March.)   **E. 830. (10.)**

[**March 15.**]—Ἔσοπτρον ᾿Αστρολογικὸν. Astrologicall Opticks, wherein are represented the Faces of every Signe, with the Images of each Degree in the Zodiack. By Johann. Regiomontanus and Johannes Angelus. [Translated by R. Turner.] pp. 184. *Printed for John Allen & R. Moon.* (15 March.)   **E. 1617. (3.)**

March 16.—An Order and Declaration of His Highness for Continuing the Committee for the Army. *Printed by Henry Hills and John Field.*
        E. 1064. (51.)

[**March 16.**]—A Second Letter to his Highness the Lord Protector, from Captain Unton Crooke, signifying the totall defeat of the Cavaliers in the West, under Sir Joseph Wagstaffe. [See above : 15 March, E. 830. (15.)] *Printed by Henry Hills and John Field.*   **E. 830. (18.)**

March 16.—A Declaration of the Free-born people of England, now in armes against the Tyrannie and Oppression of Oliver Cromwell Esq. [MS. note by Thomason : " March 16. Last night this libell was scatered up and down the streets."] *s. sh.*   **669. f. 19. (70.)**

[**March 16.**]—Certain Papers which is the Word of the Lord, as was moved from the Lord by his servants [Christopher Taylor and others] to several places and persons. (16 March.)   **E. 830. (12.)**

[**March 16.**]—The Ranters Principles & Deceits discovered and declared against, denied and disowned by us whom the world cals Quakers. [With a preface signed : R. Forneworth, i.e. Richard Farnworth.] *Printed for Giles Calvert.* (16 March.)   **E. 830. (14.)**

[**March 16.**]—To all the Ignorant people, the word of the Lord, who are under the blind guides the Priests. [A warning from the Quakers.] (16 March.)   **E. 830. (13.)**

[**March 16.**]—Devotions. By R. A., D.L. [i.e. Robert Aylett. With an engraved frontispiece representing a woman at prayer.] *Printed by T. M. for Abel Roper.* (16 March.)   **E. 1458. (3.)**

[**March 17.**]—The Voice of the Iron Rod, to the Lord Protector : being a seasonable admonition presented to him by Arise Evans. *Printed for the Author.* (17 March.)   **E. 1474. (3.)**

[**March 20.**]—A Looking-Glasse for the Quakers or Shakers, and their followers. Wherein they may behold their errours and be converted. By Sam. Morris. *Printed for Edward Thomas.* (20 March.)
        E. 830. (17.)

1655.

[**March 21.**]—The Faithfull Narrative of the late Testimony made to Oliver Cromwel and his powers on the behalf of the Lord's prisoners, in the name of the Lord Jehovah. [By Hur Horton, Christopher Crayle, Hugh Day, and other Fifth Monarchy men.] (21 March.) **E. 830. (20.)**

March 24.—A Letter from His Highnesse the Lord Protector, sent into the North of England, touching loose and idle persons and such as come from abroad to kindle fire in England. With a list of the prisoners at Salisbury and Excester, condemned to dye. *Printed by Robert Ibbitson.* **E. 833. (19.)**

[**March 26.**]—A Caveate for Sherriffs : or, a Whip for corrupt Officers. Discovering their unjust exactions, and cruell oppressions of the people. (26 March.) **E. 830. (24.)**

March 26.—The Unprofitable Servant. A sermon preached at the Assize at Chelmsford. By John Warren. *Printed for Nathanael Webb and William Grantham.* **E. 850. (15.)**

[**March 28.**]—The Countryman's Catechisme : or a helpe for housholders to instruct their families in the grounds of Christian Religion. By Robert Ram. pp. 116. *Printed for John Bartlet.* (28 March.) **E. 1533. (2.)**

[**March.**]—Honor Redivivus ; or, An analysis of Honor and Armory. By Matt. Carter. [With engraved titlepage, and numerous heraldic illustrations.] pp. 259. *Sold by Thomas Heath and Henry Herringman.* **E. 1458. (2.)**

[**March.**]—Johannis Wallisii Elenchus Geometriæ Hobbianæ. Sive, geometricorum, quæ in ipsius Elementis philosophiæ a Thoma Hobbes proferuntur, refutatio. [With two diagrams.] pp. 136. *Excudebat H. Hall, impensis Johannis Crook.* **E. 1588. (2.)**

[**April 1.**]—The Wels of Salvation opened : or, a treatise discovering the nature, preciousnesse, usefulness of Gospel-Promises. By William Spurstowe. pp. 295. *Printed by T. R. & E. M. for Ralph Smith.* (1 April.) **E. 1463. (3.)**

[**April 3.**]—A great and wonderful Victory obtained by the English Forces under General Pen and General Venables against the French and others in the West Indies. [With a wood-cut.] *Printed for Humphrey Hutchinson.* (3 April.) **E. 831. (2.)**

[**April 3.**]—Supplementum Chirurgiæ, or, The Supplement to the Marrow of Chirurgerie. By James Cooke. pp. 431. *Printed for John Sherley.* (3 April.) **E. 1516.**

April 5.—The Tryal of Col. Grove, Lieu. Col. Boules, Capt. Mason and cap. Crofts at Salisbury. With the Charge of High Treason exhibited against them. *Imprinted for Jo. Fielding.* **E. 831. (21.)**

[**April 7.**]—The Brazen Serpent lifted up on high. With some demonstrations to clear the truth from accusations, held forth by these men that

1655.

the world scornfully calleth Quakers. [By Richard Farnworth.] pp. 59. *Printed for Giles Calvert.* (7 April.)   **E. 831. (10.)**

[**April 7.**]—Chymical, Medicinal and Chyrurgical Addresses made to Samuel Hartlib. pp. 181. *Printed by G. Dawson for Giles Calvert.* (7 April.)   **E. 1509. (2.)**

[**April 9.**]—A Representation concerning the late Parliament in the year, 1654. To prevent Mistakes. (9 April.)   **E. 831. (13.)**

[**April 9.**]—The Innocent delivered out of the Snare and the Blind Guide fallen into the Pit. Or, An Answer to a booke entituled The great Mysteries of Godliness and ungodliness, put forth by Ralph Farmer against those people scornfully called Quakers. By John Audland. [See above : 23 Jan., E. 480. (2.)] *Printed for Giles Calvert.* (9 April.)   **E. 831. (11.)**

April 10.—A true Report of the great number of poor Children, and other poor people maintained in the severall Hospitalls by the pious care of the Lord Mayor, Commonalty and Citizens of the City of London. *s. sh.*   **669. f. 19. (71.)**

[**April 10.**]—God all in all, or the Highest Happines of the Saints. By Edward Buckler. pp. 144. *Printed for Luke Fawn.* (10 April.)   **E. 1442. (2.)**

[**April 10.**]—Three Great and Bloody Fights between the English and the French : the first by Gen. Pen and Gen. Venables against Monsieur de Poince, Governor of St. Christophers. The second neer St. Mallows. The third neer the Isle of Majorca, by Gen. Blake. *Printed by George Horton.* (10 April.)   **E. 831. (16.)**

April. 11.—[Instructions printed and sent down to Salisbury to the prisoners that are to be tried for their lives, for the late Insurrection there. In MS. throughout in Thomason's hand.]   **E. 903. (6.)**

April 11.—The Epitaph of a Godly Man. A sermon preached at the funerall of Adam Pemberton. By Nath. Hardy. *Printed by J. G. for Nathanaell Webb and William Grantham.*   **E. 844. (15.)**

[**April 11.**]—Emmanuel manifested : or the two Natures of Christ clearly distinguished in their acts and effects. By A. C. [i.e. Ambrose Clappe.] pp. 97. *Printed for William Larnar.* (11 April.)   **E. 1492. (3.)**

April 12.—The Tryal and Sentence of Death, to be Drawn, Hang'd and Quartered, pronounced against Mr. Mack, an Apothecary of Salisbury, Mr. John Thorp, an Inn-keeper of the same Town, Mr. Kensey, a Chyrurgeon of Newbery, and Mr. Dean and Mr. Lukes of Hungerford, upon a charge of High Treason, for conspiring to take up Arms for the King of Scots. *Printed for G. Horton.*   **E. 833. (3.)**

[**April 12.**]—A Discovery of the ground from whence the Persecution did arise in Northamptonshire against William Deusbery and Joseph Stor. (12 April.)   **E. 831. (22.)**

1655.

[**April 12.**]—The Fatall Doom ; or, The Charms of Divine Love. By
R. H. [i.e. Robert Hooke.] pp. 203. *Printed for John Williams.*
(12 April.)   **E. 1512. (2.)**

[**April 12.**]—The Jus Divinum of Presbyterie. Or, a treatise proving by
Scripture all true Ministers or Embassadors of the Gospel to be
endued with Divine Power from on high. Second edition, newly
enlarged. pp. 91. (12 April.)   **E. 1465. (3.)**

[**April 13.**]—The Quakers Shakers, or, A Warning against Quaking.
Second impression. *Printed by S. G. for Simon Waterson.* (13 April.)
                                                E. 831. (25.)

[**April 14.**]—Responsoria Bipartita. A double Reply, containing a
vindication of the antient practice of the Church, suspending the
ignorant and scandalous from the Lords Supper. As also of Ecclesiastical Presbyteries as the subject of Church Government. The first in
answer to one M. Boatmans challenge. The second part in answer to
answer to Theophilus Brabourn. By John Collings. 2 pt. [See
above : 17 Nov. 1654, E. 817. (9.)] *Printed by H. Hills for Richard
Tomlins.* (14 April.)   **E. 832. (2.)**

[**April 14.**]—Thunder from Heaven against the Back-sliders and
Apostates of the Times. By W. A. [i.e. William Aspinwall.] *Printed for
Livewell Chapman.* (14 April.)   **E. 831. (26.)**

[**April 14.**]—The Work of the Age : or, The sealed Prophecies of Daniel
opened and applied. By William Aspinwall. pp. 56. *Printed by R. I.
for Livewell Chapman.* (14 April.)   **E. 832. (1.)**

[**April 15.**]—Parnassus Biceps ; or, Several Choice Pieces of Poetry,
composed by the best Wits that were in both Universities before their
Dissolution. [Edited by Abraham Wright.] pp. 163. *Printed for
George Eversden.* (15 April.)   **E. 1679. (1.)**

[**April 15.**]—A Voice from Heaven : or a testimony against the
remainders of Antichrist yet in England, and in particular, the Court
of Tryers for approbation of Ministers. Born by Gualter Postlethwait.
[See also below : 17 Nov. 1658, E. 959. (5.)] pp. 96. *Printed for
Livewel Chapman.* (15 April.)   **E. 1498. (3.)**

[**April 17.**]—Henry Cornelius Agrippa, his Fourth Book of Occult
Philosophy. Translated by Robert Turner. pp. 217. *Printed by
J. C. for John Harrison.* (17 April.)   **E. 833. (1.)**

April 17.—The Vanity and Mischief of making Earthly, together with
the necessity and benefit of making Heavenly, Treasures our chiefe
Treasure. A sermon at Mary Spittle before the Lord Mayor and
Aldermen. By John Crodacott. *Printed for A. Kemb.* **E. 844. (11.)**

April 20.—Mercy in her Exaltation. A sermon preached at the
funeral of Daniel Taylor, in Stephens Coleman Street. [By John Goodwin.] pp. 56. *Printed by J. Macock for H. Eversden.* **E. 848. (24.)**

1655.

[April 21.]—A Narrative of the Proceedings of a great Councel of Jews, assembled in the plain of Ageda in Hungaria, to examine the Scriptures concerning Christ, 12 Oct., 1650. By Samuel Brett. *Printed for Richard Moon.* (21 April.) **E. 833. (8.)**

[April 22.]—An Iron Rod for the Naylors and Trades-men near Birmingham. The voyce of Gods holy Spirit crying in the Wildernesse. By John Sanders of Harburn. [Foretelling the coming of the "Fifth Monarchy."] *s. sh.* (22 April.) **669. f. 19. (72.)**

April 25.—[An Order by the Lord Mayor and Aldermen, at Quarter Sessions, regulating the price of Beer, Horse-Fodder, &c. and prescribing a scale of charges for Car-Men.] *Printed by James Flesher.*
669. f. 19. (76.)

April 25.—[An admonitory address, signed Martha Simmonds. MS. note by Thomason : "April 25, given about by the Quakers."] *s. sh.*
669. f. 19. (73.)

[April 25.]—A Discourse upon the Nature of Eternitie, and the condition of a Separated Soule, according to the grounds of reason and principles of Christian Religion. By William Brent. pp. 96. *Printed for Richard Moon.* (25 April.) **E. 1494. (2.)**

[April 26.]—By the Lord Protector. A Proclamation declaring His Highness pleasure and command for putting in execution the Laws, Statutes and Ordinances made against Jesuits and Priests, and for the speedy conviction of Popish Recusants. *s. sh. Printed by Henry Hills and John Field.* **669. f. 19. (74.)**

[April 26.]—The Quakers Dream, or, The Devils' Pilgrimage in England : being an infallible Relation of their Quakings, Roarings and strange Doctrines. [With wood-cuts.] *Printed for G. Horton.* (26 April.)
E. 833. (14.)

[April 27.]—The humble Representation of his late Majesties and Princes domestick Servants, signifying their distressed condition and necessitated designment for relief. *s. sh.* (27 April.)
669. f. 19. (75.)

[April 28.]—Hymen's Præludia : or, Love's Master-piece. Being the third part of that so much admired Romance Cleopatra [by Gauthier de Costes]. Rendred into English by R. Loveday. [With an engraved frontispiece.] pp. 331. [See above : 28 Nov. 1653, E. 1459. (1.)] *Printed by J. G. for R. Lowndes.* (28 April.) **E. 1459. (2.)**

[April 29.]—The true Interpretation and Etymologie of Christian Names. By Edward Lyford. pp. 237. *Printed by T. W. for George Sawbridge.* (29 April.) **E. 1549. (1.)**

[April 30.]—The History of Divine Verities. Written by John Birchensha. 4 pt. *Printed by T. C. for John Wright.* (30 April.)
E. 834.

1655.

May 1.—An Exhortation directed to the Elders of the several Congregations within this Province of Lancaster. By the Provincial Assembly at Preston. *Printed by J. M. for Luke Fawn.* **E. 850. (18.)**

[**May 1.**]—Christ Knocking at the Doore. A sermon. By Philip Tanny. *Printed by A. M. and are to be sold by Giles Calvert and Simon Miller.* (1 May.) **E. 1485. (4.)**

[**May 1.**]—The English Treasury of Wit and Language, collected out of the most and best of our English drammatick poems; methodically digested into common places for generall use. By John Cotgrave. pp. 311. *Printed for Humphrey Moseley.* (1 May.) **E. 1464.**

May 1.—A Serious Letter sent by a Private Christian to the Lady Consideration, which she is desired to communicate in Hide-Park to the Gallants of the times. *Printed and are to be sold by Mr. Butler.* **E. 835. (2.)**

[**May 2.**]—The petition of the late Risers in the West condemned at Salisbury, Exon., &c. [In MS. throughout, in Thomason's hand.] **E. 835. (5.)**

[**May 2.**]—A Defence of True Liberty from Ante-cedent and Extrinsecall Necessity, being an answer to a late book of Mr. Thomas Hobbs intituled, A Treatise of Liberty and Necessity. By John Bramhall, Bishop of Derry. pp. 253. *Printed for John Crook.* (2 May.) **E. 1450. (1.)**

[**May 4.**]—An Answer made by Sʳ. Robert Cotton, at the command of Prince Henry, to certain propositions of warre and peace, delivered to his Highness by some of his military servants. pp. 96. *Printed for William Sheares.* (4 May.) **E. 1467. (2.)**

[**May 4.**]—The French Charity: written in French by an English gentleman, upon occasion of Prince Harcourt's coming into England; and translated into English by F. S. J. E. *Printed for William Sheares.* (4 May.) **E. 1467. (3.)**

[**May 4.**]—The Quakers terrible Vision; or, The Devils Progress to the City of London. [With wood-cuts.] *Printed for G. Horton.* (4 May.) **E. 835. (10.)**

[**May 5.**]—The Boaster bared, and his Armour put off, without a Conquest, by the Quaking Principle. In an answer to Enoch Howets, called Quaking Principles dasht in pieces. By James Nayler. [See above: 21 Dec. 1654, E. 821. (2.)] *Printed for G. Calvert.* (5 May.) **E. 835. (12.)**

[**May 5.**]—Mirza. A Tragedie really acted in Persia in the last Age. Illustrated with historicall annotations. The Author R. B., Esq. [i.e. Robert Baron. In verse.] pp. 264. *Printed for Humphrey Moseley.* (5 May.) **E. 1449. (1.)**

May 6.—Joy in the Lord. A sermon preached at Pauls, by Edward Reynolds. *Printed by Tho. Newcomb for Robert Bostock.* **E. 844. (1.)**

1655.

[May 6.]—A Sermon against Murder : by occasion of the Romanists putting the Protestants to death in the Dukedome of Savoy. By William Towers. *Printed for Humphrey Mosely.* (6 May.)   **E. 835. (13.)**

[May 6.]—Saltmarsh returned from the Dead, In Amico Philalethe. Or, the Resurrection of James, the Apostle. [An exposition of the fifth chapter of the Epistle of James, by S. Gorton.] pp. 198. *Printed for Giles Calvert.* (6 May.)   **E. 836. (1.)**

May 7.—The Speech of Collonel Hugh Grove upon the Scaffold at Exeter. *Printed for Sam. Burdet.*   **E. 838. (10.)**

[May 7.]—Wits Interpreter, the English Parnassus, or, A sure guide to those Admirable Accomplishments that compleat our English Gentry. By I. C. [i.e. John Cotgrave.] 3 pt. *Printed for N. Brooke.* (7 May.)
E. 1448.

[May 8.]—An Account of Mr. Cawdry's Triplex Diatribe concerning Superstition, Wil-worship and Christmass Festivall. By H. Hammond. pp. 295. [See also below: 11 Sept. 1658, E. 1850.] *Printed by J. Flesher for Richard Royston.* (8 May.)   **E. 836. (2.)**

[May 8.]—Healths Improvement : or, Rules comprizing and discovering the Nature, Method and Manner of preparing all sorts of Food used in this Nation. By Thomas Muffett. Corrected and enlarged by Christopher Bennett. pp. 296. *Printed by Tho. Newcomb for Samuel Thomson.* (8 May.)   **E. 835. (16.)**

[May 8.]—Spiritual Flowers for Saints and Sinners, gathered out of the Garden of the sacred Scriptures. By Robert Port. pp. 175. *Printed by G. Dawson for George Sawbridge.* (8 May.)   **E. 1548. (2.)**

May 9.—Articles of Peace concluded between England and Sweden in a Treaty at Upsal. *Printed by Henry Hills and John Field.* **E. 1065. (4.)**

[May 9.]—An Antidote against Atheism. By Henry More. Second edition, enlarged. pp. 398. *Printed by J. Flesher: London; and are to be sold by William Morden, Bookseller in Cambridge.* (9 May.)
E. 1460. (1.)

[May 9.]—Vindiciæ Evangelicæ, or, The Mystery of the Gospell vindicated and Socinianisme examined, in the confutation of a Scripture Catechisme written by J. Biddle. By John Owen. pp. 683. *Printed by Leon. Lichfield : Oxford.* (9 May.)   **E. 837.**

[May 10.]—A Treatise of the Four Last Things, Death, Judgement, Hell and Heaven. By Simon Birckbek. pp. 191. *Printed by A. M. for Edward Brewster.* (10 May.)   **E. 1460. (2.)**

[May 11.]—Culpeper's Last Legacy : left and bequeathed to his dearest wife, for the publicke good. Containing sundry admirable experiences in Chyrurgery and Physick. By Nicholas Culpeper. [With an engraved portrait of the author.] pp. 265. *Printed for N. Brooke.* (11 May.)   **E. 1464. (2.)**

1655.

[May 12.]—The Author and Case of Transplanting the Irish into Connaught vindicated from the unjust Aspersions of Col. Richard Laurence. By Vincent Gookin. pp. 59. [See above: 3 Jan., E. 234. (6.), and 9 March, E. 829. (17.)] *Printed by A. M. for Simon Miller.* (12 May.)   **E. 838. (7.)**

[May 12.]—Advice sent in a Letter from an Elder Brother to a Younger, relating to remedying severall Abuses in the Common Wealth. [By Nathanael Burt.] (12 May.) *Printed for the Author.*   **E. 838. (8.)**

[May 13.]—A Mustur Roll of the evill Angels embatteld against S. Michael. Being a Collection, according to the order of time, of the chiefe of the Ancient Heretikes, with their Tenets. By R. B. [i.e. Richard Brathwait.] pp. 94. *Printed for William Sheers.* (13 May.)   **E. 1549. (2.)**

[May 14.]—A Declaration from the Children of Light, who are by the world scornfully called Quakers, against false reports, scandals and lyes in books and pamphlets put forth by Hen. Walker, R. Wood and George Horton. *Printed for Giles Calvert.* (14 May.) •   **E. 838. (11.)**

[May 14.]—A Modest Discourse of the Piety, Charity & Policy of Elder Times and Christians. By Edward Waterhouse. pp. 271. *Printed by A. M. for Simon Miller.* (14 May.)   **E. 1502. (2.)**

[May 14.]—Funerall Elegies, or, The Sad Muses in Sables, singing the Epicediums of Prince Maurice, James Duke of Lenox and Richmond, John Earl of Rivers, John Cleveland, the much cry'd up Poet. By S. H. *Printed by Tho. Wilson.* (14 May.)   **E. 838. (9.)**

[May 15.]—A Brief Explication of the last fifty Psalmes. By David Dickson. pp. 381. *Printed by T. R. and E. M. for Ralph Smith.* (15 May.)   **E. 1465. (4.)**

[May 15.]—The World to Come, or, The Kingdom of Christ asserted in two Expository Lectures on Ephes. i, 21, 22. Preached by Tho. Goodwin many years since. (15 May.)   **E. 838. (13.)**

May 16.—The Triall of Col. John Penruddock, and his Speech the day before he was beheaded. *Printed by order of the Gent. intrusted.*   **E. 845. (7.)**

[May 17.]—Interiora Regni Dei. Vidit & testatur F. Rous. pp. 290. (17 May.)   **E. 1539. (1.)**

[May 17.]—Mysticum Matrimonium quo junguntur Christus et Ecclesia. [By Francis Rous.] pp. 272. (17 May.)   **E. 1539. (2.)**

[May 17.]—A Letter to the Admired Fraternity of the Order of R. C. [Signed: Corona Honorata.] *Printed by J. C. for William Ley.* (17 May.)   **E. 1474. (4.)**

[May 17.]—The Rogue: or, The Excellencie of History displayed in the Notorious Life of Guzman de Alfarache. Written originally in Spanish

1655.

by Matheo Aleman, epitomiz'd into English by A. S., Gent. [With an engraved portrait.] pp. 222. *Printed by J. C. for the Author.* (17 May.) **E. 1449. (2.)**

May 18.—The Petition of the Prisoners in the Fleet, presented to the Lord Protector. Remonstrating the illegality of Outlaries, Arrests and Imprisonments in civill and personall actions. *Printed by T. Forcet.* **E. 843. (3.)**

[**May 18.**]—Fourteen Queries and ten Absurdities about the extent of Christ's Death, the power of the creatures, the justice of God in condemning some and saving others, presented by a Free-willer [William Pedelsden] to the Church of Christ at Newcastle, and answered by Paul Hobson, a member of the said Church. pp. 111. *Printed by Henry Hills for William Hutchison, Bookseller in Durham.* (18 May.) **E. 1492. (4.)**

[**May 18.**]—The Vindication of Sʳ John Stawell's Remonstrance against a pamphlet written by Mr. John Ash, entituled, An Answer to divers Scandalls mentioned in the humble Remonstrance of Sr. John Stawell. As also an answer to a petition of William Lawrence, with a conclusion offered unto the Lord Protector. Whereunto are annexed a letter of Sir Anthony Irbye's, and a short reply of Sr. David Watkins, relating unto some parts of the said pamphlet. [See above: Oct. 1653, E. 1072. (2.) and 15 Feb. 1655, E. 1072. (3.)] *Printed by T. R. for Henry Twyford.* (18 May.) **E. 1072. (4.)**

[**May 19.**]—A Messenger sent to remove some mistakes; or A Desirous Instrument for the promoting of Truth. By Thomas Morris. Also Robert Everards three Questions propounded to Benjamin Morley about his practice of laying on of hands, with his answer, and R. E[verard's] Reply. pp. 60. *Printed for R. E. and are to be sold by Richard Moon.* (19 May.) **E. 838. (23.)**

[**May 19.**]—The Passionate Lovers. A tragi-comedy, the first and second parts. [In verse.] By Lodowick Carlell. pp. 156. *Printed for Humphrey Moseley.* (19 May.) **E. 1449. (3.)**

[**May 20.**]—A Scripture Chronology wherein the principall Periods of Time from the Creation of the World to the death of Christ are included. By William Nisbet. pp. 312. *Printed for Joshua Kirton.* (20 May.) **E. 1501. (2.)**

[**May 21.**]—Anatomia Sambuci : or, the Anatomie of the Elder. Cutting out of it remedies for most maladies. Gathered in Latine by Dr. Martin Blochwich. Now translated [by C. Irvine]. pp. 230. *Printed for Tho. Heath.* (21 May.) **E. 1534. (2.)**

May 22.—An Order and Declaration of His Highness for collecting the Excize in Scotland. *Printed by Henry Hills and John Field.* **E. 1064. (53.)**

1655.

May 22.—An Order and Declaration of His Highness for collecting the Excise in Ireland. *Printed by Henry Hills and John Field.*

E. 1064. (52.)

[**May 23.**]—A Scripture-Map of the Wildernesse of Sin and Way to Canaan, or The Sinners Way to the Saints Rest. By Faithful Teate. pp. 462. *Printed for G. Sawbridge.* (23 May.) **E. 839.**

[**May 24.**]—Euchologia : or, The Doctrine of Practical Praying. By John Prideaux, late Bishop of Worcester. [With an engraved portrait.] pp. 307. *Printed for Rich. Marriot.* (24 May.) **E. 1515.**

[**May 24.**]—The Quacking Mountebanck, or The Jesuite turn'd Quaker. [By Daniel Lupton.] *Printed for E. B.* (24 May.) **E. 840. (4.)**

[**May 24.**]—Wo to thee, City of Oxford, *etc.* [Signed : Hester Biddle.] *s. sh.* (24 May.) **669. f. 19. (77.)**

May 25.—A Declaration of His Highness inviting the People of England and Wales to a Day of Solemn Fasting and Humiliation. *Printed by Henry Hills and John Field.* **E. 1064. (54.)**

May 25.—Instructions to be observed touching the Collection appointed by the Declaration of His Highness, inviting the people of England and Wales to a day of Solemn Fasting and Humiliation. *s. sh. Printed by Henry Hills and John Field.* **669. f. 19. (79.)**

[**May 25.**]—A Foole answered according to his Folly. An Answer to George Emmot and his Northerne Blast. By James Nayler. [See above : 14 Feb., E. 826. (27.)] *Printed & are to be sold by Giles Calvert.* (25 May.) **E. 840. (9.)**

[**May 25.**]—Apobaterion, vel in adventum Legati, veri excellentissimi Domini Marchionis de Lede, &c. carmen panegyricum. Per F. F. [i.e. Payne Fisher] ab historiis & satellitio Domini Protectoris, &c. *Typis Newcombianis excusum.* (25 May.) **669. f. 19. (78.)**

[**May 28.**]—An Honest Discourse between three Neighbours, touching the Present Government in these three Nations. *Printed for Thomas Brewster.* (28 May.) **E. 840. (10.)**

[**May 28.**]—A Philosophicall Essay towards an eviction of the Being and Attributes of God, etc. By S. W. [i.e. Seth Ward, Bishop of Salisbury.] The second impression. pp. 167. *Printed by Leonard Lichfield and are to be sold by Edward Forrest : Oxford.* (28 May.) **E. 1490. (3.)**

[**May 28.**]—The Muses Cabinet, stored with Variety of Poems. By W. W. [i.e. William Winstanley.] *Printed for F. Coles.* (28 May.) **E. 1479. (5.)**

May 29.—An Order and Declaration of His Highness for an Assessment of sixty thousand pounds per mensem, from 24 June. *Printed by Henry Hills and John Field.* **E. 1064. (55.)**

1655.

[May 29.]—A ready way to prevent Sudden Death : being a brief Relation of many misfortunes which came through hardnesse of heart and carelessnesse. By Laurence Price. *Printed for William Gilbertson.* (29 May.) **E. 1478. (3.)**

[May 29.]—The Reformed Common-wealth of Bees, presented in severall Letters to Sammuel Hartlib. With The Reformed Virginian Silk-worm. pp. 102. *Printed for Giles Calvert.* (29 May.) **E. 840. (13.)**

[May 30.]—A Treatise concerning the Broken Succession of the Crown of England. [By Robert Parsons.] pp. 167. (30 May.) **E. 482. (2.)**

[May 30.]—Jacobs Ladder, or, The Protectorship of Sion laid on the shoulders of the Almighty. With Jacob wrestling. Μονομαχία ; Jacob wrestling with the Angel. By Francis Raworth. pp. 327. *Printed by R. I. for L. Chapman.* (30 May.) **E. 1507. (2.)**

[May 31.]—Elementorum Philosophiæ sectio prima de Corpore. Authore Thoma Hobbes Malmesburiensi. [With diagrams.] pp. 304. *Excusum sumptibus Andrea Crook.* (31 May.) **E. 1450. (2.)**

[May 31.]—A Panegyrick to My Lord Protector. By E. W., Esq. [i.e. Edmund Waller.] [In verse.] *Printed for Richard Lowndes.* (31 May.) **E. 841. (2.)**

May.—The Morning-Exercise, or some short Notes taken out of the Morning-Sermons which divers Ministers preached in Giles in the Fields during the Moneth of May. By Tho. Case. pp. 115. *Printed by T. R. and E. M. for Robert Gibbs.* **E. 1706. (1.)**

[June 1.]—A third great and terrible Fire, Fire, Fire. Where ? Where ? Where ? [A tract upon the Day of Judgment.] (1 June.) **E. 841. (5.)**

[June 2.] A Glimpse of Divine Light breaking through a Cloud of Errours. Being an explanation of certain passages exhibited by Anony-mus to the Commissioners for Approbation of Publick Preachers, against Joseph Harrison. By the said Joseph Harrison. pp. 73. *Printed for N. Brook.* (2 June.) **E. 841. (7.)**

[June 4.]—The Unsearchable Riches of Christ. Twenty-two sermons by Thomas Brookes. pp. 328. *Printed by Mary Simmons for John Hancock.* (4 June.) **E. 841. (8.)**

[June 6.]—Slanders and Lyes, being cast upon the Children of Light, given forth to print by Henry Walker, which one R: Ibitson hath printed, that they deny the Resurrection, and Heaven, and Hell. Therefore for the truths sake and them that feare God, in this Paper given forth. From them whom the world calls Quakers. *s. sh.* (6 June.) **669. f. 19. (80.)**

[June 7.]—The Spirit of Bondage and Adoption. In two treatises. Whereunto is added a discourse concerning the duty of prayer in an

1655.

afflicted condition. By Simon Ford. pp. 630. *Printed by T. Maxey for Sa. Gellibrand.* (7 June.) **E. 1553.**

[June 8.]—The Second Gate ; or, The Inner Door to the Holy Tongue. Being a compendious Hebrew Lexicon. By William Robertson. pp. 551. *Printed by Evan Tyler for Humphrey Robinson.* (8 June.)
E. 1643. (1.)

[June 9.]—America ; or, An exact description of the West Indies. By N. N. [With an engraved map of America.] pp. 484. *Printed by Richard Hodgkinsonne for Edward Dod.* (9 June.) **E. 1644. (1.)**

[June 9.]—The Holy Scripture clearing itself of Scandals ; or, An Answer to a book by Richard Farnworth, a Quaker, bearing this title, Truth cleared of Scandals. By Thomas Pollard. Whereunto is added, Certain Considerations concerning those people called Quakers, by Henry Haggar. pp. 56. [See above : 27 Sept. 1654, E. 820. (3.)] *Printed by J. C. for R. Moone.* (9 June.) **E. 842. (10.)**

[June 10.]—A Collection of the several Papers sent to the Lord Protector concerning the murthers and other cruelties committed on Reformed or Protestants dwelling in Piedmont by the Duke of Savoy's Forces. [Edited by J. B. Stouppe.] *Printed for H. Robinson.* (10 June.) **E. 842. (11.)**

[June 11.]—A Fourth Volume of Familiar Letters, upon various emergent occasions. Partly philosophical, political, historical. By James Howell. pp. 126. *Printed for Humphrey Moseley.* (11 June.)
E. 1559. (1.)

[June 11.]—Harry Hangman's Honour ; or, Gloucester-shire Hangman's Request to the Smoakers or Tabacconists in London. [A satire.] (11 June.) **E. 842. (13.)**

[June 14.]—A True Relation of some passages which passed at Madrid in the year 1623 by Prince Charles, then prosecuting the match with the Lady Infanta. Also, severall observations of Ominous Presages hapning in the same year. (14 June.) **E. 842. (18.)**

[June 14.]—Three new Playes ; viz. The { Bashful Lover, Guardian, Very Woman. Written by Philip Massenger. [With an engraved portrait of the author.] 3 pt. *Printed for Humphrey Moseley.* (14 June.) **E. 1559. (2.)**

[June 16.]—The Quakers Catechism ; or, The Quakers questioned. By Richard Baxter. [See also below : 6 Aug., E. 851. (1.)] *Printed by A. M. for Thomas Underhill and Francis Tyton.* (16 June.)
E. 842. (22.)

[June 17.]—An Iron Rod put into the Lord Protectors hand to break all Antichristian Powers to pieces. By John Saunders. pp. 67. *Printed for the Author.* (17 June.) **E. 842. (23.)**

1655.

[**June 18.**]—A True Declaration of the bloody proceedings of the men in Maidstone against John Stubs and William Caton, Quakers. *Printed for Giles Calvert.* (18 June.)   **E. 843. (2.)**

[**June 18.**]—A Threefold Help to Political Observations. Three discourses: 1. Concerning the Helvetical League. 2. Declaring the state of Italy about the year 1625. 3. Touching the proceedings of the King of Sweden in his Wars in Germany. By Sir Isaac Wake. pp. 119. *Printed for Andrew Crook.* (18 June.)   **E. 1671. (2.)**

[**June 18.**]—Truths Defence against Lies. In answer to a book [by Richard Baxter] intituled The Worcestershire Petition Defended. [See above: 3 May, 1653, E. 693. (18.)] (18 June.)   **E. 843. (1.)**

[**June 19.**]—The Quakers Unmasked, and clearly detected to be but the Spawn of Romish Frogs, Jesuites and Franciscan Fryers; sent from Rome to seduce the English Nation. By William Prynne. Second edition, enlarged. *Printed for Edward Thomas.* (19 June.)   **E. 843. (6.)**

[**June 19.**]—A devout Paraphrase on the 50th Psalme. By Math: Kellison. pp. 184. *Printed at Paris.* (19 June.)   **E. 1662. (1.)**

[**June 19.**]—An Exposition upon the thirteenth chapter of the Revelation. By John Cotton. pp. 262. *Printed by M. S. for Livewel Chapman.* (19 June.)   **E. 843. (5.)**

[**June 20.**]—Antichrists Man of War, apprehended and encountred withal, by a Souldier of the Armie of the Lamb. An Answer to a book by Edmund Skipp called The Worlds Wonder, or the Quakers Blazing Starre. [By Richard Farnworth.] pp. 90. [See above: 28 Feb., E. 829. (4.)] *Printed for Giles Calvert.* (20 June.)   **E. 843. (9.)**

[**June 21.**]—A Narrative of the proceedings of the Committee for preservation of the Customes, in the case of Mr. George Cony. By Samuel Selwood. *Printed for William Sheares.* (21 June.)
      E. 844. (4.)

[**June 23.**]—A Brief Exposition upon the Second Psalme. By William Llanvædonon. pp. 63. *Printed for Livewell Chapman.* (23 June.)
      E. 844. (9.)

[**June 23.**]—Cain's Generation discover'd, in answer to an epistle to the Reader in A Short and Full Vindication of that comfortable Ordinance of Singing of Psalms put forth by Jonathan Clapham. Answered by George Whitehead. [The first edition of "A Short Vindication" is not in the Thomason collection. For the second edition see below: 9 Dec. 1656, E. 896. (8.)] *Printed for Giles Calvert.* (23 June.)
      E. 844. (12.)

[**June 23.**]—A Declaration against all Poperie. [A Quaker pamphlet.] (23 June.)   **E. 844. (10.)**

[**June 23.**]—Making light of Christ and Salvation too oft the issue of Gospel Invitations. A sermon, by Richard Baxter. pp. 66.

1655.

Printed by R. White for Nevil Simmons, Bookseller in Kederminster. (23 June.)   **E. 1606. (1.)**

[**June 24.**]—The Quakers Fiery Beacon; or, The Shaking Ranters Ghost. [An attack upon the Quakers.] *Printed for G. Horton.* (24 June.)   **E. 844. (13.)**

[**June 25.**]—Hermetical Physick : or, the right way to preserve and to restore Health. By Henry Nollius. Englished by Henry Vaughan. pp. 130. *Printed for Humphrey Moseley.* (25 June.)   **E. 1714. (1.)**

[**June 26.**]—Divine Poems, being Meditations upon several Sermons preached at Eckington in the County of Darbie by Mr. S. G. And put into Vers by William Wood. *Printed by William Du-Gard for the Author.* (26 June.)   **E. 844. (16.)**

[**June 27.**]—Reports of Speciall Cases touching severall Customs and Liberties of the City of London. Collected by Sir H. Calthrop. Whereunto is annexed divers ancient Customes and Usages of the City of London. pp. 179. *Printed for Abel Roper.* (27 June.)
                                                    E. 1681. (2.)

[**June 29.**]—Eugenius Theodidactus. The Prophetical Trumpeter sounding an Allarum to England. By John Heydon. [In verse.] pp. 156. *Printed by T. Lock for the Author.* (29 June.) **E. 1671. (3.)**

[**June 29.**]—The Innocency of the righteous seed of God cleared from all slanderous tongues. [By Richard Hubberthorne.] (29 June.)
                                                    E. 845. (4.)

[**June 30.**]—Euphrates, or the Waters of the East, being a short Discourse of that Secret Fountain, whose Water flows from Fire. By Eugenius Philalethes [i.e. Thomas Vaughan.] pp. 124. *Printed for Humphrey Moseley.* (30 June.)   **E. 1658. (1.)**

[**June.**]—The true Portraiture of a prodigious Monster, taken in the mountains of Zardana ; the following description was sent to Madrid, Oct. 20, 1654, and from thence to Don Olonzo de Cardines, Ambassador for the King of Spain, now resident at London. To the tune of, Summer Time. [A political satire, in verse. With a woodcut of a seven-headed monster with the legs of a goat.] *s. sh.* *Printed for John Andrews.*   **669. f. 19. (81.)**

[**June.**]—[Another edition.] *s. sh. Sould by Willm. Faithorne.*
                                                    669. f. 19. (82.)

[**July 2.**]—The Retired Mans Meditations ; or, The Mysterie and Power of Godlines. By Henry Vane. pp. 428. [See also below : 29 July, 1656, E. 1670. (2.)] *Printed by R. W. for T. Brewster.* (2 July.)
                                                    E. 485. (1.)

July 3.—By His Highness. A Proclamation for Relief of Godly Ministers against Suits and Molestations by Persons sequestred, ejected, or not approved. *Printed by Henry Hills and John Field.*   **669. f. 20. (1.)**

1655.

[July 3.]—The Grounds of Obedience and Government. By Thomas White. Second edition. pp. 183. [See also below : 5 Aug. 1656, E. 886. (7.)] *Printed by J. Flesher for Laurence Chapman.* (3 July.)
E. 1711. (2.)

[July 3.]—The Reward of Oppression, Tyranny and Injustice committed by the unlawful Deteiner of the Dutchie Lands of Lancaster. Declared in the case of Samuel Beck, an infant, by Margaret Beck. (3 July.)
E. 845. (9.)

July 6.—By the Protector. An Order commanding all persons of the late King's party to depart out of London and Westminster on or before 12 July. *s. sh.* *Printed by Henry Hills and John Field.*
639. f. 20. (3.)

[July 6.]—Anabaptism Routed ; or, A Survey of the Controverted Points. With a particular Answer to all that is alledged in favour of the Anabaptists by Jeremy Taylor in The Liberty of Prophesying. By John Reading. pp. 204. [See above : 28 June, 1647, E. 395. (2.)] *Printed for Thomas Johnson.* (6 July.)   E. 845. (14.)

[July 6.]—The Protector. A poem briefly illustrating the supereminency of that dignity. By George Wither. pp. 50. *Printed by J. C.* (6 July.)
E. 1565. (2.)

[July 7.]—The Covenant Sealed ; or, A Treatise of the Sacraments of both Covenants, especially the Covenant of Grace. Together with a brief Answer to Mr. Baxter's Apology in defence of the Treatise of the Covenant. By Thomas Blake. pp. 668. *Printed for Abel Roper.* (7 July.)   E. 846.

[July 7.]—The Watcher. A discovery of the ground and end of all Forms and Opinions, as hath been made manifest in several meetings betwixt the Quakers and the Baptists. By James Parnell. pp. 52. *Printed for Giles Calvert.* (7 July.)   E. 845. (18.)

[July 8.]—A tous ceulx qui vouldroyent cognoistre la voye au Royaume. Une Direction pour tourner la pensée au dedans ou la Voix de Dieu doit estre ouye. Publié par ceulx lesquels le monde appele Quakers. [By George Fox.] *Imprimé pour Giles Calvert.* (8 July.)   E. 848. (2.)

[July 8.]—Admonition à tous les Grands de la Terre, aussy bien qu'au Peuple par tout le monde ; que leur sang soit sur leurs propres testes, s'ilz ne hastent point a se repentir. [A Quaker tract.] *Imprimé pour Giles Calvert.* (8 July.)   E. 848. (1.)

[July 8.]—An Exposition upon the three first chapters of the Proverbs, delivered in lectures at Christ Church in Canterbury. By Francis Taylor. pp. 549. *Printed by E. C. for Henry Eversden.* (8 July.)   E. 847.

July 9.—To His Highness. The Petition of Godfree Goodman, Bishop late of Gloucester. [Praying that he may be restored to his position.] *s. sh.*   669. f. 20. (4.)

1655.

[July 9.]—A Warning from the Lord to this Nation. [Signed: Christopher Taylor. A Quaker tract.] (9 July.) **E. 848. (4.)**

[July 10.]—Introductio ad lectionem Linguarum Orientalium, Hebraicæ, Chaldaicæ, Samaritanæ, Syriacæ, Arabicæ, Persicæ, Æthiopicæ, Armenæ, Coptæ. Per Brianum Walton. Editio secunda. pp. 96. 112. *Imprimebat Tho. Roycroft, et venales habentur apud Timoth. Garthwait.* (10 July.) **E. 1690.**

July 12.—By the Protector. A Proclamation for perfecting the Collection for Relief of the Protestant Inhabitants of the Valleys of Lucern, Angrona, &c. *s. sh. Printed by Henry Hills and John Field.*

669. f. 20. (5.)

July 12.—By the Protector. A Proclamation giving notice that the remaining differences betwixt the English and Dutch Merchants stand referred to Commissioners to assemble at Amsterdam 20 July. *s. sh. Printed by Henry Hills and John Field.* **669. f. 20. (6.)**

July 12.—By the Protector. A Proclamation declaring that after 1 Aug. next no further use be made of any Letters of Marque granted unto any private person. *s. sh. Printed by Henry Hills and John Field.*

669. f. 20. (7.)

July 13.—An Order and Declaration of His Highnes for continuing the Committee for the Army. *Printed by Henry Hills and John Field.*

E. 1064. (56.)

[July 14.]—A True State of the Case of Liberty of Conscience in England. Together with a narrative of John Biddle's sufferings. *Printed for Richard Moone.* (14 July.) **E. 848. (12.)**

[July 15.]—A Perswasive to Peace; or, A Treatise of Christian Peace. By Thomas Whitfeld. pp. 132. *Printed by E. Tyler for John Wright.* (15 July.) **E. 1674. (1.)**

July 15.—A Warning Piece for the World, or, a Watch-word to England. Being many wonderfull visions & apparitions that appeared to one Mr. William Morgan a farmer neer Hereford, and to one John Rogers his shepherd. [With a woodcut.] *Printed for Robert Eeles.*

E. 853. (13.)

[July 17.]—Something written in answer to a book printed for E. B. in Pauls Churchyard, whose lies are denied by the Quakers; the author of it is said to be called Powel. Also a declaration against the lies printed for G. Horton. (17 July.) **E. 848. (14.)**

[July 17.]—A True Discoverie of Faith and a brief Manifestation of the Ground upon which we stand. Also an Answer to severall Queries put forth by John Reyner. [Signed: James Nayler. A Quaker tract.] *Printed for Giles Calvert.* (17 July.) **E. 848. (15.)**

1655.

[July 18.]—The Countrey Farrier. Teaching above an hundred approved
medicines to cure all sorts of cattell. With a list of the High-wayes
through England. By William Poole. [With two woodcuts.] pp. 56.
Printed by T. Forcet. (18 July.)   **E. 1669. (1.)**

[July 19.]—The Enmitie between the Two Seeds, wherein is discovered
the subtilty of the Serpents seed. By John Whithead. [A Quaker
tract.] (19 July.)   **E. 848. (19.)**

[July 19.]—Iggeret hammashkil. Or, An Admonitory Epistle unto
Mr. Rich. Baxter, and Mr. Tho. Hotchkiss, about their misapplications
of several texts of Scripture. Unto which are prefixed two dissertations. By William Robertson. pp. 174. *Printed by J. M. and T. N.
for George Sawbridge.* (19 July.)   **E. 1590. (3.)**

[July 19.]—Morall Discourses and Essayes upon severall select subjects.
By T. C. [i.e. Thomas Culpeper.] pp. 184. *Printed by S. G. for Charles
Adams.* (19 July.)   **E. 1703. (3.)**

July 20.—By the Protector. A Proclamation for putting the laws in
execution for setting Prices on Wines. *s. sh. Printed by Henry Hills
and John Field.*   **669. f. 20. (9.)**

[July 20.]—The Discovery of the great enmity of the Serpent against
the seed of the Woman. By William Dewsbury. [A Quaker tract.]
Printed for Giles Calvert. (20 July.)   **E. 848. (23.)**

[July 20.]—A Discovery of the Priests. By John Pain. [A Quaker
tract.] *Printed by Jo. Streater for Giles Calvert.* (20 July.)
                                                      E. 848. (22.)

[July 20.]—The Secret Shooting of the Wicked reproved ; or, a word to
the namelesse publisher of Strength in Weaknesse, or the Burning
Bush. By James Nayler. *s. sh.* (20 July.)   **669. f. 20. (8.)**

July 21.—A true Testimony of what was done concerning the servants
of the Lord [William Dewsbury, John Whitehead, and other Quakers],
at the Generall Assizes at Northampton. *Printed for Giles Calvert.*
                                                      E. 852. (21.)

[July 21.]—Cata-Baptism ; or, New Baptism waxing old and ready to
vanish away. Considerations touching the subject of Baptism, and an
Answer to a discourse against Infant-Baptism by W[illiam] A[llen]
under the title of Some Baptismall Abuses Briefly Discovered. By John
Goodwin. pp. 406. [See above : 23 June, 1653, E. 702. (11.)] *Printed
for H. Cripps and L. Lloyd.* (21 July.)   **E. 849.**

[July 21.]—The Spirit of Persecution again broken loose, by an attempt
to put in execution against John Biddle an abrogated Ordinance for
punishing Blasphemies and Heresies. Together with a narrative of
the proceedings upon that Ordinance against John Biddle and William
Kiffen. *Printed for Richard Moone.* (21 July.)   **E. 848. (27.)**

1655.

[July 23.]—Index Expurgatorius ; or, A Short Examination of the doctrine of Purgatory. By Am. Staveley. *Printed by J. G. for Richard Lowndes.* (23 July.) **E. 850. (2.)**

[July 24.]—An Additional Brief Narrative of a late Bloody Design against the Protestants in Ann Arundel County, and Severn, in Maryland in Virginia. By Roger Heaman. *Printed for Livewell Chapman.* (24 July.) **E. 850. (5.)**

[July 24.]—Communion with God. In two sermons. By Samuel Annesley. *Printed by Evan Tyler for Nathanael Web and William Grantham.* (24 July.) **E. 485. (2.)**

[July 24.]—Sabaudiensis in Reformatam Religionem Persecutionis brevis narratio. [The preface signed : B. M.] *Typis Tho. Newcomb, impensis Authoris.* (24 July.) **E. 850. (6.)**

[July 25.]—The Fourth Principle of Christian Religion ; or, The Foundation Doctrine of Laying on of Hands asserted by way of answer to Paul Hobson. By Tho. Tillam. pp. 61. *Printed by E. C. for Henry Eversden.* (25 July.) **E. 850. (9.)**

[July 25.]—A Voyage to East-India, wherein some things are taken notice of in our passage thither, but many more in our abode there. Observed by Edward Terry. [With a map.] pp. 545. *Printed by T. W. for J. Martin & J. Allestrye.* (25 July.) **E. 1614.**

[July 27.]—Two Letters [dated 27 and 29 July] of Mr. John Biddle, late prisoner in Newgate, but now hurried away to some remote island : one to the Lord Protector, the other to the Lord President Laurence. Wherein you have an account of his judgment concerning those opinions whereof he is accused. **E. 854. (11.)**

[July 30.]—To His Highness. The Petition of the Freeholders and other well affected people of this Commonwealth. [Praying for various legal and constitutional reforms. MS. note by Thomason : " This cast about the streets in the night."] *s. sh.* (30 July.) **669. f. 20. (10.)**

[July 30.]—Advice concerning Bills of Exchange. By John Marius. The second edition, very much enlarged. pp. 174. *Printed by W. H., and are to be sold by Nicolas Bourne.* (30 July.) **E. 1668. (1.)**

[July 31.]—Natura Exenterata : or Nature unbowelled by the most exquisite anatomisers of her. Wherein are contained her choicest secrets, digested into receipts fitted for the cure of all sorts of infirmities. [The preface signed Philiatros. With an engraved portrait of Alathea, Countess of Arundel and Surrey.] pp. 469. *Printed for, and are to be sold by H. Twiford, G. Bedell, and N. Ekins.* (31 July.) **E. 1560.**

[July.]—The Compleat Clark and Scriveners Guide. pp. 664. *Printed by T. R. for H. Twyford.* **E. 486.**

[July.]—Unum Necessarium. Or, the Doctrine and Practice of Repentance. By Jer. Taylor. [With an additional titlepage, and a folding

1655.

plate, engraved by P. Lombart.] pp. 690. [See also below : 24 April, 1658, E. 940. (1.)] *Printed by James Flesher for R. Royston.* (July.)
E. 1554.

[**Aug. 1.**]—Religio Domestica Rediviva; or, Family-Religion Revived. By Philip Goodwin. pp. 548. *Printed by R. & W. Leybourn for Andrew Kemb and Edward Brewster.* (1 Aug.) **E. 1561.**

Aug. 2.—The twelve Wonders of England : being a most strange relation of the death of Mr. Parrey, an innkeeper ; and the manner how twelve serpents were voided from him a little before his death. *Printed for G. Horton.* **E. 851. (11.)**

[**Aug. 3.**]—A Method and Instructions for the Art of Divine Meditations. By Thomas White. pp. 329. *Printed by A. M. for Joseph Cranford.* (3 Aug.) **E. 1700.**

[**Aug. 4.**]—Tentations : their nature, danger, cure. The fourth part. To which is added an appendix touching usury. By Richard Capel. pp. 298. *Printed by T. R. & E. M. for John Bartlet.* (4 Aug.) **E. 1590. (2.)**

[**Aug. 6.**]—An Answer to a Book, called The Quaker's Catechism, put out by Richard Baxter. Also some quæries for the discovering the false grounds of the literal Priest-hood of these days. [By James Nayler. See above : 16 June, E. 842. (22.) & also below : 28 Feb., 1656, E. 869. (1.)] (6 Aug.) **E. 851. (1.)**

[**Aug. 6.**]—An Elegy on the Death of the Princesse Elizabeth in Carisbrook Castle. [In MS. throughout, in Thomason's hand.] (6 Aug.)
E. 850. (23.)

Aug. 7.—A Funeral Elegie upon the Death of George Sonds, who was killed by his Brother, Freeman Sonds, 7 Aug. By William Annand, Junior. *s. sh. Printed by John Crowch.* **669. f. 20. (12.)**

[**Aug. 7.**]—The Devils Reign upon Earth. Being a relation of several Murthers lately committed, especially that of Sir Geo. Sands his son upon his own Brother. *Printed for John Andrews.* **E. 1646. (4.)**

Aug. 7.—Noah's Flood returning : or a sermon preached before the Right Honourable Christopher Pack, Lord Major of London, and the Company of Drapers. By R. Gell. *Printed by J. L. and sold by Giles Calvert.* **E. 852. (14.)**

[**Aug. 8.**]—Joannis Miltoni Angli pro se defensio contra Alexandrum Morum ecclesiasten [or rather P. Du Moulin], libelli famosi, cui titulus Regii Sanguinis clamor ad cœlum adversus parricidas Anglicanos, authorem recte dictum. pp. 204. *Typis Neucomianis.* (8 Aug.)
E. 1661. (2.)

[**Aug. 8.**]—The Proud Pharisee reproved : or the lying orator laid open. In an examination of some passages in a book entituled Precepts for Christian Practice, written by one Edw. Reyner. By Martin Mason. pp. 53. [See above : 2 March, E. 1451.] (8 Aug.) **E. 851. (6.)**

1655.

Aug. 9.—By the Protector. A Proclamation commanding due execution of the Laws against Drunkenness, Adultery and other acts of uncleannesse ; for observing the Assize of Bread, Ale and Fewel ; touching Weights and Measures ; for setting the Poor on Work, etc. *Printed by Henry Hills and John Field.* **669. f. 20. (11.)**

[**Aug. 13.**]—A Manuall of Divine Considerations, delivered and concluded by Thomas White. Translated out of the original Latine copie. pp. 181. (13 Aug.) **E. 1710. (3.)**

[**Aug. 16.**]—The Pagan Preacher silenced. Or, an answer to a treatise of Mr. John Goodwin, entituled The Pagans Debt & Dowry. By Obadiah Howe. With a verdict on the case depending between Mr. Goodwin and Mr. Howe, by George Kendal. pp. 120. *Printed by Th. Maxey, for John Rothwell.* (16 Aug.) **E. 851. (16.)**

[**Aug. 17.**]—Tabulæ suffragiales de terminandis fidei litibus, ab Ecclesia Catholica fixæ : occasione tesseræ ψευδωνύμως Romanæ inscriptæ adversus folium unum Soni Buccinæ. Authore Thoma Anglo ex Albiis [i.e. Thomas White]. pp. 354. (17 Aug.) **E. 1633. (1.)**

[**Aug. 17.**]—Two Treatises, lately delivered to the Church of God at Great Yarmouth, by John Brinsley. 2 pt. *Printed for Thomas Newberry.* (17 Aug.) **E. 1567. (1.)**

[**Aug. 17.**]—A Satyr against Hypocrites. [In verse. By John Phillips.] (17 Aug.) **E. 851. (19.)**

[**Aug. 20.**]—A second Defence of the learned Hugo Grotius ; or, a vindication of the Digression concerning him, from some fresh exceptions. By H. Hammond. *Printed by J. Flesher for Richard Royston.* (20 Aug.) **E. 852. (2.)**

[**Aug. 20.**]—A short and faithfull Account of the late Commotions in the valleys of Piedmont, within the dominions of the Duke of Savoy. With some reflections on Mr. Stouppe's collected papers touching the same businesse. [See above : 10 June, E. 842. (11.)] *Printed for W. P. and G. L.* (20 Aug.) **E. 852. (1.)**

[**Aug. 20.**]—A short Discovery of His Highness the Lord Protector's intentions touching the Anabaptists in the Army. Upon which there is propounded 35 queries for his Highness to answer to his own conscience. [MS. note by Thomason : " This Libell was scatred about the streets in the night about the midle of Aug."] (20 Aug.) **E. 852. (3.)**

Aug. 21.—By the Protector. Orders for the furtherance of Our Service as well for Our Pacquets and Letters as for Riding in Post. *Printed by Henry Hills and John Field.* **E. 1064. (57.)**

[**Aug. 21.**]—Dia Poemata : Poetick Feet standing upon Holy Ground : or, verses on certain texts of Scripture. With epigrams, &c. By E. E. [i.e. Edmund Elys.] pp. 47. *Printed by J. G. for Philip Briggs* (21 Aug.) **E. 1661. (1.)**

1655.

[**Aug. 24.**]—A Discovery of the Beast got into the seat of the False Prophet. Or, an answer to a paper set out by T. Winterton, wherein he would prove something against the Quakers, if he could. By James Nayler. *Printed for Giles Calvert.* (24 Aug.)　　**E. 852. (13.)**

[**Aug. 25.**]—Enchiridion Medicum. By Robert Bayfield. pp. 431. *Printed by E. Tyler for Joseph Cranford.* (25 Aug.)　　**E. 1563.**

[**Aug. 25.**]—Meditations upon the Marks of the true Church of Christ : or motives of credibility in behalf of the true religion. By H. W. ["Papist" : MS. note by Thomason.] pp. 266. (25 Aug.)
E. 1666. (1.)

Aug. 28.—Orders of the Lord Protector for putting into execution the Laws made against Printing Unlicensed Books. *Printed by Henry Hills and John Field.*　　**E. 1064. (58.)**

[**Aug. 28.**]—The Way to Life and Death. Laid down in a sermon, 1629, before the Lord Major of London then being. By N. Waker. pp. 96. *Printed by J. L. for Phil. Stephens.* (28 Aug.)　**E. 1639. (1.)**

[**Aug. 28.**]—Musarum Deliciæ ; or, The Muses Recreation. [Poems.] By Sʳ J. M. and Ja: S. [i.e. Sir John Mennis and James Smith.] pp. 87. *Printed for Henry Herringman.* (28 Aug.)　　**E. 1672. (1.)**

Aug. 29.—A Representation of the Government of the Borough of Evesham, in the county of Worcester, from many of the inhabitants thereof. Directed unto the Protector. [A protest against the persecution of Quakers there.] *s. sh.*　　**669. f. 20. (14.)**

[**Aug. 29.**]—The Protector. A Poem, briefly illustrating the Super-eminency of that Dignity. By George Wither. pp. 50. [MS. note by Thomason : "A second impression, enlarged."] *Printed by J. C.* (29 Aug.)　　**E. 1597. (3.)**

Aug. 30.—An Exhortation to Catechizing. By the Provincial Assembly [of Divines] at London. *Printed by T. R. and E. M. for Samuel Gelli-brand.*　　**E. 853. (32.)**

[**Aug. 30.**]—Anthropologie abstracted : or the idea of humane nature reflected in briefe philosophicall and anatomicall collections. pp. 201. *Printed for Henry Herringman.* (30 Aug.)　　**E. 1589. (2.)**

[**Aug. 31.**]—The Rape of Lucrece. By William Shakespeare. Where-unto is annexed, The Banishment of Tarquin, by J. Quarles. pp. 83. *Printed by J. G. for John Stafford and William Gilbertson.* (31 Aug.)
E. 1672. (3.)

[**Aug.**]—Romæ Ruina Finalis, Anno Dom. 1666. Sive, Literæ ad Anglos Romæ versantes datæ. [The dedication signed : J. W.] pp. 70. *Excudebat T. C., veneuntque apud Johannem Sherlæum & Sam. Thomson.*　**E. 487. (1.)**

Aug.—Culpeper Revived from the Grave ; to discover the Cheats of that Grand Impostor, call'd Aurum Potabile. [Signed : Philaretes, Tantarara, Spittlefield.]　　**E. 487. (2.)**

1655.

[**Sept. 1.**]—Some Papers given forth to the World to be read ; from them who in scorn are called Quakers. *Printed for Giles Calvert.* (1 Sept.)

E. 852. (23.)

[**Sept. 3.**]—A Salutation to the Seed of God : and a Call out of Babylon and Egypt from amongst the Magitians. With some more things added to this second impression. By James Naylor. *Printed for Giles Calvert.* (3 Sept.) **E. 852. (25.)**

Sept. 6.—'Αγάπαι ἄσπιλοι, or, The Innocent Love-Feast. A sermon preached at S. Lawrence Jury, 6 Sept., on the publick Festival of the County of Hertford. By William Clarke. *Printed for William Lee.*

E. 879. (2.)

[**Sept. 6.**]—A Compendious Introduction to the French Tongue. Illustrated by expressions and dialogues. By Peter Lainé. pp. 487. *Printed by T. N. for Anthony Williamson.* (6 Sept.) **E. 1558.**

Sept. 9.—The Male of the Flock, or a sermon preached at St. Pauls before the Lord Mayor and Aldermen of London. By Benjamin Agas. *Printed by A. N. for Henry Eversden.* **E. 861. (3.)**

[**Sept. 9.**]—The Sad and Dismal Year. Or, England's great and lamentable Flood. Being a relation of the overflowings of the Trent, Dove and Severn. *Imprinted for Arthur Reynolds.* (9 Sept.) **E. 853. (1.)**

Sept. 11.—An Act of Common Councell for the better avoiding and prevention of annoyances within the City of London, and liberties of the same. *Printed by James Flesher, Printer to the Honourable City of London.* **E. 856. (4.)**

[**Sept. 12.**]—The Whirl-wind of the Lord gone forth as a fiery flying Roule, with an alarm sounded against the inhabitants of the North Countrey. C. T. [i.e. Christopher Taylor.] *Printed for Giles Calvert.* (12 Sept.) **E. 853. (6.)**

[**Sept. 13.**]—A Call into the Way to the Kingdome. By Thomas Stubbs, one whom the world scornfully calls Quaker. *Printed for Giles Calvert.* (13 Sept.) **E. 853. (9.)**

[**Sept. 13.**]—Poems. By W. H. [i.e. William Hammond.] pp. 84. *Printed for Thomas Dring.* (13 Sept.) **E. 1604. (1.)**

[**Sept. 14.**]—The Form of a Certificate to be used by Justices of Peace and others through England and Wales in the case of Popish Recusants refusing to take the Oath of Abjuration. *s. sh.* (14 Sept.)

669. f. 20. (13.)

[**Sept. 17.**]—A New English Grammar. By J. Wharton. pp. 109. *Printed by W. Dugard, for Anthony Williamson.* (17 Sept.)

E. 1604. (2.)

[**Sept. 19.**]—A Declaration of the Marks and Fruits of the false Prophets. From them who in the world in scorn is called Quakers. (19 Sept.) **E. 853. (17.)**

1655.

[**Sept. 20.**]—A Dialogue containing a Compendious Discourse concerning the Present Designe in the West-Indies. *Printed for R. Lownds.* (20 Sept.) **E. 1619. (2.)**

[**Sept. 20.**]—Salvation from Sinne by Jesus Christ ; or, The Doctrine of Sanctification. By George Hopkins. pp. 286. *Printed by J. G. for Nathanael Web and William Grantham.* (20 Sept.) **E. 1608. (1.)**

[**Sept. 20.**]—A Warning from the Lord to the Town of Cambridge. [" By one of His servants who is despised of the world, known by the name of John Harrwood."] (20 Sept.) **E. 853. (20.)**

Sept. 21.—By the Protector. A Proclamation prohibiting Delinquents to bear Office, or to have any voice in election of any Publique Officer. *s. sh. Printed by Henry Hills and John Field.* **669. f. 20. (15.)**

[**Sept. 24.**]—Som Sober Inspections made into the Cariage and Consults of the Late-long Parliament. [By James Howell.] pp. 184. *Printed by G. C. for Henry Seile.* (24 Sept.) **E. 1656. (1.)**

[**Sept. 24.**]—A just and cleere Refutation of a false and scandalous pamphlet, entituled, Babylon's fall in Maryland, &c. And a discovery of certaine inhumane proceedings of some ungratefull people in Maryland, towards those who formerly preserved them in time of their greatest distresse. By John Langford. *Printed for the Author.* (24 Sept.) **E. 853. (25.)**

[**Sept. 24.**]—Theaurau John his Aurora in Tranlagorum in Salem Gloria. Or, the discussive of the Law and the Gospel betwixt the Jew and the Gentile in Salem Resurrectionem. [By Thomas Tany. With a preface by Robert Norwood.] pp. 57. *Printed for S. B. by Hen. Hills, and sold by Giles Calvert.* (24 Sept.) **E. 853. (26.)**

Sept. 26.—The Saints Testimony finishing through Sufferings : or, the proceedings of the Court against the servants of Jesus [Richard Farnworth, Anne Audland and other Quakers] at the Assizes in Banbury. Also a relation of Margaret Vivers. *Printed for Giles Calvert.* **E. 857. (7.)**

Sept. 26.—An Elegy upon the immature Losse of the most vertuous Lady Anne Riche. [In MS. throughout, in Thomason's hand.] 26 Sept. **E. 853. (30.)**

[**Sept. 29.**]—Englands Face in Isrels Glas : or the sinnes, mercies, judgments of both nations. By Thomas Westfeild. [Sermons. Edited by T. S.] 2 pt. *Printed for Edward Dod, and part of the impression to be vended for the use of Thomas Gibbes, gent.* (29 Sept.) **E. 854. (6.)**

Sept. 29.—A Sermon preached at the election of Alderman John Dethicke as Lord Mayor of London. By Richard Vines. *Printed for Abel Roper.* **E. 858. (4.)**

1655.

[**Sept. 29.**]—Something further in answer to John Jackson's book called Strength in Weaknesse. By James Nayler. [With "A few words in answer to a printed paper subscribed T. B."] (29 Sept.) **E. 854. (5.)**

[**Sept. 29.**]—The Queens Closet opened. Incomparable Secrets in Physick, Chirurgery, Preserving, Candying and Cookery, as they were presented to the Queen. By W. M. pp. 296. *Printed for Nathaniel Brook.* (29 Sept.) **E. 1519.**

[**Sept. 30.**]—The Reclaimed Papist ; or, The Process of a Papist Knight reformed by a Protestant Lady. [The "Prolog" is signed : J. B. V. C.] pp. 221. (30 Sept.) **E. 1650. (1.)**

[**Sept. 30.**]—A Warning to the World that are groping in the dark, after Sects, Opinions and Notions, which are all with the light condemned, and by the Children of Light declared against. By G. Fox. *Printed for Giles Calvert.* (30 Sept.) **E. 854. (7.)**

[**Oct. 1.**]—An Answer to Twenty-eight Queries, sent out by Francis Harris to those people he calls Quakers. By J. N. [i.e. James Nayler.] *Printed for Giles Calvert.* (1 Oct.) **E. 854. (8.)**

[**Oct. 2.**]—The Scriptures Vindication against the Scotish Contradictors. By one John Stalham, and the other, stiled A serious review of some principles of the Quakers, by P. E. By Richard Farneworth. [See also below : 6 June, 1657, E. 914. (1.)] *Printed for Giles Calvert.* (2 Oct.) **E. 854. (9.)**

[**Oct. 6.**]—Θεὸς Ἀνθρωποφόρος, or, God Incarnate, shewing that Jesus Christ is the Onely and the Most High God. By Edm. Porter. 4 pt. *Printed for Humphrey Moseley.* (6 Oct.) **E. 1596. (1.)**

[**Oct. 9.**]—The History of the Inquisition, composed by the Reverend Father Paul Servita. Translated out of the Italian copy. pp. 147. *Printed for Humphrey Moseley.* (9 Oct.) **E. 1596. (2.)**

[**Oct. 14.**]—An Untaught Teacher witnessed against ; or, the old Bottle's mouth opened, its wine poured forth, drunk of drunkards, denyed of them who have tasted of the new. That is to say, the unsound doctrines of Matthew Caffyn laid open. [By Thomas Lawson and John Slee.] *Printed for Giles Calvert.* (14 Oct.) **E. 854. (12.)**

[**Oct. 16.**]—To the Priests and People of England, we discharge our consciences, and give them warning. [Signed : Priscilla Cotton, Mary Cole.] *Printed for Giles Calvert.* (16 Oct.) **E. 854. (13.)**

[**Oct. 18.**]—Advice to a Son ; or directions for your better conduct through the various and most important encounters of this life. [By Francis Osborne.] pp. 151. *Printed by Hen. Hall for Thomas Robinson : Oxford.* (18 Oct.) **E. 1640. (1.)**

[**Oct. 18.**]—Σεισμὸς Μέγας, or, Heaven & Earth shaken. A treatise shewing how Kings, Princes and their Governments are turned and

II. K

1655.

changed by Jesus Christ. By John Davis. pp. 299. *Printed by T. C. for Nathaniel Brooke.* (18 Oct.)   **E. 1601. (2.)**

[**Oct. 19.**]—The Fruits of a Fast, appointed by the Churches gathered against Christ and his Kingdom. Or, a declaration of the persecution of a Messenger of the Lord by a people who go under the name of Independants, in Essex : and also of the unjust dealings of Judge Hills at the last Assizes at Chansford [i.e. Chelmsford]. By James Parnell. *Printed for Giles Calvert.* (19 Oct.)   **E. 854. (14.)**

[**Oct. 20.**]—The Holy Scriptures from Scandals are cleared. Or, an answer to a book set forth by the Baptizers ; to wit, Henry Hagger and Thomas Pollard, entituled, The Holy Scriptures clearing itself of Scandals. Also something in answer to a false Prophet called John Griffith, in a book bearing the title of True Gospel Faith. By R. F. [i.e. Richard Farnworth.] pp. 60. [See above : 25 Oct. 1654, E. 1492. (1.)] *Printed for Giles Calvert.* (20 Oct.)   **E. 855. (1.)**

[**Oct. 20.**]—A Lamentation for the Lost Sheep of the House of Israel. By Martha Simmons. *Printed for Giles Calvert.* (20 Oct.) **E. 855. (2.)**

[**Oct. 21.**]—The President of Presidents. Or, one General President for Common Assurances by Deeds. By William Sheppard. pp. 361. *Printed by Henry Hills for Humphrey Tuckey.* (21 Oct.) **E. 855. (3.)**

Oct. 22.—[A declaration of the Commissioners for Charitable Uses, inviting information respecting Abuses, etc.] *s. sh. Printed by Thomas Newcomb.*   **669. f. 20. (16.)**

[**Oct. 22.**]—The Disarmers Dexterities examined in a second Defence of the Treatise of Schisme. By H. Hammond. pp. 303. *Printed by J. Flesher for Richard Royston.* (22 Oct.)   **E. 856. (1.)**

[**Oct. 22.**]—A New Discovery of Free-State Tyranny. Four letters, together with a remonstrance of several grievances. By William Prynne. [With an engraved portrait of Prynne as frontispiece.] pp. 79. *Printed for the Author.* (22 Oct.)   **E. 488. (2.)**

[**Oct. 22.**]—Εὐχοδία, or, a Prayer-Song ; being Sacred Poems on the Birth and Passion of Our History of the Blessed Saviour. By Daniel Cudmore. [With an engraved frontispiece bearing allegorical designs.] pp. 120. *Printed by J. C. for William Ley.* (22 Oct.)   **E. 1606. (2.)**

Oct. 23.—The Petition of divers gathered Churches, and others wel affected, in and about London, for declaring the Ordinance of the Lords and Commons for punishing Blasphemies and Heresies, null and void. *Printed for William Larner, 1651 : [reprinted 23 Oct.]* **E. 856. (3.)**

[**Oct. 23.**]—Caleb's Inheritance in Canaan by Grace, not Works. An answer to a book entituled The Doctrine of Baptism, and distinction of the Covenants, lately published, by Tho. Patient. By E. W., a Member of the Army in Ireland [i.e. Edward Warren.] pp. 126. *Printed for George Sawbridge.* (23 Oct.)   **E. 856. (2.)**

1655.

[**Oct. 23.**]—The Grand Triall of True Conversion. Or, Sanctifying Grace appearing and acting first in the Thoughts. By John Bisco. pp. 444. *Printed by M. S. for G. Eversden.* (23 Oct.) **E. 1620. (1.)**

[**Oct. 24.**]—The Protector, so called, in part unvailed : by whom the Mystery of Iniquity is now working. Or a word to the good people of England, Scotland and Ireland, informing them of the abominable apostacy of the man above mentioned. By a late Member of the Army. pp. 96. (24 Oct.) **E. 857. (1.)**

Oct. 25.—By the Protector. An Order commanding all persons who have been of the late King's party to depart out of London and Westminster on or before Nov. 5. *s. sh. Printed by Henry Hills and John Field.*

669. f. 20. (17.)

Oct. 26.—A Declaration of His Highnes setting forth, on the behalf of the Commonwealth, the justice of their Cause against Spain. *Printed by Henry Hills and John Field.* **E. 1065. (1.)**

[**Oct. 26.**]—Scriptum Dom. Protectoris ex consensu atque sententia Concilii sui editum, in quo hujus Reipublicæ causa contra Hispanos justa esse demonstratur. [By John Milton.] *Excudebant Henricus Hills & Iohannes Field.* **E. 859. (2.)**

[**Oct. 27.**]—An Exercitation concerning the nature of Forgivenesse of Sin. Intended as an antidote for preventing the danger of Antinomian Doctrine. By Thomas Hotchkiss. To which is prefixed Mr. Richard Baxter's Preface. pp. 353. *Printed by T. M. for Tho. Underhill, and Math. Keinton.* (27 Oct.) **E. 1632.**

[**Oct. 27.**]—A true Tryall of the Ministers and Ministry of England ; as also a true discovery of their root and foundation, and of the called English Church, with its honours, possessions, tythes and maintenance. By Gervase Benson. *Printed for Giles Calvert.* (27 Oct.)

E. 857. (2.)

Oct. 29.—Charity Triumphant, or, the Virgin-shew : exhibited, 29 Oct., being the Lord Mayor's day. [In verse.] *Printed for Nath. Brooks.*

E. 857. (4.)

Oct. 31.—A Declaration of His Highnes by the advice of his Council, shewing the reasons of their proceedings for securing the peace of the Commonwealth upon occasion of the late insurrection and rebellion. *Printed by Henry Hills and John Field.* **E. 857. (3.)**

Oct. 31.—A Letter from a member of Parliament [Edward Hyde, Earl of Clarendon] to one of the Lords of his Highness Councell, upon occasion of the last declaration shewing the reasons of their proceedings for securing the peace of the Commonwealth. pp. 71. **E. 883. (2.)**

[**Nov. 1.**]—An Ingenious Poem called the Drunkards Prospective, or Burning-Glasses. By Joseph Rigbie. *Printed for the Author.* (1 Nov.)

E. 1606. (3.)

1655.

[**Nov. 2.**]—A Check to the Loftie Linguist. In a review of severall assertions given forth by George Scortrith, a pretended Minister of the Gospel in Lincolne. Upon a providentiall discourse betwixt him and one Robert Craven whom the world calls Quaker. [Signed : Martin Mason.] *Printed for Giles Calvert.* (2 Nov.)   **E. 857. (5.)**

[**Nov. 2.**]—Satan's Design discovered. In an answer to Thomas Moor, who calls his book An Antidote against the spreading Infections, &c. By James Nayler. pp. 58. *Printed for Giles Calvert.* (2 Nov.)
E. 857. (6.)

Nov. 3.—Articles of Peace concluded between England and France in a Treaty at Westminster. *Printed by Henry Hills and John Field.*
E. 1065. (2.)

[**Nov. 3.**]—The Bucolicks of Baptist Mantuan in ten eclogues. Translated out of Latin by Tho. Harvey. pp. 104. *Printed for Humphrey Moseley.* (3 Nov.)   **E. 1640. (4.)**

[**Nov. 4.**]—The Holy Scripture clearing itself of Scandals: or, an answer to a book written by Richard Farnworth, bearing this title, Truth cleared of Scandals. By Thomas Pollard. Whereunto is added certain considerations and queries concerning those people called Quakers, as also a postscript. By Henry Haggar. pp. 54. [See above : 27 Sept., 1654, E. 820. (3.)] *Printed by J. C. for R. Moone.* (4 Nov.) **E. 857. (8.)**

[**Nov. 5.**]—To His Highnesse the Lord Protector, the Humble Addresses of Menasseh Ben Israel. [See also below : 8 Jan., 1656, E. 863. (3.)] (5 Nov.)   **E. 490. (1.)**

[**Nov. 5.**]—Targum prius et posterius in Esteram. Nunc primum urbe donatum & in linguam Latinum translatum studio & opera Francisci Taileri. pp. 107. *Typis M. S., impensis H. Eversden.* (5 Nov.)
E. 857. (9.)

[**Nov. 6.**]—The Order of Causes of God's Fore-knowledge, Election, and Predestination, and of Man's Salvation or Damnation. As also whether Christ died for all or not for all. By Henry Haggar. The fourth edition. *Printed by James Cottrel for Richard Moone.* (6 Nov.) **E. 858. (2.)**

[**Nov. 6.**]—The Quakers wilde Questions objected against the Ministers of the Gospel, and many sacred acts and offices of Religion. With brief answers thereunto. Together with a discourse : 1. of the Holy Spirit of God. 2. of Divine Revelation. 3. of Error, Heresie and Schism. By R. Sherlock. pp. 244. *Printed by E. Cotes for R. Royston.* (6 Nov.)   **E. 858. (1.)**

[**Nov. 6.**]—The Way to the Sabbath of Rest. Or, the Soul's progresse in the work of Regeneration. Being a brief experimental discourse of the New-Birth. By a Lover of Truth and a member of the true Church. pp. 50. *Printed by John Streater for Giles Calvert.* (6 Nov.)
E. 858. (3.)

1655.

[**Nov. 7.**]—Πειθαρχία. Obedience to Magistrates, both supreme and subordinate. In three sermons preached upon the anniversarie election day of three Lord Majors successively, 29 Sept., 1653, 1654, 1655. Together with a fourth sermon tending towards a description of the corruption of the mind, preacht at Paul's, 24 June, 1655. By Richard Vines. *Printed for Abel Roper.* (7 Nov.) **E. 858. (4.)**

Nov. 8.—God's appearing for the Tribe of Levi. A sermon preached at St. Pauls 8 Nov. to the Sons of Ministers then solemnly assembled. By Geo: Hall. *Printed by Tho. Roycroft for Philemon Stephens.* **E. 859. (1.)**

[**Nov. 10.**]—Y Trydydd ar Pedwaredd Gorchymynnion. Wedi ei traethu mewn pegethau [*sic*] gan William Jones. *Printed for John Williams.* (10 Nov.) **E. 859. (3.)**

[**Nov. 12.**]—Certaine Propositions tending to the Reformation of the Parish-Congregations in England. By sundry persons, who are unfained friends to Reformation. *Printed for William Frankling, Bookseller in Norwich.* (12 Nov.) **E. 859. (4.)**

[**Nov. 13.**]—Jacob Behme's Table of the Divine Manifestation. Or, an exposition of the threefold World. (13 Nov.) **E. 859. (6.)**

[**Nov. 13.**]—Concerning the Election of Grace, or of God's Will towards Man, commonly called Predestination. Written in the German tongue by Jacob Behme. [Translated by John Sparrow.] pp. 204. *Printed by John Streater for Giles Calvert and John Allen.* (13 Nov.)
E. 859. (5.)

[**Nov. 16.**]—A Ground Voice, or some Discoveries offered to the view, with certain queries propounded to the consideration, of the whole Army in England, Scotland and Ireland. With certain Queries to the Anabaptists. (16 Nov.) **E. 860. (1.)**

[**Nov. 16.**]—The Unreasonableness of Infidelity. Four discourses. By Richard Baxter. 4 pt. *Printed by R. W. for Thomas Underhill and F. Tyton.* (16 Nov.) **E. 1562.**

[**Nov. 17.**]—Postilion, or a new Almanacke and astrologicke, prophetical, Prognostication. Calculated for the whole World. Written in High Dutch by Paulus Felghenore, and now translated into English. pp. 54. *Printed by M. S. for H. Crips and Lodo: Lloyd.* (17 Nov.)
E. 860. (2.)

Nov. 18.—A Paper from the First Fruits Office about paying the First Fruits. **669. f. 20. (18.)**

[**Nov. 19.**]—England's Compleat Law-Judge and Lawyer. [The dedication signed : "Theophilus Philopatros."] *Printed for Edmund Paxton.* (19 Nov.) **E. 860. (3.)**

[**Nov. 20.**]—The persecuted Minister, in defence of the Ministerie, the great ordinance of Jesus Christ. By William Langley. 2 pt. pp. 179. *Printed by J. G. for Richard Royston.* (20 Nov.) **E. 860. (4.)**

1655.

[**Nov. 20.**]—[A Defence of the authenticity of the posthumous publications of William Strong, by his widow Damaris Strong.]   (20 Nov.)

E. 861. (2.)

Nov. 21.—A Declaration of His Highnesse inviting the people of this Commonwealth to a Day of Solemn Fasting [on 6 Dec.].   *s. sh.   Printed by Henry Hills and John Field.*   **669. f. 20. (19.)**

[**Nov. 21.**]—The Accomplish'd Woman.   Written originally in French, since made English by the Honourable Walter Montague.   pp. 135. *Printed for Gabriel Bedell.*   (21 Nov.)   **E. 1686. (1.)**

[**Nov. 22.**]—Protection proclaimed, through the loving kindness of God in the present Government, to the three nations.   Wherein the government established in the Lord Protector and his Council is proved to be of divine institution.   By John Moore.   *Printed by J. C. for Henry Fletcher.*   (22 Nov.)   **E. 860. (5.)**

[**Nov. 23.**]—The Saints Communion with God, and God's Communion with them in Ordinances.   In severall sermons, by William Strong. [Edited by John Hering.]   pp. 212.   *Printed for George Sawbridge, and Ro. Gibbs.*   (23 Nov.)   **E. 1693. (2.)**

Nov. 24.—By the Protector.   A Declaration in order to the securing the Peace of this Commonwealth.   *s. sh.   Printed by Henry Hills and John Field.*   **669. f. 20. (20.)**

[**Nov. 26.**]—Hemerologium : or, A Register Astronomicall, Meteorologicall, Chronologicall for the Yeare 1656.   By G. Wharton.   *Printed by John Grismond.*   (26 Nov.)   **E. 1613. (3.)**

Nov. 27.—An Order and Declaration of His Highness for an Assessment of sixty thousand pounds per mensem from 25 Dec. 1655 to 24 June 1656.   *Printed by Henry Hills and John Field.*   **E. 1065. (3.)**

[**Nov. 27.**]—Goliah's Head cut off with his own Sword.   In reply to a Book, set forth under pretence of an Answer to thirty-six Queries propounded by James Parnell, whom he in scorn calls the young Quaker, by Thomas Draton.   Given forth by James Parnel.   pp. 85. *Printed for Giles Calvert.*   (27 Nov.)   **E. 861. (1.)**

[**Nov. 27.**]—The Path of the Just cleared and Cruelty and Tyranny laid open.   Or, a few words to you Priests and Magistrates of this nation, wherein your oppression and tyranny is laid open, which by you is acted against the servants of the Living God, who by the world are in derision called Quakers.   Also the ground of the imprisonment of George Whitehead and John Harwood.   From the Spirit of the Living God in me, George Whitehead.   *Printed for Giles Calvert.*   (27 Nov.)   **E. 860. (6.)**

[**Nov. 27.**]—Wit Revived : or, A New and Excellent way of divertisement, digested into most ingenious Questions and Answers.   By Asdryasdust Tossoffacan [i.e. Edmund Gayton.]   pp. 72.   *Printed for the Author.*   (27 Nov.)   **E. 1703. (1.)**

1655.

[**Nov. 28.**]—Medici Catholicon, or, a Catholick Medicine for the Diseases of Charitie. By J. C., M.D. [i.e. John Collop.] pp. 134. *Printed for Humphrey Moseley.* (28 Nov.) **E. 1637. (2.)**

[**Nov. 28.**]—The Priests Ignorance and Contrary Walkings to the Scriptures : or the Practice of the Apostles, together with thirty seven errours of the Priests, discovered. [Subscribed by Richard Farnworth and Thomas Aldam.] (28 Nov.) **E. 860. (8.)**

[**Nov. 29.**]—A Good Day well improved, or, Five Sermons upon Acts 9, 13. By Anthony Tuckney. pp. 319. *Printed by J. F. for S. Gellibrand.* (29 Nov.) **E. 1688. (1.)**

[**Nov. 30.**]—Poesis Rediviva : or Poesie Reviv'd. By John Collop. [Miscellaneous poems.] pp. 110. *Printed for Humphrey Moseley.* (30 Nov.) **E. 1640. (2.)**

[**Nov.**]—Merlini Anglici Ephemeris. Astrologicall Predictions for the Year 1656. By William Lilly. *Printed for the Company of Stationers.* **E. 1613. (1.)**

[**Nov.**]—Οὐρανοθεωρία. Celestiall Observations : or an Ephemeris of the Motions, Eclipses and Phænomenas of the Luminaries, for 1656. By John Booker. *Printed by E. Cotes.* **E. 1613. (2.)**

[**Nov.**]—A Short Introduction to the Hebrew Tongue, being a translation of John Buxtorfius' Epitome of his Hebrew Grammar. By John Davis. pp. 114. *Printed by Roger Daniel for Humphrey Moseley.* **E. 1639. (2.)**

[**Dec. 1.**]—The Reconciler of the Bible, wherein above two thousand seeming Contradictions throughout the Old and New Testament are reconciled. By J. T., Minister of the Gospel [i.e. Joannes Thaddaeus.] pp. 348. *Printed for Simon Miller.* (1 Dec.) **E. 1605. (1.)**

[**Dec. 1.**]—Wil: Bagnal's Ghost, or the Merry Devill of Gadmunton, in his perambulation of the Prisons of London. By E. Gayton. [Partly in verse.] *Printed by W. Wilson for Thomas Johnson.* (1 Dec.) **E. 861. (4.)**

[**Dec. 3.**]—A Word for God, or a Testimony on Truths behalf from several Churches and diverse hundreds of Christians in Wales, against wickednesse in high places. With a letter to the Lord Generall Cromwell. (3 Dec.) **E. 861. (5.)**

[**Dec. 5.**]—Paracelsus of the Supreme Mysteries of Nature. Englished by R. Turner. pp. 162. *Printed by J. C. for N. Brook and J. Harison.* (5 Dec.) **E. 1567. (2.)**

[**Dec. 6.**]—A few words to the people of England, who have had a day of visitation, not to slight time but prize it, least ye perish. [By Christopher Fell.] (6 Dec.) **E. 861. (6.)**

[**Dec. 7.**]—A Description of the Prophets, Apostles and Ministers of Christ. With an exhortation to the People of England to forsake them, their Blind-Guides, and to follow Christ Jesus. By Henry Clark. *Printed for Giles Calvert.* (7 Dec.) **E. 861. (8.)**

1655.

[**Dec. 7.**]—Jesus Christ, the same to-day as yesterday. Given forth in witness of the Truth, as it is in Jesus, everywhere persecuted under the reproachful name of Quaking. By George Bishop. *Printed for Giles Calvert.* (7 Dec.) **E. 861. (7.)**

[**Dec. 14.**]—Christ Exalted into his Throne, and the Scripture owned in its place. [By James Parnell.] (14 Dec.) **E. 861. (11.)**

Dec. 14.—Elisha's Lamentation for Elijah. A lecture sermon preached at St. Lawrence Church in Norwich, upon occasion of the losse of Mr. John Carter, Pastor of that Congregation. By John Collinges. *Printed by J. Streater for Richard Tomlins.* **E. 903. (4.)**

[**Dec. 15.**]—Shibboleth; or, the reformation of severall places in the translations of the French and of the English Bible. By John Despayne. Translated into English by Rob. Codrington. pp. 164. *Printed by T. W. for Anthony Williamson.* (15 Dec.) **E. 1646. (2.)**

Dec. 17.—Verses on the Speech made the 17th of Dec. by Pagan Fisher in the Middle Temple Hall. [A satire. In MS., in Thomason's hand.] **E. 498. (2.)**

[**Dec. 20.**]—Phaetons Folly or, the downfal of Pride : Being a translation [by Thomas Hall] of the second book of Ovids Metamorphosis, etc. pp. 101. *Printed for Giles Calvert.* (20 Dec.) **E. 1645. (2.)**

[**Dec. 24.**]—The Foot out of the Snare, or, A Restoration of the Inhabitants of Zion into their Place. Being a brief declaration of his entrance into that Sect called Quakers, by John Toldervy. [See below : 2 Jan. 1656, E. 863. (1.) and 21 Feb., E. 868. (13.)] pp. 52. *Printed by J. C. for Thomas Brewster.* (24 Dec.) **E. 861. (13.)**

[**Dec. 24.**]—A Rationale upon the Book of Common Prayer of the Church of England. [With an engraving of the interior of a Church during the performance of the Litany.] pp. 168. *To be sold by T. Garthwait.* (24 Dec.) **E. 1688. (2.)**

[**Dec. 29.**]—A Warning from the ¡Lord to the Teachers & People of Plimouth. From them which are scornfully called Quakers. [By Margaret Killin and Barbara Patison.] *Printed for Giles Calvert.* (29 Dec.) **E. 861. (14.)**

[**Dec. 30.**]—An Exposition with Practicall Observations upon the 22nd–26th Chapters of the Book of Job. By Joseph Caryl. pp. 826. *Printed by M. Simmons.* (30 Dec.) **E. 862.**

[**Dec. 31.**]—The Life & Death of John Fisher, Bishop of Rochester : comprising the highest and hidden transactions of Church and State, in the reign of King Henry the 8th, with divers morall, historicall and politicall animadversions upon Cardinall Wolsey, Sir Thomas Moor, etc. [By Richard Hall.] Carefully selected from severall ancient records by Tho. Baily. pp. 261. (31 Dec.) **E. 1638. (1.)**

1655.

To the following no date, except that of the year, can be assigned.

1655.—Antheologia; or, The Speech of Flowers. [By Thomas Fuller. With an engraved frontispiece representing a garden.] pp. 90. *Printed for John Stafford.* **E. 1647. (2.)**

1655.—The Compleat Cook. Expertly prescribing the most ready wayes, whether Italian, Spanish or French, for dressing of flesh and fish, ordering of sauces, or making of pastry. pp. 123. *Printed for Nath. Brook.* **E. 1531. (1.)**

1655.—Secretary Longs Letter in answer to the Kings Command concerninge the Accusation of Sir Edward Hide, and Sir Richard Greenvills concerninge the same charge. [In MS. throughout, in Thomason's hand.] **E. 482. (1.)**

1656.

Jan. 1.—A True Relation of Strange and Wonderful Sights seen in the Air, 1 Jan. *Printed for Livewel Chapman.* **E. 863. (8.)**

[Jan. 2.]—Foot yet in the Snare. An Answer to John Toldervy and others. By James Naylor. [See above: 24 Dec. 1655, E. 861. (13.) and also below: 31 Jan. 1656, E. 865. (7.)] *Printed for Giles Calvert.* (2 Jan.) **E. 863. (1.)**

[Jan. 3.]—A Relation of severall Heresies, discovering the Originall Ring-leaders, and the time when they began to spread. *Printed by J. M.* (3 Jan.) **E. 863. (2.)**

[Jan. 7.]—A Short Demurrer to the Jewes long discontinued Remitter into England. By William Prynne. 2 vols. *Printed for Edward Thomas.* (7 Jan.) **E. 483.**

[Jan. 8.]—Anglo-Judæus, or the History of the Jews, whilst here in England. Occasioned by a book written to the Lord Protector for their Readmission, by Rabbi Menasses Ben Israel, to which is also subjoyned a particular Answer by W. H. pp. 52. [See above: 5 Nov. 1655, E. 490. (1.)] *Printed by T. N. for Thomas Heath.* (8 Jan.) **E. 863. (3.)**

[Jan. 9.]—To the Lord Protector. The Humble Representation of the Promoters and Inventers of the Art of Frameworke-Knitting, that they may be incorporated by Charter under the Great Seale of England. (9 Jan.) **E. 863. (4.)**

[Jan. 9.]—The Tears of the Indians : being an account of the massacres and slaughters of above twenty millions of innocent people, committed by the Spaniards in the islands of Hispaniola, Cuba, Jamaica, &c. as also in Mexico, Peru, & other places of the West-Indies. Written in Spanish by Casaus [i.e. B. de las Casas], and made English by J. P. [i.e. John Phillips. With an engraved frontispiece representing scenes of the massacres.] pp. 134. *Printed by J. C. for Nath. Brook.* (9 Jan.) **E. 1586. (1.)**

1656.

[Jan. 12.]—A Bosome opened to the Jewes, holding forth some reasons for our receiving of them into our nation. By W. Tomlinson. *Printed for Giles Calvert.* (12 Jan.) **669. f. 20. (22.)**

[Jan. 12.]—The Mighty Day of the Lord is coming. A Warning to all to submit to Christ. By William Dewsbery. *Printed for Giles Calvert.* (12 Jan.) **E. 863. (5.)**

[Jan. 13.]—An Exhortation to Faith in Christ. By George Fox. *s. sh.* (13 Jan.) **669. f. 20. (23.)**

[Jan. 14.]—A Discovery of some fruits of the $\left.\begin{array}{l}\text{Profession} \\ \text{Religion} \\ \text{Ministry} \\ \text{Government}\end{array}\right\}$ of this Nation. With a few words to the Magistrates that does cast Christ into prison and will not suffer his brethren to visit him. *Printed for T. Simmons.* (14 Jan.) **E. 863. (6.)**

[Jan. 16.]—The Right of Dominion and Property of Liberty. As also the necessity of his Highness acceptation of the Empire. By M. H. [i.e. Michael Hawkes.] pp. 186. *Printed by T. C. and are to be sold by John Perry, and by Tho. Bruster.* (16 Jan.) **E. 1636. (1.)**

[Jan. 16.]—Something further laid open of the cruel Persecution of the People called Quakers by the Magistrates and People of Evesham. [By Humphrey Smith.] (16 Jan.) **E. 863. (7.)**

[Jan. 18.]—Wit and Drollery, Jovial Poems, never before printed. By Sir J. M. [i.e. Sir John Mennis], Ja. S. [i.e. James Smith], Sir W. D. [i.e. Sir William Davenant], J. D. [i.e. John Dryden], and other admirable Wits. [The preface signed : J. P., i.e. John Playford.] pp. 160. *Printed for Nath. Brook.* (18 Jan.) **E. 1617. (1.)**

[Jan. 22.]—Christ's Innocency pleaded against the Cry of the Chief Priests, or, A Reply unto certain papers received from William Thomas. By Thomas Speed. pp. 60. [See also below : 29 June, E. 883. (1.) and 11 July, E. 883. (5.)] *Printed for Giles Calvert.* (22 Jan.) **E. 865. (1.)**

[Jan. 22.]—Mr. Bidle's Confession of Faith touching the Holy Trinity examined and confuted. By Nicholas Estwick. pp. 477. *Printed by Tho. Maxey for Nath. Ekins.* (22 Jan.) **E. 864.**

[Jan. 22.]—Ποιμηνοπύργος. Pastorum Propugnaculum, or The Pulpits Patronage against the force of un-ordained Usurpation and Invasion. By Thomas Ball. pp. 344. *Printed by S. G. for John Wright.* (22 Jan.) **E. 863. (10.)**

Jan. 23.—[An order of the Lord Mayor for the due execution of the laws against Rogues, Vagabonds, and Beggars.] 23 Jan. *Printed by James Flesher.* **669. f. 20. (21.)**

1656.

[**Jan. 23.**]—Plain Dealing : or, The unvailing of the opposers of the Present Government and Governors. In answer of several things affirmed by Mr. Vavasor Powell and others. By Samuel Richardson. *Printed by E. C. and are to be sold by John Clarke.* (23 Jan.)
E. 865. (3.)

[**Jan. 23.**]—A Warning to all the World. By Anne Gargill. *Printed for Giles Calvert.* (23 Jan.) **E. 865. (2.)**

[**Jan. 25.**]—An Answer to some Queries put out by one John Pendarves in a Book called Arrowes against Babylon, &c. for the People called Quakers to answer. [By James Nayler.] *Printed for Giles Calvert.* (25 Jan.) **E. 865. (4.)**

[**Jan. 27.**]—An Essay on the First Book of T. Lucretius Carus De Rerum Natura. Interpreted and made English Verse by J. Evelyn. pp. 185. *Printed for Gabriel Bedle and Thomas Collins.* (27 Jan.)
E. 1572. (2.)

[**Jan. 28.**]—Animadversions upon a Letter and Paper sent to His Highness by certain Gentlemen in Wales. pp. 104. (28 Jan.)
E. 865. (5.)

[**Jan. 29.**]—Leah and Rachel, or the Two Fruitfull Sisters Virginia and Mary-Land : their present condition impartially stated. By John Hammond. *Printed by T. Mabb and are to be sold by Nich. Bourn.* (29 Jan.) **E. 865. (6.)**

[**Jan. 30.**]—Πανοπλία. Universa Arma Hieron. Or, the Christian compleatly armed. By Ralph Robinson. pp. 380. *Printed by John Streater for John Sims and Elisha Wallis.* (30 Jan.) **E. 1586. (2.)**

Jan. 31.—The Humble Representation and Address to His Highness of several Churches & Christians in South-Wales and Monmouthshire. *Printed by Henry Hills and John Field.* **E. 866. (3.)**

[**Jan. 31.**]—The Snare Broken : or, Light discovering Darknesse. Being an answer to a Book entituled, Foot yet in the Snare, by James Naylor. By John Toldervy. [See above : 2 Jan., E. 863. (1.) ; and also below : 21 Feb., E. 868. (13.)] *Printed for N. Brooks.* (31 Jan.)
E. 865. (7.)

[**Feb. 1.**]—Epicurus's Morals, collected partly out of his owne Greek Text in Diogenes Laertius, and partly out of the Rhapsodies of Marcus Antoninus, Plutarch, Cicero & Seneca, and faithfully Englished [by William Charleton. With an engraved frontispiece]. pp. 184. *Printed by W. Wilson for Henry Herringman.* (1 Feb.) **E. 865. (8.)**

[**Feb. 1.**]—Observations upon some particular persons and passages in a book [by Sir William Sanderson] intituled A Compleat History of the Lives and Reignes of Mary, Queen of Scotland and her Son James. [By Carew Raleigh.] *Printed for G. Bedell and T. Collins.* (1 Feb.)
E. 490. (2.)

1656.

[Feb. 2.]—Practical Arithmetick. By Richard Rawlyns. pp. 285.
Printed for Humphrey Moseley and Richard Tomlins. (2 Feb.)
E. 1585. (1.)

[Feb. 2.]—Villare Anglicum; or, A View of the Townes of England.
[A gazetteer.] Collected by the appointment of Sir Henry Spelman.
pp. 390. *Printed by R. Hodgkinsonne.* (2 Feb.) **E. 484.**

[Feb. 4.]—A Brief Answer to some of the Objections made against the
coming in of the Jews in this Common-wealth. [By Thomas Collier.]
Printed by Henry Hills and are to be sold by Thomas Brewster. (4 Feb.)
E. 866. (1.)

Feb. 5.—An Order and Declaration of His Highnes for continuing the
Committee of the Army. **E. 1065. (5.)**

Feb. 6.—[An Order of the Governors of the Corporation for the Poor,
respecting Vagrants, Beggars, etc.] *Printed by James Flesher.*
669. f. 20. (24.)

[Feb. 7.]—David's Psalms in metre. By John White. pp. 371.
Printed by S. Griffin for J. Rothwel. (7 Feb.) **E. 1699.**

[Feb. 9.]—Love to the Lost : and a Hand held forth to the Helpless, to
lead out of the Dark. By James Nayler. pp. 63. *Printed for Giles
Calvert.* (9 Feb.) **E. 866. (2.)**

[Feb. 10.]—The Attributes of God unfolded and applied. Delivered in
sundry sermons at Tavistocke in Devon, by Thomas Larkham. pp. 468.
Printed for Francis Eglesfield. (10 Feb.) **E. 867.**

[Feb. 11.]—Panegyricus Carolo Gustavo, Magno Suecorum Regi.
Væneunt apud Richardum Wodenothe. (11 Feb.) **E. 868. (2.)**

[Feb. 11.]—Antichrist in Man the Quakers Idol, or a faithfull discovery
of their ways and opinions. By Joshuah Miller. [See also below :
5 March, E. 869. (6.)] *Printed by J. Macock for L. Lloyd.* (11 Feb.)
E. 868. (1.)

[Feb. 12.]—Christ-mas Day, the old Heathens feasting Day, in honour
to Saturn their Idol-God. [By Hezekiah Woodward.] *Printed for
Henry Cripps.* (12 Feb.) **E. 868. (3.)**

[Feb. 12.]—The Imperious Brother. [A romance. Translated from the
Spanish by E. P.] pp. 84. *Printed by J. C. for Nathaniel Brook.*
(12 Feb.) **E. 1569. (2.)**

[Feb. 13.]—A Conference of some Christians in Church-fellowship,
about the way of Christ with His people. [By Hezekiah Woodward.]
Printed for Henry Cripps. (13 Feb.) **E. 868. (4.)**

[Feb. 14.]—A just Account upon the Account of truth and peace. [By
Hezekiah Woodward.] *Printed by Henry Cripps.* (14 Feb.)
E. 868. (5.)

1656.

[**Feb. 15.**]—An Appeal to the Churches of Christ for their Righteous Judgement in the Matters of Christ. [By Hezekiah Woodward.] *Printed for Henry Cripps.* (15 Feb.) **E. 868. (6.)**

[**Feb. 16.**]—Dæmonium Meridianum : Sathan at Noon. The Second Part. This now discovereth the slanders cast upon the Author in a pamphlet intituled, The Case of Reading rightly stated, by the Adherents of J. P[ordage]. By Christopher Fowler. pp. 60. *Printed for Fra. Eglesfield.* (16 Feb.) **E. 868. (7.)**

[**Feb. 16.**]—This is onely to goe amongst Friends. [Addresses to Quakers, by Francis Howgill and Edward Burrough.] *Printed for Thomas Simmons.* (16 Feb.) **E. 868. (8.)**

[**Feb. 17.**]—A Second Answer to Thomas Moore, to that which he calls his Defence against the poyson, &c. By James Naylor. *Printed for Giles Calvert.* (17 Feb.) **E. 868. (9.)**

[**Feb. 19.**]—The Persecution of them People they call Quakers in Lanchashire. (19 Feb.) **E. 868. (10.)**

[**Feb. 20.**]—The First Exhortation of H. N. [i.e. Hendrik Nicolas] to his Children and to the Family of Love. Likewise H. N. upon the Beatitudes and the Seven Deadly Sins. Translated out of Base-Almayne. pp. 229. *Printed for Giles Calvert.* (20 Feb.)

E. 1618. (1.)

[**Feb. 20.**]—For Manasseth Ben Israel. The Call of the Jewes out of Babylon, which is Good Tidings to the Meek. [A Quaker tract, by Margaret Fell.] *Printed for Giles Calvert.* (20 Feb.) **E. 868. (11.)**

Feb. 20.—Man's Fury subservient to God's Glory. A sermon preached to the Parliament 20 Feb. it being a day of publick thanksgiving. By John Warren. *Printed by J. G. for Nathanael Webb and William Grantham.* **E. 916. (7.)**

Feb. 20.—Mens sobria serio commendata concione habita Oxoniæ a Joh. Wallis. pp. 158. *Excudebat Leonardus Lichfield, impensis Tho. Robinson : Oxoniæ.* **E. 1639. (3.)**

[**Feb. 21.**]—A Declaration of the Difference of the Ministers of the Word from the Ministers of the World. By G. F. [i.e. George Fox.] *Printed for Giles Calvert.* (21 Feb.) **E. 868. (12.)**

[**Feb. 21.**]—The Naked Truth laid open against what is amiss, or may be mis-interpreted, in those two bookes : the one entituled The Foot out of the Snare ; and the other The Snare Broken. By John Toldervy. [See above : 24 Dec. 1655, E. 861. (13.) and 31 Jan. 1656, E. 865. (7.)] *Printed for G. Calvert.* (21 Feb.) **E. 868. (13.)**

[**Feb. 25.**]—The Golden Mean : being considerations, for a more full and frequent administration of, yet not free admission unto, the Sacrament of the Lord's Supper. By Stephen Geree. pp. 81. *Printed for Joseph Cranford.* (25 Feb.) **E. 1667. (1.)**

1656.

[**Feb. 28.**]—The Quakers Quaking Principles examined and refuted. In a briefe answer to some erroneous Tenets held forth by James Naylor in his Answer unto Mr. Baxter. By Ellis Bradshaw. pp. 63. [See above: 6 Aug. 1655, E. 851. (1.) and also below: 13 March, E. 870. (1.)] *Printed for Lodowicke Lloyd.* (28 Feb.) **E. 869. (1.)**

[**Feb. 29.**]—The Triumphant Lady: or, The Crowned Innocence. A choice and authentick piece of the famous De Ceriziers. Translated by Sir William Lower. pp. 142. *Printed for Ga. Bedell.* (29 Feb.) **E. 1617. (2.)**

[**March 1.**]—The Inheritance of Jacob discovered after his Return out of Ægypt. By Francis Howgill. [A Quaker tract.] *Printed for Giles Calvert.* (1 March.) **E. 869. (3.)**

[**March 3.**]—The Everlasting Joys of Heaven. By John Hart. [With a woodcut portrait of the author.] pp. 155. *Printed for John Andrews.* (3 March.) **E. 1680. (2.)**

[**March 4.**]—An Appendix to Mr. Perkins lies Six Principles of Christian Religion. [Signed: J. Robinson.] *Printed by J. L. for N. Bourn.* (4 March.) **E. 1615. (2.)**

[**March 4.**]—A Candle in the Dark: or, A Treatise concerning the Nature of Witches & Witchcraft. By Thomas Ady. pp. 172. *Printed for R. I.* (4 March.) **E. 869. (5.)**

[**March 5.**]—Antichrist in Man, Christ's Enemy. Clearly discovered in an answer to a book [by Joshua Miller] titled Antichrist in Man the Quakers Idol. By James Naylor. [See above: 11 Feb., E. 868. (1.)] *Printed for Giles Calvert.* (5 March.) **E. 869. (6.)**

[**March 5.**]—Moses his Prayer. Or, an exposition of the nintieth Psalme. By Samuel Smith. pp. 544. *Printed by W. Wilson.* (5 March.) **E. 1624.**

March 10.—Several Orders made by the Justices of the Peace for the City of Westminster concerning the future Licensing of Inn-keepers, the punishment of Rogues, etc. *Printed by W. G.* **E. 1065. (6.)**

[**March 11.**]—The Civil Wars of France, during the bloody reign of Charls the Ninth. [With an engraving.] pp. 272. *Printed by H. H. for W. London.* (11 March.) **E. 1696.**

[**March 13.**]—The Opinions of Divers Philosophers concerning Mans chiefest Good. By M[athias] Browne. pp. 113. *Printed for Tim. Smart.* (13 March.) **E. 1653. (3.)**

[**March 13.**]—A Publike Discovery of the Open Blindness of Babels Builders. In an answer to a book intituled A Publike Discovery of a Secret Deceipt, subscribed John Deacon. By James Naylor. [See also below: 2 Aug., E. 884. (6.)] *Printed for Giles Calvert.* (13 March.) **E. 870. (2.)**

1656.

[**March 13.**]—Wickedness Weighed : in an answer to a book called The Quakers Quaking Principle examined and refuted, set forth by Ellis Bradshaw. By James Naylor. [See above : 28 Feb., E. 869. (1.)] *Printed for Giles Calvert.* (13 March.) **E. 870. (1.)**

March 14.—A Declaration of His Highness, inviting the people of England and Wales to a Day of Solemn Fasting and Humiliation on 28 March. *s. sh. Printed by Henry Hills and John Field.*

669. f. 20. (25.)

[**March 15.**]—Englands Compleat Law-Judge and Lawyer. By Charles George Cocke. *Printed for Edmund Paxton.* (15 March.)

E. 870. (3.)

[**March 17.**]—Enochs Walk and Change, opened in a sermon at Laurence-Jury at the Funeral of the Reverend Mr. Richard Vines. By Tho. Jacombe. pp. 59. *Printed by T. R. and E. M. for Abel Roper.* (17 March.) **E. 870. (4.)**

[**March 17.**]—Lyford's Legacie ; or an Help to Young People. Preparing them for the worthy receiving of the Lord's Supper. By William Lyford. pp. 171. *Printed for Richard Royston.* (17 March.)

E. 1697.

[**March 19.**]—A Copy of a Letter written to an Officer of the Army by a true Commonwealths-man concerning the Right and Settlement of our present Government and Governors. *Printed by Tho. Newcomb.* (19 March.) **E. 870. (5.)**

[**March 20.**]—A True Testimony against the Popes Wayes, in a return to that Agreement of 42 of those that call themselves Ministers of Christ in the County of Worcester. [By Richard Farnworth.] pp. 54. *Printed for Giles Calvert.* (20 March.) **E. 870. (6.)**

[**March 21.**]—An Elegie on the miraculously learned and much lamented Bishop of Armagh [James Ussher, who died 21 March]. *Printed by Francis Leach.* **E. 875. (2.)**

[**March 21.**]—An Elegie on James Usher, Primate of Ireland. By John Quarles. *Printed by J. G. for John Stafford.* **E. 1643. (2.)**

[**March 21.**]—The Wounds of an Enemie in the House of a Friend, being a Relation of the hard Measure sustained by Miles Halhead and Thomas Salthouse. pp. 80. *Printed for Giles Calvert.* (21 March.)

E. 870. (7.)

[**March 22.**]—The Woman learning in Silence : or, The Mysterie of the Womans Subjection to her Husband. By George Fox. *Printed for Thomas Simonds.* (22 March.) **E. 870. (8.)**

[**March 24.**]—Logicke Unfolded. By T. S., Gent. [i.e. Thomas Spencer.] pp. 311. *Printed by W. H. for Nicolas Bourn.* (24 March.)

E. 1645. (1.)

1656.

[**March 24.**]—The Preacher, or the Art and Method of Preaching. By William Chappell. pp. 204. *Printed for Edw. Farnham.* (24 March.)
E. 1707. (1.)

[**March 25.**]—The Art of Simpling. An introduction to the Knowledge of Plants. By W. Coles. pp. 175. *Printed by J. G. for Nath: Brook.* (25 March.)
E. 1698. (1.)

[**March 25.**]—A Second Edition of the New Almanack for 1656, or, The Nocturnall Revised. Being annotations upon the late Mercurius Aëro-machus. (25 March.)
E. 490. (3.)

[**March 26.**]—A Relation of the Life of Christina, Queen of Sweden. Whereunto is added, Her Genius [by U. Chevreau]. Translated out of French by I. H. [i.e. James Howell?] *Printed by J. C. for Henry Fletcher.* (26 March.)
E. 870. (9.)

[**March 26.**]—A Treatise of Civil Policy ; concerning Prerogative, Right and Priviledge, in reference to the Supream Prince and the People. By Samuel Rutherford. pp. 467. *Printed by Simon Miller.* (26 March.)
E. 871.

[**March 27.**]—The English Rudiments of the Latine Tongue. By William Du-Gard. pp. 141. *Printed by W. D. and are to bee sold by Francis Eglesfield.* (27 March.)
E. 1621. (1.)

[**March 28.**]—The Diarium, or Journall : divided into 12. Jornadas in burlesque rhime or drolling verse. [By Richard Flecknoe.] pp. 104. *Printed for Henry Herringman.* (28 March.)
E. 1669. (2.)

[**March 28.**]—Vaticinia Poetica ; or rather, A fragment of some Presages long since written; which doe relate particularly to Spain, France, Rome, Italie, Venice and Great Britain. [In verse.] *Printed for Edward Blackmore.* (28 March.)
E. 1604. (3.)

[**March 29.**]—A Cloud of Witnesses, to bear witness that Jesus Christ is the Word of God, and not the Bible which is called the Scriptures. By Henry Clark. *Printed for Giles Calvert.* (29 March.) **E. 872. (2.)**

[**March 29.**]—Vestibulum linguæ Latinæ, una cum dictionario vestibulari Latino-Anglico. pp. 150. *Typis Guil. Du-Gard: veneunt apud Francis-cum Eglesfield.* (29 March.)
E. 1621. (2.)

[**March 31.**]—A Mixture of Scholasticall Divinity with Practicall. In several tractates. By Henry Jeanes. pp. 172. *Printed by H. Hall for Thomas Robinson: Oxford.* (31 March.)
E. 872. (3.)

[**March 31.**]—A Treatise concerning the Fulnesse of Christ. [By Henry Jeanes.] pp. 396. *Printed by H[enry] H[all] for Tho. Robinson: Oxford.* (31 March.)
E. 873. (1.)

[**April 3.**]—The Deceived and deceiving Quakers discovered. By Matthew Caffyn.—Antichrist made known. By William Jeffery. pp. 80. [See also below : 22 April, E. 877. (1.)] *Printed by R. I. for Francis Smith.* (3 April.)
E. 873. (2.)

1656.

[**April 3.**]—The Institutions or Fundamentals of Physick and Chirurgery. By Daniel Sennertus. Made English by N. D., B. P.   pp. 492.   *Printed for Lodowick Lloyd.*   (3 April.)   **E. 1568.**

[**April 7.**]—XXXI Select Sermons, preached on special occasions.   By William Strong.   pp. 754.   *Printed by R. W. for Francis Tyton.* (7 April.)   **E. 874** and **E. 875. (1.)**

[**April 7.**]—A Triumphant Arch erected to the Glory of the Feminine Sexe. By Monsieur de Scudery.   Englished by I. B., Gent.   pp. 229.   *Printed for William Hope and Henry Herringman*   (7 April.)   **E. 1604. (4.)**

[**April 10.**]—Finetti Philoxenis : Som choice observations of Sir John Finett touching the reception and treatment of Forren Ambassadors in England.   pp. 250.   *Printed by T. R. for H. Twyford and G. Bedell.* (10 April.)   **E. 1602. (1.)**

[**April 12.**]—An Answer to Fifteen Questions, lately published by Edward Fisher, and the suggestions therein delivered against suspending Ignorant and Scandalous Persons from the Lord's Supper.   By Giles Collier.   pp. 55.   *Printed for Edward Brewster.*   (12 April.)
                                                         E. 490. (4.)

[**April 12.**]—Three Sermons by Dr. Richard Stuart, Dean of St. Pauls. To which is added a fourth sermon, by Samuel Harsnett, Arch-Bishop of York.   pp. 165.   *Printed by Gabriel Bedel and Tho: Heath.*   (12 April.)
                                                         E. 1629. (1.)

[**April 12.**]—A Trumpet of the Lord sounded out of Sion.   By Edward Burrough.   *Printed for Giles Calvert.*   (12 April.)   **E. 875. (3.)**

[**April 14.**]—An Answer to a Scandalous Paper [by Edward Breck] wherein were some Queries given to be answered, and many slanders against those whom the world calls Quakers.   [With the " Paper " prefixed.]   *Printed for Giles Calvert.*   (14 April.)   **E. 875. (4.)**

[**April 15.**]—A Copy of a Letter, with its Answer, concerning a contest at Worcester between a Minister [— Baker] and a Quaker [Edward Born].   (15 April.)   **E. 875. (5.)**

April 17.—The Life & Death of Dr. James Usher, late Arch-Bishop of Armagh, and Primate of all Ireland.   Published in a sermon at his funeral at the Abby of Westminster.   By Nicholas Bernard.   [With an engraved portrait of Usher.]   pp. 119.   *Printed by E. Tyler, and are to be sold by J. Crook.*   **E. 1584. (2.)**

[**April 18.**]—The Picture of a New Courtier.   In which is discovered the abominable Practises and horrid hypocrisies of the Usurper [Cromwell] and his time-serving Parasites.   By J. S.   [MS. note by Thomason : " Cast about the Streets."]   (18 April.)   **E. 875. (6.)**

[**April 21.**]—A Heavenly Conference between Christ and Mary after His Resurrection.   By Richard Sibbes.   pp. 106.   *Printed by S. G. for John Rothwell.*   (21 April.)   **E. 876. (2.)**

1656.

[April 21.]—Latinæ Linguæ Janua reserata, per Joannem A. Comenium. Adjecto vocum singularum indice etymologico, per G. D. The Gate of the Latine Tongue unlocked, etc. [With an engraved portrait of the author, and three anatomical plates.] *Lat. and Eng.* pp. 721. *Printed by William Du-Gard, and are to be sold by John Clark.* (21 April.)
E. 1556.

[April 21.]—A Learned Commentary upon the fourth chapter of II. Corinthians. By Richard Sibbes. pp. 273. *Printed by S. G. for John Rothwell.* (21 April.)
E. 876. (1.)

[April 21.]—A Miracle of Miracles ; or, Christ in our Nature.—The Spirituall Mans Aime. Sermons, preached to the Honourable Society of Grayes Inne, by Richard Sibbes. pp. 66. *Printed by W. H. for John Rothwell.* (21 April.)
E. 876. (3 and 4.)

[April 22.]—The Light of Christ and the Word of Life. Laying open some Deceipts in a book titled, The deceived and deceiving Quakers discovered, subscribed by Matthew Caffin and William Jeffery. By James Nayler. [See above : 3 April, E. 873. (2.)] *Printed for Giles Calvert.* (22 April.)
E. 877. (1.)

[April 23.]—The Boasting Baptist Dismounted, and the Beast Disarmed and sorely wounded. In a reply to some papers written by Jonathan Johnson as an answer to a Letter sent him by Martin Mason. [See also below : 29 Aug., 1659, E. 995. (5.)] *Printed for Giles Calvert.* (23 April.)
E. 877. (2.)

[April 23.]—The Last and Highest Appeal ; or, An Appeal to God against the New-Religion-Makers amongst us. By Richard Carpenter. *Printed for the Author.* (23 April.)
E. 1650. (2.)

[April 25.]—The Journal or Diary of a thankful Christian. Presented in some meditations upon Numb. XXXIII. 2. By J. B. [i.e. John Beadle.] pp. 226. *Printed by E. Cotes for Tho. Parkhurst.* (25 April.)
E. 1581. (1.)

[April 26.]—Mr. Mauger's French Grammar. The second edition, enlarged. pp. 272. *Printed by R. D. for John Martin and James Allestree.* (26 April.)
E. 1581. (2.)

[April 27.]—The Abridgment of Christian Divinitie. By John Wollebius. Faithfully translated into English by Alexander Ross. The second edition with additionals. [With a portrait of Alexander Ross.] pp. 431. *Printed by T. Mab for John Saywell.* (27 April.) **E. 1682.**

[April 29.]—Vindiciæ Thesium de Sabbato ; or, A Vindication of certain passages in a Sermon of the Morality of the Sabbath from the exceptions to which they are subjected by Edward Fisher in his book called, A Christian Caveat. By Giles Collier. [See above : 7 Jan., 1650, E. 589. (2.)] *Printed for Edward Brewster.* (29 April.) **E. 490. (5.)**

1656.

April 30.—A true and faithfull Narrative, for substance, of a publique dispute between Mr. Tho. Porter & Mr. Hen. Haggar, concerning Infant-Baptism, in the parish church of Ellesmer in the County of Salop, 30 April. *Printed for John Clark.* **E. 887. (1.)**

May 1.—The Crown of Righteousness. Set forth in a sermon preached at Stephens Walbrook at the funeral of Thomas Hodges. By Thomas Watson. *Printed for Joseph Cranford.* **E. 882. (10.)**

[May 1.]—Musæum Tradescantianum: or, A Collection of Rarities preserved at South Lambeth neer London by John Tradescant. pp. 179. *Printed by John Grismond, and are to be sold by Nathanael Brooke.* (1 May.) **E. 1613. (4.)**

[May 1.]—The Yellow Book. [A religious tract addressed to women. Signed: W. B.] *Printed and are to be sold by Mr. Butler.* (1 May.) **E. 878. (1.)**

[May 1.]—The Trial of the Ladies; or, The Yellow Books Partner. [Signed: W. B.] *Printed and are to be sold by Mr. Butler.* (1 May.) **E. 878. (2.)**

[May 2.]—The Compleat Midwife's Practice. Illustrated with severall cuts in brass. By T. C., I. D., M. S., T. B., Practitioners. [With an engraved portrait of L. Bourgeois.] pp. 126. *Printed for Nathaniel Brooke.* (2 May.) **E. 1588. (3.)**

[May 2.]—Plain Scripture Proof of Infants Church-membership and Baptism. By Richard Baxter. Fourth edition. pp. 415. *Printed for T. U. F. T. and to be sold by John Wright.* (2 May.) **E. 878. (3.)**

[May 3.]—A Review of the Annotations of Hugo Grotius, in reference unto the doctrine of the Deity and Satisfaction of Christ. By John Owen. *Printed by H. Hall for Thom. Robinson: Oxford.* (3 May.) **E. 879. (1.)**

[May 5.]—Galen's Method of Physick: or, his Great Master-peece, being the very Marrow and Quintessence of all his Writings. Translatour, Peter English. pp. 344. *Printed by A. A. for George Suintoun: Edinburgh.* (5 May.) **E. 1701.**

[May 7.]—Enthusiasmus Triumphatus, or, A Discourse of the Nature, Causes, Kinds and Cure of Enthusiasme. Written by Philophilus Parresiastes [i.e. Henry More]. pp. 319. *Printed by J. Flesher.* (7 May.) **E. 1580. (1.)**

[May 7.]—A True and Lamentable Relation of the death of James Parnell, Quaker, who wilfully starved himselfe in the Prison of Colchester. *Printed by T. C. for William Gilberson.* (7 May.) **E. 879. (3.)**

[May 8.]—Kort beworp van de dry teghenwoordighe Wonderheden des Wereldts. [A commentary on the times, with special reference to Cromwell, Mazarin and the Queen of Sweden. Illustrated with an engraved plate, representing the triumph of Cromwell over Papists and Royalists.] *Ghedruckt by Johan van Souffenborgh: Ceulen.* (8 May.) **E. 879. (4.)**

1656.

[**May 8.**]—A Treatise concerning Prayer. By Thomas Hodges. pp. 151. *Printed by John Grismond.* (8 May.) 　　　　**E. 1712. (1.)**

May 8.—Zion's Birth-Register unfolded, in a sermon at Pauls. By Thomas Horton. pp. 69. *Printed for John Clark.* 　　**E. 490. (6.)**

May 11.—A Demonstration of the Day of Judgement, against Atheists & Hereticks. Preached at St. Pauls. By Anthony Burgesse. pp. 70. *Printed for T. Underhill.* 　　　　　　**E. 1715. (2.)**

[**May 12.**]—A Healing Question propounded and resolved upon occasion of the late publique Call to Humiliation. [By Sir Henry Vane, the younger.] [See also below: 16 Aug., E. 885. (8.)] *Printed for T. Brewster.* (12 May.) 　　　　　　　　　　　　　　**E. 879. (5.)**

[**May 12.**]—The Royall Game of Chesse-Play. Being the study of Biochimo, the famous Italian [i.e. Gioachino Greco. Translated by Francis Beale]. pp. 120. *Printed for Henry Herringman.* (12 May.) **E. 1612. (1.)**

[**May 13.**]—A Plain and Easie Calculation of the Name, Mark and Number or the Name of the Beast. By Nathaniel Stephens. pp. 305. *Printed by Ja. Cottrel for Matth. Keynton, Nath. Heathcote and Hen. Fletcher.* (13 May.) 　　　　　　　　　　**E. 879. (6.)**

[**May 15.**]—An Apology for the Service of Love. Being a plain Discourse about the true Christian Religion : set forth, dialogue-wise. pp. 54. *Printed for Giles Calvert.* (15 May.) 　　**E. 1610. (1.)**

[**May 15.**]—The true Bounds of Christian Freedome. By Sam. Bolton. Whereunto is annexed a discourse of John Cameron's touching the threefold covenant of God with Man. pp. 401. *Printed for P. S., and are to be sold by Austin Rice.* (15 May.) 　　　　**E. 1634. (1.)**

[**May 15.**]—Vindiciæ Judæorum ; or, A Letter in answer to certain Questions touching the reproaches cast on the Jewes. By Rabbi Menasseh Ben Israel. *Printed by R. D.* (15 May.) 　　**E. 880. (1.)**

[**May 16.**]—The Grounds and Causes of our Sufferings in Edmonds-Bury Goal in Suffolk. From George Whitehead, John Harwood, George Fox, George Rose and Henry Marshall, Quakers. *Printed for Thomas Simonds.* (16 May.) 　　　　　　　　　　**E. 880. (3.)**

[**May 16.**]—The Resurrection of John Lilburne, now a prisoner in Dover Castle. *Printed for Giles Calvert.* (16 May.) **E. 880. (2.)**
—— Second edition, with additions. *Printed for Giles Calvert.* (21 May.) 　　　　　　　　　　　　　　　　　　　**E. 880. (5.)**

[**May 19.**]—The Astrological Physitian. By Wil. Andrews. pp. 92. *Printed for George Sawbridge.* (19 May.) 　　　**E. 1674. (2.)**

[**May 19.**]—The Destruction of Troy. An Essay [in verse] upon the second book of Virgils Æneis. [By Sir John Denham.] *Printed for Humphrey Moseley.* (19 May.) 　　　　　　**E. 880. (4.)**

[**May 22.**]—The Court-Keepers Guide ; or, A Treatise needfull and usefull for the helpe of many that are imployed in the keeping of Law-dayes or

1656.

Courts Baron. By William Sheppard. Fourth edition, with additions. pp. 254. *Printed by J. G. for M. M. Gabriel Bedel and Thomas Collins.* (22 May.) **E. 1606. (4.)**

[**May 23.**]—The Visitation of the Rebellious Nation of Ireland, and a Warning from the Lord, proclaimed. [By Francis Howgill and Edward Burrough, Quakers.] *Printed for Giles Calvert.* (23 May.) **E. 880. (6.)**

[**May 26.**]—Communion with God in Ordinances the Saints Priviledge and Duty. By William Strong. [Second edition, enlarged. Edited by Lady Elizabeth Carr.] pp. 526. *Printed by R. W. for Francis Tyton.* (26 May.) **E. 1626.**

[**May 26.**]—The Lords Table, whether it is to be spread like a Table in an Inne for all comers ? That it ought not to be so done is here maintained. pp. 73. *Printed by M. S. for Henry Cripps.* (26 May.) **E. 880. (7.)**

[**May 27.**]—The Protestants Practice, or the Compleat Christian, being the true and perfect way to the Celestiall Canaan. [By Athanasius Davies.] pp. 318. *Printed by M. S. for Lodowyke Lloyd.* (27 May.) **E. 1708. (1.)**

[**May 28.**]—Foure Grand Enquiries. I. Whether this whole Nation be a Church as the Jewish Nation was ? II. Whether, by privilege of Infant-Baptism, all are to be admitted to all Church-Communions ? III. Whether there can be any Excommunication out of the Church ? IV. Whether Infants borne of parents notorious for their prophaneness may be admitted to Baptism. pp. 81. *Printed by M. S. for Henry Cripps.* (28 May.) **E. 880. (8.)**

May 29.—An Order and Declaration of His Highnesse for an Assessment of sixty thousand pounds per mensem from 24 June 1656. *Printed by Henry Hills and John Field.* **E. 1065. (7.)**

[**May 29.**]—The Siege of Antwerp, written in Latin by Famianus Strada. Englished by Tho. Lancaster. pp. 200. *Printed by W. W. for Humphrey Moseley.* (29 May.) **E. 1612. (2.)**

May 30.—By the Protector. A Proclamation concerning the Residence of the Merchant-Adventurers of England at the city of Dordrecht, and for settling the Staple there. *Printed by Henry Hills and John Field.* **669. f. 20. (26.)**

[**May 30.**]—The Doctresse. A plain and easie method of curing those diseases which are peculiar to Women. By R. B. [i.e. Richard Bunworth.] pp. 150. *Printed by J. F. for Nicholas Bourne.* (30 May.) **E. 1714. (2.)**

[**May 31.**]—Five Sermons in five several styles, or waies of preaching. First in Bp. Andrews his way. Second in Bp. Hall's way. Third in Dr. Maine's and Mr. Cartwright's way. Fourth in the Presbyterian

1656.

way. Fifth in the Independent way. With an epistle rendring an account of the author's designe in printing these his sermons. By Ab. Wright. pp. 236. *Printed for Edward Archer.* (31 May.)

E. 1670. (1.)

[May 31.]—Willsford's Arithmetick, naturall and artificiall: or Decimalls. Containing the science of numbers. By Thomas Willsford. [With an engraved portrait of the author.] pp. 335. *Printed by J. G. for Nath: Brooke.* (31 May.)   E. 1584. (1.)

[May.]—An Exact Abridgment of Publick Acts of Parliament from 1640 to the year 1656 [May]. By William Hughes. pp. 620. *Printed by T. R. for H. Twyford.*   E. 504.

[June 2.]—A Treatise of Prayer. *Printed by M. S. for Henry Cripps.* (2 June.)   E. 880. (9.)

[June 3.]—A Discovery of some Plots of Lucifer and his Council against the Children of Men. pp. 111. *Printed for T. Brewster.* (3 June.)

E. 1710. (1.)

[June 4.]—The Visible Porch, or known entrance into a Church or Christian Fellowship. By Thomas Tookey. *s. sh. Printed for Richard Moone.* (4 June.)   669. f. 20. (27.)

[June 5.]—Expeditio [i.e. that of the Duke of Buckingham] in Ream Insulam authore Edouardo Domino Herbert, Barone de Cherbury. Quam publici juris fecit Timotheus Balduinus. pp. 179. *Prostant apud Humphredum Moseley.* (5 June.)   E. 1570. (2.)

[June 5.]—The Lamb's Defence against Lyes, and a true testimony given concerning the sufferings and death of James Parnell. Also some sufferings of those people persecuted under the name of Quakers. *Printed for Giles Calvert.* (5 June.)   E. 881. (1.)

[June 7.]—Sermons. By Richard Baxter. pp. 326. *Printed by R. W. for Nevill Simmons, Bookseller in Kidderminster.* (7 June.) E. 1649. (1.)

[June 8.]—A Copy of a Letter [signed: R. G.] from an Officer of the Army in Ireland, to the Lord Protector, concerning his changing of the government. (8 June.)   E. 881. (3.)

[June 8.]—The Teachers of the World unvailed. As also certain queries touching Q. Marie's law made for defence of the Priests and Jesuits, by which the Priests and false Teachers of this nation now guard themselves. [By George Fox.] *Printed for Thomas Simmons.* (8 June.)

E. 881. (2.)

[June 10.]—Poematia. [In Latin. By Henry Birkhead.] pp. 131. *Typis L. Lichfield, impensis E. Forrest: Oxonii.* (10 June.)

E. 1379. (2.)

[June 10.]—A Vindication of the Holy Scriptures, or the Manifestation of Jesus Christ the true Messiah already come. By John Harrison. *Printed by J. M. & sold by J. Benson.* (10 June.)   E. 1685. (1.)

1656.

June 10.—The Fear of God : what it is, and exhorted to as one of the Great Lessons God calls upon men to learn. A sermon preached unto the Church of Christ meeting in Petty France by John Pendarves, a little before his death. *Printed by R. I. for Livewell Chapman.*

E. 907. (3.)

[**June 10.**]—The Method of Grace in the Justification of Sinners. Being a reply to a book written by Mr. William Eyre, entituled, Vindiciæ Justificationis Gratuitæ. By Benjamin Woodbridge. pp. 359. [See above : 10 Nov., 1653, E. 718. (5.)] *Printed by T. R. and E. M. for Edmund Paxton.* (10 June.)

E. 881. (4.)

June 11.—The Sacred Ordinance of Ordination, by Imposition of the Hands of the Presbytery. A sermon preached at the Ordination in Norwich by John Brinsley. *Printed by Rob. Ibbitson for Tho. Newberry.*

E. 1601. (3.)

[**June 12.**]—Ὑπερασπιστής, or, a Buckler for the Church of England against certaine queries propounded by Mr. Pendarvis, called Arrowes against Babylon. By William Ley. *Printed by Leon. Lichfield for Tho. Robinson.* (12 June.)

E. 882. (1.)

[**June 13.**]—The Atturneys Guide, for suing out of Fines, Concords and Recoveries. [The preface signed : I. B.] 2 pt. *Printed by F. L. for Tho. Firby.* (13 June.)

E. 1611. (1.)

[**June 13.**]—Of Christ's Testaments, viz. : Baptisme and the Supper. Written in 1642 by Jacob Behm, and Englished by John Sparrow. pp. 75. *Printed and sold by Lodowick Lloyd.* (13 June.) E. 882. (2.)

[**June 14.**]—Συλλογολογία, or, An Historical Discourse of Parliaments. [The preface signed : J. S.] pp. 80. *Printed for Thomas Firby.* (14 June.)

E. 1646. (1.)

[**June 14.**]—A Compleat Practice of Physick. By John Smith. pp. 369. *Printed by J. Streater for Simon Miller.* (14 June.) E. 1630.

[**June 15.**]—The Wise taken in their Craftiness, and their Wisdom made manifest to be Foolishness with God. Also is shewed that it is no sin for a man to stand with his hat on his head before any Emperor, King, Judge or other magistrate. By Henry Clark. *Printed for Giles Calvert.* (15 June.)

E. 882. (3.)

[**June 16.**]—Extraneus Vapulans ; or, The Observator rescued from the assaults of Hamon l'Estrange and Dr. Nicholas Bernard. By Peter Heylyn. pp. 351. *Printed by J. G. for Richard Lowndes.* (16 June.)

E. 1641. (1.)

June 17.]—A moderate Inspection into the Corruption of the pratique part of the common Law of England. Humbly offered to Oliver Lord Protector. By Ja. Freze. (17 June.) E. 882. (4.)

[**June 17.**]—Politicall Reflections upon the Government of the Turks. Nicolas Machiavel. The King of Sweden's Descent into Germany.

1656.

The Conspiracy of Piso and Vindex against Nero. The Greatness and Corruption of the Court of Rome. The Election of Pope Leo the XI. The Defection from the Church of Rome. Martin Luther vindicated. By the Author of the late Advice to a Son [i.e. Francis Osborne]. pp. 228. *Printed by J. G. for Richard Royston, and are to be sold by Thomas Robinson, Bookseller in Oxford.* (17 June.)   **E. 1631. (1.)**

June 17.—Hannam's last Farewell to the World; being a relation of the life and death of Richard Hannam, the robber. With his speech before his execution, 17 June. *Printed for Thomas Vere and William Gilbertson.*   **E. 1642. (2.)**

June 17.—The English Villain : or, the Grand Thief. Being a relation of the life and death of Richard Hanam. With the manner of the execution, and his Speech at his last farewell to the world. *Printed for John Andrews.*   **E. 1645. (3.)**

June 17.—The Speech and Confession of Richard Hannam. *Printed for G. Horton.*   **E. 882. (5.)**

June 17.—The Witty Rogue arraigned, condemned & executed. Or, the history of that incomparable thief Richard Hainam. With his speech at the place of execution. *Printed for E. S.*   **E. 882. (8.)**

[June 17.]—The Poor Man's Physician and Chyrurgion, containing above three hundred receipts for the cure of all distempers. By Lancelot Coelson. pp. 159. *Printed by A. M. for Simon Miller.* (17 June.)   **E. 1666. (2.)**

[June 17.]—A Second Vindication of Free Admission to the Lords-Supper. By John Humfrey. pp. 147. [See also below : 30 Sept., E. 889. (4.)] *Printed by F. L. for E. Blackmore.* (17 June.)   **E. 1641. (2.)**

[June 20.]—The Agreement of divers Ministers of Christ in the County of Worcester for catechizing all in their several Parishes that will consent thereunto. *Printed by R. W. for Nevil Simmons.* (20 June.)

E. 1653. (2.)

[June 20.]—The Quaker's Catechism, or, the Quakers questioned. By Richard Baxter. *Printed by A. M. for Thomas Underhill and Francis Tyton.* (20 June.)   **E. 882. (6.)**

[June 20.]—The Serpents Subtilty discovered, or a true relation of what passed in the Cathedrall Church of Rochester between divers ministers and Richard Coppin, to prevent credulity to the false representation of the said discourse published by the said R. Coppin. By Walter Rosewell. *Printed by A. M. for Jos. Cranford.* (20 June.)   **E. 882. (9.)**

[June 21.]—Medicina Magica tamen Physica; or, A Methodical Tractate of Diastatical Physick. By Samuel Boulton. pp. 195. *Printed by T. C. for M. Brook.* (21 June.)   **E. 1678. (2.)**

[June 23.]—Good Thoughts for every day of the Month. Translated out of French by Mrs. D. S. pp. 163. *Printed for Thomas Dring.* (23 June.)   **E. 1716. (1.)**

1656.

[June 25.]—Catechizing God's Ordinance. Sermons, by Zach. Crofton. pp. 132. *Printed by E. Cotes for Tho. Parkhurst.* (25 June.)

E. 1665. (1.)

[June 25.]—A Complaint to the Lord Protector by Thomas Grantham, concerning the unjust ejecting of miserable Ministers. *To be distributed by the Author.* (25 June.)

E. 1710. (2.)

June 26.—[A Declaration by the Commissioners for Charitable Uses, explaining their duties and powers.] *s. sh.*

669. f. 20. (28.)

June 26.—A Narration of a publick dipping, 26 June, in a pond of Much Leighes Parish in Essex. By Jeffry Watts.

E. 921.

[June 27.]—A Case of Conscience : Whether it be lawful to admit Jews into a Christian Commonwealth ? Resolved by Mr. John Dury. Written to Samuel Hartlib. *Printed for Richard Wodenothe.* (27 June.)

E. 882. (11.)

[June 27.]—Clavis ἐξουσιαστιχὴ : the Key of Ordination. Or, Missio potestativa. A sermon. By Aylmor Houghton. pp. 59. *Printed by R. I. for Tho. Parkhurst.* (27 June.)

E. 1665. (3.)

[June 28.]—A Warning from the Lord to the Pope. By G. F. [i.e. George Fox.] *Printed for Giles Calvert.* (28 June.)

E. 882. (12.)

[June 29.]—An Answer to a Letter written by the Ld. Bp. of Rochester [John Warner] concerning the Chapter of Original Sin in the Unum Necessarium. By Jer. Taylor. pp. 111. *Printed by E. Cotes for R. Royston.* (29 June.)

E. 1683. (1.)

[June 29.]—The Excellencie of a Free-State ; or, The Right Constitution of a Common-wealth. [By Marchamont Nedham.] pp. 246. *Printed for Thomas Brewster.* (29 June.)

E. 1676. (1.)

[June 29.]—A Sober Answer to an angry Epistle, prefixed to a book called, Christs Innocency pleaded against the Cry of the Chief Priests, written by Thomas Speed. By Christopher Fowler & Simon Ford. [See above : 22 Jan., E. 865. (1.), and also below : 18 Nov., E. 893. (1.)] *Printed for Samuel Gellibrand.* (29 June.)

E. 883. (1.)

June 30.—Joy of Angels. Delivered in a sermon before the Honourable Society of Grayes Inne. By James Rutherford. *Printed by J. G. for Henry Seile.*

E. 948. (6.)

[July 1.]—The Quakers Quaking : or the foundation of their deceit shaken. By Jeremiah Ives. pp. 55. [See also below : 18 July, E. 883. (8.)] *Printed by J. Cottrel for R. Moon.* (1 July.) E. 883. (3.)

[July 2.]—A Legal Resolution of two Important Quæries. Clearly demonstrating the bounden duty of Ministers and Vicars of Parish Churches to administer the Sacraments, as well as preach to their parishioners. By William Prynne. *Printed by F. L.* (2 July.)

E. 495. (1.)

1656.

[July 5.]—Forms the Pillars of Antichrist, but Christ in Spirit the true teacher of his people, and not Tradition. By Jonas Dell. Something in answer to a scandalous paper given forth by W. P. to the souldiers in the garrison of Holmdell in Sutherland. pp. 72. *Printed for the Author.* (5 July.)   E. 883. (4.)

[July 5.]—The Scripture's Sufficiency to determine all matters of Faith, made good against the Papist. By William Twisse. pp. 136. *Printed for Matthew Keynton.* (5 July.)   E. 1698. (2.)

[July 7.]—A Discourse of Auxiliary Beauty or Artificiall Hansomenesse. In point of Conscience between two Ladies. pp. 200. *Printed for R. Royston.* (7 July.)   E. 1594. (1.)

[July 8.]—Clamor Sanguinis Martyrum, or the Bloody Inquisition of Spain. By a Friend to the Protestant Interest. pp. 223. *Printed by A. M. for Fr. Tyton.* (8 July.)   E. 1694. (2.)

July 10.—An Order and Declaration of His Highness for continuing the Committee for the Army. *Printed by Henry Hills and John Field.*
                                                            E. 1065. (8.)

[July 11.]—Rayling Rebuked : or a defence of the Ministers of this Nation : by way of answer to the calumnies cast upon them in an epistle lately published by Thomas Speed. By William Thomas. pp. 56. [See above : 22 Jan., E. 865. (1.), and also below : 18 Nov., E. 893. (1.)] *Printed by T. M. for Edward Thomas.* (11 July.)
                                                            E. 883. (5.)

[July 12.]—The Bar against Free Admission to the Lords Supper fixed, or, An Answer to Mr. Humphrey his Rejoynder. By Roger Drake. pp. 502. [See above : 1 Dec. 1654, E. 1466. (2.)] *Printed for Philip Chetwind.* (12 July.)   E. 1593.

[July 14.]—A Testimony of God and his way and worship against all the false wayes and worships of the world. Also an answer to some of the false doctrines held forth by a professed minister in Wales [V. Powell]. By Alex: Parker. *Printed for Giles Calvert.* (14 July.)
                                                            E. 883. (6.)

[July 15.]—Mercurius Teutonicus; or, A Christian Information concerning the Last Times. Gathered out of the mysticall writings of Jacob Behmen. pp. 52. *Printed by Lodowick Lloyd.* (15 July.)
                                                            E. 490. (7.)

[July 16.]—A Visitation to the Jewes, from them whom the Lord hath visited from on high. By G. F. [i.e. George Fox.] *Printed for Giles Calvert.* (16 July.)   E. 883. (7.)

[July 18.]—Gildas Salvianus; the Reformed Pastor. Shewing the nature of the Pastoral work, especially in Private Instruction and Catechizing. By Richard Baxter. pp. 480. *Printed by Robert White for Nevil Simmons.* (18 July.)   E. 1574.

1656.

[July 18.]—Weaknes above Wickednes, and Truth above Subtilty. An answer to a book called Quakers Quaking, by Jeremiah Ives. By James Nayler. [See above: 1 July, E. 883. (3.) and also below: 30 Aug., E. 886. (2.)] *Printed for Giles Calvert.* (18 July.) **E. 883. (8.)**

[July 20.]—The Trepan : being a relation of the strange practises of Mehetabel, the wife of Edward Jones, and Elizabeth, wife of Lieutenant John Pigeon. Wherein is discovered the subtil method whereby they cheated Mr. Wessel Goodwin of a fair estate. (20 July.) **E. 884. (1.)**

[July 21.]—Examinations, Censures, and Confutations of divers Errours in the two first chapters of Mr. Hobbes his Leviathan. [By William Pike.] *Printed by Philip Wattleworth for William Hope.* (21 July.)
E. 1631. (2.)

[July 23.]—The Cry of Blood. Being a declaration of the Lord arising in those people of the City of Bristol, who are scornfully called Quakers. Subscribed by Geo. Bishop, Thomas Goldney, Henry Roe, Edw: Pyott, Dennis Hollister. pp. 143. *Printed for Giles Calvert.* (23 July.)
E. 884. (3.)

[July 23.]—Glossographia : or a Dictionary interpreting all such Hard Words as are now used in our refined English Tongue. By T. B. of the Inner Temple [i.e. Thomas Blount.] *Printed by Tho. Newcomb, and are to be sold by Humphrey Moseley.* (23 July.) **E. 1573.**

[July 23.]—Of the Mortification of Sinne in Believers. By John Owen. pp. 222. *Printed by L. Lichfield for T. Robinson: Oxford.* (23 July.)
E. 1704. (1.)

July 24.—An Order and Declaration of His Highness for an Assessment of sixty thousand pounds per mensem for six moneths from 25 Dec. *Printed by Henry Hills and John Field.* **E. 1065. (9.)**

[July 26.]—Stablishing against Quaking thrown down. An answer to a book, called Stablishing against Quaking, put forth by Giles Firmin. By Edward Burrough. [See above: 17 Feb. 1655, E. 885. (13.)] *Printed for Giles Calvert.* (26 July.) **E. 884. (4.)**

[July 26.]—The Word of Faith, improved by Eminent Ministers in their Morning Lectures at Martins in the Fields, in Feb. 1655, digested by Gabriel Sangar. pp. 234. *Printed for Francis Tyton.* (26 July.)
E. 1715. (1.)

[July 28.]—Boni ominis Votum. A Good Omen to the next Parliament, expressed upon occasion of those extraordinary Grand Juries lately summoned to serve at the summer Assizes this year 1656. [By George Wither.] *Printed for John Hardesty.* (28 July.) **E. 884. (4*.)**

[July 29.]—Animadversions upon Sir Henry Vane's book entituled The Retired Man's Meditations. By Martin Finch. pp. 179. [See above: 2 July 1655, E. 485. (1.)] *Printed for Joseph Barber.* (29 July.)
E. 1670. (2.)

1656.

July 29.—An Antidote against the Infection of the Times. Published by the appointment of the Elders and Messengers of the severall churches of Ilston, Abergevenny, Tredinog, Carmarthen, Hereford, Bredwardin, Cledock and Llangors, meeting at Brecknock, 29 and 30 July. pp. 51. *Printed for T. Brewster.* **E. 892. (10.)**

July 29.—The Proceeds of the Protector against Sir Henry Vane, 29 July to 4 Sept. **E. 937. (2*.)**

[**July 30.**]—The Horn of the He-goat broken : or an answer to a lying book, called The chasing the young Quaking Harlot out of the Citie, by Thomas Winterton. By Richard Huberthorn. *Printed for Giles Calvert.* (30 July.) **E. 883. (2.)**

[**July 30.**]—Rules for the Government of the Tongue, added as a Supplement to the Rules for governing the Thoughts and the Affections. By Edward Reyner. pp. 363. *Printed by R. I. for Thomas Newberry.* (30 July.) **E. 1594. (2.)**

[**July.**]—Three Excellent Tragœdies, viz. The Raging Turk, or Bajayet the Second, The Courageous Turk, or, Amurath the First, and The Tragœdie of Orestes. By Tho. Goff. The second edition, carefully corrected by a friend of the Authors. pp. 263. *Printed for G. Bedell & T. Collins.* **E. 1591. (2.)**

Aug. 1.—England's Remembrancers. Or, a word in season to all English men about their elections of the members for the approaching Parliament. [MS. note by Thomason : " Aug. 1st, scatred about the streets."] **E. 884. (5.)**

[**Aug. 2.**]—Parænesis ad ædificatores imperii in imperio ; in qua defenduntur jura magistratus adversus Mosem Amyraldum, et cæteros vindices potestatis Ecclesiasticæ Presbyterianæ. Authore Ludovico Molinæo. pp. 709. *Excudebat R. Daniel, prostat apud Samuelem Thomson.* (2 Aug.) **E. 496.**

[**Aug. 2.**]—A Publick Discovery of a Secret Deceit. Where may be discerned Satan transformed into the resemblance of an Angel of light in that sect commonly called Quakers. Being nineteen quæries directed to their speakers at the Bull and Mouth neer Aldersgate, and answered by that fomentor of heresie James Nayler. With a reply thereunto. By John Deacon. pp. 60. [See above : 13 March, E. 870. (2.)] *Printed for Jer. Hirones.* (2 Aug.) **E. 884. (6.)**

[**Aug. 4.**]—Here all may see that Justice and Judgement is to Rule, and the Power of God without respecting men's persons. [Signed : G. F., i.e. George Fox.] *Printed for Thomas Simmons.* (4 Aug.) **E. 884. (7.)**

[**Aug. 4.**]—Sighs for Sion. By a few of her weak and unworthy children [Abraham Cheare and others]. *Printed for Livewel Chapman.* (4 Aug.) **E. 884. (8.)**

1656.

[**Aug. 5.**]— A Lamentation for the scattered Tribes, who are exiled into captivity. By Francis Howgill. *Printed for Giles Calvert.* (5 Aug.)
E. 885. (1.)

[**Aug. 5.**]—State-Maxims. Or, certain dangerous positions destructive to the very natural right and liberty of Mankind, laid down in a book entituled The Grounds of Government and Obedience, by Tho. White. Discussed and confuted by Will Ball. [See above : 3 July, 1655, E. 1711. (2.)] *Printed by G. Dawson for T. Brewster.* (5 Aug.)
E. 886. (7.)

[**Aug. 6.**]—Lettre du Sieur Louis de Gand, Seigneur de Brachey & de Romecour, à Son Altesse [i.e. to the Lord Protector, expressing gratitude for his liberality]. (6 Aug.)
E. 498. (1.)

[**Aug. 6.**]—An Alphabet of Elegiack Groans, upon the death of that rare exemplar of youthful piety, John Fortescue, of the Inner-Temple, Esquire. By E. E. [i.e. Edmund Elys.] *Printed for Tho. Heath.* (6 Aug.)
E. 885. (2.)

[**Aug. 7.**]—The Righteousnes of God to Man, wherein he was created ; with a discovery of the fall, and of the recovery of Man. A few words to O. C. and to the officiers and souldiers of the army. With a declaration how I lived before I knew the truth. By a sufferer in the common gaol at Edmunds Bury, George Rofe. *Printed for Giles Calvert.* (7 Aug.)
E. 885. (3.)

[**Aug. 7.**]—Ex otio Negotium, or, Martiall his Epigramstranslated. With sundry Poems and Fancies, by R. Fletcher. pp. 259. *Printed by T. Mabb for William Shears.* (7 Aug.)
E. 1597. (1.)

[**Aug. 9.**]—A Declaration concerning Fasting and Prayer : of the true fast, also of the false fast. [Signed : G. F., i.e. George Fox.] *Printed for Thomas Simmons.* (9 Aug.)
E. 885. (4.)

[**Aug. 10.**]—A Confession of the Faith of several Churches of Christ in the county of Somerset. [Edited by Thomas Collier.] *Printed by Henry Hills, and sold by Thomas Brewster.* (10 Aug.)
E. 885. (6.)

[**Aug. 10.**]—Deceit brought to Day-light : in an answer to Thomas Collier, what he hath declared in a book called, A Dialogue between a Minister and a Christian. By James Nayler. [See also below : 13 Dec., E. 896. (11.)] *Printed by T. L. for Giles Calvert.* (10 Aug.)
E. 885. (5.)

[**Aug. 11.**]—Pray be not Angry : or, the Women's New Law ; with their several votes, orders, rules and precepts to the London Prentices. [By G. Thorowgood.] *Printed for George Horton.* (11 Aug.) E. 885. (7.)

[**Aug. 12.**]—The Agreement of the Associated Ministers & Churches of the Counties of Cumberland and Westmerland. pp. 59. *Printed by T. L. for Simon Waterson and Richard Scot, Bookseller in Carlisle.* (12 Aug.)
E. 498. (3.)

1656.

[**Aug. 12.**]—The Sinner Impleaded in his own Court, wherin are represented the Great Discouragements from Sinning, which the Sinner receiveth from Sin itselfe. By Tho: Pierce. pp. 390. *Printed by R. Norton for Richard Royston.* (12 Aug.)   **E. 1572. (1.)**

[**Aug. 14.**]—The Law of Conveyances, shewing the Natures, Kinds and Effects of all manner of Assurances. By John Herne. pp. 211. *Printed by T. R. for Hen. Twyford & Tho. Dring.* (14 Aug.)

E. 1597. (2.)

[**Aug. 16.**]—A Letter from a person in the countrey to his friend in the city : giving his judgement upon a book [by Sir Henry Vane], entituled A Healing Question. [See above : 12 May, E. 879. (5.)] (16 Aug.)

E. 885. (8.)

[**Aug. 18.**]—Now or Never : or, a new Parliament of Women assembled. With their declaration, articles, rules and proposals to all London prentices and others. Whereunto is added the fair Maid of the West's Love-Sonnet. *Printed for George Horton.* (18 Aug.)   **E. 885. (9.)**

[**Aug. 20.**]—The Legislative Power is Christ's peculiar Prerogative, proved from Isaiah ix, 6, 7. By W. A. pp. 52. *Printed for Livewel Chapman.* (20 Aug.)   **E. 498. (4.)**

Aug. 20.—The Magistrate's Pourtraiture drawn from the Word, and preached in a sermon at Stowe Market in Suffolk before the election of Parliament-men for the same county. By William Gurnall. *Printed for Ralph Smith.*   **E. 889. (6.)**

Aug. 20.—A True and Perfect Relation of the manner and proceeding held by the Sheriffe at Redding, being the day upon which five Knights to serve in Parliament for the said county should have been elected.

E. 891. (8.)

[**Aug. 21.**]—The True Cavalier examined by his principles, and found not guilty of Schism or Sedition. [By John Hall.] pp. 134. *Printed by Tho. Newcomb.* (21 Aug.)   **E. 885. (10.)**

Aug. 22.—[An Order of the Common Council of the City of Gloucester for " necessary reparations " to the Cathedral.]   *s. sh.*

669. f. 20. (29.)

[**Aug. 23.**]—Death in a New Dress : or Sportive Funeral Elegies. With some healths. By S. F. *Printed for Isaac Pridmore.* (23 Aug.)

E. 885. (11.)

[**Aug. 25.**]—Gospel Publique Worship : or, The Translation, Metaphrase, Analysis and Exposition of Rom. 12. By Thomas Brewer. pp. 302. *Printed by W. Godbid for Henry Eversden.* (25 Aug.)   **E. 1654. (1.)**

[**Aug. 26.**]—A Censure of Mr. John Cotton, lately of New-England, upon the way of Mr. Henden of Bennenden in Kent, expressed in some animadversions of his upon a letter of Mr. Henden's sent to Mr. Elmeston. 2. A briefe exercitation concerning the coercive power of the Magistrate

1656.

in matters of Religion, by Mr. George Petter. 3. Mr. Henden's animadversions on Mr. Elmestons's Epistle revised and chastized. pp. 56. *Printed by J. G. for John Stafford.* (26 Aug.) **E. 885. (12.)**

[**Aug. 27.**]—Suspension Discussed. Or, Church-Members Divine-Right to Christ's Table-Throne of Grace examined. By Tho. Winnel. pp. 154. *Printed by T. Lock for A. Rice.* (27 Aug.) **E. 1658. (2.)**

[**Aug. 29.**]—Coelestis Legatus : or the Coelestial Ambassadour. [An astrological treatise.] By John Gadbury. 2 pt. *Printed by E. B., and are to be sold by John Allen.* (29 Aug.) **E. 886. (1.)**

[**Aug. 30.**]—Innocency above Impudency : or, the strength of righteousness exalted above the Quakers weakness and wickedness. In a reply to a lying pamphlet, called, Weakness above Wickedness, published by J. Nayler in answer to a book entituled The Quakers Quaking. By Jeremiah Ives. [See above : 18 July, E. 883. (8.)] *Printed by J. Cottrel for R. Moon.* (30 Aug.) **E. 886. (2.)**

[**Aug. 30.**]—Musarum Deliciæ ; or, The Muses Recreation. Conteining severall pieces of poetique wit. By Sir John Mennis and James Smith. Second edition. pp. 101. *Printed by J. G. for Henry Herringman.* (30 Aug.) **E. 1649. (2.)**

Aug. 31.—The One Thing Necessary, preached in a sermon at Pauls before the Lord Major and the Aldermen of the City of London. By Thomas Watson. pp. 72. *Printed by T. R. & E. M. for Ralph Smith.* **E. 1652. (3.)**

[**Sept. 1.**]—Actæon and Diana. With a pastoral story of the nymph Oenone ; followed by the several conceited humors of Bumpkin, the huntsman, Hobbinall, the shepheard, Singing Simpkin, and John Swabber, the sea-man. [By Robert Cox. In prose and verse.] *Printed by T. Newcomb for the use of the Author.* (1 Sept.) **E. 886. (3.)**

[**Sept. 2.**]—Medicina Magnetica : or, The rare and wonderful Art of curing by Sympathy. By C. de Iryngio [i.e. C. Irvine.] pp. 110. (2 Sept.) **E. 1578. (1.)**

[**Sept. 3.**]—Gemitus Plebis : or a mournful complaint in behalf of the more weak and ignorant of the people of this nation. By C. Raie. *Printed by R. Ibbitson for Tho. Newberry.* (3 Sept.) **E. 886. (5.)**

[**Sept. 5.**]—Israels Condition and Cause pleaded ; or, Some Arguments for the Jews Admission into England. With a vindication of Mr. Peters from those foul and unjust aspersions cast upon him by W. Prynn. [The preface signed : D. L.] pp. 109. *Printed by P. W. for William Larnar and Jonathan Ball.* (5 Sept.) **E. 1677. (2.)**

Sept. 6.—By the Protector. A Proclamation commanding all persons who have been in Arms against the State to depart out of the cities of London and Westminster on or before 12 Sept. *s. sh. Printed by Henry Hills and John Field.* **669. f. 20. (30.)**

1656.

[**Sept. 6.**]—The True Faith of the Gospel of Peace contended for against the secret opposition of John Bunyan. Or, an answer to his book called, Some Gospel Truths opened. By E. B. [i.e. Edward Burrough.] *Printed for Giles Calvert.* (6 Sept.) **E. 886. (8.)**

[**Sept. 9.**]—A Vindication of Truth, as held forth in a book [by James Nayler] entituled, Love to the Lost, from the lies, slanders and deceits of T. Higgenson, in a book called, A Testimony to the true Jesus. [By James Nayler.] *Printed for Giles Calvert.* (9 Sept.) **E. 886. (8.)**

[**Sept. 11.**]—A New Discovery of some Romish Emissaries, Quakers ; as likewise of some Popish Errors, unadvisedly embraced, pursued by our Anti-Communion Ministers. By William Prynne. pp. 56. *Printed for the Author, and are to be sold by Edward Thomas.* (11 Sept.)
E. 495. (2.)

[**Sept. 12.**]—A Brief Discovery of that which is called the Popish Religion, with a word to the Inquisition discovering their seat of Injustice and Cruelty ; also a word to them who are in bondage under this deceit that upholdeth the Beasts Worship, and a word to the Pope. Given forth by A. Gargill. *Printed for Giles Calvert.* (12 Sept.)
E. 887. (2.)

[**Sept. 15.**]—The Sealed Book opened, or, A cleer Explication of the Prophecies of the Revelation. By William Child. pp. 359. *Printed by T. R. & E. M. for Anthony Williamson.* (15 Sept.) **E. 1578. (2.)**

[**Sept. 15.**]—Therapeutica Sacra, seu de curandis casibus conscientiæ circa regenerationem per fœderum divinorum prudentem applicationem libri tres. Authore Davide Dicsono. pp. 369. *Impensis Societatis Stationariorum.* (15 Sept.) **E. 887. (3.)**

[**Sept. 16.**]—Anti-Socinianism, or a brief explication of some places of holy Scripture, for the confutation of certain gross errours and Socinian heresies lately published by William Pynchion, in a dialogue of his called The Meritorious Price of our Redemption. By N. Chewney. pp. 240. [See above : 2 June, 1650, E. 606. (3.)] *Printed by J. M. for H. Twyford and T. Dring.* (16 Sept.) **E. 888. (1.)**

Sept. 17.—To all the worthy gentlemen who are duely chosen for the Parliament, which intended to meet at Westminster, 17 Sept., and to all the good people of the Commonwealth of England, the humble Remonstrance, Protestation and Appeale of severall Knights and gentlemen, duly chosen to serve their countrey in Parliament, who attended at Westminster for that purpose, but were violently kept out of the Parliament-house by armed men hired by the Lord Protector.
E. 889. (8.)

Sept. 17.—God's Work in Founding Zion. A sermon preached in the Abby Church at Westminster at the opening of the Parliament. By John Owen. *Printed by Leon. Lichfield for Tho. Robinson.* **E. 891. (2.)**

1656.

Sept. 17.—The Scorned Quaker's true and honest Account both why and what he should have spoken by commission from God, but that he had not permission from men, in the Painted Chamber before the Protector and the Parliament, 17 and 24 Sept. [By Samuel Fisher.]
E. 889. (10.)

Sept. 20.—[A MS. copy, in Thomason's hand, of a Letter from the Duke of Ormond to the Bishop of Dromore. Dated : Bruges, 20 Sept.]
669. f. 20. (42.)

Sept. 20.—The Copie of the Lord of Ormond's Letter to the Bishop of Dromore. [With a copy of a letter from Cromwell to Cardinal Mazarin, dated 26 Dec.] E. 912. (8.)

[Sept. 22.]—The Unparalleld Monarch; or, The Portraiture of a Matchless Prince, exprest in some shadows of His Highness My Lord Protector. pp. 114. *Printed by T. C.* (22 Sept.) E. 1675. (1.)

[Sept. 22.]—The Prophets Malachy and Isaiah prophecying of the great things the Lord will doe in this their day and time. To which is prefixed two epistles, by Christopher Feak and John Pendarves. *Printed for Livewell Chapman.* (22 Sept.) E. 888. (2.)

Sept. 23.—A Declaration of the Lord Protector and the Parliament for a Day of Solemn Fasting and Humiliation. *Printed by Henry Hills & John Field.* E. 1065. (10.)

[Sept. 24.]—The Banner of Truth displayed : or a testimony for Christ and against Anti-Christ. Being the substance of severall consultations, holden by a certain number of Christians, who are waiting for the visible appearance of Christ's Kingdome. pp. 91. (24 Sept.) E. 888. (4.)

Sept. 24.—The Policy of Princes in subjection to the Son, explained and applied in a sermon preached before Parliament, the day of their Publick Fast. By William Jenkyn. *Printed by A. M. for John Dallam.*
E. 888. (3.)

[Sept. 25.]—[An Address "to the honest Souldiers of the garrison of Hull," advocating Free Parliaments.] *s. sh.* (25 Sept.)
669. f. 20. (31.)

[Sept. 25.]—The Souls Turnkey, or, A Spirituall File for any Prisoner lockt up in the Dungeon and Chains of Sinne and Satan. By Edward Tuke. pp. 256. *Printed for Will. Gilbertson.* (25 Sept.) E. 1657. (1.)

[Sept. 26.]—Due Correction for Mr. Hobbes, or Schoole Discipline, for not saying his Lessons aright. In answer to his Six Lessons, directed to the Professors of Mathematicks. By the Professor of Geometry [John Wallis]. pp. 130. *Printed by Leonard Lichfield: Oxford.* (26 Sept.)
E. 1577. (1.)

[Sept. 26.]—Jacob found in a desert Land. Wherein is discovered my deliverance out of darkness into the true light and truth. By George Whitehead. *Printed for Giles Calvert.* (26 Sept.) E. 889. (1.)

II.
M

1656.

[**Sept. 26.**]—Sion's Rock exalted over all the Earth to raign. By a sufferer for the Righteous Seed sake, who is scornfully called a Quaker [George Rofe]. *Printed for Giles Calvert.* (26 Sept.)   **E. 889. (1*.)**

[**Sept. 27.**]—A Perfect Nocturnall of several proceedings between Hiel the Bethelite and his much indeered spouse Madam Policy. [A political satire.]   (27 Sept.)   **E. 889. (2.)**

[**Sept. 29.**]—Paracelsus his Dispensatory and Chirurgery. Faithfully Englished by W. D.   pp. 507.   *Printed by T. M. for Philip Chetwind, and are to be sold by Stationers.*   (29 Sept.)   **E. 1628.**

[**Sept. 29.**]—The Siege of Rhodes, made a representation by the art of prospective in scenes, and the story sung in recitative musick. [By Sir William Davenant.]   *Printed by J. M. for Henry Herringman.* (29 Sept.)   **E. 498. (6.)**

[**Sept. 30.**]—The Buddings and Blossomings of Old Truths : or, Severall practicall Points of Divinity, gathered out of St. John.   By Alexander Gross.   pp. 454.   *Printed by W. Bentley for Andrew Crook.* (30 Sept.)
                                              E. 1577. (2.)

[**Sept. 30.**]—Mr. Humphrey's Second Vindication of a disciplinary, anti-erastian, orthodox, free-admission to the Lord's-Supper, taken into consideration in a letter written by Mr. Blake. [See above : 17 June, E. 1641. (2.)]   *Printed by A. M. for Abel Roper.*   (30 Sept.)
                                              E. 889. (4.)

[**Sept.**]—A perfect List of the Names of the several Persons returned to serve in this Parliament. *Printed by Tho. Newcomb.*   **E. 498. (5.)**

[**Sept.**]—The Royall Game at Picquet. [In manuscript, in Thomason's hand.]   **E. 886. (4.)**

[**Sept.**]—A True Narrative of the late Success of the Fleet upon the Spanish Coast.   *Printed by Henry Hills & John Field.*   **E. 1065. (11.)**

[**Oct. 1.**]—A summary Collection of the principal fundamental Rights, Liberties, Proprieties of all English Freemen.   By William Prynne. [See also below : 6 Nov., E. 892. (3.)] *Printed for the Author.* (1 Oct.) **E. 889. (5.)**

[**Oct. 5.**]—The Answer of Edward Hayward, Clerk of the Survey at Chatham, to a most abusive and scandalous pamphlet, lately published by George Kendall, Clerk of the Survey at Deptford and Woolwich. *Printed by Peter Cole.*   (5 Oct.)   **E. 889. (7.)**

[**Oct. 7.**]—Heroick Education, or choice maximes and instructions for the training up of youth.   By I. B. Gent. [With an engraved portrait of William of Orange as a youth.]   pp. 148.   *Printed for William Hope, and Henry Herringman.*   (7 Oct.)   **E. 1634. (2.)**

Oct. 8.—Mans Duty in magnifying Gods Work. A sermon preached before the Parliament, 8 Oct., being a day of Publick Thanksgiving for the Victory obtained by the Navy against the Spanish Fleet in its return from the West-Indies. By John Rowe. *Printed by Robert White for Francis Tyton.*   **E. 894. (1.)**

1656.

Oct. 8.—A Sermon pressing to and directing in that great duty of Praising God. By Joseph Caryl. *Printed by M. Simmons for John Hancock.*　　　　　　　　　　　　　　　　　　**E. 899. (7.)**

[**Oct. 9.**]—The Lip of Truth opened, against a dawber with untempered morter. A few words against a book written by Magnus Bine, Priest, which he calls The scornful Quakers answered, &c. By Thomas Lawson. pp. 58. *Printed for Gile Calvert.* (9 Oct.)　**E. 889. (9.)**

[**Oct. 10.**]—A Paraenesis : Or, seasonable exhortatory to all true sons of the Church of England. By H. Hammond. pp. 240. *Printed by R. N. for Richard Royston.* (10 Oct.)　　　　　**E. 1627. (1.)**

[**Oct. 11.**]—Incomparable Company-Keeping, or A conversation on Earth in Heaven. Held forth in sundry sermons, which are now digested into a Treatise. By William Bell. pp. 131. *Printed by M. S. for George Eversden.* (11 Oct.)　　　　　　　**E. 1651. (3.)**

[**Oct. 13.**]—The History of Russia. By Giles Fletcher. [With an engraved titlepage, coloured by hand.] pp. 280. (13 Oct.)　**E. 1713.**

[**Oct. 15.**]—The Proceeds of the Protector, so called, and his Councill against Sir Henry Vane, as touching his imprisonment in the Isle of Wight. (15 Oct.)　　　　　　　　　　　**E. 889. (11.)**

[**Oct. 17.**]—Aurora. That's the Day-Spring. That is the Root or Mother of Philosophie, Astrologie & Theologie from the true ground. Or a description of Nature. By Jacob Behme. [Translated by J. Sparrow.] pp. 643. *Printed by John Streater for Giles Calvert.* (17 Oct.)　**E. 890.**

[**Oct. 20.**]—A Wonderful Pleasant and Profitable Letter written by M^{ris}. Sarah Wight to a Friend, expressing the joy is to be had in God in sore Afflictions. pp. 81. *Printed by James Cottrel for Ri. Moone.* (20 Oct.)　　　　　　　　　　　　　**E. 1681. (1.)**

[**Oct. 22.**]—A Looking-Glasse for, or, An Awakening Word to, the Officers belonging the Armies of England, Scotland and Ireland. Wherein is set before them some passages in severall of their Declarations speciously pretending for the Rights and Liberties of the People. pp. 68. (22 Oct.)　　　　　　　　　　　**E. 891. (1.)**

[**Oct. 23.**]—Englands Balme ; or, Proposals, by way of grievance & remedy, towards the Regulation of the Law and better Administration of Justice. By William Sheppard. pp. 215. *Printed by J. Cottrel for Hen. Fletcher.* (23 Oct.)　　　　　　　　**E. 1675. (2.)**

[**Oct. 23.**]—The Hypocrites Ladder or Looking-Glasses. Or, A Discourse on the nature of Hypocrisie. By Jo. Sheffeild. pp. 320. *Printed by R. I. for Tho. Newberry.* (23 Oct.)　　　**E. 1570. (1.)**

[**Oct. 23.**]—The Parliament of Women : with the merry Laws by them newly enacted. [A satire. With a woodcut.] *Printed for W. W. and are to be sold by Fra. Grove.* (23 Oct.)　　　　**E. 1636. (2.)**

Oct. 24.—Sathan Inthron'd in his Chair of Pestilence, or, Quakerism in its Exaltation. Being a narrative of James Nailer's entrance into

1656.

Bristoll, 24 Oct., together with blasphemous letters found about him. Collected by Ra. Farmer. pp. 68. [See also below: 28 March, 1657, E. 907. (2.)] *Printed for Edward Thomas.* **E. 897. (2.)**

Oct. 24.—A True Relation of a Dispute between Francis Fullwood and Thomas Salt House before the Quakers in the House of Henry Pollexfen, 24 Oct. With An answer to James Godfries Queries, by Francis Fullwood. [See also below: 28 May, 1657, E. 912. (4.)] *Printed by A. M. for Abel Roper.* **E. 892. (12.)**

Oct. 25.—The Quaker's Jesus: or the unswadling of that child, James Nailor, which a wicked toleration hath midwiv'd into the world. In a narrative of the substance of his examination before the magistrates of the city of Bristol, 25 Oct. By William Grigge. pp. 69. *Printed by M. Simmons for Joseph Cranford.* **E. 942. (2.)**

Oct. 26.—The Active and Publick Spirit handled in a Sermon preached at Pauls. By Thomas Jacomb. *Printed by T. R. for Philemon Stephens.* **E. 904. (3.)**

[Oct. 27.]—An Appeale from the Court to the Country. Made by a Member of Parliament lawfully chosen but secluded illegally by my L. Protector. (27 Oct.) **E. 891. (3.)**

[Oct. 27.]—A Brief Exposition of the Epistles of Paul to the Philippians and Colossians. By James Fergusson. pp. 262. *Printed for the Company of Stationers.* (27 Oct.) **E. 1580. (2.)**

[Oct. 28.]—The Rudiments of Grammar. The Rules composed in English Verse for the greater benefit and delight of young Beginners. By James Shirley. pp. 94. *Printed by J. Macock for R. Lownds.* (28 Oct.) **E. 1704. (2.)**

Oct. 29.—Londons Triumph; or, The Solemn Reception of Robert Tichborn, Lord Major, after his return from taking his Oath at Westminster, 29 Oct. *Printed for N. Brook.* **E. 892. (7.)**

[Oct. 29.]—The Law of Laws: or, the excellency of the Civil Law above all other humane laws whatsoever. By Ro. Wiseman. pp. 190. *Printed by J. G. for R. Royston.* (29 Oct.) **E. 889. (3.)**

Oct. 30.—God's Presence with a People the Spring of their Prosperity. A sermon preached to Parliament at Westminster, 30 Oct., a Day of Solemn Humiliation, by John Owen. *Printed by R. N. for Philemon Stephens.* **E. 891. (4.)**

[Oct. 31.]—A Lamentable Representation of the effects of the present Toleration. [Signed: U. T.] *Printed by A. M. for Thomas Underhill.* (31 Oct.) **E. 891. (5.)**

[Oct. 31.]—A Panegyrick of Christina, Queene of Swedland. Written originally in French by Mr. de Harst, and now translated by W. L., Gent. pp. 75. *Printed for Thomas Dring.* (31 Oct.) **E. 1704. (3.)**

1656.

[**Oct.**]—Here's Jack in a Box, that will conjure the Fox. Or, a new list of the new fashions now used in London. By Laurence Price. [With two woodcuts.] *Printed for Tho. Vere.* **E. 1640. (3.)**

[**Nov. 1.**]—Florus Anglicus; or, An Exact History of England, from the raign of William the Conquerour to the death of the late King. By Lambert Wood [i.e. Lambert van den Bos.] pp. 271. *Printed for Simon Miller.* **E. 1677. (1.)**

[**Nov. 1.**]—Christ Exalted, and the Scriptures owned in their place. In answer to The Quakers Apostacy, by John Timson. By William Dewsberry. *Printed for Giles Calvert.* **E. 891. (6.)**

[**Nov. 1.**]—The English Presbyterian and Independent Reconciled. Written by an English Gentleman. pp. 140. *Printed for Edward Brewster.* (1 Nov.) **E. 891. (7.)**

[**Nov. 3.**]—Adenographia : sive, Glandularum totius corporis descriptio. Authore Thomâ Whartono. pp. 287. *Typis J. G. impensis Authoris.* (3 Nov.) **E. 1579. (1.)**

[**Nov. 4.**]—The Mirrour of State and Eloquence. Represented in the Letters of Sr Francis Bacon, Lord Verulam, to Queene Elizabeth, King James and other Personages. Together with the Character of a true Christian [by Herbert Palmer. With an engraved portrait of Bacon]. pp. 103. *Printed for Lawrence Chapman.* (4 Nov.) **E. 891. (10.)**

Nov. 4.—The Peoples Need of a Living Pastor, asserted in a sermon preached at the Funerals of Mr. John Frost. By Z. C. [i.e. Zachary Crofton.] pp. 59. *Printed by E. Cotes for Thomas Parkhurst.* **E. 909. (1.)**

[**Nov. 5.**]—A Perspicuous Compendium of several Irregularities and Abuses in the present practice of the Common Laws of England. By D. W., of the Middle-Temple *Printed by T. Lock for Henry Flesher.* (5 Nov.) **E. 892. (1.)**

Nov. 5.—Mercies Memorial. A sermon before the Lord Mayor, Aldermen and Companies of the City of London. By Ralph Venning. *Printed for John Rothwell.* **E. 899. (1.)**

Nov. 5.—The Jesuit and the Monk. A sermon, preached by Richard Carpenter. *Printed by Francis Leach.* **E. 897. (5.)**

[**Nov. 5.**]—Morbus Epidemicus, or the Disease of the Latter Dayes. A sermon, by John Ramsey. *Printed by W. Godbid and are to be sold by Philip Briggs.* (5 Nov.) **E. 892. (2.)**

[**Nov. 6.**]—A Summary Collection of the principal Fundamental Rights, Liberties, Proprieties of all English Freemen. By William Prynne. [MS. note by Thomason : " A second impression, much enlarged."] pp. 64. [See above : 1 Oct., E. 889. (5.)] *Printed for the Author.* (6 Nov.) **E. 892. (3.)**

1656.

[**Nov. 6.**]—A View of many Errors and som gross absurdities in the old translation of the Psalms in English Metre. By W. B. [i.e. William Barton.] *Printed by W. D. for F. Eglesfield, Thomas Underhill and F. Tyton.* (6 Nov.) **E. 892. (4.)**

[**Nov. 7.**]—An Answer unto Thirty Quæries propounded by those called Quakers. By Thomas Rosewell. (7 Nov.) **E. 892. (5.)**

[**Nov. 7.**]—A perfect and most useful Table, beginning 150 years since, whereby the true date of any deed since that time may presently be found out with much facility. By W. H. *s. sh. Printed for W. H.* (7 Nov.) **669. f. 20. (32.)**

Nov. 8.—The Protestant's Warning-Piece ; or, the humble Remonstrance of Jeffery Corbet, published to frustrate the designes of the Incendiaries employed by the Pope and the King of Spain, to fire the City of London in 100 places and then proceed to their long intended Massacre. *s. sh.* **669. f. 20. (37.)**

[**Nov. 8.**]—The Perfect Cook : being the most exact directions for the making all kinds of pastes. By Monsieur Marnettè. [With an engraved frontispiece representing the interior of a Kitchen.] 2 pt. *Printed for Math. Brooks.* (8 Nov.) **E. 1695.**

[**Nov. 8.**]—Εἰρηνικὸν, a poeme. Wherein is perswaded the composing the differences of the faithfull in Christ Jesus. [With an engraved titlepage.] *Printed for Luke Fawne.* (8 Nov.) **E. 892. (6.)**

Nov. 9.—The Plea and Protest of Robert Winter, of Elmston in the County of Kent, for his non-payment of tythes. **E. 910. (6.)**

Nov. 9.—True Gain. A sermon preached at Pauls, by Edward Reynolds. *Printed by Tho. Newcomb for Robert Bostock.* **E. 897. (4.)**

[**Nov. 12.**]—[An Order of the Lord Mayor for the better observation of the Lord's Day and Days of Public Humiliation and Thanksgiving.] *s. sh.* (12 Nov.) **669. f. 20. (33.)**

[**Nov. 13.**]—A New Case put to an Old Lawyer, or, Lawyers look about you. [A satire.] *Printed for William Ley.* (13 Nov.) **E. 892. (8.)**

[**Nov. 14.**]—The Fulness and Freeness of Gods Grace in Jesus Christ declared. By Francis Duke. The third part. pp. 114. *Printed by T. N. for Wil. Milward and Miles Michael.* (14 Nov.) **E. 892. (9.)**

[**Nov. 15.**]—Compassion to the Captives, wherein is shewn unto them the Way of God. By George Fox. *Printed for Thomas Simmons.* (15 Nov.) **E. 892. (11.)**

[**Nov. 16.**]—[Extracts from Scripture illustrating the lives of Enoch, Noah, Abraham, Joseph and Moses, and also the " picture of a New borne Christian." With drawings of the five patriarchs. Engraved throughout.] *s. sh. To be sold by Richard Tompson.* (16 Nov.) **669. f. 20. (38.)**

1656.

Nov. 18.—By the Protector. A Proclamation for putting in execution the Laws against Transportation of Woolls, Wool-fels, Fullers-Earth, etc. *s. sh. Printed by Henry Hills and John Field.* **669. f. 20. (36.)**

[**Nov. 18.**]—An Exposition upon the thirteenth chapter of Revelation. By John Cotton. pp. 262. *Printed for Tim. Smart.* (18 Nov.)
E. 893. (2.)

[**Nov. 18.**]—The Guilty-Covered Clergy-Man Unvailed, in a Reply unto two Bundles of Wrath and Confusion, the one written by Christopher Fowler and Simon Ford, the other by William Thomas. By Thomas Speed. [A Quaker tract.] pp. 79. [See above ; 29 June, E. 883. (1.) and 11 July, E. 883. (5.)] *Printed for Giles Calvert.* (18 Nov.) **E. 893. (1.)**

[**Nov. 19.**]—A Call out of Egypt into the Glorious Light and Liberty of the Sons of God. [A Quaker tract.] By Alexander Parker. *Printed for Giles Calvert.* (19 Nov.) **E. 893. (3.)**

[**Nov. 19.**]—The Cry of the Oppressed. Some of the Sufferings of the Quakers concerning Tythes and Oaths, &c. [Signed : G. B., i.e. Gervase Benson.] *Printed for Giles Calvert.* (19 Nov.) **E. 893. (4.)**

[**Nov. 19.**]—The Safe way to Glory. By William Smyth. pp. 240. *Printed by Evan Tyler for Ed. Dod.* (19 Nov.) **E. 1686. (2.)**

[**Nov. 19.**]—A seasonable Vindication of free-admission and frequent administration of the Holy Communion, to all visible Church-members, regenerate or unregenerate. By William Prynne. pp. 74. *Printed by F. Leach for the Author.* (19 Nov.) **E. 495. (3.)**

[**Nov. 20.**]—A Treatise of the Sacrament of the Lords-Supper. By Richard Vines. pp. 376. *Printed by A. M. for Thomas Underhill.* (20 Nov.) **E. 894. (2.)**

[**Nov. 21.**]—A Catalogue of the names of the Knights, Citizens and Burgesses that have served in the last four Parlaments. With the names of such as met in the Parlament at Oxford. pp. 55. *Printed by Tho. Newcomb.* (21 Nov.) **E. 1602. (6.)**

[**Nov. 22.**]—The First Days Entertainment at Rutland-House, by Declamations and Musick : after the manner of the Ancients. [By Sir William Davenant.] pp. 91. *Printed by J. M. for H. Herringman.* (22 Nov.) **E. 1648. (2.)**

[**Nov. 25.**]—The Reduction of Episcopacie unto the Form of Synodical Government proposed as an expedient for the compremising of the now differences. By J. Usher Armachanus. *Printed by T. N. for G. B. and T. C.* (25 Nov.) **E. 894. (3.)**

[**Nov. 28.**]—Γνωστὸν τοῦ Θεοῦ καὶ γνωστὸν τοῦ Χριστοῦ, or, That which may be known of God by the Book of Nature and the Knowledge of Jesus Christ by the Book of Scripture. By Edward Wood. pp. 240. *Printed by H[enry] H[all] for Jos. Godwin and Edw. Forrest.* (28 Nov.)
E. 1648. (1.)

1656.

[**Nov. 28.**]—The Great Sins of Drunkeness and Gluttony set forth. [In verse. With an engraving representing a drunkard and a glutton.] *s. sh. Printed by T. C. for T. Crosse.* (28 Nov.)   **669. f. 20. (40.)**

[**Nov. 30.**]—Coena quasi Κοινή. The New-Inclosures broken down and the Lords Supper laid forth in a diatribe and defence thereof, against the Apology of some Ministers asserting the lawfulness of administring the Lords Supper in a select company, lately set forth by Humphrey Saunders. By William Morice. pp. 490. *Printed by W. Godbid for Richard Thrale.* (30 Nov.)   **E. 895.**

[**Nov.**]—A Brief Chronology of Great Britain, from the first discoveries of this Isle. [With an engraving representing types of the various invaders of Britain.] *s. sh. Printed by T. C. for T. Crosse.*
669. f. 20. (39.)

[**Nov.**]—The Case of William Bentley, printer at Finsbury, touching his Right to the Printing of Bibles and Psalms. *s. sh.*
669. f. 20. (34.)

[**Nov.**]—A Short Answer to a pamphlet entituled, The Case of William Bentley, etc. *s. sh.*   **669. f. 20. (35.)**

[**Dec. 1.**]—A Cry for Repentance, unto the Inhabitants of London chieflie, and unto all the World. [By George Fox.] *Printed for Thomas Simmons.* (1 Dec.)   **E. 896. (1.)**

[**Dec. 2.**]—A full Discovery and Confutation of the damnable Doctrines of the Quakers. By Jonathan Clapham. pp. 80. *Printed by T. R. & E. M. for Adoniram Byfield.* (2 Dec.)   **E. 498. (7.)**

[**Dec. 2.**]—The Grand Impostor examined; or, The Life, Tryal and Examination of James Nayler. By John Deacon. pp. 50. *Printed for Henry Brome.* (2 Dec.)   **E. 896. (2.)**

[**Dec. 3.**]—The Mysterie of Rhetorique unvail'd, wherein above 130 the Tropes and Figures are severally derived from the Greek into English. By John Smith. pp. 267. *Printed by E. Cotes for George Eversden.* (3 Dec.)   **E. 1579. (2.)**

[**Dec. 3.**]—The Skirts of the Whore discovered. A Letter sent by Denys Hollister to the Independent Baptiz'd People who call themselves a Church of Christ in Bristol but are found to be a Synagogue of Satan. Together with another letter to Thomas Ewens, a Teacher among them. Likewise an Answer to 16 Antiqueries directed to the Quakers, sent to Thomas Ewens, from whom the Antiqueries were received, though John Pendarviss a long time after published the Antiqueries by the name of Queries in a book entituled Arrows against Babylon. *Printed for Giles Calvert.* (3 Dec.)   **E. 896. (3.)**

[**Dec. 4.**]—The Rules of the Latine Grammar construed, which were omitted in the book called Lillies Rules. By Edmund Reeve. pp. 92. *Printed for Humphrey Moseley.* (4 Dec.)   **E. 896. (4.)**

1656.

[**Dec. 5.**]—Pendennis and all other standing Forts dismantled ; or, Eight Military Aphorisms, demonstrating the unprofitableness and prodigall expensivenes of all standing English Forts and Garrisons. By William Prynne. *Printed for the Author.* (5 Dec.) **E. 896. (5.)**

Dec. 5.—Copies of some few of the Papers [by George Fox, William Tomlinson, and Robert Rich] given into the House of Parliament in the time of James Naylers tryal there, which began 5 Dec.

E. 896. (13.)

[**Dec. 6.**]—A Warning to the Inhabitants of Exon., that they may forsake the wrath at hand, with some of the effects of the Priests Ministery in Devonshire. By Humphry Smith. [A Quaker tract.] [6 Dec.] **E. 896. (7.)**

[**Dec. 8.**]—Hierocles upon the Golden Verses of Pythagoras. Englished by J. Hall. pp. 177. *Printed by John Streater for Francis Eaglesfield.* (8 Dec.) **E. 1651. (1.)**

[**Dec. 9.**]—The Quakers Quaking ; or, The most just punishment inflicted on James Naylor for his blasphemies. *Printed for W. Gilbertson.* (9 Dec.) **E. 1641. (3.)**

[**Dec. 9.**]—A short and full Vindication of that sweet and comfortable ordinance of Singing of Psalmes. By Jonathan Clapham. [See above : 23 June, 1655, E. 844. (12.)] (9 Dec.) **E. 896. (8.)**

[**Dec. 10.**]—To His Highness The Lord Protector and to the Parliament. [An invective against Cathedral Churches, Church-Steeples, Bells, etc. By Samuel Chidley. With an engraved frontispiece representing the destruction of Withcomb Church in Devon by a thunderstorm during service time, 21 Oct.] (10 Dec.) **E. 896. (9.)**

[**Dec. 12.**]—Englands Lessons, set to be learned by her Rulers, Priests and People. By Henry Clark [a Quaker]. *Printed for Giles Calvert.* (12 Dec.) **E. 896. (10.)**

[**Dec. 13.**]—A Looking-Glasse for the Quakers. Being an answer to James Naylor's pretended Answer to Thomas Collier's book called A Dialogue between a Minister and a Christian. By Thomas Collier. [See above : 10 Aug., E. 885. (5.)] *Printed for Thomas Brewster.* (13 Dec.) **E. 896. (11.)**

Dec. 15.—The Libertine School'd, or, A Vindication of the Magistrates Power in Religious matters. In answer to some Fallacious Quæries scattered about the City of Limrick by a Nameless Author, about the 15 Dec. By Claudius Gilbert. pp. 57. *Printed for Francis Tyton.*

E. 923. (4.)

[**Dec. 15.**]—Omnibus Magistratibus Gubernatoribusque qui profitentur Christum, haec vobis obviantur consideranda, ab amico omnium Potentiarum justarum, Georgio Fox. (15 Dec.) **E. 896. (12.)**

1656.

[**Dec. 16.**]—Ars Notoria : The Notory Art of Solomon, shewing the Cabalistical Key of Magical Operations. Written originally in Latine, and now Englished by Robert Turner. pp. 168. *Printed by J. Cottrel and are to be sold by Martha Harison.* (16 Dec.) **E. 1655. (2.)**

[**Dec. 17.**]—The Reduction of Episcopacie unto the form of Synodical Government received in the Ancient Church. Proposed in 1641 by James Usher, Archbishop of Armagh. A true copy set forth by Nicolas Bernard. *Printed by E. C. for R. Royston.* (17 Dec.) **E. 897. (1.)**

[**Dec. 19.**]—The Triall of a Christians Sincere Love unto Christ. By William Pinke. pp. 274. *Printed by L. Lichfield for Ed. Forrest: Oxford.* (19 Dec.) **E. 1709.**

[**Dec. 20.**]—The Messiah found. Being a declaration where he is to be found, also a warning to flie from the Idol-Shepherds. By R. W. *Printed by J. C. for Giles Calvert.* (20 Dec.) **E. 897. (2*.)**

[**Dec. 20.**]—A True Relation of the life, examination and sentence of James Naylor the Quaker. [With a woodcut representing Naylor in the pillory and being whipped at the cart's tail.] *Printed for Thomas Vere.* (20 Dec.) **E. 1645. (4.)**

[**Dec. 20.**]—An Answer to a book titled Quakers Principles Quaking subscribed by Ralph Hale. By William Adamson. *Printed for Giles Calvert.* (20 Dec.) **E. 897. (3.)**

[**Dec. 22.**]—A Method for Meditation ; or, a Manuall of Divine Duties. By Ja. Ussher, Arch-bishop of Armagh. [With an engraved portrait of the author.] pp. 165. *Printed for Joseph Nevill.* (Dec. 22.) **E. 1665. (2.)**

Dec. 23.—To the Parliament. The Petition of divers of the inhabitants of the North-Riding of the County of York. [Suggesting various reforms.] 23 Dec. *s. sh. Printed by James Cottrel.* **669. f. 20. (44.)**

[**Dec. 23.**]—A Demonstration of the Resurrection of our Lord and Saviour Jesus Christ; and therein of the Christian Religion. By Richard Garbutt. pp. 168. *Printed for Samuel Gellibrand.* (23 Dec.) **E. 1693. (1.)**

[**Dec. 23.**]—A famous City turned into Stone : or a fearfull example for England to take warning by. Written by Laurence Price. *Printed for Tho. Vere.* (23 Dec.) **E. 1638. (2.)**

Dec. 23.—Moses his Death : opened and applyed in a sermon at Christ-Church in London at the Funeral of Mr. Edward Bright. By Samuel Jacombe. *Printed for Adoniram Byfield.* **E. 904. (4.)**

[**Dec. 23.**]—The Ruine of Rome, or, An Exposition upon the whole Revelation, wherein is plainely showed that the Popish Religion shall come to an utter overthrow before the end of the World. By Arthur

1656.

Dent. To which is added an Epitome of Mr. Brightman his Exposition upon the Revelation. pp. 423. *Printed by Thomas Harper for John Waterson.* (23 Dec.) **E. 1615. (1.)**

[**Dec. 24.**]—An Apologie of John, Earl of Bristol. [The dedication is dated: Caen, 8 April 1647.] pp. 96. *Printed at Caen in 1647; reprinted in London,* 1656. (24 Dec.) **E. 897. (6.)**

Dec. 26.—A true Copie of a Letter sent from a friend in Paris to his friend in London, with one inclosed [signed : O. P., and purporting to be addressed by Cromwell to Cardinal Mazarin on the subject of Catholic Toleration], casually found neer the Louvre in Paris.
E. 905. (2*.)

Dec. 26.—His Highnesse Letter to his eminency Cardinall Mazarin. [In MS., in Thomason's hand.] *s. sh.* **669. f. 20. (43.)**

[**Dec. 27.**]—The Humble Inquiry, partly approving and partly disapproving the Practice of the Law. *Printed by M[atthew] S[immons].* (27 Dec.) **E. 897. (7.)**

[**Dec. 31.**]—Barker's Delight : or the Art of Angling. The second edition, much enlarged. By Thomas Barker. pp. 52. *Printed by J. G. for Richard Marriot.* (31 Dec.) **E. 1661. (3.)**

[**Dec. 31.**]—A True and Exact Relation of the strange Finding out of Moses his Tombe in a Valley Neere unto Mount Nebo in Palestina. *Printed by J. G. for Richard Lowndes.* (31 Dec.) **E. 1660. (3.)**

Dec.—[An Advertisement of a cure for Gout and Sciatica offered by Peter Francesse.] *s. sh.* **669. f. 20. (41.)**

[**Dec.**]—A Copye of a Letter translated out of High Dutche into Frenche and imprinted at London An°. 1604, now Englished, 1607. Conteyninge a notable discourse of a Jewe yet lyvinge, and wanderinge through the world as a vagabond, whoe was an assistant at the death and passion of Jesus Christ. [In MS. throughout.] **E. 896. (6.)**

Dec.—A Tutor to Astrologie, whereunto is added an Ephemeris for the Year 1657. By W. E. pp. 96. *Printed by Joseph Moxon.*
E. 1705. (1.)

To the following no date, except that of the year, can be assigned.

1656.—Petri ab Heimbach ad Serenissimum Principem Olivarium, Magnæ Britanniæ Protectorem, Adlocutio Gratulatoria. *Ex Typographia Jacobi Cottrellii.* **E. 1069. (3.)**

1656.—Englands Golden Legacy ; or, A brief description of the blessings which the Lord hath bestowed upon our Nation. By Laurence Price. *Printed for Thomas Jenkins.* **E. 1648. (3.)**

1656.—The Illustrious Shepherdess. [A translation, by E. P., of the "Sucessos y Prodigos de Amor" by Juan Perez de Montalban.] pp. 90. *Printed by J. C. for Nath. Brook.* **E. 1588. (1.)**

1656.

1656.—Making light of Christ and Salvation too oft the issue of Gospel-Invitations. A sermon preached at Laurence Jury. By Rich. Baxter. pp. 66. *Printed by R. White for Nevil Simmons.*   **E. 1651. (2.)**

1656.—Peripateticall Institutions, in the way of that excellent philosopher Sr Kenelm Digby. The theoreticall part. Also a theologicall appendix of the beginning of the world. By Thomas White. pp. 430. *Printed by R. D., and are to be sold by John Williams.*   **E. 1692.**

1657.

[Jan. 1.]—Astrology proved harmless, useful, pious. A sermon, by Richard Carpenter. *Printed by Ja. Cottrel for John Allen and Joseph Barber.* (1 Jan.)   **E. 899. (2.)**

[Jan. 3.]—The Fiery Change; or, Almighty God His Melting and Refining of His people. By Robert Read. pp. 115. *Printed for the Author.* (3 Jan.)   **E. 899. (3.)**

[Jan. 7.]—Israels Just Judge; or, The Majestrats Brest-plate against the Darts of Pride, Envy & Hipocrisie. By Charles Hammond. [With a woodcut representing a figure of Justice.] *Printed by E. Crowch for the Author.* (7 Jan.)   **E. 899. (4.)**

Jan. 9.—The Peace of Jerusalem ; a sermon preached in the Parliament House 9 Jan., being a Day of Private Humiliation kept by the Members thereof. By Edward Reynolds. *Printed by Tho. Newcomb for George Thomason.*   **E. 904. (2.)**

[Jan. 9.]—Nature's Cabinet unlock'd. Wherein is discovered the natural Causes of Metals, Stones, Precious Earths, Juyces, Humors and Spirits. By Tho. Brown, D. of Physick. pp. 331. *Printed for Edw. Farnham.* (9 Jan.)   **E. 1687.**

[Jan. 10.]—Here are several Queries. [Respecting Astrology. By George Fox.] *Printed for Giles Calvert.* (10 Jan.)   **E. 899. (5.)**

[Jan. 14.]—A True Narrative of the Examination, Tryall and Sufferings of James Nayler. pp. 60. (14 Jan.)   **E. 899. (6.)**

[Jan. 16.]—Nature's Explication and Helmont's Vindication, or a short and sure way to a long and sound life. Being a necessary and full apology for chymical medicaments. By George Starkey. pp. 336. *Printed by E. Cotes for Thomas Alsop.* (16 Jan.)   **E. 1635. (2.)**

Jan. 18.—The Perusal of an old Statute concerning Death and Judgment. As it was delivered in a sermon at the funeral of Mrs. Frances Bedford who died 18 Jan.]. By James Bedford. *Printed by J. M. for Francis Tyton.*   **E. 941. (2.)**

[Jan. 21.]—Divine Fire-Works, hinting what the Almighty Emanuel is doing in these Whipping Times. *s. sh. Printed for the Author.* (21 Jan.)   **669. f. 20. (45.)**

1657.

Jan. 23.—By the Protection. A Proclamation of the Peace made betwixt this Common-Wealth and Portugal. *s. sh. Printed by Henry Hills and John Field.* **669. f. 20. (46.)**

[**Jan. 23.**]—A True Narrative of the late Trayterous Plot against the Lord Protector. *Printed by Tho. Newcomb.* (23 Jan.) **E. 900. (2.)**

[**Jan. 23.**]—The Humbled sinner resolved what he should do to be Saved. By Obadiah Sedgwick. pp. 282. *Printed by T. R. & E. M. for Adoniram Byfield.* (23 Jan.) **E. 900. (1.)**

[**Jan. 24.**]—A Testimony of the True Light of the World. By Geo. Fox. pp. 50. *Printed for Giles Calvert.* (24 Jan.) **E. 902. (1.)**

[**Jan. 24.**]—The West answering to the North in the fierce and cruell persecution of the manifestation of the Son of God. As appears in the following relation of the sufferings of George Fox, Edward Pyot and William Salt at Launceston [and of other Quakers in various places]. pp. 172. *Printed for Giles Calvert.* (24 Jan.) **E. 900. (3.)**

[**Jan. 26.**]—The Danger of being almost a Christian. By John Chishull. pp. 167. *Printed by A. Neile for Francis Eglesfield.* (26 Jan.) **E. 1694.**

[**Jan. 27.**]—The Difference between an Usurer and a Lawfull Prince explained in their severall Characters. (27 Jan.) **E. 902. (2.)**

[**Jan. 30.**]—Dilucidatio articulorum controversorum fidei inter Christianos Reformatos, Lutheranos, Calvinianos & Arminianos, qua luculenter patet hos omnes in essentia doctrinæ controversæ convenire. Per Lucam Morin. pp. 130. *Excudebat T. C. pro H. Robinson.* (30 Jan.) **E. 1691. (2.)**

[**Jan. 30.**]—Elijah's Mantle : or the remaines of Mr. John Tillinghast. [Nine sermons.] Published by his owne notes. pp. 466. *Printed for Livewell Chapman.* (30 Jan.) **E. 1557.**

[**Jan. 31.**]—The Compleat Bone-Setter ; whereunto is added the Perfect Oculist and The Mirrour of Health. Written originally by Francis Moulton, now Englished and enlarged by Robert Turner. pp. 175. *Printed by J. C. for Martha Harrison.* (31 Jan.) **E. 1673. (1.)**

[**Feb. 2.**]—To the Officers and Souldiers of the Army, more especially to those Officers that sit in Council at White-Hall, a sober admonition from some sighing Souls. [A tract in defence of John Biddle.] (2 Feb.) **E. 902. (4.)**

[**Feb. 6.**]—The Eagle Prophesie, or, An Explanation of the Eleventh and Twelfth Chapters of the Second Booke of Esdras. By John Birchensha. *Printed by T. C. and are to be sold by Jeremy Hierons.* (6 Feb.) **E. 902. (5.)**

[**Feb. 6.**]—The Riches of Grace Displayed in the offer and tender of Salvation to poor Sinners. By Obadiah Sedgwick. pp. 271. *Printed by T. R. & E. M. for Adoniram Byfield.* (6 Feb.) **E. 1683. (2.)**

1657.

[**Feb. 7.**]—A Learned Commentary or Exposition upon the fourth Chapter of the second Epistle of Saint Paul to the Corrinthians. To which is added : I. A Conference between Christ and Mary after his resurrection. II. The Spirituall Mans aim. III. Emanuell, or Miracle of Mirades. By Rich. Sibbs. pp. 445. *Printed by S. G. for John Rothwell.* (MS. note by Thomason : "February 7. My sad accident.")

E. 902. (6.)

Feb. 10.—The Whole Business of Sindercome from first to last, it being a perfect Narrative of his Imprisonment, Tryal and Execution, 10 Feb. *Printed by Tho. Newcomb.*

E. 903. (7.)

[**Feb. 11.**]—Love to the Captives : or, The love of God to the World. [Signed : G. R.] *Printed for Giles Calvert.* (11 Feb.) E. 903. (1.)

[**Feb. 12.**]—An Exact History of the Life of James Naylor, also how he came first to be a Quaker. By John Deacon. pp. 58. *Printed for Edward Thomas.* (12 Feb.) E. 903. (2.)

Feb. 18.—The Best Fee-Simple. Set forth in a sermon at St. Peters in Cornhil, before the gentlemen of Nottingham, 18 Feb., being the day of their publique feast. By Marmaduke James. pp. 59. *Printed by J. M. for J. Martin, J. Allestry, T. Dicas.* E. 955. (2*.)

Feb. 20.—A Declaration of the Lord Protector and Parliament for a Day of Publique Thanksgiving [for the discovery of Plots against the Lord Protector] on 20 Feb. *Printed by Henry Hills and John Field.*

E. 1065. (12.)

[**Feb. 24.**]—Conscience-Oppression : or, A Complaint of wrong done to the Peoples Rights, being a Word necessary and seasonable to all Christians in England. By J. Croope. pp. 56. (24 Feb.)

E. 903. (8.)

[**Feb. 26.**]—A Discourse of the Souls of Men, Women and Children, shewing that they are immortal, spiritual substances. By Thomas Hickes. *Printed by T. Newcomb.* (26 Feb.) E. 903. (5.)

[**Feb. 27.**]—A Catechisme for Children ; that they may come to learn of Christ the light, the truth, the way. [Signed : G. F., i.e. George Fox.] pp. 66. *Printed by Giles Calvert.* (27 Feb.) E. 1667. (3.)

[**Feb.**]—An Act for Renouncing and Disanulling the pretended Title of Charles Stuart, &c. *Printed by Henry Hills and John Field.*

669. f. 20. (47.)

[**Feb.**]—An Act for the taking away the Court of Wards and Liveries. *s. sh. Printed by Henry Hills and John Field.* 669. f. 20. (48.)

[**Feb.**]—An Act for the Security of the Lord Protector his person. *Printed by Henry Hills and John Field.* 669. f. 20. (49.)

[**Feb.**]—An Act for the Exportation of several Commodities of the Breed, Growth and Manufacture of this Commonwealth. *Printed by Henry Hills and John Field.* 669. f. 20. (50.)

1657.

[March 1.]—King Richard the Third revived. Containing a memorable Petition contrived by himself and his instruments, whiles Protector, to importune him to accept of the Kingship. [By William Prynne.] *Printed for William Leak.* (1 March.)   **E. 896. (5*.)**

March 1.—The Proviso or Condition of the Promises, being the substance of two sermons preached at Wilton, 1 March. By Tho. Drayton. pp. 68. *Printed by Tho. Newcomb.*   **E. 910. (1.)**

[March 2.]—[An Address to Cromwell, praying him to abolish Capital Punishment for Stealing. By Samuel Chidley. Printed in red ink.] (2 March.)   **E. 903. (10.)**

[March 2.]—A Cry against a Crying Sinne: or, A just Complaint to the Magistrates against killing of men meerly for Theft. By Samuel Chidley. [Printed in red ink.] *Printed for Samuel Chidley.* (2 March.)   **E. 903. (11.)**

[March 3.]—A Sad Caveat to all Quakers; containing a narration of one William Pool, Quaker. *Printed for W. Gilbertson.* (3 March.)   **E. 1645. (5.)**

[March 3.]—Prædestination as before privately, so now at last openly defended against Post-Destination in a Correptorie Correction, by way of answer to A Correct Copy of some notes concerning Gods Decrees, especially of Reprobation, by Mr. T. P. [i.e. Thomas Pierce]. By William Barlee. pp. 232. [See also below 2 May, E. 909. (9.) and 31 Aug., E. 923. (9.)] *Printed by W. H. for George Sawbridge.* (3 March.)   **E. 904. (1.)**

[March 9.]—Some Considerations humbly tendered for the satisfying and uniting the faithfull in this day, whose hearts are groaning for the deliverance of Zion, and appearance of her King. (9 March.)   **E. 746. (3.)**

March 12.—His Highnes's Commission for satisfying the Fifths of such Discoveries as have been made out before the Commissioners for Discoveries of any Manors, Lands and other things belonging to His Highness and unjustly concealed. *Printed by Thomas Newcomb.*   **E. 1065. (13.)**

March 12.—A Discovery made by the Lord Protector to the Lord Mayor, Aldermen and Common-Councell of the City of London, concerning the new attempts and designs of Charles Stewart and his party. *Printed for Thomas Vere and William Gilbertson.*   **E. 1644. (2.)**

March 12.—Justice Justified; or, The Judges Commission Opened. Two Sermons preached before the Judges of Assize, at Chard 12 March, and at Taunton 3 Aug. By James Strong. *Printed for John Stafford.*   **E. 937. (3.)**

1657.

March 15.—The Gods are Men ; or, the Mortality of persons in places of magistracy. As it was explained and applied in a sermon preached at the Assize holden at Hertford. By George Swinnocke. *Printed for N. Webb and W. Grantham.*   **E. 919. (1.)**

[March 23.]—Catholique Divinity ; or, the most solid and sententious expressions of the primitive doctors of the Church, with other ecclesiastical and civil authors, dilated upon, and fitted to the explication of Scripture. By Dr. Stuart, Dean of St. Pauls. pp. 274. *Printed for H. M. and are to be sold by Timo. Smart.* (23 March.)   **E. 1637. (1.)**

[March 24.]—On the Untimely and much lamented Death of Mrs. Anne Gray. [An elegy and epitaph, by Samuel Holland.] *s. sh.* (24 March.)
669. f. 20. (51.)

March 25.—An Act for raising of fifteen thousand pounds in Scotland per mensem for three moneths from 25 March. *Printed by Henry Hills and John Field.*   **E. 1065. (22.)**

March 25.—An Act for an Assessment at the rate of sixty thousand pounds by the moneth from 25 March to 24 June. pp. 73. *Printed by Henry Hills and John Field.*   **E. 1065. (15.)**

March 25.—An Act for the three Moneths Assessment in Ireland for the Maintenance of the Spanish War, from 25 March to 24 June. *Printed by Henry Hills and John Field.*   **E. 1065. (16.)**

[March 26.]—To the Parliament of the Commonwealth of England. [An address by Samuel Chidley, opposing the scheme of offering the Crown to Cromwell.] (26 March.)   **E. 905. (3.)**

March 26.—The Serious Attestation of many thousands religious and well-disposed people living in London, Westminster and parts adjoyning. [Professing loyalty to the Commonwealth.] 26 March. *s. sh.*
669. f. 20. (52.)

[March 26.]—Certain Disputations of Right to Sacraments, and the true nature of Visible Christianity. By Richard Baxter. pp. 541. *Printed by William Du-Gard for Thomas Johnson.* (26 March.)
E. 906.

[March 28.]—The Throne of Truth exalted over the Powers of Darkness, from whence is judged the Mouth of Ralph Farmer, an unclean and blood-thirsty Priest of Bristol, opened in blasphemy in a late noysome Pamphlet entituled, Satan enthron'd in his Chair of Pestilence ; or, Quakerism in its Exaltation. By Geo. Bishope. pp. 111. [See above : 24 Oct. 1656, E. 897. (2.)] *Printed for Giles Calvert.* (28 March.)
E. 907. (2.)

[March 28.]—The History of the French Academy. Written in French by Mr. Paul Pellison. [Translated by H. S.] pp. 258. *Printed by J. Streater for Thomas Johnson.* (28 March.)   **E. 1595. (1.)**

1657.

March 31.—Οἱ Ἐλεήμονες ἐλεηθήσονται, or God's Mercy for Man's Mercy. Opened in a sermon at the Spittle, 31 March, before the Lord Major. By Thomas Jacomb. *Printed for Philemon Simmons.* **E. 912. (13.)**

[**March.**]—The Arraignment and Condemnation of Cap. Bridges Bushell, declaring the occasion and manner how a Soldier was by him slain, about nine years since, for which at the Lent-Assizes, 1657, he received the Sentence of Death. *Printed for Marmaduke Boat.* **E. 910. (8.)**

[**March.**]—English Liberty and Property asserted in pursuance of the Statute Laws of this Common-wealth, discovering Israels Sin in chusing a King, by several Questions humbly propounded to the grave Senators at Westminster. *Printed for Livewell Chapman.* **E. 905. (2.)**

[**March.**]—The Third Part of a Seasonable, Legal and Historical Vindication of the good old Fundamental Liberties of English Free-men. By William Prynne. pp. 402. *Printed by Francis Leach.*
E. 905. (1.)

[**April 1.**]—An Exposition with Practicall Observations upon the 4th to 9th Chapters of the Proverbs, as they were delivered in severall Expository Lectures at Christ-Church in Canterbury. By Francis Taylor. pp. 817. *Printed by E. Cotes and are to be sold by George Eversden.* (1 April.)
E. 908.

[**April 1.**]—The Triumph and Unity of Truth, in two Treatises. By John Robinson. [With an engraved emblematical frontispiece.] pp. 172. *Printed for Thomas Johnson.* (1 April.) **E. 1595. (2.)**

[**April 2.**]—A Judicious View of the Businesses which are at this time between France and the House of Austria. Translated out of French by a Person of Honour. pp. 239. *Printed by W. Wilson for Henry Herringman.* (2 April.) **E. 1598. (2.)**

[**April 6.**]—The most wonderful and true Relation of Master John Macklain, who being one hundred and sixteen years of age, was miraculously restored to a youthful vigour and complexion. [With a woodcut.] *Printed for T. Vere & W. Gilberson.* (6 April.)
E. 1635. (3.)

[**April 6.**]—A Stay in Trouble, or the Saints Rest in the Evil Day. By Alexander Pringle. 2 pt. *Printed by Anne Maxey for William Weekly.* (6 April.) **E. 1592. (1.)**

[**April 9.**]—Two Treatises: the first, The Young-Mans Memento, the second, Now if Ever. By John Chishull. pp. 260. *Printed by A. N. & are to be sold by F. Eglesfield.* (9 April.) **E. 1684. (1.)**

[**April 15.**]—The Priests Fruits made manifest and the Fashions of the world, and the Lust of Ignorance. By G. F. [i.e. George Fox.] *Printed for Thomas Simmons.* (15 April.) **E. 909. (2.)**

1657.

[April 20.]—The Downfall of the Fifth Monarchy. Or, the personal reign of Christ on Earth, confuted. *Printed for John Andrews.* (20 April.)   **E. 1637. (3.)**

[April 20.]—The People's Impartiall and Compassionate Monitor, about hearing of Sermons. Or, the World's Preachers and Proselytes lively painted out, upon occasion of hearing two famous divines. By R. Younge. *Printed by J. B. for James Crumpe.* (20 April.)
                                                                E. 1583. (1.)

[April 20.]—The Universal Character, by which all the Nations in the World may understand one anothers Conceptions, reading out of one Common Writing their own Mother Tongues. By Cave Beck. [With an engraving representing a European, an Asiatic, an African and an American.] pp. 192. *Printed by Tho. Maxey for William Weekley.* (20 April.)   **E. 1591. (1.)**

[April 23.]—A Warning to all Teachers of Children, which are called School-Masters and School-Mistresses. By G. F. [i.e. George Fox.] *Printed for Thomas Simmons.* (23 April.)   **E. 909. (3.)**

[April 23.]—A Warning-Piece for the Slumbring Virgins. In some awakening meditations upon Matth. xxvi. 41. By Geo. Scortreth. pp. 175. *Printed for Thomas Brewster.* (23 April.)   **E. 1638. (3.)**

[April 24.]—The Godly Mans Ark or City of Refuge in the day of his Distresse, discovered in divers sermons. By Ed. Calamy. pp. 254. *Printed for Jo. Hancock.* (24 April.)   **E. 1616. (1.)**

[April 24.]—The True Light hath made manifest Darknesse : or, Sion builded up and Babylon cast downe. With a true Answer of what the Baptist Teachers objected against John Moon. By John Moone. *Printed for G. Calvert.* (24 April.)   **E. 909. (4.)**

[April 25.]—The first and second Priesthood declared according to the Scriptures, that both Priests, Professors and People may come to see with the Light of Christ which Priesthood this belongs to. [By Humphrey Smith.] (25 April.)   **E. 909. (6*.)**

[April 25.]—The Priests and Professors Catechisme, for them to try their Spirits, whether it be after the Doctrine of Godliness, or after the Traditions of men. By G. F. [i.e. George Fox.] *Printed for Giles Calvert.* (25 April.)   **E. 909. (5.)**

[April 25.]—A Testimony of the Light within. The Truth cleared from Scandals, and some of the Errors of two Cornish Teachers testified against. By Alexander Parker. *Printed for Giles Calvert.* (25 April.)
                                                                E. 909. (6.)

[April 26.]—An Attest of the Housholders within the Parish of St. Buttolphs, Aldgate, unto the Innocency of Mr. Zach. Crofton. Wherein wee acquit our selves from the guilt and odium of prosecuting him

1657.

and rescue him from the clamours of Incivility charged upon him. *Printed for James Nuthall.* (26 April.) **E. 909. (7.)**

[**April 30.**]—Ἡ Προβολὴ τῆς Ἀληθείας. Or, the Bul-warke of Truth, being a treatise of God, of Jesus Christ, of the Holy Ghost, and of the Trinity in Unity, against Atheists and Hereticks. By Robert Bayfeild. [With an engraved portrait of the author.] pp. 228. *Printed by T. R. for Edw. Dod.* (30 April.) **E. 1636. (3.)**

[**April.**]—To the Parliament. The Petition of the Real Lenders upon the Publick Faith, the Clothiers, and all others in the counties of Essex and Suffolk that are unpaid. [Praying for payment.] *s. sh.* **669. f. 20. (54.)**

[**April.**]—The lamentable Estate and distressed case of the deceased Sir William Dick [stated to have suffered imprisonment for debt after having lost all his possessions in his country's service. Illustrated with three engraved plates, by William Vaughan]. **669. f. 20. (53.)**

[**April.**]—An Invective against the Pride of Women. [In verse.] *s. sh.* **669. f. 20. (56.)**

May 1.—A Manifesto of Prince Charles Lodwick, Count Palatin of the Rhin, and Vicar of the Holy Empire, containing his ancient and patrimoniall right to the sayed Vicarship, within the Circles of the Rhin, Suabland and the Franconian territories. Wherein ther are divers reflections upon the Aurea Bulla and the fundamentall lawes of the Empire. *Printed for Richard Lownds.* **E. 916. (9.)**

[**May 1.**]—An Appeal to the Consciences of the chief Magistrates of this Commonwealth, touching the Sabbath-day. By William Saller and John Spittlehouse. *Printed for the Author.* (1 May.) **E. 909. (8.)**

[**May 1.**]—Philosophy reformed & improved in four profound tractates. The one discovering the Mysteries of Nature, by Osw. Crollius. The other three discovering the Mysteries of the Creation, by Paracelsus. Both made English by H. Pinnell. [Withan engraved portrait of Paracelsus.] pp. 296. *Printed by M. S. for Lodowick Lloyd.* (1 May.) **E. 1589. (1.)**

[**May 2.**]—The Divine Philanthropie defended against the declamatory attempts of certain late-printed papers intitl'd A Correptory Correction [by William Barlee]. By Thomas Pierce. pp. 216. [See above : 3 March, E. 904. (1.)] *Printed for Richard Royston.* (2 May.) **E. 909. (9.)**

May 3.—The Defeat of the Barbary Fleet, or a letter of advice [signed : N. N. M.] relating the Victory which the Republique of Venice obtained against the Turk in the Chanel of Scio under the command of the Lord Lazaro Mosenigo. *Printed for Richard Lowndes.* **E. 916. (5.)**

[**May 4.**]—The Trappan Trapt, or, The true Relation of a Cunning, Cogging and Cheating Knight, alias Knave. Wherein is discovered

1657.

his mischievous and Machivillian mischiefs plotted against Mr. John Marriot. By W. B. *Printed by Joseph Moxon.* (4 May.) **E. 910. (2.)**

[May 4.]—Poems, Elegies, Paradoxes and Sonnets. [By Henry King, Bishop of Chichester.] pp. 151. *Printed by J. G. for R. Marriot and H. Herringman.* **E. 1656. (2.)**

[May 5.]—Truth, the Strongest of all, witnessed forth in the Spirit of Truth, against all Deceit : and pleading its owne cause against a very great number of slanders held forth by the Independants and in particular by one John Bunion, in two severall bookes put forth by him against the people called Quakers [i.e. " Some Gospel Truths opened " and " A Vindication "]. By Edward Burrough. pp. 63. *Printed for Giles Calvert.* (5 May.) **E. 910. (3.)**

[May 7.]—The Priests Wickednesse and Cruelty laid open and made manifest by Priest Smith of Cressedge, persecuting the Servants of the Lord. *Printed for Giles Calvert.* (7 May.) **E. 910. (4.)**

[May 7.]—The Walks of Islington and Hogsdon with the Humours of Woodstreet-Compter. A Comedy. By Tho. Jordan. *Printed by Tho. Wilson.* (7 May.) **E. 910. (5.)**

[May 9.]—Brachy-Martyrologia; or, A Breviary of all the greatest Persecutions which have befallen the Saints and People of God. Paraphras'd by Nicholas Billingsly. [In verse.] pp. 213. *Printed by J. C. for Austin Rice.* (9 May.) **E. 1608. (2.)**

May 10.—An Epistle to all People on the Earth, and the Ignorance of all the World, of the Birth that must be silent, and of the Birth that is to speak, which declares God ; and the difference betwixt Silence and Speaking. [Subscribed G. F., i.e. George Fox.] *Printed for Giles Calvert.* (10 May.) **E . 910. (7.)**

May 14.—The Office of Publick Advice, newly set up in several places in and about London and Westminster, by authority. [A prospectus.] *s. sh. Printed by Thomas Newcomb.* **669. f. 20. (59.)**

[May 14.]—Daphnis and Chloe. A Most Sweet and Pleasant Pastorall Romance for Young Ladies. By Geo. Thornley. [Translated from Longus.] pp. 229. *Printed for John Garfield.* (14 May.)
E. 1652. (2.)

[May 16.]—Questions propounded by the Natural Man by way of reasoning, and answered by the Spiritual Man. [Signed : R. W.] (16 May.)
E. 910. (9.)

[May 17.]—A Standard set up, whereunto the true Seed and Saints of the most High may be gathered together. Subscribed W. Medley. (17 May.) **E. 910. (10.)**

[May 18.]—The Life and Adventures of Buscon, the Witty Spaniard. Put into English by a person of honour. To which is added, The

1657.

Provident Knight. By Don Francisco de Quevedo. pp. 319. *Printed by J. M. for Henry Herringman.* (18 May.) **E. 1585. (2.)**

[May 21.]—Enchiridion Medicum. An Enchiridion of the Art of Physick. Written in Latine by John Sadler. Translated by Robert Turner. pp. 208. *Printed by J. C. for R. Moone and Henry Fletcher.* (21 May.) **E. 1678. (1.)**

[May 22.]—The Literal Mans Learning: or, The Light of Saints Perfection in the Life of Grace. [By Daniel Lewes.] *Printed for the Author.* (22 May.) **E. 910. (11.)**

[May 23.]—Βασανισταί, or, The Triers or Tormenters tried and cast, by the Laws both of God and of Men. By John Goodwin. [See also below : 30 July, E. 920. (1.)] *Printed for Henry Eversden.* (23 May.) **E. 910. (12.)**

[May 23.]—Time well improved, or, Some Helps for Weak Heads in their Meditations. Whereunto is added the Verses used by the Bellmen of London in their nightly Perambulations. [By Samuel Rowlands.] pp. 236. *Printed for Henry Fletcher.* (23 May.) **E. 1706. (2.)**

May 25.—The Petition presented unto the Lord Protector [by Parliament, with regard to the forming of a Constitution]. See also below : 26 June, E. 1065. (18*.) *Printed by Henry Hills and John Field.* **E. 1065. (18.)**

[May 25.—Concerning Good-Morrow and Good-Even : the Worlds Customs ; but by the Light which into the world is come, by it made manifest to all who be in the darkness. [Signed : G. F., i.e. George Fox.] *Printed for Thomas Simmons.* (25 May.) **E. 910. (13.)**

[May 25.]—The Logicians School-Master ; or, A Comment upon Ramus Logick. By Alexander Richardson. Whereunto are added his Prelections on Ramus his Grammer, Taleus his Rhetorick, also his Notes on Physicks, Ethicks, Astronomy, Medicine and Opticks. pp. 488. *Printed by Gertrude Dawson and are to be sold by Samuel Thomson.* (25 May.) **E. 1063. (2.)**

[May 25.]—Several Works of Mr. John Murcot. Together with his life and death. Published by Mr. Winter, Mr. Chambers, Mr. Eaton, Mr. Carryl and Mr. Manton. pp. 695. *Printed by R. White for Francis Tyton.* (25 May.) **E. 911.**

[May 26.]—A Prohibition to all persons who have set up any offices called by the names of Addresses, Publique Advice or Intelligence in London. By Oliver Williams. *s. sh. Printed for the Author.* (26 May.) **669. f. 20. (57.)**

[May 26.]—The Filacers Office, or, the measne processe Filacers make out before Appearance, the Nature and Forms of their Several Writs'

1657.

and the manner of their Proceedings thereupon. [The prefatory epistle signed : J. B.] pp. 242. *Printed for Tho. Firby.* (26 May.)

E. 1655. (1.)

[**May 26.**]—The Ground of High Places : and the End of High Places : and a rest for the people of God above all the High Places of the Earth. [Signed : G. F., i.e. George Fox.] *Printed for Thomas Simmons.* (26 May.)
E. 912. (2.)

May 27.—Paracelsus of the Chymical Transmutation, Genealogy and Generation of metals and minerals. Whereunto is added Philosophical and Chemical Experiments of Raymund Lully. Translated into English by R. Turner. pp. 166. *Printed for Rich: Moon, and Hen. Fletcher.* (May 27.)
E. 1590. (3.)

May 28.—An Order of Parliament for a Day of Publike Thanksgiving on 3 June for the success of the Navy under General Blake against the Spaniard, 28 May. *Printed by Henry Hills & John Field.*

E. 1065. (14.)

[**May 28.**]—A Description of the State and Condition of all Mankinde upon the face of the whole Earth. Shewing what Man was in his creation before transgression, and what he is in transgression. By Edward Burrough. *Printed for Giles Calvert.* (May 28.) **E. 912. (3.)**

[**May 28.**]—The Hidden things of Esau brought to light, and reproved, in an answer to a book entituled A true Relation of a Dispute between Francis Fulwood and Thomas Salthouse before the congregation of them called Quakers, in the house of Henry Pollexpher [*sic*]. By Thomas Salthouse. [See above : 24 Oct. 1546, E. 892. (12.)] *Printed for Giles Calvert.* (28 May.)
E. 912. (4.)

[**May 29.**]—This is to all Officers and Souldiers of the Armies in England, Scotland and Ireland, and to all magistrates and them in authority in these nations. [Signed : by G. F., i.e. George Fox.] *Printed for Thomas Simmons.* (29 May.)
E. 912. (5.)

[**May 29.**]—The Two Constant Lovers in Scotland. [A ballad.] *s. sh.* (29 May.)
669. f. 20. (55.)

[**May 30.**]—Death's Advantage ; opened in a sermon preached the last summer, at Northampton, at the funeral of Peter Whalley, Mayor of the said town. Now published by Edward Reynolds. *Printed by Tho. Newcomb for George Thomason.* (30 May.)
E. 912. (6.)

[**May 30.**]—Certain Elegies upon the death of Peter Whalley, late Major of Northampton. [A collection, by various authors.] (30 May.)
E. 912. (7.)

[**May 31.**]—An Examination of the Political Part of Mr. Hobbs his Leviathan. By George Lawson. pp. 214. *Printed by R. White for Francis Tyton.* (31 May.)
E. 1591. (3.)

1657.

[**May.**]—Killing Noe Murder. Briefly discourst in three Quæstions. By William Allen. [Attributed by Professor Firth to the joint authorship of Colonel Edward Sexby and Colonel Silius Titus. See "The English Historical Review." Vol. XVII., 1902. pp. 308–309. See also below : 21 Sept., E. 925. (12.)]   **E. 501. (4.)**

[**May.**]—The Immortality of the Human Soul, demonstrated by the Light of Nature. In two dialogues. [By W. Charleton. With a portrait of the author.] pp. 188. *Printed by William Wilson for Henry Herringman.*   **E. 501. (3.)**

[**May.**]—The Christians Spiritual Conflict. [In verse.] *s. sh.*
669. f. 20. (58.)

[**June 1.**]—Letters of Affaires, Love and Courtship. By Monsieur de Voiture. English'd by J. D. [i.e. John Davies.] pp. 370. *Printed for T. Dring and J. Starkey.* (1 June.)   **E. 1607. (1.)**

[**June 3.**]—Nuntius a Mortuis ; hoc est stupendum iuxta ac tremendũ colloquiũ, inter manes Henrici VIII. & Caroli I. in Ecclesia Windsoriensi, ubi sub eodem marmore cõtumulati sunt. *Londini, sumptibus R. P., et veneunt Parisiis.* (3 June.)   **E. 912. (10.)**

June 4.—A Disputation concerning Church-Members and their children, in answer to xxi questions, wherein the state of such children when adult, together with their duty towards the Church, is discussed. By an Assembly of Divines meeting at Boston in New England, 4 June, 1657. *Printed by J. Hayes for Samuel Thomson.*   **E. 987. (3.)**

[**June 5.**]—Christ tempted : the Divel conquered. Or, a short exposition on a part of the fourth chapter, St. Matthew's Gospel. Together with two Sermons preached before the University at Oxford. By John Gumbleden. pp. 79. *Printed for Simon Miller.* (5 June.) **E. 912. (11.)**

[**June 6.**]—Of Peace and Contentment of Minde. By Peter Du Moulin the Sonne. pp. 475. *Printed for Humphrey Moseley.* (6 June.) **E. 1571.**

[**June 6.**]—The Reviler rebuked : or a re-inforcement of the charge against the Quakers, which Richard Farnworth attempted to answer in his pretended Vindication of the Scriptures. By John Stalham. pp. 308. [See above : 2 Oct. 1655, E. 854. (9.), and also below : 23 July, E. 919. (7.)] *Printed by Henry Hills and John Field.* (6 June.)   **E. 914. (1.)**

June 8.—A String of Pearls. A sermon preached at the funeral of Miss Mary Blake. By Thomas Brooks. pp. 172. *Printed by R. I. for John Hancock.*   **E. 1589. (3.)**

—— The second edition. pp. 222. *Printed by R. I. for John Hancock.* July, 1660.   **E. 1919. (1.)**

[**June 8.**]—An History of the Constancy of Nature, wherein, by comparing the latter Age with the former, it is maintained that the World doth not decay universally in respect of itself. By John Jonston of Poland. pp. 180. *Printed for John Streater.* (8 June.) **E. 1653. (1.)**

1657.

[**June 9.**]—Χωνευτήριον τῆς Σιῶν. The Refinement of Sion : or, the old orthodox Protestant doctrine justified, and defended against several exceptions of the Antinomians. By Anthony Warton. pp. 233. *Printed by John Streater.* (9 June.) E. 914. (2.)

[**June 9.**]—An Exposition with practical observations continued upon the twenty-seventh, the twenty-eighth and twenty-ninth chapters of the Booke of Job. By Joseph Caryl. pp. 628. *Printed by M. S. for Elisha Wallis.* (9 June.) E. 913.

June 9.—Sensuality Dissected ; or, the Epicure's Motto opened in a sermon preached to divers Citizens of London, born in the county of Kent, in Paul's Church. By Tho. Case. pp. 92. *Printed by T. N. for R. Gibbs.* E. 1705. (2.)

June 11.—Paul's last Farewel. A sermon preached at the funerall of Thomas Blake, by Anthony Burgesse. With a funeral oration by Samuel Shaw. *Printed for Abel Roper.* E. 937. (1.)

[**June 11.**]—The Spirit's Touchstone : or the teachings of Christ's Spirit on the hearts of believers. By J. R., late Student of Merton Colledge in Oxford [i.e. Job Roys]. pp. 351. *Printed for Simon Miller.* (11 June.) E. 1663.

June 13.—[An Act respecting the working of the Act providing for the Assessment from 25 March to 24 June, 1657.] *Printed by Henry Hills & John Field.* E. 1065. (17.)

[**June 13.**]—Pacis Consultum : A Directory to the Publick Peace, briefly describing the antiquity, extent, practice and jurisdiction of several Countrey-Corporation-Courts, especially the Court-Leet. By Judge Jenkings. pp. 135. *Printed by J. C. for H. Fletcher.* (13 June.) E. 1672. (2.)

[**June 15.**]—Ψυχομαχία, or, The Soules Conflict. Pourtrayed in eight severall sermons by Henry Beesley. pp. 236. *Printed for Henry Brome.* (15 June.) E. 1607. (2.)

[**June 15.**]—A Witness to the Saints in England and Wales, to whom our God has given Grace and Glory and the shield of his salvation. By some of the Mourners in Zion. (15 June.) E. 915. (2.)

[**June 17.**]—Of Schisme : the true nature of it discovered and considered, with reference to the present differences in Religion. By John Owen. pp. 280. *Printed by L. L. for T. Robinson: Oxford.* (17 June.) E. 1664. (2.)

[**June 20.**]—Sion's Praises. Opened in a sermon preached before the Lord Mayor of London, on the day of solemn thanksgiving unto God for his preservation of that great city from pestilence, fire and other dangers. By Edward Reynolds. *Printed by Tho. Newcomb for George Thomason.* (20 June.) E. 915. (4.)

1657.

June 23.—The City Remembrancer. A sermon preached in Pauls. By Edmund Calamy. pp. 74. *Printed by S. G. for John Baker.*

E. 1676. (2.)

[**June 23.**]—The Man in the Moone discovering a Word of Knavery under the Sunne. *Printed for Charles Tyus.* (23 June.) E. 1620. (2.)

June 24.—An Act for an Assessment at the rate of five and thirty thousand pounds by the moneth upon England, six thousand pounds upon Scotland, and nine thousand pounds upon Ireland, for three years from 24 June. *Printed by Henry Hills and John Field.* E. 1065. (21.)

[**June 24.**]—The Deputy Divinity. A discourse of Conscience. By Henry Carpenter. pp. 120. *Printed for N. Webb & W. Grantham.* (24 June.) E. 1711. (1.)

[**June 25.**]—The Βίος πάντων εἰδέοτος, or The Vision of Eternity, held forth in answer to some Antiquæries which were given forth from Ægypt by one of Babel's builders, a pretended Minister of Christ, living at Beudly, that is called Mr. Henry Osland. By John Humphryes. *Printed for Giles Calvert.* (25 June.) E. 915. (6.)

June 26.—An Act for the Adjournment of this present Parliament from 26 June, unto 20 Jan. next. *Printed by Henry Hills & John Field.*

E. 1065. (40.)

June 26.—A Proclamation by His Highness and the Parliament [requiring all persons "to conform and submit themselves unto the Government"]. *s. sh. Printed by Henry Hills and John Field.*

669. f. 20. (60.)

June 26.—To His Highness the Lord Protector. The Additional Petition [of Parliament, with regard to the forming of a Constitution. See above : 25 May, E. 1065. (18.)] *Printed by Henry Hills & John Field.*

E. 1065. (18*.)

[**June 27.**]—An Appendix to a Seasonable Vindication of free-admission to and frequent administration of the Lord's Holy Communion to all visible Church-members, regenerate or unregenerate. By William Prynne. (27 June.) E. 916. (1.)

[**June 27.**]—De Morbis Foemineis. The Womans Counsellour ; or, the Feminine Physitian. Translated out of Massarius by R. T. Φιλομαθής. pp. 211. *Printed for John Streater.* (27 June.) E. 1650. (3.)

[**June 27.**]—A Treatise of Fruit-Trees. [By Ralph Austen.] The second edition ; with the addition of many new experiments and observations. pp. 348. *Printed by Henry Hall, Printer to the University, for Thomas Robinson : Oxford.* (27 June.) E. 915. (7.)

[**June 28.**]—The Ancient of dayes is come, the Judgment is set, glad Tydings is proclaimed. Isa. 55. 1, 2. Written by a Lover of Peace and Truth, J. G. [Appended is " A Paper written unto all friends in obedience to the Lord by J. B."] (28 June.) E. 916. (2.)

1657.

[June 30.]—The Fort-Royal of Christianity defended.   Or, A Demonstration of the Divinity of Scripture.   With a Discussion of some of the great Controversies in Religion.   By Thomas Gery.   2 pt.   *Printed by T. C. for Nathanael Web.*   (30 June.)   **E. 1702.**

June.—An Act for continuing the Subsidie of Tunnage and Poundage and for reviving an Act for the Better Packing of Butter.   *Printed by Henry Hills & John Field.*   **E. 1065. (20.)**

[June.]—An Act for the Improvement of the Revenue of the Customs and Excize.   (June.)   *Printed by Henry Hills & John Field.*   **E 1065. (28.)**

June.—An Additional Act for the better improving the Receipts of the Excize.   [With a Book of Values of Merchandize.]   pp. 61.   *Printed by Henry Hills & John Field.*   **E. 1065. (19.)**

[June.]—An Act for the Attainder of the Rebels in Ireland.   *Printed by Henry Hills & John Field.*   **E. 1065. (39.)**

[June.]—An Act for the assuring and setling of Lands and Estates in Ireland.   *Printed by Henry Hills & John Field.*   **E. 1065. (38.)**

[June.]—An Act for the better suppressing of Theft upon the Borders of England and Scotland.   *Printed by Henry Hills & John Field.*

E. 1065. (37.)

[June.]—An Act giving licence for Transporting Fish in Forreign Bottoms.   *Printed by Henry Hills & John Field.*   **E. 1065. (35.)**

[June.]—An Act for the taking away of Purveyance and Compositions for Purveyance.   *Printed by Henry Hills & John Field.*   **E. 1065. (34.)**

[June.]—An Act against Vagrants.   *Printed by Henry Hills and John Field.*   **E. 1065. (33.)**

[June.]—An Act for quiet enjoying of Sequestred Parsonages and Vicaridges by the present Incumbent.   *Printed by Henry Hills & John Field.*   **E. 1065. (32.)**

[June.]—An Act for discovering, convicting and repressing of Popish Recusants.   *Printed by Henry Hills and John Field.*   **E. 1065. (31.)**

[June.]—An Act for the Better Observation of the Lords-Day.   *Printed by Henry Hills & John Field.*   **E. 1065. (30.)**

[June.]—An Act for punishing of such persons as live at high rates and have no visible estate or calling answerable thereunto.   *Printed by Henry Hills & John Field.*   **E. 1065. (29.)**

[June.]—An Act for Indempnifying of such persons as have acted for the service of the Publique.   *Printed by Henry Hills & John Field.*

E. 1065. (27.)

[June.]—An Act for the Preventing of the Multiplicity of Buildings in and about the suburbs of London and within ten miles thereof.   *Printed by Henry Hills & John Field.*   **E. 1065. (26.)**

1657.

[**June.**]—An Act for Limiting and setling the Prices for Wines. *Printed by Henry Hills & John Field.* **E. 1065. (24.)**

[**June.**]—An Act touching several Acts and Ordinances made since 20 April, 1653, and before 3 Sept., 1654. *Printed by Henry Hills & John Field.* **E. 1065. (23.)**

[**June.**]—Instructions agreed upon in Parliament for Commissioners for surveying the Forests of Sherwood, Needwood, Kingswood, Ashdown and Endfield Chase. *Printed by Henry Hills & John Field.* **E. 1065. (25.)**

[**July 1.**]—Antidotum contra Naufragium Fidei & Bonæ Conscientiæ. Concio habita ad Academicos Cantabrig. in Ecclesia S. Mariæ 9 die Octobris 1627. Authore Rich. Sibbs. *Excudebat J. G. pro Nath. Webb & Guliel. Grantham.* (1 July.) **E. 703. (2.)**

[**July 1.**]—A Declaration of the Ground of Error & Errors, Blasphemy, Blasphemers and Blasphemies, and the ground of Inchantings and seducing Spirits, and the doctrine of Devils. By G. F. [i.e. George Fox. MS. note by Thomason : " Alias Goose, Quaker."] *Printed for Giles Calvert.* (1 July.) **E. 916. (4.)**

[**July 3.**]—The History of Magick. Written in French by G. Naudæus. Englished by John Davies. pp. 306. *Printed for John Streater.* (3 July.) **E. 1609. (1.)**

[**July 4.**]—Of Communion with God the Father, Sonne, and Holy Ghost, each Person distinctly, in Love, Grace and Consolation : or, the Saints Fellowship with the Father, Sonne and Holy Ghost, unfolded. By John Owen. pp. 320. *Printed by A. Lichfield for Philemon Stevens : Oxford.* (4 July.) **E. 916. (6.)**

[**July 7.**]—Fides Divina : The Ground of True Faith asserted. Or, A useful and brief Discourse, shewing the insufficiency of humane and the necessity of Divine Evidence. Being a transcript out of several authors extant. pp. 107. *Printed for the Author.* (7 July.) **E. 1598. (3.)**

[**July 10.**]—The Expert Physician : learnedly treating of all Agues and Feavers whether simple or compound. By Bricius Bauderon, translated into English by B. W., Licentiate in Physick. [With a portrait of Bauderon.] pp. 160. *Printed by R. I. for John Hancock.* (10 July.) **E. 1616. (2.)**

[**July 11.**]—Ecclesia Vindicata : or the Church of England Justified : 1. In the way and manner of her Reformation. 2. In officiating by a Publick Liturgie. 3. In prescribing a set form of Prayer to be used by Preachers before their sermons. 4. In her right and patrimony of Tithes. 5. In retaining the Episcopal Government. And therewith,

1657.

6. The Canonical Ordination of Priests and Deacons. By Peter Heylyn. 2 vol. *Printed by E. Cotes for Henry Seile.* (11 July.) **E. 917** and **918.**

[July 11.]—A Theological Concordance of the Synonymous Terms in the Holy Scriptures. By R. Bennet. pp. 220. *Printed by J. Streater, and are to be sold by G. Sawbridge.* (11 July.) **E. 1609. (2.)**

[July 11.]—A Treatise of the Divine Promises. By Edward Leigh. Fourth edition, enlarged. pp. 402. *Printed by A. Miller for Henry Mortlocke.* (11 July.) **E. 1605. (2.)**

July 14.—An Order of His Highness for continuing the Committee for the Army and for the more orderly paiment of the Assessment. *Printed by Henry Hills & John Field.* **E. 1065. (36.)**

July 17.—Divine Blossomes. A Prospect or Looking-Glass for Youth. [Poems.] By Francis Cockin, alias Cokayne. pp. 118. *Printed by W. G. for E. Farnham.* (17 July.) **E. 1652. (1.)**

July 18.—Sad News from the County of Kent, shewing how 40 Armed, Resolute, Desperate Fellows plundered Sir Nicholas Crisps House. *Printed for Richard Harper.* **E. 922. (2.)**

[July 20.]—A Discovery of two unclean Spirits. Or, two Priests (Henry Hean and William Wilton) by their fruits made manifest to be out of the way of Truth and out of the life of Godliness. By A. H. [i.e. Anthony Holder.] *Printed for Giles Calvert.* (20 July.) **E. 919. (5.)**

[July 21.]—Nonnihil de Febribus, a Guilielmo Slatholmo. pp. 148. *Typis J. B. venalisque habetur apud Philemonem Stephans.* (21 July.)

E. 1611. (2.)

[July 23.]—The Rebukes of a Reviler fallen upon his own head. In an answer to a book put forth by one John Stelham. [By Richard Hubberthorne and Edward Burrough.] pp. 75. [See above : 6 June, E. 914. (1.), and also below : 15 Oct., E. 926. (3.)] *Printed for Giles Calvert.* (23 July.) **E. 919. (7.)**

[July 24.]—A Measure of the Times : and a full & clear description of the Signes of the Times, and of the changing of the times, and of the reign of Antichrist. By Edw: Burrough. *Printed for Thomas Simmons.* (24 July.) **E. 919. (6.)**

[July 25.]—The Holy Feasts and Fasts of the Church, with meditations and prayers pious and proper for them. And some also upon the Sacraments, and other subjects of sacred consideration. By Dr. W. Brough. pp. 456. *Printed by J. G. for John Clark.* (25 July.)

E. 1622.

[July 28.]—Jegar-Sahadutha : an Oyled Pillar set up for posterity against the present wickednesses and cruelties of this Serpent power now up in England. Or a heart appeale to Heaven and Earth, in a relation of the

1657.

sufferings of John Rogers in close prison and banishment, for the cause of Jesus. [By John Rogers.] (28 July.) **E. 919. (9.)**

[July 28.]—Methodus Gratiæ Divinæ in traductione hominis peccatoris ad vitam, septuaginta thesibus succincte & elaborate explicata. Authore Thoma Parkero. pp. 62. *Impensis Abelis Roper.* (28 July.) **E. 1670. (3.)**

July 29.—A Soveraign Remedy for all Kindes of Grief. Applyed in a sermon at the funeral of Mr. John Langham, who dyed 29 July 1657. By Th. B. [i.e. Thomas Burroughs.] *Printed by S. G. for John Baker.* **E. 926. (4.)**

[July 29.]—Of Perfection. The great Mystery of Antichrist unfolded, by the rising of the sun of righteousnesse. By Ambrose Rigge. (29 July.) **E. 919. (10.)**

[July 30.]—The Great Accuser cast down. Or, a publick trial of Mr. John Goodwin at the bar of Religion and Right Reason. Being a full answer to a book of his entituled The Triers tried and cast, &c. By Marchamont Nedham. pp. 130. [See above : 23 May, E. 910. (12.) and also below : 25 Aug., E. 923. (7.)] *Printed by Tho. Newcomb for George Sawbridge.* (30 July.) **E. 920. (1.)**

[Aug. 1.]—The Best Name on Earth. Together with severall other sermons. By Tho. Fuller. [With an engraved portrait of the author, and an engraved frontispiece.] pp. 144. *Printed by R. D. for John Stafford.* (1 Aug.) **E. 1582. (1.)**

[Aug. 1.]—A Treatise of Conversion. Preached, and now published for the use of those that are strangers to a true conversion, especially the grosly ignorant and ungodly. By Richard Baxter. pp. 307. *Printed by R. W. for Nevil Simmons, Bookseller in Kiderminster, and sold by Joseph Nevil in Paul's Churchyard.* (1 Aug.) **E. 920. (2.)**

[Aug. 2.]—A Scribe, Pharisee, Hypocrite ; and his Letter answered, Separates churched, Dippers sprinkled : or, A Vindication of the Church of England in many Orthodox Tenets. Whereunto is added a Narration of a publick dipping, 26 June 1656, in a pond of Much Leighes Parish in Essex, with a censure thereupon. By Jeffry Watts. pp. 623. *Printed for Edward Dod & Thomas Johnson.* (2 Aug.) **E. 921.**

Aug. 3.—A Sermon preached at the Assizes at Taunton, 3 Aug. By James Strong. *Printed for John Stafford.* **E. 937. (3.)**

[Aug. 4.]—The Expert Doctors Dispensatory. The whole Art of Physick restored to practice. [By Petrus Morellus. Translated by Nicholas Culpeper.] To which is added, by Jacob à Brunn, a Compendium of the Body of Physick. [With an engraved frontispiece

1657.

representing "The Doctor's Dispensatory" and "The Apothecary's shop."] pp. 471. *Printed for N. Brook.* (4 Aug.)   **E. 1565. (1.)**

Aug. 6.—A Full and the Truest Narrative of the most horrid, barbarous and unparalled Murder committed on the Person of John Knight, by Nathaniel Butler, 6 Aug. Also of the tryall, condemnation and sentence pronounced against him. *Printed by T. Mabb for J. Saywell.*   **E. 925. (1.)**

Aug. 6.—Blood washed away by Tears of Repentance : being an Exact Relation of that horrid Murther committed on the person of John Knight, by Nathaniel Butler. Written with his owne hand. *Printed by W. G. for Isaac Pridmore & Henry Marsh.*   **E. 925. (2.)**

Aug. 6.—Heavens Cry against Murder, or, A true Relation of the bloudy & unparallel'd Murder of John Knight by one Nath. Butler. *Printed for Henry Brome.*   **E. 923. (1.)**

[Aug. 8.]—Quatuor Novissima : or, Meditations upon the Four Last Things, delivered in four common-place discourses. By Thomas Longland. pp. 128. *Printed by A. Maxey for J. Rothwell.* (8 Aug.)
                                                                E. 1633. (2.)

[Aug. 10.]—[Orders, by the Company of Woodmongers, for the regulation of their trade.] *s. sh.* (10 Aug.)   **669. f. 20. (64.)**

Aug. 11.—An Elegie on the Death of Robert Blake. By George Harrison. *s. sh. Printed for John Bartlet.*   **669. f. 20. (61.)**

[Aug. 12.]—Chiliasto-mastix redivivus, sive Homesus enervatus. A confutation of the Millenarian Opinion, where you also have many Texts of Scripture vindicated from the vain Glosses of one Dr. Homes. By Tho. Hall. pp. 102. *Printed for John Starkey.* (12 Aug.)
                                                                E. 1654. (2.)

Aug. 13.—[A Proclamation by the Lord Protector appointing 21 Aug. as a " Day of Solemn Fasting and Humiliation."] *s. sh. Printed by Henry Hills and John Field.*   **669. f. 20. (62.)**

[Aug. 14.]—Considerations on Mr. Harrington's Common-wealth of Oceana. [By Matthew Wren. See also below : 28 March 1660, E. 1853. (1.)] pp. 94. *Printed for Samuel Gellibrand.* (14 Aug.)
                                                                E. 1659. (2.)

Aug. 15.—Petitions for a reprieve, from John Bernard to the Protector, the Lord Mayor, and the people in general. *s. sh.* **669. f. 20. (63.)**

[Aug. 15.]—A Word from the North sounded into the South, heard and received of many. By Thomas Howseyor. [A Quaker tract, addressed to the County of Kent.] *Printed for Giles Calvert.* (15 Aug.)
                                                                E. 923. (2.)

[Aug. 19.]—A Little Cabinet richly stored with all sorts of Heavenly Varieties and Soul-reviving Influences. Being an abridgment of the

1657.

Substance of the true Christian Religion. By Robert Purnell. pp. 467. *Printed by R. W. for Thomas Brewster.* (19 Aug.) **E. 1575.**

[Aug. 22.]—Catechising, Gods Ordinance. By Zachary Crofton. Second edition, enlarged. pp. 132. *Printed by R. I. for Thomas Parkhurst.* (22 Aug.) **E. 1673. (2.)**

[Aug. 24.]—Paraphrasis poetica Psalmorum Davidis. Auctore Arturo Ionstono. Accesserunt ejusdem Cantica Evangelica, Symbolum Apostolicum, Oratio Dominica, Decalogus. pp. 180. *Excudebat R. Daniel, & venales prostat apud S. Thomson.* (24 Aug.) **E. 1662. (2.)**

[Aug. 24.]—A Standard lifted up, and an Ensigne held forth to all Nations ; shewing what the Testimony of God is, and of his people, who are in scorn called Quakers. By Edward Burrough. *Printed for Giles Calvert.* (24 Aug.) **E. 923. (6.)**

Aug. 25.—[An Order by the Protector appointing 3 Sept. as a Day of Public Thanksgiving for the victories at Dunbar and Worcester.] *s. sh. Printed by Henry Hills and John Field.* **669. f. 20. (65.)**

[Aug. 25.]—A Letter of Addresse [signed : D. F.] to the Protector, occasioned by Mr. Needhams reply to Mr. Goodwins Book against the Triers. By a Person of Quality. [See above : 23 May, E. 910. (12.) and 30 July, E. 920. (1.)] (25 Aug.) **E. 923. (7.)**

Aug. 30.—A State of Glory for Spirits of Just Men upon Dissolution demonstrated. A sermon preached in Pauls Church. By Tho. Goodwin. pp. 71. *Printed by J. G. for Robert Dawlman.* **E. 928. (2.)**

[Aug. 31.]—The Divine Purity defended, or, A Vindication of some Notes concerning God's Decrees from the Censure of D. Reynolds in his Epistolary Præface to Mr. Barlee's Correptory Correction. By Thomas Pierce. pp. 133. [See above : 3 March, E. 904. (1.)] *Printed by R. Norton for Richard Royston.* (31 Aug.) **E. 923. (9.)**

[Aug. 31.]—Les Provinciales : Or, the Mysterie of Jesuitisme, discover'd in certain Letters, written upon occasion of the present differences at Sorbonne, between the Jansenists and the Molinists. [By Louis de Montalte, i.e. Blaise Pascal.] Faithfully rendred into English. [With a second titlepage, engraved.] pp. 509. *Printed by J. G. for R. Royston.* (31 Aug.) **E. 1623.**

[Aug. 31.]—The Use and Practice of Faith. Delivered in the Publick Lectures at Ipswich, by Mr. Matthew Lawrence. pp. 624. *Printed by A. Maxey for William Weekly, Bookseller at Ipswich, and are to be sold by John Rothwell and Robert Littleberry.* (31 Aug.) **E. 924.**

[Aug.]—A Glance at the Glories of Sacred Friendship. By E. B. [Mainly in verse.] *s. sh. Printed by R. D. for Humphrey Mosely.*
669. f. 20. (66.)

1657.

[**Aug.**]—Schism dispach't, or, a rejoynder [by S. W., i.e. John Sergeant] to the replies of Dr. Hammond and the Ld. of Derry [John Bramhall]. pp. 666. [See also below : 19 July, 1659, E. 991.]

E. 1555.

[**Sept. 1.**]—Enchiridion Judicum. Or, Jehosaphat's Charge to his Judges. Opened in a Sermon before the Judges of the County Palatine of Lancast. Together with Catastrophe Magnatum, or King David's Lamentation at Prince Abner's Incineration, in a sermon preached at the funeral of John Atherton, High Sheriffe of the county Palatine of Lanc. By John Livesey. pp. 327. *Printed by R. I. for Tho. Parkhurst.* (1 Sept.)   E. 1582. (2.)

Sept. 2.—Mardike Fort, put into the possession of Major Gen. Morgan, 2 Sept. [An engraved plate, by Thomas Jenner after Wenceslaus Hollar, with a "particular account" of Mardike.] *s. sh. Printed by M. S. for T. Jenner.*   669. f. 20. (67.)

[**Sept. 4.**]—Solutio Quæstionis veteris et novæ. Sive, De Legati delinquentio Judice competente dissertatio. Authore Richardo Zoucheo. pp. 168. *Excudebat Hen. Hall, impensis Tho. Robinson : Oxoniæ.* (4 Sept.)   E. 1712. (2.)

[**Sept. 5.**]—Doctor Hammond his Ἐκτενέστερον, or, A greater Ardency in Christs love of God at one time than another proved to be utterly irreconcileable with his fulnesse of habituall grace. By Henry Jeanes. [See also below : 9 Nov. 1659, E. 1009.] *Printed by Henry Hall for Thomas Robinson: Oxford.* (5 Sept.)   E. 925. (3.)

[**Sept. 8.**]—The Grounds of the Lawes of England. By M. H. [i.e. Michael Hawke.] pp. 474. *Printed for H. Twyford, T. Dring, J. Place and W. Place.* (8 Sept.)   E. 1569. (1.)

[**Sept. 8.**]—A brief Relation of the Inhumane cruelties of the Turks, perpetrated on the Commander and company of the ship Lewis of London. (8 Sept.)   E. 925. (5.)

Sept. 10.—[An Order of the Protector appointing 30 Sept. as a Day of Solemn Fasting.] *s. sh. Printed by Henry Hills and John Field.*

669. f. 20. (68.)

[**Sept. 11.**]—Χοροθεολόγον, or, Two Breife but Usefull Treatises, the one touching the Office and Quality of the Ministry of the Gospell, the other of the Nature and Accidents of Mixt Dancing. By Joseph Bentham. pp. 56. *Printed by Tho. Roycroft for Philemon Stephens.* (11 Sept.)   E. 925. (6.)

[**Sept. 18.**]—The Testimony of the Lord concerning London, with a Warning to all sorts of People in it. By E. B. [i.e. Edward Burrough.] *Printed for Giles Calvert.* (18 Sept.)   E. 925. (9.)

1657.

[Sept. 19.]—Dagons-Downfall ; or, The great Idol digged up Root and Branch. [By Roger Crab.] (19 Sept.) **E. 925. (10.)**

Sept. 21.—A Sermon touching the use of Humane Learning. Preached in Mercers Chappel, at the funeral of Mr. John Langley, late Schoolmaster of Paul's School. By Ed. Reynolds. *Printed by T. N. for George Thomason.* **E. 746. (1.)**

[Sept. 21.]—A Golden-Chain, or, A Miscelany of Divine Sentences. Collected by Edward Bulstrode. pp. 207. *Printed by F. L. for W Lee, D. Pakeman and G. Bedel.* (21 Sept.) **E. 1618. (2.)**

[Sept. 21.]—Killing is Murder : or, An Answer to a Treasonous Pamphlet entituled, Killing is no Murder [by Edward Sexby and Silius Titus. See above : May, E. 501. (4.)]. *Printed for Joseph Moor.* (21 Sept.) **E. 925. (12.)**

[Sept. 25.]—A Review of the true nature of Schisme, with a vindication of the Congregationall Churches in England from the imputation thereof unjustly charged on them by Mr. D. Cawdrey. By John Owen. pp. 181. *Printed by Henry Hall for Thomas Robinson : Oxford.* (25 Sept.) **E. 1664. (1.)**

[Sept. 30.]—Fur pro Tribunali. Examen dialogismi cui inscribitur Fur Prædestinatus. Accesserunt Oratio de Doctrina Neo-Pelagiana, etc. Authore Georgio Kendallo. pp. 488. *Excudebat Hen. Hall impensis Tho. Robinson : Oxoniæ.* (30 Sept.) **E. 1642. (1.)**

[Oct. 1.]—The King of Spains Cabinet Councel Divulged ; or, A Discovery of the Prevarications of the Spaniards for obtaining the Universal Monarchy. pp. 158. *Printed by J. H. for J. S. and are to be sold by Simon Miller.* (1 Oct.) **E. 1659. (3.)**

[Oct. 2.]—Gods House, with the nature and use thereof. By Simon Gunton. pp. 130. *Printed for Thomas Dring.* (2 Oct.) **E. 1684. (2.)**

[Oct. 3.]—A Just and Lawful Trial of the Teachers & professed Ministers of England. By E. B. [i.e. Edward Burrough.] *Printed for Thomas Simmonds.* (3 Oct.) **E. 925. (14.)**

[Oct. 7.]—A Suddain Flash, timely discovering some reasons wherefore the stile of Protector should not be deserted by these nations. By Britan's Remembrancer [i.e. George Wither. A poem]. pp. 70. *Printed for J. S.* (7 Oct.) **E. 1584. (3.)**

[Oct. 10.]—A Rod discovered, found and set forth to whip the Idolaters till they leave off their Idolatry. By Henry Clark. pp. 77. *Printed for the Author.* (10 Oct.) **E. 926. (1.)**

[Oct. 11.]—A Reviving Word from the Quick and the Dead to the Scatter'd Dust of Sion. [Signed by Edward Edmonds and others.] pp. 69. *Printed for Giles Calvert.* (11 Oct.) **E. 926. (2.)**

[Oct. 14.]—The Penitent Murderer. Being an Exact Narrative of the Life and Death of Nathaniel Butler, who became a convert after he had

1657.

most cruelly murdered John Knight. By Randolph Yearwood. pp. 80.
Printed by T. Newcomb for J. Rothwell. (14 Oct.) **E. 1660. (2.)**

[**Oct. 15.**]—Marginall Antidotes, to be affixed over against the lines of
R. H. [i.e. Richard Hubberthorn] and E. B. [i.e. Edward Burrough]
their pamphlet, entituled, The Rebukes of a Reviler. By John Stalham.
[See above: 23 July, E. 919. (7.)] *Printed for Edward Brewster.*
(15 Oct.) **E. 926. (3.)**

[**Oct. 19.**]—The Entrance of Mazzarini. Or, some memorials of the State
of France between the death of the Cardinall of Richelieu and the
beginning of the late Regency. Collected and digested out of forraign
writers. By an indifferent hand [i.e. Thomas Tanner.] p. 114. *Printed
by H. H. for Thom. Robinson : Oxford.* (19 Oct.) **E. 1627. (2.)**

[**Oct. 20.**]—Gospel-Separation separated from its Abuses ; or the Saints
Guide in Gospel-Fellowship. By R. L. [i.e. Richard Lawrence.] pp. 141.
Printed for Giles Calvert. (20 Oct.) **E. 1613. (5.)**

[**Oct. 21.**]—A Vindication of the Orthodoxe Protestant Doctrine against
the Innovations of Dr. Drayton and Mr. Parker. [By John Tendring.]
pp. 77. *Printed for Richard Royston.* (21 Oct.) **E. 926. (5.)**

[**Oct. 21.**]—A Winding-Sheet for Popery. By Richard Baxter. *Printed
by Robert White, for Nevil Simmons, Book-seller in Kederminster.* (21 Oct.)
E. 1602. (5.)

[**Oct. 22.**]—A True Testimony of Faithfull Witnesses recorded, wherein
the wicked designs of several of the Rulers of the County of Somerset
are witnessed against, by those who are reproachfully called Quakers.
By Robert Wastfeild. pp. 98. *Printed for Giles Calvert.* (22 Oct.)
E. 926. (6.)

[**Oct. 22.**]—The Wofull Cry of Unjust Persecutions and grievous Oppressions of the People of God in England, in scorn called Quakers. By E. B.
[i.e. Edward Burrough.] *Printed for Giles Calvert.* (22 Oct.) **E. 927. (1.)**

[**Oct. 27.**]—Hobbiani Puncti Dispunctio ; or, The Undoing of Mr. Hobs's
Points: in answer to Mr. Hobs's Στιγμαὶ, id est, Stigmata Hobbii.
By John Wallis. *Printed by Leonard Lichfield for Tho. Robinson :
Oxford.* (27 Oct.) **E. 1602. (2.)**

[**Oct. 27.**]—Lignum Vitæ. Libellus ad utilitatem cujusque animæ in
altiorem vitæ perfectionem suspirantis. Authore Richardo Brathwait.
[With an allegorical engraving as frontispiece.] pp. 679. *Excudebat
Joh. Grismond.* (27 Oct.) **E. 1566.**

[**Oct. 30.**]—Legis Fluvius ; or, The Fountain of the Law opened. By
A. G. pp. 141. *Printed by J. C. for T. Rooks.* (30 Oct.) **E. 1647. (1.)**

[**Oct. 31.**]—The Devils Cabinet broke open : or, A New Discovery of the
High-way Thieves, being a Seasonable Advice of a Gentleman lately
converted from them, to Travellers to avoyd their Villanies. *Printed
for Henry Marsh.* (31 Oct.) **E. 927. (4.)**

1657.

[**Oct. 31.**]—A Loving Salutation to the seed of Abraham among the Jewes. By M. F. [i.e. Margaret Fell.] *Printed for Tho. Simmons.* (31 Oct.)   **E. 927. (3.)**

[**Oct.**]—Cleaveland's Petition to the Lord Protector [praying that he may no longer be persecuted for his previous loyalty to the King]. *s. sh. Printed for William Sheares.* (Oct.)   **669. f. 20. (69.)**

[**Oct.**]—[A Copy of the Petition of John Cleveland to the Protector. In MS. throughout in Thomason's hand.]   **E. 746. (4.)**

[**Nov. 2.**]—Hosannah to the Son of David : or, A Testimony to the Lord's Christ, more especially intended for the Quakers, wherein the reclaiming them from the Error of their way is modestly endevoured. [By John Jackson.] pp. 168. *Printed by William Godbid.* (2 Nov.)   **E. 927. (5.)**

Nov. 3.—Abraham's Image in one of his Sonnes. A sermon at the Funeral of John Dethick, in West Newton. By William Knapp. *Printed by Peter Cole.*   **E. 937. (2.)**

[**Nov. 7.**]—The Saints Support & Comfort, in the Time of Distress and Danger, with divers other treatises. By John Cotton, of Boston in New-England. pp. 135. *Printed and are to be sold by Thomas Basset.* (7 Nov.)   **E. 927. (6.)**

[**Nov. 7.**]—The Perfect Husbandman, or the Art of Husbandry. By C. H. [i.e. C. Heresbachius], B. C. [i.e. C. Googe] and C. M. [i.e. C. Markham.] pp. 385. *Printed and are to be sold by Thomas Basset.* (7 Nov.)   **E. 928. (1.)**

[**Nov. 17.**]—The Office of a Justice of Peace, together with instructions, how and in what manner Statutes shall be expounded. Written by W. Fleetwood. pp. 164. *Printed by Ralph Wood, for W. Lee, D. Pakeman, and G. Bedell.* (17 Nov.)   **E. 1668. (2.)**

[**Nov. 18.**]—The Lords Supper briefly vindicated, and demonstrated by Scripture to be a Grace-begetting ordinance. By William Prynne. [See also below : 18 May, 1658, E. 946. (2.)] pp. 60. *Printed and are to be sold by Edward Thomas.* (18 Nov.)   **E. 928. (3.)**

[**Nov. 18.**]—Some Prison Meditations, being a Free-Gift Sermon, mainly touching the Religious Robbers of the former, later and present times. [By Thomas Taylor.] *Printed for Giles Calvert.* (18 Nov.)
                                                                 E. 929. (1.)

[**Nov. 21.**]—A Discourse upon the nationall Excellencies of England. By R. H. [i.e. Richard Hawkins.] pp. 248. *Printed by Tho. Newcomb for Henry Fletcher.* (21 Nov.)   **E. 1583. (2.)**

[**Nov. 21.**]—Jus Fratrum, the Law of Brethren. Touching the power of parents to dispose of their estates to their children or to others. Shewing the variety of customes in several counties. By John Page. pp. 114. *Printed by I. M. for Henry Fletcher.* (21 Nov.)   **E. 1669. (3.)**

1657.

[**Nov. 23.**]—A Word to the Officers of the Army. [Signed : T. Z., i.e. Thomas Zachary.] *Printed for Giles Calvert.* (23 Nov.)

E. 929. (4.)

[**Nov. 25.**]—The Cause of Stumbling removed from all that will receive the Truth. By Richard Hubberthorne. *Printed for Thomas Simmons.* (25 Nov.)

E. 929. (5.)

[**Nov. 25.**]—Love's Entercours between the Lamb & his Bride, Christ and his Church. Or, a clear explication and application of the Song of Solomon. By William Guild. pp. 287. *Printed by W. Wilson for Ralph Smith.* (25 Nov.)

E. 1583. (3.)

[**Nov. 26.**]—Omnibus, vel ullis illorum in mundo Regibus aut Gubernatoribus vocatis, haec in amore promulgantur, ut a tenebris ad lucem convertantur. Haec sunt ab iis, qui per derisores mundi vocati sunt Anglicé Quakers. [By George Fox.] (26 Nov.)

E. 929. (6.)

[**Nov. 28.**]—A New Catalogue of the Dukes, Marquesses, Earls, Viscounts, Barons of England, Scotland and Ireland, also the Baronets. Whereunto is added the Honours that the Lord Protector hath bestowed to this present. Collected by T. W. [i.e. Thomas Walkley.] pp. 175. *Printed for Thomas Walkley.* (28 Nov.)

E. 1602. (3.)

[**Nov. 28.**]—The Prerogative of Popular Government. A Politicall Discourse in two books. By James Harrington. pp. 218. *Printed for T. Brewster.* (28 Nov.)

E. 929. (7.)

[**Nov. 28.**]—Pierides, or the Muses Mount. [Poems.] By Hugh Crompton. pp. 150. *Printed by J. G. for Charles Web.* (28 Nov.)

E. 1660. (1.)

[**Nov. 29.**]—A Practical Commentary on the Epistle of Jude delivered in Sunday Lectures at Stoke-Newington. By Thomas Manton. pp. 567. *Printed by J. M. for Luke Fawn.* (29 Nov.)

E. 930.

[**Nov.**]—A Discourse of the Knowledg of Beasts ; wherein all that hath been said for and against their ratiocination, is examined. By Monsieur [Cureau] de la Chambre, Counsellor to the King of France, and his physitian in ordinary. Translated into English. pp. 304. *Printed by Tho. Newcomb for Humphrey Moseley.*

E. 1829. (1.)

[**Nov.**]—The Holy Life of Mon\[r\]. de Renty, a late nobleman of France, and sometimes Councellor to King Lewis the 13\[th\]. Written in French by John Baptist S. Jure, and faithfully translated into English by E. S. [With an engraved portrait of Baron de Renti.] pp. 358. *Printed for John Crook.*

E. 1587. (2.)

[**Nov.**]—The Judgement of the late Arch-bishop of Armagh and Primate of Ireland, of the extent of Christ's death and satisfaction. With a vindication of him, and a declaration of his judgement in several other subjects. By N. Bernard. [With an engraved portrait of Usher.] pp. 192. *Printed for John Crook.*

E. 1587. (1.)

1657.

[**Nov.**]—The Saints Delight. To which is annexed a Treatise of Meditation. By Thomas Watson. pp. 403. *Printed by T. R. & E. M. for Ralph Smith.* **E. 1610. (2.)**

[**Nov.**]—Sixteen pence in the Pound; or, A Table shewing the present worth of one Pound Annuity for any time under 100 yeares. By John Newton. **E. 1602. (4.)**

[**Dec. 2.**]—Perjury the proof of Forgery; or, Mr. Crofton's Civilitie justified by Cadmans Falsitie. [A vindication of Zachary Crofton from the charge of having whipped his maid Mary Cadman.] By Alethes Noctroff [i.e. Crofton.] *Printed for James Nuthal in the Minories.* (2 Dec.) **E. 931. (1.)**

Dec. 4.—The Comfort and Crown of Great Actions. A sermon preached before the Honourable East India Company. By Edward Reynolds. *Printed by Tho. Newcomb for George Thomason.* **E. 934. (4*.)**

Dec. 6.—The Great Case of Tythes truly stated. By a Countery-man, A. P. [i.e. Anthony Pearson, a Quaker.] *Printed for Giles Calvert.* (6 Dec.) **E. 931. (2.)**

Dec. 7.—Confidence questioned; or, A Brief Examination of some Doctrines delivered by Thomas Willes in a sermon preached by him at Margrets New-Fish-Street. By Jeremiah Ives. [See also below : 17 Jan., 1658, E. 934. (3.)] *Printed for Daniel White.* **E. 932. (2.)**

[**Dec. 7.**]—The Doctrins and Principles of the Priests of Scotland contrary to the Doctrine of Christ and the Apostles. By George Weare, John Hart [and other Quakers]. pp. 56. *Printed for Giles Calvert.* (7 Dec.) **E. 931. (3.)**

[**Dec. 8.**]—A Lamentation for the Deceived People of the World, but in particular to them of Alesbury. By Jeane Bettris, Quaker. (8 Dec.) **E. 931. (4.)**

[**Dec. 10.**]—The Examination of Tilenus before the Triers : in order to his intended Settlement in the office of a publick preacher in the commonwealth of Utopia. Together with a short essay [in Latin], by way of annotations, upon the Fundamental Theses of Mr. Thomas Parker. [By N. N., i.e. Laurence Womock.] pp. 283. *Printed for R. Royston.* (10 Dec.) **E. 1625.**

[**Dec. 10.**]—Malice against Ministry manifested by the defence of Zach. Crofton unto the false and frivolous charge against him exhibited. *Printed for James Nuthall.* (10 Dec.) **E. 931. (5.)**

Dec. 10.—Mistris Shawe's Tomb-Stone. Being remarkable passages in the life and death of Dorothy Shaw, who slept in the Lord 10 Dec. pp. 104. *Printed for Nathanael Brooks.* **E. 1926. (1.)**

[**Dec. 11.**]—Reponse aux Questions de Mr. Despagne adressées à l'Eglise Françoise de Londres. [By William Herbert.] pp. 74. *Chez Jean Baker.* (11 Dec.) **E. 746. (2.)**

1657.

[**Dec. 19.**]—Caro-Carita.   A treatise discovering the true nature of Charity.   By L. W.   pp. 90.   *Printed by T. M., for Stephen and Thomas Lewis.*   (19 Dec.)   **E. 1716. (2.)**

[**Dec. 20.**]—A Call and a Warning to all Priests, Professors and People. By John Gould.   [A Quaker tract.]   *Printed for Thomas Simmons.* (20 Dec.)   **E. 932. (1.)**

[**Dec. 24.**]—The True Christian Religion againe discovered.   [A defence of the Quakers.   By Edward Burrough.]   *Printed by Roger Norton Junior for Giles Calvert.*   (24 Dec.)   **E. 932. (3.)**

[**Dec. 25.**]—The Banner of Gods Love and Ensign of Righteousness spread over his people.   By Ambrose Rigge.   *Printed for Giles Calvert.* (25 Dec.)   **E. 932. (4.)**

[**Dec. 27.**]—Of Bowings.   By George Fox.   *Printed for Thomas Simmons.*   (27 Dec.)   **E. 932. (5.)**

[**Dec.**]—A Collection of Offices or Forms of Prayer in cases ordinary and extraordinary.   Together with the Psalter according to the Kings Translations.   *Printed by G. Flesher for R. Royston.*   **E. 1600.**

[**Dec.**]—The Judgement of the late Arch-Bishop of Armagh [James Usher], of Babylon being the present See of Rome, with a Sermon of Bishop Bedels of Laying on of Hands.   Published by Nicholas Bernard. [See also below : 20 April, 1657, E. 938. (4.)]   pp. 380.   *Printed for John Crook.*   (Dec.)   **E. 1783. (1.)**

To the following no date, except that of the year, can be assigned.

1657.—Two Assize Sermons preached at Bridgnorth in the year 1657. By Mich. Thomas.   pp. 128.   *Printed by W. Wilson for Humphrey Moseley.*   **E. 1790. (1.)**

1657.—Deaths Advantage ; opened in a Sermon preached at North-ampton at the Funeral of Peter Whalley.   By Edward Reynolds. *Printed by Tho. Newcomb for George Thomason.*   **E. 501. (2.)**

1657.—Dialling Universal : performed by an easie and most speedy way. By G. S.   *Printed by R. and W. Leybourn for Thomas Pierrepont.*
                                                E. 956. (3.)

1657.—An Examination of the political part of Mr. Hobbs his Leviathan. By George Lawson.   pp. 214.   *Printed by R. White for Francis Tyton.*
                                                E. 1723. (2.)

1657.—Psalterium Carolinum.   The Devotions of his Sacred Majestie in his solitudes and sufferings, rendred in verse.   [From the Εἰκων Βασιλικη by T. Stanley.]   Set to music for 3 voices and an organ or theorbo, by John Wilson.   5 pts.   *Printed for John Martin and James Allestrey.*   **E. 1076.**

1658.

[Jan. 1.]—Brittish and Out-landish Prophesies.   By Thomas Pugh. pp. 183.   *Printed by Lodowick Lloyd.*   (1 Jan.)   **E. 932. (6.)**

[Jan. 1.]—Observations, Censures and Confutations of divers Errors in the 12, 13 and 14 Chap. of Mr. Hobs his Leviathan.   [By William Lucy, Bishop of St. David's.]   pp. 235.   *Printed by T. F. for H. Robinson.* (1 Jan.)   **E. 1691. (1.)**

[Jan. 3.]—Ovid's Invective or Curse against Ibis.   Translated into English verse.   By John Jones.   pp. 164.   *Printed by J. G. for Ric. Davis: Oxford.*   (3 Jan.)   **E. 1657. (2.)**

Jan. 4.—Redeeming the Time.   A sermon preached at Preston at the funerall of the Lady Margaret Houghton.   By Isaac Ambrose.   *Printed by T. C. for Nath. Webb and William Grantham.*   **E. 945. (3*.)**

[Jan. 7.]—Christ and His Church; or, Christianity Explained, with a Justification of the Church of England.   By Edward Hyde.   pp. 723. *Printed by R. W. for Richard Davis.*   (7 Jan.)   **E. 933.**

[Jan. 10.]—An Admonitory Letter written by an Old Minister of the New Combinational Church and sent to divers Ejected Ministers. *Printed by J. G. for Richard Lowns.*   (10 Jan.)   **E. 934. (1.)**

[Jan. 11.]—Entertainment of the Cours : or, Academical Conversations. Compiled by Monsieur de Marmet and rendered into English by Thomas Saintserf.   [With an engraved frontispiece.]   pp. 207.   *Printed by T. C.*   (11 Jan.)   **E. 1599. (1.)**

[Jan. 12.]—Replies made to the Antiqueries of Thomas Lye, wherein the Parish-Ministers call and maintenance are debated.   By H. L., a friend to the Quakers [i.e. Henry Lavor.]   pp. 71.   *Printed for Daniel White.* (12 Jan.)   **E. 934. (2.)**

[Jan. 17.]—The Confident Questionist Questioned ; or, The Examination of the doctrine delivered by Thomas Willes in certain Queries.   Published by Jeremiah Ives.   Examined in Counter-Queries.   By N. E.   pp. 56. [See above : 7 Dec. 1657, E. 932. (2.), and also below : 24 Feb., E. 936. (1.)]   *Printed for Tho. Newberry.*   (17 Jan.)   **E. 934. (3.)**

[Jan. 19.]—The Rights of the People concerning Impositions.   [By Sir Henry Yelverton.]   pp. 117.   *Printed for William Leak.*   (19 Jan.)   **E. 1647. (3.)**

Jan. 20.—The Speech of the Lord Fiennes, Commissioner of the Great Seal, made before His Highness and Parliament.   *Printed by Henry Hills and John Field, Printers to His Highness.*   **E. 934. (6.)**

[Jan. 20.]—[A Petition from Samuel Vassall to Parliament for the payment of a debt due to him from the Commonwealth.]   *s. sh.* 4°.   **E. 934. (5.)**

[Jan. 24.]—The Christian in Compleat Armour, or, a Treatise of the Saints Warre against the Devil.   The Second Part.   By William Gurnal.   pp. 676.   *Printed for Ralph Smith.*   (24 Jan.)   **E. 901.**

1658.

[Jan. 25.]—A Catalogue of the Names of those Honourable Persons who are now Members of this present House of Lords. *s. sh.* (25 Jan.)

669. f. 20. (70.)

[Jan. 25.]—To the Parliament. The Petition of diverse Citizens and Inhabitants in and about the City of London. [Praying for the establishment of various rights and reforms.] *s. sh.* (25 Jan.)

669. f. 20. (71.)

[Jan. 30.]—The Preacher sent : or, A Vindication of the Liberty of Publick Preaching by some men not ordained. In answer to two Books : 1. Jus Divinum Ministerii Euangelici, by the Provincial Assembly of London. 2. Vindiciæ Ministerii Euangelici, by John Collings. Published by John Martin, Sam. Petto, Frederick Woodal. pp. 359. [See above : 6 June, 1651, E. 630. (3.), and also below : 22 May, E. 946. (4.) and 2 Sept., E. 952. (2.)] *Printed for Livewell Chapman.* (30 Jan.)

E. 1592. (2.)

[Jan.]—The Coat of Armes of Sir John Presbyter. [A satire.] *s. sh.*

669. f. 20. (79.)

[Feb. 1.]—To the Protector and Parliament of England. [An address, by George Fox, advocating reform in the Law and Church of England.] pp. 63. *Printed for Giles Calvert.* (1 Feb.) **E. 934. (7.)**

[Feb. 2.]—A Confession and Profession of Faith in God by his People who are in scorn called Quakers. By R. Farnsworth. *Printed for Giles Calvert.* (2 Feb.) **E. 935. (1.)**

[Feb. 3.]—A Narrative of the great success God hath been pleased to give his Highness forces in Jamaica against the King of Spains forces. Together with a true relation of the Spaniards losing their Plate Fleet, as it was communicated in a letter [dated : 3 Feb.] from the Governour of Jamaica [Edward Doyley]. *Printed by Henry Hills and John Field.*

E. 948. (5.)

[Feb. 3.]—The Law of God the Rule for Law-makers. The ground of all just Laws and the corruption of English Laws and Lawyers discovered, by George Fox. *Printed for Giles Calvert.* (3 Feb.) **E. 935. (2.)**

[Feb. 5.]—Three Sermons preached by Dr. Richard Stuart. To which is added a fourth sermon, by Samuel Harsnett, Arch-bishop of York. The second edition. pp. 165. *Printed for G. Bedel and T. Collins.* (5 Feb.)

E. 1629. (2.)

[Feb. 9.]—A Description of the whole World with some General Rules touching the use of the Globe. By Robert Fage. [With a map.] pp. 70. *Printed by J. Owsley & sold by Peter Stent.* (9 Feb.) **E. 1595. (3.)**

[Feb. 16.]—The Stumbling-Block of Disobedience and Rebellion, cunningly laid by Calvin in the Subjects way, discovered, censured and removed. By P. H. [i.e. Peter Heylyn.] pp. 307. *Printed by E. Cotes for Henry Seile.* (16 Feb.) **E. 935. (3.)**

1658.

[**Feb. 20.**]—Whether it be better to turn Presbyterian, Romane, or to continue what I am, Catholique in matter of Religion? By Thomas Swadlin. *Printed for the Author.* (20 Feb.) **E. 935. (4.)**

[**Feb. 24.**]—Confidence Encountred ; or, A Vindication of the lawfulness of Preaching without Ordination. In answer to a book by N. E., intituled, The Confident Questionist Questioned. By Jer. Ives. pp. 58. [See above : 17 Jan., E. 934. (3.)] *Printed for the Author.* (24 Feb.)
E. 936. (1.)

Feb. 26.—A Most Exact and True Relation extracted out of the Registers and Publick Instruments, whereby those passages are laid open which hapned since the Pacification made at Roschilt 26 Feb. between the Kings of Denmark and Norway and the King of Sweden. Also at Coppenhagen and elsewhere between the Danish Commissioners and the Sweedish Ambassadors. *Printed by J. C. for John Crooke.*
E. 977. (8.)

Feb. 27.—By the Protector. A Proclamation commanding all Papists and other persons who have been of the late Kings Party to depart out of London and Westminster on or before 8 March. *s. sh. Printed by Henry Hills and John Field.* **669. f. 20. (72.)**

Feb. 27.—By the Protector. A Proclamation commanding all Papists and other persons who have been of the late King's party, to repair unto their places of abode and not to remove above five miles from the same. *s. sh. Printed by Henry Hills and John Field.*
669. f. 20. (73.)

[**Feb. 27.**]—Comfort and Counsel for Dejected Souls, or, A Treatise concerning Spiritual Dejection. By John Durant. The Fourth Edition. pp. 259. *Printed for R. I. and are to be sold by Charles Tyus.* (27 Feb.) **E. 1599. (2.)**

[**Feb.**]—A Narrative of the late Parliament. By a Friend to the Common Wealth. **E. 935. (5.)**

[**Feb.**]—The Mystery of Dreames historically discoursed. By Philip Goodwin. pp. 361. *Printed by A. M. for Francis Tyton.* **E. 1576.**

[**March 2.**]—A knot of Fooles. [By Thomas Brewer. A satire, in verse. With a woodcut on the titlepage.] *Printed for Francis Grove.* (2 March.) **E. 936. (2.)**

[**March 3.**]—Demophilos ; or, The Assertor of the Peoples Liberty. By William Prynne. [Another edition of " A Summary Collection of the Principal Fundamental Rights, etc.," published in 1656.] pp. 63. *Printed for Francis Coles.* (3 March.) **E. 936. (3.)**

[**March 4.**]—A Messenger from the Dead ; or Conference, full of stupendious horrour, between the Ghosts of Henry the 8. and Charls the First in Windsore-Chappel. *Printed for Thomas Vere and William Gilbertson.* (4 March.) **E. 936. (4.)**

1658.

March 5.—Funerals made Cordials : in a sermon preached at the interment of the Right Honorable Robert Rich. By John Gauden. pp. 124.
Printed by T. C. for Andrew Crook.   **E. 946. (1.)**

March 9.—By the Protector. A Proclamation declaring the right of
the Fellowship and Company of English Merchants for Discovery of
New Trades, commonly called the Muscovia Company, to the sole fishing for Whales upon the Coasts of Green-land and Chery-Island. *s. sh.*
Printed by Henry Hills and John Field.   **669. f. 20. (78.)**

March 10.—By the Protector. A Proclamation for the better levying
and payment of the Duty of Excise. *s. sh.* *Printed by Henry Hills and
John Field.*   **669. f. 20. (77.)**

[**March 11.**]—A True Copy of a Petition [praying for a satisfactory settle-
ment of the questions of taxation, the Militia, and the regular assembling
of Parliament] signed by many people inhabiting in and about the
City of London, intended to have been delivered to the late Parliament.
Now presented, with a brief Apology in the behalf of the Petitioners, by
E. H. *Printed for the Author.* (11 March.)   **E. 936. (5.)**

March 14.—The Pious Votary and Prudent Traveller. A Farewell-
Sermon occasioned by the voyage of Nathanael Wych, President to the
East-Indies. Preached in S. Dionys Back-church by Nath. Hardy.
pp. 52. *Printed by J. G. for John Clark.*   **E. 938. (3.)**

[**March 19.**]—A Petitionary Epistle to the Lord Protector and People
of the Commonwealth to continue in unity. [Signed : N. T.]
(19 March.)   **E. 936. (7.)**

March 19.—To the Inhabitants and Souldery of London. [A letter
giving warning of a " great and dreadful judgement suddenly to
approach, a judgement by fire and sword." MS. note by Thomason : " Scatered about the street, 19 March."] *s. sh.*

                                                    669. f. 20. (75.)

[**March 21.**]—Preparation to Conversion ; or, Faith's Harbinger. A
rare Epistle, writ by a Person of Quality before his Death. *Printed by
Thomas Newcomb.* (21 March.)   **E. 1599. (3.)**

March 22.—The Judges Charge. Delivered in a sermon before M.
Justice Hale and M. Sergeant Crook, Judges of Assize, by Rich. Parr.
Printed by J. C. for Nathaniel Brook.   **E. 947. (2.)**

March 24.—[A MS. note by Thomason, written on a blank leaf, as
follows : " March 24. This day I did cease my elaborat Collection,
because the number was soe exceedinge few and inconsiderable and not
now worth my labour, & the yeare 1658 beginning to-morrow I did
prefer put an end to my great paynes and charges."]   **E. 936. (8*.)**

[**March 24.**]—A Plea for the Lords, and House of Peers : or a full,
necessary, seasonable enlarged vindication of the just antient hereditary
right of the Lords, Peers, and Barons of this Realm to sit, vote, judge

1658.

in all the Parliaments of England. By William Prynne. pp. 518. *Printed for the Author.* (24 March.) **E. 749.**

[**March 24.**]—Religious Principles in Verse. *Printed for Richard Wood-nothe.* (24 March.) **E. 936. (8.)**

[**March 24.**]—Seven Particulars : I. Against Oppressors. II. Magistrates Work and Honor, *etc.* By W. T. [i.e. William Tomlinson.] *Printed for Giles Calvert.* (24 March.) **E. 936. (9.)**

[**March 24.**]—A Wedding Ring fit for the Finger. A sermon at a wedding in Edmonton. By William Secker. pp. 56. *Printed for Thomas Parkhurst.* (24 March.) **E. 1648. (4.)**

[**March.**]—The Delinquents Passport; or, a plea upon his Highness Proclamation commanding all Delinquents to return home to their own country. [In verse.] *s. sh.* **669. f. 20. (76.)**

[**March.**]—[An account of a trade dispute respecting the printing of Sir George Crookes Reports.] *s. sh.* **669. f. 20. (74.)**

[**April 1.**]—The Snare of the Devill discovered; or, A true relation of the sad condition of Lydia the wife of John Rogers in Wapping, how she wanting money the Devil appeared to her in the shape of a man and a contract was made between them. *Printed for Edward Thomas.* (1 April.) **E. 1833. (2.)**

April 8.—By the Protector. A Proclamation prohibiting Horse-Races in England or Wales for Eight Moneths. *s. sh. Printed by Henry Hills and John Field.* **669. f. 21. (1.)**

[**April 10.**]—A Model for the maintaining of Students of choice abilities at the Universities, and principally in order to the Ministry. [Signed : Matthew Poole.] (10 April.) **E. 937. (4.)**

[**April 13.**]—The Crucifying of the World by the Cross of Christ. By Richard Baxter. pp. 254. *Printed by R. W. for Nevill Simmons, Bookseller in Kederminster, and Nathaniel Ekins, in Pauls Church-Yard.* (13 April.) **E. 937. (5.)**

[**April 13.**]—A Discourse of Disputations concerning Religion; with Animadversions on a Publick Disputation at Killingworth between John Bryan and John Onley. By John Ley. pp. 126. *Printed for Nathaniel Webb and William Grantham.* (13 April.) **E. 938. (1 & 2.)**

[**April 13.**]—A Lamentable Narration of the sad Disaster of a great part of the Spanish Plate-Fleet that perished neare St. Lucas, by the valour and prowess of Generals Mountague and Blake, in the yeare 1657. [In verse.] *s. sh. Printed by T. P. for N. B.* (13 April.) **669. f. 21. (2.)**

[**April 14.**]—Abel being Dead yet speaketh; or, The Life & Death of John Cotton, late of Boston in New-England. By John Norton. pp. 51. *Printed by Tho. Newcomb for Lodowick Lloyd.* (14 April.) **E. 937. (6.)**

1658.

[April 15.]—The coming of God in Mercy, in Vengeance ; beginning with
fire to convert or consume this so sinful City London.   By Walter
Gostelo.   *Printed for the Author.*   (15 April.)   **E. 1833. (1.)**

[April 20.]—Respondet Petrus ; or, The Answer of Peter Heylyn to
Dr. Bernard's book entituled, The Judgement of the late Primate of
Ireland.   To which is added an Appendix in answer to certain passages
in Mr. Sandersons History of the Life of K. Charles.   [See above :
Nov. 1657, E. 1587. (1.)]   pp. 157.   *Printed for R. Royston and
R. Marriot.*   (20 April.)   **E. 938. (4.)**

[April 20.]—Richard Baxter's Account of his present Thoughts concerning the Controversies about the Perseverance of the Saints.
Occasioned by misreports of his book called The Right Method for
Peace of Conscience.   [See above : 17 Oct., 1653, E. 1514.]   *Printed
for Tho. Underhill and F. Tyton.*   (20 April.)   **E. 939. (1.)**

[April 21.]—The Blessed Peace-Maker and Christian Reconciler.   By
Claudius Gilbert.   pp. 131.   *Printed for Francis Titon.*   (21 April.)
                                                          E. 939. (3.)

[April 21.]—A Pleasant Walk to Heaven.   By Claudius Gilbert.
pp. 67.   *Printed for Francis Titon.*   (21 April.)   **E. 939. (2.)**

[April 21.]—A Soveraign Antidote against Sinful Errors.   By Claudius
Gilbert.   pp. 158.   *Printed by R. W. for Francis Titon.*   (21 April.)
                                                          E. 939. (4.)

[April 24.]—Vindiciæ Fundamenti ; or, A threefold defence of the
Doctrine of Original Sin.   The first against the exceptions of Robert
Everard in his book entituled The Creation and Fall of man, the second
against the Examiners of the late Assemblies Confession of Faith,
the third against the allegations of Jeremy Taylor in his Unum
Necessarium.   By Nathaniel Stephens.   pp. 239.   [See above : July,
1655, E. 1554.]   *Printed by T. R. and E. M. for Edmund Paxton.*
(24 April.)   **E. 940. (1.)**

[April 27.]—A Strange Metamorphosis in Tavistock.   A reply to a
pamphlet called Judas.   (27 April.)   **E. 940. (2.)**

[April 27.]—A Treatise of Conversion.   By Richard Baxter.   pp. 307.
*Printed by R. W. for Nevil Simmons, Bookseller in Kederminster, and
Nathaniel Ekins in Paul's Churchyard.*   (27 April.)   **E. 941. (1.)**

[April 27.]—The Way to Bliss.   By Elias Ashmole.   pp. 220.   *Printed
by John Grismond for Nath. Brook.*   (27 April.)   **E. 940. (3.)**

[April 30.]—Principles of Christian Doctrine, illustrated with Questions
and Scripture-Answers.   By John Warren.   Third edition.   *Printed
for N. Webb and W. Grantham.*   (30 April.)   **E. 1853. (2.)**

[April 30.]—The Shepherd of Israel.   Sermons on the twenty-third
Psalm.   Together with the doctrine of Providence practically handled,

1658.

on Matth. x. 29–31. By Obadiah Sedgwick. pp. 432. *Printed by D. Maxwell for Sa. Gellibrand.* (30 April.) **E. 942. (1.)**

[April.]—Christ the Perfect Pattern of a Christian's Practice. Being the substance of severall sermons preached by Mr. Ralph Robinson. pp. 284. *Printed by J. S. & are to be sold by John Sims.* **E. 1818. (1.)**

[April.]—Directions and Perswasions to a Sound Conversion. By Richard Baxter. pp. 534. *Printed by A. M. for Nevil Simmons, Bookseller in Kederminster, and Joseph Cranford in Pauls Churchyard.* **E. 1717.**

[April.]—Endoxa, or some probable Inquiries into Truth, both divine and humane. Together with a Stone to the Altar : or short disquisitions on a few difficult places of Scripture. As also, a calm Ventilation of Pseudo-doxia Epidemica [by Sir Thomas Browne]. By John Robinson. [See also below : 1 June, E. 752. (1.)] pp. 151. *Printed by J. Streater for Francis Tyton.* (April.) **E. 1821. (1.)**

[April.]—Of Schism, Parochial Congregations in England, and Ordination by Imposition of Hands. By Giles Firmin. pp. 157. *Printed by T. C. for Nathanael Webb.* **E. 1819. (1.)**

[April.]—Sincerity and Hypocrisy. Or, the sincere Christian, and Hypocrite, in their lively colours, standing one by the other. By W. S. [i.e. William Sheppard.] pp. 416. *Printed by A. Lichfield for Rob. Blagrave : Oxford.* **E. 1822. (1.)**

[April.]—Τελείωσις : or, An Exercitation upon Confirmation. The second edition, with an appendix annexed. By Jonathan Hanmer. pp. 166. [See also below : 7 June, E. 947. (3.)] *Printed by S. Griffin for John Rothwell.* **E. 1819. (2.)**

[May 1.]—A Plea for the Lords, and House of Peers : or, a full vindication of the just, antient, hereditary right of the Lords, Peers, and Barons of this realm, to sit, vote, judge in all the Parliaments of England. By William Prynne. pp. 518. *Printed for the Author.* (1 May.) **E. 944.**

[May 1.]—An Ephemerides of the cœlestial motions for XIII years, beginning anno 1659, ending anno 1671. By Vincent Wing. *Printed by R. & W. Leybourn for the Company of Stationers.* (1 May.) **E. 943.**

May 1.—A Patterne for all. A Sermon preached at the interment of the Earle of Warwick. By Edmund Calamy. *Printed for Edward Brewster.* **E. 947. (1.)**

[May 1.]—The Yellow Book. [By W. B. Second edition.] *Printed and sold by Tho. Butler and by Tho. Brewster.* (1 May.) **E. 945. (1.)**

[May 1.]—A New Trial of the Ladies. Or, the Yellow Book's Partner. [By W. B. Second edition.] *Printed and sold by Tho. Butler and by Tho. Brewster.* (1 May.) **E. 945. (2.)**

1658.

[**May 2.**]—A Declaration of his Highness, for a collection towards the relief of divers Protestant Churches driven out of Poland; and of twenty Protestant families driven out of the confines of Bohemia. *Printed by Henry Hills and John Field.* (2 May.) **E. 1073. (1.)**

[**May 2.**]—By the Committee for the affairs of the poor Protestants in the Valleys of Piedmont. [A report, together with an account of the persecution of the Protestants in Poland.] *Printed by Hen. Hills and John Field.* (2 May.) **E. 1073. (2.)**

[**May 5.**]—Of Saving Faith : that it is not only gradually, but specifically distinct from all Common Faith. The agreement of Richard Baxter with that adversary, that hath maintained my assertion by a pretended confutation in the end of Serjeant Shephard's book of Sincerity and Hypocrisie. pp. 96. [See above : April, E. 1822. (1.)] *Printed by R. W., for Nevill Simmons, Bookseller in Kederminster, and Nathaniel Ekins in Paul's Churchyard.* **E. 945. (3.)**

[**May 8.**]—The dreadfull danger of Sacrilege held forth in this one Proposition, namely, the with-holding of tithes from a Minister that labours in the Word and Doctrine, is a great and grievous sin. *s. sh.* (8 May.) **669. f. 21. (3.)**

[**May 10.**]—A Voyce from the Temple. Written and published to goe abroad in the Army among those that are called Anabaptists. By Jonas Dell. pp. 96. *Printed for the Author.* (10 May.) **E. 945. (4.)**

[**May 14.**]—The Subjection of all Traytors, Rebels, as well Peers as Commons in Ireland, to the Laws, Statutes, and Trials by Juries of good and lawful men of England in the Kings Bench at Westminster, for Treasons perpetrated by them in Ireland, or any foreign Country. Being an argument at law made in the Court of King's Bench in the case of Connor Magwire, an Irish Baron. By William Prynne. pp. 72. *Printed by J. Leach for the Author.* (14 May.) **E. 945. (5.)**

[**May 16.**]—A distinct and faithful Accompt of all the moneys collected in England, Wales and Ireland, for the relief of the poor distressed Protestants in the valleys of Piemont. Together with a brief accompt [by Sam. Morland] of the present state of affairs in those parts. pp. 116. *Printed by Hen. Hills and John Field.* (16 May.)

E. 1073. (3.)

May 18.—By the Protector. A Declaration, inviting persons to send over all sorts of necessary provisions to Mardike. *s. sh. Printed by Henry Hills and John Field.* **669. f. 21. (4.)**

[**May 18.**]—Holy things for Holy Men : or, the Lawyers Plea non-suited. In some Christian reproofe and pitie expressed towards Mr. Prynn's book, intituled, The Lord's Supper briefly vindicated. By S. S., Minister of the Gospel. [See above : 18 Nov., 1657, E. 928. (3.)] *Printed for Tho. Parkhurst.* (18 May.) **E. 946. (2.)**

1658.

[May 22.]—A New Method of Rosie Crucian physick. By John Heydon. pp. 62. *Printed for Thomas Lock.* (22 May.)
E. 946. (3.)

[May 22.]—Vindiciæ Ministerii Evangelici revindicatæ : or, the Preacher pretendedly Sent, sent back again. By way of reply to a late book, in the defence of gifted brethren, preaching, published by Mr. John Martin, Mr. Samuel Petto, Mr. Frederick Woodale, so far as anything in their book pretends to answer a book called, Vindiciæ Ministerii Evangelici. By John Collinges. pp. 134. [See above : 30 Jan., E. 1592. (2.) and also below : June, 1659, E. 1728. (2.)] *Printed by S. G. for Richard Tomlins.* (22 May.)
E. 946. (4.)

[May 24.]—The Horrible and Bloody Conspiracy undertaken by many Desperate Persons to introduce the Interests of Charles Stewart. *Printed for Thomas Vere and William Gilbertson.* (24 May.)
E. 1881. (1.)

May 28.—[A satirical document purporting to be an Order from "the Commissioners for the Survey of the Highwaies" requiring persons to appear "with shovell and pik-axe at the gravel-pits near Palmers Green."
669. f. 21. (5.)

[May 29.]—A Discourse of the Empire, and of the election of a King of the Romans, the greatest businesse of Christendom now in agitation ; as also of the Colledge of Electors, their particular interests, and who is most likely to be the next Emperour. [By James Howell.] pp. 109. *Printed by F. L. for Rich. Lowndes.* (29 May.)
E. 1823. (1.)

[May 31.]—The Confession of Faith, together with the larger and lesser Catechismes. Composed by the Reverend Assembly of Divines, sitting at Westminster [in Jan. 1647]. The second edition. *Printed by E. M. for the Company of Stationers, and sold by John Rothwel.* (31 May.)
E. 751. (1.)

[May 31.]—The humble Advice of the Assembly of Divines now [Jan. 1647] sitting at Westminster, concerning a larger Catechism. The second edition. pp. 108. *Printed by S. Griffin, for the Company of Stationers and J. Rothwell.* (31 May.)
E. 751. (3.)

[May.]—Castigations of Mr. Hobbes his last Animadversions, in the case concerning Liberty and Universal Necessity. By John Bramhall, Bishop of Derry. pp. 573. *Printed by E. T. for J. Crook.* E. 1757.

[May.]—Choice and Rare Experiments in Physick and Chirurgery. By Thomas Collins. pp. 210. *Printed by J. T. for Francis Eglesfield.*
E. 1887. (1.)

[May.]—Circumspect Walking, describing several rules as so many steps in the way of Wisdome. By Thomas Taylor. pp. 189. *Printed for A. K. and R. I. and are to bee sold by Elisha Wall's.* E. 1769. (1.)

1658.

[May.]—The Crafty Whore; or, the Mistery and Iniquity of Bawdy Houses. [With an engraved frontispiece.] pp. 112. *Printed for Henry Marsh.*　　　**P.C. 21. a. 24.**

[May.]—The False Teacher tried and cast. [A sermon.] By John Brinsley. pp. 78. *Printed by J. T. for Thomas Newberry.*

E. 1821. (2.)

[May.]—Hydrotaphia, Urne-Buriall, or, A Discourse of the Sepulchrall Urnes lately found in Norfolk. Together with the Garden of Cyrus. By Thomas Browne. pp. 102. *Printed for Hen. Brome.* **E. 1821. (3.)**

[May.]—The Policy of the Jesuits. pp. 77. **E. 1894. (1.)**

[May.]—The Practice of the Exchequer Court. By Sr T. F. [i.e. Sir Thomas Fanshaw.] pp. 160. *Printed by T. R. for T. Twyford and W. Place.*　　　**E. 1928. (1.)**

[May.]—A Prospective of the Naval Triumph of the Venetians over the Turk. By Gio: Francesco Busenello. [Translated from the Italian by Sir Thomas Higgons. In verse.] pp. 62. *Printed for Henry Herringman.*　　　**E. 1826.**

[May.]—Satyrical Characters and handsome Descriptions, in Letters, written to severall persons of quality. By Monsieur de Cyrano Bergerac. Translated out of the French. pp. 174. *Printed for Henry Herringman.*　　　**E. 1756. (2.)**

[May.]—Suspension reviewed, stated, cleered and setled upon plain Scripture-Proof. Defending a private sheet written by the author upon this subject, against a publique pretended refutation of the same by Mr. W. in his book, entituled, Suspension discussed. By Samuel Langley. pp. 222. *Printed by J. Hayes for Thomas Underhill.*

E. 1823. (2.)

[May.]—The Tempestuous Soul calmed by Jesus Christ : being an extract of several sermons preached by Anthony Palmer. pp. 94. *Printed for Edward Brewster.*　　　**E. 1826. (3.)**

[May.]—Topica Sacra. Spiritual Logick ; some Helps to Faith, etc. By Thomas Harrison. pp. 175. *Printed for Francis Titon.*

E. 1769. (2.)

[May.]—Vox Dei & Hominis. A Survey of Effectual Calling. Being the substance of several sermons. By J. Votier. pp. 320. *Printed by T. C. for Nathanael Webb and William Grantham.* **E. 1756. (1.)**

[May.]—Witty Apophthegms delivered upon severall occasions by King James, King Charles, the Marquess of Worcester, Francis Lord Bacon and Sir Thomas Moore. [With an engraved frontispiece, bearing portraits of the said five.] pp. 168. *Printed for Edward Farnham.*

E. 1892. (1.)

[June 1.]—Pseudodoxia Epidemica : or, enquiries into very many received tenents and commonly presumed truths. By Thomas Brown. The

1658.

fourth edition. pp. 468. [See above: April, E. 1821. (1.)] *Printed for Edward Dod, and sold by Andrew Cook.* (1 June.) **E. 752. (1.)**

June 3.—An Order and Declaration of his Highness the Lord Protector and his Privy Council, appointing a Committee for the Army, and Receivers General for the third six moneths Assessment, commencing 24 June. *Printed by Henry Hills and John Field.* **E. 1073. (4.)**

[**June 7.**]—A Discourse of the Visible Church: in a debate of this question, viz. Whether the visible Church may be considered to be truely a Church of Christ without respect to saving grace? Also an appendix occasioned by Mr. Hanmore his Exercitation of Confirmation. By Francis Fulwood. 2 pt. [See above: April, E. 1819. (2.)] *Printed by Tho. Ratcliffe for Abel Roper.* (7 June.) **E. 947. (3.)**

June 7.—Dr Hewit's Letter to Dr Wilde, on the day before he suffered death. **669. f. 21. (6.)**

June 8.—The Tryals of Sir Henry Slingsby and John Hewet, for high treason, in Westminster Hall. Together with the Lord President's speech before the sentence of death was pronounced, 2 June. As also the manner of the execution on Tower Hill, 8 June. **E. 753. (5.)**

June 8.—The true and exact Speech and Prayer of Doctor John Hewytt, upon the scaffold on Tower-Hill immediately before his execution. **E. 948. (2.)**

June 8.—An Elegie upon the most eminent Doctor John Hewit. [With an engraving, representing his execution.] **669. f. 21. (7.)**

[**June 10.**]—A Visit to the Spirit in Prison; and an invitation to all people to come to Christ. By Saraah Blackborow. *Printed for Thomas Simmons.* (10 June.) **E. 948. (1.)**

June 14.—By the Protector. A Proclamation of assistance to the Merchant Adventurers of England, for the better carrying on of their trade, and for punishing of Offendors against the same. *s. sh. Printed by Henry Hills and John Field.* **669. f. 21. (8.)**

[**June 14.**]—A Remedy for Uncleanness. Or certain queries propounded to his Highness the Lord Protector [concerning the lawfulness of Polygamy]. By a Person of quality. (14 June.) **E. 948. (3.)**

[**June 14.**]—Graphice. The Use of the Pen and Pensil. Or, the most excellent art of Painting: in two parts. By William Sanderson. [With engraved portraits of the author, of King Charles I., and of Maria Ruten, wife of Antony Van Dyck.] pp. 87. *Printed for Robert Crofts.* (14 June.) **E. 1077.**

[**June 15.**]—The Actors' Vindication. Containing three brief treatises, viz. I. Their Antiquity. II. Their antient Dignity. III. The true Use of their Quality. Written by Thomas Heywood. *Printed by G. E. for W. C.* (15 June.) **E. 948. (4.)**

II.   P

1658.

[June 25.]—Annotations upon the five Books immediately following the historicall part of the Old Testament. The third part. By Arthur Jackson. [With an engraved portrait of the author.] 2 vol. *Printed by Roger Daniel for the Author.* (25 June.) **E. 754 and 755.**

[June.]—The Accomplished Courtier. Consisting of institutions and examples, by which courtiers and officers of State may square their transactions prudently and in good order and method. By H. W., Gent. pp. 140. *Printed for Thomas Dring.* **E. 1824. (1.)**

[June.]—Advice to a Son. By Francis Osborn. The second part. pp. 189. *Printed for Tho. Robinson: Oxford.* **E. 1887. (2.)**

[June.]—A Brief Receipt, Moral & Christian, against the Passion of the Heart. A sermon, by J. H., Minister of Froome [i.e. John Humfrey.] pp. 101. *Printed for E. Blackmore.* **E. 1895. (1.)**

[June.]—Conciones sex ad Academicos Oxonienses Latine habitæ. Authore Henrico Wilkinson. pp. 410. *Excudebat A. Lichfield, impensis Tho. Robinson : Oxonii.* **E. 1768. (1.)**

[June.]—The Enchanted Lovers : a pastoral, by Sʳ William Lower. [In verse.] pp. 104. *Printed by Adrian Vlack : Hage.* **E. 1905. (1.)**

[June.]—La Fida Pastora. Comœdia pastoralis. Autore FF. Anglo-Britanno. [The Faithful Shepherdess of John Fletcher, translated into Latin verse by Sir Robert Fanshawe, with additions by the translator. With an engraved frontispiece.] pp. 103. *Typis R. Danielis. Impensis G. Bedell & T. Collins.* **E. 1823. (3.)**

[June.]—A Greek English Lexicon, containing the derivations and various significations of all the words in the New Testament. By T. C., late of C.C.C. in Oxford. pp. 428. *Printed by Lodowick Lloyd.* **E. 1720. (1.)**

[June.]—Latham's Faulconry, or, the Faulcons Lure and Cure. 2 pt. [Illustrated with woodcuts.] *Printed by Ric. Hodgkinsonne for Thomas Rooks.* **E. 1867.**

[June.]—Mr. Wingate's Arithmetick, containing a perfect method. Digested into a more familiar methode, and augmented by John Kersey. pp. 640. *Printed for Philemon Stephens.* **E. 1844. (1.)**

[June.]—The Modern Assurancer, or the Clark's Directory. Containing the practick part of the Law. By J. H. [i.e. John Herne.] pp. 278. *Printed for Henry Twyford and Nath. Brook.* **E. 1825. (1.)**

[June.]— A New Treatise proving a Multiplicity of Worlds. By Peter Borell. [Translated from the French by D. Sashott.] pp. 200. *Printed by John Streater.* **E. 1891. (2.)**

[June.]—Of Temptation. By John Owen. pp. 184. *Printed by H. Hall for T. Robinson : Oxford.* **E. 2112. (1.)**

July 3.—A Declaration of His Highnesse the Lord Protector for a Day of Publick Thanksgiving. *Printed by Henry Hills and John Field.* **E. 1073. (5.)**

1658.

July 4.—The Perfection, Authority and Credibility of the Holy Scriptures. Discoursed in a sermon before the University of Cambridge, 4 July. By Nathanael Ingelo. The second edition. pp. 182. *Printed by E. T. for Luke Fawn.* **E. 1792. (1.)**

July 13.—Concio Oxoniæ habita, pro Gradu Doctoris, à Gulielmo Burt. pp. 75. *Excudebat Hen. Hall, impensis Thomæ Robinson : Oxoniæ.*
E. 2110. (1.)

[July 25.]—The Cruelty of the Spaniards in Peru. Exprest by instrumentall and vocal musick, and by art of perspective in scenes, &c. Represented daily at the Cockpit in Drury Lane. [By Sir William Davenant.] *Printed for Henry Herriagman.* (25 July.)
E. 756. (22.)

[July.]—Christ's Valedictions ; or, Sacred Observations on the Last Words of Our Savior delivered on the Crosse. By Jenkin Lloyd. pp. 220. *Printed by D. M. for D. Pakeman.* **E. 1895. (2.)**

[July.]—Considerationes modestæ et pacificæ controversiarum, de Justificatione, Purgatorio, Invocatione Sanctorum et Christo Mediatore, Eucharistia. Per Gulielmum Forbesium. Opus posthumum. pp. 466. *Typis Thomæ Roycroft. Impensis J. Martin, Jacobi Allestrye & Tho. Dicas.*
E. 1772.

[July.]—The Divine Right and Original of the Civill Magistrate from God, as it is drawn by S. Paul, Rom. xiii. 1., illustrated and vindicated. By Edward Gee. pp. 372. *Printed for George Eversden.* **E. 1774.**

[July.]—Electa Thargumico-Rabbinica ; sive annotationes in Exodum. Authore Christophoro Cartwrighto. pp. 551. *Typis T. M. prostant apud Matt. Keinton.* **E. 1773.**

[July.]—An exact Abridgement of the Reports of Sir George Crook, one of the Judges of both Benches. pp. 333. *Printed for Tho. Warren and J. Streeter.* **E. 1730.**

[July.]—The Gospel New-Creature ; wherein the work of the Spirit is opened. By A[nthony] Palmer. pp. 265. *Printed for Edward Brewster.*
E. 1826. (2.)

[July.]—The Grotian Religion discovered, at the invitation of Mr. Thomas Pierce in his Vindication. With a preface vindicating the Synod of Dort from the calumnies of the new Tilenus, etc. By Richard Baxter. pp. 119. [See also below : 31 Jan. 1660, E. 1013. (2.)] *Printed by R. W. for Nevill Simmons, Bookseller in Kederminster, and are to be sold by Tho. Brewster and John Starkey.* **E. 1868. (2.)**

[July.]—Hymen's Preludia : or Loves Master-Piece. Being the seventh part of that so much admir'd romance, intituled, Cleopatra. Written originally in the French [by Gauthier de Costes, Seigneur de La Calprenède], and now rendred into English by J. C. [i.e. John Coles]. pp. 325. *Printed for Humphrey Moseley and for John Crook.* **E. 1827. (1.)**

1658.

[July.]—Jacobi Wardei de Hibernia & antiquitatibus ejus Disquisitiones. Editio secunda.   Accesserunt Rerum Hibernicarum regnante Henrico VII. Annales.   [Illustrated with engraved plates.]   pp. 356. 168. *Typis E. Naylor, impensis Jo. Crook.*   **E. 1770.**

[July.]—Mans Master-Piece, in the exercise of a Christian Duty.   By P. T., K^t. [i.e. Sir Peter Temple.]   pp. 251.   *Printed for Joseph Barber and Samuel Speed.*   **E. 1886.**

[July.]—Ter Tria ; or, The Doctrine of the Three Sacred Persons.   By Faithfull Teate.   [In verse.]   pp. 190.   *Printed for George Sawbridge.*
                                                         E. 1901. (1.)

[July.]—Vox Coeli ; or, Philosophical, Historicall and Theological Obser-vations of Thunder.   By Robert Dingley.   pp. 174.   *Printed by M. S. for Henry Cripps.*   **E. 1868. (1.)**

Aug. 24.—The Holy Longing.   A sermon at the funeral of Jacob Stock. By Thomas Watson.   pp. 55.   *Printed by E. M. for Ralph Smith.*
                                                         E. 1864. (2.)

[Aug.]—Astrological Institutions.   Being a perfect Isagoge to the whole Astral Science.   By a Student in Physick and Astrologie.   [With engravings of the signs of the Zodiack.]   pp. 200.   *Printed by J. C. for Samuel Speed.*   **E. 1825. (2.)**

[Aug.]—A Brief Exposition of the First and Second Epistles General of Peter.   By Alexander Nisbet.   pp. 360.   *Printed for the Company of Stationers.*   **E. 1775. (1.)**

[Aug.]—Culpeper's Semeiotica Uranica : or an Astrological Judgement of Diseases.   By Nicholas Culpeper.   The third edition.   [With an engraved portrait of the author.]   pp. 224.   *Printed for Nath. Brooke.*
                                                         E. 1726. (1.)

[Aug.]—Euclides Metaphysicus, sive De Principiis Sapientiæ, Stoecheidea. E.   Authore Thoma Anglo ex Albiis East-Saxonum [i.e. Thomas White.]   pp. 198.   *Typis J. M., impensis Jo. Martin, Ja. Allestry & Tho. Dicas.*   **E. 1884. (1.)**

[Aug.]—Exercitatio Geometrica de Geometria Indivisibilium & Pro-portione Spiralis ad Circulum.   Authore Thoma Anglo ex Albiis East-Saxonum [i.e. Thomas White.]   **E. 1884. (2.)**

[Aug.]—The Fables of Esop in English.   Whereunto are added the Fables of Avian, also the Fable of Alphonse, with the Fables of Poge the Florentine.   [Illustrated with woodcuts.]   pp. 284.   *Printed by J. Owsley and P. Lillicrap for Abell Roper.*   **E. 1889.**

[Aug.]—The French Gardiner, instructing how to cultivate all sorts of Fruit-Trees and Herbs in Gardens.   First written by R. D. C. D. W. B. D. N. [i.e. Nicolas de Bonnefons], and now transplanted into English by Philocepos [i.e. John Evelyn.   With an engraved frontis-piece.]   pp. 294.   *Printed for John Crooke.*   **E. 1890.**

1658.

[Aug.]—Miscellanea ; sive Meditationes, Orationes, &c. Authore Edmundo Elis. pp. 59. **E. 1891. (1.)**

[Aug.]—The Mysteries of Love & Eloquence ; or, The Arts of Wooing and Complementing. [By Edward Phillips. With an engraved frontispiece representing the " Theater of Courtship " and " Love's Library."] pp. 358. *Printed for N. Brooks.* **E. 1735.**

[Aug.]—Nature's Secrets. Or the admirable and wonderfull history of the generation of Meteors. By Thomas Willsford. [With an engraved portrait of the author.] pp. 199. *Printed for Nath. Brook.* **E. 1775. (2.)**

[Aug.]—Nine Select Sermons. By the late John Hewytt. [With an engraved portrait of the author.] pp. 217. *Printed for Henry Eversden and Tho. Rooks.* **E. 1776. (2.)**

[Aug.]—Repentance and Conversion, the Fabrick of Salvation. Being the last sermons preached by John Hewyt. With other of his sermons. Also an advertisement concerning some sermons lately printed, and pretended to be the Doctors, but are disavowed by Geo. Wild, Jo. Barwick. pp. 230. *Printed by J. C. and are to be sold by Samuel Speed.* **E. 1776. (1.)**

[Aug.]—Of the Right of Churches, and of the Magistrates power over them. By Lewis du Moulin. pp. 394. *Printed by R. D. and are to be sold by Sa. Thomson.* **E. 2115.**

[Sept. 1.]—Animi Medela, seu de beatitudine & miseria. Authore Johanne Stearne. pp. 516. *Typis Gulielmi Bladen.* (1 Sept.) **E. 951.**

[Sept. 1.]—Αὐτοκατάκρισις, or Self-Condemnation, exemplified in Mr. Whitfield, Mr. Barlee, and Mr. Hickman. With occasional reflexions on Mr. Calvin, Mr. Beza, Mr. Zuinglius, Mr. Piscator, Mr. Rivet, and Mr. Rollock : but more especially on Doctor Twisse and Master Hobbs. With an additional advertisement of Mr. Baxter's late book, entituled The Grotian Religion discovered, &c. By Thomas Pierce. pp. 212. *Printed by J. G. for R. Royston.* (1 Sept.) **E. 950. (2.)**

[Sept. 1.]—The Christian's rescue from ·the Grand Error of the Heathen, touching the fatal necessity of all events, and the dismal consequences thereof, which have slily crept into the Church. By Thomas Pierce. pp. 74. *Printed by J. G. for Richard Royston.* (1 Sept.) **E. 949. (1.)**

[Sept. 1.]—The Divine Philanthropie defended against the declamatory attempts of certain late-printed papers [by William Barlee] intitl'd A Correptory Correction. The second edition. By Thomas Pierce. pp. 212. *Printed for Richard Royston.* (1 Sept.) **E. 949. (2.)**

[Sept. 1.]—Ἑαυτοντιμωρούμενος, or the Self-Revenger, exemplified in Mr. William Barlee. By way of rejoynder to the first part of his Reply. By Thomas Pierce. pp. 163. *Printed by R. Daniel for Richard Royston.* (1 Sept.) **E. 950. (1.)**

1658.

[**Sept. 1.**]—A Glass of Justification ; or, the Work of Faith with Power, wherein the Apostles' doctrine touching Justification without the Deeds of the Law is opened. By William Allen. pp. 170. *Printed by G. Dawson for Francis Smith.* (1 Sept.) **E. 948. (7.)**

[**Sept. 2.**]—Exercitationes aliquot Metaphysicæ de Deo. Per Thomam Barlow. Editio secunda. pp. 329. *Excudebat A. Lichfield, impensis Jos. Godwin & Tho. Robinson : Oxoniæ.* (2 Sept.) **E. 952. (1.)**

[**Sept. 2.**]—Quo Warranto ; or a moderate enquiry into the warrant-ableness of the Preaching of Gifted and Unordained persons. Being a vindication of the late Jus Divinum Ministerii Evangelici from the exceptions of Mr. John Martin, Mr. Sam. Petts, Mr. Frederick Woodal, in their late book intituled, The Preacher sent. By Matthew Poole pp. 163. [See above : 30 Jan., E. 1592. (2.) and also below : June 1659, E. 1728. (2.)] *Printed by J. H. for J. Rothwell and S. Thomson.* (2 Sept.) **E. 952. (2.)**

[**Sept. 3.**]—Peplum Olivarii. Or, a Good Prince bewailed by a Good People. Represented in a Sermon upon the death of Oliver, late Lord Protector [3 Sept.]. By George Lawrence. *Printed by E. M. for Samuel Thomson.* **E. 459. (4.)**

Sept. 3.—The Tenth Worthy ; or, several Anagrams in Latine, Welsh and English, upon the name of that most highly renowned Worthy of Worthies, Oliver, late Lord Protector. Together with some elegeical verses upon his death. [By Thomas Davies.] *s. sh.* **669. f. 21. (12.)**

[**Sept. 3.**]—Upon the much lamented Departure of the High and Mighty Prince, Oliver, Lord Protector, &c. A funeral elegie. [Signed : " Jo. Row. C. C. C.," i.e. John Rowland.] *s. sh.* **669. f. 21. (11.)**

[**Sept. 3.**]—Salt upon Salt : made out of certain ingenious verses upon the late Storm and the Death of his Highness ensuing. By Geo. Wither. pp. 65. *Printed for L. Chapman.* **E. 1827. (2.)**

[**Sept. 3.**]—An exact Book of Entries of the most select Judiciall Writs used in the Common Law. Translated from the originall manuscript, which was collected by Robert Moyle. By J. H. Gent. pp. 414. *Printed for Robert Crofts.* (3 Sept.) **E. 757.**

[**Sept. 3.**]—An Exposition continued upon the xx–xxix chapters of the prophet Ezekiel. By William Greenhill. pp. 592. *Printed for Livewell Chapman, and are to be sold by Henry Mortlock.* (3 Sept.) **E. 954.**

[**Sept. 3.**]—The Fast Friend : or, a Friend at Mid-Night. Set forth in an exposition on Luke xi. 5–11. By Nehemiah Rogers. pp. 464. *Printed for Geo. Sawbridge.* (3 Sept.) **E. 953.**

[**Sept. 3.**]—A Treatise of the Power of Godlinesse. By Thomas White. pp. 423. *Printed by R. I. for Joseph Cranford.* (3 Sept.) **E. 1848.**

1658.

[**Sept. 4.**]—[A Proclamation by " the Privy Council, the Lord Mayor, Aldermen and Citizens of London, the Officers of the Army, and numbers of other principal gentlemen," declaring Richard Cromwell Lord Protector.] *s. sh. Printed by Henry Hills for John Field.* (4 Sept.) **669. f. 21. (9.)**

Sept. 4.—By the Protector. A Proclamation signifying His Highness pleasure that all men being in office of Government, at the decease of his most dear Father, Oliver, late Lord Protector, shall so continue till His Highness further direction. *s. sh. Printed by Henry Hills and John Field.* **669. f. 21. (14.)**

Sept. 5.—God's Arraignment of Adam : declared in a sermon preached at St. Paul's before the Lord Major. By Thomas Cartwright. *Printed for John Baker.* **E. 960. (1.)**

Sept. 6.—A Voyce from Heaven, speaking good words concerning Saints departed. A sermon preached at South-Weal in Essex, at the funeral of Thomas Goodwin. By G. B., Preacher of the word at Shenfield in Essex [i.e. George Bownd.] *Printed by S. Griffin for J. Kirton.* **E. 972. (8.)**

[**Sept. 11.**]—The Account Audited and Discounted ; or, a Vindication of the Diatribe against Doctor Hammonds Paradiatribees. By D. C. [i.e. Daniel Cawdrey.] pp. 438. [See above : 8 May, 1655, E. 863. (2.)] *Printed by Ralph Wood for M. Wright.* (11 Sept.) **E. 1850.**

[**Sept. 18.**]—Bestowe one Penny for the Lord's sake. And buy this Paper for the Poor's sake, *etc.* [An exhortation to charity.] *s. sh.* (15 Sept.) **669. f. 21. (10.)**

Sept. 17.—A Letter written by the Prince Elector of Brandenbourgh unto the King of France, declaring the reasons inducing his Electoral Highnes to take up Arms against the King of Sweden. Translated out of the Latine coppies. *Printed by J. C. for John Crooke.* **E. 965. (2.)**

Sept. 24.—By the Protector. A Declaration of His Highness for a day of Publique Fasting and Humiliation. *s. sh. Printed by Henry Hills and John Field.* **669. f. 21. (15.)**

Sept. 25.—By His Highness. A Proclamation for the better encouragement of Godly Ministers and others, and their enjoying their dues and liberty according to law. *s. sh. Printed by Henry Hills and John Field.* **669. f. 21. (13.)**

[**Sept. 25.**]—A Catalogue of the most vendible Books in England, alphabetically digested under heads. [By William London. See also below : 31 May, E. 1025. (17.)] (25 Sept.) **E. 955. (1.)**

[**Sept. 28.**]—The Agreement of the Associated Ministers of the County of Essex, proposed to their particular Congregations. With a word of exhortation to brotherly union. The second edition. pp. 51. *Printed for Edward Brewster.* (28 Sept.) **E. 955. (2.)**

1658.

Sept. 29.—The Watch Charged. A sermon preached at Bridgewater on a day set apart for Ordination. By John Chetwind. pp. 88. *Printed by Roger Daniel and are to be sold by Edward Brewster.* **E. 1862. (1.)**

[**Sept.**]—Additional Annotations, or a collection of all the additions to the third impression of that most excellent work intituled, Annotations upon all the Books of the Old and New Testament. By the labour of certain learned Divines, thereunto appointed by authority of Parliament. pp. 504. *Printed by Evan Tyler.* **E. 1777.**

[**Sept.**]—Confirmation and Restauration the necessary means of Reformation and Reconciliation for the healing of the Divisions of the Churches. By Richard Baxter. pp. 380. *Printed by A. M. for Nevil Simmons, Bookseller in Kederminster, and are to be sold by Joseph Cranford in Pauls Churchyard.* **E. 2111. (1.)**

[**Sept.**]—A Few Sighs from Hell, or, The Groans of a Damned Soul. By John Bunyan. pp. 251. *Printed by Ralph Wood for M. Wright.* **C. 59. a. 2.**

[**Sept.**]—A Further Discovery of the Mystery of Jesuitisme, in a collection of several pieces. [By Pierre Jarrige.] 6 pt. *Printed for R. Royston.* **E. 1842. (1.)**

[**Sept.**]—The History of the Romans, by Lucius Florus. With annotations by M[eric] Casaubon. [With an engraved titlepage.] pp. 455. *Printed by R. B. for Daniel Pakeman.* **E. 1849. (1.)**

[**Sept.**]—Holy Meditations upon God. By Thomas Gery. pp. 108. *Printed by T. C. for Nathanael Webb and William Grantham.* **E. 1892. (2.)**

[**Sept.**]—Ludovici Molinæi Epistola ad Amicum, in qua Gratiam Divinam seque defendit adversus objecta Johannis Dallæi in præfatione Libri in Epicritam. pp. 211. *Excudebat R. Daniel, prostat apud Samuelem Thomson.* **E. 1894. (2.)**

[**Sept.**]—A Perfect Guide for a studious young Lawyer. Being Presidents for Conveyances and other business of the like kind. Collected together out of the labours of the Lord Coke, the Lord Hobart, the Lord Richardson, Justice Haughton, Justice Reve, Justice Bacon, Sir William Denny, Master Godfrey, and Master Jermy. By Thomas Fidell. pp. 277. *Printed by Tho. Roycroft for John Place.* **E. 1726. (2.)**

[**Sept.**]—Φλεβοτομιογραφία, or, A Treatise of Phlebotomy. Written originally in French by Da. de Plumis Campi [i.e. David de Planis Campy]. Rendered into English by E. W., Well-wisher to Physick and Chirurgery. pp. 176. *Printed by John Streater for John Place and William Place.* **E. 1929. (1.)**

[**Sept.**]—Tap's Arithmetick. Second edition, corrected and amplyfied, by P. Ray. pp. 491. *Printed by J. Streater for J. Wright.* **E. 1778.**

1658.

[Oct. 1.]—نظم الجوهر Contextio Gemmarum, sive, Eutychii Patriarchæ Alexandrini Annales. Illustriss. Johanne Seldene chorago. Interprete Edwardo Pocockio. [With an engraved portrait of Selden.] Arab. & Lat. 2 tom. *Impensis Humphredi Robinson: Oxoniæ.* (1 Oct.)

E. 758 and 759.

[Oct. 10.]—Meanes to prevent Perishing. Or, the Usefulnesse of the Saving Knowledge of God. By W. S. a servant of the Lord Jesus. pp. 66. *Printed and are to be sold by Fr. Smith.* (10 Oct.) E. 955. (3.)

[Oct. 12.]—A Declaration of the Faith and Order owned and practised in the Congregational Churches in England. Agreed upon by their Elders and Messengers in their Meeting at the Savoy, 12 Oct. [MS. note by Thomason: "By Philip Nie and his Confederat Crew of Independants."] *Printed for D. L.* E. 968. (4.)

Oct. 12.—A true Relation of a very strange and wonderful thing that was heard in the air, 12 Oct., by many hundreds of people; namely three cannons shot off, a peal of musquets followed, and drums beating all the while. *Printed for L. Chapman.* E. 955. (4.)

[Oct. 20.]—Horometria : or the Compleat Diallist. By Thomas Stirrup. The second edition. [With diagrams.] pp. 181. *Printed by R. & W. Leybourn for Thomas Pierrepont.* (20 Oct.) E. 956. (2.)

[Oct. 20.]—The Sector on a Quadrant ; or, a treatise containing the description and use of three several Quadrants. By John Collins. Also, an Appendix touching Reflective Dyalling [by John Lyon]. With large cuts of each quadrant printed from the plates graved by Henry Sutton. pp. 364. *Printed by J. Macock : to be sold by George Hurlock, William Fisher, and Henry Sutton.* (20 Oct.) E. 956. (1.)

[Oct. 29.]—A Chain of Scripture Chronology ; from the Creation of the World to the Death of Jesus Christ. By Tho. Allen. [Illustrated with scenes from Scripture history.] pp. 240. *Printed by Tho. Roycroft, and sold by Francis Tyton, and Nath. Ekins.* (29 Oct.) E. 957.

[Oct. 29.]—Syon's Redemption, and Original Sin vindicated. Being an answer to a book by Hezekiah Holland. By George Hammon. pp. 200. *Printed by G. Dawson for the Author.* (29 Oct.) E. 958.

[Oct.]—Balzac's Remaines, or his last Letters : written to severall eminent persons in France. [With an engraved portrait of the author.] pp. 432. *Printed for Thomas Dring.* E. 1779.

[Oct.]—Comes Facundus in Via. The Fellow-Traveller. Furnished with short stories and the choicest speeches of wit and mirth for discourse or private entertainment. By Democritus Secundus. pp. 309. *Printed for Hum. Robinson.* E. 1885.

Oct.—Eliah's Abatement ; or, Corruption in the Saints. A sermon preached at the funeral of Gualter Roswell. By Tho. Case. pp. 135. *Printed by E. T. for Luke Fawn.* E. 1882. (1.)

1658.

[Oct.]—The History of Christina Alessandra, Queen of Swedland. By John Burbury. *Printed for T. W.*   **E. 1851.**

Oct.—Hymen's Præludia: or Loves Master-Piece. Being the eighth part of that so much admir'd romance intituled, Cleopatra. Written originally in the French [by Gauthier de Costes, Seigneur de La Calprenède], and now rendred into English by J. W. [i.e. James Webb.] pp. 273. *Printed for Humphrey Moseley.*   **E. 1828. (1.)**

[Oct.]—Joannis Miltoni Pro Populo Anglicano Defensio, contra Salmasii Defensionem Regiam. Editio auctior. pp. 171. [See also below: Dec. 1660, E. 1926. (2.)] *Typis Neucombianis.*   **E. 1900. (1.)**

[Oct.]—Naps upon Parnassus. [Verses, by Samuel Austin.] (Two exact Characters, one of a Temporizer, the other of an Antiquarian.) *Printed for N. Brook.*   **E. 1840. (1.)**

[Oct.]—The Scriptures Stability proved and applied. By Robert Perrot. pp. 199. *Printed by S. G. for John Rothwell and John Hancock.*
                                                            E. 1928. (2.)

[Oct.]—A Sure Guide to the French tongue. By Paul Cogneau. The fourth edition, much amplifi'd. pp. 320. *Printed by S. G. for Joshua Kirton.*   **E. 1828. (2.)**

[Oct.]—A Treatise of Self-Judging, in order to the worthy receiving of the Lords Supper. By Anthony Burgesse. pp. 218. *Printed by J. H. for T. Underhill and M. Keinton.*   **E. 1904. (1.)**

[Nov. 4.]—An Apology for the Discipline of the Ancient Church, in answer to the Admonitory Letter lately published. By William Nicolson. pp. 241. *Printed for William Leake.* (4 Nov.)   **E. 959. (1.)**

[Nov. 13.]—A Probable Expedient for present and future Publique Settlement. By a Well-wishing Phylopater [William Prynne.] (13 Nov.)   **E. 959. (2.)**

[Nov. 16.]—The Faithfull Christian's Gain by Death. Opened in a sermon at the funeral of the Countess of Manchester. By Simeon Ashe. *Printed by A. M. for George Sawbridge.* (16 Nov.)
                                                            E. 959. (3.)

[Nov. 17.]—A Pretended Voice from Heaven, proved to bee the voice of Man, and not of God. Or, an answer to a treatise called, A Voice from Heaven, written by Mr. Gualter Postlethwait, an unordained preacher. Together with a brief answer to the arguments for popular ordination, brought by the Answerers of Jus Divinum Ministerii Evangelici, in their book called, The Preacher Sent. By Ezekiel Charke. pp. 126. [See above: 15 April 1655, E. 1498. (3.), and 30 Jan. 1658, E. 1592. (2.)] *Printed for Andrew Kembe.* (17 Nov.)
                                                            E. 959. (5.)

[Nov. 18.]—Innocents no Saints: or, a Paire of Spectacles for a dark-sighted Quaker. Being a rejoynder to a paper lately published

1658.

intituled, Innocency cleared from Lies. In vindication of Samuel Smith, from the calumnies of those pretended Innocents. By E. D. *Printed for Francis Tyton.* (18 Nov.) **E. 960. (3.)**

[**Nov. 18.**]—A Vindication of the Essence and Unity of the Church-Catholick visible. In answer to the objections made against it by Mr. John Ellis, junior, and by Mr. Hooker in his Survey of Church Discipline. The second edition. By Samuel Hudson. [With a preface by E. Calamy.] pp. 317. *Printed by J. B. and are to be sold by Andrew Kembe, Edward Brewster and Thomas Bassett.* (18 Nov.) **E. 960. (2.)**

Nov. 19.—A Contention for Truth, in two publique disputations at Clement Dane Church, 19 and 26 Nov., between Mr. Gunning and Mr. Denne, concerning the Baptisme of Infants. *Printed by J. Moxon for Francis Smith and John Sweeting.* **E. 963. (1.)**

Nov. 23.—The True Manner of the Conveyance of His Highnesse Effigies from Sommerset House to Westminster, 23 Nov. *Printed for Thomas Vere and William Gilbertson.* **E. 1866. (2.)**

[**Nov. 25.**]—An Antidote against Hen. Haggar's Poysonous Pamphlet, entituled, The Foundation of the Font discovered. By Aylmar Houghton. pp. 334. [See above: 17 Aug. 1653, E. 711. (1.)] *Printed for Tho. Parkhurst.* (25 Nov.) **E. 961.**

[**Nov.**]—Αὐθέντης, or, A Treatise of Self-Deniall. By Theophilus Polwheile. pp. 424. *Printed for Thomas Johnson, and are to be sold by Richard Scott, Bookseller in Carlisle.* **E. 1733.**

[**Nov.**]—The Copy of the Covenant of Grace. By Robert Bidwell. pp. 410. *Printed by E. T. for Thomas Johnson.* **E. 2117.**

[**Nov.**]—Διονυσίου Οἰκουμένης Περιήγησις. Dionysii Orbis Descriptio, commentario critico & geographies, ac tabulis illustrata a Guilielmo Hill. pp. 313. *Excudebat R. Daniel, impensis Humphredi Robinson.* **E. 1780.**

[**Nov.**]—Mount Ebal Levell'd ; or, Redemption from the Curse. By Elkanah Wales. pp. 324. *Printed by R. Trott for T. Johnson.* **E. 1923. (1.)**

[**Nov.**]—Of the Divine Originall, Authority and Power of the Scriptures. With some considerations on the late Biblia Polyglotta. By John Owen. pp. 349. *Printed by Henry Hall for Thomas Robinson : Oxford.* **E. 1866. (1.)**

[**Nov.**]—XVI Sermons preached in the University of Oxford, and at Court. By Rich. Gardiner. pp. 308. *Printed by James Cottrel for Joseph Barber and Samuel Speed.* **E. 1840. (2.)**

[**Nov.**]—Τὸ Πνεῦμα ξωπυροῦν, or, Sparkes of the Spirit, being motives to sacred theorems and divine meditations. [By Athanasius Davies.] Divine meditations. pp. 339. *Printed for Edward Thomas.* **E. 1903.**

1658.

Dec. 2.—The Everlasting Covenant. Delivered in a sermon at St. Paul's before the gentlemen of Nottinghamshire, the day of their yearly fast. By Marmaduke James. *Printed by J. M. for J. Martin.* **E. 955. (2*.)**

[**Dec. 14.**]—Two Books of Mr. Sydrach Simpson, viz., I. Of Unbelief. II. Not going to Christ for Life and Salvation. pp. 255. *Printed by Peter Cole.* (14 Dec.) **E. 962. (1.)**

[**Dec. 15.**]—Two Books of Mr. Sydrach Simpson, viz., I. Of Faith. II. Of Covetousness. pp. 281. *Printed by Peter Cole.* (15 Dec.) **E. 962. (2.)**

Dec. 16.—A Declaration of His Highness for a day of Solemn Fasting and Humiliation. *s. sh. Printed by Henry Hills and John Field.* **669. f. 21. (16.)**

Dec. 17.—An Antidote against Immoderate Mourning for the Dead, being a Funeral Sermon preached at the Burial of Mr. Thomas Bewley, junior. By Sa. Clarke. pp. 55. *Printed by E. M. for George Calvert.* **E. 1015. (5.)**

Dec. 24.—A Letter [dated 24 Dec.] written by the Prince Elector of Brandenborough unto Richard, Lord Protector of the Common-Wealth. Translated out of the Latine copy printed at Hamborough. **E. 972. (7.)**

[**Dec. 29.**]—A True Relation of the most horrid Murders committed by Abigail Hill, of St. Olaves Southwark, on the persons of foure Infants whom she undertooke to nurse. *Printed for F. Coles.* (29 Dec.) **E. 1881. (2.)**

To the following no date, except that of the year, can be assigned.

1658.—The Coming of God in Mercy, in Vengeance ; beginning with fire to convert or consume, at this so sinful City London. By Walter Gostelo. [MS. note at end, signed Ro. Bathurst : " The poor melancholick Author of this booke, after the death of Cromwell, finding that his prophecies in this, but especially his former book, could not now come to pass ; but that he should be counted for a deluded phantastick person, avoyded all company and discourse about any of these matters, which had before so strongly possessed him, and with which he so vehemently endeavoured to possess the world, and shortly after, for shame & griefe dyed at Prestcot (as I think) in Cropredy parish near Banbury. He had been milliner to K. Charles I. & would talk soberly and rationally of any other matter but this."] *Printed for the Author.* **E. 1612. (3.)**

1658.—Διονυσίου Οἰκουμένης Περιήγησις. [In Greek and Latin.] Grammaticarum in Dionysii Περιήγησιν Annotationum Systema. [With eight engraved maps.] pp. 83. *Excudebat Tho. Newcomb.* **E. 1761. (1.)**

1658.
1658.—An English-Greek Grammar. By J. C., Gent. pp. 62.
E. 1720. (2.)
1658.—An Epitome of Stenographie. By Job Everardt. [With an allegorical engraved frontispiece.] pp. 90. *Printed by M. S. for Lodo-wick Lloyd.* E. 1845. (1.)
1658.—Homerus Ἑβραΐζων, sive, Comparatio Homeri cum Scriptoribus Sacris. Autore Zach. Bogan. pp. 439. *Excudebat H. Hall, impensis T. Robinson: Oxoniæ.* E. 1767.
[1658.]—A Postscript concerning Sacrilege. [A fragment: being pp. 119–134 of a larger work.] E. 945. (5*.)
1658.—Pro Sacris Scripturis adversus hujus temporis Fanaticos Exerci-tationes Apologeticæ quatuor. [By John Owen.] pp. 118. *Excudebat A. Lichfield, impensis T. Robinson: Oxonii.* E. 1866. (1.*)
1658.—Some things relating to the thirtie Tyrants of Athens togeather with their names: with the adition of the names of some of the cheife Traytors & Tyrants of England. [Extracts from Raleigh's History of the World; together with a list of the " regicides," and the following note:—" Which, with these aditions of mine, I was very desirous to have published, but noe printer then durst venture upon it. Anno 1658 Geo: Thomason." In MS. throughout, in Thomason's hand.]
E. 945. (6.)

1659.

[Jan. 1.]—The Bloody Almanack, or, Astrological Predictions and Monethly Observations for the Year, 1659. *Printed for John Reynor.* (1 Jan.) E. 993. (19.)
Jan. 2.—The Servant doing and the Lord Blessing. A sermon preached at the funeral of Richard Pepys, Lord Chief Justice in Ireland, who deceased 2 Jan. By Edward Worth. *Printed by William Bladen: Dublin.* E. 974. (3.)
[Jan. 4.]—The Saints Gods Precious Treasure. A sermon at the funeral of Darcy Wyvil. By Thomas Case. pp. 80. *Printed for Robert Gibs.* (4 Jan.) E. 1904. (2.)
[Jan. 6.]—Four Books on the Eleventh of Matthew. By Jeremiah Burroughs. pp. 1646. *Printed by Peter Cole.* (6 Jan.)
E. 963. (2.), E. 964, E. 965. (1.)
[Jan. 12.]—A Practicall Discourse concerning Gods Decrees. By Edward Bagshawe. *Printed by Hen. Hall for Tho. Robinson: Oxford.* (12 Jan.)
E. 965. (3.)
Jan. 27.—The Speech of the Lord Protector made to both Houses of Parliament at their first meeting, 27 Jan.; also the Speech of Nathaniel Lord Fiennes made at the same time. *Printed by Henry Hills and John Field.* E. 968. (1 and 2.)

1659.

[**Jan. 28.**]—A Brief Relation containing an Abreviation of the Arguments urged by the late Protector against the Government of this Nation by a King. [See also below : 24 Feb., E. 968. (7.)] (28 Jan.)

E. 965. (4.)

[**Jan.**]—The Arraignment of Ignorance. As also the excellency, profit and benefit of Heavenly Knowledge. By W. G., Minister of the Word at Lymington. pp. 198. *Printed for Luke Fawn.*   E. 1760. (1.)

[**Jan.**]—J. A. Commeni Orbis Sensualium Pictus. Commenius's Visible World ; or, A picture of all the chief things that are in the world. Translated into English by Charles Hoole. [With an engraved portrait of the author and numerous illustrative engravings.] pp. 309. *Printed for J. Kirton.*   E. 2116. (1.)

[**Jan.**]—The Hidden Treasures of the Art of Physick. By John Tanner. pp. 543. *Printed for George Sawbridge.*   E. 1847.

[**Jan.**]—Five new Playes, viz. The English Moor, or The Mock-Marriage ; The Love-sick Court, or The Ambitious Politique ; Covent Garden Weeded ; The New Academy, or The New Exchange ; The Queen and Concubine. By Richard Brome. 5 pt. *Printed for A. Crook.*

E. 1782.

[**Feb. 1.**]—Expositions and Sermons upon the ten first chapters of Matthew. By Christopher Blackwood. pp. 901. *Printed by Henry Hills for Francis Tyton and John Field.* (1 Feb.)   E. 966.

Feb. 1.—Imitation and Caution for Christian Women ; or, The life and death of Mrs. Mary Bewley, who departed this life 1 Feb. *Printed by E. M. for George Calvert.*   E. 968. (10.)

[**Feb. 1.**]—A Key for Catholics, to satisfie all whether the cause of the Roman or Reformed Churches be of God. By Richard Baxter. pp. 460. [See also below : Sept., E. 1841. (2.)] *Printed by R. W. for Nevill Simmons, Bookseller in Kederminster, and Thomas Johnson in St. Pauls Churchyard.* (1 Feb.)   E. 967.

[**Feb. 8.**]—A Declaration to the People, concerning the great and present Expedition. With the gallant Resolutions of the Parliament. With the Order and Instructions of His Highness thereupon, in order to the restoring and preservation of Free-Trade and Commerce. As also a list of the English Fleet designed for the Sound. *s. sh. Printed for G. E. Horton.* (8 Feb.)   669. f. 21. (17.)

Feb. 11.—The Unhappy Marksman ; or, A Perfect and Impartial Discovery of that late murther committed by George Strangwayes on his brother-in-law John Fussel, 11 Feb. *Printed by T. N. for R. Clavell.*

E. 972. (10.)

[**Feb. 12.**]—The Petition and Narrative of George Wither. (12 Feb.)

E. 761. (12.)

1659.

Feb. 13.—Ψυχησημία, or, The greatest Loss. A discourse occasioned by the loss of Humphery Chetham, who died 13 Feb. By James Livesey. pp. 199. *Printed by J. B. for Thomas Parkhurst.* **E. 1738. (1.)**

Feb. 15.—The Petition of many thousand Citizens of London to the Parliament [respecting their rights and liberties]. Together with the Parliaments Answer. *Printed for Livewell Chapman.* **E. 968. (6.)**

[Feb. 15.]—To Parliament. The Petition of the Marchants trading to the Dominion of the King of Spain. [Praying " that during the War with Spain all wines and fruits of the growth of any of the King of Spains dominions may be prohibited to be imported."] *s. sh. Printed by Joseph Moxon.* (Feb. 15.) **669. f. 21. (18.)**

[Feb. 16.]—The Leveller ; or, The Principles & Maxims concerning Government and Religion which are asserted by those that are commonly called Levellers. *Printed for Thomas Brewster.* (16 Feb.)
E. 968. (3.)

[Feb. 16.]—XXV Queries modestly and humbly propounded to the People of England. *Printed for L. Chapman.* (16 Feb.)
E. 968. (5.)

Feb. 23.—A Reply to the Danish Papers presented to Parliament 23 Feb., concerning the question whether England should not assist the Swede as well as the Dutch do the Dane. **E. 972. (2.)**

[Feb. 23.]—Nuncius Astrologus. Demonstrating the success that may be expected from the present Controversie between the two Northern Kings, deduced from the Nativity of His Majesty of Denmark. By John Gadbury. [With an engraved portrait of the author, and another of Frederick III., King of Denmark.] pp. 53. *Printed by J. Cottrel for F. Cossinet.* (23 Feb.) **E. 2112. (4.)**

[Feb. 24.]—A Moderate Answer to certain Immoderate Quæries laid down in a paper entituled, A Brief Relation, containing an Abreviation of the Arguments urged by the late Protector against the Government of this Nation by a King. By Charles Noble. [See above : 28 Jan., E. 965. (4.)] *Printed for Henry Marsh.* (24 Feb.) **E. 968. (7.)**

[Feb. 24.]—The Dutch Tutor ; or, A New Book of Dutch and English. pp. 79. *Printed for William Fisher.* (24 Feb.) **E. 2116. (2.)**

[Feb. 26.]—An Expedient for the Preventing any Difference between His Highness and the Parliament. *Printed for Giles Calvert.* (26 Feb.)
E. 968. (9.)

[Feb. 26.]—A Call to the Officers of the Army. *Printed for Livewell Chapman.* (26 Feb.) **E. 968. (8.)**

[Feb.]—Advice to a Daughter [by John Heydon], in opposition to the Advice to a Son [by Francis Osborne]. Second edition. With a word of advice to T. P. [i.e. Thomas Pecke]. pp. 186. *Printed by T. J. for F. Cossinet.* **E. 1882. (2.)**

1659.

[Feb.]—Anatomy Lectures at Gresham Colledge. By Dr. Thomas Winston. pp. 256. *Printed by R. Daniel for Thomas Eglesfield.*

E. 1746. (2.)

[Feb.]—'Επιδιόρθωσις, or, A modest Enquiry into the Nature and State of Churches, in order to their Through-Reformation. By Thomas Boyer. pp. 75. *Printed by R. W. for Nathaniel Ekins.* E. 1929. (2.)

[Feb.]—The Gospels Glory, without prejudice to the Law. By Richard Byfield. pp. 378. *Printed by E. M. for Adoniram Byfield.*

E. 1864. (1.)

[Feb.]—A Miscellany of sundry Essayes, Paradoxes, etc. By Francis Osborn. pp. 260. *Printed by John Grismond.* E. 1900. (2.)

[Feb.]—The Resurrection rescued from the Souldiers Calumnies. Two sermons, by Robert Jones. pp. 100. *Printed for Richard Lownds.*

E. 1902. (1.)

[Feb.]—The School-Masters Auxiliaries, to remove the Barbarians Siege from Athens ; advanced under two guides. The first, leading by rule and reason to read and write English dexterously. The second, asserting the Latine tongue in prose and verse. By R. L. [i.e. Richard Lloyd.] 3 pts. *Printed by T. R.* E. 1830. (1.)

[Feb.]—Ζωολογία : or the History of Animals, as they are useful in Physick and Chirurgery. Divided into four parts. By John Schroder. [Translated by T. B., i.e. T. Bateson.] pp. 159. *Printed by E. Cotes for R. Royston.* E. 1759. (1.)

[Feb.]—Rhan o waith Mr. Rees Prichard. Some part of the Works of Mr. Rees Prichard. [In verse.] pp. 157. *Printiedig yn Llundain, ag a werthir gan Thomas Brewster.* E. 1829. (2.)

[March 2.]—America Painted to the Life. The True History of the Spaniards Proceedings, as also of the advancement of Plantations into those parts. By Ferdinando Gorges. [With an engraved frontispiece representing a female figure symbolical of America, and an engraved map.] 4 pt. *Printed for Nathaniel Brook.* (2 March.) E. 969.

[March 2.]—The Cause of God and of these Nations sought out and lifted up into sight. [A tract against Monarchy.] (2 March.)

E. 968. (11.)

[March 2.]—Five Disputations of Church-Government and Worship. By Richard Baxter. pp. 492. *Printed by R. W., for Nevill Simmons, Bookseller in Kederminster, and Thomas Johnson in Pauls Churchyard.* (2 March.) E. 970.

[March 2.]—Influences of the Life of Grace ; or, A Practical Treatise concerning the means of improving Spiritual Dispositions. By Samuel Rutherfurd. pp. 438. *Printed by T. C. for Andrew Crook, and James Davies.* (2 March.) E. 971.

1659.

March 2.—Two Sermons preached at Christ-Church in the City of Dublin, before the General Convention of Ireland ; the first at the first meeting of the said Convention, 2 March, the second at a publique fast appointed by the said Convention, 9 March. By Sem Coxe. *Printed by William Bladen: Dublin.*   **E. 1026. (2.)**

[**March 2.**]—A Spiritual Journey of a Young Man towards the Land of Peace. Translated out of Dutch. pp. 206. *Printed by J. Macock.* (2 March.)   **E. 972. (1.)**

[**March 3.**]—The sad Suffering Case of Major-General Rob. Overton, prisoner in the Isle of Jersey. By J. R.   *Printed for L. Chapman.* (3 March.)   **E. 972. (4.)**

[**March 3.**]—The Plain Case of the Common-Weal neer the Desperate Gulf of the Common-Woe. *Printed for Livewell Chapman.* (3 March.)
                    E. 972. (5.)

[**March 3.**]—An Oration of Agrippa to Octavius Cæsar Augustus against Monarchy, taken out of the LII Book of Dion the Philosopher. Put into English by A. R. *Printed for Livewell Chapman.* (3 March.)
                    E. 972. (3.)

[**March 4.**]—The Way to the Peace and Settlement of these Nations. By Peter Cornelius Van Zurick-Zee [i.e. Peter Corneliszoon Plockhoy.] *Printed for Deniel White.* (4 March.)   **E. 972. (6.)**

[**March 12.**]—The Ancient Land-Mark, Skreen or Bank betwixt the Prince or Supreame Magistrate and the People of England, by the Right of Inheritance which the Nobility & Baronage have to sit in the House of Peers. *Printed by T. W. for Daniel White.* (12 March.)
                    E. 972. (9.)

[**March 20.**]—The Sinfulnesse of Evil Thoughts. A discourse. By Jo. Sheffield. pp. 312. *Printed by J. H. for Samuel Gellibrand.* (20 March.)   **E. 1863. (1.)**

[**March 21.**]—The Figg-less Figg-Tree; or, The Doome of a Barren and Unfruitful Profession lay'd open in an Exposition upon that Parable. By Nehemiah Rogers. pp. 502. *Printed by J. S. for George Sawbridge.* (21 March.)   **E. 973.**

[**March 26.**]—Forraign and Domestick Prophecies, both Antient and Modern. In Welsh and English. pp. 183. *Printed by Lodowick Lloyd.* (26 March.)   **E. 974. (1.)**

[**March 27.**]—Beheaded Dr. John Hewytts Ghost pleading for exemplarie justice against the arbitrarie injustice of his Judges. [By William Prynne.] (27 March.)   **E. 974. (2.)**

[**March 27.**]—The Whole Body of Christian Religion. By Hieron. Zanchius. pp. 404. *Printed by John Redmayne.* (27 March.)
                    E. 1897.

II.   Q

1659.

[**March 28.**]—Christ and the Church ; or, Parallels, in three books By Henry Vertue. pp. 430. *Printed by Tho. Roycroft.* (28 March.)

E. 975.

[**March 31.**]—Diatribæ de Æterno Divini Beneplaciti circa Creaturas Intellectuales Decreto pars prima. Authore Thoma Aylesbury. pp. 473. *Excudebat Joannes Field : Cantabrigiæ.* (31 March.)   **E. 976.**

March.—A Seasonable Speech made by a Member of Parliament in the House of Commons concerning the Other House.   **E. 974. (6.)**

[**April 6.**]—Tythes Vindicated from Anti-Christianisme and Oppression. Wherein is proved that paying and receiving of Tythes doe not deny Christ to be come in the flesh, as the Kentish Petitioners to the Parliament, anno 1651, and with them now the Quakers, doe affirm. By G[iles] Firmin. *Printed for Nath. Webb and William Grantham.* (6 April.)   **E. 974. (4.)**

April 7.—The Good Angel of Stamford, or an Extraordinary Case of an Extraordinary Consumption, in a True and Faithful Narrative of Samuel Wallas, recovered by the Power of God and Prescription of an Angel, 7 April.   **E. 999. (4.)**

[**April 8.**]—To His Excellency the Lord Fleetwood and the General Council of Officers of the Armies of England, Scotland and Ireland. The Humble Address of the Inferiour Officers and Souldiers of the late Lord Pride's Regiment. [An address of loyalty to the Commonwealth and opposition to the Royalist cause.] *Printed by T. Lock.* (8 April.)   **E. 974. (5.)**

April 11.—Mary Magdalens Love to Christ, opened in a sermon preached at the Funeral of Mistris Elizabeth Thomason. By Edw. Reynolds. pp. 68. [With MS. Elegies appended.]   **E. 1820.**

[**April 12.**]—Of the Becoming Man, or of the Incarnation of Jesus Christ. Of Christ's Suffering, Death and Resurrection. Of the Tree of Christian Faith. By Jacob Boehme. [Translated by John Sparrow.] pp. 239. *Printed by J. M. for Lodowick Lloyd.* (12 April.)   **E. 977. (1.)**

April 13.—The Things of Peace : or, some means thereof and motives thereto. Propounded in a sermon preached before the Associated Ministers of the County of Somerset, at their general meeting at Wells. By Richard Warre. pp. 86. *Printed by D. Maxwell for Edward Brewster.*   **E. 1023. (17.)**

[**April 13.**]—A Sermon prepared to be preached at the funerall of Walter Norbane, Esq. (13 April). By W. Haywood. *Printed for Richard Thrale.*   **E. 1027. (16.)**

[**April 14.**]—To Parliament. The Petition of the Workmen-Printers, Freemen of the City of London. [Protesting against the monopoly for printing Bibles, at present possessed by Henry Hills and John Field.] *s. sh.* (14 April.)   **669. f. 21. (19.)**

1659.

[April 14.]—Englands Slavery, or Barbados Merchandize, represented in a Petition to Parliament by Marcellus Rivers and Oxenbridge Foyle, on behalf of themselves and three-score and ten more Free-born Englishmen sold uncondemned into slavery. (14 April.) **E. 1833. (3.)**

April 17.—A Sermon preached at St. Pauls Church. By Nath. Ingelo. pp. 144. *Printed for L. Fawn.* **E. 1787. (2.)**

[April 20.]—A Second Narrative of the Late Parliament. pp. 55. *Printed in the Fifth Year of Englands Slavery under its New Monarchy.* (20 April.) **E. 977. (3.)**

April 20.—An Invocation to the Officers of the Army for preventing their owne and the ruine of the Good Old Cause. In a Letter presented to them 20 April. **E. 979. (1.)**

[April 21.]—To His Highnes Richard, Lord Protector. The Humble Representation of the Field-Officers and Captains of the Trained-Bands of the City of London. [Declaring their loyalty to the cause of the Common-Wealth.] (21 April.) **E. 977. (4.)**

[April 22.]—By the Lord Protector. A Proclamation about dissolving Parliament. *s. sh. Printed by Henry Hills and John Field.*
669. f. 21. (20.)

[April 23.]—By the Lord Protector. A Proclamation commanding all Papists, and all other Persons who have been of the late King's party or his Son's, to depart out of the Cities of London and Westminster, and late lines of Communication, within three days. *s. sh. Printed by Henry Hills and John Field.* **669. f. 21. (22.)**

[April 23.]—By the Lord Protector. A Proclamation commanding all Papists, and all other persons who have been of the late King's party, or his Son's, to repair unto their places of abode, and not to remove above five miles from the same. *s. sh. Printed by Henry Hills and John Field.* **669. f. 21. (21.)**

[April 23.]—A Declaration of the present Sufferings of above 140 Quakers, who are now in Prison. *Printed for Thomas Simmons.* (23 April.) **E. 977. (7.)**

[April 24.]—Irenicum; or, An Essay towards a Brotherly Peace & Union between those of the Congregational and Presbyterian Way. By Discipulus De Tempore Junior. [The preface signed: D. T.] pp. 75. *Printed for Nathanael Webb and William Grantham.* (24 April.)
E. 978. (1.)

[April 25.]—The Abuse of Gods Grace. By Nicholas Claget. pp. 284. *Printed by A. Lichfield for Thomas Robinson and Samuel Pocock: Oxford.* (25 April.) **E. 978. (2.)**

April 25.—To the Rt. Hon. the Ld Fleetwood, to be communicated to the Officers of the Army, the Humble Representation of divers well-affected Persons of the City of Westminster. [In support of the

1659.

Good   Old   Cause.   Presented   25   April.]   *Printed   for   Livewell Chapman.*   **E. 979. (5.)**

April 26.—The Humble Remonstrance of the Non-Commission Officers and Private Soldiers of Major General Goffs Regiment present to Lord Fleetwood and the General Council of Officers at Wallingford House. [Professing loyalty to the Good Old Cause.]   **E. 979. (6.)**

April 26.—A true Copie of a Paper delivered to Lt. G. Fleetwood, to be communicated to the General Council of Officers ; from a People who through Grace have been hitherto kept from the great Apostacie of this day [i.e. the Quakers]. Wherein the Good Old Cause is stated, according to the Armies own declarations. Delivered 26 April. *Printed for Livewell Chapman.*   **E. 979. (4.)**

[April 26.]—A Plain Word of Truth to all the Officers and Souldiers of the Army. [Warning them of the reviving strength of the Royalist party.]   *s. sh.*   (26 April.)   **669. f. 21. (23.)**

[April 26.]—To His Excellencie the Lord Charls Fleetwood, and the rest of the Officers of the Army. From several thousands of faithful friends to the Good Old Cause in and about London. [Complaining of their neglect of their duty to the Country and the Cause.]   *s. sh. Printed by J. C. for Livewel Chapman.* (26 April.)   **669. f. 21. (24.)**

April 26.—De memoria sapientum peritura. Concio latine habita ad theologos Londinenses in solenni & anniversario eorum conventu, 26 Apr. Authore Guil. Jenkyn. *Excudebat R. White, impensis Sa. Gellibrand.*   **E. 985. (28.)**

April 27.—To the Officers and Souldiers of the Armies of England, Scotland and Ireland. The Petition and Advice of divers well-affected to the Good Old Cause, inhabitants in and about the borough of Southwark.   **E. 980. (1.)**

[April 27.]—A Faithful Memorial of that remarkable Meeting of many Officers of the Army in England at Windsor Castle. As also a discovery of the goodness of God in answering their suit. By William Allen. *Printed for Livewel Chapman.* (27 April.)   **E. 979. (3.)**

[April 27.]—An Account from Paris of the Articles of Peace concluded betwixt the two Crownes France and Spaine.   *s. sh.*   (27 April.)
                                                          669. f. 21. (25.)

[April 28.]—Twelve plain Proposals offered to the Honest and Faithful Officers and Souldiers of our English Army. [Urging them to stand to or fall with the Good Old Cause, for otherwise "nothing can keep off Kingship."]   *s. sh.   Printed by J. C. for Livewel Chapman.* (28 April.)
                                                          669. f. 21. (26.)

[April 28.]—Some Reasons humbly proposed to the Officers of the Army for the speedy Re-admission of the Long Parliament. *Printed for L. Chapman.* (28 April.)   **E. 979. (8.)**

1659.

[**April 28.**]—The Compleat Husband-man; or, A discourse of the whole Art of Husbandry. By Samuel Hartlib. pp. 141. *Printed and are to be sold by Edward Brewster.* (28 April.) **E. 979. (10.)**

[**April 29.**]—קְבוּ צְדָק יְהוָה or, The Plain Doctrine of the Justification of a Sinner in the sight of God. By Charles Chauncy. pp. 306. *Printed by R. I., for Adoniram Byfield.* (29 April.) **E. 979. (11.)**

[**April 30.**]—Huc Ades, Hæc Animo ; or, A Serious and perhaps Seasonable Advice to the Souldier of the Three Nations. By T. L., Esq. [Urging loyalty to the Commonwealth.] (30 April.) **E. 980. (3.)**

[**April.**]—Animadversiones in libros Novi Testamenti. Authore Nortono Knatchbull. pp. 331. *Typis Guil. Godbid.* **E. 1731. (1.)**

[**April.**]—Certamen Epistolare, or the Letter-Combate. Managed by Peter Heylyn with 1. Mr. Baxter. 2. Dr. Barnard. 3. Mr. Hickman, and 4. J. H., of the City of Westminster, Esq. With 5. An appendix to the same, in answer to some passages in Mr. Fuller's late Appeal. pp. 397. *Printed by J. M. for H. Twyford, T. Dring and J. Place.* **E. 1722.**

[**April.**]—The History of the Life and Death of his most Serene Highness, Oliver, late Lord Protector. By S. Carrington. pp. 272. *Printed for Nath. Brook.* **E. 1787. (1.)**

[**April.**]—Historie & Policie re-viewed, in the heroick transactions of Oliver, late Lord Protector, from his cradle to his tomb : declaring his steps to princely perfection, as they are drawn in lively parallels to the ascents of the great Patriarch Moses, in thirty degrees, to the height of honour. By H. D., Esq. [i.e. H. Dawbeny.] pp. 306. *Printed for Nathaniel Brook.* **E. 1799. (2.)**

[**April.**]—The History of the English & Scotch Presbytery, wherein is discovered their Designes and Practices for the Subversion of Government in Church and State. Written in French by an eminent Divine of the Reformed Church [Isaac Basire?] and now Englished [by Matthew Playford]. pp. 324. *Printed in Villa Franca* [i.e. London.] **E. 1785.**

[**April.**]—The Holy Life of Philip Nerius, Founder of the Congregation of the Oratory. [Translated from the Latin of Antonio Gallonio, by Jacobus Baccius.] To which is annexed a relation written by S. Augustine of the Miracles in his dayes, and a relation of sundry Miracles wrought at the Monastery of Port-Royall, in Paris, A.D. 1656. Translated out of a French copie published at Paris, 1656. pp. 427. *At Paris.* **E. 1727.**

[**April.**]—Lovedays Letters, Domestick and Forrein, to several persons, occasionally distributed in Subjects Philosophicall, Historicall & Morall. By R. Loveday. pp. 280. *Printed by J. G. for Nath. Brook.* **E. 1784. (1.)**

[**April.**]—Speculum Patrum : A Looking-Glasse of the Fathers, wherein you may see each of them drawn, characterized and displayed in

1659.

their colours. By Edward Larkin. pp. 322. *Printed for Henry Eversden.* **E. 1786.**

[April.]—Θανατολογία, seu de Morte dissertatio. Authore Johanne Stearne. pp. 288. *Typis Gulielmi Bladen, Dublinii, et prostat venalis apud Georgium Sawbridg, Londini.* **E. 1862. (2.)**

[May 1.]—De Monarchia Absoluta dissertatio politica. [By Edward Bagshaw the elder.] *Excudebat Hen. Hall, impensis Tho. Robinson: Oxoniæ.* (1 May.) **E. 980. (4.)**

[May 2.]—A Declaration of the Well-affected to the Good Old Cause, for the return and session of the Long Parliament interrupted by the late Protector. Directed to the surviving Members of that Parliament. *s. sh. Printed by J. C.* (2 May.) **669. f. 21. (27.)**

[May 2.]—A Declaration of the Faithful Soldiers of the Army to all the honest People of the Nation, shewing their resolution to stand by the Good Old Cause. (2 May.) **E. 980. (7.)**

[May 2.]—The Armies Dutie; or, Faithfull Advice to the Souldiers. Two Letters written unto Lord Fleetwood. (2 May.) **E. 980. (12.)**

[May 2.]—The Humble Desires of a Free Subject and true Lover of the Liberties of the Three Nations, to unite them in Love and Amity. *Printed for Fr. Coles.* (2 May.) **E. 980. (8.)**

[May 2.]—The Honest Design: or, The true Commonwealth-Man. Offering a word in order to a Settlement. *Printed for L. Chapman.* (2 May.) **E. 980. (11.)**

[May 2.]—The Nativity of Carolus Gustavus, King of Sweden, astrologically handled. Published, for the better information of William Lilly, by Merlinus Verax. (2 May.) **E. 980. (13.)**

[May 2.]—A Beam of Light, shining in the midst of much Darkness and Confusion; being an essay towards the stating the Best Cause under Heaven, viz. the Cause of God. By Chr. Feake. pp. 59. *Printed by J. C. for Livewell Chapman.* (2 May.) **E. 980. (5.)**

[May 2.]—Pour enclouer le Canon. [A treatise, by James Harrington, on behalf of government by Commonwealth.] *Printed for Henry Fletcher.* (2 May.) **E. 980. (6.)**

[May 3.]—A List of the Names of the Long Parliament, of 1640. Likewise of the Parliament Holden at Oxford. As also of the Parliaments holden at Westminster, 1653, 1654, 1656, and of the late Parliament dissolved 22 April. With a catalogue of the Lords. pp. 70. (3 May.) **E. 1836. (4.)**

[May 3.]—Five Proposals presented to the General Council of the Officers of the Armies of England Scotland and Ireland. [In support of the Good Old Cause, and urging that " the Old Parliament may have the door opened unto them."] *s. sh. Printed by J. C. for L. Chapman.* (3 May.) **669. f. 21. (28.)**

1659.

[May 3.]—Certain Queries upon the Dissolving of the late Parliament, likewise upon the present proceedings of the Army. (3 May.)
E. 980. (14.)

[May 4.]—A Perambulatory Word to Court, Camp, City and Country ; or, An Arrow, shot at randome. [In defence of the Good Old Cause.] *Printed by J. C. for Livewell Chapman.* (4 May.) **E. 980. (15.)**

[May 4.]—A faithful Remembrance and Advice to the General Council of Officers from divers in Cornwal and Devon. [Urging allegiance to the Good Old Cause.] *Printed for Livewell Chapman.* (4 May.)
E. 980. (16.)

[May 4.]—On the most noble James, Earl of Annandale. [An epitaph, in verse ; signed : T. S.] *s. sh.* (4 May.) **669. f. 21. (29.)**

[May 5.]—A Declaration of the Faithfull Souldiers of the Army, shewing their resolution to stand by the Good Old Cause. (5 May.) **E. 980. (18.)**

[May 5.]—A Catechisme containing the Chief Heads of Christian Religion. By John Davenport and William Hooke. pp. 54. *Printed by John Brudenell for John Allen.* (5 May.) **E. 1920. (1.)**

[May 5.]—Chymia Cœlestis. Drops from Heaven ; or, Pious Meditations and Prayers. By Ben. Parry. pp. 121. *Printed for Humphrey Moseley.* (5 May.) **E. 1883. (1.)**

[May 5.]—A Seasonable Word ; or, certain Reasons against a Single Person. Tender'd to the consideration of the Lord Fleetwood and the Officers and Souldiers of the Army. Proving the sinfulnesse of that Accursed Thing. *Printed by J. C. for Livewell Chapman.* (5 May.)
E. 980. (17.)

May 6.—A Declaration of the Officers of the Army, inviting the Members of the Long Parliament to return to the Exercise and Discharge of their Trust. *Printed by Henry Hills, for him and William Mountfort.* **E. 980. (20.)**

May 7.—A Declaration of Parliament. 7 May. [Describing the proceedings which lead to the return of the members of the Long Parliament, and asserting their determination to stand by the Good Old Cause.] *s. sh. Printed by John Field.* **669. f. 21. (30.)**

May 7.—A True and Perfect Narrative of what was done between Mr. Prynne, the Secluded Members, the Army Officers, and those now sitting both in the Commons and elsewhere, 7 and 9 May. By William Prynne. pp. 99. **E. 767. (1.)**

May 9.—By the Lord Lieutenant of Ireland, Henry Cromwell. [A Proclamation commanding all civil and military officers to check promptly all signs of disaffection to the Government.] *s. sh. Printed at Dublin by William Bladen, and reprinted at London.* **669. f. 21. (38.)**

May 10.—[A Resolution of Parliament, calling in all arrears of Duties for Customs, Excise, etc.] *s. sh. Printed by John Field.* **669. f. 21. (31.)**

1659.

[**May 10.**]—A Seasonable Word to the Parliament-Men. Likewise a watchword, how they prefer not again such persons to places of trust who have lately betrayed the Priviledges of Parliaments, and the just Rights of the People, into the hands of a single person By John Canne. *Printed by J. C. for L. Chapman.* (10 May.) **E. 983. (1.)**

May 11.—An Act for enabling and authorising certain persons to be Justices of the Peace and Sheriffs. *Printed by John Field.*

E. 1074. (1.)

May 12.—The Petition and Addresse of the Officers of the Army to the Parliament of the Common-wealth. [Praying for the maintenance of the government as established by Cromwell.] *Printed by Henry Hills for him and Francis Tyton.* **E. 983. (7.)**

[**May 12.**]—Twelve Queries humbly proposed to the consideration of the Parliament & Army, for the better security of, and advantage to the present Government. By divers well-affected persons. [An attack upon certain public officials. The names are supplied in MS. by Thomason.] (12 May.) **E. 933. (3.)**

[**May 12.**]—The Censures of the Church Revived. In the defence of a Paper published by the first Classis within the Province of Lancaster, since printed under the title Excommunicatio Excommunicata, or a Censure of the Presbyterian Censures in the Classis at Manchester. pp. 353. *Printed for George Eversden.* (12 May.) **E. 980. (22.)**

May 13.—The Petition of divers Inhabitants of the County of Hertford, who have faithfully adhered to the Good Old Cause. Presented to Parliament May 13. Together with the Parliament's answer thereunto, [Praying for the restoration of "such faithfull officers in the Armie and Nation that have been illegally displaced, or forced by their consciences to quit their employments."] *s. sh. Printed for Tho. Brewster.*

669. f. 21. (32.)

[**May 13.**]—The Re-publicans and others spurious Good Old Cause, briefly and truly anatomized. By William Prynne. (13 May.)

E. 983. (6.)

[**May 13.**]—The true Good Old Cause rightly stated, and the false uncased. [MS. note by Thomason: "I believe by Mr. Prin." See also below: 16 May, E. 983. (11.)] (13 May.) **E. 983. (6*.)**

May 13.—The true and 'exact Particulars of the Articles of Peace & Mariage agreed, confirmed and published at the heads of both the Armies of the two great Monarchs of Europe, his most Catholick Majesty of Spain, and the most Christian King of France. (13 May.)

E. 984. (4.)

[**May 13.**]—A Body of Divinity : or Institutions of Christian Religion ; framed out of the word of God and the writings of the best Divines.

1659.

Written in Latine by William Bucanus. Translated into English by Robert Hill. pp. 858. *Printed for Daniel Pakeman, Abel Roper and Richard Tomlins.* (13 May.) **E. 982.**

[May 13.]—The First General Epistle of St. John the Apostle unfolded & applied. The second part, in thirty and seven lectures on the second chapter from the third to the last verse. By Nath: Hardy. pp. 755. *Printed for Joseph Cranford.* (13 May.) **E. 981.**

May 14.—[An Act of Parliament "that this present Easter Term be continued to all intents and" purposes, as if Judges authorized by Act of Parliament sate in Court.] *s. sh. Printed by John Field.*
669. f. 21. (31*.)

[May 14.]—A Short Catechism about Baptism. By John Tombes. *Printed by Henry Hills.* (14 May.) **E. 1854. (1.)**

[May 14.]—Several Cases of Conscience concerning Astrologie, answered. By a Friend to the Truth. [Signed : J. A.] *Printed for John Allen.* (14 May.) **E. 1856. (1.)**

May 16.—The Out-cry and just Appeale of the inslaved people of England, made to the Parliament for the Common-wealth of England. Presented by J. Freeze. **E. 983. (17.)**

[May 16.]—The Continuation of this Session of Parliament justified, and the action of the Army touching that affair defended : and objections to both answered. By J. S. (16 May.) **E. 983. (10.)**

[May 16.]—The Common-wealth of Israel, or a brief account of Mr. Prynne's Anatomy of the Good Old Cause. By H. S. [i.e. H. Stubbe. See above : 13 May, E. 983. (6*.)] *Printed for Tho. Brewster.* (16 May.) **E. 983. (11.)**

May 16.—A Discourse upon this Saying : "The Spirit of the Nation is not yet to be trusted with Liberty ; lest it introduce Monarchy, or invade the Liberty of Conscience." [Signed : Ja. Harrington.] *Printed by J. C. for Henry Fletcher.* **E. 983. (12.)**

[May 16.]—To Parliament. The Petition of the peaceable and well-affected People of the three Nations. [A satire, attacking William Prynne.] *s. sh.* (16 May.) **669. f. 21. (33.)**

[May 16.]—Shufling, Cutting and Dealing, in a game at Pickquet : being acted from the year 1653 to 1658 by O. P. [i.e. Oliver Protector] and others, with great applause. [By Henry Nevile. A political satire, in the form of an imaginary game of cards.] (16 May.) **E. 983. (9.)**

[May 17.]—The Character or Ear-Mark of Mr. William Prinne. In which are contained many seasonable exhortations to the same. (17 May.) **E. 983. (16.)**

May 18.—A Declaration of the Lord Protector and Parliament, for a day of solemn fasting and humiliation to be observed within the Commonwealth. *Printed by I. S.* **E. 983. (8.)**

1659.

May 18.—An Act enabling such Commissioners of Sewers as acted on the 19th of April 1653, to act as Commissioners of Sewers. *s. sh.* *Printed by John Field.* **669. f. 21. (34.)**

May 18.—Articles of Impeachment of transcendent crimes committed by Col. Philip Jones. Exhibited by Mr. Bledry Morgan, and read in Parliament, 18 May. Together with Col. Philip Jones's answer thereunto. **E. 983. (31.)**

May 18.—A Letter of Addresse from the Officers of the Army in Scotland. Directed to the Speaker of the Parliament of the Commonwealth of England. *Printed by John Field.* **E. 983. (19.)**

May 18.—To the Parliament, the Army, and all the wel-affected in the Nation, who have been faithful to the Good Old Cause. [Signed : Isaac Penington, the younger ; 18 May.] **E. 893. (21.)**

[May 18.]—A Publick Plea opposed to a Private Proposal. Or, eight necessary queries presented to the Parliament and Armies consideration, in this morning of freedom, after a short, but a sharp night of tyranny and oppression. By one who hates both treason and traitors. *Printed for L. Chapman.* (18 May.) **E. 983. (18.)**

[May 19.]—An Act impowering Judges for Probate of Wills, and granting Administrations. *s. sh.* *Printed by John Field.* **669. f. 21. (36.)**

[May 19.]—An Act appointing Judges for the Admiralty. *s. sh.* *Printed by John Field.* **669. f. 21. (37.)**

[May 19.]—The Church-Sleeper Awakened. A discourse on Acts, 20. 9, being the substance of two sermons. By Joseph Eyres. pp. 71. *Printed by W. Godbid for Joseph Cranford.* (19 May.) **E. 1902. (2.)**

[May 20.]—A Relation of a Quaker that to the shame of his profession, attempted to bugger a mare near Colchester. [Satirical verse. By Sir John Denham ?] *s. sh.* (20 May.) **669. f. 21. (35.)**

[May 21.]—The World in a Maize, or Oliver's Ghost. [A satire in prose and verse. With a woodcut.] (21 May.) **E. 983. (23.)**

[May 23.]—Secret Reasons of State in reference to the affairs of these nations at the interruption of this present Parliament, anno 1653, discovered. With other matters worthy of observation, in Jo: Streater's case, this being a narrative of his two years troubles at the beginning of the late Monarchie erected by General Cromwel. (23 May.) **E. 983. (24.)**

[May 23.]—The Case of Colonel Matthew Alured ; or, a short account of his sufferings. Submitted to the consideration of the Parliament and Army. *Printed for L. Chapman.* (23 May.) **E. 983. (25.)**

[May 23.]—An Epitomie of Tyranny in the Island of Guernzey. In relation to a certaine deputation and address made to Richard, late

1659.

Protector. With the said addresse itself, lately presented to him by Peter and William de Beauvoir. Discovering their evil designs against the government of a Commonweath. (23 May.) **E. 983. (26.)**

May 25.—His late Highnes's Letter to the Parlament of England, shewing his willingness to submit to this present Government. Read in the House, 25 May. *s. sh. Printed by D. Maxwell.*

669. f. 21. (39.)

[May 25.]—An Observation and Comparison between the Idolatrous Israelites and Judges of England. A Word to the Army. A memorandum, with twelve propositions, tendered to the Army. By H. N., a well-known wisher to Englands freedome and prosperity. *Printed for L. Chapman.* (25 May.) **E. 983. (29.)**

May 26.—An Act for appointing Commissioners for bringing in the arrears of the Revenue due to the Commonwealth. *Printed by John Field.* **E. 1074. (2.)**

May 26.—To Parliament. The Petition and Representation of divers well-affected of the County of South-hampton. [Praying that the existing form of Government should be secured and maintained. With the answer of Parliament.] *s. sh. Printed by R. W. for Francis Tyton.*

669. f. 21. (40.)

[May 26.]—A Treatise of the Covenant of Grace. The substance of divers sermons preached by John Cotton, at Boston in N. E. Second edition. pp. 259. *Printed by Ja. Cottrel for John Allen.* (26 May.)

E. 1920. (2.)

[May 26.]—Eighteen new Court-Quæries humbly offered to the serious consideration of the good honest hearted people of the Three Nations. By several wel-wishers to our Settlement. (26 May.) **E. 984. (1.)**

[May 27.]—Quærees on the Proposalls of the Officers of the Armie to the Parliament. (27 May.) **E. 984. (3.)**

[May 27.]—Scripture Baptism and Church-Way with True-Seekers. (27 May.) **E. 984. (5.)**

[May 28.]—Trade's Destruction is England's Ruine, or Excise decryed. Wherein is manifested the irregularity and inequality of raising money by way of Excise to defray the charge of the nation. By W. C., a Lover of his Country. (28 May.) **E. 984. (6.)**

[May 28.]—The Throne of David : or an exposition of the Second of Samuell, wherein is set downe the patterne of a pious and prudent Prince. By William Guild. [Edited by John Owen.] pp. 339. *Printed by W. Hall for Rob. Blagrave: Oxford.* (28 May.)

E. 984. (8.)

[May 28.]—A Way propounded to make the poor in these and other nations happy, by bringing together a fit people unto one household Government. By Peter Cornelius, Van-Zurik-Zee. [MS. note by

1659.

Thomason : " I believe this pamphlet was made by Mr. Hugh Peeters ; who hath a man named Cornelius Glover."] *Printed for G. C.* (28 May.)   **E. 984. (7.)**

[**May 30.**]—Margery Good-Cow, that gave a gallon of milk and kickt down the pail, what did she merit ? Speak, gentlemen. Or, a short discourse shewing that there is not a farthing due from this nation to old Oliver for all his pretended services : and if anything be given his son, it must be in respect to his own personal virtues. (30 May.)

E. 984. (9.)

[**May 30.**]—England's Confusion : or a true and impartial relation of the late traverses of State in England. Together with a description of the present power ruling there by the name of a Parliament, under the mask of the Good Old Cause. (30 May.)   **E. 985. (1.)**

[**May 30.**]—One Sheet, or, if you will, a Winding Sheet for the Good Old Cause, in order to a decent funerall, in case of a second death. By W. P?, Philopolites. [See also below : 31 May, 669. f. 21. (42.)] (30 May.)   **E. 984. (12.)**

[**May 30.**]—The Case between the City of London and Robert Campion. [Respecting money lent to the City.] *s. sh.* (30 May.)

669. f. 21. (41.)

[**May 30.**]—A Declaration to all the world of our Faith, and what we believe who are called Quakers. [Signed : Edw: Burrough.] *Printed for Thomas Simmons.* (30 May.)   **E. 984. (11.)**

[**May 30.**]—Works of Darknes brought to Light. Or a glance on the mystery of iniquity carried on in these three nations by the Jesuits. By S. W. (30 May.)   **E. 984. (10.)**

May 31.—An Act for constituting Commissioners for ordering and managing the affairs of the Admiralty and Navy. *Printed by John Field.*

E. 1074. (3.)

[**May 31.**]—Mola Asinaria : wherein is demonstrated what slavery the nation must subject itself to by allowing the lawfulness and usurped authority of the pretended Long Parliament now unlawfully and violently held at Westminster. By William Prynne. [Supposititious. See following entry.] (31 May.)   **E. 985. (4.)**

[**May 31.**]—The New Cheaters Forgeries detected, disclaimed. By Will. Prynne. [Concerning two supposititious pamphlets, " A Sheet, or if you will, a Winding Sheet for the Good Old Cause. By W. P. Philopolites," and " Mola Asinaria. By William Prynne." [See above : 30 May, E. 984. (12.) and 31 May, E. 985. (4.).] *Printed for Edward Thomas.* (31 May.)   **669. f. 21. (42.)**

[**May.**]—Bibliotheca Regia ; or, The Royal Library. Containing a collection of such of the Papers of His Late Majesty King Charles as have escaped the wrack and ruines of these times, not extent in the

1659.

Reliquiæ Carolinæ or the Exact Collection of Edward Husbands. [With an engraved portrait of the King, and an allegorical engraved plate representing the storm-tossed Ship of State.] 2 vols. *Printed for Henry Seile.* **E. 1718. (19.)**

[May.]—A Character of King Charles II. Written by a Minister of the Word. *Printed by D. Maxwell.* **E. 1836. (3.)**

[May.]—A Character of England. With reflections upon Gallus Castratus. Third edition. [By John Evelyn.] pp. 66. *Printed for John Crooke.* **E. 1902. (3.)**

[May.]—Confessio Fidei in Conventu Theologorum elaborata. Unà cum Catechismo duplici Majori Minorique. pp. 229. *Excudebat Johannes Field: Cantabrigiæ.* **E. 1913. (1.)**

[May.]—The Doctrine of the Law and Grace unfolded. By John Bunyan. pp. 389. *Printed for M. Wright.* **E. 1878. (1.)**

[May.]—England described: or the several counties & shires thereof briefly handled. Some things also premised, to set forth the glory of this nation. By Edward Leigh. pp. 234. *Printed by A. M. for Henry Marsh.* **E. 1792. (2.)**

[May.]—The Life of Adam. Written in Italian by Giovanno Francesco Loredano. Renderd into English by J. S. pp. 86. *Printed for Humphrey Moseley.* **E. 1909. (1.)**

[May.]—Παμβοτανολογία, or, A Compleat Herball. By Robert Lovell. pp. 671. *Printed by William Hall for Rich. Davis: Oxford.*
E. 1858, & 59.

[May.]—A Survey of the Law. Containing Directions how to prosecute and defend Personal Actions, usually brought at Common Law. By William Glisson and Anthony Gulston. pp. 401. *Printed for Henry Brome.* **E. 1788.**

[May.]—Susannas Apologie against the Elders. Or, A Vindication of Susanna Parr, one of those two women lately excommunicated by Mr. Lewis Stucley. Composed and published by her selfe. pp. 114.
E. 1784. (2.)

[June 1.]—Government described: viz. what Monarchie, Aristocracie, Oligarchie and Democracie is. Together with a brief model of the government of the common-wealth or Free-State of Ragouse. By J. S. (1 June.) **E. 985. (7.)**

[June 1.]—A Lively Pourtraicture of the Face of this Common-wealth, exactly drawn by Lewis the Fourth of France. [A tract advocating the restoration of Charles II.] (1 June.) **E. 985. (6.)**

[June 2.]—A Catalogue of the Names of this present Parliament, interrupted April 19, 1653. *s. sh. Printed for D. Maxwell.* (2 June.)
669. f. 21. (43.)

1659.

[June 2.]—Twenty four Queries touching the Parliament & Army, and the interest of the Royal Party, and others of this nation. By several Friends to Publick Good. (2 June.) **E. 985. (8.)**

[June 2.]—A Word to purpose: or, a Parthian Dart, shot back to 1642, and from thence shot back again to 1659, and now sticks fast in two substantial queries: 1. Concerning the legality of the second ·meeting of some of the Long-Parliament Members. Also, a fool's bolt shot into Wallingford House, concerning a Free State. [See also below : 22 June, E. 988. (11.)] (2 June.) **E. 985. (9.)**

[June 2.]—A Journall of all Proceedings between the Jansenists and the Jesuits, from the first coming abroad of the Provincial Letters to the publication of the Censures of the Clergy of France passed upon a book [by G. Pirot] entituled An Apology for the Casuists. [Signed : H. H.] *Printed by W. W., and sold by William Place.* (2 June.) **E. 985. (7*.)**

[June 3.]—Democritus turned Statesman : or twenty quæries between jest and earnest, proposed to all true-hearted Englishmen. (3 June.) **E. 985. (12.)**

[June 4.]—To Parliament. The hearty Congratulations and humble Petition of thousands of well-affected Inhabitants of the County of Kent, and City of Canterbury. [Praying that the existing form of Goverment should be secured and maintained.] *s. sh. Printed for Livewell Chapman.* **669. f. 21. (45.)**

[June 4.]—The first and second Parts of Invisible John made Visible : or, a Grand Pimp of Tyranny portrayed in Barkstead's arraignment at the barre. Whereunto is added his barbarous cruelty to Dr. John Hewyt and others. (4 June.) **E. 985. (11.)**

[June 6.]—No Return to Monarchy ; and Liberty of Conscience secured, without a Senate, or any imposing power over the people's representatives. Humbly tendered to the consideration of the Parliament, upon occasion of the Army's thirteenth proposal. *Printed for Thomas Brewster.* (6 June.) **E. 985. (16.)**

[June 6.]—An Alarum to the City and Souldiery. [Concerning an alleged plot of the Fifth Monarchy Men to overpower the Army, set fire to the City and massacre the populace.] *s. sh.* (6 June.) **669. f. 21. (44.)**

[June 6.]—A Lively Character of some pretending Grandees of Scotland to the good old cause. (6 June.) **E. 985. (15.)**

[June 6.]—Three Propositions from the Case of our Three Nations. [In favour of the restoration of Charles II.] (6 June.) **E. 985. (17.)**

[June 6.]—Twenty seven Queries relating to the general good of the three nations, which will please madmen nor displease rational men. (6 June.) **E. 985. (13.)**

1659.

[June 6.]—University Queries, in a gentle touch by the by. *Printed at Cambridge.* (6 June.) **E. 985. (14.)**

[June 7.]—A Vindication of Sir Henry Vane from the lyes and calumnies of Mr. Richard Baxter. In a monitory letter to the said Mr. Baxter. By a true friend and servant of the Commonwealth. *Printed for Livewel Chapman.* (7 June.) **E. 985. (21.)**

[June 8.]—The Sentinels Remonstrance ; or a Vindication of the Souldiers to the People of this Commonwealth, &c. By W. B. *s. sh.* (8 June.) **669. f. 21. (46.)**

[June 9.]—A Dialogue betwixt the Ghosts of Charls I., late King of England, and Oliver, the late usurping Protector. (9 June.)
E. 985. (24.)

[June 9.]—A Collection of several passages concerning his late Highnesse Oliver Cromwell in the time of his sickness. Wherein is related many of his expressions upon his deathbed, together with his prayer within two or three days before his death. Written by one that was then groom of his bed-chamber. [Attributed to Charles Harvey.] *Printed for Robert Ibbitson.* (9 June.) **E. 985. (22.)**

[June 9.]—A true and impartial Narrative of the most material debates and passages in the late Parliament, together with the rise and dissolution of it. By a Member of that Parliament, who is none of the present Parliament. *Printed for Thomas Brewster.* (9 June.)
E. 985. (25.)

[June 9.]—Long Parliament Work, if they wil please to do't, for the good of the Common-wealth : or, the humble desires of the well-affected, revived. Tender'd to the consideration of the Parliament, Army, and others, in xx proposals. *Printed by T. L. for G. Calvert.* (9 June.)
E. 985. (23.)

[June 9.]—The Declaration and Proclamation of the Army of God owned by the Lord of Hosts in many victories. Whereunto is annexed 17 necessary proposals for settling of good judges in every city, taking off the excise, and payment of the souldiers. Second edition enlarged with new additions. *Printed by J. Clowes for the Authour.* (9 June.)
E. 985. (26.)

[June 9.]—Killing no Murder. By William Allen [i.e. Edward Sexby and Silius Titus.] A new edition. See above : May, 1657, E. 501. (4.)] (9 June.) **E. 763. (1.)**

[June 10.]—To Parliament. The Petition of the Sentinels in the Regiment formerly belonging to Major General Goffe. [Praying that their arrears of pay may be made good to them, *etc.*] *s. sh.* (10 June.)
669. f. 21. (47.)

[June 10.]—Reasons for the Continuance of the Process of Arrest, for the Good of the Commonwealth. *s. sh.* (10 June.) **669. f. 21. (48.)**

1659.

[**June 10.**]—A Vindication of the Laws of England as they are now established. Together with some proposals to the Parliament for the regulation of them. By a Lover of the Laws. *Printed for John Starkey.* (10 June.) **E. 986. (1.)**

[**June 10.**]—Ἀσύστατα. The repugnancy and inconsistency of the maintenance of an Orthodox Ministery, and tolleration of heretical opinions. (10 June.) **E. 986. (2.)**

[**June 13.**]—A Letter of Comfort to Richard Cromwell Esq., sent him since the alteration of his titles and our government. From a servant of his late Highness. (13 June.) **E. 986. (8.)**

[**June 13.**]—The New Lord's Winding-Sheet : or, An Arrow shot at randome to the Tower of London. With the articles, charge and voting of Col. Barkestead from his command in the Tower, and the appointing Colonel Fitz in his place. (13 June.) **E. 986. (7.)**

[**June 13.**]—A Pair of Spectacles for this purblinde nation, with which they may see the Army and Parliament, like Simeon and Levi, walk hand in hand together. By H. M., a true friend to this nation's liberties. (13 June.) **E. 986. (9.)**

[**June 13.**]—Endlesse Queries : or an end to queries laid down in 36 merry mad queries for the people's information. (13 June.)
E. 986. (10.)

[**June 13.**]—The Poor Man's Mite unto the more large contributions of the Liberal, at this day freely added, in testimony of that respect which is born unto the faithful and their interest, as it's laid up and hid in Jesus. *Printed for Livewell Chapman.* (13 June.)
E. 986. (3.)

[**June 13.**]—A Secret Word to the Wise : or, Seventeen Queries humbly proposed to the well-affected people of the Good Old Cause. (13 June.)
E. 986. (6.)

[**June 13.**]—The Unhappy Marks-man : or, Twenty three Queries offered to the consideration of the people of these nations. (13 June.)
E. 986. (5.)

[**June 13.**]—Bibliotheca Militum : or the Souldiers Publick Library, lately erected for the benefit of all that love the Good Old Cause, at Wallingford-House. [A satire.] (13 June.) **E. 986. (4.)**

[**June 14.**]—A Common-wealth or Nothing ; or, Monarchy and Oligarchy prov'd parallel in tyranny. In XII. queries. *Printed for Livewell Chapman.* (14 June.) **E. 986. (17.)**

[**June 14.**]—The Dispersed United : or, Twelve Healing Questions, tending to stop the reproaches cast upon those that submitted unto the several governments that have been exercised over this Commonwealth since the interruption of this present Parliament 20 April 1653. (14 June.)
E. 986. (17*.)

1659.

[**June 14.**]—Loyal Queries. Humbly tendred to the consideration of the Parliament and Army. [Advocating the restoration of Charles II.] (14 June.) **E. 986. (15.)**

[**June 14.**]—Nineteen Cases of Conscience submissively tendred to Mr. Hugh Petrs [*sic*] and the rest of his fellow commissioners, the Triars. By sundry weak Brethren. (14 June.) **E. 986. (16.)**

[**June 14.**]—A Proposition in order to the proposing of a Commonwealth or Democracie. [A list of names which it is desired should be added to " the Committee to receive Mr. Harrington's Propositions for settling the Government of this Commonwealth," should Parliament. appoint such a Committee. See also below : 17 June, E. 986. (24.)] *s. sh.* (14 June.) **669. f. 21. (49.)**

[**June 14.**]—Several Resolves prepared by the Commanding Junto to pass the House. [A satire.] (14 June.) **E. 986. (11.)**

[**June 15.**]—A true Narrative of the Occasions and Causes of the late Lord Gen. Cromwell's anger and indignation against Col. George Joyce, & his proceedings against him. [See also below : 28 June, E. 988. (17.)] (15 June.) **669. f. 21. (50.)**

[**June 15.**]—A Short Discourse concerning the work of God in this nation, and the duty of all good people, both governors and governed, in this their day. *Printed by R. W. for Francis Tyton.* (15 June.) **E. 986. (19.)**

[**June 16.**]—France no friend to England. Or, the resentments of the French upon the success of the English. Wherein much of the private transactions between Cardinal Mazerin and the late Protector Oliver, are discovered. Translated out of French [from the " Très humble et très importante Remonstrance," published anonymously by Cardinal de Retz]. (16 June.) **E. 986. (21.)**

June 16.—To Parliament. The humble Representation and desires of divers Freeholders and others inhabiting within the County of Bedford. [Praying that tithes may be abolished, toleration exercised in matters of religion, and " the Militia speedily settled in the hands of such persons who have manifested the continuance of their integrity to the Good Old Cause."] *s. sh. Printed for Thomas Brewster.*

669. f. 21. (51.)

[**June 16.**]—Loyalty Banished : or England in Mourning. Being a narrative of the proceedings between divers members of Parliament and M. Wil. Prynne. As also Mr. Prynne's demands to the Parliament in the name of all the Commons of England. (16 June.) **E. 986. (20.)**

[**June 16.**]—Declarations and Pleadings in English : being the most authentique form of proceeding in Courts of Law. Collected by Richard Brownlow. pp. 288. *Printed by Tho. Roycroft for Henry Twyford.* (16 June.) **E. 768.**

1659.

[June 16.]—A Scourge for a Denn of Thieves. [By Peter Chamberlen. A proposal for raising money to pay off the arrears of pay owing to the army.] *Printed by J. C. for the Author.* (16 June.) **E. 986. (23.)**

[June 16.]—Several new Cheats brought to publique view ; or, the Good Old Cause turn'd to a new cheat. (16 June.) **E. 986. (22.)**

[June 16.]—The History of Sr Francis Drake. Exprest by instrumental and vocall musick, and by art of perspective in scenes, &c. [By Sir William Davenant.] *Printed for Henry Herringman.* (16 June.)
E. 764. (1.)

[June 17.]—Ambitious Tyrany clearly demonstrated; in England's unhappy and confused Government. Proposed to the serious consideration of those that may endeavour to remedie it. (17 June.)
E. 988. (3.)

[June 17.]—An Answer to a Proposition in order to the proposing of a Commonwealth or Democracy. Proposed by friends to the Commonwealth by Mr. Harrington's consent. [By W. Prynne. See above : 14 June, 669. f. 21. (49.)] (17 June.) **E. 986. (24.)**

[June 17.]—A Baker's-Dozen of plain down-right queries, harmlesse and honest : propounded to all that expect benefit from this present Power. By George Gregorie. (17 June.) **E. 988. (2.)**

[June 17.]—A Brief Admonition of some of the inconveniences of all the three most famous Governments known to the world : with their comparisons together. [The dedication signed : J. H.] (17 June.)
E. 988. (1.)

June 17.—Divine Arithmetick, or the right art of numbring our dayes. Being a sermon preached at the funerals of Mr. Samuel Jacomb. By Symon Patrick. [With a collection of funeral poems by various authors.] pp. 80. *Printed by R. W. for Francis Tyton.* **E. 989. (1.)**

[June 17.]—The Jews Sabbath antiquated, and the Lord's Day instituted by Divine Authority. By Edm. Warren. pp. 263. *Printed by David Maxwel, for W. Weekly of Ipswich, and sold by John Rothwel, and also by Nath. Web and Will. Grantham.* (17 June.) **E. 986. (26.)**

[June 17.]—A Light shining out of Darknes : or occasional queries submitted to the judgment of such as would enquire into the true state of things in our times. [By Henry Stubbe or Sir Henry Vane.] (17 June.)
E. 987. (2.)

[June 17.]—The Parable of the Tares expounded & applyed, in ten sermons preached before his late Majesty King Charles. By Peter Heylin. To which are added three other sermons of the same author. pp. 395. *Printed by J. G. for Humphrey Moseley.* (17 June.) **E. 987. (1.)**

[June 17.]—A Congratulation to our newly restored Parliament of the Commonwealth of England. [In verse, signed : W. H.] *s. sh.* *Printed by J. T.* (17 June.) **669. f. 21. (52.)**

1659.

June 18.—An Act of Assessment. *Printed by John Field and Henry Hills.* **E. 1074. (4.)**

[**June 20.**]—An Animadversion upon the late Lord Protector's Declaration, for the distressed Churches of Lesna, &c. Together with a seasonable caution against the petition of the Kentish Anabaptists for too large a toleration in religion. (20 June.) **E. 988. (5.)**

[**June 20.**]—The Army Mastered; or Great Britains Joy: briefly presented to those true patriots of their country now assembled in Parliament, by thousands well-affected to the lawful authority of these nations. *s. sh.* (20 June.) **669. f. 21. (53.)**

June 21.—To Parliament. The Petition of divers Free-holders and others, inhabitants in the County of Hartford. [Praying that the Good Old Cause may be maintained, tithes abolished and the laws revised.] *s. sh. Printed for Thomas Brewster.* **669. f. 21. (55.)**

June 21.—Chaos. [A discourse on government. Dated 21 June.] *Printed for Livewel Chapman.* **E. 988. (22.)**

June 21.—Real Comforts extracted from moral and spiritual principles. Presented in a sermon preached at the funeral of Mr. Thomason Ball. With a narrative of his life and death. By John Howes. pp. 54. *Printed by S. Griffin for R. Royston.* **E. 988. (29.)**

June 22.—An additional Act for bringing in all arrear, and also the growing dutie of Excise, new Impost, Customes, Subsidies and Prize-Goods until the first day of October. *Printed by John Field and Henry Hills.* **E. 1074. (5.)**

[**June 22.**]—A Copie of Quæries, or a comment upon the life and actions of the Grand Tyrant and his complices, Oliver, the first and last of that name. (22 June.) **E. 988. (10.)**

[**June 22.**]—Lilburn's Ghost, with a whip in one hand, to scourge tyrants out of authority; and balme in the other, to heal the sores of our, as yet, corrupt state. *Printed for Livewell Chapman.* (22 June.)
E. 988. (9.)

[**June 22.**]—A Shield against the Parthian Dart, or, a word to the purpose shot into Wallingford-House, answered, in defence of the present actions of State here in England that produced the late change of Government. By J. S. [See above: 2 June, E. 985. (9.)] (22 June.) **E. 988. (11.)**

[**June 22.**]—White-Hall's Petition to Parliament: that he may enjoy his former priviledges. [A political satire, in verse.] *s. sh.* (22 June.)
669. f. 21. (54.)

[**June 23.**]—England's Safety in the Law's Supremacy. (23 June.)
E. 988. (13.)

[**June 23.**]—Love, Kindness and due Respect by way of warning to the Parliament, that they may not neglect the great opportunity now put

1659.

into their hands for the redemption and freedom of these nations. From J. Hodgson. *Printed for Giles Calvert.* (23 June.)
                                                                    E. 988. (12.)

June 24.—A Declaration of the King of Denmark, to the Emperour, the King and State of Poland and the Elector of Brandenburgh, in relation to the Treaty concluded at the Haghe the 21 May. *Printed by E. C., for Henry Eversden.*   **E. 770. (1.)**

June 24.—Articles of Impeachment exhibited against Col. Robert Gibbons and Cap. Richard Yeardley, late Governors of the Isle of Jersey. [Preceded by a letter signed : A. B., and dated 24 June.] *Printed for G. Horton.*   **E. 989. (20.)**

[June 24.]—The Bishop of Armagh's Direction, concerning the Liturgy and Episcopall Government. Being thereunto requested by the House of Commons. Now reprinted. (24 June.)   **E. 988. (15.)**

[June 24.]—A Seasonable Question soberly proposed, argued and resolved. ["Whether such as have received moneys from the late Protectors, by way of bargain, sallary or reward, ought to be compelled to refund the same."] (24 June.)   **E. 988. (14.)**

[June 25.]—England's Changeling. Or, the Time Servers laid open in their colours. Being a discovery of the new cheat of the thing called the Good Old Cause. By one that hopes to see better times. [In verse. The dedicatory poem signed : H. W.] (25 June.)   **E. 988. (16.)**

June 27.—[A Resolution of Parliament, "that the payment of tithes shall continue as now they are, unless Parliament shall finde out some other more equal and comfortable maintenance for the Ministry."] Protesting against the payment of tithes. *s. sh. Printed by John Field and Henry Hills.*   **669. f. 21. (56.)**

June 27.—The Copie of a Paper presented to the Parliament. [Against Tithes.] *Printed by A. W. for Giles Calvert.*   **E. 988. (24.)**

[June 27.]—Ten Considerable Quæries concerning Tithes. By William Prynne. *Printed for Edward Thomas.* (27 June.)   **E. 767. (2.)**

June 28.—An Act for impresting of Seamen. *Printed by John Field and Henry Hills.*   **E. 1074. (7.)**

June 28.—An Act for setling the Militia of the City of Westminster, and liberties thereof, and places adjacent. *Printed by John Field and Henry Hills.*   **E. 1074. (6.)**

[June 28.]—Innocencie Vindicated. Or, a brief answer to part of a scandalous paper, entituled, A true Narrative of the occasion and causes of the late Lord General Cromwel's anger against Lieutenant Colonel Joyce. By Jo. Rix, once Lieutenant to the said Lt. Colonel Joyce. [See above : 15 June, 669. f. 21. (50.)] *Printed by J. C.* (28 June.)   **E. 988. (17.)**

1659.

[**June 28.**]—A Commonwealth, and Commonwealths-men, asserted and vindicated. Wherein the necessity of putting their principles into speedy practice is briefly repeated. *Printed for Henry Fletcher.* (28 June.) **E. 988. (19.)**

[**June 28.**]—Eight and thirty Queries touching things past, present, and to come. *Printed for Richard Andrews.* (28 June.)
E. 988. (21.)

[**June 29.**]—The Moderate Man's Proposall to the Parliament about Tithes, in behalf of the Magistrate, Minister and People. *Printed by A. W. for Giles Calvert.* (29 June.) **E. 988. (23.)**

[**June 29.**]—Sundry Things from severall hands concerning the University of Oxford : viz. I. A Petition from some well-affected therein. II. A Modell for a Colledge Reformation. III. Queries concerning the said University, and severall persons therein. *Printed by Thomas Creake.* (29 June.) **E. 988. (25.)**

[**June 30.**]—A New Conference between the Ghosts of King Charles and Oliver Cromwell. Faithfully communicated by Adam Wood. *Printed for Robert Page.* (30 June.) **E. 988. (28.)**

[**June 30.**]—An Answer to a Letter sent to a gentleman of the Middle Temple, concerning the late changes of the times. And also a clear way discovered whereby a million of money may be brought into the publick treasury. By Tho. Le White. *Printed by J. Clowes.* (30 June.)
E. 988. (26.)

[**June 30.**]—A Defence and Justification of Ministers Maintenance by Tythes. And of Infant-Baptism, Humane Learning and the Sword of the Magistrate. In a reply to a paper sent by some Anabaptists to Immanuel Bourne ; with a short Answer to Anthony Peirson's Great Case of Tythes. pp. 157. [See above : 6 Dec. 1657, E. 931. (2.)] *Printed for John Allen.* (30 June.) **E. 1907. (1.)**

[**June 30.**]—A Little View of this Old World, in two books. I. A Map of Monarchy. II. An Epitome of Papacy. A work fitted to the press five years agone, and now published, by Tho. Palmer. pp. 192. *Printed for Livewell Chapman.* (30 June.) **E. 1912. (1.)**

[**June 30.**]—A Seasonable Advertisement to the people of England. Whether a Monarchy or Free State be better, in this juncture of time ? *Printed for Thomas Matthews.* (30 June.) **E. 988. (30.)**

[**June.**]—Arcana Dogmatum Anti-Remonstrantium ; or, The Calvinists Cabinet unlock'd. In an Apology for Tilenus against a pretended Vindication of the Synod of Dort. At the provocation of Master R. Baxter, held forth in the Preface to his Grotian Religion. Together with a few soft drops let fall upon the Papers of Master Hickman. [By Lawrence Womock. See above : July, 1658, E. 1868. (2.)] pp. 562. *Printed for Richard Royston.* **E. 1854. (2.)**

1659.

[June.]—The Considerator Considered; or, A Brief View of certain Considerations upon the Biblia Polyglotta. By Bri. Walton [afterwards Bishop of Chester]. pp. 293. *Printed by Thomas Roycroft.*
　　　　　　　　　　　　　　　　　　　　　　　　　　　　E. 1860.

[June.]—The English Case, exactly set down by Hezekiah's Reformation. In a Court Sermon at Paris by Dr. Steward. Published for the vindication of the Church of England from the Romanists charge of Schism, and commended to the consideration of the late author of The Grotian Religion discovered. [See above : July, 1658, E. 1868. (2.)] pp. 71. *Printed for T. Garthwait.* **E. 2106. (2.)**

[June.]—Habakkuks Prayer applyed to the Churches present occasions. By Samuel Balmford. pp. 109. *Printed by E. M. for Adoniram Byfield.* **E. 1910. (2.)**

[June.]—Ἡ Κατήχησις τῆς Χριστιανικῆς Θρησκείας συντομωτέρα, sive, Catachesis Religionis Christianæ compendiosior. Opera Joannis Harmari. [In Greek and Latin.] pp. 67. *Typis Joannis Macock & impensis J. H.*
　　　　　　　　　　　　　　　　　　　　　　　　　　　E. 1911. (1.)

[June.]—Knowledge & Practice ; or a plain discourse of the chief things necessary to be known, believ'd & practised in order to Salvation. By Samuel Cradock. pp. 634. *Printed by J. Hayes for John Rothwell.*
　　　　　　　　　　　　　　　　　　　　　　　　　　　E. 1724.

[June.]—Mary Magdalen's Tears wip't off; or, The Voice of Peace to an Unquiet Conscience. [By T. Martin.] pp. 116. *Printed by J. C. for T. Garthwait.* **E. 1913. (2.)**

[June.]—The Pastor and the Clerk; or, A Debate [real] concerning Infant-Baptisme. By John Ellis. pp. 207. *Printed for Elisha Wallis.*
　　　　　　　　　　　　　　　　　　　　　　　　　　　E. 1909. (2.)

[June.]—Unio Reformantium, sive Examen Hoornbecki de Independentismo. Per Johannem Beverley. pp. 185. *Excudebat J. H. pro S. Thomson.* (June.) **E. 1910. (1.)**

[June.]—A Vindication of the Preacher Sent. Or, a Warrant for publick Preaching without Ordination. In answer to two books. 1. Vindiciæ Ministerii Evangelici revindicatæ. By Dr. Colling. 2. Quo Warranto. By Mr. Pool. With a reply to the exceptions of Mr. Hudson and Dr. Collings against the Epistle to the Preacher Sent. Published by Frederick Woodal, Samuel Petto. pp. 213. [See above : 22 May, 1658, E. 946. (4.) and 2 Sept., 1658, E. 952. (2.)] *Printed by J. T. [for] Livewell Chapman.* **E. 1728. (2.)**

[June.]—An Advice against Libertinism. By Edward Reynell. pp. 113. *Printed for Abel Roper.* **E. 2106. (1.)**

[June.]—Barker's Delight : or, The Art of Angling. By Thomas Barker. Second edition, much enlarged. pp. 52. *Printed for Humphrey Moseley.*
　　　　　　　　　　　　　　　　　　　　　　　　　　　E. 1908. (1.)

1659.

[June.]—Βουλευτήριον, or, A Practical Demonstration of County Judicatures. Wherein is amply explained the Judiciall and Ministeriall Authority of Sheriffs. By Will. Greenwood. pp. 397. *Printed by T. R. for John Place.* **E. 1789.**

[June.]—The Golden Grove; or, A Manual of Daily Prayers. Also Festival Hymns. By Jeremy Taylor. Fourth edition. pp. 171. *Printed by J. F. for R. Royston.* **E. 1937. (1.)**

[June.]—Panacea; or, The Universal Medicine. Being a discovery of the wonderfull vertues of Tobacco, taken in a pipe. [With an engraved frontispiece, representing a student smoking.] By Dr. Everard. 2 pt. *Printed for Simon Miller.* **E. 1907. (2.)**

[June.]—The Scale or Ladder of Perfection, written by Walter Hilton, a Carthusian, famous in the reigne of Henry the 6th. Printed first in the year 1494. pp. 312. *Printed by T. R.* **E. 1791.**

[June.]—The Third Part of the Young Clerk's Guide. [A legal handbook.] By Sir R. H. [i.e. Sir Richard Hutton?] pp. 320. *Printed for Humphrey Tuckey.* **E. 1908. (2.)**

[June.]—The Vanity of Judiciary Astrology, or Divination by the Stars. Lately written in Latin by Petrus Gassendus. Translated into English by a Person of Quality. [With an engraved portrait of the author.] pp. 162. *Printed for Humphrey Moseley.* **E. 1728. (1.)**

[June.]—The Last Remains of Sir John Suckling, being a full collection of all his Poems and Letters. [With an engraved portrait of Suckling.] pp. 97. *Printed for Humphrey Moseley.* **E. 1768. (2.)**

[June.]—The Ephesian Matron. [A romance. By Walter Charleton.] pp. 124. *Printed for Henry Herringman.* **E. 2107. (1.)**

[June.]—The Learned Maid. A logick exercise written by Anna Maria à Schurman of Utrecht. [With an engraved portrait of the author. The translator's dedication signed: C. B.] pp. 55. *Printed by John Redmayne.* **E. 1910. (3.)**

[June.]—The Legend of Captain Jones. [In verse. By David Lloyd.] pp. 71. *Printed for Humphrey Moseley.* **E. 2113. (1.)**

[June.]—Pharonnida : a heroick poem. By William Chamberlayne. 2 pt. *Printed for Robert Clavell.* **E. 1771.**

[July 2.]—A Prophecy lately found amongst the collections of famous Mr. John Selden. Faithfully rendred in the originall Latine, and translated. (2 July.) **E. 989. (2.)**

[July 2.]—The President of Presidents: or an Elegie on the death of John Bradshaw. [A satire, signed : T. B. Bradshaw died 31 Oct. 1659.] *s. sh.* (2 July.) **669. f. 21. (57.)**

[July 2.]—A Dialogue betwixt an Excise-Man and Death. [A satire, in verse. With a woodcut.] *s. sh. Printed by I. C.* (2 July.) **669. f. 21. (58.)**

1659.

July 6.—The Petition of divers well-affected persons, delivered 6 July to the Supreme Authority, the Parliament of the Commonwealth. With the Parliament's answer thereunto, and sense thereupon. [Proposals "for securing the government of this Commonwealth."] *Printed for Thomas Brewster.* **E. 989. (11.)**

[**July 6.**]—Bloody Babylon Discovered; or, The Mystery of Iniquity Reveal'd. Written long since, and now published. By Christianus Londinatus. pp. 116. (6 July.) **E. 1928. (3.)**

[**July 6.**]—A New Modell, or the conversion of the infidell terms of the Law, for the better promoting of mis-understanding according to common sence. The first century. [A satire.] (6 July.) **E. 989. (8.)**

[**July 6.**]—Several Proposals offered to the consideration of the Keepers of the Liberties of the people of England, in reference to a settlement of peace and truth in this nation. As also a narrative, chiefly to make known two or three sums of money concealed, and many of the actings of the proposer, Samuel Duncon, from the year 1640 to the year 1652. *Printed by James Cottrel.* (6 July.) **E. 989. (9.)**

[**July 6.**]—Paul's Churchyard. Libri theologici, politici, historici, nundinis Paulinis, una cum Templo, prostant venales. Juxta seriem alphabeti democratici. Done into English for the Assembly of Divines. [A political satire, by Sir John Birkenhead.] 2 pts. (6 July.) **E. 989. (7.)**

[**July 6.**]—Twenty Quaking Queries, having been clowded and now brought forth to light. By Mad-Tom. [A satire.] *Printed for Robert Page.* (6 July.) **E. 989. (6.)**

July 7.—An Act for setling the Militia for the City of London, and liberties thereof. *Printed by John Field and Henry Hills.* **E. 1074. (8.)**

July 7.—[A Declaration of Parliament, forbidding Scottish Sheriffs to try civil cases.] *s. sh. Printed by John Field and Henry Hills.* **669. f. 21. (60.)**

[**July 7.**]—James Nailor's Recantation, penned, and directed by himself, to all the people of the Lord, gathered and scattered. *Printed for Edward Farnham.* (7 July.) **E. 989. (10.)**

[**July 7.**]—Water upon the Flame: by xx Queries propounded to the consideration of all God's People, principally to the Fifth Monarchy Men, commonly so called. (7 July.) **E. 989. (12.)**

July 10.—A Relation of the Cruelties and Barbarous Murthers and other mis-demeanours committed by some Foot-Souldiers upon some of the Inhabitants of Enfield, Edmonton, Southmyms and Hadley, 10 July. **E. 993. (10.)**

July 12.—An Act of Indempnity and Free Pardon. *Printed by John Field and Henry Hills.* **E. 1074. (9.)**

1659.

[July 12.]—A Caution against Sacriledge: or sundry queries concerning Tithes. By one that hath no propriety in tithes, and humbly tendred to this present Parliament. *Printed by Abraham Miller for Thomas Underhill.* (12 July.) **E. 989. (18.)**

[July 12.]—The great and grievous Oppression of the Subject, exhibited in a remonstrance to the Parliament. Wherein is set forth the unjust dealings of the two Corporations of Hull and Headon in the County of York. By Robert Raikes. *Printed for the Author.* (12 July.) **E. 989. (14.)**

[July 12.]—A Rod for the Lawyers, who are hereby declared to be the grand robbers & deceivers of the nation. To which is added a word to the Parliament and a word to the Army. By William Cole. (12 July.) **E. 989. (15.)**

July 13.—An Act against Delinquents. *Printed by John Field and Henry Hills.* **E. 1074. (10.)**

July 13.—An Act for enabling Judges to hold an Assize at Durham. *Printed by John Field.* **E. 1074. (11.)**

[July 13.]—Speculum Libertatis Angliæ re restitutæ: or the Looking-Glasse of England's Libertie really restored. Being the representation of the just and equitable constitution of a real Commonwealth. [The preface signed: R. M.] *Printed by J. B., and are to be sold by Richard Skelton.* (13 July.) **E. 989. (19.)**

[July 13.]—Golden Remains of Mr. John Hales of Eton College. [With engraved titlepage and frontispiece by W. Hollar.] 3 pt. *Printed for Tim. Garthwait.* (13 July.) **E. 769.**

July 14.—An Act for setling the Militia within the hamblets of the Tower of London. *Printed by John Field and Henry Hills.* **E. 1074. (12.)**

July 14.—An Act for setling the Militia for the borough of Southwark, and parishes adjacent. *Printed by John Field and Henry Hills.* **E. 1074. (13.)**

[July 14.]—Truth seeks no Corners. Or, Seven Cases of Conscience humbly presented to the Army and Parliament. (14 July.) **E. 989. (21.)**

[July 15.]—Fourty four Queries to the life of Queen Dick [i.e. Richard Cromwell]. By one who will at any time work a job of journey-work to serve his countrey. (15 July.) **E. 986. (18.)**

[July 15.]—Vox vere Anglorum; or, Englands Loud Cry for their King. Written by a hearty Well-willer to the Common-weale. [A plea for the restoration of Charles II.] (15 July.) **E. 763. (3.)**

[July 15.]—The Cry of Oppression, occasioned by the Priests of Englands Pulpit-guard, which is a Popish Law made by Queen Mary to guard her

1659.

Friars and Jesuits. With a true discovery of the unjust proceedings of those called Magistrates of Bathe. By Thomas Morford. (15 July.)

E. 989. (23.)

[July 16.]—The Court Career. Death shaddow'd to life, or Shadowes of Life and Death. A Pasquil dialogue [between the shades of Charles I. and Oliver Cromwell]. (16 July.) **E. 989. (26.)**

[July 16.]—Concordia Discors; or, The Dissonant Harmony of Sacred Publique Oathes lately taken by many time-serving Officers. By William Prynne. *Printed for Edward Thomas.* (16 July.) **E. 767. (3.)**

[July 16.]—The Order of Causes, of God's Fore-knowledge, Election, and Predestination, and of Man's Salvation or Damnation. By Henry Haggar. The fifth edition. *Printed for Francis Smith.* (16 July.) **E. 989. (25.)**

[July 18.]—A Letter written and presented to the late Lord Protector, then Lord General, and the Councel of War : but smothered in his hands. [Satirising "the Law of England" and "Tythe Piggs."] *s. sh. Printed by J. C. for the Authour.* (18 July.) **669. f. 21. (59.)**

[July 18.]—Chaos, or a discourse wherein is presented to the view of the Magistrate, and all others who shall peruse the same, a frame of government by way of a Republique. By a well-willer to the Publique Weale. [Second edition.] pp. 54. *Printed for Livewel Chapman.* (18 July.) **E. 989. (27.)**

[July 18.]—An Exposition with practicall Observations continued upon the thirtieth and thirty-first chapters of the Booke of Job : being the substance of thirty-seven lectures, delivered at Magnus neare the Bridge, London. By Joseph Caryl. pp. 769. *Printed by M. Simmons for Elisha Wallis.* (18 July.) **E. 990.**

[July 18.]—An Indictment against Tythes, or tythes no wages for gospel-ministers. By John Osborne. *Printed for Livewel Chapman.* (18 July.) **E. 989. (28.)**

[July 19.]—An Act for appointing Judges for the Admiralty. *s. sh. Printed by John Field.* **669. f. 21. (62.)**

[July 19.]—An Act for reviving an Act impowering Judges for Probate of Wills, and granting Administrations. *s. sh. Printed by John Field.* **669. f. 21. (61.)**

[July 19.]—The Dispatcher Dispatched. Or, an Examination of the Romanists Rejoynder to the Replies of D. H[ammond]. Being a Third Defence of the Treatise of Schisme, wherein is inserted a View of their Possession and Orall Tradition in the way of M. White. By H. Hammond. pp. 821. [See above : Aug. 1657, E. 1555.] *Printed for Richard Royston.* (19 July.) **E. 991, 992.**

July 22.—An Act for Householders to give an account of lodgers, horses, arms and ammunition. *Printed by John Field.* **E. 1074. (14.)**

1659.

July 22.—[Two Resolutions of Parliament concerning the attendance of Members.] *s. sh. Printed by John Field.* **669. f. 21. (63.)**

[**July 22.**]—The Interest of England stated ; or, A faithful and just Account of the Aims of all Parties now pretending. [By John Fell, Bishop of Oxford.] [See also below : 17 Aug., E. 763. (5.)] (22 July.) **E. 763. (4.)**

[**July 24.**]—A Relation of the Riotous Insurrection of divers Inhabitants of Enfield and places adjacent Humbly offered to the consideration of Parliament. *s. sh.* (24 July.) **669. f. 21. (64.)**

[**July 25.**]—The Hammer of Persecution : or, The Mystery of Iniquity, in the Persecution of many good people in Scotland under the Government of Oliver, late Lord Protector. By Rob. Pittilloh. *Printed for L. Chapman.* (25 July.) **E. 993. (4.)**

[**July 25.**]—The Swedish Cloak of Religion : or, A Politick Discourse between two Citizens of Elbing. Wherein is laid open how the whole Palatinate of Marienburgh is made desolate by the introduction of a new Church-Government. First printed in the German language and now faithfully Englished. *Printed for Isaac Pridmore & Henry Marsh.* (25 July.) **E. 993. (5.)**

July 26.—An Act for setling the Militia in England and Wales. *Printed by John Field.* **E. 1074. (15.)**

[**July 28.**]—Articles of High Crimes and Grand Misdemeanors exhibited against Lt. Col. Tho. Kelsey. *Printed for Livewel Chapman.* (28 July.) **E. 993. (8.)**

[**July 28.**]—A Discourse, shewing that the Spirit of Parliaments is not to be trusted for a Settlement : lest it introduce Monarchy and Persecution for Conscience. By James Harrington. *Printed by J. C. for Henry Fletcher.* (28 July.) **E. 993. (9.)**

[**July 30.**]—England Anatomized : her Disease discovered, and the Remedy prescribed, in a Speech by a Member of the [so-called] Parliament. (30 July.) **E. 993. (12.)**

[**July.**]—Golden Apples ; or, Seasonable and Serious Counsel from the Sanctuary to the Rulers of the earth. Collected out of the writings of the most orthodox Divines, both Presbyterians and Independents. By Sam. Clarke. pp. 210. *Printed by Tho. Ratcliffe for Tho. Underhill.* **E. 1881. (3.)**

[**July.**]—Gospel-Marrow, the Great God giving himself for the Sins of Men : or, The Sacred Mystery of Redemption, with Justification and Sanctification, opened and applied. To which is added, Three Links of a Golden Chain, etc. By John Brinsley. 2 pt. *Printed by S. Griffin for Richard Tomlins.* **E. 1852.**

[**July.**]—A Holy Commonwealth, or Political Aphorisms, opening the true Principles of Government : for the healing of the mistakes, and resolving

1659.

the doubts that most endanger and trouble England at this time.   By Richard Baxter.   pp. 517.   *Printed for Thomas Underhill and Francis Tyton.*   **E. 1729.**

[July.]—Parnassi Puerperium ; or, Some Well-wishes to Ingenuity, in the translation of Owen's Epigrams, Martial de Spectaculis, Sir Tho. More, etc.   By Tho. Pecke.   pp. 184.   *Printed by J. Cottrel for Thomas Bassett.*   **E. 1861. (1.)**

[July.]—A Paraphrasticall Explication of the twelve Minor Prophets. By Da. Stokes.   pp. 618.   *Printed for Thomas Davies.*   **E. 1721.**

[July.]—Sacred Eloquence :   or, The Art of Rhetorick, as it is layd down in Scripture.   By John Prideaux, late Lord Bishop of Worcester.   pp. 134.   *Printed by W. Wilson for George Sawbridge.*

E. 1790. (2.)

[July.]—Sonus Buccinæ ; sive, Tres Tractatus de Virtutibus Fidei et Theologiæ.   Authore Thoma Anglo, ex Albiis Est-Saxonum [i.e. Thomas White].   pp. 431.   *Sumptibus Joannis Kinckii & Sociorum : Coloniæ Agrippinæ.*   **E. 1877.**

[Aug. 1.]—A Friendly Letter of Advice to the Souldiers from a Quondam Member of the Army.   [Signed : J. F.]   (1 Aug.)   **E. 993. (13.)**

[Aug. 1.]—Walk, Knaves, walk.   A discourse intended to have been . spoken at Court, and now publish'd for the satisfaction of all those that have participated of the sweetness of publike Employments.   By Hodg Turbervil.   (1 Aug.)   **E. 993. (14.)**

Aug. 2.—An Act appointing Commissioners for Sequestrations.   *Printed by John Field.*   **E. 1074. (17.)**

Aug. 2.—An Act enabling the Commissioners for the City of London to raise three moneths assessment for paying incident charges to the Militia.   *Printed by John Field.*   **E. 1074. (16.)**

Aug. 2.—A Letter from Sir George Booth to a friend of his, shewing the Reasons of his present Engagement in defence of his Countries Liberties, &c.   *s. sh.*   **669. f. 21. (66.)**

Aug. 2.—Sir George Booth's Letter, shewing the Reasons of his present Engagement, together with an Answer to the said Letter, invalidating the said Reasons.   **E. 993. (35.)**

[Aug. 4.]—The Case of Thomas Elwood, Bricklayer, and Richard Higginson, Mercer, late Alderman of London.   [Signed : "Thomas Elwood." In relation to an action of ejectment.]   *s. sh.*   (4 Aug.)

669. f. 21. (65.)

[Aug. 4.]—Duke Hamilton's Ghost, or the Underminer countermined. [In verse.]   (4 Aug.)   **E. 993. (17.)**

Aug. 5.—An Act for holding an Assize for the County of Lancaster. *Printed by John Field.*   **E. 1074. (18.)**

1659.

[**Aug. 8.**]—Babylon the Great described, with some plain Queries further to discover her. By Isaac Pennington the younger. pp. 56. *Printed for Lodowick Lloyd.* (8 Aug.) **E. 770. (2.)**

Aug. 9.—An Express from the Knights and Gentlemen now engaged with Sir George Booth. To the City and Citizens of London, and all other Free-men of England. [With a letter from Sir George Booth to a friend of his in London, dated 9 Aug.] *s. sh.* **669. f. 21. (68.)**

[**Aug. 12.**]—A Declaration of the Maids of the City of London, &c. [A satire.] *s. sh.* (12 Aug.) **669. f. 21. (67.)**

Aug. 13.—An Act for the speedy bringing in of second moyeties upon the sale of lands forfeited to the Commonwealth for treason. *Printed by John Field.* **E. 1074. (19.)**

Aug. 13.—The Copy of a Letter from an Officer under the Lord Lambert giving an Account of a Rising in Derby of Col. Charles White, his proclaiming Booth's Declaration, and how they were dispersed, 13 Aug. *Printed for Thomas Brewster.* **E. 995. (3.)**

Aug. 14.—A Letter from an Officer of the Army in Ireland to a Kinsman of his in the English Army. [Exhorting him and his comrades " to return to duty and reason."] *s. sh.* **669. f. 21. (69.)**

[**Aug. 15.**]—An ancient and true Prophesie of all those Transactions that have already happened, also what is to come. Written in verse, in the latter end of the Raign of Queen Elizabeth and found in Sir Robert Cotton's Library. *Printed for R. Page.* (15 Aug.) **E. 993. (23.)**

[**Aug. 15.**]—The Londoners Last Warning. [A tract, advocating the restoration of Charles II.] (15 Aug.) **E. 993. (24.)**

Aug. 16.—A Declaration of Sir George Booth at the General Rendesvouz, near the City of Chester, with the number both of Horse and Foot, their advance to the City and the joyning of Colonel Ireland with their Army. *Printed for G. Horton.* **E. 993. (34.)**

[**Aug. 17.**]—Interest will not Lie; or, A View of England's True interest. In refutation of a pamphlet [by John Fell, Bishop of Oxford] entituled The Interest of England Stated. By Marchamont Nedham. [See above : 22 July, E. 763. (4.) & also below : 7 Nov., E. 772. (2.)] *Printed by Thomas Newcomb.* (17 Aug.) **E. 763. (5.)**

Aug. 19.—A Bloudy Fight between the Parliaments Forces and Sir George Booth's on Priest-Moor in the County of Shropshire, with the particulars thereof. *Printed for G. Horton.* **E. 995. (1.)**

Aug. 19.—One and Twenty Chester Queries, or, Occasional Scruples, reflecting upon the late Affairs in Cheshire. [Referring to Booth's rising and defeat.] **E. 995. (20.)**

Aug. 19.—A Dialogue betwixt Sir George Booth and Sir John Presbyter, at their meeting near Chester, wherein the machinations

1659.

depending upon that affair are discovered. [A satire referring to Booth's rising.] *Printed for William Wild.* **E. 995. (22.)**

[**Aug. 20.**]—A Few Proposals offered to the Parliament holding forth a Medium or Essay for the Removing of Tythes. *Printed for L. Chapman.* (20 Aug.) **E. 993. (29.)**

[**Aug. 20.**]—A Declaration of the Christian Free-Born Subjects of the once flourishing Kingdom of England, making out the Principles relating both to their Spiritual and Civil Liberties which they conceive they are bound to maintain. (20 Aug.) **E. 993. (30.)**

Aug. 23.—A True Narrative of the manner of the taking of Sir George Booth at Newport-Pannel, being disguised in Womans Apparel, 23 Aug. *Printed for Thomas Richardson.* **E. 995. (4.)**

[**Aug. 23.**]—The Fifth Monarchy, or Kingdom of Christ, in opposition to the Beast's, asserted. *Printed for Livewel Chapman.* (23 Aug.) **E. 993. (31.)**

[**Aug. 25.**]—Michael opposing the Dragon; or, A Fiery Dart struck through the Heart of the Kingdom of the Serpent. pp. 298. (25 Aug.) **E. 994.**

Aug. 27.—An Act for Sequestrations. *Printed by John Field.* **E. 1074. (20.)**

Aug. 27.—[An Order of Parliament, suspending the proceedings of the Commissioners for the Militia with respect to "the raising of money, or charging the people with horse, foot, or arms."] *s. sh. Printed for John Field.* **669. f. 21. (70.)**

[**Aug. 28.**]—Proposals for Reformation of Abuses and Subtilties in Practise against the Law. By William Gery. *Printed for William Shears.* (28 Aug.) **E. 993. (27.)**

[**Aug. 29.**]—The Quaker Quasht and his Quarrel Quelled, in an Answer to a railing pamphlet written by Martin Mason of Lincoln, intituled The Boasting Baptist Dismounted. By Jonathan Johnson. pp. 52. [See above: 23 April, 1656, E. 877. (2.)] *Printed for Francis Smith.* (29 Aug.) **E. 995. (5.)**

Aug. 29.—Questions propounded to George Whitehead and George Fox, who disputed by turns against one University-Man in Cambridge, 29 Aug. **E. 764. (3.)**

[**Aug. 31.**]—Aphorisms Political. By James Harrington. [See also below: 17 Oct., E. 763. (7.)] *Printed by J. C. for Henry Fletcher.* (31 Aug.) **E. 995. (8.)**

[**Aug. 31.**]—A Model of a Democraticall Government humbly tendered to consideration, by a Friend and Wel-Wisher to this Common-Wealth. *Printed for W. P.* (31 Aug.) **E. 995. (9.)**

[**Aug. 31.**]—A Review of the Certamen Epistolare betwixt Pet. Heylin and Hen. Hinckman, wherein the exceptions of the Dr. against Mr. H.'s arguments are all taken off, and our first Reformers are proved

1659.

not to hold with the Arminians. Also a Reply to Mr. Pierce his late virulent Letter to the aforesaid Dr. By Theophilus Churchman [i.e. Peter Heylin]. pp. 182. [See also below : 15 Sept. 1660, E. 1044. (12.)] *Printed at London for John Adams, Bookseller in Oxford.* (31 Aug.) **E. 1873. (1.)**

[**Aug.**]—The Nativity of the late King Charls, astrologically and faithfully performed ; with reasons in art of the various success and misfortune of his whole life. By John Gadbury. pp. 126. *Printed by James Cottrel.* **E. 1725. (1.)**

[**Aug.**]—Aristippus ; or, Mon^{sr} de Balsac's Masterpiece. Being a Discourse concerning the Court. Englished by R. W. pp. 159. *Printed by Tho. Newcomb for Nat. Eakins and Tho. Johnson.*
E. 2105. (1.)

[**Aug.**]—A Compendious View, or cosmographical and geographical Description, of the whole World. By Tho. Porter. [With an engraved frontispiece and an engraved map of the world.] pp. 138. *To be sold by Robert Walton.* **E. 1863. (2.)**

[**Aug.**]—The Compleat Midwife's Practice enlarged. The second edition. By R. C., I. D., M. S., T. B. [With a portrait of Louise Bourgeois, and four other engraved plates.] pp. 309. *Printed for Nath. Brook.*
E. 1723.

[**Aug.**]—Considerations touching the likeliest means to remove Hirelings out of the church. The author J. M. [i.e. John Milton.] pp. 153. *Printed by T. N. for L. Chapman.* **E. 2110. (2.)**

[**Aug.**]—The Dying Man's Testament to the Church of Scotland ; or, a Treatise concerning Scandal. By James Durham. Published by John Carstares. To which is prefixed an excellent preface of famous Mr. Blair. pp. 432. *Printed for the Company of Stationers.* **E. 1796.**

[**Aug.**]—Epicteti Enchiridion, una cum Cebetis Tabula, Græce & Latine : cum notis Merici Casauboni. Ejusdem Enchiridii paraphrasis Græca. Item paraphraseos versio. pp. 208. *Typis Tho. Roycroft. Impensis Rob. Beaumont.* **E. 1800. (2.)**

[**Aug.**]—A New Survey of the Justice of the Peace his office. By W. S., Serjeant at Law [i.e. William Sheppard.] pp. 230. *Printed by J. S.*
E. 1871. (1.)

[**Aug.**]—Panthalia : or the Royal Romance. A discourse stored with infinite variety in relation to State-Government. Faithfully and ingenuously rendred. [By Richard Brathwait. With an engraved portrait of Charles II.] pp. 303. *Printed by J. G. and are to be sold by Anthony Williamson.* **E. 1797.**

[**Aug.**]—Politicaster ; or, A comical discourse in answer unto Mr. Wren's Monarchy Asserted, against Mr. Harrington's Oceana. By James Harrington. pp. 50. [The first edition of " Monarchy Asserted " is not in

1659.

the Thomason collection. For the second edition see below : 28 March, 1660, E. 1853. (1.)] *Printed by J. C. for Henry Fletcher.* **E. 2112. (2.)**

[**Aug.**]—A Short Catechism. [On religion.] **E. 1845. (3.)**

[**Aug.**]—The Way, step by step, to sound and saving Conversion. With a clear discovery of the two states, viz : Nature, & Grace. By Robert Purnell. pp. 128. *Printed by T. Childe and L. Parry for Edw. Thomas.*

E. 1800. (1.)

[**Sept. 2.**]—Peter Patern, or, The perfect Path to Worldly Happiness, as it was delivered in a Funeral Sermon preached at the interrment of Mr. Hugh Peters. By I. C., Translator of Pineda upon Job, and one of the Triers. [A satire.] [See also below : 26 Sept., E. 999. (8.)] (2 Sept.) **E. 995. (11.)**

Sept. 3.—By the Parliament. [A Proclamation, calling upon John Mordant, Major General Edward Massey, the Earl of Lichfield, Sir Thomas Leventhorp, William Compton, Thomas Fanshawe, and Major General Richard Brown, " all of them violently suspected to be engaged in the same treasonable design with Sir George Booth," to render themselves to the Parliament or Council of State.] *s. sh. Printed by John Field.* **669. f. 21. (71.)**

[**Sept. 3.**]—A Word of Settlement in these Unsettled Times, containing some necessary encouragements for the godly People of this Nation, in the time of present danger from the Cavaliers and their Adherents. *Printed for Giles Calvert.* (3 Sept.) **E. 995. (12.)**

[**Sept. 12.**]—The Anabaptist's Faith and Belief, open'd. [A satire, in verse.] *s. sh.* (12 Sept.) **669. f. 21. (72.)**

[**Sept. 12.**]—Englands Settlement upon the two solid foundations of the Peoples Civil and Religious Liberties. (12 Sept.) **E. 995. (17.)**

[**Sept. 19.**]—Epistolium-Vagum-Prosa-Metricum ; or, An Epistle at Randome in prose and metre. Intended for two or three of the Authors Friends in Authority to mediate in Parliament the redress of his grievances. By George Wither. (19 Sept.) **E. 763. (6.)**

[**Sept. 19.**]—An Essay toward Settlement upon a sure foundation, being a testimony for God in this perillous time by a few who have been bewailing their own abominations, etc. [With twenty signatures.] [See also below : 29 Sept. 669. f. 21. (78.)] *s. sh. Printed for Giles Calvert.* (19 Sept.) **669. f. 21. (73.)**

Sept. 20.—[An Order of Parliament prohibiting Governors of Hospitals from granting or renewing leases.] *s. sh. Printed by John Field.*

669. f. 21. (74.)

[**Sept. 20.**]—Διαπολιτεία. A Christian Concertation with Mr. Prin, Mr. Baxter, Mr. Harrington for the True Cause of the Commonwealth. Or, an Answer to Mr. Prin's Perditory Anatomy of the Republic, to Mr. Baxter's Purgatory Pills for the Army, etc.

1659.

By John Rogers. pp. 124. [See also below : 7 Nov., E. 772. (2.)]
Printed for Livewel Chapman. (20 Sept.) **E. 995. (25.)**

[**Sept. 20.**]—Excise anotomiz'd, and Trade epitomiz'd ; declaring that
unequall Imposition of Excise to be the only cause of the ruine of Trade
and universall impoverishment of this whole Nation. By Z. G., a well
wisher of the Common Good. *Printed for F. Cossinet.* (20 Sept.)
E. 999. (1.)

[**Sept. 20.**]—Cheerfull Ayres or Ballads, first composed for one single
Voice and since set for three Voices. By John Wilson. Cantus
Primus.—Cantus Secundus.—Bassus. 3 pt. *Printed by W. Hall
for Ric. Davis : Oxford.* (20 Sept.) *obl.* **E. 996, 997, 998.**

[**Sept. 21.**]—A Dialogue between Riches, Poverty, Godliness, Gravity,
Labour and Content : fit for the perusal of all that are Sober-minded in
this time of Unsetledness. By a Friend to the Publique. *Printed for
Nehemiah Bradford.* (21 Sept.) **E. 999. (2.)**

Sept. 22.—A True Narrative of the Proceedings in Parliament from
22 Sept. untill this present 2 Dec. pp. 72. *Printed by John
Redmayne.* **E. 1010. (24.)**

[**Sept. 22.**]—M. Harrington's Parallel Unparallel'd : or, A Demonstration upon it, and the Parable opened. [By John Rogers.] [See below :
18 Oct., E. 770. (3.)] (22 Sept.) **E. 999. (3.)**

[**Sept. 22.**]—The New Letany. [A political satire, in verse.] *s. sh.*
(22 Sept.) **669. f. 21. (75.)**

[**Sept. 23.**]—A General, or, No General over the Present Army of the
Common-wealth : in twenty two Queries briefly handled. (23 Sept.)
E. 999. (6.)

[**Sept. 23.**]—Truth brought to Light ; or, a Discovery of some of the
Frauds committed by the late Collectors. Contained in the insuing
Breviate of the proceedings of a charge exhibited against them, by
Robert Turner. *Printed by John Clowes.* (23 Sept.)
669. f. 21. (76.)

[**Sept. 26.**]—Now or Never : or, The Princely Calendar. Being a
Bloudy Almanack for the Time present and to come. [For the year
1660.] *Printed for G. Horton.* (26 Sept.) **E. 999. (7.)**

[**Sept. 26.**]—Peters's [i.e. Hugh Peters] Resurrection by way of Dialogue
between him and a Merchant : occasioned upon the publishing a
pretended Sermon at his Funeral. [See above : 2 Sept., E. 995. (11.)]
(26 Sept.) **E. 999. (8.)**

[**Sept. 27.**]—To Parliament. The Petition of the Common-Council of
the City of London. [For the maintenance of their charter and
privileges in the election of the Lord-Mayor.] *s. sh. Printed for John
Johnson.* (27 Sept.) **669. f. 21. (77.)**

1659.

Sept. 28.—An Act for the Continuance of the Customs and Excise. *Printed by John Field.* **E. 1074. (21.)**

[**Sept. 28.**]—A True Catalogue, or, An Account of the several places and most eminent persons in the three Nations and elsewhere, where and by whom Richard Cromwell was proclaimed Lord Protector of the Commonwealth. pp. 76. (28 Sept.) **E. 999. (12.)**

[**Sept. 28.**]—A Modest Plea for an Equal Common-wealth against Monarchy, in which the Genuine Nature of a Free-State is briefly stated. [By William Spriggs.] pp. 102. [See also below : 17 Oct., E. 1010. (9.)] *Printed for Giles Calvert.* (28 Sept.) **E. 999. (11.)**

[**Sept. 29.**]—Mene Tekel, or, The Council of Officers of the Army against the Declarations &c. of the Army. By Geo. Bishop. pp. 50. *Printed and are to be sold by Tho. Brewster.* (29 Sept.) **E. 999. (13.)**

[**Sept. 29.**]—A Word to the Twenty Essayes towards a Settlement, &c. [See above : 19 Sept., 669. f. 21. (73.)] (29 Sept.) **669. f. 21. (78.)**

[**Sept.**]—An Essay in the defence of the Good Old Cause. By Henry Stubbe. pp. 140. **E. 1841. (1.)**

[**Sept.**]—The Golden Book of St John Chrysostom, concerning the Education of Children. Translated out of the Greek by J. E., Esq. [i.e. John Evelyn]. pp. 96. *Printed by D. M. for G. Bedel and T. Collins.* **E. 1931. (1.)**

[**Sept.**]—Malice Rebuked ; or, A Character of Richard Baxters Abilities, and a vindication of Sir Henry Vane from his aspersions in his Key for Catholicks. By Henry Stubbe. pp. 60. [See above : 1 Feb., E. 967.] **E. 1841. (2.)**

[**Sept.**]—The Middle State of Souls, from the hour of Death to the Day of Judgment. By Thomas White. pp. 260. **E. 1879.**

[**Sept.**]—A Modest Plea for an Equal Common-wealth, against Monarchy. [By William Spriggs.] pp. 136. *Printed for Giles Calvert.* **E. 1802. (1.)**

[**Sept.**]—Of Corporations, Fraternities and Guilds. With Forms and Precedents of Charters of Corporation. By William Shepheard. pp. 187. *Printed for H. Twyford, T. Dring and J. Place.* **E. 1912. (2.)**

[**Sept.**]—The Whole Faith of Man. By Will. Jeffery. Second edition, much enlarged. pp. 176. *Printed by G. Dawson, for Francis Smith in Flying Horse Court, and Stephen Dagnal of Alisbury.* **E. 1804. (1.)**

Oct. 1.—A Declaration of the Parliament for a day of Thanksgiving [on 6 Oct.]. *Printed by John Field.* **E. 1074. (22.)**

[**Oct. 3.**]—The True Magistrate, or, The Magistrate's Duty and Power in matters of Religion. *Printed for Thomas Brewster.* (3 Oct.) **E. 1000. (1.)**

Oct. 5.—The Representation and Petition of the Officers of the Army to the Parliament. *Printed by Henry Hills.* **E. 1000. (5.)**

1659.

Oct. 5.—A Letter from the Lord Lambert and other Officers to General Monck, inviting the Officers to subscribe the Representation presented to Parliament. With a Modest Answer thereunto by General Monck.
E. 1000. (22.)

[**Oct. 6.**]—Seek and You shall Find; or, Certaine Queryes of Highest Import, conducing to the laying a foundation of a more righteous Government. (6 Oct.) **E. 1000. (4.)**

Oct. 6.—A Sermon preached before the Parliament and the Officers of the Army in Christ Church London, being the Publick Day of Thanksgiving for the suppression of the Northern Insurrection. By Nathanael Homes. *Printed by J. B. for Edward Brewster.* **E. 1001. (1.)**

[**Oct. 7.**]—The Northern Queries from the Lord Gen. Monck his Quarters, sounding an Allarum to all Loyall Hearts and Free-born English-men. *Printed in the Year of Englands Confusions, and are to be sold at the Sign of Wallingford House, right against a Free Parliament.* (7 Oct.) **E. 1005. (15.)**

[**Oct. 10.**]—Merlinus Gallicus; or, A Prediction for the year 1660. By François Missonne. *Printed by T. J. for Fr. Cossinet.* (10 Oct.)
E. 1831. (1.)

Oct. 11.—An Act against the Raising of Moneys upon the people, without their consent in Parliament. *Printed by John Field.*
E. 1074. (23.)

Oct. 11.—A Letter from Ma. Gen. Overton, Governour of Hull, and the Officers under his command. Directed for Lieut. General Fleetwood, to be communicated to the Officers of the Army. *s. sh.*
669. f. 21. (83.)

Oct. 11.—A True Relation of the State of the Case between the ever Honourable Parliament and the Officers of the Army. By a Lover of his Countrey and Freedom, E. D. *Printed by J. C.* **E. 1000. (12.)**

Oct. 12.—An Act appointing Commissioners for the government of the Army. *Printed by John Streater.* **669. f. 21. (79.)**

Oct. 12.—A late Letter from the Citty of Florence written by Signor Fabricio Pisani touching these present Distempers of England.
E. 1013. (2.)

Oct. 13.—A Declaration published in the North of England, also a Declaration of the Generall-Council of Officers at Wallingford-House. *Printed for N. Crook.* **E. 1005. (6.)**

Oct. 13.—A Letter from General Monck from Dalkeith, to be communicated to the Parliament. **E. 1000. (23.)**

Oct. 14.—A Letter to the Lord Lambert from a Lover of Peace and Truth, being a most faithful Advice how to chuse the safest way to the happy Ending of all our Distractions. Also, a Declaration from the King of Scots, how the Army shall be fully satisfied all their Arrears. **E. 1000. (15.)**

1659.

[**Oct. 14.**]—Ludgates Late Petition to the Parliament and the Prison of the Fleets Letter to Mr. Caril answered. (14 Oct.) **E. 1000. (9.)**

[**Oct. 14.**]—The Peace-Maker, or Christian Reconciler. Being the Breathings of a Troubled Spirit, considering the Calamities of England, Scotland and Ireland. By a Lover of Truth and Peace (14 Oct.)
E. 1000. (10.)

[**Oct. 16.**]—The Quaker no Papist, in answer to The Quaker Disarmed. Or, A brief reply and censure of Mr. Thomas Smith's frivolous Relation of a Dispute held betwixt himself and certain Quakers at Cambridge. By Hen. Denne. [See also below : 3 Nov., E. 764. (2.)] *Printed and are to be sold by Francis Smith.* (16 Oct.) **E. 1000. (13.)**

[**Oct. 17.**]—A Declaration of the Proceedings of the Parliament and Army. *Printed for Emanuel Richardson.* (17 Oct.) **E. 1000. (14.)**

[**Oct. 17.**]—A Cure for the State. Or, an excellent Remedy against the Apostacy of the Times. [A satire, in the form of a medical prescription.] *s. sh.* (17 Oct.) **669. f. 21. (80.)**

Oct. 17.—A Modest Reply, in answer to the Modest Plea for an Equal Common-wealth against Monarchy [by William Spriggs], in three Letters [dated 17 Oct., 29 Oct., 5 Nov.] to a worthy Gentleman. [See above : 28 Sept., E. 999. (11.)] **E. 1010. (9.)**

[**Oct. 17.**]—A Plea for the Peoples Good Old Cause. By way of answer to Mr. James Harrington his CXX Political Aphorismes in his second edition. By Capt. William Bray. [See above : 31 Aug., E. 995. (8.)] *Printed by J. C., and are to be sold by Francis Smith.* (17 Oct.)
E. 763. (7.)

[**Oct. 18.**]—A Parallel of the Spirit of the People with the Spirit of Mr. Rogers, and an appeal thereupon unto the Reader, whether the Spirit of the People or the Spirit of men like Mr. Rogers be the fitter to be trusted with the Government. By James Harrington. [See above : 22 Sept., E. 999. (3.)] *Printed by J. C., for Henry Fletcher.* (18 Oct.) **E. 770. (3.)**

Oct. 18.—A True Relation of the Proceedings against certain Quakers at the Generall Court of the Massachusets holden at Boston in New-England. *s. sh. Printed by A. W.* **669. f. 23. (69.)**

[**Oct. 19.**]—The Acts and Monuments of our late Parliament. By J. Canne. (19 Oct.) **E. 1000. (19.)**

[**Oct. 20.**]—Considerations upon the late transactions and proceedings of the Army, in reference to the Dissolution of the Parliament. *s. sh. Printed for Isaac Pridmore.* (20 Oct.) **669. f. 21. (81.)**

[**Oct. 20.**]—The Rendezvouz of General Monck upon the Confines of England. Also, A Declaration of the Lords, Knights and Gentry in the Northern Parts, and their adhering to General Monck. (20 Oct.) *Printed for Richard Foster : York ; reprinted at London.* **E. 1005. (11.)**

1659.

Oct. 20.—A Declaration of the Officers of the Army in Scotland to the Churches of Christ in the three Nations. *Printed by Christopher Higgins : Edinburgh.* **E. 1005. (7.)**

Oct. 20.—Three Letters from the Lord General Monck, viz. to Mr. Speaker, to the Lord Fleetwood, to the Lord Lambert. *Printed by Christopher Higgins : Edinburgh.* **E. 1005. (4.)**

[**Oct. 20.**]—An excellent Receipt to make a compleat Parliament, or, if you please a New Senate, fitted to the English-man's palate. [A satire, in the form of a medical prescription.] *s. sh.* (20 Oct.)
669. f. 21. (82.)

[**Oct. 21.**]—One and Thirty new Orders of Parliament, and the Parliaments Declaration : published for the satisfaction of the people of England, Scotland and Ireland. [A satire.] (21 Oct.)
E. 1000. (20.)

Oct. 22.—A Letter of the Officers of the Army in Scotland to the Officers of the Army in England. *Printed by Christopher Higgins : Edinburgh ; reprinted at London.* **E. 1005. (14.)**

Oct. 23.—A Declaration of the Commander in Chief of the Forces in Scotland, with a Declaration of the Officers of the Army in Scotland to the Churches of Christ in the three Nations. *Printed by Christopher Higgins : Edinburgh.* **E. 1000. (18.)**

[**Oct. 24.**]—The Army's Plea for their present Practice : tendered to the consideration of all ingenuous and impartial men. *Printed by Henry Hills.* (24 Oct.) **E. 1000. (24.)**

Oct. 25.—A Letter from a person of quality in Edenburgh, to an Officer of the Army, wherein is given a true accompt of Generall Monck's proceedings. *s. sh. Printed by Sarah Griffin for Thomas Hewer.*
669. f. 21. (86.)

[**Oct. 25.**]—The Grand Concernments of England ensured by a constant Succession of Free Parliaments, with some smart Rebukes to the Army. pp. 70. (25 Oct.) **E. 1001. (6.)**

[**Oct. 25.**]—A Mite of Affection, manifested in 31 Proposals offered to the People within this Common-wealth ; tending and tendred unto them for a Settlement in this the day of the Worlds Distraction and Confusion. [Signed : E. B., i.e. E. Billing or E. Burrough.] *Printed for Giles Calvert.* (25 Oct.) **E. 1001. (5.)**

[**Oct. 25.**]—A New Map of England, or, Forty six Quæries. By I. B. (25 Oct.) **E. 1001. (3.)**

[**Oct. 25.**]—The Parliaments Plea : or XX. Reasons for the Union of the Parliament & Army presented to Publick Consideration. (25 Oct.)
E. 1001. (7.)

[**Oct. 25.**]—Peace and not Warre : or, The Moderator. Truly stating the Case of the Common-Wealth, as to several of the Councils and

1659.

Transactions from 1636 to 1659. By John Harris. *Printed for Nath. Brook.* (25 Oct.) **E. 1000. (25.)**

[Oct. 25.]—The Plague of Athens. By Tho. Sprat. [A poem.] *Printed by T. Childe and L. Parry for Henry Brome.* (25 Oct.) **E. 770. (4.)**

[Oct. 26.]—The Christian Commonwealth : or, The Civil Policy of the Rising Kingdom of Jesus Christ. By John Eliot. *Printed for Livewell Chapman.* (26 Oct.) **E. 1001. (10.)**

[Oct. 26.]—A Letter to an Officer of the Army concerning a select Senate mentioned by them in their Proposals to the late Parliament. By Henry Stubbe. pp. 76. *Printed for T. B.* (26 Oct.)
E. 1001. (8.)

Oct. 27.—A Declaration of the General Council of the Officers of the Army, agreed upon at Wallingford. [See also below : 8 Nov., E. 1006. (2.)] *Printed by Henry Hills.* (29 Oct.) **E. 1001. (12.)**

Oct. 27.—The Declaration of the Officers of the Army opened, examined & condemned. By E. D. pp. 50. **E. 1010. (16.)**

Oct. 29.—A true Copy of a Message sent to General Monck from severall Officers of the Army [praying Monck "not to go to war precipitately "]. *s. sh.* **669. 22. (1.)**

Oct. 31.—By the Committee of Safety. A Proclamation declaring the continuance of Justices, Sheriffs, and other Officers. *Printed by Henry Hills and John Field.* **669. f. 21. (85.)**

[Oct. 31.]—The Anatomy of Secret Sins, Presumptuous Sins, Sins in Dominion & Uprightness ; delivered in divers sermons preached at Mildreds in Bread-street. By Obadiah Sedgwick. pp. 297. *Printed by T. R. for Adoniram Byfeild.* (31 Oct.) **E. 1003.**

[Oct. 31.]—The Good Man's Epitaph briefly explained and applyed in a sermon at the Funeral of Mr. John Drury. By Thomas Cartwright. *Printed by D. Maxwel for John Baker.* (31 Oct.) **E. 1001. (16.)**

[Oct. 31.]—Navigation by the Mariners Plain Scale new plain'd : or, A Treatise of Geometrical and Arithmetical Navigation. By John Collins. 4 pt. *Printed by Tho. Johnson for Francis Cossinet.* (31 Oct.)
E. 1002.

[Oct. 31.]—Baron Tomlin's learned Speech to the Sheriffs of London and Middlesex, when they came to be sworn at the Exchequer. [A satire.] (31 Oct.) **E. 1001. (13.)**

[Oct. 31.]—The Lord Henry Cromwels Speech in the House. [A satire.] (31 Oct.) **E. 1001. (15.)**

[Oct. 31.]—Mr. John Iretons Oration at the Choosing of the new Lord Mayor. [A satire.] (31 Oct.) **E. 1001. (14.)**

[Oct.]—Cheiragogia Heliana. A manuduction to the Philosopher's Magic Gold. To which is added : Ἄντρον Μίτρας ; Zoroaster's Cave. By Geo. Thor. pp. 96. *Printed for Humphrey Moseley.* **E. 1911. (2.)**

1659.

[Oct.]—Excellentissimi viri Dni. Johannis Wallæi Medica omnia ad chyli & sanguinis circulationem eleganter concinnata. In lucem nunc primum proferre voluit C. Irvinus. pp. 288. *Excudebat J. C. & prostant venales apud T. Davies & T. Sadler.* **E. 1725. (2.)**

[Oct.]—The Nullity of Church-Censures : or, A Dispute written by Thomas Erastus wherein is proved that Excommunication and Church-Senates exercising the same are not of Divine Institution. pp. 93. *Printed for G. L.* **E. 1783. (2.)**

[Oct.]—Dia, a poem. [With other poems.] To which is added, Love made Lovely. By William Shipton. pp. 172. *Printed for Charles Tyus.* **E. 2113. (2.)**

[Nov. 1.]—A Declaration of the Commander-in-Chief of the Forces in Scotland, and of the Officers of the Army under his command, in vindication of the Liberties of the People, and the Priviledges of Parliament. *s. sh. Printed by Christopher Higgins : Edinburgh.* (1 Nov.)
669. f. 21. (84.)

Nov. 1.—The Humble Representation of some Officers of the Army to the Right Honourable Lieutenant General Fleetwood. **E. 1005. (8.)**

[Nov. 1.]—Eighteen Sermons preached in Oxford, 1640, by the late Reverend James Usher, Lord Primate of Ireland. With a Preface concerning the Author, by Stanly Gower. pp. 464. *Printed for John Rothwell.* (1 Nov.) **E. 1004.**

[Nov. 1.]—A Treatise of Gavelkind, both name and thing, shewing the true Etymologie and Derivation of the one, the Nature, Antiquity, and Original of the other. By William Sommer. pp. 216. *Printed by R. & W. Leybourn for the Author.* (1 Nov.) **E. 1005. (1.)**

[Nov. 1.]—Twelve Seasonable Quæries proposed to all True Zealous Protestants and English Free-Men, occasioned by our late and present Revolutions. (1 Nov.) **E. 1005. (5.)**

[Nov. 2.]—The Advice or Remonstrance of several thousands in the County of Durham, Northumberland, and the adjacent parts of Westmerland and Cumberland, with the north part of Yorkshire, to the Lord General Monk, and those with him. *Printed by Hen. Hills.* (2 Nov.) **669. f. 21. (87.)**

[Nov. 3.]—The Declaration of the Lords, Gentlemen, Citizens, Free-holders and Yeomen of this once happy Kingdom of England. [Explaining that they have taken up arms "in defence of ourselves, and others who will pertake with us in the vindication and maintenance of the freedom of Parliaments."] *s. sh.* (3 Nov.)
669. f. 21. (88.)

[Nov. 3.]—A Narrative of the Proceedings of the Committee of the Militia of London concerning a Letter in part resolved to be sent to

1659.

General Monck, and the Officers under his command in Scotland. [With the names of "the promoters of the letter" and of "the dissenters."] *s. sh.*　　　**669. f. 22. (6.)**

[**Nov. 3.**]—A Gagg for the Quakers. With an Answer to Mr. Denn's Quaker no Papist. [See above : 16 Oct., E. 1000. (13.)] *Printed by J. C.* (3 Nov.)　　　**E. 764. (2.)**

[**Nov. 3.**]—Unio Reformantium ; or, The Presbyterian and Independent vindicated from the Contradictious Way of Free-Admission. In answer to John Timpson and William Morice. By John Beverley. pp. 175. *Printed by Ja. C. for John Allen.* (3 Nov.)　　　**E. 1803. (1.)**

[**Nov. 4.**]—An Apology for the Royal Party : written in a Letter to a Person of the late Councel of State. By a Lover of Peace and of his Countrey. With a Touch at the pretended Plea for the Army. [By John Evelyn.] (4 Nov.)　　　**E. 763. (11.)**

[**Nov. 4.**]—A short, legal, medicinal, usefull, safe, easie Prescription to recover our Kingdom, Church, Nation from their present dangerous, distractive, destructive Confusion. By William Prynne. [See also below : 26 Nov., E. 1010. (8.)] *Printed and are to be sold by Edward Thomas.* (4 Nov.)　　　**E. 772. (1.)**

[**Nov. 5.**]—By the Committee of Safety. A Proclamation inhibiting all Meetings for the raysing or drawing together of forces, without order of the said Committee or the Lord Fleetwood. *s. sh.* *Printed by Henry Hills and John Field.*　　　**669. f. 22. (2.)**

[**Nov. 5.**]—The Game is up : or, XXXI new Quæries and Orders fitted for the present State of Affairs. (5 Nov.)　　　**E. 1005. (12.)**

Nov. 5.—A Sermon, being the last which was preached by Bishop Brownrigg, Bishop of Exon. pp. 76. *Printed for Robert Crofts.*

　　　E. 2107. (3.)

Nov. 6.—A Proclamation touching the Election of fit persons to serve in Parliament. By the King. Given at our Court [at Brussels] the sixth of Nov. *s. sh.* *Printed for M. B.*　　　**669. f. 24. (9.)**

[**Nov. 7.**]—Certamen Brittanicum, Gallico Hispanicum. A true relation of a Conference holden between Charles Stuart, King of Scots, Don Lewis de Haro and the Cardinall Mazarine. (7 Nov.)　**E. 1005. (16.)**

Nov. 7.—The Treaty of Peace between the Crowns of France and Spain. *Printed by Tho. Newcomb & are to be sold by G. Bedell & T. Collins.*

　　　E. 774. (7.)

[**Nov. 7.**]—A Brief, Necessary Vindication of the Old and New Secluded Members from the false calumnies of John Rogers in his Un-Christian Concertation with Mr. Prynne, and of M. Nedham in his Interest will not Lie. By William Prynne. pp. 62. [See above : 20 Sept., E. 995. (25.) and 17 Aug., E. 763. (5.)] *Printed and are to be sold by Edward Thomas.* (7 Nov.)　　　**E. 772. (2.)**

1659.

[**Nov. 7.**]—Valerius and Publicola : or, The true Form of a Popular Commonwealth extracted e puris naturalibus. By James Harrington. *Printed by J. C. for Henry Fletcher.* (7 Nov.) **E. 1005. (13.)**

[**Nov. 7.**]—The Amourous Fantasme. A tragi-comedy [in verse]. By Sir William Lower. [With an engraved frontispiece.] pp. 96. *Printed by John Ramzey : Hage.* (7 Nov.) **E. 2108. (1.)**

[**Nov. 7.**]—The Arraignment of the Divel, for stealing away President Bradshaw. [In verse.] *s. sh.* (7 Nov.) **669. f. 22. (3.)**

Nov. 8.—The Lord General Fleetwoods Answer to the Humble Representation of Collonel Morley and some other late Officers of the Army. **E. 1010. (6.)**

Nov. 8.—Three Speeches made to the Lord Maior, Aldermen and Common-Council of London by the Lord Whitlock, Lord Fleetwood, Lord Disbrowe at Guild-Hall. **E. 1010. (5.)**

[**Nov. 8.**]—The Armies Declaration examined and compared with their Declaration May 6, discovering some of their Contradictions, Lies and Designes. [See above : 6 May, E. 980. (20.) and 27 Oct., E. 1001. (12.)] (8 Nov.) **E. 1006. (2.)**

[**Nov. 8.**]—The Form of the New Commissions by which the Forces act, that are under the command of Charles Fleetwood Esq., with some observations thereupon ; the power by which Monck acteth is vindicated, and the Nation thereby undeceived. *s. sh.* (8 Nov.) **669. f. 22. (4.)**

[**Nov. 8.**]—Armilla Catechetica. A Chain of Principles, or, an orderly concatenation of Theological Aphorismes and Exercitations. By John Arrowsmith. pp. 490. *Printed by John Field : Cambridge.* (8 Nov.) **E. 1007.**

[**Nov. 8.**]—Hypo[c]rites Unmasked, or, The Hypocrisie of the New Usurpers discovered. In a few Questions propounded to the Army, wherein the Parliament and their General Monck are vindicated from the aspersions cast upon them by their enemies. *Printed for Goodman Constant and are to be sold at the Sign of the Faithful Souldier, right against Turn-Coat-Hall.* (8 Nov.) **E. 1005. (18.)**

[**Nov. 8.**]—A Light shining out of Darknes ; or, Occasional Queries submitted to the judgment of such as would enquire into the true state of things in our times. With a brief Apologie for the Quakers. [By Henry Stubbe.] pp. 186. (8 Nov.) **E. 770. (5.)**

[**Nov. 8.**]— A Treatise of Self-Denyall. By Richard Baxter. pp. 339. *Printed by Robert White for Nevil Simmons.* (8 Nov.) **E. 1006. (3.)**

[**Nov. 9.**]—The Morning Exercise methodized ; or certain chief heads and points of the Christian Religion opened and improved in divers sermons by several Ministers of the City of London in the monthly course of the Morning Exercise at Giles in the Fields, May. [Edited by Thomas Case.] pp. 697. *Printed by E. M. for Ralph Smith.* (9 Nov.) **E. 1008.**

1659.

[Nov. 9.]—The Refuter Refuted, or Doctor Hammonds Ἐκτενέστερον defended against the impertinent Cavils of Mr. Henry Jeanes. By William Creed. pp. 644. [See above : 5 Sept., 1657, E. 925. (3.)] *Printed for R. Royston.* (9 Nov.) **E. 1009.**

[Nov. 9.]—A Guild-Hall Elegie, upon the Funeralls of that Infernal Saint John Bradshaw, President of the High Court of Justice. *s. sh.* (9 Nov.) **669. f. 22. (5.)**

[Nov. 11.]—A proper new Ballad on the Old Parliament. Or, the second part of Knave out of Doores. *s. sh.* (11 Nov.) **669. f. 22. (7.)**

[Nov. 12.]—Englands Alarm, the State-Maladies and Cure. By J. H., a Lover of Englands Peace. [In verse.] *Printed by Tho. Johnson.* (12 Nov.) **E. 1010. (1.)**

[Nov. 12.]—A Seasonable Enquiry after the sure way to Peace in England, directed principally to the Army. (12 Nov.)
E. 763. (12.)

[Nov. 12.]—Decrees and Orders of the Committee of Safety of the Commonwealth of Oceana. [A satire.] (12 Nov.) **E. 1010. (3.)**

[Nov. 13.]—Hell broke loose ; or, An History of the Quakers both old and new. By Thomas Underhill. pp. 50. *Printed for Simon Miller.* (13 Nov.) **E. 770. (6.)**

[Nov. 14.]—A Continuation of the Acts and Monuments of our late Parliament from June 9 to July 7. By J. Canne. [A satire.] (14 Nov.) **E. 1010. (4.)**

[Nov. 14.]—A Word of seasonable and sound Counsell, laid down in severall proposals. Humbly tendred unto those that are in eminent places. As an Essay in order to a well-grounded unity. *s. sh. Printed for Francis Smith.* (14 Nov.) **669. f. 22. (9.)**

[Nov. 15.]—The Remonstrance of the Apprentices in and about London. [Advocating the Restoration of Charles II.] *s. sh.* (15 Nov.)
669. f. 22. (10.)

Nov. 16.—A Narrative of the Northern Affairs, touching the Proceedings of General Monck and the Lord Lambert. **E. 1010. (19.)**

[Nov. 16.]—The Remonstrance of the Noblemen, Knights, Gentlemen and Commons of the late Eastern, Southern and Western Associations, who desire to shew themselves faithfull to the Good Old Cause. *s. sh.* (16 Nov.) **669. f. 22. (11.)**

[Nov. 20.]—A Negative Voyce : or, A Check for your Check, being a Message of Non-concurrence, for the Ballancing-House or Co-ordinate Senate, fairly discussing the Security it can give to the Good Old Cause. (20 Nov.) **E. 1010. (10.)**

[Nov. 21.]—Eighteen Questions propounded, to put the great Question between the Army and their dissenting Brethren out of Question. By Jer. Ives. *Printed by G. D. for Francis Smith.* (21 Nov.) **E. 1010. (12.)**

1659.

[**Nov. 21.**]—Erastus Junior, or, A Fatal Blow to the Clergie's Pretensions to Divine Right. By Josiah Web. *Printed and are to be sold by Livewell Chapman.* (21 Nov.) **E. 1010. (11.)**

[**Nov. 22.**]—Bradshaws Ultimum Vale, being the last Words that are ever intended to be spoke of him, as they were delivered in a Sermon preach'd at his Interrment. By J. O. D. D. Time-Server General of England. [A satire.] *Printed at Oxford.* **E. 1011. (1.)**

Nov. 23.—[An Order of Common Council appointing the 2nd of Dec. to be kept as a Fast Day.] *s. sh. Printed by James Flesher.*
669. f. 22. (11*.)

Nov. 24.—An Act for the more certain and constant supply of the Soldiery with pay ; and the preventing of any further oppression or damage to the people by Free-quarter or Billet. 12 Maii 1649. [With an Order for its republication, by the Committee of Safety, dated 24 Nov.] *Printed by Henry Hills and John Field.*
E. 1074. (24.)

Nov. 24.—The Out-Cries of the Poor, Oppressed and Imprisoned ; presented to the Council of Officers, by William Pryor and Thomas Turner. *Printed by G. D. for Francis Smith.* **E. 1010. (23.)**

Nov. 24.—A Narrative of the Proceedings of the Northern Armies under the present Conduct of Generall Monck and the Lord Lambert. *Printed for G. Horton.* **E. 1010. (25.)**

[**Nov. 24.**]—Tumulus Decimarum ; or, The History of Tythes. By H. P. *Printed for Giles Calvert.* (24 Nov.) **E. 1010. (13.)**

[**Nov. 24.**]—Resolves of the Committee of Safety. Whereunto is added, the Saints Dictionary. [A satire, chiefly on ecclesiastical topics.] (24 Nov.) **E. 1872. (1.)**

[**Nov. 25.**]—A Timely Warning and Friendly Admonition to the Forces in Scotland under Generall Monck. By some Members of the Army under the command of Major General Lambert. (25 Nov.)
E. 1010. (18.)

[**Nov. 26.**]—A Reply to Mr. William Prinne, his unsafe Expedient for the settlement of these Nations by restoring the ancient Nobility. [See above : 4 Nov., E. 772. (1.)] *Printed for Francis Smith.* (26 Nov.)
E. 1010. (8.)

Nov. 29.—His Majesty's Gracious Message to General Monck, Commander in Chief of His Majesties Army in Scotland, and to the Lords, Knights, Gentlemen, &c. sitting in Council at Edenburgh. [From "Our Court at Orleance."] *s. sh. Printed at Paris.* **669. f. 22. (22.)**

[**Nov. 29.**]—A Letter [dated from Edinburgh] sent by General Monck to Vice Admiral Goodson, to be communicated to the rest of the Officers of the Fleet, in answer to a Letter with some proposals lately sent to him from them. *s. sh. Printed by John Johnson.* **669. f. 22. (20.)**

1659.

[**Nov.**]—The Christians Dayly Practice; or, A practical discourse of Prayer. By Sampson Tounesend. pp. 124. *Printed by E. M. for George Calvert.*   **E. 1803. (2.)**

[**Nov.**]—A Compendious History of the Turks: containing an exact account of the Originall of that People. By Andrew Moore. pp. 1434. *Printed by John Streater.*   **E. 1742–45.**

[**Nov.**]—A Discourse of the true Gospel Blessedness in the New Covenant. By Tho. Collier. pp. 134. *Printed by H. Hills, for the Author.*

E. 1801. (2.)

[**Nov.**]—Modus tenendi Parliamentum; or, The Old Manner of holding Parliaments in England. [With a Catalogue of the names of the Speakers of the Commons.] By W. Hakewel. pp. 220. *Printed by J. G. for Abel Roper.*   **E. 1930. (1.)**

[**Nov.**]—Parkerus Illustratus; sive, Annotata quædam in ommes lxx. Thomæ Parkeri theses De Traductione Hominis Peccatoris ad Vitam. Omnia Richardo Baxtero opposita ab authore Philo-Tileno. [See above: 28 July 1657, E. 1670. (3.)] pp. 143. *Excudebat D. M. sumptibus Joannis Baker.*   **E. 1911. (3.)**

[**Nov.**]—Πέλαγος, or, An Improvement, of the Sea, upon the nine nautical verses in the 107 Psalm. By Daniel Pell. pp. 610. *Printed for Livewell Chapman.*   **E. 1732.**

[**Nov.**]—The Practice of Godlines. By Henry Lukin. Second edition. pp. 116. *Printed by A. M. for Tho. Underhill.*   **E. 2107. (2.)**

[**Nov.**]—The Second Part of the Garden of Eden. Or, An accurate description of all Flowers and Fruits growing in England. By Sir Hugh Plat. pp. 159. *Printed for William Leak.*   **E. 1804. (2.)**

[**Nov.**]—The Substance of Christian Religion. By William Ames. pp. 307. *Printed by T. Mabb for Thomas Davies.*   **E. 1738. (2.)**

Nov.]—Καιροὶ χαλεποί. A Word in Season, for a Warning to England. By Thomas Willes. pp. 430. *Printed by Tho. Ratcliff for Tho. Underhill.*   **E. 1734.**

[**Nov.**]—A Century of Select Hymns, collected out of Scripture. By W. B., Ministre of the Gospel at Martins in Leicester [i.e. William Barton.] pp. 108. *Printed by T. R. for Francis Eglesfield, Thomas Underhill and Francis Tyton.*   **E. 2104. (1.)**

[**Nov.**]—Ratts Rhimed to Death. Or, The Rump-Parliament hang'd up in the Shambles. [Ballads.] pp. 89.   **E. 1761. (2.)**

Dec. 1.—By the Committee of Safety. [A Proclamation "prohibiting the contrivance or subscription of any petitions or papers for the promoting of designs dangerous to the peace of the Commonwealth."] *s. sh. Printed by Henry Hills and John Field.*   **669. f. 22. (13.)**

[**Dec. 1.**]—To the Army. [An exhortation to humility: by Isaac Penington, the younger.] *s. sh.* (1 Dec.)   **669. f. 22. (12.)**

1659.

[**Dec. 2.**]—Select Ayres and Dialogues for one, two, and three voyces; to the theorbo-lute or basse-viol. [Edited by John Playford. With an engraved frontispiece.] pp. 114. *Printed by W. Godbid for John Playford.* (2 Dec.) **E. 1078.**

[**Dec. 3.**]—Legislative Power in Problemes. Published for the information of all those who have constantly adhered to the Good Cause, and for the reformation of all those who had embraced the Bad Cause. By Peter Chamberlin. *Printed by John Clowes.* (3 Dec.) **E. 1079. (1.)**

Dec. 5.—To our right worthy and grave Senatours, the Lord Mayor, Aldermen and Commonalty of the City of London in Common Council assembled. The Petition and Address of divers Young Men, on the behalf of themselves and the Apprentices in and about this City. [Praying "that the two great pillars of the land, Magistracy and Ministry, may be asserted and encouraged," and that a new Parliament may be summoned.] *s. sh.* **669. f. 22. (14.)**

Dec. 6.—To the General Council of Officers. The Representation of divers Citizens of London and others well affected to the peace of the Commonwealth. [Praying "that, as the only way left us for our preservation, you would speedily withdraw the force from the Parliament House door, leaving the Members lately interrupted to return to the discharge of their trust."] *Printed by John Clowes.*

669. f. 22. (17.)

Dec. 6.—A Letter to the Lord Mayor, sent to him from the Committee appointed to disperse the General Remonstrance and Protestation of the 16th of November last to be by him communicated to the Aldermen and Common-Councel. *s. sh. Printed by J. C.* **669. f. 22. (16.)**

[**Dec. 7.**]—Magna Charta : containing that which is very much the sence and agreement of the good people of these nations, notwithstanding their differences relating to Worship. Humbly tendred to those that are in eminent place, as some further essay in order to a well grounded unity, peace and settlement. [Signed : J. C.] *s. sh. Printed for Francis Smith.* (7 Dec.) **669. f. 22. (15.)**

Dec. 9.—A Declaration by the Committee of Safety, touching the payment of the duties of Custome and Excise. *Printed by Henry Hills and John Field.* **E. 1074. (25.)**

[**Dec. 9.**]—Beatis Manibus invictissimi herois Olivarii Cromwelli Magni, Magnæ Britanniæ Protectoris parentatio. Scripta ab Equite Polono. [With an engraved frontispiece bearing the arms of Cromwell.] *Excudebat J. B. impensis Edvardi Brewster.* (9 Dec.) **E. 1079. (2.)**

[**Dec. 12.**]—The Engagement and Remonstrance of London, subscribed by 23,500 hands. [Demanding the dispersal, within twelve hours, of " all such troups and companies as do not properly belong to the Guard

1659.

of this City," and the release from prison of certain citizens.] *s. sh.*
(12 Dec.)   **669. f. 22. (18.)**

[**Dec. 12.**]—To the Lord Mayor, Aldermen and Commons of the City of
London, in Common Council assembled. The Petition and Address of
the Sea-men and Water-men in and about London. ["Praying
that a free and legal Parliament may be convened, the Militia
of the City raised, etc." By William Prynne.] *s. sh.* (12 Dec.)
                                                            669. f. 22. (8.)

[**Dec. 13.**]—To our worthy and grave Senators, the Lord Mayor, and
Aldermen, to be suddenly communicated and consulted with the
Commonalty of the City of London, in Common-Councell assembled.
The further Petition and Remonstrance of the Freemen and Prentices
of the City of London. [Praying them to continue the work of
"arraying a Militia for the defence of the City," and expressing their
earnest desires for the establishment of a "Free Parliament."] *s. sh.*
(13 Dec.)   **669. f. 22. (19.)**

Dec. 13.—A Perfect Narrative of the Grounds & Reasons moving some
Officers of the Army in Ireland to the securing of the Castle of Dublin
for the Parlament. *Printed by Tho. Newcomb.*   **E. 1013. (16.)**

[**Dec. 13.**]—A Faithfull Searching Home Word, intended for the view
of the remaining Members of the former Old Parliament, shewing the
Reasonableness of their first Dissolution. (13 Dec.)   **E. 774. (1.)**

Dec. 14.—By the Committee of Safety. A Proclamation touching the
summoning of a Parliament. *s. sh.* *Printed by Henry Hills and John
Field.*   **669. f. 22. (24.)**

Dec. 14.—[An Order of Common Council, for preserving the peace of
the City at the forthcoming meeting of Parliament.] *s. sh.* *Printed by
James Flesher.*   **669. f. 22. (23.)**

Dec. 14.—An Account of the Affairs in Ireland, in reference to the
late change in England ; with a Declaration of several Officers of the
Army in Ireland, holding forth their steadfast resolution to adhere to
the Parliament. *Printed at Dublin: and reprinted at London, for Nath.
Brook.*   **669. f. 22. (40.)**

[**Dec. 14.**]—The Grand Cheat cryed up under-hand by many in the
factious and giddy part of the Army. By one that was a member of
the Army whilst they were obedient to the Authority. *s. sh.* (14 Dec.)
                                                            669. f. 22. (21.)

Dec. 15.—A Letter sent from Ireland for the Right Honourable William
Lenthall. [By Theophilus Jones and others.] *Printed by John Streater
& John Macock.*   **E. 1013. (8.)**

Dec. 16.—By the Committee of Safety. A Proclamation requiring the
departure of the persons herein mentioned [i.e. "those who have been in

1659.

actual Arms under the late King and his Sonne " out of London]. *s. sh.*
Printed by Henry Hills and John Field. **669. f. 22. (25.)**

Dec. 17.—A Sermon preached in the Temple Chappel at the Funeral of
Dr. Brounrig, the late Bishop of Exceter ; with an account of his
life and death. By John Gauden. [With an engraved portrait of
Brownrig as frontispiece.] pp. 251. *Printed by J. Best for Andrew
Crook.* **E. 1737. (1.)**

[Dec. 19.]—An Admonition of the greatest Concernment in the present
Juncture ; particularly to the Citizens of London, touching their election
of Common Councill men ; and to them, touching their election of
Members to serve in the Parliament, pretended to be shortly convened.
s. sh. (19 Dec.) **669. f. 22. (27.)**

[Dec. 19.]—The Final Protest and Sense of the Citie. ["The Army
proposes to pillage and murther us ; the Mayor, and his worthy advisers,
Ireton &c., are to hold our hands whiles they give the blow," *etc.*]
s. sh. (19 Dec.) **669. f. 22. (26.)**

Dec. 20.—[A Declaration by the Common Council, vindicating the
Lord Mayor and others from "certain scandalous aspersions, contained
in a pamphlet entitled, The Final Protest and Sense of the Citie." See
above : 19 Dec., 669. f. 22. (26.)] *s. sh. Printed by James Flesher.*
669. f. 22. (28.)

Dec. 20.—A Letter [signed : N. L.] sent from Portsmouth, from a very
worthy person there to a friend of his in London. [Describing the
raising of the siege of Portsmouth.] *s. sh.* **669. f. 22. (30.)**

Dec. 22.—The Agreement of the General Council of Officers of the
Armies of England, Scotland and Ireland. [See also below : 23 Dec.,
669. f. 22. (32.)] *s. sh. Printed by Henry Hills.* **669. f. 22. (31.)**

[Dec. 22.]—London's Out-cry to her Sister-Cities of England. [In verse.]
s. sh. (22 Dec.) **669. f. 22. (29.)**

Dec. 23.—The Resolve of the Citie. [Protesting against the terms of
the "Agreement of the general Council of Officers." See above :
22 Dec., 669. f. 22. (31.)] *s. sh.* **669. f. 22. (32.)**

[Dec. 23.]—A Cordial Confection, to strengthen their hearts whose
courage begins to fail, by the Armies late dissolving the Parliament.
It is wrapt up in an epistolary discourse occasionally written to Mr. R.
Hamon by George Wither. *Printed by James Cottrel.* (23 Dec.)
E. 763. (13.)

Dec. 27.—An Act for further Continuance of the Customs and Excise.
Printed by John Streater. **E. 1074. (26.)**

Dec. 27.—[A Resolution of Parliament respecting absent Members.]
s. sh. Printed by John Streater. **669. f. 22. (37.)**

Dec. 27.—[Orders of Parliament, dated 27 and 29 Dec. ; 1. "That no
Forces shall be raised but by authority of this present Parliament."

1659.

2. "That it be referred to the Commissioners for Management of the Army, to dispose of the Militia Forces."] *s. sh. Printed by John Streater and John Macock.* **669. f. 22. (44.)**

Dec. 27.—A Brief Narrative of the manner how divers Members of the House of Commons coming upon 27 Dec. to discharge their Trusts for the several Counties for which they serve were forcibly shut out by pretended Orders of the Members now sitting at Westminster. *Printed for Edward Thomas.* **E. 1011. (4.)**

Dec. 27.—A seasonable Letter of Advice delivered to the Major of London as he was sitting at Common Councell at Guild-Hall, and by him read on the Bench. [Signed : C. D.] *s. sh.* **669. f. 22. (35.)**

Dec. 27.—To the High Sheriffs and Justices of the Peace for the County of Cornwall, met at Truro. The humble Remonstrance and Petition of the Gentlemen and Freeholders of the said County. [Protesting against the violence of the Army, and praying for a " Free Parliament."] *s. sh.* **669. f. 22. (53.)**

[Dec. 27.]—A Letter from Gen. Monck in Scotland to the Commissioners of Parliament in Ireland, touching his present actings. *s. sh. Printed at Dublin : and reprinted at London, for Nath. Brook.* (27 Dec.) **669. f. 22. (38.)**

[Dec. 27.]—The Petition of Richard Cromwell, late Lord Protector, to the Councel of Officers at Walingford House. [A satire.] *s. sh.* (27 Dec.) **669. f. 22. (34.)**

[Dec. 27.]—The Golden Speech of Queen Elizabeth to her last Parliament, 30 Nov. 1601. *s. sh. Printed by Tho. Milbourn.* (27 Dec.) **669. f. 22. (33.)**

Dec. 28.—A Declaration of Sir Hardresse Waller, Major General of the Parliament's Forces in Ireland, and the Council of Officers there. [On the duty of thankfulness to God "for the late dispensations of His gracious appearances ;" and appointing the following Tuesday a day of Public Thanksgiving.] *s. sh. Dublin, printed by William Blades: and reprinted at London by John Macock.* **669. f. 22. (70.)**

[Dec. 28.]—Two Letters from Vice-Admiral John Lawson : the one to the Lord Mayor of London [declaring the resolution of the Navy that " the Parliament being now returned to the exercise of their authority," they " are bound to yield obedience to them "], the other to the Commissioners for the Militia of London [expressing his confidence in them and the willingness of the Navy to assist them]. *s. sh.* **669. f. 22. (42.)**

[Dec. 28.]—The Noble English Worthies. [A ballad in praise of General Monk.] *Printed by Tho. Milbourn.* (28 Dec.) **669. f. 22. (36.)**

1659.

Dec. 29.—[Votes of a Common Council upon a report by Alderman Fowke with respect to "the imminent and extraordinary danger" of the City of London, to raise six regiments of trained-bands, etc. With the names of the officers appointed to them.] *s. sh.* **669. f. 22. (45.)**

Dec. 29.—A true Copy of the Letter sent from the Lord Mayor, Aldermen and Common-Council, directed to the Right Honorable George Moncke. [Expressing their approval of his resolution to vindicate the civil and religious liberties of the country.] *s. sh.*
669. f. 22. (58.)

Dec. 29.—A Letter sent from General Monck, at Coldstreame, to the Right honorable William Lenthall. *Printed by John Streater and John Macock.* **E. 1013. (6.)**

Dec. 29.—A Letter sent from Col. John Disbrowe, superscribed to the Speaker of the Parliament. *Printed by John Streater & John Macock.*
E. 1011. (5.)

[**Dec. 29.**] Six New Queries. [Relating to the Army and Parliament. With a MS. note in Thomason's hand : "N.B. G. T.," i.e. by George Thomason ?] *s. sh.* (Dec. 29.) **669. f. 22. (41.)**

[**Dec. 29.**]—A New-Years-Gift for Mercurius Politicus. [A satire in verse. By William Kilburne.] *s. sh. Printed by Thomas Milbourn.* (29 Dec.) **669. f. 22. (39.)**

[**Dec. 30.**]—Six Important Quæres, propounded to the Re-sitting Rump of the Long Parliament, to be resolved by them before they presume to act any further. [By William Prynne ?] *s. sh.* (30 Dec.)
669. f. 22. (43.)

[**Dec. 30.**]—A Declaration from the People called Quakers to the Present Distracted Nation of England. (30 Dec.) **E. 1011. (3.)**

Dec. 30.—A Sermon preached at the Funeral of Mrs. Dorothy Litster. By Edward Smith. *Printed by T. R. for Will. Palmer.*
E. 1013. (19.)

Dec. 31.—The humble Remonstrance of the County of Cornwall. [Praying for a Free Parliament.] *s. sh. Printed by Nathaniel Thomas.*
669. f. 23. (13.)

Dec. 31.—An Extract of a Letter from York concerning the Lord Fairfax's raising that County in arms against illegal taxes and free-quarter, and for the freedom of Parliament as it was in 1648. *s. sh.*
669. f. 22. (52.)

Dec. 31.—A Letter sent from Col. Will. Lockhart at Dunkirk for the Right Honorable William Lenthall. *Printed by John Streater and John Macock.* **E. 1013. (3.)**

[**Dec. 31.**]—To the Supreme Authority, the Parliament of England, &c. The Petition of Charles Fleetwood Esq. [A satire.] *s. sh.* (31 Dec.)
669. f. 22. (46.)

1659.

[Dec. 31.]—The Cities New Poet's Mock-Show. [A satire, in verse. Signed : M. T.] *s. sh.* (31 Dec.)   **669. f. 22. (48.)**

[Dec. 31.]—The Re-surrection of the Rump : or Rebellion and Tyranny revived. The third edition. [A satire, in verse.] *s. sh.* (31 Dec.)
669. f. 22. (47.)

[Dec.]—Foelix scelus, Querela piorum, et Auscultatio Divina. Sermons, by Zachary Crofton. pp. 408. *Printed for Tho. Parkhurst.*
E. 1870. (1.)

[Dec.]—Frier Bacon his Discovery of the Miracles of Art, Nature and Magick. Translated out of Dr. Dees own copy by T. M. pp. 51. *Printed for Simon Miller.*   **E. 1932. (1.)**

[Dec.]—The Hearts Ease ; or, A Remedy against all Troubles. By Symon Patrick. pp. 221. *Printed by R. W. for Francis Tyton.*
E. 1801. (1.)

[Dec.]—The History of the Propagation & Improvement of Vegetables by the concurrence of Art and Nature. By Robert Sharrock. [With an engraved plate illustrating methods of grafting, etc.] pp. 150. *Printed by A. Lichfield for Tho. Robinson : Oxford.*   **E. 1731. (2.)**

[Dec.]—Proverbs English, French, Dutch, Italian and Spanish. All Englished and alphabetically digested by N. R. pp. 151. *Printed for Simon Miller.*   **E. 1935. (1.)**

[Dec.]—Quæstionum Juris Civilis Centuria, in decem classes distributa opera Richardi Zouchei. pp. 511. *Excudebat Gul. Hall, impensis Thomæ Robinson : Oxoniæ.*   **E. 1893.**

[Dec.]—The Sinners Hope. Being the substance of severall sermons, preached by Henry Newcome. pp. 187. *Printed by E. C. for George Eversden.*   **E. 1764. (2.)**

To the following no date, except that of the year, can be assigned.

1659.—The Life and Raigne of King Charles. By Lambert Wood [i.e. Lambert van den Bos. With an engraved portrait of Charles I.] pp. 199. *Printed for Simon Miller.*   **E. 1760. (2.)**

1659.—Architectonice. The Art of Building : or, An Introduction to all young Surveyors in common structures. By Thomas Wilsford. *Printed for Nath. Brook.*   **E. 1748. (2.)**

1659.—Culpeper's School of Physick. pp. 461. *Printed for N. Brook.*
E. 1739.

1659.—The Worlds Idol. Plutus : a comedy, by Aristophanes. Translated by H. H. B. [i.e. H. H. Burnell ?]. Together with his notes, and a short discourse upon it. *Printed by W. G. for Richard Skelton, Isaac Pridmore and H. Marsh.*   **E. 1925. (1.)**

1660.

Jan. 1.—A Letter sent from the Lord Fairfax, at Popleton, for the Right Honorable William Lenthall. *Printed by John Streater and John Macock.* **E. 1013. (5.)**

[**Jan. 1.**]—The Parable of the Prodigal, delivered in divers Sermons. By Obadiah Sedgwick. pp. 368. *Printed by D. Maxwel for Sa. Gellibrand.* (1 Jan.) **E. 1011. (7.)**

Jan. 2.—[A Resolution of Parliament "that all Officers who were in the late Rebellion," i.e. of Sir George Booth, "who shall submit themselves to Parliament before 9 Jan. shall be pardoned."] *s. sh. Printed by John Streater and John Macock.* **669. f. 22. (50.)**

Jan. 2.—A Letter from a Captain of the Army to an Honourable Member of Parliament, dated at Tadcaster. *Printed by John Streater and John Macock.* **E. 1013. (9.)**

[**Jan. 2.**]—The Apprentices Hue-and-Cry after their Petition. [A satire, in verse.] *s. sh.* (2 Jan.) **669. f. 22. (49.)**

[**Jan. 2.**]—Thomas Campanella, an Italian Friar and second Machiavel, his advice to the King of Spain for attaining the universal Monarchy of the World. Translated by Ed. Chilmead. With an admonitorie preface by William Prynne. pp. 232. *Printed for Philemon Stephens.* (2 Jan.) **E. 1012. (1.)**

[**Jan. 3.**]—A Free Parliament proposed by the City to the Nation. (3 Jan.) *s. sh.* **669. f. 22. (56.)**

[**Jan. 3.**]—The Lord Lambert's Letter to the Speaker. [A satire.] (3 Jan.) **E. 1013. (1.)**

[**Jan. 4.**]—Seven additional Quæres in behalf of the secluded Members. [By William Prynne.] (4 Jan.) **E. 765. (1.)**

Jan. 5.—[A Resolution of Parliament, "that the Members who stand discharged from voting or sitting as Members of this House in the years 1648, 1649, do stand duely discharged from sitting as Members of this Parliament."] *s. sh. Printed by John Streater and John Macock.* **669. f. 22. (59.)**

[**Jan. 5.**]—Anti-Quakerism, or, a Character of the Quaker's Spirit. *s. sh.* (5 Jan.) **669. f. 22. (57.)**

[**Jan. 5.**]—The Quaker-Jesuite, or, Popery in Quakerisme. By William Brownsword. *Printed by J. M. and are to be sold by Miles Harrison, Bookseller in Kendal.* (5 Jan.) **E. 1013. (4.)**

[**Jan. 5.**]—Englands Murthering Monsters set out in their Colours, in a dialogue between Democritus and Heraclitus. [A satire, in verse. Signed: G. P.] *s. sh.* (5 Jan.) **669. f. 22. (54.)**

[**Jan. 5.**]—A New-Years-Gift for the Rump. [A satire, in verse.] *s. sh. Printed at Oxford for G. H.* (5 Jan.) **669. f. 22. (55.)**

1660.

Jan. 7.—[An Order of Parliament for the due and strict observance of the Lord's Day.] *s. sh.* *Printed by John Streater and John Macock.*
669. f. 22. (60.)

Jan. 7.—Londons Glory ; or, The Riot and Ruine of the Fifth Monarchy Men. Being a relation of their desperate attempts in the City of London, 7 to 9 Jan. *Printed for C. D.* **E. 1874. (3.)**

[Jan. 9.]—The Rota : or, A Model of a Free-State or equall Commonwealth. [By James Harrington.] *Printed for John Starkey.* (9 Jan.)
E. 1013. (7.)

[Jan. 10.]—A Sober and Serious Representation to such as are or may be in power, tending to the happy settlement of these distracted Nations. *s. sh.* (10 Jan.) **669. f. 22. (62.)**

Jan. 10.—To the Right Honourable the Council of State. The Report of all the Births, Baptizings and Burials within the City of London, 10 to 17 Jan. [The form only is printed ; the figures of the returns are supplied in MS. by Thomason.] **E. 1079. (3.)**

[Jan. 11.]—A Hymne to the Gentle-Craft, or Hewson's Lamentation. [A satire, in verse.] *s. sh.* *Printed for Charls Gustavus.* (11 Jan.)
669. f. 22. (64.)

[Jan. 11.]—The Rump roughly but righteously handled, in a new ballad. *s. sh.* (11 Jan.) **669. f. 22. (63.)**

[Jan. 12.]—A Declaration of the People of England for a Free-Parliament. *s. sh.* (12 Jan.) **669. f. 22. (65.)**

Jan. 12.—A Letter from the Lord Gen. Monck to Major General Overton : together with Maior Gen. Overtons Answer thereto. *Printed by James Cottrel.* **E. 1013. (21.)**

Jan. 12.—A Declaration of a small Society of Baptized Believers, undergoing the name of Free-Willers, about the City of London. [By Henry Adis.] *s. sh.* *Printed for the Author.* **669. f. 22. (66.)**

[Jan. 12.]—The Heart of New-England rent at the Blasphemies of the present Generation ; or, a brief tractate concerning the doctrine of the Quakers. By John Norton. pp. 83. *Printed by J. H. for John Allen.* (12 Jan.) **E. 1909. (3.)**

[Jan. 12.]—The Recantation and Confession of John Lambert, Esq. Taken from his Mouth by C. Prince. [A satire.] *Printed for Charls Gustavus.* (12 Jan.) **E. 1013. (10.)**

[Jan. 12.]—Things just and necessary which the Parliament must do, if ever they would prosper. *s. sh.* (12 Jan.) **669. f. 22. (61.)**

Jan. 13.—The humble desires of the County and Burrough of Leicester, delivered to Gen. Monck at St. Albans, 13 Jan. [Praying for the recall of the secluded Members of Parliament, and for the setting in order of the nation's affairs by the Parliament.] *s. sh.* *Printed for Henry Chase.* **669. f. 23. (29.)**

1660.

[**Jan. 13.**]—The Case of the old Secured, Secluded and now Excluded Members stated. By William Prynne. (13 Jan.) **E. 765. (2.)**

[**Jan. 13.**]—Proposals to the Officers of the Army, and to the City of London for the taking off of all Excise, Taxes and Custom. By W. W. Gent. *Printed for R. Ibbitson.* (13 Jan.) **E. 1013. (11.)**

Jan. 13.—Joannis [Gauden] Episcopi Exoniensis Consilia et voce & scripto tradita XLIIII. fratribus filiisque sacris ordinibus initiatis, Januarii 13. [In Latin and English.] *Typis J. Flesher, & prostant apud Andr. Crook.* **E. 1079. (4.)**

Jan. 14.—A Letter from Exeter, advertising the state of affairs there. [Giving the text of a protest to Parliament, passed at a meeting of the Gentry of the County of Devon, urging the recall of the excluded Members.] *s. sh. Printed for Thomas Creake.* **669. f. 22. (74.)**

[**Jan. 14.**]—A Declaration of some of those people in or near London, called Anabaptists. [A statement of their religious and political creed.] *s. sh. Printed by Thomas Milbourn for Samuel Cleaver.* (14 Jan.) **669. f. 22. (67.)**

[**Jan. 16.**]—A Letany for the New-Year, with a description of the New State. [Verses satirising the Rump Parliament.] *s. sh.* (16 Jan.) **669. f. 22. (68.)**

[**Jan. 16.**]—The Out-cry of the London Prentices for Justice to be executed upon John Lord Hewson. [A satire.] *Printed for Gustavus Adolphus.* (16 Jan.) **E. 1013. (12.)**

Jan. 17.—The Occasion and Manner of Mr. Francis Wolleys death, slaine by the Earle of Chesterfield at Kensington, 17 Jan. **669. f. 23. (18.)**

[**Jan. 17.**]—The Gang, or the Nine Worthies and Champions, Lambert &c. [Verses satirising the leading Parliamentarians.] *s. sh. Printed for Charls Gustavus.* (17 Jan.) **669. f. 22. (71.)**

[**Jan. 17.**]—The Hang-mans last Will and Testament: with his Legacy to the Nine Worthies, viz. Col. Lambert, Creed, &c. [A satire, in verse.] *s. sh. Printed for Charls Gustavus.* (17 Jan.) **669. f. 22. (72.)**

[**Jan. 17.**]—A New Ballade to an Old Tune, Tom of Bedlam. [Beginning "Make room for an honest Red-coat." A satire against the Army.] *s. sh.* (17 Jan.) **669. f. 22. (69.)**

[**Jan. 18.**]—A Brief Account of the Meeting, Proceedings and Exit of the Committee of Safety. [A satire.] *Printed for Thomas Williamson.* (18 Jan.) **E. 1013. (13.)**

[**Jan. 18.**]—Vanity of Vanities. Or, Sir Harry Vane's Picture. [A satirical ballad.] *s. sh. Printed for Charls Gustavus.* (18 Jan.) **669. f. 22. (73.)**

[**Jan. 19.**]—A Plea for Sir George Booth and the Cheshire Gentlemen. By W. P. [i.e. William Prynne.] *s. sh.* (19 Jan.) **669. f. 23. (1.)**

1660.

[Jan. 19.]—Three Seasonable Quæres proposed to all those Cities, Counties and Boroughs whose citizens have been excluded and disabled to sit in the Commons House by those now acting at Westminster. *s. sh. Printed for Edward Thomas.* (19 Jan.)   **669. f. 23. (3.)**

[Jan. 19.]—The Declaration of Sir Charls Coot, Lord President of Conaught, and the Officers and Souldiers under his Command. *Printed for Tho. Vere and W. Gilbertson.* (19 Jan.)   **E. 1013. (14.)**

[Jan. 19.]—To the Divines in the City of London. [An anonymous address, requesting the Clergy to take into consideration the unhappy state of the nation.] *s. sh.* (19 Jan.)   **669. f. 23. (4.)**

[Jan. 19.]—The Breech Wash'd by a Friend to the Rump. [In verse.] *s. sh. Printed at Oxford for Carolus Gustavus.* (19 Jan.)

          669. f. 23. (2.)

[Jan. 20.]—A Declaration of many thousand well-affected persons in London and Westminster, expressing their adherence to this present Parliament. *s. sh.* (20 Jan.)   **669. f. 23. (5.)**

[Jan. 20.]—Fortunate Rising ; or, the Rump Upward. [In verse.] *s. sh. Printed for Henry James.*   **669. f. 23. (7.)**

[Jan. 20.]—A Seasonable Speech made by Alderman Atkins in the Rump-Parliament. [A satire.] (20 Jan.)   **E. 1013. (15.)**

[Jan. 20.]—To His Excellency General Monck. The Petition of the Lady Lambert. [A satire.] *s. sh.* (20 Jan.)   **669. f. 23. (6.)**

[Jan. 21.]—The Rump Dock't. [In verse.] *s. sh.* (21 Jan.)

          669. f. 23. (8.)

Jan. 22.—A Letter to General Monk, expressing the sense of many thousands of Old Parliamenters and Old Puritanes. [Praying for the recall of the secluded members of Parliament.] *s. sh.* (22 Jan.)

          669. f. 23. (25.)

Jan. 23.—A Declaration of the Parliament assembled at Westminster. [With regard to its proposed system of Government.] *Printed by John Streater & John Macock.*   **E. 1013. (24.)**

Jan. 23.—A Letter of General George Monck's, dated at Leicester, and directed unto Mr. Rolle to be communicated unto the rest of the Gentry of Devon. [See also below: 28 Jan., 669. f. 23. (23.), and E. 1015. (1.) ; 3 Feb., E. 1015. (10.), and 4 Feb., E. 1015. (11.)] *Printed by John Redmayn.*   **E. 1013. (20.)**

[Jan. 23.]—The Remonstrance of the County of Gloucester, that no new Laws ought to be imposed, nor any Taxes taken, without the consent of the People in a Free-Parliament. *s. sh.* (23 Jan.)   **669. f. 23. (9.)**

[Jan. 23.]—A Seasonable Exhortation of sundry Ministers in London to the People of their respective Congregations. *Printed by E. M. for Samuel Gellibrand.* (23 Jan.)   **E. 1013. (17.)**

1660.

[**Jan. 23.**]—A Curtain-Conference betwixt John Lambert and his Lady. [A political satire.] *s. sh.* *Printed for W. L.* (23 Jan.)

669. f. 23. (10.)

Jan. 24.—An Apologie and Vindication of the Major part of the Members of Parliament excluded from sitting and speaking for themselves and the Common-wealth. *Printed by Tho. Ratcliffe.*

E. 1013. (18.)

Jan. 24.—The humble Address of the County of Northampton, presented to Gen. Monk on his arrival at Northampton. [Praying for a Free Parliament and its privileges.] *s. sh.* *Printed by D. Maxwell.*

669. f. 23. (11.)

[**Jan. 25.**]—The honest Cryer of London. [A satire.] *s. sh.* *Printed for George Thompson.* (25 Jan.) **669. f. 23. (12.)**

Jan. 26.—An Act for an Assessment of one hundred thousand Pounds by the moneth upon England, Scotland and Ireland, for six months. pp. 92. *Printed by John Streater and John Macock.* **E. 1074. (27.)**

[**Jan. 26.**]—To the Rt. Hon. William Lenthal. [An address from the County of Berks, praying for a Free Parliament and the recall of the Members secluded in 1648.] *s. sh.* *Printed for Edward Thomas.* (26 Jan.) **663. f. 23. (15.)**

[**Jan. 26.**]—Chipps of the Old Block ; or, Hercules cleansing the Augæan Stable. [A satire, in verse.] *s. sh.* *Printed at the Hague, for S. Browne.* (26 Jan.) **669. f. 23. (14.)**

[**Jan. 26.**]—To the Company of Grocers. The Petition of Major Salloway. [A satire on Richard Salwey's imprisonment in the Tower and subsequent release.] *s. sh.* *Printed for Henry James.* (26 Jan.)

669. f. 23. (16.)

Jan. 28.—To His Excellency Gen. Monck. A Letter from the Gentlemen of Devon [advocating a Free Parliament] in answer to his Lordships of 23 Jan. [See above : 23 Jan., E. 1013. (20.)] *s. sh. Printed for Y. E.* **669. f. 23. (23.)**

Jan. 28.—A Letter to General Monck in answer to his of the 23rd of Jan. directed to Mr. Rolle. By one of the Excluded Members of Parliament. [Signed : R. M. See above : 23 Jan., E. 1013. (20.)] *Printed for R. Lowndes.* **E. 1015. (1.)**

[**Jan. 28.**]—Κλεὶς Προφητείας, or, The Key of Prophecie : whereby the Mysteries of all the Prophecies from the Birth of Christ until this present are unlocked, and the speedy Resurrection of King Charls the II. out of banishment is foreshewn. (28 Jan.) **E. 774. (2.)**

[**Jan. 28.**]—The Common-Wealths Catechism. [An anti-monarchical tract.] By Lyon Freeman. *Printed by John Clowes.* (28 Jan.)

E. 1870. (2.)

1660.

Jan. 29.—A Letter sent to General Monk to St. Albons, wherein the Antient Government of England is vindicated. [Signed: H. N.] *Printed for the Author.* **E. 1015. (2.)**

Jan. 30.—A Letter agreed unto by the County of Suffolk, presented to the Lord Mayor of London, 30 Jan. [Praying for a Free Parliament.] *s. sh. Printed for Thomas Dring.* **669. f. 23. (22.)**

Jan. 30.—A Full Declaration of the true State of the Secluded Members Case, in Vindication of themselves and their privileges against the Vote of their Discharge. pp. 54. *Printed and are to be sold by Edward Thomas.* **E. 1013. (22.)**

[Jan. 30.]—A Declaration by the Officers in Ireland concerning their late Actings there. *s. sh. Printed by William Bladen: Dublin; reprinted at London by James Cottrel.* (30 Jan.) **669. f. 23. (17.)**

[Jan. 31.]—The Declaration of the County of Norfolk [praying for a Free Parliament and the recall of the Members secluded in 1648]. *s. sh.* (31 Jan.) **669. f. 23. (21.)**

Jan. 31.—To the Parliament of the Commonwealth. The humble Address and Congratulation of many thousands of Watermen belonging to the Thames. [Professing loyalty.] 31 Jan. *s. sh. Printed by John Streater and John Macock.* **669. f. 23. (28.)**

[Jan. 31.]—A Letter of Advice to his Excellency the Lord General Monck, tending to the Peace and Welfare of this Nation. [Signed: T. J.] (31 Jan.) **E. 1013. (23.)**

[Jan. 31.]—Advice to Gen. Monck. [In verse.] *s. sh.* (31 Jan.) **669. f. 23. (19.)**

[Jan. 31.]—The New Discoverer Discover'd. By way of Answer to Mr. Baxter his Pretended Discovery of the Grotian Religion. By Thomas Pierce. pp. 309. [See above: July 1658, E. 1868. (3.)] *Printed by J. G. for Richard Royston.* (31 Jan.) **E. 1014. (2.)**

[Jan. 31.]—A New-Years-Gift for Women. Being a true Looking-Glass wherein they may see their duties. By William Hill. pp. 230. *Printed by T. N. for the Author.* (31 Jan.) **E. 2114.**

[Jan. 31.]—Roome for a Justice; or The Life and Death of Justice Waterton. [A ballad.] *s. sh. Printed for Charles Gustavus.* (31 Jan.) **669. f. 23. (20.)**

[Jan. 31.]—Θεάνθρωπος; or, God-Man: being an Exposition upon the first eighteen verses of the first chapter of the Gospel according to St. John. By John Arrowsmith. pp. 311. *Printed for Humphrey Moseley and William Wilson.* (31 Jan.) **E. 1014. (1.)**

[Jan.]—David Restored. Or, An Antidote against the Prosperity of the Wicked and the Afflictions of the past. By Edward Parry, late L. Bishop of Killaloe. pp. 311. *Printed for Joseph Godwin: Oxford.* **E. 1812. (1.)**

1660.

[Jan.]—Devotions of the Ancient Church, in seaven pious prayers with seaven administrations. pp. 224. *Printed for R. Royston.*
E. 1835. (1.)

[Jan.]—A Dying Fathers Living Legacy to his Loving Son. By F. S., Gent. pp. 137. *Printed for the Authour.* E. 2105. (2.)

[Jan.]—Elenchi motuum nuperorum in Anglia pars prima. Ab autore Geor. Batio recognita & aucta. [With an engraved portrait of Charles I.] pp. 256. *Typis J. Flesher & prostant apud R. Royston.*
E. 1759. (2.)

[Jan.]—Five Seasonable Sermons. By Paul Knell. pp. 188.
E. 1766. (2.)

[Jan.]—The Hang-mans Lamentation for the losse of Sir Arthur Haslerigge, dying in the Tower. Being a dialogue between Esquire Dun and Sir Arthur Haslerig. [A satire.] *Printed for Thomas Vere and William Gilbertson.* E. 1869. (3.)

[Jan.]—Hell, with the Everlasting Torments thereof asserted. By Nich. Chewney. pp. 120. *Printed by J. M. for Tho. Dring.*
E. 1802. (2.)

[Jan.]—Καταβάπτισται κατάπτυστοι. The Dippers dipt. Seventh edition. By Daniel Featley. pp. 258. *Printed by E. C. for N. Bourne.*
E. 1012. (2.)

[Jan.]—A Resolution of a seasonable Case of Conscience, being part of a letter to a Person of Quality, by a Son of the Church of England. *Printed by W. Hall for J. Godwin.* E. 1812. (2.)

[Jan.]—A Thousand Notable Things of sundry sorts, enlarged. [By Thomas Lupton.] pp. 371. *Printed for M. Wright.* E. 1747.

[Feb. 1.]—Roome for Cuckolds; or, My Lord Lamberts Entrance into Sodome and Gomorrah. [A satirical ballad.] *s. sh. Printed for L. M.* (1 Feb.) 669. f. 23. (27.)

Feb. 2.—An Act for constituting Commissioners for ordering and managing the affairs of the Admiralty and Navie. *Printed by John Streater and John Macock.* E. 1074. (28.)

[Feb. 2.]—To His Excellency General Monk. The Congratulation and Address of the County of Bucks. [Praying for a Free Parliament.] *s. sh.* (2 Feb.) 669. f. 23. (24.)

Feb. 2.—To His Excellency General Monck. The Unanimous Representation of the Apprentices and Young Men of London. [Praying for a Free Parliament.] Delivered to His Excellency at St. Albans. *s. sh. Printed by Thomas Ratcliffe.* 669. f. 23. (33.)

[Feb. 2.]—The Declaration of the County of Kent. [Praying for " a Full and Free Parliament."] *s. sh.* (2 Feb.) 669. f. 23. (31.)

1660.

[**Feb. 2.**]—A Translate of a Letter from Don Lewis de Harro, Minister of State to His Majesty of Spaine, sent unto the King of Scots at Brussels concerning the affaires in England.   (2 Feb.)

669. f. 23. (30.)

[**Feb. 2.**]—Anglorum Singultus : or, The Sobbs of England poured out. To be presented to his Excellency Generall George Monke.   *Printed for D. L.*   (2 Feb.)   **E. 774. (3.)**

[**Feb. 2.**]—A Coffin for the Good Old Cause ; or, A Sober Word by way of Caution to the Parliament and Army.   *Printed for the Author.* (2 Feb.)   **E. 1015. (3.)**

[**Feb. 2.**]—A Legal Vindication of the Liberties of England against illegal Taxes and pretended Acts of Parliament.   By William Prynne. The second Edition enlarged.   pp. 80.   *Printed for Edward Thomas.* (2 Feb.)   **E. 772. (4.)**

[**Feb. 2.**]—A Letter to the House, from the Laird Wareston.   [A satire, signed : Archibald Johnson.]   *s. sh.*   *Printed by Edward Mason.* (2 Feb.)   **669. f. 23. (26.)**

[**Feb. 2.**]—A Receipt for the State-Palsie, or, A Direction for the Setling the Government of the Nation, delivered in a sermon.   By S. S. *Printed for Henry Mortlocke.*   (2 Feb.)   **E. 1015. (4.)**

[**Feb. 3.**]—The Remonstrance of the Soldiery to the Lord Mayor and Common Councell of London.   [Tendering their services to assist in obtaining a Free Parliament.]   *s. sh.*   (3 Feb.)   **669. f. 23. (32.)**

[**Feb. 3.**]—Animadversion upon Generall Monck's Letter to the Gentry of Devon.   By M. W.   [See above : 23 Jan., E. 1013. (20.)]   (3 Feb.)

E. 1015. (10.)

[**Feb. 3.**]—The Pedigree and Descent of General George Monck.   *Printed for W. Godbid.*   (3 Feb.)   **E. 1015. (9.)**

[**Feb. 3.**]—Moderation : or Arguments and Motives tending thereunto, humbly tendred to the Parliament.   Together with a brief Touch of the reputed German Anabaptists and Munster Tragedy.   By S. T. *Printed by Henry Hills.*   (3 Feb.)   **E. 1015. (8.)**

[**Feb. 3.**]—Mutiny maintained : or, Sedition made good from its Unity, Knowledge, Wit, Government.   Being a Discourse, directed to the Armies Information.   (3 Feb.)   **E. 774. (5.)**

[**Feb. 3.**]—The Qualifications of Persons, declared capable by the Rump Parliament to elect or be elected Members to supply their House.   [A satire.]   (3 Feb.)   **E. 1015. (6.)**

[**Feb. 4.**]—The fair Dealer : or, A Modest Answer to the Sober Letter of General Monck.   By a Gent. of Devon.   [Signed : J. Trev.   See above : 23 Jan., E. 1013. (20.)]   *Printed for James Hanzen.*   (4 Feb.)

E. 1015. (11.)

1660.

Feb. 6.—The Lord General Monck, his Speech delivered in Parliament. *Printed by J. Macock.*   **E. 1015. (12.)**

Feb. 7.—An additionall Act for Sequestrations. *Printed by John Streater and John Macock.*   **E. 1074. (29.)**

Feb. 8.—To the Lord Maior and Common Councell of London. The Petition of divers well-affected Housholders and Freemen of the said City. [Praying for a " Full and Free Parliament."] *s. sh. Printed by J. H.*   **669. f. 23. (34.)**

[**Feb. 8.**]—Irelands Fidelity to the Parliament of England. In answer to a Paper, intituled The Petition of the Officers and Soldiers in the Fort of Duncannon. *Printed by Tho. Newcomb.* (8 Feb.)   **E. 1015. (13.)**

[**Feb. 8.**]—The Wayes and Meanes whereby an equal & lasting Commonwealth may be suddenly introduced and perfectly founded with the Free Consent of the People of England. By James Harrington. *Printed for J. S.* (8 Feb.)   **E. 1015. (14.)**

Feb. 9.—A Letter of General Monck to the Speaker [enquiring whether he shall destroy the Gates and Portcullises of the City of London]. *s. sh. Printed by John Macock.*   **669. f. 23. (39.)**

[**Feb. 9.**]—[A Petition to Gen. Monk from the County of Warwick, for a Free Parliament and its privileges.] *s. sh. Printed for R. L.* (9 Feb.)   **669. f. 23. (35.)**

Feb. 9.—A Letter of the Apprentices of Bristoll to the Apprentices of London, together with their Declaration for a Free Parliament. *Printed for I. Pridmore.*   **E. 1015. (20.)**

[**Feb. 9.**]—A Letter from Sir Hardress Waller and several other Gentlemen at Dublin to Lieutenant General Ludlowe, with his Answer to the same. *Printed for John Allen.* (9 Feb.)   **E. 774. (6.)**

Feb. 9.—That wicked and Blasphemous Petition of Praise-God Barbone and his Sectarian Crew, presented to the Parliament 9 Feb., anatomized. *Printed for Philo-Monarchæus.*   **E. 1019. (15.)**

[**Feb. 9.**]—The Red-Coats Catechisme, or Instructions to be learned by every one that desires to be one of the Parliaments Janizaries. (9 Feb.)   **E. 1015. (15.)**

[**Feb. 9.**]—The Royall Virgine; or, The Declaration of several Maydens in and about the city of London. [Praying for the restoration of Charles II.] *s. sh. Printed for Virgin Hope-well.* (9 Feb.)   **669. f. 23. (36.)**

Feb. 10.—The most Heavenly and Christian Speech of the King of Sweden, Carolus Gustavus Adolphus on his Death-Bed, 10 Feb. Faithfully translated out of High-Dutch. *Printed for Tho. Vere.*   **E. 1017. (22.)**

1660.

Feb. 11.—A Letter from the Lord General Monck and the Officers under his Command to the Parliament.   *Printed by John Macock.*

E. 1015. (17.)

[**Feb. 11.**]—An exact Accompt of the Receipts and Disbursements expended by the Committee of Safety, upon the emergent occasions of the nation. [A political satire.]   *Printed for Jer. Hanzen.*   (11 Feb.)

E. 1079. (3*.)

Feb. 11.—A Psalme sung by the People before the bone-fires made in London on 11 Feb.   [A ballad, satirising the Rump.]   *s. sh.*

669. f. 23. (43.)

Feb. 12.—A Pattern of Mercy.   Opened in a sermon at St. Pauls before the Lord Mayor and the Lord General Monck.   By Tobias Conyers. *Printed by M. I.*   **E. 774. (8.)**

Feb. 13.—By the Parliament.   [A Proclamation ordering John Lambert to appear before the Council of State, to explain his Contempt of an Order of Parliament commanding him to repair to his house at Holmeby.] *s. sh.   Printed by John Streater and John Macock.*   **669. f. 23. (37.)**

Feb. 13.—The Declaration of the County of Oxon to General Monck. [Praying for a Free Parliament.]   Delivered at his in quarters Broad Street, London.   *s. sh.   Printed for John Starkey.*

669. f. 23. (42.)

Feb. 13.—The Declaration of Thomas Lord Fairfax and the County and City of York.   [Praying for a Free Parliament.]   *s. sh.   Printed for James Williamson.*   **669. f. 23. (47.)**

Feb. 13.—A true copy of a Letter written by the Marquis of Dorchester to the Lord Roos.   [Challenging him to a duel.]   [See also below : 19 and 20 March, 669. f. 24. (22 and 27.)]   **669. f. 23. (38.)**

[**Feb. 13.**]—Epistola Veridica ad homines φιλοπρωτέvοντας, cui additur oratio pro statu Ecclesiæ.   [Signed : N. Y.   By John Hinckley.] (13 Feb.)   **E. 1015. (18.)**

[**Feb. 13.**]—The Signal Loyalty and Devotion of Gods true Saints and Pious Christians towards their Kings.   By William Prynne.   pp. 96. *Printed by T. C. and L. P. and are to be sold by Edward Thomas.* (13 Feb.)   **E. 772. (5.)**

[**Feb. 14.**]—Peace to the Nation.   [An account of the proceedings of General Monck.]   *s. sh.*   (14 Feb.)   **669. f. 23. (41.)**

[**Feb. 14.**]—No Droll, but a Rational Account, making out the probable Fall of the present, with the Rise and Succession of a Free Parliament. (14 Feb.)   **E. 1015. (19.)**

[**Feb. 14.**]—To the Supreme Authority of the Nation.   A Petition of many thousands of Quakers, Fifth-Monarchy Men, Anabaptists, &c. [A satire.]   *s. sh.   Printed by D. Maxwell.*   (14 Feb.)

669. f. 23. (40.)

1660.

[**Feb. 15.**]—The Declaration of the County and Citty of Lincolne. [Praying for a Free Parliament.] *s. sh. Printed for H. M.* (15 Feb.)
669. f. 28. (45.)

[**Feb. 15.**]—The Petition of the Rump to the City of London. [A satire.] *s. sh.* (15 Feb.)
669. f. 23. (44.)

[**Feb. 16.**]—A Letter and Declaration of the County of York to Generall Monck. [Desiring the recall of the secluded Members and the establishment of a Free Parliament.] *s. sh. Printed at York, reprinted at London for John Starkey.* (16 Feb.)
669. f. 23. (48.)

Feb. 16.—A Letter from divers of the Gentry of the County of Lincolne to General Monck. [With a declaration desiring a Free Parliament.] *s. sh. Printed for Richard Lowndes.*
669. f. 23. (51.)

Feb. 16.—The Declaration of Sir Charls Coot and the rest of the Council of Officers of the Army in Ireland concerning the Re-admission of the Secluded Members. *Printed by William Bladen : Dublin ; reprinted at London by J. Macock.*
E. 1016. (7.)

[**Feb. 16.**]—The Message of John Lambert, in answer to the Proclamation. [A satire. See above : 13 Feb., 669. f. 23. (37.)] *s. sh. Printed for James Dukeson.* (16 Feb.)
669. f. 23. (46.)

[**Feb. 17.**]—The Noble Monk ; or, An acrostical panegyrick to General George Monk. *s. sh. Printed by Thomas Milbourn.* (17 Feb.)
669. f. 23. (49.)

[**Feb. 18.**]—A Letter [signed : T. S.] to General Monck. [Complaining of the proceedings of the Rump.] *s. sh.* (18 Feb.)
669. f. 23. (50.)

[**Feb. 18.**]—A Word in Season to General Monk, the City and the Nation. [Advocating a Free Parliament.] *s. sh. Printed at the Hague [London] for S. B.* (18 Feb.)
669. f. 23. (52.)

[**Feb. 20.**]—Considerations by way of Sober Queries, whether the state of the three nations have been bettered or made worse by the sitting of the remnant of the old Parliament. By Thomas Le White. *s. sh. Printed for the Author.* (20 Feb.)
669. f. 23. (53.)

[**Feb. 20.**]—A Plea for Limited Monarchy, as it was established in this Nation before the late War. An Addresse to General Monck. [See also below : 17 July, E. 765. (4.)] *Printed by T. Mabb for William Shears.* (20 Feb.)
E. 765. (3.)

Feb. 21.—The Speech and Declaration of Generall Monck delivered at White-hall to the Members of Parliament, before the Re-admission of the formerly Secluded Members. *Printed by S. Griffin for John Playford.*
E. 1016. (2.)

Feb. 21.—A Letter from General Monck and the Officers here to the respective Regiments and other Forces in England, Scotland and

1660.

Ireland. [Desiring their adherence to the plan of dissolving the Rump and electing a Free Parliament.] *Printed by John Macock.*

669. f. 23. (54.)

Feb. 21.—Sir Arthur Hesilrigs Lamentation upon his being voted from sitting in this long-expected Parliament. [A satire.] *Printed by Edw. Mason.* **E. 1016. (4.)**

[**Feb. 22.**]—The Declaration of the County of Bedford. [Desiring a Free Parliament.] *s. sh.* (22 Feb.) **669. f. 23. (55.)**

Feb. 22.—A Letter sent from a Merchant in Dublin declaring the alteration of Affaires there in summoning a Convention of Estates to sit at Dublin. *Printed for Thomas Pool.* **669. f. 23. (74.)**

[**Feb. 22.**]—The Parliament-Complement; or, The Re-Admission of the Secluded Members. [A satirical ballad.] *s. sh. Printed for James Nidale.* (22 Feb.) **669. f. 23. (56.)**

Feb. 23.—[An Order of Parliament "that all the Militias in the respective counties, and the powers given to them, be revoked."] *s. sh. Printed by John Streater and John Macock.* **669. f. 23. (59.)**

[**Feb. 23.**]—A Declaration of the counties of Chester, Salop, Stafford, &c. against all Assemblies which impose Taxes upon the People without their consent by their representatives in a Free Parliament. *s. sh. Printed for Thomas Poole.* (23 Feb.) **669. f. 23. (60.)**

Feb. 23.—A Letter from Sir Henry Vane to Sir Arthur Hasilrig. [A satire.] *Printed for John Frost.* **E. 1016. (8.)**

[**Feb. 23.**]—The Copy of a Letter from a Lincolnshire Gentleman sent to his Friend in London. (23 Feb.) **E. 1016. (3.)**

[**Feb. 23.**]—Learne of a Turk, or Instructions and Advise sent from the Turkish Army at Constantinople to the English Army at London. By M. B. (23 Feb.) **E. 1016. (6.)**

[**Feb. 23.**]—Νεοφυτο-'Αστρολόγος. The Novice-Astrologer Instructed. In a New-Years-Gift to William Lilly, occasioned by his Merlin for the ensuing year. [By John Gadbury?] pp. 65. *Printed for E. C.* (23 Feb.) **E. 2112. (3.)**

[**Feb. 23.**]—An Outcry after the late Lieut. Gen. Fleetwood. [A satire upon Fleetwood.] *s. sh. Printed by Henry Mason.* (23 Feb.) **669. f. 23. (58.)**

[**Feb. 23.**]—The Rump Ululant. [A satirical ballad.] *s. sh.* (23 Feb.) **669. f. 23. (57.)**

Feb. 24.—An Act for making void the Acts appointing Commissioners for government of the Army, and for making Charles Fleetwood Commander in Chief of the Land Forces. *Printed by John Streater and John Macock.* **E. 1074. (30.)**

1660.

[**Feb. 24.**]—To the Parliament. The Petition of the Mayor and Commons of London in Common Council assembled, that the Militia of London may be forthwith settled in the hands of Citizens of known integrity and interest in the city. *s. sh. Printed by John Redmayn.* (24 Feb.) **669. f. 23. (61.)**

Feb. 25.—An Act for the continuance of the Customs and Excise, from the last day of February until the twenty fourth day of June. [See also below : 7 March, E. 1074. (34.)] *Printed by John Streater and John Macock.* **E. 1074. (31.)**

Feb. 25.—[An Order of Parliament " that the Circuits for holding of Assize for England and Wales be not held this present vacation of Lent."] *Printed by John Streater and John Macock.* **669. f. 23. (63.)**

[**Feb. 25.**]—To the Parliament. The Illegal and Immodest Petition of Praise-God Barebone. [A satire.] *s. sh. Printed by Henry Mason.* (25 Feb.) **669. f. 23. (62.)**

Feb. 27.—[An Order of Parliament for "Officers of the Army forthwith to repair to their respective Charges."] *Printed by John Streater and John Macock.* **669. f. 23. (65.)**

Feb. 27.—To His Excellency General Monck. The humble Addresse and Thanks of the Gentry and other Free-Holders in the County of Hartford. [Praying for a Free Parliament.] *s. sh. Printed by John Brudenell.* **669. f. 23. (67.)**

Feb. 27.—A Letter from Shrewsbury, setting forth the design which the Anabaptists and Quakers had to secure the Castle and to have received five hundred more unto them in opposition to the Parliament. *Printed for T. H.* **669. f. 23. (71.)**

[**Feb. 27.**]—A Letter [signed : S. E.] from a Person of Honour in France concerning the late transactions in England in reference to the Rights of the People in Electing of Parliaments. *s. sh. Printed for Thomas Pool.* (27 Feb.) **669. f. 23. (64.)**

[**Feb. 27.**]—Your Servant, Gentlemen, or, What think you of a Query or two more? [Queries satirising the Parliament.] (27 Feb.) **E. 1016. (9.)**

[**Feb. 28.**]—A Serious Manifesto of the Anabaptist and other congregational Churches, touching the present transactions of the affairs of this Commonwealth both in Church and State. *s. sh. Printed for Henry Hardy.* (28 Feb.) **669. f. 23. (65*.)**

Feb. 28.—A Letter sent to the Lord Mayor of London by Lieut. Col. Kiffen, Capt. Gosfright, Capt. Hewling and Lieut. Lomes, touching the seizing of their persons. Also shewing the forgery and falsehood of a pamphlet intituled, A Manifesto and Declaration of the Anabaptists. *Printed by Henry Hill.* **669. f. 23. (72.)**

1660.

Feb. 28.— Κάκουργοι, sive Medicastri : Slight Healers of Publick Hurts, set forth in a sermon preached in St. Pauls Church.   By John Gauden. pp. 112.   *Printed for Andrew Crook.*   **E. 1019. (4.)**

Feb. 28.—The Wall & Glory of Jerusalem, a sermon preached in St. Pauls Church London, before the Lord Mayor.   By Edward Reynolds. *Printed by Tho. Newcomb for George Thomason.*   **E. 1017. (6.)**

[Feb. 28.]—Saint George and the Dragon.   [A satirical ballad.]   *s. sh.* (28 Feb.)   **669. f. 23. (66.)**

Feb.—Furor Poeticus, i.e. Propheticus.   A Poetick-Phrensie, occasioned by a report of the Parliaments restauration by General George Moncke in February.   By G. W. [i.e. George Wither.]   *Printed by James Cottrel.* **E. 1818. (2.)**

[Feb.]—The Perfect Politician; or, A full view of the life and actions of O. Cromwel.   [With an engraved portrait of Cromwell.]   pp. 359. *Printed by J. Cottrel for William Roybould and Henry Fletcher.* **E. 1869. (1.)**

[Feb.]—England's Worthies.   Select lines of the most Eminent Persons from Constantine the Great to the death of Oliver Cromwel.   By William Winstanley.   [With an engraved frontispiece bearing the portraits of the subjects of the biographies.]   pp. 613.   *Printed for Nathaniel Brooke.*   **E. 1736.**

[Feb.]—De obligatione conscientiæ prælectiones decem, Oxonii in Schola Theologica habitæ anno MDCXLVII. a Roberto Sanderson, nunc vero Episcopo Lincolniensi.   pp. 384.   *Typis R. N.   Impensis Jo. Martin, Ja. Allestry & Tho. Dicas.*   **E. 1754.**

[Feb.]—Diatribæ duæ medico-philosophicæ, prior de fermentatione, altera de febribus.   Studio Thomæ Willis.   [With an allegorical engraving.] pp. 376.   *Typis T. Roycroft, impensis J. Martin, J. Allestry & T. Dicas.* **E. 1888.**

[Feb.]—Examinatio Grammaticæ Latinæ, in usum Scholarum.   Authore Carolo Hoole.   pp. 140.   *Typis T. Mabb.*   **E. 1860. (2.)**

[Feb.]—Four Sermons, preach'd by John Towers, L. Bishop of Peterburgh. pp. 214.   *Printed for Thomas Rooks.*   **E. 1861. (2.)**

[Feb.]—The Life and Death of Robert Harris, late President of Trinity Colledge in Oxon.   Published by W. D. [i.e. William Dunham.] pp. 119.   *Printed for S. B. and are to be sold by J. Bartlet.* **E. 1794. (1.)**

[Feb.]—Manuductio : or, A Leading of Children by the Hand through the Principles of Grammar.   By Ja. Shirley.   Second edition, enlarged.   pp. 243.   *Printed for Richard Lowndes.*   **E. 1931. (2.)**

[Feb.]—The Scales of Commerce and Trade, ballancing betwixt the Buyer and Seller.   By Thomas Willsford.   pp. 217.   *Printed by J. G. for Nath. Brook.*   **E. 1748. (1.)**

1660.

[Feb.]—The Scarlet Gown: or the History of all the present Cardinals of Rome. Written originally in Italian and translated by H. C., Gent. [i.e. Henry Cogan]. pp. 113. *Printed for Humphrey Moseley.*
E. 1748. (3.)

March 1.—The Second Addresse from the Gentlemen of the County of Northampton to the Lord Generall Monck. [Tendering their thanks to him "for that the Secluded Members are restored to the freedome of their places," and urging him not to slacken his endeavours "for the perfecting this good work so happily begun."] *s. sh.*
669. f. 24. (13.)

[March 1.]—Fanatique Queries propos'd to the present Assertors of the Good Old Cause. *Printed for Praise-God-Barebones.* (1 March.)
E. 1016. (10.)

[March 1.]—The Rump serv'd in with a Grand Sallet. [A satirical ballad.] *s. sh.* (1 March.)
669. f. 23. (70.)

March 2.—An Act for Repeal of two Acts for Sequestrations. *Printed by John Streater and John Macock.*
E. 1074. (32.)

[March 2.]—A Declaration of Old Nick, to the whole world, but chiefly to the Quakers of Great Britain. *s. sh. Printed by George Morgan.* (2 March.)
669. f. 23. (68.)

[March 2.]—A Phanatique Prayer by Sir H. V. [i.e. Sir Henry Vane. A satire.] (2 March.)
669. f. 23. (73.)

March 3.—A Letter sent from the Commissioners of Scotland to the Lord General Monck, in the Behalf of themselves and the whole Nation. *Printed for Daniel White.*
E. 1017. (5.)

[March 3.]—The Readie & Easie Way to establish a Free Commonwealth. The author J. M. [i.e. John Milton. See also below: 26 March, E. 1019. (5*.) and May, E. 1915. (2.)] *Printed by T. N. and are to be sold by Livewell Chapman.* (3 March.)
E. 1016. (11.)

[March 4.]—A Declaration of the Nobility and Gentry of the County of Worcester, adhering to the late King. [Asserting that they "neither do nor will harbour any thought of rancor or revenge against any person which hath been of a contrary judgement" to them; and that "their chief desire is for the peace and unity of the nation."] *s. sh. Printed for Charles Adams.* (4 March.)
669. f. 24. (1.)

March 4.—A Letter from the King of Denmark to Mr. William Lilly, occasioned by the Death of his Patron the King of Sweden. [A satire.] *Printed for Gustavus Montelion.*
E. 1017. (33.)

March 5.—Colonell John Lambert's Speech at the Council of State. *Printed by Iohn Redmayne.*
E. 1017. (27.)

March 5.—An Extract of a Letter [signed: T. R.] from a person of quality at Bruxel to a private friend. [Declaring that the King of Scots is promised such active support by the Courts of Spain, France

II.   U

1660.

and Holland, " as will undoubtedly bring a bloudy warre into England, unless the Parliament do in love to themselves and Country prevent it, by a peaceable restoration of the King to his owne Right."]   *s. sh.* *Printed for Thomas Bassett.*   **669. f. 24. (6.)**

[March 6.]—The Coppy of a Letter to Generall Monck.   (6 March.)
E. 1016. (13.)

[March 6.]—A Letter to the Lord General Monk containing the instrumental Causes of the ruine of Governments.   [Signed : John Maudit.] (6 March.)   **E. 1016. (12.)**

[March 6.]—Orthodox State-Queries, presented to all those who retain any sparks of their ancient loyalty.   [In favour of the restoration of Charles II.]   *s. sh.*   *Printed for Philo-Basileuticus Verax.*   (6 March.)
669. f. 24. (2.)

[March 6.]—The Proceedings, Votes, Resolves, and Acts of the late half-quarter Parliament, called The Rump : as it was taken out of their own journal-books.   [A satire.]   *Printed for John Thomason.*   (6 March.)
E. 1074. (33.)

[March 6.]—To the Right Honourable the Parliament of England. The Petition of Arthur Haslerig.   [A satire.]   *Printed for Any Body.* (6 March.)   **669. f. 24. (3.)**

March 7.—An Act for explanation of certain Clauses and Provisos in an Act of this present Parliament, entituled, An Act for the continuance of the Customs and Excise, from the last of February until the 24th day of June.   [See above : 25 Feb., E. 1074. (31.)]   *Printed by John Macock and John Streater.*   **E. 1074. (34.)**

[March 7.]—The History of the Second Death of the Rump.   [A satirical ballad.]   *s. sh.*   (7 March.)   **669. f. 24. (5.)**

[March 7.]—My Lord Whitlocks Reports on Machiavil ; or his Recollections for the use of the Students of Modern Policy.   *Printed for Thomas Bateman.*   (7 March.)   **E. 1016. (14.)**

[March 7.]—The Second Part of Saint George for England.   [In praise of General Monk and the defeat of the Rump Parliament.]   *s. sh.* (7 March.)   **669. f. 24. (4.)**

[March 8.]—Englands Monarchy asserted, and proved to be the Freest State throughout the World.   *Printed by W. G. for Richard Lowndes.* (8 March.)   **E. 1016. (16.)**

[March 8.]—A Short Discourse upon the Desires of a Friend : wherein it is made evident what alone can be the perfect Settlement of this Nation.   *Printed for H. H.*   (8 March.)   **E. 1016. (15.)**

[March 8.]—To the Honourable Citie of London.   The Petition of Philip Skippon, Esq.   [A satire.]   *s. sh.*   *Printed for William Waterson.* (8 March.)   **669. f. 24. (7.)**

1660.

[**March 9.**]—Quæsumus te, &c. or, The Supplement to the New Letany for these Times : being a further expedient to the perfecting of a Reformation in the three nations, but chiefly of the City of London. [A satirical ballad.] *Printed for Cauda Draconis : in English, the Rump.* (9 March.) **E. 1017. (2.)**

[**March 9.**]—Select City Quæries : discovering several Cheats, Abuses and Subtilties of the City Bawds, Whores and Trapanners. By Mercurius Philalethes. 2 pt. (9 & 19 March.) **E. 1017. (1.) & (23.)**

March 10.—Newes from Brussels, in a Letter from a neer Attendant on His Maiesties Person, 10 March. [By Marchamont Nedham.]
E. 1017. (38.)

March 11.—A Letter from several Ministers in and about Edinburgh to the Ministers of London concerning the Re-establishing of the Covenant. *Printed at Edinburgh for Christopher Higgens, and reprinted at London for Richard Hills.* **E. 1017. (11.)**

March 12.—An Act and Declaration for putting the Lawes against Priests and Jesuites in speedy and effectuall execution. *Printed by John Streater and John Macock.* **E. 1074. (35.)**

March 12.—An Act for the setling the Militia for the City of London and liberties thereof. *Printed by John Streater and John Macock.*
E. 1074. (36.)

March 12.—An Act for setling the Militia within England and Wales. pp. 58. *Printed by John Streater and John Macock.* **E. 1074. (37.)**

[**March 12.**]—The Apology of Robert Tichborn and Iohn Ireton, being a serious Vindication of themselves and the Good Old Cause. [A satire.] *Printed for every body but the light-heel'd Apprentices and headstrong Masters of this wincing City of London.* (12 March.) **E. 1017. (3.)**

March 12.—Sir Tho. Soame vindicated by a Vote of the late Parliament, of 12 March, for the discharging of two former Votes of 1 June, 1649. With a recital of the said Votes so discharged. *Printed by James Cottrel.*
669. f. 24. (51.)

March 13.—Ireland's Declaration : being a Remonstrance of the Generality of the Good People of Ireland. [Acknowledging Charles II. to be rightfully King of England, Scotland and Ireland, and undertaking to assist in procuring his restoration, on certain conditions.] *s. sh.*
669. f. 24. (20.)

March 13.—Be Merry and Wise ; or, A Seasonable Word to the Nation, shewing the Cause, the Growth, the State, and the Cure of our present Distempers. **E. 765. (6.)**

March 13.—A Conference held in the Tower of London between two Aldermen, Praise-God Lean-Bone, and the Lord Lambert, concerning the King of Scots and the present Parliament. [A satire.] **E. 1017. (9.)**

1660.

[March 13.]—The Last Will and Testament of Carolus Gustavus, King of Sweden. Translated by Thomas Scot. [A satire.] *Printed for William Leadsom.* (13 March.)   **E. 1017. (6*.)**

[March 13.]—The Life and Approaching Death of William Kiffin, extracted out of the Visitation Book by a Church Member. *Printed for Thomas Bateman.* (13 March.)   **E. 1017. (4.)**

[March 13.]—No New Parliament: or, some Queries or Considerations humbly offered to the present Parliament Members. By a Friend to them and their Cause. [See also below: 14 March, E. 1017. (15.)] (13 March.)   **E. 1017. (8.)**

March 13.—A Speech made to the Lord General Monck at Clotheworkers Hall in London, 13 March, at which time he was there entertained by that Worthie Companie. [In verse.] *s. sh.* **669. f. 24. (8.)**

March 14.—An Act for approbation and admission of Ministers of the Gospel to Benefices and Publick Lectures. *Printed by John Streater and John Macock.*   **E. 1074. (38.)**

March 14.—Rump Enough: or Quære for Quære, in answer to a pamphlet, entituled No New Parliament. [See above: 13 March, E. 1017. (8.)] *Printed for any man that loves Peace.* 14 March.   **E. 1017. (15.)**

[March 14.]—An Heroical Song on the Atchievements of His most excellent Highnesse James, Duke of York, Admiral of Castile. *s. sh. Printed by Henry Blunt.* (14 March.)   **669. f. 24. (10.)**

[March 14.]—A Phanatique League and Covenant, solemnly enter'd into by the Assertors of the Good Old Cause. [A parody of the "Solemn League and Covenant."] *s. sh. Printed for G. H. the Rump's Pamphleteer General.* (14 March.)   **669. f. 24. (11.)**

[March 14.]—A Phanatick Play. The First Part, as it was represented before and by the Lord Fleetwood, Sir Arthur Hasilrig, Sir Henry Vane, the Lord Lambert and others, last night. (14 March.)   **E. 1017. (10.)**

[March 14.]—The Rumps Last Will and Testament, which the Executors herein named have thought good to publish and exhibite. (14 March.)   **E. 1017. (12.)**

[March 15.]—Englands Faiths Defender vindicated: or, A Word to clear a most foul Aspersion, which hath been cast upon Charles II., that he should have renounced the Protestant Religion and Church of England and have embraced Popery. *Printed for Charles King.* (15 March.)   **E. 1017. (17.)**

March 15.—An Act for bringing in the revenue of Delinquents and Popish Recusants. *Printed by John Streater and John Macock.*

E. 1074. (39.)

March 15.—An Act for recovery of Publique Debts, and other Duties belonging to the Common-Wealth. *Printed for John Streater and John Macock.*   **E. 1074. (40.)**

1660.

[March 15.]—Articles of High Treason, made and enacted by the late Half-Quarter Usurping Convention : and now presented to publick view. *Imprinted for Erasmus Thorowgood, and are to be sold at the signe of the Roasted Rump.* (15 March.)　　　　　**E. 1017. (16.)**

[March 15.]—The Black Book opened, or Traytors arraigned and condemned by their own Confession. Being a tragical discourse between a noble cavalier and a select number of those pure refined diabolical saints, called King-Killers. As it is to be acted at the Red Bull in St. Johns Street by a Company of Blind Bloomsbury Fidlers, the ablest now extant. *s. sh. Printed for Theodorus Microcosmus.* (15 March.)
669. f. 24. (12.)

[March 15.]—A Brief Confession or Declaration of Faith set forth by many of us, who are falsely called Ana-Baptists. *Printed by G. D. for F. Smith.* (15 March.)　　　　　**E. 1017. (14.)**

March 15.—The Jesuits Grand Design upon England clearly discovered in a Letter lately written from a Father of that Society, 15 March. [Signed : J. M.]　　　　　**E. 1019. (16.)**

[March 15.]—A Letter unto Mr. Stubs in answer to his Oceana weighed. *Printed for J. S.* (15 March.)　　　　　**E. 1017. (13.)**

March 16.—Policy, no Policy : or, The Devil Himself confuted, being an answer to a clause of a Letter written to a Person of Quality at Brussels, wherein the King and his Court there are fully discovered, 16 March. [Signed : B. T.]　　　　　**E. 1019. (17.)**

March 16.—An Act for dissolving the Parliament begun 3 Nov. 1640, and for the calling and holding of a Parliament at Westminster, 25 April. *Printed by John Streater and John Macock.*　**E. 1074. (42.)**

March 16.—An Act for taking the accompts and redressing of grievances concerning the Tythes and Church-Livings in Wales ; and for advancement of religion and learning there. *Printed by John Streater and John Macock.*　　　　　**E. 1074. (41.)**

March 16.—The Grand Memorandum : or a true and perfect Catalogue of the Secluded Members of the House of Commons sitting 16 March, being the day of their Dissolution. Also a perfect Catalogue of the Rumpers. Together with the names of such as were the King's Judges, and condemned Him to death. *s. sh. Printed for Edward Husbands.*　　　　　**669. f. 24. (37.)**

[March 16.]—A Pertinent Speech made by an Honourable Member of the House of Commons, tending to the establishment of Kingly Government. (16 March.)　　　　　**E. 1017. (18.)**

[March 16.]—News from the Royall Exchange : or Gold turned into Mourning : from Exit tyrannus regum ultimus anno libertatis Angliæ restitutæ primo, Januarii 30. 1648, to Ecce ! Exit non tyrannus, sed regum hominumq ; optimus anno Angliæ felicitatio ultimo. [Verses in favour of the restoration of Charles II.] *s. sh.* (16 March.)　**669. f. 24. (15.)**

1660.

[March 16.]—No Fool to the old Fool. [A satire on the Parliament. Signed : Tho. Scot.] (16 March.) *s. sh.* **669. f. 24. (16.)**

[March 16.]—Poor John : or a Lenten Dish. Being the soliloquies of John Lambert, now prisoner in the Tower of London. [A satire.] *s. sh.* (16 March.) **669. f. 24. (14.)**

March 17.—By the Council of State. [A Proclamation requiring all "reduced and disbanded officers " to quit London.] *s. sh. Printed by Abel Roper and Thomas Collins.* **669. f. 24. (23.)**

March 17.—By the Council of State. [A Proclamation enjoining a general submission to the existing Government.] *s. sh. Printed by Abel Roper and Thomas Collins.* **669. f. 24. (24.)**

March 17.—By the Council of State. [A Proclamation requiring all Papists and such as have borne arms for the late King, to repair to their places of abode ; and instructing all Officers of Ports and Commanders of Ships to apprehend all suspicious persons either leaving or entering the country.] *s. sh. Printed by Abel Roper and Thomas Collins.* **669. f. 34. (25.)**

[March 17.]—The Character of the Rump. (17 March.) **E. 1017. (20.)**

[March 17.]—An Exit to the Exit Tyrannus ; or, upon erasing that ignominious and scandalous Motto which was set over the place where King Charles the First statue stood, in the Royall Exchange, London. [In verse.] *s. sh.* (17 March.) **669. f. 24. (18.)**

[March 17.]—A Free-Parliament-Letany. [A satire, in verse.] *s. sh.* (17 March.) **669. f. 24. (19.)**

[March 17.]—King Charles vindicated, or, The grand Cheats of the Nation discovered. By W. L. a lover of his Country. *Printed for Theodorus Microcosmus.* (17 March.) **E. 1017. (19.)**

[March 17.]—The Qualifications of the succeeding Parliament. [A scheme for the establishment of a " free and full Parliament," to which none may be elected "that is an enemy to Kingly Government." *s. sh.* (March 17.) **569. f. 24. (17.)**

[March 17.]—The Form of Writs to be issued forth under the Great Seal of England, for the election of Knights, Citizens and Burgesses to sit and serve in the Parliament which is to be holden in Westminster, 25 April. *s. sh. Printed by John Redmayne.* (19 March.) **669. f. 24. (21.)**

[March 19.]—A Conference held between the Old Lord Protector and the New Lord General, truly reported by Hugh Peters. [A satire.] (19 March.) **E. 1017. (24.)**

March 19.—A Plant of Paradise. Being a sermon preached at the funeral of John-Goodhand Holt. By R. M. [i.e. R. Mossom.] *Printed by R. N.* **E. 1025. (4.)**

1660.

[March 19.]—Select City Quæries. Part 2. [See above: 9 March, E. 1017. (1.)]   **E. 1017. (23.)**

[March 19.]—A true and perfect Copy of the Lord Roos his Answer to the Marquesse of Dorchester's Letter written 25 Feb. [With reference to a challenge sent to Lord Roos by the Marquess of Dorchester, his father-in-law, on account of his ill-treatment of Lady Roos.] [See above: 13 Feb., 669. f. 23. (38.)] *s. sh.* (19 March.)

669. f. 24. (22.)

March 20.—The Reasons why the Lrd. Marquiss of Dorchester printed his Letter the 25th of Feb., dated the 13th of the same moneth. Together with my Answer to a printed paper called, A true and perfect Copy of the Lord Roos his Answer to the Marquiss of Dorchester's Letter, written the 25th of Feb. *s. sh. Printed the 20th of March, the day after the printing the Lord Roos his Answer &c., the date whereof by him purposely omitted.*   **669. f. 24. (27.)**

[March 20.]—A Letter from His Ma^{ty} King Charles II., to his Peers the Lords in England. *Printed for Charles Gustavus.* (20 March.)

669. f. 24. (28.)

[March 20.]—A Letter from a Lover of his Country to his Friend in Surrey concerning the Election of Members to serve in this approaching Parliament. [Signed : H. O.] (20 March.)   **E. 1017. (25.)**

[March 20.]—A Declaration of the Lord Broghill and the Officers of the Army of Ireland, in the Province of Munster. [For a " full and free Parliament."] *s. sh. Dublin, printed by William Bladen; and reprinted at London by John Macock.* (20 March.) **669. f. 24. (26.)**

March 20.—True and good News from Brussels, containing a Soveraigne Antidote against the Poysons and calumnies of the Present Time. In a Letter from a Person of Quality. [Signed : W. S.] **E. 1019. (12.)**

[March 21.]—England's Directions for Members' Election. [Satirical verses on the Members of the Rump Parliament.] *s. sh.* (21 March.)

669. f. 24. (29.)

[March 21.]—The King Advancing; or, Great Brittains Royal Standard. [A poem in Latin, with an English translation.] *Printed for Charles Prince.* (21 March.)   **E. 1017. (28.)**

[March 21.]—The Lamentation of a Bad Market : or, Knaves and Fools foully foyled and fallen into a pit of their own digging. *Printed at the Charge of John Lambert, Charles Fleetwood, Arthur Hesilrig and —— Hewson the Cobler, and are to be distributed to the fainting Brethren.* (21 March.)   **E. 1017. (26.)**

[March 21.]—The Loyal Subjects Teares for the Sufferings and Absence of their Sovereign, Charles II. *Printed for Charles King.* (21 March.)

E. 1017. (29.)

1660.

[March 22.]—A Warning Piece to all His Majesties Subjects of England, containing the Motives by which some of them have been drawn into Rebellion against their lawful King. *Printed for Charles King.* (22 March.)　　　　　　　　　　　　　　　　　**E. 1017. (34.)**

[March 22.]—The Arraignment of the Anabaptists Good Old Cause, with the manner and proceedings of the Court of Iustice against him. [A satire.] *Printed by John Morgan.* (22 March.)　　**E. 1017. (32.)**

[March 22.]—The Rump held forth last first-day in a Brotherly Exercise, at the Bull and Mouth in Aldersgate. (22 March.)
　　　　　　　　　　　　　　　　　　　　　　　E. 1017. (35.)

March 23.—To the Lord General Monck. The humble Gratulation and Acknowledgment of Colonel Robert Broughton, and several others his countrymen. *s. sh.*　　　　　　　　　　**669. f. 24. (39.)**

[March 23.]—The Age of Wonders, or Miracles are not ceased. Being a true but strange Relation of a Child born at Burslem who, before it was three quarters old, spoke and prophesied strange and wonderful things touching the King. *Printed for Nehemiah Chamberlain.* (23 March.)
　　　　　　　　　　　　　　　　　　　　　　　E. 1017. (37.)

[March 23.]—Arsy Versy: or the second Martyrdom of the Rump. [Satirical verse.] *s. sh.* (23 March.)　　　　**669. f. 24. (31.)**

[March 23.]—A Letter intercepted, in which the two different Forms of Monarchy and Popular Government are briefly controverted. By N. D. Gent. [See also below : 29 March, E. 1019. (5.)] (23 March.)
　　　　　　　　　　　　　　　　　　　　　　　E. 1017. (36.)

[March 23.]—No King but the Old King's Son. Or, a Vindication of Limited Monarchy as it was established in this Nation before the late War between the King and Parliament. *s. sh. Printed for Theophilus Microcosmus.* (23 March.)　　　　**669. f. 24. (30.)**

March 24.—By the Council of State. [A Proclamation ordering the arrest of such persons as "do attempt the debauching and alienating the affections of some in the Army."] *s. sh. Printed by Abel Roper and Tho. Collins.*　　　　　　　　　　　**669. f. 24. (40.)**

[March 24.]—Alderman Bunce his Speech to the Lord Maior, Aldermen and Common-Council of London, touching the King's Resolution to accept of honourable Conditions from a Free-Parliament for his Admitment. *Printed by T. S. for O. H.* (24 March.) **E. 1017. (41.)**

[March 24.]—The Case stated touching the Soveraign's Prerogative and the Peoples Liberty. *Printed for Charles King.* (24 March.) **E. 1017. (40.)**

March 24.—The Fanatique Powder-Plot. Or, the Design of the Rumpers and their adherents to destroy both Parliament and People. With a Caution against Forged Intelligence. *s. sh.* **669. f. 24. (38.)**

March 24.—A Necessary and Seasonable Caution, concerning Elections. *s. sh.* (24 March.)　　　　　　　　　　**669. f. 24. (32.)**

1660.

[March 24.]—A Panegyrick to his Excellency the Lord Generall Monck. By Sir William Davenant. [In verse.] *s. sh. Printed for Henry Herringman.* (24 March.) **669. f. 24. (33.)**

[March 24.]—The Spirit of the Fanatiques dissected, and the solemne League and Covenant solemnly discussed in 30 Queries. By William Collinne. *Printed for F. Wallis.* (24 March.) **E. 1017. (39.)**

March 25.—The Fear of God and the King. Press'd in a sermon preached at Mercers Chappell. By Matthew Griffith. pp. 106. *Printed for Tho. Johnson.* **E. 1918. (1.)**

[March 25.]—The Door of Salvation opened by the Key of Regeneration. A treatise, by George Swinnocke. pp. 465. *Printed by John Best for Tho. Parkhurst.* (25 March.) **E. 1817.**

[March 26.]—King Charles His Speech to the Six Eminent Persons who lately arrived at Brussels, to treat with His Majesty touching His Restoration to the Royal Throne and Dignity of his Father. *s. sh. Printed at Antwerp.* (26 March.) **669. f. 24. (36.)**

[March 26.]—The Royal Pilgrimage, or the Progresse and Travels of King Charles the Second through the most and greatest Courts of Europe. Byan Eye Witnesse. *Printed by John Morgan.* (26 March.) **E. 1019. (2.)**

[March 26.]—Englands Redemption : or, A Path Way to Peace, plainly demonstrating that we shall never have any setled State until Charles II. enjoy the Crown. *Printed for Charles King.* (26 March.) **E. 1019. (1.)**

March 26.—The Censure of the Rota upon Mr. Milton's Book, entituled, The Ready and Easie Way to Establish a Free Commonwealth. [By James Harrington.] [See above : 3 March, E. 1016. (11.)] *Printed by Paul Giddey.* **E. 1019. (5*.)**

[March 26.]—Certain Considerations ; being the legitimate issue of a true English Heart, presented to the several Corporations in this Nation to regulate their Election of Members to serve in the next Parliament. (26 March.) **E. 765. (8.)**

[March 26.]—The Character of a Phanatique. *s. sh. Printed for Henry Marsh.* (26 March.) **669. f. 24. (35.)**

[March 26.]—The Rump Desparing [*sic*], or, The Rump Proverbs and Lamentations. (26 March.) **E. 1017. (43.)**

[March 26.]—Seasonable and Healing Instructions, humbly tendered to the Freeholders, Citizens and Burgesses of England and Wales, to be seriously recommended by them to their respective Knights, Citizens and Burgesses elected and to be elected for the next Parliament. *s. sh.* (26 March.) **669. f. 24. (34.)**

1660.

[March 26.]—A Second Part of the Mixture of Scholasticall Divinity with Practical, in several Tractates. By Henry Jeanes. Whereunto are annexed several Letters of the same Author and Dr. Jeremy Taylor concerning Original Sin, together with a Reply unto Dr. Hammonds Vindication of his Grounds of Uniformity. *Printed by H. Hall for Thomas Robinson: Oxford.* (26 March.)   **E. 1018.**

March 28.—By the Council of State. [A Proclamation calling attention to the Act of Parliament whereby all Papists, and all persons who have assisted in any war against the Parliament, since 1 Jan. 1641, are declared ineligible for Parliament. *Printed by Abel Roper and Tho: Collins.*   **669. f. 24. (48.)**

March 28.—By the Council of State. [A Proclamation requiring Livewell Chapman, who "having, from a wicked design to engage the nation in blood, caused several seditious and treasonable books to be published, doth now obscure and hide himself," to appear before the Council.] *s. sh. Printed by Abel Roper and Thomas Collins.*   **669. f. 24. (47.)**

March 28.—A Dialogue betwixt Tom and Dick. Presented to his Excellency [General Monk] and the Council of State, at Drapers-Hall in London, 28 March. [A ballad in praise of General Monk.] *s. sh.*   **669. f. 24. (49.)**

March 28.—A Speech Spoken to the Lord General Monk, by one representing the genius of England, at Drapers-Hall, 28 March. [In verse.]   **669. f. 24. (45.)**

March 28.—A Speech made to the Lord General Monck and the Councel of State at Drapers-Hall in London, 28 March, at which time they were entertained by that honourable Company. Spoken by Walter Yeokney. [In verse. With a note: "The Reader may take notice that the other Speech is a forged cheat, and disowned by Walter Yeokney."] *s. sh. Printed for Henry Broome.*

        669. f. 24. (46.)

[March 28.]—Colonel John Okie's Lamentation, or, a Rumper cashiered. [A satirical ballad.] *s. sh.* (28 March.)   **669. f. 24. (43.)**

[March 28.]—M^{ris} Rump brought to bed of a Monster. [A satire on the Rump Parliament.] *s. sh. Printed by Portcullis Damgate for Theod. Microcosmus.* (28 March.)   **669. f. 24. (44.)**

[March 28.]—Monarchy Asserted, in vindication of the Considerations upon Mr. Harrington's Oceana. By M[atthew] Wren. Second edition. pp. 189. [See above : 14 Aug. 1657, E. 1659. (1.) and Aug. 1659, E. 2112. (2.)] *Printed by T. R. for Francis Bowman of Oxford; and to be sold by J. Martin, J. Allestry and T. Dicas in St. Pauls Churchyard.* (28 March.)   **E. 1853. (1.)**

March 28.—News from Hell; or the Relation of a Vision. [A satire, in verse.] *s. sh.* 28 March.   **669. f. 24. (42.)**

1660.

[March 29.]—Sir Politique uncased, or, A Sober Answer to a Juggling Pamphlet entituled A Letter Intercepted, by N. D. Gent. By D. N. Gent. [See above: 23 March, E. 1017. (36.)] (29 March.)
E. 1019. (5.)

March 29.—The Pursuit of Peace. Briefly explained and plainly propounded in a sermon preached unto a solemne assembly of the parishioners of Botolphs Algate, on the composure of their late unhappie differences. By Z. C. [i.e. Zachary Crofton.] pp. 53. *Printed by T. Fawcet for James Nuthall.* **E. 1025. (19.)**

March 30.—The King's Declaration to all his loving Subjects. Given at Brussels, 30 March. *s. sh. Printed for Richard Parker.*
669. f. 24. (41.)

[March 30.]—His Majesties Gracious Message to all his loving Subjects in the Kingdom of Ireland upon their exemplary Return to their Obedience. *Printed for Charls Prince.* (30 March.) **E. 1019. (7.)**

[March 30.]—King Charles the II. his Restitution the best Cure for Englands Confusion. By Ed[ward] Mat[hews]. (30 March.)
E. 1019. (8.)

[March 30.]—The Standard of Common Liberty : or, The Petition of Right, exhibited to K. Charles the I. by the Parliament, with his most gracious Assent, 7 June, 1628. (30 March.) **E. 1019. (9.)**

[March 30.]—The Tragical Actors ; or, the Martyrdome of the late King Charles. [A satirical dialogue between Cromwell, Cornet Joyce, Bradshaw, Haselrig and Vane.] *Printed for Sir Arthur.* (30 March.)
E. 1019. (6*.)

March 30.—A Just Vindication of the Questioned Part of the Reading of Edward Bagshaw, had in the Middle Temple Hall 24 Feb. 1639. (30 March.) **E. 1019. (6.)**

March 31.—A Letter out of Flanders, from a Person of Honour, who lately transported himself purposely to kisse the hands of King Charles the Second, to a Nobleman in England. [Signed : G. S.] *Printed for Miles Thatcher.* **E. 1019. (11.)**

[March 31.]—England's Vote for a Free Election of a Free Parliament. [A poem.] *s. sh.* **669. f. 24. (50.)**

[March 31.]—A Jewell of Earthly Joy ; or, Familie Observations directing all true-hearted Christians to the keeping of the Commandments of God. By W. P. *Printed by T. F. for Francis Coles.* (31 March.) **E. 1856. (2.)**

March.—Beames of Former Light, discovering how evil it is to impose doubtfull and disputable formes or practises upon Ministers. [By Philip Nye.] pp. 241. *Printed by R. I. for Adoniram Byfield.*
E. 1794. (2.)

1660.

[**March.**]—Ecclesiæ Anglicanæ Θρηνωδία, in qua perturbatissimus Regni & Ecclesiæ status sub Anabaptistica Tyrannide lugetur. Dictante Johanne Gough. pp. 159. *Typis W. G. & prostant venales apud Rich. Thrale.* E. 1814. (2.)

March.—A Guide for the Penitent. [By Brian Duppa, Bishop of Winchester.] pp. 55. *Printed by James Flesher for Richard Royston.* E. 1835. (2.)

[**April 2.**]—The Private Debates, Conferences and Resolutions of the late Rump, imparted to publick view. (2 April.) E. 1019. (10.)

April 2.—A Letter from an Eminent Person in Gloucester, giving an account of the late passages there, in reference to Maior Gen. Massey. *Printed by James Cottrel.* E. 1019. (20.)

[**April 2.**]—Ad Populum ; or a Lecture to the People. With a Satyre against Separatists. By A. C. Generosus [i.e. Abraham Cowley. In verse.] (2 April.) E. 1822. (2.)

[**April 2.**]—The Grand Rebels detected, or, The Presbyter unmasked. (2 April.) E. 1019. (13.)

[**April 2.**]—The Life and Death of M^{ris} Rump. [A satire on the Rump Parliament.] *s. sh. Printed for Theodorus Microcosmus.* (2 April.) 669. f. 24. (52.)

[**April 3.**]—Treason Arraigned, in answer to Plain English, being a trayterous and phonatique pamphlet which was condemned by the Counsel of State. (3 April.) E. 1019. (14.)

April 4.—A Collection of His Majesties gracious Letters, Speeches, Messages and Declarations since 4 April [to 25 Oct.]. pp. 109. *Printed by John Bill.* E. 191.

April 4.—A Speech to the Lord General Monck at Skinners-Hall. Spoken by Mr. W. Bard. [In verse.] *s. sh. Printed for John Towers.* 669. f. 24. (55.)

[**April 5.**]—The Muses Congratulatory Address to the Lord General Monck. [In verse. Signed : T. B.] *s. sh.* (5 April.) 669. f. 24. (54.)

[**April 5.**]—The Army's Declaration ; being a true Alarum in answer to a false and fiery one made lately by a Member of that destable (*sic*) Rump. By a member of the Army now in London. *Printed for prevention of Sedition and Mutiny.* (5 April.) E. 1019. (18.)

[**April 5.**]—Double your Guards ; in answer to a bloody and seditious pamphlet entituled An Alarum to the Armies of England, Scotland and Ireland. (5 April.) E. 1019. (19.)

April 6.—A plain-dealing and plain-meaning Sermon preach't in Bristol the day appointed for Publique Fasting and Humiliation. [By Ralph Farmer.] *Printed by S. Griffin, and are to be sold by Thomas Wall : Bristol.* E. 1025. (5.)

1660.

[April 9.]—The Downfall of Mercurius Britannicus, Pragmaticus, Politicus, that three headed Cerberus. [A satire in verse.] *s. sh.* *Printed in the year that the Saints are disappointed.* (9 April.) **669. f. 24. (56.)**

April 9.—The Remonstrance & Address of the Armies of England, Scotland, and Ireland, to the Lord General Monck. [With a list of the signatories.] *Printed by John Macock.* **E. 1021. (1.)**

April 10.—A Letter from the King to F. M. [From Brussels.] *s. sh.* **669. f. 24. (53.)**

April 10.—A Speech made to the Lord General Monck and the Council of State, at Goldsmiths Hall in London, the tenth day of April. [In verse. By Thomas Jordan.] *s. sh.* *Printed for H. B.* **669. f. 24. (59.)**

April 10.—The Speech spoken to the Lord General Monck at Goldsmiths-Hall, April the tenth. By Walter Yolkney. [In verse.] *s. sh.* *Printed for John Towers.* **669. f. 24. (58.)**

[April 10.]—Free-Parliament Quæres proposed to Tender Consciences. By Alazonomastix Philalethes. (10 April.) **E. 1019. (23.)**

[April 10.]—A Word for All : or, The Rump's Funerall Sermon, held forth by Mr. Feak to a Conventicle of Fanatiques at Bedlam upon the last Dissolution of the Half quarter Parliament. (10 April.) **E. 1019. (22.)**

[April 10.]—A Word in due Season to the ranting Royalists and the Rigid Presbiterians. *s. sh.* (10 April.) **669. f. 24. (57.)**

April 11.—By the Council of State. [A Proclamation announcing the escape of Colonel John Lambert from imprisonment in the Tower, and offering a reward for his apprehension.] *s. sh.* *Printed by Abel Roper and Tho: Collins.* **669. f. 24. (60.)**

[April 11.]—An Examination of the Grounds or Causes which are said to induce the Court of Boston in New-England to make that Order of Banishment upon pain of Death against the Quakers. By Isaac Penington, the Younger. pp. 99. *Printed for L. Lloyd.* (11 April.) **E. 1020. (5.)**

[April 11.]—Historia Quinqu-Articularis : or, A Declaration of the Judgement of the Western Churches, and more particularly of the Church of England, in the five Controverted Points reproched by the name of Arminianism. By Peter Heylin. 3 pt. *Printed by E. C. for Thomas Johnson.* (11 April.) **E. 1020. (1.)**

[April 11.]—Select City Queries. Part III. By Mercurius Philalethes. (11 April.) **E. 1019. (24.)**

April 12.—Bacchus Festival, or a New Medley. Being a musical Representation at the Entertainment of the Lord General Monck at Vintners-Hall, 12 April. [In verse.] *s. sh.* **669. f. 24. (63.)**

April 12.—Fame's Genius. Or, a Panegyrick upon the Lord General Monck. At Vintners-Hall, 12 April. [In verse. By C. Southaick.] *s. sh.* *Printed for J. Jones.* **669. f. 24. (62.)**

1660.

April 12.—A Speech made to his Excellency George Monck, General, &c. the twelfth day of April, at a Solemn Entertainment at Vinteners-Hal. [In verse. By Thomas Jordan.] *s. sh.* **669. f. 24. (61.)**

[**April 12.**]—Dagon Demolished : or, twenty admirable examples of God's displeasure against the subscribers of the late Engagement against our lawfull sovereign King Charls the second and the whole House of Peeres. By John Vicars. *Printed by T. Mabb, for Edward Thomas.* (12 April.) **E. 1021. (2.)**

April 12.—An Antidote against Immoderate Sorrow for the death of our friends. Delivered in a sermon, preached at the funeral of Sr William Button, Baronet. By Francis Bayly. *Printed by W. Godbid for Richard Thrale.* **E. 1026. (5.)**

April 13.—By the Council of State. [A Proclamation declaring "that it is not in their intention or thoughts to retrench or abate any part of the Arrears due to the Souldiers."] *Printed by Abel Roper and Tho. Collins.* **669. f. 24. (64.)**

April 13.—By the Council of State. [A Proclamation forbidding any Subject of the Commonwealth to receive Letters of Marque from Foreign Powers.] *s. sh. Printed by Abel Roper and Tho. Collins.*
669. f. 24. (65.)

April 16.—Comfortable Newes from Breda in a Letter to a Person of Honour. [Signed : T. L. Containing an alleged personal assurance from Charles II. that he had made no treaties prejudicial to English Protestants.] *s. sh. Printed for Henry Seile.* **669. f. 25. (6.)**

[**April 16.**]—A great and bloody Plot discovered against his Royal Majesty Charles. [With a woodcut.] *Printed for Samuel Chamberlain.* (16 April.) **E. 1021. (5.)**

[**April 16.**]—The Mystery of Prophesies revealed, by which the restoring of K. Charls the Second to the government of these Three Nations, is fully convinced by several prophesies in the Scriptures. (16 April.)
E. 1021. (6.)

[**April 16.**]—A Declaration of the Knights and Gentry in the County of Dorset, who were in his late Majesties Army. [Disclaiming all association with the "heady and intemperate sort of people which falsely terme themselves Royallists," and declaring their readiness to submit to the Parliament.] *s. sh.* (16 April.) **669. f. 24. (66.)**

[**April 16.**]—A Changling no company for Lovers of Loyaltie. Or, the Subjects lesson in poynt of sacred submission to and humble comply-ance with God and the King. [A sermon, by W. H.] *Printed by M. Simmons for Thomas Parkhurst.* (16 April.) **E. 1021. (4.)**

[**April 16.**]—A Serious Admonition to those Members of Parliament that sate alone without the Secluded Members. With another to those Souldiers yet living that secluded the major part of the House of

1660.

Commons. Together with a vindication of the Presbyterians. By a Minister of the Gospel. [Signed: A. B.] *Printed for Thomas Parkhurst.* (16 April.) **E. 1021. (3.)**

April 17.—The Declaration and Address of the Gentry of Essex, who have adhered to the King and suffered Imprisonment or Sequestration during the late Troubles. *s. sh. Printed for Gabriel Bedell & Thomas Collins.* **669. f. 25. (1.)**

[**April 17.**]—Serious sober State-Considerations relating to the government of England and the garrison of Dunkirk in Flanders. By Theophilus Verax, a Dunkirker. *Printed by W. G.* (17 April.) **E. 1021. (7.)**

[**April 19.**]—An Elegy consecrated to the inestimable Memory of Charles the First. *s. sh. Printed by R. W. for R. G.* (19 April.) **669. f. 24. (68.)**

[**April 19.**]—King Solomon's infallible Expedient for Three Kingdoms Settlement. A sermon preached at Gloucester, the Lord's day before their election of Burgesses for Parliament. By Samuel Keme. *Printed by J. S. for G. Sawbridge.* (19 April.) **E. 1021. (9.)**

[**April 20.**]—A Declaration of the Nobility and Gentry that adhered to the late King, now residing in and about London. [Disclaiming "any violent thoughts or inclinations to revenge," and declaring their readiness to submit to the Council of State, "in expectation of the future Parliament."] *s. sh. Printed by Roger Norton.* (20 April.) **669. f. 24. (69.)**

[**April 20.**]—The Declaration of the Gentry of the County of Kent, who have adhered to the King, and suffered imprisonment or sequestration during the late troubles. [Asserting their readiness " to acquiesce in the Resolutions of the ensuing Parliament."] *s. sh. Printed for Gabriel Bedell.* (20 April.) **669. f. 24. (67.)**

[**April 20.**]—Expedients for Publique Peace. Shewing the necessity of a National Union, and the way to it in this time of danger. (20 April.) **E. 1021. (8.)**

April 20.—No Blinde Guides. In answer to a seditious pamphlet of J. Milton's, intituled, Brief Notes upon a late Sermon titl'd, The Fear of God and the King, by Matthew Griffith. [By Sir Roger L'Estrange.] *Printed for Henry Broome.* **E. 187. (2.)**

April 21.—By the Council of State. [A Proclamation forbidding anyone to join with Colonel John Lambert, who is declared a traitor.] *s. sh. Printed by Abel Roper and Tho. Collins.* **669. f. 24. (70.)**

April 21.—By the Council of State. [A Proclamation requiring Colonel John Hewson, and others who have joined with Colonel Lambert, " to appear and render themselves to the Council within three days."] *s. sh. Printed by Abel Roper and Tho. Collins.* **669. f. 24. (71.)**

1660.

April 22.—A Vindication of the Roman Catholicks of the English Nation from some aspersions lately cast upon them. In a letter from a Protestant Gentleman in the countrey to a Citizen of London.   **E. 1023. (11.)**

April 23.—Iter Boreale. Attempting somthing upon the successful and matchless march of the Lord General George Monck, from Scotland to London, the last winter. By a Rural Pen. [A poem. By Robert Wild.] *Printed on St. George's Day, for George Thomason.*   **E. 1021. (10.)**

April 23.—Physician cure thy self : or an answer to a seditious pamphlet, entitled, Eye-Salve for the English Army, &c. [See above : 17 Sept., 1647, E. 407. (16.)]   *Printed for H. B.*   **E. 1021. (15.)**

April 25.—A Perfect List of the Parliament begun at Westminster 25 Aprill. *Printed for Robert Pawley.*   **E. 765. (9.)**

April 26.—[A Resolution of Parliament, appointing "a day of Thanksgiving to the Lord for raising the Lord General, and other persons who have been instrumental in delivery of this nation from thraldome and misery."] *s. sh. Printed by John Macock and Francis Tyton.*   **669. f. 24. (73.)**

[April 26.]—A Declaration of the Knights and Gentry of the County of Hertford, that adhered to the late King. [Affirming their confidence in General Monck, and their readiness to "abide by the wisdome of the approaching Parliament."] *s. sh. Printed for Daniel Pakeman.* (26 April.)   **669. f. 24. (72.)**

April 26.—A Packet of severall Letters being intercepted and taken on Thursday night last, 26 April, which were sent from John Lambert Esq. to many of the Phanaticks in the country. *Printed for John Morgan.*
            E. 1021. (13.)

[April 26.]—A Discourse for a King and Parliament. By a moderate and Serious Pen. [Signed : W. C.] *Printed for G. Bedell and T. Collins.* (26 April.)   **E. 1021. (12.)**

[April 27.]—Council humbly propounded for the speedy settlement of these long disturbed nations. Wherein is offered such a King, such a Church-Government, such liberty for tender consciences, as that the Royalist, Presbiterian and persons of different judgements may acquiess in. *Printed by M. Simmons, for H. C.* (27 April.)   **E. 1021. (14.)**

[April 28.]—A Declaration of the Gentry of the County of Salop, who were of the late King's party. [Disdaining "all animositie and revengeful remembrance of sides or parties in the late war," and affirming their intention "to submit to the determination of the Parliament." *s. sh. Printed for Daniel Pakeman.* (28 April.)   **669. f. 24. (74.)**

[April 28.]—A Declaration of the Nobility, Knights and Gentry of the County of Oxon which have adhered to the late King. [Disclaiming "all purpose of Revenge," and promising to "acquiesce in the Determinations of ensuing Parliaments."] *s. sh. Printed for Thos. Bassett.* (28 April.)   **669. f. 25. (2.)**

1660.

[April 30.]—A Character of Charles the Second. [By Sir Samuel Tuke or George Morley, Bishop of Winchester.] *Printed for Gabriel Bedell.* (30 April.) **E. 765. (10.)**

[April 30.]—Englands Genius pleading for King Charles to the Parliament and to the Lord Monck. [In verse.] *s. sh. Printed for J. Jones.* (30 April.) **669. f. 25. (3.)**

April 30.—A Declaration and Vindication of the Lord Mayor, Aldermen and Commons of the City of London in Common Councell assembled. *Printed by James Flesher.* **E. 1023. (2.)**

April 30.—The Meanes and Method of Healing in the Church. A sermon preached before the House of Peers. By Edward Reynolds. *Printed by Tho. Ratcliffe for George Thomason.* **E. 983. (32.)**

April 30.—Μεγαλεῖα Θεοῦ. God's great demonstrations and demands of justice, mercy and humility. A sermon preached before the House of Commons, at their fast. By John Gauden. pp. 67. *Printed by J. Best for Andrew Crook.* **E. 1023. (12.)**

April 30.—A Sermon of Repentance. Preached before the House of Commons at their fast. By Richard Baxter. *Printed by R. W. and A. M. for Francis Tyton and Jane Underhil.* **E. 1023. (14.)**

April 30.—The Good Catholick no bad Subject : or a letter from a Catholick gentleman to Mr. Richard Baxter, modestly accepting the challenge by him made in his Sermon of Repentance preached before the House of Commons, 30 April. **E. 1027. (13.)**

[April 30.]—Brethren in Iniquity : or a Beardless Pair. Held forth in a dialogue betwixt Tichburn and Ireton, prisoners in the Tower of London. [A political satire.] *Printed for Daniel Webb.* (30 April.) **E. 1021. (16.)**

[April.]—An Admonition moving to Moderation. By John Gaule. pp. 125. *Printed by Henry Lloyd and Roger Vaughan.* **E. 1916. (1.)**

[April.]—An Apology in the behalf of the Sequestred Clergy. Presented to Parliament. By R. Mossom. [See also below : 31 May, E. 1026. (1.)] *Printed for William Grantham.* **E. 1029. (5.)**

[April.]—Catholic Unity ; or, The only way to bring us all to be of one Religion. By Rich. Baxter. pp. 379. *Printed by R. W. for Thomas Underhill and Francis Tyton.* **E. 1898.**

[April.]—A Continuation of the Grand Conspiracy by the Insolent Usurper and the Regal Intruder. Two sermons, by J. A., a Suffering Son of the Church of England. pp. 80. Imperfect ; wanting pp. 31–43. *Printed for R. Royston.* **E. 1936. (1.)**

[April.]—De Plenitudine Mundi brevis & philosophica dissertatio, in qua defenditur Cartesiana Philosophia contra sententias Francisci Baconi Baronis de Verulamio, Th. Hobbii & Sethi Wardi. Authore Gilberto Clerk. pp. 110. *Apud Jo. Martin, Ja. Allestry & Th. Dicas.* **E. 1917. (1.)**

1660.

[**April.**]—Herberts French and English Dialogues. pp. 247. *Printed by D. Maxwell for T. Davis and T. Sadler.* **E. 1809. (1.)**

[**April.**]—Mensa Mystica; or a Discourse concerning the Sacrament of the Lord's Supper. By Simon Patrick. pp. 464. *Printed by A. M. for F. Tyton.* **E. 1752.**

[**April.**]—Metamorphosis Anglorum; or, Reflections historical and political, upon the late Changes of Government in England. pp. 112. *Printed for William Palmer.* **E. 2109. (1.)**

[**April.**]—Occult Physick. By W. W., Philosophus [i.e. William Williams. With an engraved portrait of the author.] pp. 160. *Printed by Thomas Leach, and are to be sold by W. Palmer.* **E. 1737. (2.)**

[**April.**]—The Politique Poet to the wise Reader. [A poem in MS., in Thomason's hand.] **E. 184. (8.)**

[**April.**]—Reflections upon some persons and things in Ireland, by letters to and from Dʳ Petty. With Sir Hierome Sankey's Speech in Parliament. pp. 185. *Printed for John Martin, James Allestreye and Thomas Dicas.* **E. 1915. (1.)**

[**April.**]—The True Catholick described, and the Vanity of the Papists discovered. By Richard Baxter. pp. 335. *Printed by A. M. for T. Underhill.* **E. 1899.**

[**April.**]—The Uncharitable Informer charitably informed that Sycophancy is a Sin. By Faithfull Teate. pp. 81. *Printed by William Bladen: Dublin.* **E. 1921. (1.)**

May 1.—Two Letters from his Majesty. The one to the Speaker of the Commons, the other to the Lord Generall Monck, with his Majestie's Declaration inclosed. Together with the resolve of the House thereupon, 1 May. *Printed by Edward Husbands and Tho. Newcomb.* **E. 1075. (1.)**

May 1.—King Charls II. his Declaration to all his Loving Subjects of the Kingdome of England, dated from his Court at Breda in Holland, and read in Parliament 1 May. *Printed by W. Godbid for John Playford.* **E. 765. (11.)**

May 1.—His Majestie's Gracious Letter and Declaration, sent to the House of Peers from Breda, and read in the House, 1 May. *Printed by John Macock and Francis Tyton.* **E. 1023. (3.)**

[**May 1.**]—The Answer of the Lord Mayor, Aldermen and Common-Council of the City of London to his Majestie's Gracious Letter and Declaration sent by the Lord Mordant; and a present of ten thousand pounds from the City to the King, and their declaration to submit to his Majestie's Government. *Printed for Samuel Styles.* **E. 1023. (5.)**

1660.

[May 1.]—Maiestie Irradiant, or The Splendor Displayd, of our Soveraigne King Charles. By Anthony Sadler. *s. sh.* (1 May.)
669. f. 25. (4.)

May 1.—Solomon in Solio : Christus in Ecclesia. Concio habita in Templo B. Mariæ Oxon., a Johanne Wall. pp. 51. *Excudebat H. Hall, impensis R. Davis : Oxoniæ.* E. 1920. (3.)

[May 2.]—A Letter to the King's Majesty from the Commons of England, in answer of his Majestie's gracious Letter to that House. *Printed by Edward Husbands and Thomas Newcomb.* E. 1075. (2.)

May 2.—To his Excellency the Lord General Monck, the humble Address of the Officers of your Excellencies Army. *s. sh. Printed by William Godbid for John Playford.* 669. f. 25. (5.)

[May 2.]—The famous History of the most renowned Christian worthy Arthur, King of the Britaines, and his famous Knights of the Round Table. [With two woodcuts. The dedication signed : M. P.] (2 May.)
E. 1022. (2.)

[May 2.]—A Happy Handfull, or Green Hopes in the Blade ; in order to a Harvest of the several shires, humbly petitioning or heartily declaring for peace. [A collection of petitions, remonstrances and declarations from various parts of the Kingdom.] pp. 83. *Printed for John Williams.* (2 May.) E. 1021. (17.)

[May 2.]—Laudensium Apostasia : or a dialogue in which is shewen that some Divines risen up in our Church since the greatness of the late Archbishop, are in sundry points of great moment, quite fallen off from the doctrine received in the Church of England. By Henry Hickman. pp. 94. *Printed by D. Maxwell for Sa. Gellibrand.* (2 May.)
E. 1022. (5.)

[May 2.]—The Perfect and Experienced Farrier. Shewing a most exact and speedy way of curing all sorances and diseases incident to horses and other cattle. By Robert Barret. *Printed by T. Fawcet for Fr. Coles.* (2 May.) E. 1022. (3.)

[May 2.]—Some few Queries and Considerations proposed to the Cavaliers, being of weighty importance to them. [By Isaac Penington, the Younger.] (2 May.) E. 1022. (1.)

[May 2.]—Truth and Innocency prevailing against Error and Insolency. By way of answer to Mr. Hezekiah Holland. Whereunto is added a second part, being an answer to one Mr. Simon Hendon. By George Hammon. pp. 216. *Printed for the Author.* (2 May.)
E. 1022. (4.)

May 3.—The Humble Answer of the House of Peers to his Majestie's gracious Letter and Declaration. *Printed by John Macock and Francis Tyton.* E. 1025. (10.)

1660.

[May 3.]—A Parly between the Ghosts of the late Protector and the King of Sweden at their meeting in Hell. *Printed for Lo. Whimbleton.* (3 May.)　　　　　　　　　　　　　　　　　　　**E. 1023. (1.)**

May 5.—[A Declaration of Parliament "that by reason of the extraordinary and important affairs of the Kingdom, there will be no proceedings this next Easter-term in the ordinary courts of law.] *s. sh.　Printed by Edward Husbands & Thomas Newcomb.*
　　　　　　　　　　　　　　　　　　669. f. 25. (7.)

[May 5.]—A Letter to a Member of the House of Commons, speaking his humble desires of the receiving the King, without dishonourable conditions, according to his just rights, and the confirming the antient privileges of Parliament. (5 May.)　　　　**E. 1023. (4.)**

May 7.—Vox & Votum Populi Anglicani. Shewing how deeply the nation resents the thought of capitulating now, with his Majestie, and holding him, as we say, at armes-end, if they could. In a letter to the Earle of Manchester. By T. C., Esquire.　　**E. 1025. (2.)**

May 7.—[A Declaration of Parliament that all Sheriffs, Justices of the Peace and Constables that were in office on 25 April shall be continued in their respective offices.] *s. sh.　Printed by John Macock & Francis Tyton.*　　　　　　　　　　　　**669. f. 25. (8.)**

[May 7.]—An Epistle [signed : N.] narrative of the barbarous and illegall arrest of Freder. Turvill Esquire, by Sixteen Bailiffs. (7 May.)
　　　　　　　　　　　　　　　　　　E. 1023. (7.)

[May 7.]—William Lilly, Student in Astrologie, his past and present opinion touching Monarchy in these nations. [A satire on Lilly.] (7 May.)　　　　　　　　　　　　　　　　**E. 1023. (6.)**

May 8.—[A Proclamation of Parliament, acknowledging Charles II. as the rightful King.] *s. sh.　Printed by Edward Husbands and Thomas Newcomb.*　　　　　　　　　　　　**669. f. 25. (11.)**

—— [Another edition.] *s. sh.　Printed by John Macock & Francis Tyton.*
　　　　　　　　　　　　　　　　　　669. f. 25. (12.)

[May 8.]—Dolor ac Voluptas invicem cedunt. Or, Englands Glorious Change, by calling home of King Charles the Second. [Signed : T. W. In verse.] *s. sh.* (8 May.)　　　　　　**669. f. 25. (10.)**

[May 8.]—The Great Memorial : or, A List of those pretended Judges who sentenced our late King, and also of the Witnesses sworn against the said King. [With an engraved portrait of Charles I.] *s. sh. Printed for Edward Thomas.* (8 May.)　　　　**669. f. 25. (9.)**

May 8.—[A Declaration of the Commons that the Act for securing the Protestant Religion & the General Act for Oblivion, Indemnity & Free Pardon are under consideration.] *s. sh.　Printed by Edward Husbands & Thomas Newcomb.*　　　　　　　**669. f. 25. (13.)**

1660.

[May 8.]—Judge Jenkins Remonstrance [maintaining the divine right of Kingship] to the Lords and Commons of Parliament, 21 Feb., 1647. *Reprinted.* (8 May.) **E. 1023. (8.)**

[May 8.]—A Letter from a Friend, occasioned by the receipt of his Majestie's most gracious Expresses and Declaration. (8 May.)
E. 1023. (9.)

May 8.—Britain's Royal Star : or an astrological demonstration of England's future felicity, deduced from the position of the Heavens at the first proclamation of King Charles the Second, 8 May. Together with an examination and refutation of that nest of sedition, published by Mr. H. Jessey, in his pamphlet falsely intituled, The Lord's loud call to England, &c. By John Gadbury. [See below : 14 Aug., E. 1038. (8.)] *Printed for Sam. Speed.* **E. 1050. (1.)**

May 9.—[An Order of Parliament that the Arms of the Commonwealth, wherever they are standing, be taken down, and the King's Arms set up in stead thereof.] *s. sh. Printed by John Macock & Francis Tyton.*
669. f. 25. (16.)

May 9.—[Resolutions of the Lords and Commons that all Ministers do pray for the King, the Duke of York, & the rest of the royal progeny.] *s. sh. Printed by John Macock & Francis Tyton.* **669. f. 25. (15.)**

May 9.—[An Order of the Lords that no Peer be charged upon any Act for the Trained Bands or Militia.] *s. sh. Printed by John Macock and Francis Tyton.* **669. f. 25. (17.)**

[May 9.]—A Ballad of a Countrey Wedding. By King James the Fifth [or rather the First] of Scotland. *s. sh.* (9 May.)
669. f. 25. (14.)

May 10.—St. Paul's Thanksgiving : a sermon preached before the House of Peers in the Abby-Church, Westminster, the day of solemn Thanksgiving. By James Buck. *Printed by J. G. for John Playford.*
E. 1033. (2.)

May 10.—A Sermon preached before the House of Commons. By John Price. *Printed by J. G. for Richard Royston.* **E. 1027. (1.)**

May 10.—Right Rejoycing : discovered in a sermon preached before the Lord Maior. By Richard Baxter. pp. 51. *Printed by R. W. and A. M. for Francis Tyton and Jane Underhil.* **E. 1025. (11.)**

May 10.—England's Gratulation for the King and his Subjects happy Union. First preacht on the Day of Publique Thankgiving. By R. Mossom. *Printed by Tho. Newcomb for William Grantham.*
E. 1033. (12.)

[May 10.]—Musa Ruralis. In Adventum Caroli II. vota, suspiria, gaudia, & rursum vota. Quae effudit Alex. Huissus. [Verses in Latin and English.] *Excudebat Thomas Milbourn.* (10 May.)
E. 765. (12.)

1660.

[May 10.]—O. Cromwell's Thankes to the Lord Generall [Monk], faithfully presented by Hugh Peters in another conference Together with an Hue and Cry after Mercurius Politicus. [A satire.] *Printed by M. T.* (10 May.) **E. 1023. (10.)**

[May 10.]—The Prayer of Collonel John Lambert in Captivity. [A satire.] *s. sh.* (10 May.) **669. f. 25. (18.)**

[May 11.]—Certain Letters evidencing the King's stedfastness in the Protestant Religion. Sent from the Princess of Turenne and the Ministers of Charenton to some persons in London. *Printed by Thomas Newcomb for Gabriell Bedell and Thomas Collins.* (11 May.) **E. 1079. (5.)**

[May 11.]—A Declaration and Vindication of the Nobility, Gentry and others of the County of Kent, that they had no hand in the Murther of our King. *s. sh. Printed for H. Brome.* (11 May.) **669. f. 25. (19.)**

May 11.—The Grand Statute; or, The Law of Death unalterable. A sermon preached at the funerals of Mr. John Cope in St. Mary-Bothaw, London. By John Kitchin. *Printed for Francis Kitchin and John Garway.* **E. 1040. (17.)**

May 12.—[An Order of the Lords commanding those who have in their possession any Jewels, Plate, Pictures or other Goods belonging to his Majesty to bring them to the Lords' Committees.] *s. sh. Printed by John Macock & Francis Tyton.* **669. f. 25. (20.)**

[May 14.]—Britain's Triumph for her imparallel'd Deliverance, and her joyfull celebrating the Proclamation of her most gracious King, Charles the Second. [A poem. Signed: G. S.] *Printed for W. Palmer.* (14 May.) **E. 1023. (13.)**

[May 14.]—Englands Joy for the coming in of our Gratious Soveraign King Charles the II. [In verse.] *s. sh. Printed for H. Brome.* (14 May.) **669. f. 25. (22.)**

May 14.—[An Order of Parliament for the continuance in office of all Commissioners of the Army, Navy & Revenue that were in office 25 April.] *s. sh. Printed by Edward Husbands and Thomas Newcomb.* **669. f. 25. (21.)**

[May 14.]—Lilly lash't with his own Rod. Or, An Epigram on the quaint skill of that Arch Temporizing Astrologer Mr. William Lilly. [In verse.] *s. sh.* (14 May.) **669. f. 25. (23.)**

[May 15.]—The Royal Oake. Or, an historical description of the royal progress, wonderful travels, miraculous escapes of his Sacred Majesty Charles the II. By John Danverd. *Printed for G. Horton.* (15 May.) **E. 1023. (15.)**

May 15.—A Sermon preached at Dorchester at the Proclaiming of His Majesty Charles the II. By Gilbert Ironsyde. *Printed for Robert Clavell.* **E. 1034. (15.)**

May 15.—The Strong Man ejected by a Stronger then he. A sermon preached at Gloucester, the day King Charles the Second was proclaimed.

1660.

By William Bartholomew. *Printed by W. Godbid for Richard Thrale.* **E. 1033. (3.)**

[May 15.]—Lambert's last game plaid. Set out in a mock Comedy betwixt John Lambert, Col. Cobbet, young Haslerig, and Major Creed, at their lodgings in the Tower, and a merry conceited fellow called Roger. *Printed for Richard Andrew.* (15 May.) **E. 1023. (16.)**

May 16.—Instructions lately agreed on by the Lords and Commons in Parliament for the Commissioners sent by them to the Hague, unto the King's Majesty. Together with the speech made thereupon by the honorable Denzell Holles, one of the Commissioners. *Printed for Robert Clavel.* **E. 1027. (9.)**

[May 16.]—The Subjects Desire to see our Gracious King Charles the Second, his Safe Arrival. [In verse. Signed : M. D.] *Printed for H. B.* (16 May.) **669. f. 25. (24.)**

[May 16.]—Jacobi Usserii Armachani Chronologia Sacra. Editionem accurante Thoma Barlow. pp. 213. *Excudebat W. Hall, impensis Rich. Davis, Eduardi & J. Forrest: Oxoniæ.* (16 May.) **E. 1024. (1.)**

[May 16.]—Jacobi Usserii Armachani de Romanæ Ecclesiæ Symbolo Apostolico vetere diatriba. *Excudebat G. Hall, impensis J. S. & venales prostant apud Ric. Davis, Ed. Forrest, & Joh. Forrest: Oxonii.* (16 May.) **E. 1024. (2.)**

[May 16.]—Politica Sacra & Civilis : or, a Model of Civil and Ecclesiasticall Government. The first part. By George Lawson. pp. 264. *Printed for John Starkey.* (16 May.) **E. 1024. (3.)**

[May 16.]—A Private Conference between Mr. L. Robinson and Mr. T. Scott, occasioned upon the publishing his Majesties Letters and Declaration. [A satire.] *Printed for Isack Goulden.* (16 May.) **E. 1025. (1.)**

May 17.—[An Order of Parliament to stop the demolishing or committing waste in the houses and lands of the King that are not sold.] *s. sh. Printed by John Macock & Francis Tyton.* **669. f. 25. (27.)**

May 17.—[An Order and Declaration of the Commons concerning the collection of the arrears of the Assessments.] *s. sh. Printed by Edward Husbands and Thomas Newcomb.* **669. f. 25. (26.)**

May 17.—The Dressing up of the Crown. A sermon preached at St. Edmunds Bury, when His Majestie was proclaimed King. By Laurence Womock. *Printed by W. H. for Will. Sheares.* **E. 1029. (2.)**

[May 17.]—Away with't quoth Washington, or, The Phanatick General vindicated over the left Shoulder. [In verse.] *Printed for J. Phanatick.* (17 May.) **669. f. 25. (25.)**

[May 17.]—A Third Conference between O. Cromwell and Hugh Peters in Saint James's Park ; wherein the horrible plot is discovered about

1660.

the barbarous murder of King Charles the I. [A satire.] *Printed by Tho. Mabb.* (17 May.)   **E. 1025. (3.)**

May 18.—[An Order of the Lords for seizing the persons and estates of those who sat in Judgment upon the late King.] *s. sh. Printed by John Macock and Francis Tyton.*   **669. f. 25. (29.)**

May 18.—God Save the King; or, A sermon preached at Lyme-Regis, at the Solemn Proclamation of Charles II. By Ames Short. [With an engraved portrait of the King.] pp. 87. *Printed for W. Roybould.*

                                                           E. 1919. (2.)

[May 18.]—Upon the Declaration of His Majesty King Charles of England the Second. [In verse. Signed : Nathaniel Richards.] *s. sh. Printed for J. G.* (18 May.)   **669. f. 25. (28.)**

[May 21.]—The Three Royall Cedars, Or, Great Brittains Glorious Diamonds. Being a narrative of the proceedings of Charles, King of Great Britain, France and Ireland, James, Duke of York, and Henry, Duke of Gloucester, since their too-much-lamented exile in Flanders. By E. Sanders. *Printed by G. Horton.* (21 May.)   **E. 1025. (6.)**

[May 22.]—His Sacred Majesty Charles the II. his Royal Title anagramatiz'd. [With a poem eulogizing General Monk and Thomas Allen, Lord Mayor of London, by J. Rowland.] *s. sh.* (22 May.)

                                                           669. f. 25. (30.)

[May 22.]—A Hue and Cry after the High Court of Injustice. Or, the arraignment and sentence of those traitors who condemned the late King's Majesty to death. With a perfect list of all their names, whose estates are to be sequestered for the same, for the use of his Majesty. [With a woodcut portrait of Charles I.] *Printed for John Andrews.* (22 May.)   **E. 1025. (8.)**

[May 22.]—The Last Counsel of a Martyred King to his Son. [A letter written by Charles I. to his son, dated 26 Nov. 1648; together with an account of the death of Charles I., and an elegy.] By J. D., Esq. *Printed for J. Jones.* (22 May.)   **E. 1025. (7.)**

May 22.—A Panegyrick to his Excellency the Lord General Monck. By Richard Farrar. [In verse.] *s. sh. Printed by John Macock.* (22 May.)   **669. f. 25. (31.)**

[May 23.]—The Royal Martyrs : or, A List of the Lords and Gentlemen that were slain in the late Wars in defence of their King and Country. *s. sh. Printed by Thomas Newcomb.* (23 May.)   **669. f. 25. (32.)**

[May 23.]—The State Martyrologie. A List of some worthy Persons who have suffered violent Deaths for their Loyalty to King Charles the Second. [With engraved portraits.] *s. sh. Printed by T. Creake.* (23 May.)   **669. f. 25. (33.)**

May 23.—The Royal Joy. Or, a sermon of congratulation made upon the occasion of the first news of the Proclamation of Charles II, brought

1660.

to His Majesty in the town of Breda. Preached in the Walloon Church of the said town. By Anthony Hulsius. *Printed by John Bill.*

E. 1048. (10.)

May 24.—His Majestie's Letter to the Lord General Monck, to be communicated to the Officers of the Army. From his Majestie's Court at the Hague. *Printed by John Macock.* E. 1025. (12.)

[**May 24.**]—[To the King's most excellent Majesty. To his Highnesse the Duke of York. To his Highnesse the Duke of Glocester. Three congratulatory poems, by Martin Llewellyn.] (24 May.)

E. 1080. (1.)

May 24.—The Kings Return. A sermon preached at Winchcomb upon the Kings-Day, by Clement Barksdale. *Printed for R. Royston.*

E. 1033. (5.)

May 24.—God Save the King. A sermon of Thanksgiving for His Majesties happy Return to his Throne. Preached in the Parish-Church of East Coker. By William Walwyn. [With an engraved portrait of the King as frontispiece.] *Printed for Henry Brome.*

E. 1033. (10.)

May 24.—The Bowing the Heart of Subjects to their Sovereign. A sermon by Francis Walsall. *Printed for John Sherley.*

E. 1033. (6.)

[**May 24.**]—Englands Jubilee; or, Her happy Return from Captivity. A sermon preached at St. Botolphs Aldersgate, by John Douch. *Printed for R. Royston.* (24 May.) E. 1033. (1.)

May 24.—A Sermon preach't at Christs-Church Dublin before the General Convention of Ireland. By Henry Jones. *Printed by J. C. for J. Crook.* E. 1041. (3.)

May 24.—Votiva Tabula; or, A Solemn Thanksgiving for the Restauration of Charls the II. Two sermons, preached 24 May and 28 June, contrived into one. By James Warwell. pp. 88. *Printed for R. Royston, and are to be sold by Samuel Woomock bookseller in Burry.*

E. 1033. (4.)

[**May 25.**]—Sol Angliae Oriens Auspiciis Caroli II. Regum Gloriosissimi. [Congratulatory Latin poems, with versions in Hebrew, Chaldee, Syriac, Samaritan, Ethiopic, Arabic, Persian and Greek. By Edmund Castell.] *Typis Tho. Roycroft, impensis Jo. Martin, Ja. Allestry & Tho. Dicas.* (25 May.) E. 184. (1.)

[**May 28.**]—Fifteen Loyal Queries for the Kings most excellent Majesty and the three Kingdoms. With a lash for the quondam jugler of State, W. L. Sp. [i.e. William Lenthall, Speaker], and the rest of the grand traytors. By J. Bramstone. *Printed for G. Horton.* (28 May.)

E. 1025. (13.)

[**May 28.**]—Lucifers Life-guard: containing a list of the Antichristian

1660.

Imps who have been Murderers and Destroyers of the best Religion, the best Government and the best King that ever Great Britain enjoyed. *s. sh.* (28 May.)   **669. f. 25. (34.)**

May 29.—The Earl of Manchester's Speech to His Majesty, in the name of the Peers, at his arrival at White-Hall. With His Majestie's gracious answer thereunto. *Printed by John Macock and Francis Tyton.*
                                                    E. 1027. (3.)

May 29.—The Speech of Sir Harbottle Grimston, Baronet, Speaker of the House of Commons, to the King's most excellent Majesty. Delivered in the Banquetting-House at Whitehal. *Printed by Edward Husbands and Thomas Newcomb.*   **E. 1025. (15.)**

May 29.—A Congratulatory Poem on the miraculous and glorious return of that unparallel'd King, Charles the II. By Alex. Brome. *Printed for Henry Brome.*   **E. 1027. (4.)**

May 29.—Postliminia Caroli II. The Palingenesy, or Second-Birth, of Charles the Second to his kingly life ; upon the day of his first. By Abiel Borfet. *Printed for M. Wright.*   **E. 1027. (10.)**

[**May 29.**]—Upon the joyfull and welcome Return of his Sacred Majestie Charles the Second, to his due and indubitate right of Government. A panegyrick [in verse]. By Tho. Mayhew. *Printed for Abel Roper.* (29 May.)   **E. 1025. (14.)**

May 29.—Davids Recognition, with a parallel between his and our present Soveraigns Sufferings and Deliverances. A sermon preached at Grymston, celebrating the 30 Anniversary of his Majestie's Nativity. By R. Feltwell. *Printed for the Author.*   **E. 1033. (7.)**

May 29.—Solomons Blessed Land. A sermon preached before an extraordinary Assembly at Newark upon Trent, on the Birth-day of Charles II. By Samuel Brunsell. *Printed by E. C. for Henry Seile.*
                                                    E. 1033. (9.)

May 29.—A Thanksgiving Sermon for the blessed Restauration of Charles II. Preach'd at Upton by William Towers. *Printed by R. D., for Thomas Rooks.*   **E. 1034. (1.)**

May 30.—A Proclamation against Vicious, Debauch'd, and Prophane Persons. By the King. *s. sh. Printed by Christopher Barker and John Bill.*   **669. f. 25. (36.)**

May 30.—God Save the King : or pious and loyal joy, the subject's duty, for their Soveraign's safety. Opened in a sermon at Aldermanbury, the day after his Majestie's triumphant entrance into London. By Anthony Walker. *Printed by M. S. for Thomas Parkhurst.*
                                                    E. 1030. (5.)

[**May 31.**]—Good Newes from the Netherlands ; or, A Congratulatory Panegyrick composed by a true Lover of his King and Country. [In verse ; signed : W. L.] *s. sh.* (31 May.)   **669. f. 25. (35.)**

1660.

[**May 31.**]—Ode upon the blessed Restoration and Returne of his Sacred Majestie Charles the Second. By A. Cowley. *Printed for Henry Herringman.* (31 May.) **E. 1025. (18.)**

[**May 31.**]—Oliver Cromwell, the late great Tirant, his Life-Guard : or the names of those who complied and conspired with him all along in his horrid designes, to bring this nation to universal ruine. *Printed for Francis Coles.* (31 May.) **E. 1026. (4.)**

[**May 31.**]—The late Warre parallel'd. Or, a brief relation of the five years civil warres of Henry the Third. By Edward Chamberlain. *Printed for John Starkey.* (31 May.) **E. 1026. (3.)**

[**May 31.**]—A Catalogue of new Books, by way of supplement to the former. Being such as have been printed from that time, till Easter Term. [By W. L., i.e. William London. See above : 25 Sept. 1658, E. 955. (1.)] *Printed by A. M. and sold by Luke Fawn and Francis Tyton.* (31 May.) **E. 1025. (17.)**

[**May 31.**]—A Leaf pull'd from the Tree of Life : medicinall for the healing of England's divisions. Or, a glimpse of the excellency of a Kingly Government. By John Moore. *Printed for E. Brewster.*

E. 1026. (7.)

[**May 31.**]—A Plea for Ministers in Sequestrations ; wherein Mr. Mossom's Apology for the Sequestred Clergy is duly considered and discussed. [See above : April, E. 1029. (5.)] *Printed for Thomas Parkhurst.* (31 May.) **E. 1026. (1.)**

[**May 31.**]—The Tragedy of Christopher Love at Tower-Hill. By the ingenious author of Iter Boreale [i.e. Robert Wild. In verse.] *Printed for R. Crofts.* (31 May.) **E. 1025. (16.)**

[**May.**]—England's black Tribunall. Set forth in the Triall of K. Charles I. Also the several Dying Speeches of the Nobility and Gentry as were put to death for their Loyalty to their King from 1642 to 1658. [With an engraved portrait of Charles I. by R. Gaywood.] pp. 232. *Printed for J. Playford.* **E. 1805. (1.)**

[**May.**]—Ten Charges of Government in England from May 1659 to May 1660. Observed by Dr. Turner. [In MS. throughout, in Thomason's hand.] *s. sh.* **E. 1917. (2.)**

[**May.**]—The Dignity of Kingship Asserted, in answer to Mr. Milton's Ready and Easie way to establish a Free Common-Wealth. By G. S., a Lover of Loyalty [i.e. George Searle ?] pp. 221. [See above : 3 March, E. 1016. (11.)] *Printed by E. C. for H. Seile.* **E. 1915. (2.)**

[**May.**]—The Accomplisht Cook, or the Art and Mystery of Cookery. By Robert May. [With a portrait of the author, and illustrations.] pp. 447. *Printed by R. W. for Nath. Brooke.* **E. 1741.**

[**May.**]—Apples of Gold for Young Men and Women, and a Crown of Glory for Old Men and Women. By Thomas Brooks. Third edition. pp. 359. *Printed by R. I. for John Hancock.* **E. 1918. (2.)**

1660.

[**May.**]—Golden Remains ; or, Three Sermons of R. Stuart, Dean of Westminster. pp. 167. *Printed for H. Brome.* **E. 1936. (2.)**

[**May.**]—Symptomes of Growth and Decay to Godlinesse. By Francis Smith. pp. 230. *Printed by G. Dawson, for F. S.* **E. 2114. (2.)**

June 1.—By the King. A Proclamation for quieting Possessions. *s. sh. Printed by Christopher Barker and John Bill* **669. f. 25. (38.)**

June 1.—By the King. A Proclamation against the Rebels in Ireland. *s. sh. Printed by Christopher Barker and John Bill.* **669. f. 25. (27.)**

[**June 1.**]—A Letter farther and more fully evidencing the King's stedfastnesse in the Protestant Religion. Written by Mounsieur de l'Angle, Minister of the Protestant Church at Rouen, to a friend in London. *Printed by A. W. for Joshua Kirton.* (1 June.) **E. 1027. (2.)**

[**June 1.**]—The Shaking of the Olive-Tree. The Remaining Works of Joseph Hall, late Bishop of Norwich. [With an engraved portrait of the author.] pp. 502. *Printed by J. Cadwel, for J. Crooke.* (1 June.) **E. 185. (1.)**

June 2.—An exact and true Relation of the wonderfull Whirle-Wind on 2 June, at Worthington, Worthington Hall, and at Tongue, and some other places in the County of Leicester. *Printed by T. F. for Fr. Coles.* **E. 1030. (6.)**

[**June 3.**]—England's Season for Reformation of Life. A sermon delivered in St. Paul's Church on the Sunday next following his Sacred Majesties Restauration. By Tho. Pierce. *Printed for Timothy Garthwait.* **E. 1027. (17.)**

[**June 3.**]—To the King, upon his Majestie's happy Return. By a Person of Honour. [A poem.] *Printed by J. M. for Henry Herringman.* **E. 1080. (2.)**

[**June 4.**]—An Act for Continuance of Process and Judicial Proceedings. *Printed by John Macock and Francis Tyton.* **E. 1075. (3.)**

June 4.—A Noble Salutation and a faithful Greeting unto thee, Charles Stuart, who art now proclaimed King of England, Scotland, France and Ireland. From George Fox, the younger. A copy of this was delivered by Richard Hubberthorn unto the King's hand at Whitehal. 4 June. *Printed for Robert Wilson.* **E. 1027. (14.)**

[**June 4.**]—The Martyrdom of King Charls I. Or his Conformity with Christ in his Sufferings. In a sermon preached at Bredah, before his Sacred Majesty King Charls the Second and the Princess of Orange. By the Bishop of Downe [Jeremy Taylor]. *Printed at the Hague* 1649, *and reprinted at London by W. Godbid.* (4 June.) **E. 1027. (5.)**

June 5.—By the King. A Proclamation for setting apart a Day of Solemn and Publick Thanksgiving throughout the whole Kingdom. *s. sh. Printed by Christopher Barker and John Bill.* **669. f. 25. (40.)**

1660.

June 5.—Great Britains Resurrection; or, England's Complacencie in her Royal Soveraign King Charles the Second. A sermon preached in the lecture at Gloucester. By Richard Eedes. *Printed by Ja. Cottrel for Henry Fletcher.* **E. 1034. (6.)**

[**June 5.**]—The Restauration. Or, a poem on the return of Charles the II. to his Kingdoms. By Arthur Brett. *Printed by J. H. for Samuel Thomson.* (5 June.) **E. 1027. (7.)**

June 6.—By the King. A Proclamation to summon the Persons therein named, who assisted in that horrid and detestable Murder of His Majesties Royal Father, to render themselves within fourteen days, under pain of being excepted from Pardon. *s. sh. Printed by John Bill & Christopher Barker.* **669. f. 25. (41.)**

[**June 6.**]—L'Estrange his Apology, with a short view of some late transactions leading to the happy settlement of these Nations under Charles the II. By R. L. S. [i.e. Sir Roger L'Estrange.] pp. 157. *Printed for Henry Browne.* (6 June.) **E. 187. (1.)**

[**June 6.**]—Upon the Blessed Return of King Charles the Second. Presented to his Majesty by a Person of Honour the next day. [A collection of poems, signed : John Lawson.] *s. sh.* (6 June.) **669. f. 25. (39.)**

[**June 7.**]—Epinicia Carolina. Or an essay upon the return of his sacred Majesty, Charles the Second. By S. W., of the Inner Temple. [A poem.] *Printed for Robert Gibbs.* (7 June.) **E. 1027. (8.)**

June 8.—An Ordinance of the Lords and Commons for an Assessment of seventy thousand pounds by the moneth, upon England, for three moneths for the supply of the present occasions of the King's Majesty and for the payment of the armies and navies. pp. 85. *Printed by Edward Husbands and Thomas Newcomb.* **E. 1075. (6.)**

[**June 8.**]—An Act for removing and preventing all questions and disputes concerning the assembling and sitting of this present Parliament. *Printed by John Bill and Christopher Barker.* (8 June.) **E. 1075. (4.)**

June 9.—To the Kings most Excellent Majesty. [An address from the County of Somerset.] *s. sh. Printed for R. Royston.* **669. f. 25. (43.)**

[**June 9.**]—To the King upon His Majestie's happy Return. [A poem. By Edmund Waller.] *Printed for Richard Marriot.* (9 June.) **E. 1080. (3.)**

[**June 10.**]—A Panegyrick to the King. By Thomas Higgons. [In verse.] *Printed for Henry Herringman.* (10 June.) **E. 1080. (4.)**

[**June 11.**]—Ad Augustissimum Majestatem Caroli Secundi Sylvæ II. [Laudatory verses, in Latin, by James Windet.] (11 June.) **E. 765. (13.)**

1660.

[**June 11.**]—To the King's Most Excellent Majesty : on his return to the government of his Kingdoms. [A poem, by Clement Ellis. With a MS. note by Thomason : " The gift of the Author, my son George's Tutor."]   *Printed by James Cottrel for Humphry Robinson.*   (11 June.)
E. 1080. (5.)

June 12.—To the Kings most Excellent Majesty.   The Humble Address of the County of Dorset.   *s. sh.   Printed for R. Clavel.*
669. f. 25. (44.)

[**June 12.**]—The Charges issuing forth of the Crown Revenue of England and Wales.   With the several officers of his Majestie's Courts, Customs, Castles, Forts, Parks, Chases, with their several fees and allowances. And also the valuation of the Bishops and Deanes lands.   By Captain Lazarus Haward.   *Printed for M. Wright.*   (12 June.)   E. 1027. (11.)

[**June 14.**]—An Act for putting in execution an Ordinance [for Assessment] mentioned in this Act.   *Printed by John Bill and Christopher Barker.*
E. 1075. (5.)

[**June 14.**]—To the best of Monarchs, his Maiesty Charles the Second, a Gratulatory Poem.   [Signed : S. Holland.]   *s. sh.   Printed by S. Griffin for M. Wallbancke.*   (14 June.)
669. f. 25. (42.)

June 15.—By the King.   A Proclamation concerning His Majesties gracious Pardon, in pursuance of His Majesties former Declaration. *s. sh.   Printed by John Bill and Christopher Barker.*   669. f. 25. (47.)

June 15.—By the King.   A Proclamation for Recalling of Commissions at Sea.   *Printed by John Bill & Christopher Barker.*   669. f. 25. (45.)

[**June 15.**]—To the King's most Sacred Majesty upon his happy and glorious return.   An endeavoured poem.   By Samuel Willes.   *Printed by T. R. for John Baker.*   (15 June.)   E. 1027. (15.)

[**June 17.**]—Anglia Rediviva.   A poem on his Majestie's most joyfull reception into England.   *Printed by R. Hodgkinsonne for Charles Adams.* (17 June.)
E. 1029. (3.)

[**June 17.**]—Gospel-Revelation.   In three treatises.   By Jeremiah Burroughs.   pp. 370.   *Printed for Nath. Brook and Thomas Parkhurst.* (17 June.)
E. 1029. (1.)

[**June 17.**]—The Saints Happinesse.   Together with the severall steps leading thereunto, delivered in divers lectures on the Beatitudes. By Jeremiah Burroughs.   Being the last sermons that ever he preached. pp. 662.   *Printed by M. S. for Nathaniel Brook, and for Thomas Parkhurst.*   (17 June.)
E. 1028.

[**June 17.**]—Samuel in Sackcloth.   Or, a sermon assaying to restrain our bitter animosities, and commending a spirit of moderation.   By S. S. *Printed by R. I. for Henry Mortlock.*   (17 June.)
E. 1029.

June 18.—His Majestie's gracious Message to the House of Commons [concerning the Bill of Indemnity].   *Printed by John Bill and Christopher Barker.*
E. 1075. (7.)

1660.

[**June 18.**]—The Thrice Welcome and happy Inauguration of our Sovereign King Charles II. to the Crown and Kingdoms of Great Britain and Ireland. In the first place, the author's supplication to the King's Majesty, in order to the reformation of religion. In the second part, the subjects' duty to their Sovereign. By Geo. Willington. [See also below : 6 Sept., E. 1043. (8.)] *Printed by R. D.* (18 June.)
E. 1030. (1.)

June 18.—Two Votes [of the House of Lords] concerning the King and Queenes Houses and Lands. *s. sh. Printed by John Bill and Christopher Barker.* **669. f. 25. (46.)**

[**June 18.**]—The Golden Apophthegms of King Charles I. and Henry, Marq. of Worcester, both divine and morale, as they were delivered upon several occasions in the time of the late unhappy War. By Tho. Bayly. *Printed by John Clowes.* (18 June.) **E. 184. (3.)**

June 19.—The Loyal Addresse of the Gentry of Gloucestershire to the Kings most Excellent Majesty. *s. sh. Printed for Humphrey Tuckey.*
669. f. 25. (48.)

[**June 19.**]—Astræa Redux. A poem on the happy Restoration & Return of his Sacred Majesty Charles the Second. By John Driden. *Printed by J. M. for Henry Herringman.* (19 June.) **E. 1080. (6.)**

June 20.—[A Congratulatory Address to the King from the County of Northampton.] *s. sh. Printed for John Martin, James Allestry & Thomas Dicas.* **669. f. 25. (49.)**

[**June 21.**]—The Humble and Penitent Petition of William Jenkin, now Minister of Christ-Church, London, then prisoner to the Rump Parliament. Presented to them in the year 1651, with their resolves thereupon. (21 June.) **E. 1030. (2.)**

[**June 21.**]—The Rump ; or, A collection of Songs and Ballads made upon those who would be a Parliament and were but a Rump of an House of Commons. pp. 191. *Printed for H. Brome and H. Marsh.* (21 June.) **E. 1833. (4.)**

[**June 25.**]—Poem upon His Sacred Majesties most happy Return to His Dominions. By Sʳ William Davenant. *Printed for Henry Herringman.* (25 June.) **E. 184. (2.)**

[**June 25.**]—Englands Joy, expressed in an 'Επινίκιον, to His Excellency the Lord General Monck. [Signed : J. H.] *Printed for M. B.* (25 June.) **669. f. 25. (50.)**

[**June 25.**]—'Ανάλυσις. The Loosing of St. Peter's Bands ; setting forth the true sense and solution of the Covenant, in point of conscience, so far as it relates to the government of the Church by Episcopacy. By John Gauden. [See also below : 19 July, E. 765. (4.) ; 6 Aug., E. 187. (3.), and 23 Nov., E. 1050. (2.)] *Printed by J. Best for Andrew Crook.* (25 June.) **E. 1030. (4.)**

1660.

[June 25.]—The Reduction of Episcopacie unto the form of Synodical Government received in the Antient Church. Proposed as an expedient for the compremising of the now differences. By Ja. Usher, Armachanus. *Printed by T. N. for G. B. and T. C.* (25 June.)   **E. 1030. (3.)**

June 26.—To his most Sacred Maiestie, Charles the Second, the Humble Congratulations of the Nobility and Gentry of the County of Rutland. *s. sh. Printed by S. Griffin for Robert Pawley.*   **669. f. 25. (55.)**

[June 26.]—To his sacred Majesty, Charles the Second, on his happy Return. [A poem. By Thomas Edwards.]   (26 June.)

E. 1080. (7.)

[June 26.]—An humble Caution concerning the danger of removing godly and approved Ministers out of Sequestrations. *Printed by Thomas Ratcliffe.* (26 June.)   **E. 1030. (7.)**

June 28.—A Form of Prayer, with Thanksgiving, to be used of all the King's Majestie's loving subjects for His Majestie's happy return to his Kingdoms. *Printed by John Bill and Christopher Barker.*

E. 1030. (9.)

June 28.—Davids Deliverance and Thanksgiving. A sermon preached before the King at Whitehall the Day of Solemn Thanksgiving for the Happy Return of His Majesty. By Gilbert Sheldon. pp. 50. *Printed for Timothy Garthwait.*   **E. 1035. (1.)**

June 28.—Sions Hallelujah ; set forth in a sermon preached before the House of Peers in the Abbie Church of Westminster. By Tho. Hodges. *Printed by J. Best, for Andrew Crook.*   **E. 1034. (11.)**

June 28.—Divine Efficacy without Humane Power. A sermon preached before the House of Commons at St. Margaret's Church. By Edward Reynolds. *Printed by Tho. Ratcliffe for George Thomason.*

E. 988. (27.)

June 28.—Davids Devotions upon his Deliverances, set forth in a sermon at All-Saints in Derby. By Joseph Swetnam. *Printed for H. M.*   **E. 1037. (1.)**

June 28.—England's Royal Stone at the Head of the Corner. A sermon preached in the Cathedral Church at Gloucester. By John Nelme. *Printed by Ja. Cottrel for Henry Fletcher.*   **E. 1034. (9.)**

June 28.—Englands Sorrows turned into Joy. A sermon. By John Whynnell. [With an engraved portrait of Charles II. as frontispiece.] *Printed by T. M. for H. Brome.*   **E. 1033. (8.)**

June 28.—Hosannah ; a Thanksgiving-Sermon. By J. M., Presb. Anglic. [i.e. John Martin.] *Printed by H. Hall for Rich. Davis: Oxford.*   **E. 184. (4.)**

June 28.—Judah's Return to their Allegiance : and David's Returne to his Crown and Kingdom. A sermon preached at St. Mary Woolchurch. By William Creed. *Printed by J. C. for Timothy Garthwait.*

E. 1033. (11.)

1660.

June 28.—Obedience perpetually due to Kings. A sermon to Mr. Peter Gunning's Congregation in Exeter Chappel near the Savoy. By William Towers. *Printed by R. D. for Thomas Rooks.*

E. 1040. (6.)

June 28.—Παράλληλα, or, The Loyall Subjects Exultation for the Royall Exiles Restauration. A sermon preached at All-Saints Church in Northampton. By Simon Ford. *Printed by Abraham Miller for Samuel Gellibrand.* **E. 1038. (5.)**

[June 30.]—A Glimpse of Joy for the happy Restoring of the Kings most Excellent Majesty. [In verse.] *s. sh. Printed for John Andrews.* (30 June.) **669. f. 25. (53.)**

[June 30.]—A Panegyrick to his renowned Majestie Charles the Second. [In verse. Signed : T. F.] *Printed for Henry Marsh.* (30 June.)

669. f. 25. (51.)

[June 30.]—A Pair of Prodigals returned ; or, England and Scotland agreed. [In verse.] *s. sh.* (30 June.) **669. f. 25. (52.)**

[June.]—The History of His Sacred Majesty Charles II. [By John Dauncy. With an engraved portrait of the King.] pp. 236. *Printed for James Davies.* **E. 1935. (2.)**

[June.]—Aminta : the famous pastorall. By Torquato Tasso. Translated into English verse by John Dancer. Together with divers ingenious poems. pp. 134. *Printed for Joh. Starkey.* **E. 1836. (2.)**

[June.]—Arnaldo ; or, The Injur'd Lover. An excellent new romance. By Girolamo Brusoni. Made English by T. S. pp. 190. *Printed for Thomas Dring.* **E. 1841. (3.)**

[June.]—Euchologia ; or, The Doctrine of Practical Praying, by John Prideaux, late Bishop of Worcester. Second edition, enlarged. pp. 273. *Printed for George Sawbridge.* **E. 1932. (2.)**

[June.]—Honor redivivus ; or, An analysis of Honor and Armory. By Matt. Carter. [Illustrated with woodcuts and engravings.] pp. 251. *Printed for Henry Herringman.* **E. 1922. (1.)**

[June.]—The Idea of the Law charactered from Moses to King Charles. Whereunto is added the Idea of Government and Tyranny. By John Heydon. pp. 208. *Printed for the Author.* **E. 1916. (2.)**

[June.]—The Learned Man defended and reform'd. A discourse asserting the Right of the Muses. Written in Italian by Daniel Bartolus ; Englished by Thomas Salusbury. pp. 402. *Printed by R. & W. Leybourn for Thomas Dring.* **E. 1831. (2.)**

[June.]—The Plain Way of Peace and Unity in Matters of Religion. By John Durie. *Printed for Fr. Tyton.* **E. 1808. (1.)**

[June.]—Poems, viz. : 1. A Panegyrick to the King. 2. Songs and Sonnets. 3. The Blind Lady, a comedy. 4. The Fourth Book of Virgil. 5. Statius his Achilleis, with annotations. 6. A Panegyrick

II.

Y

1660.

to Generall Monck. By the Honorable Sr Robert Howard. pp. 285.
Printed for Henry Herringman.   **E. 1824. (2.)**

[**June.**]—Le Prince d'Amour ; or, The Prince of Love. [By Sir Benjamin
Rudyerd.] With a collection of several ingenious poems and songs by the
Wits of the age. pp. 184. *Printed for William Leake.* **E. 1836. (1.)**

[**June.**]—Θυσιαστήριον, vel Scintilla Altaris. Being a pious Reflection on
Primative Devotion in the Feasts and Fasts of the Church of England.
By Edward Sparke. The second edition. [With engraved plates.]
pp. 644. *Printed by W. G. and R. W.*   **E. 1763.**

[**July 2.**]—The Oath of Allegiance. *s. sh.* (2 July.) **669. f. 25. (54.)**

[**July 3.**]—Some Considerations offered to publique view, in behalf of the
many thousand persons interested in publique Sales. *Printed for Giles
Calvert.* (3 July.)   **E. 1030. (11.)**

[**July 3.**]—Something against Swearing and concerning the Oath of
Allegiance and Supremacy. By Richard Hubberthorne and George
Fox the Younger. *s. sh. Printed for G. C.* (3 July.) **669. f. 25. (56.)**

[**July 4.**]—The Character of a Presbyter, or Sr John anatomized. *Printed
for John Calvin.* (4 July.)   **E. 1030. (12.)**

July 5.—London's Glory represented by Time, Truth and Fame : at the
triumphs and entertainment of his Majesty Charls the II., the two
Houses of Parliament, &c., at Guildhall, 5 July. [By John Tatham.]
Printed by William Godbid.   **E. 1030. (13.)**

[**July 7.**]—Britannia Rediviva. [Gratulatory poems on the restoration
of Charles II.] pp. 150. *Excudebat A. & L. Lichfield : Oxoniæ.* (7 July.)
        E. 1030. (16.)

[**July 8.**]—The Beatitudes ; or, A Discourse upon part of Christs Famous
Sermon on the Mount. By Thomas Watson. pp. 655. *Printed for
Ralph Smith.* (8 July.)   **E. 1031.**

[**July 10.**]—Academiæ Cantabrigiensis Σῶστρα. Sive, Ad Carolum II
reducem Gratulatio. pp. 116. *Excudebat Joannes Field : Cantabrigiæ.*
(10 July.)   **E. 1032. (3.)**

[**July 10.**]—A True Relation of the Tryal and Horrid Murder of Col.
Eusebius Andrewe by John Bradshaw, President of the pretended
High-Court of Justice and others of the same Court. By Francis
Buckley. pp. 77. *Printed for Daniel Pakeman.* (10 July.)
        E. 1032. (1.)

[**July 12.**]—To His Majesty, upon His happy Arrival in our late dis-
composed Albion. By R. Brathwait. [In verse.] *Printed for Henry
Brome.* (12 July.)   **E. 1032. (5.)**

July 13.—Britains Glory ; being a relation of the Solemnity wherewith
the English Nation residing in Livorne entertained the Joyful Tidings
of His Majesties Return to his Royal Throne. *Printed for Edw. Farnham.*
        E. 1040. (5.)

1660.

[**July 13.**]—Royal and other Innocent Bloud crying aloud to Heaven for due vengeance. By George Starkey. *Printed by A. Warren for Daniel White.* (13 July.)

E. 1032. (7.)

[**July 13.**]—An Essay to a continuation of Iter Boreale, attempting something upon the happy influence which the successefull march of the Lord Generall Monck out of the North had upon the Arts and Sciences. By a Lover of Learning. [By Robert Wild. In verse.] *Printed for Robert Smith.* (13 July.)

E. 1032. (6.)

[**July 14.**]—The Oaths of Supremacy & Allegiance, which have lain dead for many years, now taken by both Houses of Parliament and all Officers and Souldiers. *Printed for William Sheares.* (14 July.)

E. 1032. (9.)

[**July 14.**]—The English Episcopacy and Liturgy asserted by the Great Reformers abroad and the most Glorious and Royal Martyr the late King His Opinion and Suffrage for them. *Printed by Tho. Leach for Henry Seile.* (14 July.)

E. 1032. (10.)

[**July 14.**]—Gods Working and Brittains Wonder. A sermon congratulating the most happy establishment of His Sacred Majesty Charls the II. on his Throne. By Will. Price. *Printed by W. Godbid for Peter Dring.* (14 July.)

E. 1034. (5.)

[**July 14.**]—The Devils Cabinet-Councell discovered; or, The Mistery and Iniquity of the Good Old Cause. pp. 55. *Printed by H. Brugis for Henry Marsh.* (14 July.)

E. 2111. (2.)

[**July 14.**]—The Picture of the Good Old Cause drawn to the Life in the Effigies of Master Prais-God Barebone. [An engraved portrait of Barebone, with printed matter.] *s. sh.* (14 July.)

669. f. 25. (57.)

[**July 17.**]—The Royal Chronicle, wherein is contained an historical Narration of His Majesties Royal Progress, etc. *Printed for G. Horton.* (17 July.)

E. 1034. (2.)

[**July 17.**]—Advise to a Friend discontented at some proceedings in His Majesties Royall Court. By F. G. *Printed by Thomas Creake.* (17 July.)

E. 1034. (4.)

July 17.—An Eccho to the Plea for limited Monarchy. By the same Author. [See above: 20 Feb., E. 765. (3.)] *Printed by T. M for William Shears.*

E. 765. (4.)

[**July 17.**]—The Hangmans joy, or the Traytors Sorrow. Being a very merry dialogue between the Hangman and the Haltermaker. *Printed for John Andrews.* (17 July.)

E. 1842. (2.)

[**July 17.**]—The Lamentation of a Bad Market: or, The Disbanded Souldier. [In verse.] *s. sh. Printed for Charles Gustavus.* (17 July.)

669. f. 25. (58.)

1660.

[July 19.]—The Anatomy of Dr. Gaudens Idolized Non-sence and Blasphemy in his pretended Analysis of the Covenant. [See above : 25 June, E. 1030. (4.)] (19 July.) **E. 765. (14.)**

[July 19.]—The Case of Mr. Hugh Peters, impartially communicated to the view and censure of the whole World : written by his own hand. *Printed for Samuel Speed.* (19 July.) **E. 1034. (10.)**

[July 19.]—De Efficacia Gratiæ Convertentis determinatio habita Cantabrigiæ per Sam. Gardiner. *Per Johannem Field : Cantabrigiæ.* (19 July.) **E. 1034. (8.)**

[July 19.]—Divers Politique Discourses of the Duke of Rohan. Render'd into English by G. B., Esq. [i.e. George Bridges]. pp. 70. *Printed by Thomas Ratcliffe for G. Bedell and T. Collins.* (19 July.) **E. 1764. (1*.)**

[July 19.]—The Memoires of the Duke of Rohan. Englished by George Bridges. pp. 224. *Printed by E. M. for Gabriel Bedell and Thomas Collins.* (19 July.) **E. 1764. (1.)**

[July 19.]—A Visitation of Love unto the King and those call'd Royallists, consisting of an answer to several Queries proposed to the Quakers. By Edward Burrough. *Printed and are to be sold by Robert Wilson.* (19 July.) **E. 1034. (7.)**

[July 20.]—In mirabilem Caroli II. restitutionem carmen gratulatorium. [By Christopher Wase.] *Impressit D. Maxwell, sumptibus Caroli Adams.* (20 July.) **E. 1080. (8.)**

July 20.—The Earle of Bristoll his Speech in the House of Lords, upon the Bill of Indempnity. **E. 765. (15.)**

July 22.—The Life of Faith. A sermon preached before the King at White-hall. By Richard Baxter. pp. 70. *Printed by R. W. and A. M. for Francis Tyton and Jane Underhill, London, and by Nevill Simmons at Kederminster.* **E. 1038. (7.)**

July 23.—By the King. A Proclamation concerning the Times of holding the Summer Assizes. *Printed by John Bill and Christopher Barker.* **669. f. 25. (59.)**

July 23.—[A Proclamation concerning the Herring Fishery.] *s. sh.* *Printed for Jane Bourne.* **669. f. 25. (61.)**

[July 24.]—To the Kings most Excellent Majesty. The Humble Addresse of the Clergy of Kent. *s. sh.* **669. f. 25. (76.)**

[July 24.]—A Catalogue of the Peers of the Kingdome of England. *s. sh.* (24 July.) **669. f. 25. (60.)**

[July 24.]—A Mirror, wherein the Rumpers and Fanaticks may see their deformity. *Printed for Robert Pawley.* (24 July.)

E. 1034. (14.)

[July 25.]—Anagram of his Excellency the Lord Generall Monck. [With a poem, by W. Drummond.] *s. sh.* (25 July.)

669. f. 25. (63.)

1660.

[July 25.]—Don Pedro de Quixot, or in English the Right Reverend Hugh Peters. The names of the Rumps twelve Chaplains extra-ordinary. [A satire; with an engraved portrait of Hugh Peters.] *s. sh. Printed for T. Smith.* (25 July.) **669. f. 25. (62.)**

[July 25.]—Haslerig & Vain; or, A dialogue between them in the Tower of London, being a lamentation of both their vile actions, with all their damnable plots against the late King Charles. [A satire.] By T. H. *Printed for William Gilbertson.* (25 July.) **E. 1849. (2.)**

[July 25.]—The Rebels Plea; or, Mr. Baxters judgement concerning the late Wars. [By Thomas Tomkins.] *Printed by Thomas Mabb for Henry Brome.* (25 July.) **E. 1034. (17.)**

[July 25.]—A Scandalous, Libellous and Seditious Pamphlet entituled The Valley of Baca, or the Armies Interest pleaded, answered. (25 July.) **E. 1034. (16.)**

[July 26.]—Εἰκὼν Βασιλικὴ, or, The True Pourtraicture of His Majesty Charls the II., from his birth unto this present year 1660. By David Lloyd. [With engraved portraits of the King, the Duke of York, the Duke of Gloucester and General Monk.] 3 pt. *Printed for H. Brome and H. Marsh.* (26 July.) **E. 1922. (2.)**

[July 26.]—A Brief Confession of Faith lately presented to King Charles the Second: set forth by many of us who are falsely called Ana-Baptists. *s. sh. Printed for Francis Smith.* (26 July.) **669. f. 25. (65.)**

[July 26.]—Censura Cleri, or, A Plea against Scandalous Ministers not fit to be restored to the Churches Livings. By a true Lover of the Church of England in Doctrine [John Barnard]. *Printed for Giles Calvert.* (26 July.) **E. 1035. (2.)**

[July 26.]—The Fanatick History; or, An Exact Relation of the Old Anabaptists and New Quakers. [By Richard Blome. With an engraved portrait of Charles II.] pp. 224. *Printed for J. Sims.* (26 July.) **E. 1832. (2.)**

[July 26.]—Jews in America; or, Probabilities that those Indians are Judaical. By Tho. Thorowgood. An Accurate Discourse is premised of Mr. John Elliot touching their origination. pp. 89. *Printed for Henry Brome.* (26 July.) **E. 1032. (8.)**

[July 26.]—Argyles Arraignment; or, Treachery displayed. [In verse.] *s. sh.* (26 July.) **669. f. 25. (64.)**

July 27.—His Majestie's gracious Speech to the House of Peers, con-cerning the speedy passing of the Bill of Indempnity & Oblivion. *Printed by Christopher Barker and John Bill.* **E. 1075. (8.)**

[July 27.]—The English Devil; or, Cromwel and his Monstrous Witch discover'd at White-Hall. *Printed by Robert Wood for George Horton.* (27 July.) **E. 1035. (3.)**

1660.

July 28.—The Rates of Merchandise, that is to say, the subsidy of Tonnage, subsidy of Poundage, and the subsidy of Woollen or old Drapery, as they are rated and agreed on by the Commons House. pp. 58. *Printed by Edward Husbands and Thomas Newcomb.* **E. 1075. (10.)**

July 28.—A Letter [signed : W. L., London, 28 July] from one of the Persons under censure of Parliament, written upon the publishing of His Majesties late Speech in the Upper House. With an Answer [signed : R. E., Oxford, 31 July]. *Printed for William Shears.* **E. 765. (5.)**

[July 28.]—A Modest Discourse concerning the Ceremonies heretofore used in the Church of England, shewing the unlawfulness of them in the worship of God. *Printed by T. R. for Nathanael Webb.* (28 July.) **E. 1035. (4.)**

[July 30.]—The Case of Oliver St. John, Esq. Concerning his Actions during the late Troubles. (30 July.) **E. 1035. (5.)**

[July 30.]—Funebria Floræ ; the Downfall of May-Games. Occasioned by the generall complaint of people in this Interval of Settlement. [A satire.] By Tho. Hall. *Printed for Henry Mortlock.* (30 July.) **E. 1035. (7.)**

[July 30.]—The Traytors Tragedy ; or, their great Plot and treasonable design discovered. [A satire.] *Printed for R. Cotton.* (30 July.) **E. 1035. (6.)**

[July 31.]—A Subsidy granted to the King of Tonnage and Poundage, and other sums of money payable upon Merchandize exported and imported. An Act for continuing the Excise until the twentieth of August. An Act for the present nominating of Commissioners of Sewers. *Printed by John Bill and Christopher Barker.* (31 July.) **E. 1075. (9.)**

July 31.—A Sermon preached at a Visitation held at Lin in Norfolk, 24 June 1633. By William Strode. *Printed by W. Wilson for Samuel Brown.* **E. 1035. (8.)**

[July.]—Stemma Sacrum. The Royal Progeny delineated, shewing His Sacred Majesties Royal and Lawful Descent to his Crown. By Giles Fleming. [With an engraved genealogical tree.] *Printed for Robert Gibbs.* **E. 1914. (1.)**

[July.]—An Exact History of the several changes of Government in England from the horrid Murther of King Charles I. to the happy Restauration of King Charles II. Being the second part of Florus Anglicus, by J. D. [i.e. John Dauncy]. pp. 392. *Printed for Simon Miller.* **E. 1917. (3.)**

[July.]—Cromwell's Bloody Slaughter-house ; or, His Damnable Designes in contriving the Murther of King Charles I. discovered. By a Person of Honor. [By John Gauden.] pp. 131. *Printed for James Davis.* **E. 1933. (2.)**

1660.

[July.]—The Long Parliament revived : or an Act for the continuation and the not dissolving the Long Parliament but by an Act of Parliament. With undenyable reasons deduced from the s^d Act to prove that that Parliament is not yet dissolved. Also Mr. Wm. Prin his 5 arguments fully answered whereby he endeavours to prove it to be dissolved by the King's death. By a true lover and great sufferer for his King and Country [Sir William Drake. In MS. throughout, in Thomason's hand ; with a note : "This was printed afterwards." For the printed copy, see below : 23 Oct., E. 1046. (12.)]. **E. 1030. (15.)**

[July.]—The Mystery of the Good old Cause briefly unfolded. In a catalogue of such Members of the late Long Parliament that held offices, contrary to the Self-denying Ordinance. pp. 56. **E. 1923. (2.)**

[July.]—The Benefit of Afflictions. By Edward Reynell. *Printed for Abel Roper.* **E. 1914. (2.)**

[July.]—Celestial Amities ; or, A Soul Sighing for the Love of her Saviour. By Edward Reynell. pp. 190. *Printed by J. M. for Abel Roper.* **E. 1914. (3.)**

[July.]—The Character of Italy ; or, The Italian Anatomiz'd by an English Chyrurgion. pp. 93. *Printed for Nath. Brooke.* **E. 2109. (3.)**

[July.]—The Character of Spain ; or, An Epitome of their Virtues and Vices. pp. 93. *Printed for Nath. Brooke.* **E. 2109. (2.)**

[July.]—A Discourse and Defence of Arms and Armory. By Edward Waterhouse. pp. 232. *Printed by T. R. for Samuel Mearne.* **E. 1839. (1.)**

[July.]—The Law of Charitable Uses, wherein the Statute of 43 Eliz. cap. 4 is explained. By John Herne. pp. 151. *Printed by T. R. for Timothy Twyford.* **E. 1921. (2.)**

[July.]—מסורה Masorah, seu Critica Divina, or, a Synoptical Directorie on the Sacred Scriptures. By Ferdinando Parkhurst. pp. 188. *Printed by Thomas Newcomb for G. Bedel, T. Collins and James Magnes.* **E. 1832. (1.)**

[July.]—Moor's Arithmetick, in two books. By Jonas Moore. 5 pt. *Printed by J. G. for Nath. Brook.* **E. 1753.**

[July.]—A Plaine & Profitable Catechisme. Whereunto is added a Sermon upon Exod. xxiii. 2. By James Bacon. pp. 235. *Printed by W. Hall for R. Davis : Oxford.* **E. 1853. (3.)**

[July.]—The Sage Senator delineated ; or, A Discourse of the qualifications, endowments, offices, duty and dignity of a Perfect Politician. By J. G., Gent. [i.e. John Grimefield ?] pp. 216. *Printed by Ja. Cottrel for Sam. Speed.* **E. 1766. (1.)**

[July.]—A Treatise concerning Religions, in refutation of the opinion which accounts all indifferent. Rendred into English out of the French copy of Moyses Amyraldus. pp. 539. *Printed by M. Simons for Will. Nealand, Bookseller at Cambridge.* **E. 1846. (1.)**

1660.

[**Aug. 1.**]—A List of Knights made since his Majestie came to London.
s. sh. Printed by S. Griffin. (1 Aug.)   **669. f. 25. (66.)**

[**Aug. 1.**]—Historical Reflections on the Bishop of Rome. By John
Wagstaff. *Printed by Hen. Hall for Ric. Davis, Oxford; and are to
be sold by S. Thompson in St. Paul's Churchyard.* (1 Aug.)
E. 1035. (9.)

[**Aug. 2.**]—A Brief View of the late troubles begun by a prevailing faction
in the Long Parliament. Deduced to the auspicious coming in of
General Monck and the Restitution of King Charles II. By William
Younger. pp. 149. *Printed for Robert Gibbs.* (2 Aug.)
E. 1873. (2.)

[**Aug. 2.**]—A Declaration of Maj: Gen. Harrison, prisoner in the Tower
of London; with his Rules and Precepts to all Publike Churches and
Private Congregations; and an Answer thereunto. Also, the Resolution of the Fifth-Monarchy-Men, Anabaptists, Quakers and others.
Printed for Nathaniel Tomkins. (2 Aug.)   **E. 1035. (10.)**

[**Aug. 2.**]—Strange and True Newes from Gloucester; or, A perfect
relation of the Power of God shewed for injustice at Fairford, where
an innumerable company of Froggs and Toads overspread the Orchards
and Houses of the Lord of the Town. [See also below: 20 Sept.,
E. 1045. (5.)] *Printed by J. C. for N. T.* (2 Aug.)   **E. 1035. (12.)**

[**Aug. 3.**]—Reasons shewing the necessity of Reformation of the Publick
Doctrine, Worship, Rites and Ceremonies, Church-Government, and
Discipline. By divers Ministers. [Edited by Cornelius Burges.] pp.
63. [See also below: 5 Sept., 1660, E. 1043. (7.) and 13 Dec. 1661,
E. 2106. (3.)] *Printed by Ja. Cottrel.* (3 Aug.)   **E. 764. (4.)**

[**Aug. 4.**]—Three Royal Poems upon the return of Charles the II., James
Duke of York, Henry Duke of Glocester. *Printed by Edward Cole.*
(4 Aug.)   **E. 1080. (9.)**

[**Aug. 6.**]—Serious Observations lately made touching His Majesty in
Hebrew; translated into English, The King hath prepared a Refreshing,
hee hath crushed it out of the Rock by degrees. Published by H.
Walker. *Printed by R. I. and are to be sold by William Gilbertson.*
(6 Aug.)   **E. 1035. (14.)**

[**Aug. 6.**]—The Form and Manner of Making & Consecrating Bishops,
Priests and Deacons, according to the Appointment of the Church of
England. *Printed by Robert Barker and John Bill.* (6 Aug.)
E. 1035. (15.)

[**Aug. 6.**]—Ἀνάληψις, or, Saint Peters Bonds abide. A consideration of
John Gauden's Sence and Solution of the Solemn League and Covenant.
By Zech. Crofton. Third edition. [See above: 25 June, E. 1030. (4.)
and also below: 8 Aug., E. 1038. (4.)] *Printed for Ralph Smith.*
(6 Aug.)   **E. 187. (3.)**

1660.

[Aug. 6.]—A Copie of the proceedings of some worthy and learned Divines touching Innovations in the Doctrine and Discipline of the Church of England. *Printed by A. W.* (6 Aug.) **E. 1038. (3.)**

[Aug. 6.]—Articles of High-Treason against Major General Harrison, Sir Arthur Hasilrig, Sir Henry Vane, and Mr. Thomas Scot. *Printed for Marm. Johnson.* (6 Aug.) **E. 1035. (13.)**

[Aug. 6.]—The Case is Altered ; or, Dreadful news from Hell. In a discourse between the Ghost of Oliver Croomwel and Joan his wife, at their late meeting neer the Scaffold on Tower-hill. [With a woodcut representing the heads of Cromwell and his wife.] *Printed for John Andrews.* (6 Aug.) **E. 1869. (2.)**

[Aug. 6.]—Via Recta ad Vitam Longam ; or, A Treatise wherein the best manner of living for attaining to a long life is demonstrated. By Tob. Venner. The fourth impression, amplified with many profitable additions. [With an engraved portrait of Venner as frontispiece.] pp. 404. *Printed for Abel Roper.* (6 Aug.) **E. 1036.**

Aug. 7.—The Kings Majesties most gracious Letter and Declaration to the Bishops, Deans and Prebends. [With reference to the stipends of Vicars and Curates.] *s. sh. Printed for John Jones.* **669. f. 25. (69.)**

[Aug. 7.]—Honest, Plain, Down-right-dealing with the People called Episcopal-Men and Presbyterians. By George Fox. *Printed for Robert Wilson.* (7 Aug.) **E. 1037. (2.)**

[Aug. 8.]—An Answer to A Quakers Seventeen Heads of Queries containing in them seventy seven Questions [by William Emerson]. By John Bewick. pp. 165. *Printed by T. R. for Andrew Crook.* (8 Aug.) **E. 1038. (1.)**

[Aug. 8.]—Cromwell's Conspiracy. A tragy-comedy, by a Person of Quality. *Printed for the Author.* (8 Aug.) **E. 1038. (2.)**

[Aug. 8.]—A Reply to the Answer of Anonymus to Doctor Gauden's Analysis of the Sense of the Covenant and to a tract of Mr. Zach. Crofton. By John Rowland. pp. 52. [See above : 6 Aug., E. 187. (3.)] *Printed for T. J.* (8 Aug.) **E. 1038. (4.)**

[Aug. 8.]—The Second Part of the Signal Loyalty and Devotion of Gods true Saints towards their Christian Kings & Emperors. Manifested in a chronological method. By William Prynne. pp. 321. *Printed by T. Childe and L. Parry for Edward Thomas.* (8 Aug.) **E. 1037. (3.)**

[Aug. 8.]—The White Robe ; or, The Surplice Vindicated as a most ancient and decent Ornament of the Ministry. Sermons, by Thomas Westfield, Bishop of Bristol. pp. 252. *Printed by J. C. for Samuel Speed.* (8 Aug.) **E. 2104. (2.)**

[Aug. 9.]—God Save the King. A justification by the Word of God of the Kings proffer for Liberty of Conscience in matters disputable. By Theophilus Brabourn. *Printed for the Author, and are to be sold by*

1660.

Booksellers in London, and by William Nowell bookseller in Norwich.
(9 Aug.)   **E. 1038. (6.)**

[**Aug. 9.**]—The Phanaticks Plot discovered : being a true Relation of
their* strange Proceedings in Glocestershire and other counties. [In
verse.] *s. sh. Printed for Samuel Burdet.* (9 Aug.)   **669. f. 25. (67.)**

Aug. 10.—His Majesties Gracious Letter directed to the Presbytery of
Edinburgh, and by them to be communicated to the rest of the
Presbyteries of this Kirk. *s. sh. Printed at Edinburgh and reprinted
for George Calvert.*   **669. f. 26. (24.)**

Aug. 13.—By the King. A Proclamation against Fighting of Duells.
s. sh. Printed by John Bill & Christopher Barker.   **669. f. 25. (71.)**

Aug. 13.—By the King. A Proclamation for calling in and suppressing
of two books written by John Milton ; the one intituled, Johannis
Miltoni Angli pro Populo Anglicano Defensio, and the other [" Εἰκονο-
κλάστης"] in answer to a Book intituled, The Pourtraicture of his
Sacred Majesty in his Solitude and Sufferings. *s. sh. Printed by John
Bill and Christopher Barker.*   **669. f. 25. (70.)**

Aug. 13.—By the King. A Proclamation for publishing a former Proclamation of the 30th of May last entituled, A Proclamation against
Vitious, Debauch'd and Prophane persons, in all Churches and Chappels
throughout England and Wales. *s. sh. Printed by John Bill & Christopher Barker.*   **669. f. 25. (73.)**

Aug. 14.—By the King. A Proclamation for Restoring and Discovering
his Majesties Goods. *s. sh. Printed by John Bill & Christopher Barker.*
                                                   669. f. 25. (72.)

[**Aug. 14.**]—The Lords Loud Call to England ; being a true relation of
some Judgments of God by Earthquake, Lightening, etc. By H. J.
[i.e. Henry Jessey.] [See above : 8 May, E. 1050. (1.) and also below :
20 Sept., E. 1045. (5.)] *Printed for L. Chapman and Fr. Smith.*
(14 Aug.)   **E. 1038. (8.)**

[**Aug. 14.**]—The Rebels Almanack, calculated for the use of all Loyal
Subjects. [A satire.] *Printed for George Horton.* (14 Aug.) **E. 1040. (1.)**

[**Aug. 14.**]—Three Decads of Sermons lately preached to the University
at St. Mary's Church in Oxford. By Henry Wilkinson. 3 pt. *Printed
by H. H. for Thomas Robinson : Oxford.* (14 Aug.)   **E. 1039.**

Aug. 16.—Exultationis Carmen. To the King's most excellent Majesty,
upon his most desired return. By Rachel Jevon. Presented with her
own hand, 16 Aug. *Printed by John Macock.*   **E. 1080. (11.)**

Aug. 16.—Carmen θριαμβευτικὸν. A Rachele Jevone compositum. [A
Latin version of the preceding.] *Typis Joannis Macock.* **E. 1080. (10.)**

[**Aug. 16.**]—Via ad Pacem Ecclesiasticum, monstratore B. Paulo, Phil. iii.
15, 16. [By Gulielmus Phalerius.] *Excudebat Robertus White, pro
Richardo Davis bibliopolâ Oxoniensi.* (16 Aug.)   **E. 1040. (2.)**

1660.

[**Aug. 17.**]—Mr. Pryns Letter and Proposals to King Charles [respecting the Drinking of Healths], and his Majesties Gracious Resolves [respecting Drinking and Duelling]. *Printed for Nathaniel Cotes.* (17 Aug.) **E. 1040. (4.)**

[**Aug. 17.**]—An Expedient for taking away all Impositions and for raising a Revenue without Taxes. By Francis Cradocke. *Printed for Henry Seile.* (17 Aug.) **E. 187. (4.)**

[**Aug. 17.**]—The Blazing-Star ; or, Nolls Nose newly revived. By Collonel Baker. [A satire, in verse.] *Printed for Theodorus Microcosmus.* (17 Aug.) **E. 1040. (3.)**

[**Aug. 20.**]—Boscobel ; or, The history of His Sacred Majesties preservation after the Battle of Worcester, 3 Sept. 1651. By Thomas Blount. [With an engraved plate, representing Boscobel House.] pp. 55. *Printed for Henry Seile.* (20 Aug.) **E. 1838. (2.)**

[**Aug. 20.**]—A Meditation for the 30th Day of January, the Anniversary of the Murther of K. Charles the I. Written and wept by M. de R. of the Middle Temple. *s. sh.* (20 Aug.) **669. f. 25. (74.)**

[**Aug. 20.**]—An Act for continuing of the Excise till the five and twentieth day of December, one thousand six hundred and sixty. *Printed by John Bill and Christopher Barker.* **E. 1075. (11.)**

[**Aug. 20.**]—An Apology for Purchases of Lands late of Bishops, Deans and Chapters. pp. 4. (20 Aug.) **669. f. 25. (75.)**

[**Aug. 20.**]—No Necessity of Reformation of the Publick Doctrine of the Church of England. By John Pearson. [See also below : 11 Sept., E. 1044. (4.) and 13 Sept., E. 764. (5.)] *Printed by J. G. for Nathaniel Brook.* (20 Aug.) **E. 1040. (7.)**

[**Aug. 20.**]—The League illegal. Wherein the late Solemn League and Covenant is examined and confuted. Written long since in Prison by Daniel Featley ; published by John Faireclough, vulgò Featley. pp. 60. [See also below : 23 Nov., E. 1050. (2.)] *Printed for R. Royston.* (20 Aug.) **E. 1040. (8.)**

[**Aug. 20.**]—Ahivah's Petition to his Majesty for the Saints' Liberties. *s. sh.* (20 Aug.) **669. f. 25. (68.)**

[**Aug. 21.**]—A Declaration of the Presbiterians concerning His Majesties Royal Person and the Government of the Church of England. *Printed for T. Dacres.* (21 Aug.) **E. 1040. (9.)**

[**Aug. 21.**]—Oliver Cromwell the late great Tirant his Life-Guard ; or, the Names of those who conspired with him in his Horrid Designs. *Printed for Francis Coles.* (21 Aug.) **E. 1040. (10.)**

[**Aug. 22.**]—The Triumphs of Paris at the Reception and entrance of Their Majesties of France. *Printed by Sarah Griffin.* (22 Aug.) **E. 1040. (11.)**

1660.

[**Aug. 24.**]—The Free-born English Mans Plea for Justice. Being a survey of the controversies touching late Purchased Titles. By William Jackson. *Printed by Edward Cole.* (24 Aug.)   **E. 1040. (14.)**

[**Aug. 24.**]—The Purchasers Pound ; or, The Return to Lambeth-Fair of Knaves and Thieves with all the Sacred Ware. [A satire on the Church, in verse. With a woodcut on the titlepage, representing a banquet.] *Printed for John Jones.* (24 Aug.)   **E. 1040. (13.)**

[**Aug. 24.**]—The Two Grand Traytors Lamentation ; or, Strange News from the Tower of London. Being the speeches of Col. Hacker and Col. John Barkstead. [A satire.] *Printed for J. Wilts.* (24 Aug.)

   E. 1040. (15.)

[**Aug. 24.**]—We have brought our Hoggs to a fair Market ; or, The Iron Age turned into Gold. By J. A., a lover of his countryes welfare. *Printed for Thomas Mills.* (24 Aug.)   **E. 1040. (12.)**

Aug. 26.—Evangelical Worship is Spiritual Worship. A sermon preached before the Lord Major, at Paul's Church. By Matthew Poole. *Printed for Sa. Thomson.*   **E. 1044. (1.)**

[**Aug. 27.**]—A Panegyrick to the King's Most Excellent Majesty. By Charles Cotton. *Printed by Tho. Newcomb.* (27 Aug.)

   E. 1080. (11*.)

[**Aug. 27.**]—The Judgement of Foraign Divines, as well from Geneva as other parts, touching the Discipline, Liturgie and Ceremonies of the Church of England. Whereunto is added a letter from Mr. John Calvin to Mr. Knox concerning the English Common-Prayer. (27 Aug.)

   E. 1040. (16.)

[**Aug. 28.**]—The Art of Water-Drawing ; or, A Compendious Abstract of all sorts of Water-Machines. [By R. Dacres.] *Printed for Henry Brome.* (28 Aug.)   **E. 1040. (19.)**

[**Aug. 28.**]—The Due Way of composing the differences on foot, preserving the Church. By Herbert Thorndike. pp. 70. *Printed by A. Warren for John Martin, James Allestry and Thomas Dicas.* (28 Aug.)

   1838. (3.)

[**Aug. 28.**]—Gallicantus, seu Præcursor Gallicinii primus. Containing two addresses, the one to the King, the other to the Parliament. By R. Lanceter. *Printed for Nathaniel Ranew.* (28 Aug.)

   E. 1041. (1.)

[**Aug. 28.**]—The Lamentation of the Safe Committee. Or, Fleetwood's Teares, Hewson's Last, Desborough's Cart, met together at Hangmans-Fayre. [A satire.] *Printed for William Gilbertson.* (28 Aug.)

   E. 1844. (2.)

Aug. 29.—His Majestie's gracious Speech to Parliament at the passing of the Act of Free Pardon, Indemnity and Oblivion, and several other Acts. *Printed by John Bill and Christopher Barker.*   **E. 1043. (1.)**

1660.

Aug. 29.—The Speech which the Speaker of the House of Commons [Sir Harbottle Grimston] made unto the King in the House of Lords, at his passing of the Bills therein mentioned, 29 Aug. *Printed by Edward Husband and Tho. Newcomb.* **E. 1043. (2.)**

[**Aug. 29.**]—A Dispute against the English-Popish Ceremonies obtruded upon the Church of Scotland. [By George Gillespie.] pp. 366. (29 Aug.) **E. 1041. (2.)**

[**Aug. 30.**]—An Act for the speedy provision of Money for disbanding and paying off the forces of this Kingdom both by sea and land. *Printed by John Bill and Christopher Barker.* (30 Aug.) **E. 1075. (13.)**

[**Aug. 30.**]—An Act of Free and General Pardon, Indempnity and Oblivion. *Printed by John Bill and Christopher Barker.* (30 Aug.) **E. 1075. (12.)**

[**Aug. 30.**]—A Discourse of Praying with the Spirit, and with the Understanding. Preached in two sermons, 1659. By Henry Leslie, Bishop of Down and Connor. Whereunto is annexed a letter of Jer. Taylor concerning the same subject. *Printed for John Crook.* (30 Aug.) **E. 1041. (4.)**

[**Aug. 31.**]—An Act for Confirmation of Judicial Proceedings. *Printed by John Bill and Christopher Barker.* (31 Aug.) **E. 1075. (14.)**

[**Aug. 31.**]—An Act for restraining the taking of excessive Usury. *Printed by John Bill and Christopher Barker.* (31 Aug.) **E. 1075. (13*.)**

[**Aug. 31.**]—Examinatio & Emendatio Mathematicæ Hodiernæ. Authore Thoma Hobbes. [With four engraved diagrams.] pp. 187. *Excusum sumptibus Andreæ Crooke.* (31 Aug.) **E. 188.**

[**Aug.**]—A Narrative of the Proceedings of the Commissioners appointed by O. Cromwell for Ejecting Scandalous and Ignorant Ministers, in the case of Walter Bushnell. pp. 256. [See also below: 12 Sept., E. 187. (5.)] *Printed for R. Clavell.* **E. 1837. (1.)**

[**Aug.**]—Analecta Sacra : sive Excursus Philologici super diversis S. Scripturæ locis. Pars posterior. Authore Joan. Doughteio. pp. 357. *Excudebat R. W., sumptibus, Joannis Baker.* **E. 1816. (1.)**

Aug.—Books lately printed, to acquaint those that are studious what are extant, divers of them being printed this moneth. [An advertisement.] *Printed for J. Rothwel. s. sh.* fol. **E. 1044. (6.)**

[**Aug.**]—A Caveat against Seducers, as it was preached by Richard Standfast. Whereunto are annexed The Blind Mans Meditations, by the same author. pp. 77. *Printed by H. Mortlock.* **E. 1816. (2.)**

[**Aug.**]—The Drinking of the Bitter Cup ; or, The hardest lesson in Christ's School, learned and taught by Himself, Passive Obedience. By John Brinsley. pp. 303. *Printed by E. C. for Joseph Cranford.* **E. 1838. (1.)**

[**Aug.**]—Λόγοι Ὡραῖοι. Three Seasonable Sermons, by Tho. Stephens. pp. 122. *Printed by J. C. for John Crooke.* **E. 1839. (2.)**

1660.

[**Aug.**]—New Experiments Physico-Mechanicall touching the Spring of the Air and its effects. By the Honorable Robert Boyle, Esq. [With an engraved plate.] pp. 399. *Printed by H. Hall for Tho. Robinson: Oxford.* **E. 1834.**

[**Aug.**]—Of the Daily Practice of Piety; also Devotions & Praiers in time of Captivity. pp. 192. *Printed by J. F. for R. Royston.* **E. 1880.**

[**Aug.**]—The Practical Part of Love. Extracted out of the extravagant and lascivious life of a fair but subtle female. pp. 84. **E. 1793. (2.)**

[**Aug.**]—The Silent Soul, with soveraign antidotes against the most Miserable Exigents. By Thomas Brooks. pp. 372. *Printed by R. I. for John Hancock.* **E. 1876. (1.)**

[**Aug.**]—A Vindication of the Lords Prayer. By Meric Casaubon. pp. 112. *Printed by T. R. for Thomas Johnson.* **E. 1921. (3.)**

Sept. 1.—By the King. A Proclamation for the Apprehension of Edmund Ludlow, Esquire, commonly called Colonel Ludlow. *s. sh. Printed by John Bill & Christopher Barker.* **669. f. 25. (77.)**

[**Sept. 1.**]—De Atramentis cujuscunque generis. Auctore Petro Maria Canepario. pp. 568. *Excudebat J. M. Impensis Jo. Martin, Ja. Alestry, Tho. Dicas.* (1 Sept.) **E. 1042.**

Sept. 2.—The Speech and Confession of Hugh Peters, with the manner how he was taken. *Printed for George Horton.* **E. 1043. (9.)**

Sept. 3.—The Speech of Major John Harris at the place of execution near St. Mary Axe. With his confession touching the most horrid murder of our late King Charles. *Printed for Nathaniel Bryan.* **E. 1043. (3.)**

[**Sept. 3.**]—The London Printers Lamentation; or, The Press opprest and overprest. (3 Sept.) **E. 765. (16.)**

[**Sept. 4.**]—The King's Supremacy asserted. Or, a Remonstrance of the King's Right against the pretended Parliament. By Robert Sheringham. pp. 128. *Printed formerly in Holland, and now reprinted by W. Godbid.* (4 Sept.) **E. 1043. (5.)**

Sept. 4.—[Orders by the Commissioners under the Act for the Speedy Provision of Money for Disbanding and Paying of the Forces, to the Aldermen and Common-Council-men of the different Wards, for the better execution of the Act. See above: 30 Aug., E. 1075. (13.)] *s. sh.* **669. f. 26. (3.)**

[**Sept. 4.**]—A Declaration or Remonstrance to his Majestie's loyal and faithful Subjects; touching Brokers, Usurers, Scrivenors and Solicitors. *Printed for George Horton.* (4 Sept.) **E. 1043. (4.)**

[**Sept. 4.**]—The Common Prayer-Book unmasked. Wherein is declared the unlawfulnesse and sinfulnesse of it. Published by divers Ministers of God's Word. pp. 68. [See also below: 11 Sept., E. 1044. (3.)] *Newly reprinted.* (4 Sept.) **E. 1043. (6.)**

1660.

[Sept. 5.]—Conscientious, Serious Theological and Legal Quæres propounded to the twice-dissipated, self-created, Anti-Parliamentary Westminster Juncto and its Members. By William Prynne. *Printed and are to be sold by Edward Thomas.* (5 Sept.) **E. 772. (3.)**

[Sept. 5.]—Reasons humbly offered, why the Bill brought in by the Adventurers in the Fenns should not passe before the adjournment of the Parliament. *s. sh.* (5 Sept.) **669. f. 26. (1.)**

[Sept. 5.]—Reasons shewing that there is no need of such a Reformation of the publique Doctrine, Worship, Church-government, as is pretended by Reasons offered to the serious consideration of this present Parliament, by divers Ministers in England. By H. S., D.D. [i.e. Henry Savage.] [See above : 3 Aug., E. 764. (4.)] *Printed for Humphrey Robinson.* (5 Sept.) **E. 1043. (7.)**

[Sept. 6.]—The Manner of the Solemnity of the Coronation of His Majesty King Charles. [With an engraved portrait of Charles II. and a set of verses addressed to him. The Coronation described is that of Charles I.] *s. sh. Printed by T. C. and are to be sold by W. Gilbertson.* (6 Sept.) **669. f. 26. (2.)**

[Sept. 6.]—A Presentation of wholesome Informations unto the King of England, &c. Being a defence pleaded in answer to a certain accusation, in a printed book called, The thrice happy Welcom of King Charles the Second, by one George Willington, against us whom in derision the accuser calls Quakers. By Edward Burroughs. [See above : 18 June, E. 1030. (1.)] *Printed at London ; and are to be sold by Richard Moon, Bookseller in Bristol.* (6 Sept.) **E. 1043. (8.)**

[Sept. 7.]—The Path-Way to Justification. By Thomas Kilcopp. [A sermon.] (7 Sept.) **E. 1043. (11.)**

[Sept. 7.]—A Rope for Pol ; or a hue and cry after Marchemont Nedham, the late scurrulous news-writer. Being a collection of his blasphemies and revilings against the King's Majesty, published in his weekly Politicus. (7 Sept.) **E. 1043. (10.)**

[Sept. 8.]—[Proposals " on the behalf of the Purchasers of Bishops, and Deans and Chapters Lands."] *s. sh.* (8 Sept.) **669. f. 26. (4.)**

[Sept. 10.]—Acts of Parliament now in force, establishing the Religion of the Church of England. *Printed for Robert Pawley.* (10 Sept.) **E. 1044. (2.)**

[Sept. 10.]—A Breife Description or Character of the Religion and Manners of the Phanatiques in generall, scil. Anabaptists, Independents, Brownists, Enthusiasts, Levellers, Quakers, Seekers, Fift-Monarchy-Men, & Dippers. pp. 52. (10 Sept.) **E. 1765. (1.)**

Sept. 10.—Jus Poli et Fori, or, God and the King. Judging for Right against Might, as it was delivered in a sermon before His Majesties

1660.

Judges of Assize in the Cathedrall Church of Lincolne. By Edward
Boteler. pp. 70. *Printed for G. Bedell & T. Collins.*   **E. 1813. (1.)**

[**Sept. 11.**]—Scarbrough Spaw, or, description of the nature and vertues
of the Spaw. By Robert Wittie. pp. 254. *Printed for, and are to be
sold by Charles Tyus, on London Bridge, and by Richard Lambert, in
York.* (11 Sept.)   **E. 1830. (2.)**

[**Sept. 11.**]—Several Treatises of Worship & Ceremonies. By William
Bradshaw. pp. 122. *Printed for Cambridge and Oxford, and are to be
sold in Westminster Hall and in Paul's Churchyard.* (11 Sept.)

E. 1044. (5.)

[**Sept. 11.**]—Some Necessity of Reformation of the Publick Doctrine of
the Church of England. Or, a reply to Dr. Pearson's No Necessity of
Reformation of the Publick Doctrine of the Church of England. By
William Hamilton. [See above: 20 Aug., E. 1040. (7.)] *Printed by
John Sherley.* (11 Sept.)   **E. 1044. (4.)**

[**Sept. 11.**]—Thou shalt fear God, and reverence my Sanctuary. A sharp
rebuke, or a rod for the enemies of Common Prayer that wrote the
book of unmasking it with lies. By Thomas Hicks. [See above: 4
Sept., E. 1043. (6.)] *Printed by R. L.* (11 Sept.)   **E. 1044. (3.)**

[**Sept. 12.**]—An Answer of Humphrey Chambers to the charge of Walter
Bushnel published in a book entituled, A Narrative of the Proceedings
of the Commissioners appointed by O. Cromwel for ejecting scandalous
and ignorant Ministers. [See above: Aug., E. 1837. (1.)] *Printed for
Thomas Johnson.* (12 Sept.)   **E. 187. (5.)**

[**Sept. 12.**]—Exercitationes duæ: altera theologica de Presbyteris &
Episcopis, altera Academica de philosophia veterum, ejusque usu. Per
Edvardum Bagshaw. *Excudit A. M. pro Simone Millero.* (12 Sept.)

E. 1044. (7.)

Sept. 13.—His Majesties most gracious Speech, together with the Lord
Chancellor's, to the two Houses of Parliament. *Printed by John Bill
and Christopher Barker.*   **E. 1075. (16.)**

Sept. 13.—The Speech which the Speaker of the House of Commons [Sir
Harbottle Grimston] made unto the King in the House of Lords, at his
passing of the Bills therein mentioned, on the day of their adjournment,
13 Sept. *Printed by Edward Husbands and Tho. Newcomb.* **E. 1044. (8.)**

Sept. 13.—An Act for the confirming and restoring of Ministers.
Printed by John Bill and Christop   rker. (17 Sept.) **E. 1075. (17.)**

Sept. 13.—A Cordial Elegy & Epitaph upon the death of Henry Duke
of Glocester, 13 Sept. [With a woodcut representing the Duke's
catafalque.] *Printed for George Horton.*   **E. 1045. (7.)**

Sept. 13.—An Elegie on the Death of the most illustrious Prince, Henry
Duke of Glocester. By Martin Lluelyn. *Printed by Hen. Hall for Ric.
Davis: Oxford.*   **E. 1080. (13.)**

1660.

[Sept. 13.]—An Eligie up the Death of the noble and vertuous Prince, Henry Duke of Gloucester. *s. sh. Printed for Thomas Parkhurst.*
669. f. 26. (8.)

Sept. 13.—Some Teares dropt ore the Herse of the incomparable Prince Henry, Duke of Gloucester. [Verses.] *s. sh. Printed by W. Godbid for Henry Brome and Henry Marsh.* 669. f. 26. (7.)

Sept. 13.—Threnodia : on the death of the Duke of Glocester. By Arthur Brett. *Printed by H. Hall : Oxford.* E. 1047. (1.)

Sept. 13.—Epicedia Academiæ Oxoniensis in obitum Henrici Ducis Glocestrensis. pp. 70. *Typis Lichfieldianis : Oxoniæ.* E. 1048. (4.)

Sept. 13.—[An Elegy, in Hebrew, on the death of Henry, Duke of Gloucester. By Thomas Smith, of Queens College, Cambridge.] *s. sh.*
669. f. 26. (26.)

Sept. 13.—Threni Cantabrigienses in funere duorum Principum, Henrici Glocestrensis [13 Sept.] & Mariæ Arausionensis [24 Dec.]. *Excudebat Joannes Field : Cantabrigiæ.* E. 1082. (6.)

[Sept. 13.]—No Sacrilege nor Sin to alienate or purchase Cathedral Lands as such. By Cornelius Burges. The third edition, revised and abbreviated for the service of Parliament. With a Postscript to Dr Pearson [and his No Necessity of Reformation of the Publick Doctrine of the Church]. pp. 71. [See above : 20 Aug., E. 1040. (7.), and also below : 15 Sept., E. 1044. (10.), and 20 Sept., E. 1045. (4.)] *Printed by James Cottrel.* (13 Sept.) E. 764. (5.)

[Sept. 14.]—A Remonstrance to the Presbyterians concerning the Government established in the Church of England ; and a vindication of Episcopacy. *Printed for G. Horton.* (14 Sept.) E. 1044. (9.)

Sept. 15.—By the King. A Proclamation for the preventing of the Exportation of Wools, Wool-Fells, Woollen-Yarn, Fullers-Earth, and other Scouring-Earths, out of this Kingdom. *Printed by John Bill and Christopher Barker.* 669. f. 26. (5.)

[Sept. 15.]—An Act for the speedy disbanding of the Army and Garrisons of this Kingdome. *Printed by John Bill and Christopher Barker.* (15 Sept.) E. 1075. (15.)

[Sept. 15.]—Antisacrilegus : or a defensative against the plausible Pest, or guilded Poyson, of that nameless paper, supposed to be the plot of Dr. C. Burges and his partners, which tempts the King's Majestie by the offer of Five hundred thousand pounds, to make good, by an Act of Parliament, to the purchasers of Bishop's, Dean's and Chapter's lands. By John Gauden. [See above : 13 Sept., E. 764. (5.)] *Printed by J. B. for Andrew Crook.* (15 Sept.) E. 1044. (10.)

[Sept. 15.]—Fratres in Malo ; or the Matchles Couple, represented in the writings of Mr. Edward Bagshaw and Mr. Henry Hickman. By way of answer to a scandalous letter, bearing the name of Mr. Bagshaw ;

II. z

1660.

and to a slanderous libel, fictitiously subscribed Theophilus Churchman, but proved to be written by Henry Hickman. All in vindication of Dr. Heylin and Mr. Pierce. By one of the meanest of their Admirers, M. O., Bachelour of Arts. [See above : 31 Aug., 1659, E. 1873. (1.)] *Printed by R. Wilks, and are to be sold by the Booksellers of London and Oxford.* (15 Sept.) **E. 1044. (12.)**

[**Sept. 15.**]—The Great Question concerning things indifferent in Religious Worship, briefly stated. [By Edward Bagshaw, the Younger.] (15 Sept.) **E. 1044. (11.)**

[**Sept. 16.**]—A Perfect Description of Antichrist and his false Prophet. Wherein is plainly shewed that Oliver Cromwell was Antichrist, and John Presbiter or John Covenanter his false Prophet. Written in 1654. By Abraham Nelson. *Printed by T. F.* (16 Sept.)
E. 1044. (13.)

Sept. 16.—Spiritual Wisdom improved against Temptation. In a sermon preached at Stepney. By Matthew Meade. *Printed for Thomas Parkhurst.* **E. 1045. (12.)**

Sept. 17.—[Further Orders by the Commissioners under the Act for the speedy provision of Money for Disbanding and Paying of the Forces, to the Aldermen and Common-Council-men of the different Wards. See above : 4 Sept., 669. f. 26. (3.)] **669. f. 26. (6.)**

[**Sept. 17.**]—The most vile and lamentable Confession of Hugh Peters of all his Bloody Advices given to the late Oliver Cromwel. *Printed for John Andrews.* (17 Sept.) **E. 1842. (3.)**

Sept. 17.—Relation de l'entrée magnifique de Monsieur le Prince de Ligne dans la ville de Londres, en qualité d'Ambassadeur extraordinaire de sa Majesté Catholique. *A Londres, par Jean Redmayne, et les vend au même lieu, en la maison Lovellian.* **E. 1045. (8.)**

[**Sept. 18.**]—An Act for raising sevenscore thousand pounds, for the compleat Disbanding of the whole Army, and paying off some part of the Navy. *Printed by John Bill and Christopher Barker.* (18 Sept.)
E. 1075. (20.)

[**Sept. 18.**]—An Act for supplying and explaining certain defaults in an Act entituled, An Act for the speedy provision of Money for Disbanding and paying off the Forces of this Kingdom, both by land and sea. [See above : 30 Aug., E. 1075. (13.)] *Printed by John Bill and Christopher Barker.* (18 Sept.) **E. 1075. (19.)**

[**Sept. 18.**]—An Act for the encouraging and increasing of Shipping and Navigation.—An Act to prevent frauds and Concealments of His Majestie's Customs and Subsidies. *Printed by John Bill and Christopher Barker.* (18 Sept.) **E. 1075. (18.)**

[**Sept. 19.**]—The Kingdom's Remembrancer : or the Protestation, Vow and Covenant, Solemne League and Covenant, animadverted, so far as

1660.

it concerns Religion. By W. Wickins. *Printed for John Rothwell.* (19 Sept.) **E. 1045. (2.)**

[**Sept. 19.**]—The Warrant for bowing at the name Jesus, truly produced and briefly examined. By William Wickins. (19 Sept.) **E. 1045. (1.)**

[**Sept. 20.**]—An Act for the regulating of the trade of Bay-making in the Dutch Bay-Hall in Colchester. *Printed by John Bill and Christopher Barker.* (20 Sept.) **E. 1075. (21.)**

[**Sept. 20.**]—An Answer to Dr. Burges his Word by way of Postscript, in vindication of No Necessity of Reformation of the Publick Doctrine of the Church of England. By John Pearson. [See above : 13 Sept., E. 764. (5.)] *Printed by J. G. for Nathaniel Brook.* (20 Sept.)
E. 1045. (4.)

[**Sept. 20.**]—An Answer to the Solemne League and Covenant; presented to the publick view of all loyall Subjects. *Printed for George Horton.* (20 Sept.) **E. 1045. (3.)**

[**Sept. 20.**]—The Lying-Wonders, or rather the Wonderful Lyes, lately published in a lying pamphlet called, Strange and True News from Gloucester. With some observations on another such like pamphlet, The Lord's loud Call to England. By Robert Clark. [See above : 2 Aug., E. 1035. (12.) and 14 Aug., E. 1038. (8.)] (20 Sept.)
E. 1045. (5.)

[**Sept. 20.**]—A Perfect Narrative of the Phanatick Wonders seen in the West of England. Sent in a letter [from Fairford, signed : G. Brown]. *Printed for Charles Gustavus.* (20 Sept.) **E. 1045. (6.)**

[**Sept. 22.**]—By the King. A Proclamation for apprehension of Edward Whalley and William Goffe. *Printed by Christopher Barker and John Bill.* **669. f. 26. (9.)**

[**Sept. 24.**]—The Scotch Covenant condemned, and the King's Majesty vindicated, in some animadversions on a paper intituled, The Form and Order of the Coronation of Charles the II. at Scoon, 1651, by R. Dowglas. Written by a Loyall Orthodox Hand. [See above : 1 Jan., 1651, E. 793. (2.)] *Printed for the Author.* (24 Sept.) **E. 1045. (11.)**

[**Sept. 24.**]—Certain Scruples and Doubts of Conscience about taking the Solemne League and Covenant; first printed in 1643. Now reprinted and in all love tendered to the consideration of Sir Lawrence Bromfield and Mr. Zach. Grofton [Crofton] with all others who are conscientious as well as zealous. (24 Sept.) **E. 1045. (10.)**

[**Sept. 24.**]—A Charge of High-Treason, prepared by the London Apprentices against Col. Hewson; and the strange apparitions that appeared unto him, immediately after his being taken near Plymouth. [With a woodcut representing the vision.] *Printed for C. Gustavus.* (24 Sept.) **E. 1045. (9.)**

[**Sept. 24.**]—A Poem to His most Excellent Majesty Charles the Second.

1660.

By H. Beeston. Together with another by Hen. Bold. *Printed by Edward Husbands and Thomas Newcomb.* (24 Sept.) **E. 1080. (12.)**

[**Sept. 24.**]—A Short Catechisme for all the Kings Loyal Subjects. *Printed for William Gilbertson.* (24 Sept.) **E. 1874. (1.)**

Sept. 25.—[A Proclamation by the King, forbidding the publication of " Almanacks and Prognostications " without licence.] *s. sh.*
669. f. 26. (16.)

Sept. 25.—Ourania : the high and mighty Lady the Princess Royal of Aurange congratulated on her most happy arrival. [Verses.] *s. sh. Printed by W. Godbid.* **669. f. 26. (12.)**

Sept. 26.—By the King. A Proclamation for Payment of the Duty of Excise, together with the Arrears thereof. *s. sh. Printed by John Bill and Christopher Barker.* **669. f. 26. (11.)**

Sept. 26.—By the King. A Proclamation for speeding the payment of the Arrears of Seventy thousand pounds for three moneths Assessments, due and payable the first of August last past. *s. sh. Printed by John Bill and Christopher Barker.* **669. f. 26. (10.)**

[**Sept. 27.**]—Defensio Fidei ; seu, Responsio succincta ad Argumenta quibus impugnari solet Confessio Anglicana. Opera Johannis Elis. pp. 157. *Typis Roberti White & sumptibus Johannis Symmes.* (27 Sept.)
E. 2108. (2.)

Sept. 29.—By the King. A Proclamation for the due Payment of the Subsidy and Aulnage upon all Woollen Clothes and Draperies. *s. sh. Printed by John Bill and Christopher Barker.* **669. f. 26. (14.)**

Sept. 29.—By the King. A Proclamation for the suppressing of disorderly and unseasonable Meetings in Taverns and Tipling Houses, and also forbidding Footmen to wear Swords or other weapons, within London, Westminster and their Liberties. *Printed by John Bill and Christopher Barker.* **669. f. 26. (13.)**

[**Sept. 29.**]—Presbyterial Ordination vindicated. The arguments of Dr. Davenant modestly examined, with a discourse concerning imposed Forms of Prayer and Ceremonies. By G. F. [i.e. Giles Firmin?] *Printed for Nathanael Webb.* (29 Sept.) **E. 1045. (17.)**

[**Sept. 29.**]—The Royall Exchange. A Comedy acted at the Black-Friers by his Majestie's Servants. Written by Mr. Richard Brome. *Printed for Henry Brome.* (29 Sept.) **E. 1045. (18.)**

Sept. 30.—Church Reformation ; a discourse pointing at some Vanities in Divine Service. Delivered in two sermons at Bridgnorth. By Mich. Thomas. *Printed for Jo. Martin, Ja. Allestry and Tho. Dicas.*
E. 1055. (17.)

[**Sept.**]—A Collection of several Letters and Declarations sent by General Monck unto King Charles II., the Lord Lambert, the Lord

1660.

Fleetwood, and the rest of the General Council of Officers of the Army ; as also unto that part of the Parliament called the Rump, the Committee of Safety, the Lord Mayor and Common Council, the Congregated Churches in and about London. **E. 1045. (16.)**

[Sept.]—The Rights of the Crown of England, as it is established by Law. Written in the time of the late King, by Edward Bagshaw. pp. 126. *Printed by A. M. for Simon Miller.* **E. 1749. (1.)**

[Sept.]—Arithmetick: vulgar, decimal, instrumental, algebraical. By William Leybourn. [With an engraved portrait of the author.] pp. 392. *Printed by R. and W. Leybourn, and are to be sold by George Sawbridge.* **E. 1755. (1.)**

[Sept.]—Britannia Baconica ; or, The Natural Rarities of England, Scotland & Wales historically related according to the precepts of the Lord Bacon. By J. Childrey. pp. 184. *Printed for the Author.* **E. 1837. (2.)**

[Sept.]—The Circles of Proportion and the Horizontall Instrument, &c. Both invented, and the uses of both written in Latine, by W. Oughtred. Translated into English by W. F. [i.e. William Forster], and now much amplifyed and explained, by A. H., Gent. [i.e. Arthur Haughton]. [With plates and diagrams.] pp. 254. *Printed by W. Hall for R. Davis: Oxford.* **E. 1793. (1.)**

[Sept.]—Exercitationes duæ, quarum prior de Passione Hysterica, altera de Affectione Hypochondriaca. Authore Nathanaele Highmoro. pp. 184. *Excudebat A. Lichfield, impensis R. Davis: Oxon.* **E. 1933. (1.)**

[Sept.]—A Help to Prayer and Meditation. By Zachary Bogan. pp. 337. *Printed by W. H. for Thomas Robinson.* **E. 1906.**

[Sept.]—The Last Visitation, Conflicts and Death of Mr. Thomas Peacock. Published by E. B. [i.e. Edward Bagshaw], from the copie of Mr. Robert Bolton. pp. 69. *Printed for William Miller.* **E. 2103. (1.)**

[Sept.]—New Atlantis. Begun by the Lord Verulam, Viscount St. Albans, and continued by R. H., Esquire. Wherein is set forth a Platform of Monarchical Government. pp. 101. *Printed for John Crooke.* **E. 1797. (2.)**

[Oct. 1.]—The Unbishoping of Timothy and Titus and of the Angel of the Church of Ephesus. By William Prynne. pp. 36, 123. *First printed 1636 ; reprinted 1660 ; to be sold by Edward Thomas.* (1 Oct.) **E. 190. (1.)**

[Oct. 2.]—The Best Way to make England the richest Kingdome in Europe, by advancing the Fishing-Trade, and imploying ships and mariners. By T. Gentleman, Fisherman and Mariner. (2 Oct.) **E. 1080. (13.)**

[Oct. 2.]—A Landskip: or a brief prospective of English Episcopacy.

1660.

Drawn by three skilfull hands [viz. by Viscount Falkland, N. Fiennes and Sir H. Vane, The Younger] in Parliament, anno 1641. (2 Oct.)

E. 1045. (13.)

[**Oct. 3.**]—The Welsh Hubub, or the Unkennelling and Earthing of Hugh Peters, that Crafty Fox. [A satire, in verse.] *s. sh. Printed by P. Lillicrap.* (3 Oct.) 669. f. 26. (17.)

[**Oct. 4.**]—An humble Addresse of the Provinciall Synod of Fife in Scotland, to his Majesty, after the receipt of his most gracious Letter to the several Presbyteries of the Church of Scotland.

E. 1047. (4.)

[**Oct. 4.**]—A true Narrative, in a letter [signed : C. H.] written to Col. B. R. a Member of Parliament, of the apprehension of the grand traytor Thomas Scot. *Printed by Matthew Inman and are to be sold by James Magnes.* (4 Oct.) E. 1046. (1.)

Oct. 7.—His Majesties gracious Commission to search into and examine the pretended sales and purchases of the Honours, Mannors, Lands and Hereditaments of and belonging to his Majestie, his royal mother, the archbishops, bishops, and other ecclesiastical persons. *Printed for Rich. Marriot and John Playford.* E. 1075. (24.)

[**Oct. 8.**]—The Black Remembrancer for the year 1661. Written by Thomas Riders. *s. sh. Printed by Tho. Johnson.* (8 Oct.)

669. f. 26. (18.)

[**Oct. 8.**]—Some Treasure fetched out of Rubbish : or, three treatises concerning the imposition and use of significant ceremonies in the worship of God. [By J. Cotton and R. Nichols.] pp. 75. (8 Oct.)

E. 1046. (2.)

Oct. 10.—A List of His late Majesties Unjust Judges, and others who are to be tried for their horrid treason, by a speciall Commission at the Session House in the Old Bayly, beginning the tenth day of October. *s. sh. Printed for John Stafford and Edward Thomas.*

669. f. 26. (20.)

Oct. 10.—The Manner of the Arraignment of those twenty-eight persons who were appointed to be tried at the Sessions House in the Old Bayly. *Printed for J. S. and Edward Thomas.* E. 1046. (5.)

Oct. 10.—The Tryal of the pretended Judges that signed the warrant for the murther of King Charles the I. E. 1046. (4.)

Oct. 10.—An exact and most impartial Accompt of the Trial of nine and twenty Regicides, the murtherers of his late Majesty, 10 to 19 Oct. pp. 287. *Printed for Andrew Crook, and Edward Powel.* E. 1047. (3.)

Oct. 10.—A Looking Glass for Traytors, being the manner of the Tryall of those barbarous wretches who compassed the death of King Charles the First. [With an engraving representing the interior of

1660.

the Old Bailey during the trial.] *s. sh.* *Printed for Thomas Vere and William Gilbertson.* **669. f. 26. (25.)**

Oct. 11.—An Exact Catalogue of all Printed Books and Papers written by William Prynne before, during and since his imprisonments. *Printed for Michael Sparke, 1643 ; reprinted for Edward Thomas by T. Childe and L. Parry.* (11 Oct.) **E. 190. (2.)**

Oct. 13.—[An Order from the King to the Archbishop of Canterbury, respecting the letting of Church Lands.] *s. sh.* **669. f. 26. (21.)**

Oct. 13.—[An Order from the King to the Archbishop of York, respecting the letting of Church Lands.] *s. sh.* **669. f. 26. (22.)**

Oct. 13.—The Tryall and Condemnation of John Cooke, and Hugh Peters, for their severall High-treasons, at the Sessions-house in the Old-baily, 13 Oct. *Printed for John Stafford and Edward Thomas.* **E. 1046. (6.)**

Oct. 13.—A true and perfect Relation of the Grand Traytors execution, as at severall times they were drawn, hang'd, and quartered at Charing Crosse and at Tiburne [13 to 19 Oct.]. Together with their severall confessions. [With woodcuts representing the beheading of Charles II, and the execution of the regicides.] *s. sh.* *Printed for William Gilbertson.* **669. f. 26. (31.)**

Oct. 13.—The Speeches and Prayers of Major General Harrison, 13 Oct., Mr. John Carew, 15 Oct., Mr. Justice Cooke, Mr. Hugh Peters, 16 Oct., Mr. Tho. Scott, Mr. Gregory Clement, Col. Adrian Scroop, Col. John Jones, 17 Oct., Col. Daniel Axtell & Col. Fran. Hacker, 19 Oct., and the times of their Death. pp. 96. **E. 1053. (1.)**

Oct. 14.—A Peace-Offering in the Temple ; or a seasonable plea for unity among dissenting brethren. In a sermon at St. Paul's. By Richard Henchman. *Printed by Thomas Roycroft for William Grantham.* **E. 1048. (3.)**

Oct. 15.—The Tryall and Condemnation of Col. Daniel Axtell, who guarded the High Court of Injustice, Col. Francis Hacker, who guarded His Sacred Majesty to the Scaffold, Cap. Hewlet, who was proved to be the man that butchered His Majesty : at the Sessions House in the Old Baily, 15 Oct. *Printed for H. Deacon.* **E. 1046. (8.)**

[Oct. 17.]—The Right of the Church asserted, against the power usurped over it. By J. Gailhard. *Printed for J. Rothwell.* (17 Oct.) **E. 1046. (7.)**

Oct. 18.—By the King. A Proclamation to restrain the abuses of Hackney Coaches in the Cities of London and Westminster and the Suburbs thereof. *Printed by John Bill and Christopher Barker.* **669. f. 26. (23.)**

[Oct. 20.]—The Tryall of Traytors, or the Rump in the Pound. [A woodcut representing a Pound, in which are various animals, clothed :

1660.

with descriptive verses, satirising the chief members of the Rump
Parliament.] *s. sh. Printed for John Clowes and John Jones.* (20 Oct.)

669. f. 26. (19.)

[**Oct. 22.**]—Monarchy Revived, in the most illustrious Charles the
Second, whose life and reign is exactly described in the ensuing dis-
course. By Francis Eglesfield. pp. 334. *Printed by R. Daniel for
Francis Eglesfield.* (22 Oct.) **E. 1934. (1.)**

[**Oct. 22.**]—A serious Consideration of the Oath of the Kings Supremacy.
By John Tombes. [See also below : 2 March, 1661, E. 1084. (1.) and
(2.)] *Printed by Henry Hills.* (22 Oct.) **E. 1046. (10.)**

[**Oct. 22.**]—A Sermon by Hugh Peters, preached before his death ; as
it was taken by a faithful hand. *Printed by John Best.* (22 Oct.)

E. 1046. (9.)

[**Oct. 23.**]—A true and briefe Narrative of all the several parts of the
Common Prayer Book, cleared from aspersion. *Printed by R. L. for the
Author.* (23 Oct.) **E. 1046. (11.)**

[**Oct. 23.**]—The Long Parliament revived. Or, an Act for the continuation and the not dissolving the Long Parliament, called by King Charles
the First in the year 1640, but by an Act of Parliament. With
undeniable reasons deduced from the said Act to prove that that
Parliament is not yet dissolved. Also Mr. Will. Prynne his Five
Arguments fully answered, whereby he endevours to prove it to be
dissolved by the King's death. By Tho. Phillips, Gent. [pseud., i.e. Sir
William Drake.] [See also below : 28 Nov., E. 1050. (8.) ; 3 Dec.,
E. 1053. (2.) ; and 7 Dec., E. 1053. (5.)] *Printed for the Author.*
(23 Oct.) **E. 1046. (12.)**

[**Oct. 23.**]—A Funeral Sermon thundred forth by John Feak in his
private congregation, for the loss of their dearly beloved champion,
Maj. Gen. Harison. [A satire.] *Printed for I. P.* (23 Oct.)

E. 1046. (13.)

[**Oct. 23.**]—A Sermon preached at the Funerall of the Lady Elizabeth
Capell, Dowager. By Edm. Barker. *Printed by I. R. for John Williams.*
(23 Oct.) **E. 1046. (14.)**

Oct. 25.—His Majestie's Declaration to all his loving subjects of England
and Wales, concerning Ecclesiastical Affairs. *Printed by John Bill and
Christopher Barker.* **E. 1075. (22.)**

Oct. 27.—The Speech of Francis Lovelace Esquire, Recorder of Canterbury, to the King's Majestie, at his coming to Canterbury. *Printed by
S. Griffin for Matthew Walbancke.* **E. 1048. (8.)**

Oct. 28.—The Lord's Property in His Redeemed People. Opened in a
sermon at St. Paul's Church, London. By Edward Reynolds. *Printed
by T. R. for George Thomason.* **E. 1048. (2.)**

Oct. 28.—A Sermon preached at the Consecration of Gilbert [Sheldon],

1660.

Bishop of London, Humphry [Henchman], Bishop of Sarum, George [Morley], Bishop of Worcester, Robert [Sanderson], Bishop of Lincolne, George [Griffith], Bishop of St. Asaph, at St. Peter's, Westminster. By John Sudbury. *Printed for R. Royston.* **E. 1048. (9.)**

Oct. 29.—The King of Terrors Metamorphosis. A Sermon preached at the Funeral of Mrs. Elizabeth Nicoll. [Preface dated: 29 Oct.] *Printed by M. S. for Hen. Cripps.* **E. 1053. (4.)**

[**Oct. 30.**]—An Apology for the ancient right and power of the Bishops to sit and vote in Parliaments. With an Answer to the reasons maintained by Dr. Burgesse and others against the votes of Bishops; a Determination at Cambridge of Dr. Davenant, Englished; the Speech in Parliament made by Dr. Williams, Archbishop of York, in defence of the Bishops; two Speeches in the House of Lords by Viscount Newarke, 1641. pp. 120. *Printed by W. Godbid for Richard Thrale.* (30 Oct.) **E. 1047. (2.)**

Oct. 30.—The Churches Patience and Faith in Afflictions, delivered in a sermon at the Funerall of Cecilia, Lady Peyton, in the Parish Church of Southfleet in Kent. By George Eves. *Printed for G. Bedell & T. Collins.* **E. 1057. (8.)**

[**Oct.**]—Virtus Rediviva. A Panegyrick on King Charles I., by Thomas Forde. With severall other pieces from the same pen. Concluding with a Panegyrick on His Sacred Majesties Return. pp. 254. *Printed by R. & W. Leybourn for William Grantham and Thomas Basset.* **E. 1806.**

[**Oct.**]—[A Petition to Parliament from "the Purchasers of Bishops and Deans and Chapters Lands." Praying for the confirmation of the sales, etc.] *s. sh.* **669. f. 26. (15.)**

[**Oct.**]—The Compleat History of the Warrs in Scotland under the conduct of James Marquesse of Montrose. [Translated from the Latin of George Wishart, Bishop of Edinburgh.] Now newly corrected and enlarged. [With an engraved portrait of Montrose as frontispiece.] pp. 231. **E. 1874. (2.)**

[**Oct.**]—A Brief Character of the Low-Countries under the States. [By Owen Felltham.] pp. 100. *Printed for H. S. and are to be sold by Rich. Lowndes.* **E. 2108. (3.)**

[**Oct.**]—Christian Reformation: being an earnest Perswasion to the speedy practise of it. By Richard Parr. pp. 306. *Printed by J. G. for Nathaniel Brook.* **E. 1749. (2.)**

[**Oct.**]—An Introduction of the Rudiments of Arithmetick. By W. Jackson. *Printed by R. J. for F. Smith.* **E. 2110. (3.)**

[**Oct.**]—The Life of S. Augustine. The first part. Written by himself in the first ten books of his Confessions, faithfully translated. pp. 208. *Printed by J. C. for John Crook.* **E. 1755. (2.)**

1660.

[**Oct.**]—Methodi Practicæ Specimen.   An Essay of a Practical Grammar ; or an Enquiry after a more easie and certain help to the making and speaking of Latine.   By Christopher Wase.   pp. 79.   *Printed by D. Maxwel and are to be sold by Charles Adams.*   E. 1750. (2.)

[**Oct.**]—The Mystery of Faith opened up.   Or, some Sermons concerning Faith.   By Andrew Gray.   pp. 178.   *Printed for Thomas Johnson.*
                                        E. 1871. (2.)

[**Oct.**]—The Nonsuch Professor in his Meridian Splendor, or the Singular Actions of Sanctified Christians.   Laid open in seaven sermons at Allhallows Church in the Wall.   By William Secker.   pp. 434.   *Printed by M. S. for Thomas Parkhurst.*   E. 1750. (1.)

[**Oct.**]—A Treatise of Divine Meditation.   By John Ball.   pp. 284. *Printed for H. Mortlock.*   E. 1875. (1.)

[**Nov. 1.**]—A breife Relation of some of the most remarkable pasages of the Anabaptists in High and low Germany in the year 1521 &c. Gathered out of the writings of Sleyden and others.   By George Pressick.   (1 Nov.)   E. 1047. (5.)

[**Nov. 1.**]—Complaints concerning Corruptions and Grievances in Church-Government.   By certain peaceably affected Presbyters of the Church of England.   (1 Nov.)   E. 1047. (6.)

Nov. 2.—[An Address to Charles II. on matters of Religion, signed Martin Mason, and dated from Lincoln.]   *s. sh.   Printed for Robert Wilson.*   669. f. 26. (33.)

Nov. 2.—[An Address to both Houses of Parliament, on matters of Religion, signed Martin Mason, and dated from Lincoln.]   *s. sh.   Printed for Robert Wilson.*   669. f. 26. (34.)

[**Nov. 3.**]—The Solemn League and Covenant discharg'd : or, St. Peters Bonds not only loosed but annihilated.   [By John Russell.]   Attested by John Gauden.   [See also below : 23 Nov., E. 1050. (2.)]   *Printed for Henry Brome.*   (3 Nov.)   E. 1048. (1.)

Nov. 9.—The Speech which the Speaker of the House of Commons made unto the King in the Banqueting-House at Whitehall.   *Printed by John Bill.*   E. 1075. (23.)

[**Nov. 14.**]—The Royal Standard of King Charles the II., presented to the publick view of all true subjects, Presbyterians, Independants and others.   Written [in French] by the Lady Charlette, Countess of Bregy. And now translated into English.   *Printed for G. Horton.*   (14 Nov.)
                                        E. 1048. (5.)

Nov. 15.—[A Resolution and Declaration by the House of Commons, " that the Priviledge of Protection from Arrest doth belong to the Members of this House and their menial Servants onely."]   *s. sh. Printed by John Bill.*   669. f. 26. (29.)

1660.

Nov. 15.—A Cedars Sad and Solemn Fall. Delivered in a sermon at the Parish Church of Waltham Abbey by Thomas Reeve, at the Funeral of James late Earl of Carlisle. *Printed for William Grantham.*
E. 1056. (2.)

[**Nov. 15.**]—Don Juan Lamberto : or, a comical history of the late times. The first part. By Montelion, Knight of the Oracle, &c. [Ascribed to John Phillips, and to Thomas Flatman.] *Sold by Henry Marsh.* (15 Nov.)
E. 1048. (6.)

Nov. 16.—To the Kings Majesty. The humble and grateful acknowledgement of many Ministers of the Gospel, in and about London, for his gracious concessions in his late Declaration concerning Ecclesiastical Affairs. *s. sh. Printed for Joh. Rothwel.*
669. f. 26. (28.)

[**Nov. 17.**]—The Loyal Remembrancer : or, a poem dedicated to the Queen's Majesty. [By S. C.] *Printed by R. Wood, 1650 : but not permitted to be publick till now.*
E. 1048. (7.)

Nov. 19.—The Prologue to His Majesty, at the first play presented at the Cock-pit in Whitehall, being part of that noble entertainment which their Majesties received from his Grace the Duke of Albemarle. [In verse.] *s. sh. Printed for G. Bedell and T. Collins.*
669. f. 26. (30.)

[**Nov. 21.**]—Irenicum. A weapon-salve for the Churche's wounds : or, the divine right of particular forms of Church Government, discussed and examined. By Edward Stillingfleete. pp. 416. *Printed by R. W. for Henry Mortlock.* (21 Nov.)
E. 1049.

[**Nov. 23.**]—The Muse's Joy for the Recovery of that weeping Vine, Henretta Maria, the Queen-Mother, and her royal branches. [A poem. By John Crouch.] *Printed for Tho. Batterton.* (23 Nov.)
E. 1050. (3.)

[**Nov. 23.**]—’Ανάληψις ἀνελήφθη. The Fastning of St. Peter's Fetters by Seven Links, or Propositions. Or, the efficacy and extent of the Solemn League and Covenant asserted and vindicated, against the doubts and scruples of Dr. John Gauden's Anonymous Questionist ; St. Peter's bonds not only loosed, but annihilated by Mr. John Russel ; The League Illegal, falsely fathered on Dr. Daniel Featley ; and the reasons of the University of Oxford for not taking the Solemn League and Covenant. By Zech. Crofton. pp. 259. [See above : 23 June, E. 1030. (4.), 20 Aug., E. 1040. (8.) and 3 Nov., E. 1048. (1.)] *Printed for Ralph Smith.* (23 Nov.)
E. 1050. (2.)

Nov. 25.—Cordifragium, or, The Sacrifice of a Broken Heart, open'd, offer'd, own'd and honour'd. Presented in a sermon at St. Pauls. By Francis Walsall. *Printed by Abraham Miller for John Sherley.*
E. 1081. (4.)

[**Nov. 26.**]—Considerations touching the Liturgy of the Church of

1660.

England.   In reference to his Majestie's late gracious Declaration, and in order to an happy union in Church and State.   By John Gauden. [See also below : 5 Jan., 1661, E. 1055. (7.) and 15 Feb., 1661, E. 1082. (7.)]   *Printed by J. G. for John Playford.*   (26 Nov.)   **E. 1050. (6.)**

[**Nov. 26.**]—Observations upon the last actions and words of Maj. Gen. Harrison.   *Printed by H. Lloyd and R. Vaughan.*   (26 Nov.)
E. 1050. (5.)

[**Nov. 26.**]—Hugh Peters last Will and Testament.   [A satirical ballad.] *s. sh.*   (26 Nov.)   **669. f. 26. (32.)**

[**Nov. 27.**]—Several Arguments against Bowing at the Name of Jesus. By a Learned Author.   (27 Nov.)   **E. 1050. (7.)**

[**Nov. 28.**]—The Long Parliament is not revived by Tho. Philips.   Or, an answer to Tho. Philips his Long Parliament Revived.   By R. C. [See above : 23 Oct., E. 1046. (12.)]   *Printed for N. W.*   (28 Nov.)
E. 1050. (8.)

[**Nov. 29.**]—A Grant of certain Impositions upon Beer, Ale, and other Liquors, for the encrease of his Majestie's Revenue during his life. *Printed by John Bill.*   (29 Nov.)   **E. 1075. (26.)**

[**Nov. 29.**]—A Fannatick's Mite cast into the King's Treasury : being a sermon printed to the King, because not preach'd before the King. By Henry Adis.   *Printed for the Author an Upholdster.*   (29 Nov.)
E. 1050. (9.)

[**Nov. 29.**]—A Seasonable Vindication of the Supream Authority and Jurisdiction of Christian Kings, Lords, Parliaments.   Transcribed out of the Works of John Hus and John Fox his Acts and Monuments, by William Prynne.   *Printed by T. Childe and L. Parry for Edward Thomas.*   (29 Nov.)   **E. 190. (3.)**

Nov. 30.—His Majestie's gracious Declaration for the settlement of his Kingdome of Ireland, and satisfaction of the severall interests of Adventurers, Souldiers, and other his Subjects there.   *Printed by J. Bill.*   **E. 1075. (25.)**

[**Nov. 30.**]—Romanism Discussed, or, An Answer to the nine first Articles of H. T. [i.e. Henry Turberville] his Manual of Controversies. By John Tombes.   pp. 227.   *Printed by H. Hills and are to be sold by Jane Underhill & Henry Mourtlock.*   (30 Nov.)   **E. 1051.**

[**Nov.**]—The Arraignment of Pride.   By W. Gearing.   pp. 270.   *Printed by R. White for Francis Tyton.*   **E. 1762. (1.)**

[**Nov.**]—Christ a Christians Onely Gain.   Sermons, by Richard Vines. pp. 235.   *Printed for Thomas Johnson.*   **E. 2103. (2.)**

[**Nov.**]—A Cluster of Grapes taken out of the Basket of the Woman of Canaan.   Or, Counsel and Comfort for Beleeving Soules.   Being the summe of certain sermons.   By John Durant.   pp. 206.   *Printed for L. C. and are to bee sold by H. Mortlock.*   **E. 1746. (1.)**

1660.

[**Nov.**]—A Collection of Letters, made by Sr Tobie Mathews K^t. With a character of the Lady Lucy, Countesse of Carleile, by the same author. To which are added many letters of his own. [Edited by John Donne. With an engraved portrait of the author.] pp. 356. *Printed for Henry Herringman.* **E. 1798.**

[**Nov.**]—The Common Law Epitomiz'd. By William Glisson and Anthony Gulston. pp. 401. *Printed for Henry Brome.* **E. 1807.**

[**Nov.**]—The Epitome of Man's Duty. A discourse upon Micah VI. 8. [By Simon Patrick.] pp. 131. *Printed by R. W. for Francis Tyton.* **E. 1751. (2.)**

[**Nov.**]—An Historical and Geographical Description of the Country & River of the Amazones in America. Written in French by the Count of Pagan, and translated by William Hamilton. [With an engraved map.] pp. 153. *Printed for John Starkey.* **E. 1805. (2.)**

[**Nov.**]—The Horn Exalted ; or, Roome for Cuckolds. A treatise concerning the word Cuckold, and why such are said to wear Horns. pp. 84. *Printed for John Cadwel at the Royal Exchange.* **E. 1808. (3.)**

[**Nov.**]—Jewish Hypocrisie, a Caveat to the present Generation. By Symon Patrick. pp. 413. *Printed by R. W. for Francis Tyton.* **E. 1751. (1.)**

[**Nov.**]—Medicus Microcosmus. Autore Daniele Beckhero. Editio nova auctior. pp. 304. *Prostant apud J. Martin, J. Allestry & T. Dicas.* **E. 1896.**

[**Nov.**]—A Spiritual Treasure, containing our Obligations to God and the Vertues necessary to a Perfect Christian. By D. J. Q. pp. 530. *Printed by T. R. for Thomas Dring.* **E. 1740.**

[**Nov.**]—Viro honoratissimo Edvardo Hide, & Carmen Gratulatorium. [By Robert Whitehall. Latin and English verse.] *s. sh.* **669. f. 26. (27.)**

[**Nov.**]—The Visions and Prophecies, concerning England, Scotland and Ireland, of Ezekiel Grebner. pp. 82. *Printed for Henry Herringman.* **E. 1936. (3.)**

[**Dec. 1.**]—The Compleat History of Independency. By Clem. Walker. 4 pt. *Printed for Ric. Royston and Ric. Lownds.* (1 Dec.) **E. 1052.**

Dec. 2.—A Sermon preached in S. Peter's Westminster, at the Consecration of John [Cosin], Lord Bishop of Durham, William [Lucy], Lord Bishop of S. David's and others. By W. S., B. D. [i.e. William Sancroft.] *Printed by T. Roycroft for Robert Beaumont.* **E. 1055. (4.)**

[**Dec. 3.**]—King Charles I. his Imitation of Christ. Or the parallel lines of our Saviour's and our King's Sufferings. Drawn through fourty six texts of Scripture. In an English and French poem. By J. W. *Printed by T. L.* (3 Dec.) **E. 1080. (14.)**

1660.

[**Dec. 3.**]—The Long Parliament twice Defunct: or, an Answer to a seditious Pamphlet [by Sir William Drake] intituled The Long Parliament Revived. [See above: 23 Oct., E. 1046. (12.)] *Printed for Henry Brome.* (3 Dec.) **E. 1053. (2.)**

[**Dec. 5.**]—The Dragons Forces totally routed by the Royal Shepherd. [The same woodcut as that published with " The Tryall of Traytors, or the Rump in the Pound," 20 Oct., 669. f. 26. (19.), altered by giving the figures their animal instead of their human names. With satirical verses.] *s. sh.* (5 Dec.) **669. f. 26. (35.)**

[**Dec. 6.**]—Andromana ; or, The Merchant's Wife. [A tragedy, in verse.] By J. S. [i.e. James Shirley.] *Printed for John Bellinger.* (6 Dec.)
E. 184. (6.)

[**Dec. 6.**]—The Worthy Communicant. Or, a discourse of the nature, effects and blessings consequent to the worthy receiving of the Lord's Supper. By Jeremy Taylor, Bishop Elect of Down and Connor. pp. 576. *Printed by R. Norton for John Martin, James Allestry and Thomas Dicas.* (6 Dec.) **E. 1758.**

[**Dec. 7.**]—Another Word to Purpose against The Long Parliament Revived [by Sir William Drake]. By C. C. of Grays Inn. [See above: 23 Oct., E. 1046. (12.)] *Printed for Thomas Dring.* (7 Dec.)
E. 1053. (5.)

[**Dec. 10.**]—The Loyall Mourner, shewing the Murdering of King Charles the First, fore-shewing the Restoring of King Charles the Second ; in an Elegy written in 1648, now printed. By Anthonie Sadler. *Printed by T. C. for L. Sadler.* (10 Dec.) **E. 1053. (6.)**

[**Dec. 10.**]—Panem Quotidianum: or, A short Discourse tending to prove the legality and expediency of Set Forms of Prayer in the Churches of Christ. By William Annand. *Printed for Edward Brewster.* (10 Dec.) **E. 1053. (7.)**

[**Dec. 12.**]—Christmas Revived : or an Answer to certain Objections made against the Observation of a Day in memory of our Saviour Christ his Birth. By John Reading. *Printed for John Andrews and John Garway.* (12 Dec.) **E. 1053. (9.)**

[**Dec. 13.**]—The Ladies Champion, confounding the Author of the Wandring Whore. By Eugenius Theodidactus. (13 Dec.)
E. 1053. (10.)

[**Dec. 14.**]—The true Characters of the Educations, Inclinations, and several Dispositions of all those bloody and barbarous persons who sate as Judges upon the life of our late King Charls I. [With an engraved frontispiece, representing the beheading of Charles I., and the execution of the regicides.] *Printed for Edward Thomas.* (14 Dec.)
E. 1080. (15.)

[**Dec. 14.**]—The Strange and Wonderfull Prophesie of David Cardinal

1660.

of France, touching King Charles II. *Printed by J. C. for S. R.* (14 Dec.)   **E 1053. (11.)**

[**Dec. 15.**]—The Old Anabaptists grand Plot discovered : with their Covenant, League and Articles. *Printed for George Horton.* (15 Dec.)   **E. 1053. (12.)**

[**Dec. 16.**]—The Hinge of Faith and Religion ; or, A Proof of the Deity against Atheists. By L. Cappel. Translated out of French by Philip Marinel. pp. 184. *Printed for Thomas Dring.* (16 Dec.)   **E. 1845. (2.)**

Dec. 17.—By the King. A Proclamation commanding all Cashiered Officers and Soldiers, and other persons who cannot give a good account for their being here, to depart out of the Cities of London and Westminster. *s. sh. Printed by John Bill.*   **669. f. 26. (37.)**

Dec. 17.—[An Order of the House of Commons, for the care of Maimed Soldiers.] *s. sh. Printed by John Bill.*   **669. f. 26. (36.)**

[**Dec. 17.**]—The Covenanters Plea against Absolvers, or, A Discourse shewing why those who took the Solemn League and Covenant cannot judge their Consciences discharged from the Obligation of it, by anything said by Dr. Featly, Dr. Gauden or any other. By Theophilus Timorcus. pp. 87. *Printed by T. B.* (17 Dec.)   **E. 1053. (13.)**

[**Dec. 20.**]—Featlæi Παλιγγενεσία, or, Doctor Daniel Featley revived. Proving that the Protestant Church is the onely Catholick and true Church. With a succinct account of his life and death. Published by John Featley. pp. 86. *Printed for Nath. Brook.* (20 Dec.) **E. 1937. (2.)**

[**Dec. 20.**]—Fair Play in the Lottery ; or, Mirth for Money. In several witty passages and conceits of Persons that came to the Lottery. By E. F., Gent. [i.e. Edward Ford.] *Printed by H. Brugis.* (20 Dec.)   **E. 1865. (2.)**

[**Dec. 24.**]—By the King. A Proclamation for continuing the Officers of Excise, during His Majesties pleasure. *Printed by John Bill.*   **669. f. 26. (41.)**

Dec. 24.—Elegy on the death of Her Highness Mary, Princess Dowager of Aurange. [By Henry Bold.] *Printed for Edward Husbands.*   **669. f. 26. (55.)**

Dec. 24.—In Mortem Serenissimæ principis Mariæ ad Regem Elegia. [By J. van Vliet.] *s. sh.*   **669. f. 26. (42.)**

Dec. 24.—Epicedia Academiæ Oxoniensis in Obitum Serenissimæ Mariæ, Principis Arausionensis. *Excudebat A. & L. Lichfield : Oxoniæ.*   **E. 1082. (4.)**

Dec. 24.—Threni Cantabrigienses in furere Mariæ Aransionensis. *Excudebat Joannes Field : Cantabrigiæ.*   **E. 1082. (6.)**

[**Dec. 27.**]—Κέρδιστον Δῶρον. King Charles the Second presented to

1660.

the Houses of Parliament as the Strength, Honour and Peace of the Nations. Eight sermons. By Richard Burney. pp. 133. *Printed by I. Redmayne for the Authour.* (27 Dec.) **E. 1054. (2.)**

Dec. 29.—His Majestie's Gracious Speech, together with the Lord Chancellor's, to both Houses of Parliament, the day of their dissolution; as also that of the Speaker of the House of Commons at the same time. *Printed by John Bill.* **E. 1075. (28.)**

[**Dec. 30.**]—Æneas his Descent into Hell : as it is inimitably described by the Prince of Poets in his Æneis. Made English by John Boys. pp. 232. *Printed by R. Hodgkinsonne.* (30 Dec.) **E. 1054. (3.)**

[**Dec.**]—Articles to unite the Catholicks and Evangelicks, agreed on and sent to the Pope by the Elector of Ments. [Stated in a MS. note, on the authority of the Secretary to the Palsgrave, to be : "a kinde of Libell, at the publishing whereof the Court of Mentz is much offended."] **E. 1055. (5.)**

[**Dec.**]—[A MS. copy of the preceding, in Thomason's hand.] **669. f. 26. (43.)**

[**Dec.**]—Claudii Salmasii ad Johannem Miltonum Responsio. pp. 304. [See above : 6 April, 1650, E. 1393. ; and Oct., 1658, E. 1900. (1.)] *Typis T. Roycroft, impensis J. Martin, J. Allestry & T. Dicas.* **E. 1926. (2.)**

[**Dec.**]—Englands Deliverance ; or, The great and bloody plot discovered, contrived against the King's Majesty, the Queen, and all the Royal Progeny. *Printed for T. Vere and W. Gilbertson.* **E. 1846. (2.)**

[**Dec.**]—[Two Latin poems, in the form of acrostics, in praise of Charles II. and James, Duke of York. By Philip Woulfe.] *s. sh.* **669. f. 26. (38.) and (39.)**

[**Dec.**]—To the Commons of England. The Petition of Sir Nicholas Crisp. [Praying for the repayment of money lent in the service of Charles I.] *s. sh.* **669. f. 26. (40.)**

[**Dec.**]—A brief Introduction to the Skill of Musick. In two books. [By John Playford.] The third edition. To which is added, The Art of Descant, by Dr. Tho. Campion. With annotations thereon by Mr. Chr. Simpson. [With an engraved portrait of John Playford.] pp. 136. *Printed by W. Godbid for John Playford.* **E. 1795. (2.)**

[**Dec.**]—Choice Proverbs and Dialogues in Italian and English. Published by P. P., an Italian, and Teacher of the Italian Tongue. pp. 304. *Printed by E. C. for Robert Horn.* **E. 1865. (1.)**

[**Dec.**]—Humane Industry ; or, A History of most Manual Arts. [By Thomas Powell.] pp. 188. *Printed for Henry Herringman.* **E. 1762. (2.)**

[**Dec.**]—A Seasonable Vindication of the Supream Authority and Jurisdiction of Christian Kings, Lords, Parliaments over Delinquent Prelates.

1660.

By William Prynne. *Printed by T. Childe and L. Parry & are to be sold by Edward Thomas.* **E. 1054. (4.)**

[**Dec.**]—Some Motives and Incentives to the Love of God. By the Honble. Robert Boyle. Second edition, much corrected. pp. 174. *Printed for Henry Herringman.* **E. 1808. (2.)**

To the following no date, except that of the year, can be assigned.

1660.—The faithful yet imperfect Character of a glorious King, King Charles I., his Country's & Religion's Martyr. By a Person of Quality. [With an engraved portrait of Charles I.] pp. 71. *Printed for Richard Royston.* **E. 1799. (1.)**

1660.—Veritas Inconcussa; or, A most certain Truth asserted, that King Charles I. was no Man of Blood, but a Martyr for his People. By Fabian Philipps. [With an engraved portrait of the King.] pp. 237. *Printed by Richard Hodgkinson in 1649, reprinted by Thomas Newcomb for William Place.* **E. 1925. (2.)**

1660.—The Bishop of Armaghe's Direction concerning the Lyturgy and Episcopall Government, being thereunto requested by the House of Commons, and then presented in the year 1642. *Printed for the general good.* **E. 1030. (10.)**

1660.—Χριστολογία μετρική · sive Hymnus ad Christum. Opera Joannis Harmari. [In Greek and Latin.] *Typis Joannis Macock.*
E. 1911. (1*.)

1660.—A Door of Hope; or, A Call and Declaration for the gathering together of the first ripe Fruits unto the Standard of our Lord, King Jesus. **E. 764. (7.)**

1660.—A Mirrour for Anabaptists, in three rational discourses that may put the blush upon them. By Thomas Gery. *Printed for Nath. Webb and W. Grantham.* **E. 1892. (3.)**

1660.—Poems, by William Earl of Pembroke. Whereof many of which are answered by way of repartee, by Sir Benjamin Ruddier. pp. 118. *Printed by Matthew Inman and are to be sold by James Magnes.*
E. 1924. (3.)

1660.—Several Cases of Conscience discussed in ten lectures in the Divinity School at Oxford. By Robert Sanderson, now Lord Bishop of Lincoln. pp. 363. *Printed by Tho. Leach for John Martin, James Allestry and Tho. Dicas.* **E. 1765. (2.)**

1660.—The Whole Duty of Man, necessary for all Families. With Private Devotions for severall Occasions. [Attributed to Richard Allestree; also to Dorothy, Lady Pakington; and others.] pp. 482. *Printed for Timothy Garthwait.* **E. 1781.**

1660.—The Gentlemans Calling. [By the author of "The Whole Duty of Man": with a prefatory epistle signed: H. H., i.e. Humphrey Hench

1660.

man. With two engraved titlepages, and two engraved illustrations representing Jeremiah and Zedekiah. For the authorship see the preceding entry.] pp. 176. *Printed for T. Garthwait.* **E. 1795. (1.)**

1660.—The Young Sea-man's Guide; or, The Mariners Almanack for 1661. By Timothy Gadbury. *Printed for Fr. Cossinet.* **E. 1924. (1.)**

1661.

[Jan. 1.]—[A portrait of Charles II., engraved by Peter Williamson. With an inscription in verse by John Ogilby.] *s. sh. Printed for John Williams.* (1 Jan.)   **669. f. 26. (44.)**

[Jan. 1.]—[A portrait of Henrietta Anna, Duchess of Orleans, engraved by Peter Williamson, after a painting by David Klöcker von Ehrenstrahl. With an inscription in verse.] *s. sh. Printed for John Williams.* (1 Jan.)   **669. f. 26. (45.)**

[Jan. 2.]—An Act for taking away the Court of Wards and Liveries, and Tenures in Capite, and by Knights-Service, and Purveyance, and for settling a revenue upon his Majesty in lieu thereof. *Printed by John Bill.* (2 Jan.)   **E. 1075. (27.)**

[Jan. 2.]—The Several Speeches, Disputes and Conferences betwixt the Actors in that most horrid Tragedy against our late King Charles and divers of the Independant party in the Common Dungeon at Newgate. *Printed for George Horton.* (2 Jan.)   **E. 1055. (1.)**

[Jan. 3.]—The History of the Life and Death of Hugh Peters, that Arch-traytor. [With a wood-cut.] *Printed for Fr. Coles.* (3 Jan.)
        E. 1055. (2.)

[Jan. 4.]—A Perfect & exact account of all the Holy-Daies in the Yeare. *Printed for I. Stafford and F. Coles.* (4 Jan.) **E. 1055. (3.)**

[Jan. 5.]—Rhetorick Restrained, or, Dr. John Gauden his Considerations of the Liturgy of the Church of England considered and clouded. By Thomas Bolde, Exon. [See above : 26 Nov. 1660, E. 1050. (6.)] *Printed for Tho. Parkhurst.* (5 Jan.)   **E. 1055. (7.)**

Jan. 6.—A Sermon preached in St. Peter's Westminster at the Consecration of Gilbert [Ironside], Lord Bishop of Bristoll, Edward [Reynolds], Lord Bishop of Norwich and others. By Richard Allestry. *Printed for Jo. Martin Ja. Allestry and Tho. Dicas.*   **E. 1057. (6.)**

Jan. 9.—An Advertisement as touching the Fanaticks late Conspiracy and Outrage attempted partly in the City. *Printed by H. Lloyd & R. Vaughan.*   **E. 1055. (15.)**

Jan. 9.—A Judgment & Condemnation of the Fifth-Monarchy-Men their late Insurrection. By a Moderate Gentleman.   **E. 1055. (13.)**

1661.

Jan. 9.—The last farewel to the rebellious sect called the Fifth Monarchy-Men, with the total dispersing of that Damnable and Seditious Sect. **E. 1055. (12.)**

Jan. 9.—The Plotters unmasked, Murderers no Saints, or, A Word in season to all those that were concerned in the late Rebellion. By John Clarke. **E. 1055. (11.)**

Jan. 9.—A Renuntiation and Declaration of the Ministers of Congregational Churches in London against the late Horrid Insurrection. *Printed by Peter & Edward Cole.* **E. 1055. (18.)**

Jan. 9.—Rebellion Unmasked, or a sermon preached at Poplar upon occasion of the late Rebellious Insurrection in London. By Thomas Marriot. *Printed by I. R. for Thomas Johnson.* **E. 1055. (21.)**

Jan. 10.—By the King. A Proclamation prohibiting all unlawfull and seditious Meetings and Conventicles under pretence of Religious Worship. *s. sh. Printed by John Bill.* **669. f. 26. (47.)**

[Jan. 10.]—The Just Devil of Woodstock, or, A True Narrative of the several Apparitions and Punishments inflicted upon the Rumpish Commissioners sent thither, 16 Oct. 1649. (10 Jan.) **E. 1055. (10.)**

[Jan. 10.]—To my Lady Morton on New Years Day 1650, at the Louver in Paris. [Verses, by Edmund Waller.] *s. sh. Printed by Henry Herringman.* (10 Jan.) **669. f. 26. (46.)**

Jan. 13.—Christian Concord: or, S. Pauls Parallel between the Body Natural and Mystical exemplified in a sermon preacht in the Cathedral Church of S. Paul. By Matthew Griffith. *Printed by W. G. for T. Firby.* **E. 1081. (6.)**

Jan. 16.—By the King. A Proclamation for quieting the Post-Master-General in the execution of his office. *s. sh. Printed by John Bill.* **669. f. 26. (48.)**

[Jan. 17.]—By the King. A Proclamation prohibiting the seizing of any persons, or searching houses without warrant, except in time of actual insurrections. *s. sh. Printed by John Bill.* **669. f. 26. (49.)**

[Jan. 17.]—An Act for the better ordering the selling of Wines by retail, and for preventing abuses in the mingling, corrupting, and vitiating of Wines, and for setting and limiting the prices of the same.—An Act for the levying of the arrears of the Twelve Moneths Assessment commencing 24 June 1659, and the Six Moneths Assessment commencing 25 Dec. 1659.—An Act for granting unto the King's Majesty four hundred and twenty thousand pounds, by an Assessment of threescore and ten thousand pounds by the moneth, for six moneths, for disbanding the remainder of the Army, and paying off the Navy. *Printed by John Bill.* (17 Jan.) **E. 1075. (29.)**

[Jan. 17.]—An Act for further supplying and explaining certain defects in an Act, intituled, An Act for the speedy provision of money for dis-

1661.

banding and paying off the forces of this Kingdom, both by sea and land.—An Act for the raising of seventy thousand pounds for the further supply of his Majesty.—An Act for the Attainder of several persons guilty of the horrid murther of his late sacred Majestie King Charles the First.—An Act for confirmation of leases and grants from Colledges and Hospitals.—An Act for prohibiting the exportation of Wooll, Woolsels, Fuller's Earth, etc. *Printed by John Bill.* (17 Jan.)
E. 1075. (30.)

[Jan. 17.]—An Act for confirmation of Marriages.—An Act for prohibiting the planting, setting, or sowing of Tobacco in England and Ireland.—An Act for erecting and establishing a Post-Office. *Printed by John Bill.* (17 Jan.)
E. 1075. (31.)

[Jan. 17.]—A Short Direction for the performance of Cathedrall Service. By E. L. [i.e. Edward Lowe. With the music of the chants, etc.] *Printed by William Hall for Richard Davis: Oxford.* (17 Jan.) E. 1924. (2.)

[Jan. 18.]—The Phanatiques Creed, or A Door of Safety ; in answer to a bloody pamphlet intituled A Door of Hope. *Printed for Henry Brome.* (18 Jan.)
E. 1055. (14.)

[Jan. 18.]—The Pretended Saint and the Prophane Libertine, well met in Prison ; or, A Dialogue between Robert Titchburne and Henry Marten, Chamber-Fellowes in Newgate. *Printed for J. Stafford.* (18 Jan.)
E. 1873. (3.)

[Jan. 19.]—A Discourse concerning the Solemne League and Covenant. By an Episcopall Divine. [Signed : J. D.] (19 Jan.)
E. 1055. (16.)

[Jan. 21.]—A Full Relation or Dialogue between a Loyallist and a converted Phanattick. *Printed for F. Coles.* (21 Jan.)
E. 1875. (2.)

Jan. 22.—Proclamation against all Meetings of Quakers, Anabaptists, &c. [Dated at Edinburgh.]
669. f. 26. (56.)

Jan. 23.—The Charge of High Treason, Murders, Oppressions and other Crimes exhibited to the Parliament of Scotland against the Marquess of Argyle and his Complices. *Printed for Richard Lowndes.*
E. 1083. (1.)

Jan. 23.—The Grand Indictment of High-Treason exhibited against the Marquess of Argyle by His Maiesties Advocate to the Parliament of Scotland. With the Marquesses answers.   E. 1087. (1.)

Jan. 23.—The Marques of Argyll his Defences against the Grand Indytement of High Treason exhibited against him to the Parliament in Scotland. pp. 96.
E. 1087. (3.)

Jan. 24.—The Character of an Anabaptist. As it was presented to some Lords of His Majesty's Privy Council, for His Majesty, 24 Jan. *s. sh.* *Printed by J. Clowes for P. C.*   669. f. 26. (51.)

1661.

Jan. 25.—By the King. A Proclamation for observation of the thirtieth day of January as a Day of Fast and Humiliation, according to the late Act of Parliament for that purpose. *s. sh. Printed by John Bill.* **669. f. 26. (50.)**

[**Jan. 25.**]—De Adoratione Dei versus Altare : or, Bowing towards the Altar vindicated. By Eleazar Duncon. *Printed & are to be sold by Timothy Garthwait.* (25 Jan.) **E. 1055. (19.)**

[**Jan. 26.**]—The holy Sisters Conspiracy against their Husbands and the City of London, designed at their last Farewell of their Meeting-houses in Coleman-street. [A satire against the Fifth-Monarchy Men.] *Printed by T. M.* (26 Jan.) **E. 1055. (20.)**

[**Jan. 26.**]—England's Restitution, or The Man, the Man of Men, the States-man. Delivered in several sermons in the Parish Church of Waltham Abbey. By Thomas Reeve. pp. 164. *Printed by John Redmayne for William Grantham.* (26 Jan.) **E. 1056. (1.)**

[**Jan. 26.**]—England's Backwardnesse, or a lingring Party in bringing back a lawful King. Delivered in a sermon at Waltham Abbey Church. By Thomas Reeve. *Printed for William Grantham.* (26 Jan.) **E. 1056. (3.)**

Jan. 27.—The Proceedings observed in the Consecration of the Twelve Bishops at St. Patrick's Church, Dublin. By Dudley Loftus. *Printed by J. C. for John Crook.* **E. 764. (6.)**

Jan. 27.—An Antheme sung at the Consecration of the Archbishops and Bishops of Ireland, at St. Patricks in Dublin. *s. sh.* **669. f. 26. (61.)**

Jan. 28.—The Marquess of Argile his Answer to his Charge sent unto him in the Castle of Edinburgh. **E. 1083. (4.)**

[**Jan. 28.**]—The Humble Apology of some commonly called Anabaptists with their Protestation against the late wicked Insurrection. *Printed by Henry Hills & are to be sold by Francis Smith.* (28 Jan.) **E. 1057. (1.)**

[**Jan. 28.**]—Private Forms of Prayer, fitted for the late sad times. Particularly, a Form of Prayer for the Thirtieth of January. pp. 357. *Printed by Thomas Mabb for William Not.* (28 Jan.) **E. 1872. (2.)**

[**Jan. 28.**]—Exercitationes Pathologicæ, in quibus morborum penè omnium natura, generatio & caussae sedulo inquiruntur a Gualtero Charltono. pp. 208. *Apud Tho. Newcomb.* (28 Jan.) **E. 1056. (4.)**

[**Jan. 29.**]—By the King. A Proclamation for restraint of killing, dressing, and eating of Flesh in Lent, or on Fish-dayes appointed by the Law to be observed. *Printed by John Bill.* **669. f. 26. (52.)**

[**Jan. 29.**]—An Elegie and Epitaph on King Charles I. written a day or two after his Martyrdom, for the suspition of which the Author lay

1661.

two years in the Gate-house, saying alwayes God bless King Charles the Second. *Printed for J. Williams.* (29 Jan.)   **E. 1057. (3.)**

[**Jan. 29.**]—Ministers Dues and People's Duty, shewing what People owe unto their Ministers. By Sam. Clark. pp. 52. *Printed by A. M. for William Miller.* (29 Jan.)   **E. 1057. (4.)**

[**Jan. 29.**]—The Way to True Peace, or a Calm, Seasonable and Modest word to the Independents, Phanaticks, Anabaptists, Presbyterians, Quakers, Papists and Fifth Monarchists. *Printed for John Clowes.* (29 Jan.)   **E. 1057. (2.)**

[**Jan. 30.**]—A Form of Common Prayer to be used upon the thirtieth of January, being the Anniversary-Day appointed by Parliament to implore the Mercy of God, that neither the Guilt of that Sacred and Innocent Bloud nor those other Sinns by which God was provoked to deliver up both us & our King into the hands of cruel men, may be visited upon us or our Posterity. *Printed by John Bill.* (30 Jan.)
    E. 1057. (5.)

Jan. 30.—Curse not the King. A sermon preached at St. Martin's in the Fields, the Anniversary Day of Humiliation for the Horrid Murder of Charles the I. By John Meriton. *Printed by J. Macock for Henry Herringman.*   **E. 1084. (7.)**

Jan. 30.—Lacrymæ Ecclesiæ; or, The mourning of Hadadrimmon for Englands Josiah. Delivered in two sermons, at the solemn Fasting & Humiliation for the Martyrdom of King Charles the First. By Wil. Hampton. *Printed for Wil. Hope.*   **E. 1086. (9.)**

[**Jan. 30.**]—To the King of these Nations. The humble Representation of several Societies, commonly called by the name of Anabaptists, where in short they declare their innocency, suffering, & resolutions. *s. sh.* (30 Jan.)   **669. f. 26. (53.)**

[**Jan. 31.**]—Mercurius Benevolens. Not Prag. nor Pol. not he, nor he. But a well-wishing Mercury. [In verse.] *Printed for Hen. Brome.* (31 Jan.)   **E. 1057. (7.)**

[**Jan.**]—The Character of Sr. Arthur Haslerig, the Church-thief. By F. B. Gent. *s. sh.*   **669. f. 26. (54.)**

[**Jan.**]—Justice Restored; or, A Guide for Justices of Peace. Second edition, enlarged. pp. 158. *Printed by Th. Roycroft for H. Twyford, T. Dring and J. Place.*   **E. 1930. (2.)**

[**Jan.**]—A Vade Mecum, or Table containing the substance of such Statutes wherein any one or more parties of the Peace are enabled to act. By Wal. Young. Sixth edition. pp. 186. *Printed for Rich. Best and are to be sold by H. Twyford, Tho. Dring and John Place.*
    E. 1883. (2.)

1661.

[**Feb. 1.**]—An Historical Discourse, briefly setting forth the nature of Procurations, and how they were anciently paid. By J. S. [i.e. John Stephens.] pp. 146. *Printed by R. Hodgkinson.* (1 Feb.)

E. 1057. (9.)

[**Feb. 2.**]—Justa sive Inferiæ Regicidarum: or, Tyburns Revels, presented before Protector Cromwell, Lord President Bradshaw, Lord Deputy Ireton. By Squire Dun, Mercury and Chorus. [A satire, in verse.] *s. sh. Printed for R. B.* (2 Feb.)   **669. f. 26. (58.)**

[**Feb. 2.**]—On the Death of that Grand Impostor Oliver Cromwell. [Verses. MS. note by Thomason : " This poem was printed the 3ᵈ day after that Cromwell, Bradshaw & Ireton were hanged at Tiburn, and their boddies turned into a hole under the Gallows."]   *s. sh. Printed for J. Williams.* (2 Feb.)   **669. f. 26. (57.)**

[**Feb. 2.**]—Zimri's Peace : or, The Traytor's Doom & Downfall. Being the substance of two sermons preached at Apethorp in the County of Northampton. By John Ramsey. *Printed for Charles Adams.* (2 Feb.)   **E. 1057. (10.)**

[**Feb. 5.**]—A Collection out of the Book called Liber Regalis, touching the Coronation of the King and Queen together. *Printed by R. D. for Charls Adams.* (5 Feb.)   **E. 1081. (3.)**

[**Feb. 5.**]—An Epistle recommended to all the Prisons in this City & Nation. Wherein is asserted the Lawfulness of an Oath. By Henry Den. [See also below : 2 March, E. 1084. (2.)] *Printed for Francis Smith.* (5 Feb.)   **E. 1081. (1.)**

[**Feb. 5.**]—The Thracian Wonder. A Comical History, as it hath been several times acted with great applause. By John Webster and William Rowley. *Printed by Tho. Johnson, & are to be sold by Francis Kirkman.* (5 Feb.)   **E. 1081. (2.)**

[**Feb. 6.**]—The Second Humble Addresse of those who are called Anabaptists in the County of Lincoln, presented to His Majesty. [Praying for the redress of their grievances.] *s. sh. Printed by Simon Dover.* (6 Feb.)   **669. f. 26. (59.)**

[**Feb. 6.**]—The Speeches of Oliver Cromwell, Henry Ireton and John Bradshaw, intended to have been spoken at their Execution, 30 Jan., but for many weightie Reasons omitted. [A satire.] *Printed and are to be sold at the Old Exchange.* (6 Feb.)   **E. 1081. (5.)**

[**Feb. 6.**]—Treasons by the Laws of England. A brief Collection of what is Treason by Law. *s. sh. Printed by Roger Norton for Robert Pawley.* (6 Feb.)   **669. f. 26. (60.)**

[**Feb. 7.**]—A Discovery of some Sins of the Ministry made in a Confession, published some years since by divers Ministers, and now made publick again. (7 Feb.)   **E. 1878. (2.)**

1661.
Feb 11.—The Petition and Address of the General Court sitting at Boston in New-England unto Charles the Second, presented 11 Feb.
E. 1085. (2.)

[**Feb. 11.**]—Short Meditations on, with a briefe Description of the Life and Death of Oliver Cromwell. By J. D. Durnovariæ. *Printed by T. M. for Robert Clavel.* (11 Feb.) E. 1082. (1.)

Feb. 12.—The Marquess of Argyle his Petition to the Parliament of Scotland. pp. 62. E. 1087. (2.)

[**Feb. 12.**]—Lent-Preachers at Court. [A list.] *s. sh. Sold by T. Garthwait.* (12 Feb.) 669. f. 26. (62.)

[**Feb. 12.**]—The Great Case of Conscience opened about the Lawfulness of Swearing. By Ieremiah Ives. [See also below : 2 March, E. 1084. (2.) and 13 March, E. 1085. (5.)] *Printed by S. D. for Francis Smith.* (12 Feb.) E. 1082. (2.)

[**Feb. 12.**]—The holding the Bishop and Presbyter equall vindicated from Heresie. By Luke Cranwell. *Printed by A. M. for John Sherley.* (12 Feb.) E. 1082. (3.)

Feb. 12.—A Wonder in Staffordshire. Of a strange and horrible apparition of the Divell appearing to one James Fisher, a Phrenatick, neare Brummingham, 12 Feb. *Printed for Francis Coles.*
E. 1085. (10.)

[**Feb. 13.**]—A Collection of so much of the Statutes in force as contain and enjoyn the taking of the several Oaths of Supremacy and Allegiance. [The preface signed : W. B.] *Printed by Robert White.* (13 Feb.)
E. 1082. (5.)

[**Feb. 15.**]—The Liturgical Considerator considered : or a brief view of Dr. Gauden's Considerations touching the Liturgy of the Church of England. By G. F. [i.e. Giles Firmin. See above : 26 Nov. 1660, E. 1050. (6.)] *Printed for Ralph Smith.* (15 Feb.) E. 1082. (7.)

Feb. 17.—Tandem bona causa triumphat. Or, Scotland's late misery bewailed and the Honour and Loyalty of this Antient Kingdom asserted in a sermon preached before the Parliament of Scotland. By John Paterson. *Printed at Edinburgh and reprinted at London for James Thrale.* E. 1085. (11.)

Feb. 20.—Act [of the Scottish Parliament] condemning the transactions concerning the King's Majesty whilst he was at Newcastle in the years 1646 and 1647. *s. sh. Printed by Evan Tyler : Edinburgh.*
669. f. 27. (4.)

Feb. 22.—Act and Proclamation [of the Scottish Parliament] that none come from Ireland without sufficient Testimonial. *s. sh. Printed by Evan Tyler : Edinburgh.* 669. f. 26. (67.)

[**Feb. 23.**]—The Controversie between Episcopacy and Presbytery stated and discussed. By J. Gailhard. *Printed for the Author.* (23 Feb.)
E. 1083. (3.)

1661.

[**Feb. 26.**]—Placita Latinè Rediviva : A Book of Entries ; containing perfect and approved Presidents of Counts, Declarations, Barrs, Avowries, Replications, Pleas in Abatement, Issues, Judgments. By R. A. [i.e. R. Aston] of Furnival's-Inn. pp. 520. *Printed for H. Twyford, T. Dring and John Place.* (26 Feb.) **E. 193.**

Feb. 26.—A Serious View of Presbyters Re-ordination by Bishops. In a letter written unto a Minister in Warwickshire. [By Zachary Crofton.] *Printed for Ralph Smith.* **E. 1084. (10.)**

[**Feb.**]—A Collection of such Statutes as do enjoyn the observation of Lent. *s. sh. Printed for R. Pawley.* **669. f. 26. (66.)**

[**Feb.**]—A Perfect Catalogue of all the Archbishops & Bishops in England and Wales, established by King Charles the Second. *s. sh. Printed for R. Pawley.* **669. f. 26. (63.)**

[**Feb.**]—Hodder's Arithmetick. By James Hodder. [With an engraved portrait of the author.] pp. 214. *Printed by R. Davenport for Tho. Rooks.* **E. 1901. (2.)**

[**Feb.**]—Lux Mercatoria. Arithmetick Natural and Decimal. By Noah Bridges. [With an engraved portrait of the author.] pp. 349. *Printed by R. I. for Thomas Johnson.* **E. 1815.**

[**Feb.**]—Πανζωορυκτολογία, sive Panzoologicomineralogia. Or, a Compleat History of Animals and Minerals. By Robert Lovell. 2 vols. *Printed by Hen. Hall for Jos. Godwin : Oxford.* **E. 1810, 11.**

[**Feb.**]—The Principles of Law reduced to Practice. By W. Phillipps. pp. 167. *Printed for Hen. Twyford, Thomas Dring & John Place.* **E. 1905. (2.)**

[**Feb.**]—The Royal Robe ; or, A Treatise of Meeknesse. By James Barker. pp. 252. *Printed by E. M. for Robert Gibbs.* **E. 1857. (1.)**

[**Feb.**]—Speculum Speculativum : or, A Considering-Glass, being an Inspection into the present and late sad condition of these Nations. By George Wither. [In verse.] pp. 166. **E. 1814. (1.)**

[**Feb.**]—Lent. [An allegorical engraving, with explanatory verses.] *s. sh. Printed by M. S. for Thomas Jenner.* **669. f. 26. (65.)**

[**Feb.**]—Shrovetyde. [An allegorical engraving, with explanatory verses.] *s. sh. Printed by M. S. for Thomas Jenner.* **669. f. 26. (64.)**

[**March 1.**]—Anti Baal-Berith : or, The binding of the Covenant and all Covenanters to their good Behaviours, by a just Vindication of Dr. Gaudens Analysis, against the Cacotomy of a nameless and shameless Libeller the worthy Hyperaspistes of Dr. Burges, also against the pittyful cavils of Mr. Zach. Grafton [i.e. Zachary Crofton. By John Gauden]. pp. 295. [See above : 23 Nov., 1660, E. 1050. (2.), and also below : 14 March, E. 1085. (6.)] *Printed by John Best for Andrew Crook.* (1 March.) **E. 1083. (5.)**

1661.

[**March 2.**]—A Fannatick's Testimony against Swearing, being an Answer to four Books published by John Tombes, Jeremiah Ives, Theophilus Brabourne and Henry Den. By Henry Adis. pp. 50. [See above : 22 Oct. 1660, E. 1046. (10.), 12 Feb. 1661, E. 1082. (2.), 5 Feb., E. 1081. (1.) ; and also below : 18 March, E. 1085. (8.)] *Printed by S. Dover.* (2 March.) **E. 1084. (2.)**

[**March 2.**]—A Supplement to the Serious Consideration of the Oath of the King's Supremacy. By John Tombes. [See above : 22 Oct. 1660, E. 1046. (10.)] *Printed by Henry Hills.* (2 March.) **E. 1084. (1.)**

[**March 4.**]—The Several Statutes in force for the observation of Lent : and Fish-dayes at all other times of the Year. [The preface signed : W. B.] *Printed by Robert White.* (4 March.) **E. 1084. (3.)**

[**March 5.**]—The Petition of Theophilus Brabourn unto the Honourable Parliament, that Bishops may be required in their Office to own the Kings Supremacy. *Printed for the Author.* (5 March.)

E. 1084. (5.)

[**March 5.**]—A Strange and True Relation of several Wonderful and Miraculous Sights seen in the Air, 15 Feb. and this present March. *Printed for J. Jones.* (5 March.) **E. 1084. (4.)**

[**March 6.**]—A Fannaticks Letter sent out of the Dungeon of the Gate-House Prison of Westminster to all his Brethren at liberty. By Henry Adis. *Printed by S. Dover for the Author.* (6 March.)

E. 1084. (6.)

[**March 7.**]—An Imperfect Pourtraicture of his Sacred Majestie Charls the II. Written by a Loyal Subject. [With an engraved portrait.] *Printed for Henry Herringman.* (7 March.) **E. 1084. (8.)**

March 8.—By the King. A Proclamation declaring his Majesties Pleasure touching his Royal Coronation. *s. sh. Printed by John Bill.*

669. f. 26. (68.)

[**March 8.**]—Minors no Senators : or, A Brief Discourse proving Infants under 21 years of age to be uncapable of being elected Members of Parliament. By William Prynne. *Printed for Edward Thomas.* (8 March.) **E. 1084. (11.)**

[**March 8.**]—A Parallel of the Liturgy with the Mass-Book, the Breviary and other Romish Rituals. By Robert Bayly. pp. 80. (8 March.)

E. 1084. (9.)

[**March 10.**]—The Second Part of the Interest of England in the Matter of Religion. [An advocacy of Protestantism.] By J. C. [i.e. John Corbet.] pp. 132. *Printed for George Thomason.* (10 March.)

E. 1857. (2.)

[**March 11.**]—Englands Warning-Piece, or, The most strange and wonderfull Predictions of Cleombrotus, a heathen Jew, prophesied in the year 1272, upon the Raignes of 29 Kings of England ; from Edward

1661.

the I. to Charles the Fifth, 1799. *Printed for Francis Coles.* (11 March.) **E. 1085. (1.)**

[March 12.]—Common-Prayer-Book no Divine Service ; or, XXVIII Reasons against forming and imposing any Humane Liturgies. By Vavasor Powell. Third edition, enlarged. *Printed for Livewell Chapman.* (12 March.) **E. 1085. (3.)**

[March 12.]—An Impartial Character of that famous Polititian Cardinal Mazarine. (12 March.) **E. 1085. (4.)**

March 13.—The Last Proceedings of the Parliament in Scotland against the Marquesse of Argyle. *Printed by T. M. for T. J.* **E. 1086. (5.)**

[March 13.]—A Caution to the Sons of Sion : being an Answer to Jeremiah Ives his Book intituled The great Case of Conscience opened. By Samuel Hodgkin. [See above : 12 Feb., E. 1082. (2.)] *Printed for the Author.* (13 March.) **E. 1085. (5.)**

[March 14.]—Berith Anti-Baal, or Zach. Croftons Appearance before the Prelate-Justice of Peace. By way of Rejoinder to Doctor John Gauden's Reply or Vindication of his Analysis. pp. 68. [See above : 1 March, E. 1083. (5.)] *Printed by. M. S. for Ralph Smith.* (14 March.) **E. 1085. (6.)**

March 16.—Joyful News for all Christendom, being a happy Prophesie of the Turks advancing to the Christian Borders. *Printed for J. Jones.* **E. 1086. (8.)**

[March 18.]—A New Meeting of Ghosts at Tyburn, being a Discourse of Oliver Cromwell, John Bradshaw, Henry Ireton and others. *Printed in the Year of the Rebellious Phanaticks downfall.* (18 March.) **E. 1085. (7.)**

[March 18.]—Of the Lawfulness of the oath of Allegiance to the King and of the other oath to his Supremacy. By Theophilus Brabourn. [See above : 2 March, E. 1084. (2.)] *Printed for the Author.* (18 March.) **E. 1085. (8.)**

March 19.—By the King. A Proclamation for the Publishing of an Act of Parliament late made for the better Ordering and selling of Wines by Retail. *s. sh. Printed by John Bill.* **669. f. 26. (71.)**

March 19.—The Loyall Subjects Lamentation for Londons Perversenesse in the malignant choice of some Rotten Members on 19 March. *s. sh.* **669. f. 27. (3.)**

[March 19.]—The Manner of Creating the Knights of the Order of the Bath according to the Custom used in England in Time of Peace. *Printed for Phil. Stephens.* (19 March.) **E. 1085. (9.)**

March 20.—By the King. A Proclamation touching the speedy calling to accompt of all such persons whose Accompts are excepted in the Act of Oblivion. *s. sh. Printed by John Bill.* **669. f. 27. (2.)**

1661.

March 21.—Strange News from the West, being a true and perfect Account of several Miraculous Sights seen in the Air, 21 March. *Printed for J. Jones.* **E. 1086. (6.)**

March 22.—A Sermon preached before the Kings Majesty at Whitehall. By John Hacket. *Printed by W. Wilson for John Place.*
E. 1086. (7.)

[**March 23.**]—Bo-Peep, or the Jerking Parson catechising his Maid. A pleasant Ballad. *s. sh. Printed for the Belman of Algate.* (23 March.)
669. f. 26. (72.)

March 24.—Εὔκαιρον Σύμβολον. A seasonable Watch-word to all sober Christians. A sermon preach'd in the Cathedral Church of St. Paul. By Chr. Shute. *Printed for John Williams.* **E. 1087. (8.)**

[**March 25.**]—The Cavaleers Letany. [Satirical verses.] *Printed for Robert Crofts.* (25 March.) **669. f. 27. (1.)**

[**March 25.**]—The Merry conceited Humours of Bottom the Weaver. As it hath been often publikely acted by some of his Majesties Comedians. [An adaptation of scenes from Shakespeare's "A Midsummer Night's Dream."] *Printed for F. Kirkman & H. Marsh.* (25 March.) **E. 1085. (13.)**

[**March 25.**]—The Presbyterian Lash, or, Noctroff's Maid Whipt. A Tragy-Comedy as was lately acted in the Pye Tavern at Aldgate. The first Part. [A satire on Zachary Crofton, by Francis Kirkman.] *Printed for the use of Mr. Noctroffs friends.* (25 March.)
E. 1085. (12.)

[**March 28.**]—Semper Iidem : or a Parallel betwixt the ancient and modern Phanatics. *Printed for Richard Lownds.* (28 March.)
E. 1086. (1.)

March 29.—By the King. A Proclamation prohibiting the Planting of Tobacco in England and Ireland. *s. sh. Printed by John Bill.*
669. f. 27. (5.)

[**March 29.**]—A Plea for Tolleration of Opinions and Perswasions in Matters of Religion, differing from the Church of England. By John Sturgion. *Printed by S. Dover for Francis Smith.* (29 March.)
E. 1086. (3.)

[**March 29.**]—St. George for England : or, A Relation of the Manner of the Election of the Knights of the Order of the Garter. *Printed for James Thrale.* (29 March.) **E. 1086. (2.)**

[**March 30.**]—A Declaration of the Sad and Great Persecution of the People of God, called Quakers, in New-England. [Signed : E. B., i.e. Edward Burrough.] *Printed for Robert Wilson.* (30 March.)
E. 1086. (4.)

[**March.**]—The true Copy of a Letter sent to the Kings Majestie by W. Cowell. *s. sh. Printed by J. C. for the Author.* **669. f. 26. (70.)**

1661.

[**March.**]—The Cavaleers Complaint. [In verse.] *s. sh. Printed for Robert Crofts.* **669. f. 26. (69.)**

[**March.**]—The Female Duel, or, The Ladies Lookingglass, representing a Scripture Combate carried on between a Roman Catholick Lady and the wife of a Dignified person in the Church of England. By Tho. Toll. pp. 248. *Printed by H. Bell & P. Lillicrap.* **E. 1813. (2.)**

[**March.**]—Lues Venerea; or, A Perfect Cure of the French Pox. By John Wynell. pp. 76. *Printed for the Author and are to be sold by H. Brome.* **E. 1855. (2.)**

[**March.**]—A Proposition for the Advancement of Experimental Philosophy. By A. Cowley. pp. 61. *Printed by J. M. for Henry Herringman.* **E. 1856. (3.)**

[**March.**]—Regulæ de Genere Nominum, de nominibus Heteroclitis, de præteritis & supinis Verborum. Ex Vossio, Farnabio aliisque collectæ. *Excudebat J. H. pro J. Allen.* **E. 1881. (4.)**

[**March.**]—The Vanity of Dogmatizing: or, Confidence in Opinions, manifested in a Discourse of the Shortness and Uncertainty of our Knowledge. By Jos. Glanvill. pp. 250. *Printed by E. C. for Henry Eversden.* **E. 1855. (1.)**

April 2.—The City's Remonstrance and Addresse to the King's most excellent Majesty. *Printed by R. D. for Tho. Rooks.* **E. 1086. (10.)**

April 3.—The Speech of the Lord Mayor of London, with the humble address of the Military Forces of the same City to the Kings most excellent Majesty. With His Majesties gracious Answer. *Printed for Tho. Rooks.* **E. 1086. (15.)**

[**April 4.**]—The Divine Dirge of a dying Swan, or a Priestly Poem entitled De anima immortali carmen. By Fr. Tucker. *Printed by Peter Lillicrap.* (4 April.) **E. 1086. (12.)**

[**April 4.**]—The True Presbyterian without Disguise: or, A Character of a Presbyterian's Wayes and Actions, in verse. (4 April.) **E. 1086. (11.)**

[**April 6.**]—A Dialogue between the two Giants in Guildhall, Colebrond and Brandamore, concerning the late Election of Citizens to serve in Parliament for the City of London. *Printed for the Authors.* (6 April.) **E. 1086. (13.)**

April 8.—To the Constables of St. Clements Danes, of Covent Garden and St. Martins in the Fields. [An Order of the Knight Marshall respecting regulations to be observed at the King's Coronation.] *s. sh. Printed by John Bill.* **669. f. 27. (6.)**

[**April 8.**]—A Sober and Temperate Discourse concerning the Interest of Words in Prayer, the just Antiquity and Pedigree of Liturgies. By

1661.

H. D., M.A. [i.e. Henry Daubeny.] pp. 114. *Printed for W. A.*
(8 April.)   **E. 1086. (14.)**

[**April 11.**]—A True Copie of the List of the Kings most Royall Proceedings through London, as it will be marshalled. *s. sh.* *Printed for*
Richard Williams. (11 April.)   **669. f. 27. (8.)**

[**April 11.**]—The Cavaliers Thanksgiving. Written by a sober Cavalier,
T. H. [In verse.] *Printed by I. C. for the Author.* (11 April.)
                                                             E. 1087. (4.)

[**April 11.**]—The Cities Feast to the Lord Protector. [A satirical
ballad.] *s. sh.* *Printed for Henry Marsh.* (11 April.) **669. f. 27. (7.)**

[**April 11.**]—The Folly and Wisdom of the Ancients : being two Letters
of Artaxerxes, as they are recorded by Josephus. *Printed for F. Smith.*
(11 April.)   **E. 1087. (5.)**

April 13.—By the King. A Proclamation requiring all Cashiered
Officers and Souldiers of the late Army to depart and not come within
twenty miles of London until 20 May next. *s. sh.* *Printed by John*
Bill.   **669. f. 27. (9.)**

[**April 13.**]—Hell's Higher Court of Justice ; or, The Triall of the three
Politick Ghosts, viz. Oliver Cromwell, King of Sweden and Cardinal
Mazarine. (13 April.)   **E. 1087. (6.)**

April 14.—The Traytors Unvailed, or, A brief account of that horrid
and bloody designe intended by the Anabaptists and Fifth Monarchy
[Men], upon 14 April.   **E. 1087. (10.)**

[**April 14.**]—A true Discovery of a Bloody Plot contrived by the
Phanaticks against the Proceedings of the City of London in order to
the Coronation of King Charles the Second, with the manner how it
should have been acted on Sunday last [14 April]. *Printed for John*
Jones.   **E. 1087. (9.)**

[**April 15.**]—A Knot Untied: or, Allegiance sworn to the King no
breach of Allegiance due unto God. *Printed for Henry Eversden.*
(15 April.)   **E. 1087. (7.)**

April 17.—The History of St. George of Cappadocia, the Institution of
that most noble Order of St. George commonly called the Garter, with
the names of the Knights already installed & to be installed on the
17 April.   **E. 1087. (14.)**

[**April 18.**]—An Antidote against Melancholy : made up in Pills. Com-
pounded of Witty Ballads, Jovial Songs and Merry Catches. [With
an engraved illustration.] pp. 76. *Printed by Mer. Melancholicus.*
(18 April.)   **E. 1087. (11.)**

April 19.—By the King. A Proclamation for the better regulating His
Majesties Royal Proceeding to Whitehall, 22 April next, being the day
before His Majesties Coronation. *s. sh.* *Printed by John Bill.*
                                                            669. f. 27. (10*.)

1661.

April 19.—By the King. A Proclamation for recalling and prohibiting Sea-men from the services of Forraign Princes and States. *s. sh. Printed by John Bill.* **669. f. 27. (11.)**

[**April 19.**]—A Proclamation by His Majesties Commissioners for executing his Declaration for the Settlement of Ireland. *s. sh. Printed by William Bladen: Dublin; reprinted at London.* (19 April.) **669. f. 27. (10.)**

[**April 19.**]—The Cities Loyalty Display'd: or the Four Famous and renowned Fabricks in the City of London exactly described. (19 April.) **E. 1087. (12.)**

[**April 19.**]—A Perfect Catalogue of all the Knights of the Order of the Garter from the first Institution of it, until this present. Collected and continued by J. N. *Printed for Anne Seile.* (19 April.) **E. 1087. (13.)**

[**April 20.**]—The Compleat Gentleman : fashioning him absolute in the most Necessary and Commendable Qualities. By Henry Peacham. The third impression much inlarged. pp. 455. *Printed by E. Tyler for Richard Thrale.* (20 April.) **E. 1088. (1.)**

[**April 20.**]—The Knavish Merchant, now turn'd Warehouseman, charactarized, or, A severe Scourge for an unjust, cruel, and unconscionable Adversary. By Philadelphus Verax. [An attack upon Richard Neave in defence of Thomas Crocker.] (20 April.) **E. 1088. (2.)**

[**April 20.**]—Q. F. F. Q. S. A New Fiction, As Wee were. [A satire, in verse, signed : J. C.] *Printed by J. C. for the Author.* (20 April.) **E. 1088. (3.)**

April 22.—The Relation of his Majestie's entertainment passing through the City of London to his Coronation, 22 April, with a description of the triumphal arches and the solemnity. By John Ogilby. *Printed by Tho. Roycroft for Rich. Marriott.* **E. 1080. (16.)**

April 22.—A Speech spoken by a Blew-Coat Boy of Christs Hospital to King Charles the Second in his passage from the Tower to White-hall. *Printed by John Hayes.* **E. 1088. (5.)**

April 22.—The Speech spoken by Sir William Wylde to King Charles II. in his Passage from the Tower to White-hall. *Printed by William Godbid for Edward Powell.* **E. 1088. (4.)**

April 22.—Neptune's Address [in verse] to his Majesty Charls the Second, congratulating his happy Coronation. In several designements and shews upon the water before Whitehall, at his Majestie's return from the Land-Triumphs. By John Tatham. *Printed by William Godbid for Edward Powel.* **E. 1080. (18.)**

April 23.—By the King. A Proclamation concerning His Majesties Coronation Pardon. *s. sh. Printed by John Bill.* **669. f. 27. (12.)**

1661.

April 23.—The Form of His Majesties Coronation-Feast to be solemnized at Westminster Hall, 23 April. *s. sh. Printed for R. Crofts.*

669. f. 27. (15.)

April 23.—A Narrative of the Manner of celebrating his Majesties Coronation in the City of Bath, by the citizens thereof. [A letter, signed : John Ford.] *s. sh. Printed for Edward Thomas.*

669. f. 27. (16.)

April 23.—Of the Celebration of the King's Coronation-Day, in the famous City of Bath. [A letter, signed : William Smith.]

E. 1088. (7.)

April 23.—Robin Hood and his Crew of Souldiers. A Comedy acted at Nottingham on the day of His Majesties Coronation. *Printed for James Davis.* **E. 1088. (6.)**

April 23.—A Sermon preached at the Coronation of King Charles II., at Westminster. By George [Morley], Bishop of Worcester. [With an engraved portrait of the King in Coronation Robes.] pp. 62. *Printed by R. Norton for T. Garthwait.* **E. 184. (5.)**

April 23.—A Sermon preached at the Collegiate Church at Manchester. By Richard Heyrick. *Printed for Ralph Shelmerdine.* **E. 1088. (9.)**

April 23.—The Coronation. A poem, by R. Whitehall. *Printed for John Playford.* **E. 184. (7.)**

April 23.—Festa Georgiana, or the Gentrie's & Countrie's Joy for the Coronation of the King. [A poem.] **E. 1080. (17.)**

April 23.—The Fortunate Change: being a Panegyrick to his Majesty King Charls the Second immediately on his Coronation. By Carew Reynell. [In verse.] *Printed for Henry Herringman.*

E. 1080. (19.)

April 23.—Gloria Britanica : or, A Panegyrick on his Sacred Majesties Passage thorow the City of London to his Coronation. [In verse.] *Printed by J. B. for Andrew Crook.* **E. 1088. (8.)**

April 23.—Heroick Stanzas on his Majestie's Coronation. By Sam. Pordage. *Printed for Peter Dring.* **E. 1080. (24.)**

[April 23.]—An humble Monitory to Charles II. By Thomas Warmstrey. [In verse.] *s. sh. Printed by Matthew Inman for James Magnes.* (23 April.) **669. f. 27. (14.)**

April 23.—A Hymne, called Englands Hosanna to God for the Restoration of Charles II. By Daniel Harcourt. *s. sh.* **669. f. 27. (20.)**

April 23.—Monarchiæ Encomium ; or, A Congratulation of the Kings Coronation. By Tho. Malpas. pp. 62. *Printed by T. Leach ; and are to be sold by William Palmer in Fleetstreet, and by Joan Malpas in Sturbridge in Worcestershire.* (23 April.) **E. 1856. (5.)**

1661.

April 23.—On the Thunder happening after the solemnity of the Coronation of Charles II. [In verse.] *s. sh. Printed for K. Crofts.*

669. f. 27. (13.)

April 23.—A Poem upon His Majesties Coronation. *Printed for Gabriel Bedel and Thomas Collins.*

E. 1080. (21.)

April 23.—St. George's Day sacred to the Coronation of his Majesty Charles the II. By Hen. Bold. [A poem.] *Printed for R. Crofts.*

E. 1080. (23.)

April 23.—To his Sacred Majesty, A Panegyrick on his Coronation. By John Dryden. [In verse.] *Printed for Henry Herringman.*

E. 1080. (22.)

April 23.—A Triumphant Panegyrick in honour of King Charles the Second his Coronation. [In verse.] *s. sh. Printed for Thomas Ratcliffe.*

669. f. 27. (19.)

April 23.—Verses on the blessed and happy Coronation of Charles the II. [By John Rich.] *Printed and are to be sold by John Ratcliffe, Bookseller in Plymouth.*

E. 1080. (20.)

[April.]—Jerusalems Glory, or, the Saints Safetie in eying the Churches Security. Being an Invitation to all the different minded men in the World to become one. By Thomas Watson. pp. 104. *Printed by J. C. for the Authour.*

E. 1856. (4.)

[April.]—The Scotch Covenant newly revived, in a conference between Mr. Crofton and a Converted Scotch Parson. [A satire.]

E. 1878. (3.)

[April.]—Two most strange Wonders. The one, a relation of an Angel appearing to James Wise, Minister in Yorkshire; the other being a judgment which befell Dorothy Matley of Ashover, who having couzened a poor lad of two pence, the ground opened and swallowed her. *Printed for W. Gilbertson.*

E. 1874. (4.)

May 17.—An Ode on the Fair Weather that attended His Majesty on His Birth. *s. sh. Printed by John Clowes for the Author.*

669. f. 27. (17.)

May.—A Petition for Peace: with the Reformation of the Liturgy. As it was presented to the Bishops by the Divines appointed to treat with them about the Alteration of it. [By Richard Baxter.] pp. 95.

E. 1089. (1.)

[May.]—A Countrey Song, intituled The Restoration. *s. sh.*

669. f. 27. (18.)

[Sept.]—An Accompt of all the Proceedings of the Commissioners of both Perswasions for the Review of the Book of Common Prayer. pp. 126. *Printed for R. H.*

E. 1089. (2.)

II.

2 B

1661.

[**Oct.**]—'Ορθολατρεία, or, A Brief Discourse concerning Bodily Worship. By Simon Gunton. pp. 103. *Printed for G. Bedell and T. Collins.*

E. 1934. (2.)

[**Nov.**]—Montelion, 1661 ; or, the Prophetical Almanack. [A satire, by John Philipps. With woodcuts.] *Sold by Henry Marsh.* **E. 1876. (2.)**

[**Nov.**]—A Rationale upon the Book of Common Prayer. By Anth. Sparrow. [With an engraved titlepage and a frontispiece representing congregations at worship.] pp. 408. *Printed for T. Garthwait.*

E. 1938.

[**Dec. 13.**]—A Defence of the Liturgy of the Church of England. An answer to the book [by Cornelius Burges] entituled Reasons shewing the Necessity of Reformation of the Publick Doctrine and Worship, &c. pp. 79. [See above : 3 Aug., 1660, E. 764. (4.)] *Printed for T. Garthwait.* (13 Dec.) **E. 2106. (3.)**

[**Dec. 20.**]—Θεάνθρωπος, or, God made Man. A tract proving the Nativity of our Saviour to be on the 25 of December. By John Selden. pp. 91. *Printed by J. G. for Nathaniel Brooks.* (20 Dec.)

E. 1809. (2.)

To the following no date, except that of the year, can be assigned.

1661.—A Poem on St. James's Park, as lately improved by his Majesty. By Edmund Waller. [With another poem. " Of our late War with Spaine, and first victory at sea near St. Lugar."] *Printed for Gabriel Bedel and Thomas Collins.* **E. 1080. (25.)**

1661.—Effata Regalia. Aphorismes, divine, moral, politick, scattered in the Books, Speeches, Letters, &c. of Charles the First. Collected by Richard Watson. pp. 354. *Printed for Robert Horn.* **E. 1843.**

NEWSPAPERS

1641–1663.

1641.

Nov.—The Heads of Severall Proceedings. 22–29 Nov. **E. 201. (1.)**
Dec.—The Heads of Severall Proceedings. 29 Nov.–6 Dec.
                                                            E. 201. (2.)
—— Diurnall Occurrences. 13–27 Dec. **E. 201. (3.) and (4.)**

1642.

Jan.—Diurnall Occurrences. 27 Dec.–24 Jan. **E. 201.**
——— The Diurnall Occurrances in Parliament. 17–24 Jan.
                                                            E. 201. (11.)
—— A Perfect Diurnall. 24–31 Jan. **E. 201. (12.)**
Feb.—A Continuation of the True Diurnall. 14–28 Feb.
                                                    E. 201. (18.) and (19.)
—— Diurnall Occurrences. (*John Thomas.*) 7–14 Feb. **E. 201. (14.)**
—— Diurnall Occurrences. (*I. G.*) 7–14 Feb. **E. 201. (16.)**
—— Irelands True Diurnall. 11 Jan.–3 Feb. **E. 201. (9.)**
—— A Perfect Diurnall. 21–28 Feb. **E. 201. (20.)**
—— The True Diurnall Occurrances. (*I. Hammond.*) 31 Jan.–14 Feb.
                                                    E. 201. (13.) and (15.)
March.—A Continuation of the true Diurnall of all the Passages.
    28 Feb.–28 March. **E. 201.**
—— A Continuation of the true Diurnall of Passages. 7–14, 21–28
    March. **E. 201.**
—— A Continuation of the true Diurnall of Proceedings. 7–21 March.
                                                            E. 201.
—— A Perfect Diurnall. 28 Feb.–28 March. **E. 201.**
—— A True Diurnall. (*Bladen.*) 12 Feb.–8 March. **E. 201. (17.)**
——— A True Diurnall of the Passages in Parliament. 14–21 March.
                                                    E. 201. (29.) and (31.)
April.—A Perfect Diurnall. 28 March–4 April. **E. 202. (1.)**
May.—The Heads of all the Proceedings. 23–30 May. **E. 202. (2.)**
June.—Diurnall Occurrences. 30 May–13 June, 20–25 June. **E. 202.**
—— A Perfect Diurnall. 13–28 June. **E. 202.**
—— Remarkeable Passages. 30 May–6 June. **E. 202. (4.)**
—— Some Speciall Passages. 24 May–2 June, 13–28 June. **E. 202.**

1642.

July.—A Diurnall and Particular.   16–26 July   E. 202. (21.)

—— A Perfect Diurnall.   (*W. Cooke.*)   27 June–25 July.   E. 202.

—— A Perfect Diurnall.   (*J. Thomas.*)   11–25 July.   E. 202.

—— Some Speciall Passages.   3–26 July.   E. 202.

—— A True and Perfect Diurnall of . . . passages in Lancashire.
3–9 July.   E. 154. (39.)

Aug.—Certaine Speciall and Remarkable Passages.   22–26 Aug.
E. 114. (23.)

—— A Continuation of certaine Speciall and Remarkable Passages.   25–
30 Aug.   E. 114. (34.)

—— A Continuation of the True Diurnall.   8–15 Aug.   E. 202. (35.)

—— An Exact and True Diurnall.   (*W. Cook.*)   8–29 Aug.   E. 202.

—— A Perfect Diurnall.   (*T. Cook.*)   25 July–15 Aug.   E. 202.

—— A Perfect Diurnall.   (*J. Jonson.*)   25 July–1 Aug.   E. 202. (27.)

—— A Perfect Diurnall.   (*W. Cooke.*)   25 July–29 Aug.   E. 202.

—— A Perfect Diurnall.   (*T. Fawcet.*)   8–15 Aug.   E. 202.

—— A Perfect Diurnall of the Passages in Parliament.   (*Walter Cook
and Robert Wood.*)   8–22 Aug.   E. 239.

—— Some Speciall Passages from Hull, Anlaby and Yorke.   1 Aug.
E. 108. (33.)

—— Some Speciall Passages from London, Westminster, *etc.*   1–9 Aug.
E. 109. (35.)

—— Some Speciall and considerable Passages.   9–16 Aug.   E. 112

—— Speciall Passages from divers parts.   16–23 Aug.   E. 113.

—— Speciall Passages and Certain Informations.   23–30 Aug.   E. 114.

Sept.—A Continuation of certaine Speciall and Remarkable Passages.
30 Aug.–9 Sept., 16–29 Sept.   E. 116, 240.

—— A Continuation of True and Speciall Passages.   22–29 Sept.
E. 119. (6.)

—— England's Memorable Accidents.   12–26 Sept.   E. 240.

—— An Exact and True Diurnall.   29 Aug.–5 Sept.   E. 202. (42.)

—— A Perfect Diurnall.   (*W. Cooke.*)   29 Aug.–5 Sept.
E. 202. (41.)

—— A Perfect Diurnall of the Passages in Parliament.   (*William Cooke.*)
5–12, 19–26 Sept.   E. 239, 240.

—— A Perfect Diurnall of the Passages in Parliament.   (*Francis Coles.*)
5–26 Sept.   E. 239, 240.

—— A Perfect Diurnall of the Passages in Parliament.   (*Walter Cook
and Robert Wood.*)   29 Aug.–26 Sept.   .   E. 239, 240.

—— A Perfect Diurnall of the Passages in Parliament.   (*Walt. Cook and
Robert Wood.*)   12–26 Sept.   E. 240. (3.) and (11.)

1642.

Sept.—A Perfect Diurnall of the Passages in Parliament. (*Walt. Cook and Rob. Woodner.*) 12–19 Sept.   **E. 240. (6.)**

—— A Perfect Diurnall of the Proceedigns [*sic*] in Parliament. (*Robert Wood and Wil. Cooke.*) 12–19 Sept.   **E. 240. (4.)**

—— Remarkable Passages. 5–12 Sept.   **E. 202. (44.)**

—— Speciall Passages. 30 Aug.–27 Sept.   **E. 115, 116, 118.**

—— A True and Perfect Diurnall. 29 Aug.–6 Sept.   **E. 202. (43.)**

Oct.—A Continuation of Certaine Speciall and Remarkable Passages. (*F. Leach & F. Coles.*) 29 Sept.–1 Oct., 8–15, 24–28 Oct.

     E. 240, 121, 122, 124.

—— A Continuation of Certaine Speciall and Remarkable Passages. (*R. Wood.*) 3–12, 10–14 Oct.   **E. 121, 122.**

—— A Continuation of Certaine Speciall and Remarkable Passages. (*Marke Wallace.*) 10–14 Oct.   **E. 122. (14.)**

—— Englands Memorable Accidents. 26 Sept.–31 Oct.   **E. 240.**

—— A Perfect Diurnall. 26 Sept.–3 Oct.   **E. 202. (45.)**

—— A Perfect Diurnall of the Passages in Parliament. (*William Cooke.*) 3–10, 24–31 Oct.   **E. 240.**

—— A Perfect Diurnall of the Passages in Parliament. (*Francis Coles.*) 26 Sept.–17 Oct.   **E. 240.**

—— A Perfect Diurnall of the Passages in Parliament. (*Walter Cook and Robert Wood.*) 26 Sept.–24 Oct.   **E. 240.**

—— A Perfect Relation or Summarie of all the Declarations, *etc.* 19 Sept.–11 Oct.   **E. 240.**

—— Speciall Passages. 27 Sept.–25 Oct.   **E. 119, 121, 123, 124.**

—— The Weekly Intelligence. 11, 18 Oct.   **E. 121, 123.**

Nov.—A Collection of Speciall Passages. 2 Nov.   **E. 242. (2.)**

—— A Continuation of certain Speciall and Remarkable Passages. (*F. Leach & F. Coles.*) 31 Oct.–24 Nov.   **E. 242.**

—— A Continuation of certain Speciall and Remarkable Passages. (*John White.*) 4–24 Nov.   **E. 127, 242.**

—— A Continuation of certain Speciall and Remarkable Passages. (*I. Coule.*) 17–24 Nov.   **E. 242. (24.)**

—— Englands Memorable Accidents. 31 Oct.–28 Nov.   **E. 242.**

—— A Grand Diurnall of the Passages in Parliament. 21–28 Nov.

     E. 242. (29.)

—— A Perfect Diurnall of the Passages in Parliament. (*Francis Coles.*) 31 Oct.–7 Nov., 14–28 Nov.   **E. 242.**

—— A Perfect Diurnall of the Passages in Parliament. (*Walter Cook and Robert Wood.*) ˉ–28 Nov.   **E. 242.**

—— Speciall Passages. 25 Oct.–29 Nov.   **E. 126–128.**

1642.

Dec.—A Continuation of certain Speciall and Remarkable Passages.
(*F. Leach & F. Coles.*)　26 Nov.–1 Dec.　　　**E. 242, 244.**

—— A Continuation of certain Speciall and Remarkable Passages.
(*W. Cooke & R. Wood.*)　26 Nov.–30 Dec.　　**E. ¡242, 244.**

—— Englands Memorable Accidents.　28 Nov.–26 Dec.　**E. 242, 244.**

—— A Perfect Diurnall of the Passages in Parliament. (*Francis Coles.*)
28 Nov.–5 Dec., 12–26 Dec.　　　　　**E. 242, 244.**

—— A Perfect Diurnall of the Passages in Parliament. (*Walter Cook
and Robert Wood.*)　28 Nov.–12 Dec.　　**E. 242, 244.**

—— Speciall Passages.　29 Nov.–13 Dec., 20–27 Dec.

E. 129, 130, 83.

1643.

Jan.—Certaine Informations.　16–30 Jan.　　　**E. 85, 86.**

—— A Continuation of certain Speciall and Remarkable Passages.
(*F. Leach & F. Coles.*)　2–26 Jan.　　　**E. 244, 245.**

—— A Continuation of certain Speciall and Remarkable Passages.
(*W. Cook & R. Wood.*)　5–26 Jan.　　　**E. 245.**

—— The Daily Intelligencer.　30 Jan.　　　**E. 86. (37.)**

—— Englands Memorable Accidents.　26 Dec.–16 Jan.　**E. 244, 245.**

—— The Kingdomes Weekly Intelligencer.　27 Dec.–31 Jan.

E. 84–86.

—— Mercurius Aulicus.　1–28 Jan.　　**E. 244, 86, 245, 246.**

—— A Perfect Diurnall of the Passages in Parliament. (*Francis Coles.*)
26 Dec.–30 Jan.　　　　　**E. 244, 245.**

—— A Perfect Diurnall of the Passages in Parliament. (*Walter Cook
and Robert Wood.*)　26 Dec.–9 Jan., 16–30 Jan.　**E. 244, 245.**

—— Speciall Passages.　27 Dec.–31 Jan.　　**E. 84–86.**

Feb.—Certaine Informations.　30 Jan.–27 Feb.　　**E. 88–90.**

—— A Continuation of certain Speciall and Remarkable Passages.
(*F. Leach & F. Coles.*)　30 Jan.–23 Feb.　**E. 245, 89, 90.**

—— A Continuation of certain Speciall and Remarkable Passages.
(*W. Cook & R. Wood.*)　26 Jan.–23 Feb.　　**E. 245, 246.**

—— The Kingdomes Weekly Intelligencer.　31 Jan.–28 Feb.

E. 88–91.

—— Mercurius Aulicus.　29 Jan.–25 Feb.　　**E. 246.**

—— A Perfect Diurnall of the Passages in Parliament. (*Francis Coles.*)
30 Jan.–27 Feb.　　　　　**E. 246.**

—— A Perfect Diurnall of the Passages in Parliament. (*Walter Cook
and Robert Wood.*)　30 Jan.–13 Feb., 20–27 Feb.　**E. 246.**

—— Speciall Passages.　7–28 Feb.　　　**E. 89–91.**

1643.

March.—Certaine Informations. 6–27 March. **E. 93, 94.**

—— A Continuation of Certaine Speciall and Remarkable Passages. (*W. Cook & R. Wood.*) 23 Feb.–2 March, 9–16 March. **E. 246.**

—— A Continuation of Certaine Speciall and Remarkable Passages. (*F. Leach & F. Coles.*) 23 Feb.–9 March, 23–30 March.
E. 91, 92, 94.

—— The Kingdomes Weekly Intelligencer. 28 Feb.–28 March.
E. 92–94.

—— Mercurius Aulicus. 26 Feb.–25 March. **E. 86, 247, 92, 247.**

—— A Perfect Diurnall of the Passages in Parliament. (*Francis Coles.*) 27 Feb.–27 March. **E. 246, 247.**

—— A Perfect Diurnall of the Passages in Parliament. (*Walter Cook and Robert Wood.*) 27 Feb.–27 March. **E. 246, 247.**

—— Speciall Passages. 28 Feb.–14 March, 21–28 March. **E. 92–94.**

April.—Certaine Informations. 27 March–24 April.
E. 94, 95, 97, 99.

—— A Continuation of Certain Speciall and Remarkable Passages. (*W. Cook & R. Wood.*) 30 March–6 April, 13–20 April. **E. 247.**

—— A Continuation of Certain Speciall and Remarkable Passages. (*F. Leach & F. Coles.*) 30 March–27 April. **E. 95–99.**

—— The Kingdomes Weekly Intelligencer. 28 March–18 April.
E. 94, 96, 97.

—— Mercurius Aulicus. 26 March–29 April. **E. 96, 100, 101.**

—— A Perfect Diurnall of the Passages in Parliament. (*Francis Coles.*) 27 March–24 April. **E. 247.**

—— A Perfect Diurnall of the Passages in Parliament. (*Walter Cook and Robert Wood.*) 27 March–24 April. **E. 247.**

—— Speciall Passages. 4–25 April. **E. 96, 97, 99.**

May.—Certaine Informations. 24 April–1 May. **E. 100. (10.)**

—— A Continuation of certain Speciall and Remarkable Passages. (*W. Cook & R. Wood.*) 4–18 May. **E. 249.**

—— A Continuation of certain Speciall and Remarkable Passages. (*F. Leach & F. Coles.*) 27 April–25 May. **E. 100, 101, 104.**

—— The Kingdomes Weekly Intelligencer. 25 April–30 May.
E. 100–104.

—— Mercurius Aulicus. 30 April–27 May. **E. 102–105.**

—— Mercurius Civicus. 4–25 May. **E. 101–104.**

—— Mercurius Rusticus. 20, 27 May. **E. 103, 105.**

—— A Perfect Diurnall of the Passages in Parliament. (*Francis Coles.*) 24 April–29 May. **E. 247, 249.**

—— A Perfect Diurnall of the Passages in Parliament. (*Walter Cook and Robert Wood.*) 24 April–29 May. **E. 247, 249.**

—— Speciall Passages. 25 April–9 May, 16–30 May. **E. 100, 101, 104.**

1643.

June.—Certaine Informations. 12–26 June. **E. 55, 56.**

—— A Continuation of certain Speciall and Remarkable Passages.
25 May–16 June. **E. 104–106.**

—— A Coranto from beyond Sea. 9 June. **E. 105. (20.)**

—— The Kingdomes Weekly Intelligencer. 30 May–20 June.
E. 105, 55.

—— Mercurius Aulicus. 28 May–24 June. **E. 106, 55–59.**

—— Mercurius Civicus. 25 May–16 June. **E. 104–106.**

—— Mercurius Rusticus. 3, 10, 24 June. **E. 105, 106, 62.**

—— The Parliament Scout. 20–27 June. **E. 56. (7.)**

—— The Parliament Scouts Discovery. 9–15 June. **E. 106. (16.)**

—— A Perfect Diurnall of the Passages in Parliament. (*Francis Coles.*)
29 May–19 June. **E. 249.**

—— A Perfect Diurnall of the Passages in Parliament. (*Walter Cook
and Robert Wood.*) 29 May–19 June. **E. 249.**

—— Speciall Passages. 30 May–13 June. **E. 105.**

July.—Certaine Informations. 26 June–17 July. **E. 59, 60.**

—— A Continuation of certain Speciall and Remarkable Passages.
29 June–6 July, 20–27 July. **E. 59, 61.**

—— The Kingdomes Weekly Intelligencer. 27 June–25 July.
E. 59, 61.

—— Mercurius Aulicus. 25 June–29 July. **E. 60–64.**

—— Mercurius Civicus. 6–28 July. **E. 60–62.**

—— The Parliament Scout. 29 June–27 July. **E. 59–61.**

—— A Perfect Diurnall of some Passages in Parliament. 26 June–
31 July. **E. 249.**

—— Speciall Passages continued. 18–28 July. **E. 61, 62.**

—— Wednesday's Mercury. 19 July. **E. 61.**

—— The Weekly Accompt. 3–10 July. **E. 249. (25.)**

Aug.—A Continuation of certain Speciall and Remarkable Passages.
10–25 Aug. **E. 65.**

—— The Kingdomes Weekly Intelligencer. 25 July–15 Aug.
E. 63–65.

—— Mercurius Aulicus. 30 July–12 Aug. **E. 65.**

—— Mercurius Civicus. 27 July–17 Aug. **E. 63, 65.**

—— The Parliament Scout. 27 July–24 Aug. **E. 63–65.**

—— A Perfect Diurnall of some Passages in Parliament. 31 July–
28 Aug. **E. 249, 250.**

—— Wednesday's Mercury. 31 July–2 Aug. **E. 63.**

—— The Weekly Accompt. 27 July–3 Aug. **E. 63.**

1643.

Sept.—A Continuation of Certain Speciall and Remarkable Passages.
21–29 Sept.   **E. 250. (15.)**

—— Mercurius Aulicus.   27 Aug.–30 Sept.   **E. 67–70.**

—— Mercurius Britanicus.   5–26 Sept.   **E. 67, 68.**

—— Mercurius Civicus.   7–28 Sept.   **E. 67, 69.**

—— The Parliament Scout.   7–29 Sept.   **E. 67–69.**

—— A Perfect Diurnall of some Passages in Parliament.   28 Aug.–25 Sept.   **E. 250.**

—— The True Informer.   23–30 Sept.   **E. 67, 69.**

—— The Weekly Account.   28 Aug.–20 Sept.   **E. 250.**

Oct.—Certaine Informations.   16–30 Oct.   **E. 71, 73.**

—— A Continuation of certain Speciall and Remarkable passages.
29 Sept.–13 Oct.   **E. 69, 70.**

—— Mercurius Aulicus.   1–28 Oct.   **E. 71–75.**

—— Mercurius Britanicus.   26 Sept.–26 Oct.   **E. 69–73.**

—— Mercurius Civicus.   28 Sept.–26 Oct.   **E. 69–73.**

—— Mercurius Rusticus.   14 Oct.   **E. 70.**

—— New Christian Uses upon the Weekly True Passages.   7 Oct.
                                       E. 70. (5.)

—— The Parliament Scout.   29 Sept.–27 Oct.   **E. 69–71, 73.**

—— A Perfect Diurnall of some Passages in Parliament.   25 Sept.–30 Oct.   **E. 250, 252.**

—— The Scottish Dove.   13–27 Oct.   **E. 71, 72.**

—— The Scottish Mercury.   [13 Oct.]   **E. 70. (24.)**

—— The True Informer.   30 Sept.–28 Oct.   **E. 70–73.**

—— The Weekly Account.   27 Sept.–25 Oct.   **E. 70–72.**

—— The Welch Mercury.   21–28 Oct.   **E. 73.**

Nov.—Britanicus Vapulans.   4 Nov.   **E. 74. (23.)**

—— Certaine Informations.   30 Oct.–27 Nov.   **E. 75–77.**

—— The Compleate Intelligencer.   2–28 Nov.   **E. 74–77.**

—— Informator Rusticus.   27 Oct.–3 Nov.   **E. 74. (15.)**

—— The Kingdomes Weekly Intelligencer.   7–28 Nov.   **E. 75–77.**

—— The Kingdomes Weekly Post.   9–28 Nov.   **E. 75–77.**

—— Mercurius Aulicus.   29 Oct.–25 Nov.   **E. 75–77.**

—— Mercurius Britanicus.   26 Oct.–30 Nov.   **E. 74–77.**

—— Mercurius Civicus.   26 Oct.–30 Nov.   **E. 74–77.**

—— Mercurius Urbanus.   [9 Nov.]   **E. 75. (16.)**

—— The Parliament Scout.   27 Oct.–24 Nov.   **E. 74–76.**

—— A Perfect Diurnall of some Passages in Parliament.   30 Oct.–27 Nov.   **E. 252.**

—— Remarkable Passages.   1–25 Nov.   **E. 75, 77.**

—— The Scottish Dove.   27 Oct.–24 Nov.   **E. 73–76.**

1643.

Nov.—The True Informer.   28 Oct.–25 Nov.   **E. 74–77.**

—— The Weekly Account.   25 Oct.–29 Nov.   **E. 73–77.**

—— The Welch Mercury.   28 Oct.–11 Nov.   **E. 74, 75.**

Dec.—Certaine Informations.   27 Nov.–4 Dec., 18–23 Dec.   **E. 77, 79.**

—— The Kingdomes Weekly Intelligencer.   28 Nov.–26 Dec.

E. 77–79.

—— The Kingdomes Weekly Post.   28 Nov.–20 Dec.   **E. 77, 78.**

—— Mercurius Aulicus.   26 Nov.–30 Dec.   **E. 78–81.**

—— Mercurius Britanicus.   30 Nov.–28 Dec.   **E. 77–79.**

—— Mercurius Civicus.   30 Nov.–28 Dec.   **E. 77–79.**

—— Mercurius Rusticus.   16 Dec.   **E. 78.**

—— The Parliament Scout.   24 Nov.–29 Dec.   **E. 77–79.**

—— A Perfect Diurnall of some Passages in Parliament.   27 Nov.–
25 Dec.   **E. 252.**

—— Remarkable Passages.   9–29 Dec.   **E. 78, 79.**

—— The Scottish Dove.   24 Nov.–29 Dec.   **E. 77–79.**

—— The True Informer.   25 Nov.–30 Dec.   **E. 77–80.**

—— The Weekly Account.   29 Nov.–27 Dec.   **E. 77–79.**

1644.

Jan.—Certaine Informations.   1–8, 15–29 Jan.   **E. 81, 29, 30.**

—— A Continuation of certain Speciall and Remarkable Passages.
29 Dec.–17 Jan.   **E. 81, 29.**

—— The Kingdomes Weekly Intelligencer.   26 Dec.–28 Jan.

E. 81, 29, 30.

—— The Kingdomes Weekly Post.   10 Jan.   **E. 81.**

—— Mercurius, etc.   17 Jan.   **E. 29. (7.)**

—— Mercurius Aulicus.   31 Dec.–27 Jan.   **E. 29–32.**

—— Mercurius Britanicus.   28 Dec.–11 Jan.   **E. 81.**

—— Mercurius Civicus.   28 Dec.–25 Jan.   **E. 81, 29, 30.**

—— Occurrences of certain Speciall and remarkable Passages in Parliament.   5–19 Jan.   **.E. 81, 29.**

—— The Parliament Scout.   29 Dec.–26 Jan.   **E. 80, 81, 29, 30.**

—— A Perfect Diurnall of some Passages in Parliament.   25 Dec.–
29 Jan.   **E. 252.**

—— The Scottish Dove.   29 Dec.–26 Jan.   **E. 81, 29, 30.**

—— The Spie.   23–30 Jan.   **E. 31.**

—— The True Informer.   30 Dec.–20 Jan.   **E. 81, 29.**

1644.

Jan.—The Weekly Account. 27 Dec.–10 Jan., 17–31 Jan.

           E. 80, 81, 31.

Feb.—Anti-Aulicus. 6–8 Feb.   **E. 31. (17.) and (22.)**

—— Certaine Informations. 29 Jan.–21 Feb.   **E. 32, 33.**

—— A Continuation of certain Speciall and Remarkable Passages. 1–29
    Feb.   **E. 32–34.**

—— The Kingdomes Weekly Intelligencer. 28 Jan.–29 Feb.

           E. 32–34.

—— Mercurius, etc. 31 Jan.–6 Feb.   **E. 31. (18.)**

—— Mercurius Anglicus. 31 Jan.–20 Feb.   **E. 31, 33.**

—— Mercurius Aulicus. 28 Jan.–24 Feb.   **E. 33–37.**

—— Mercurius Britanicus. 29 Jan.–26 Feb.   **E. 31–34.**

—— Mercurius Civicus. 25 Jan.–29 Feb.   **E. 31–34.**

—— Mercurius Veridicus. 6–27 Feb.   **E. 33, 34.**

—— The Military Scribe. 20–27 Feb.   **E. 34.**

—— Occurrences of certain speciall and remarkable Passages in Parlia-
    ment. 17–23 Feb.   **E. 32, 34.**

—— The Parliament Scout. 2–25 Feb.   **E. 31–35.**

—— A Perfect Diurnall of some Passages in Parliament. 29 Jan.–
    26 Feb.   **E. 252.**

—— The Scottish Dove. 2–23 Feb.   **E. 32–34.**

—— The Spie. 30 Jan.–27 Feb.   **E. 31, 33, 34.**

—— The True Informer. 27 Jan.–3 Feb., 10–24 Feb. **E. 31, 33, 34.**

—— The Weekly Account. 7–29 Feb.   **E. 33, 34.**

March.—Britaines Remembrancer. 12–26 March.   **E. 38, 39.**

—— A Continuation of certain Speciall and Remarkable Passages. 1–28
    March.   **E. 36–39.**

—— The Kingdomes Weekly Intelligencer. 29 Feb.–21 March.

           E. 35–38.

—— Mercurius Aulicus. 25 Feb.–30 March.   **E. 37–42.**

—— Mercurius Britanicus. 26 Feb.–25 March.   **E. 35–39.**

—— Mercurius Britanicus. [Counterfeit.] 12–25 March. **E. 37–39.**

—— Mercurius Civicus. 29 Feb.–28 March.   **E. 35–39.**

—— Mercurius Veridicus. 27 Feb.–5 March, 12–26 March.

         E. 35, 38, 39.

—— The Military Scribe. 27 Feb.–26 March.   **E. 35, 37–39.**

—— Occurrences of certain speciall and remarkable Passages in Parlia-
    ment. 23 Feb.–1 March, 15–29 March.   **E. 35, 37–39.**

—— The Parliament Scout. 1–22 March.   **E. 36–38.**

—— A Perfect Diurnall of some Passages in Parliament. 4–25 March.

           E. 252.

1644.

March.—The Scottish Dove. 23 Feb.–29 March. **E. 35–39.**

—— The Spie. 27 Feb.–28 March. **E. 35, 37–39.**

—— The True Informer. 9–30 March. **E. 37–39.**

—— The Weekly Account. 29 Feb.–27 March. **E. 35, 37–39.**

April.—Britaines Remembrancer. 26 March–2 April. **E. 40. (11.)**

—— A Continuation of certain Speciall and Remarkable Passages. 28 March–25 April. **E. 40–43.**

—— The Kingdomes Weekly Intelligencer. 2–30 April. **E. 42–44.**

—— Mercurius Aulico-Mastix. 12 April. **E. 42. (15.)**

—— Mercurius Aulicus. 31 March–27 April. **E. 43–47.**

—— Mercurius Britanicus. 25 March–29 April. **E. 40–44.**

—— Mercurius Britanicus. [Counterfeit.] 25 March–1 April. **E. 40.**

—— Mercurius Civicus. 28 March–25 April. **E. 40–43.**

—— Mercurius Veridicus. 28 March–10 April. **E. 40, 42.**

—— The Military Scribe. 26 March–2 April. **E. 40.**

—— Occurrences of certain speciall and remarkable Passages in Parliament. 5–26 April. **E. 40, 42–44.**

—— The Parliament Scout. 28 March–26 April. **E. 40–44.**

—— A Perfect Diurnall of some Passages in Parliament. 25 March–29 April. **E. 252.**

—— The Scottish Dove. 29 March–26 April. **E. 40, 42–44.**

—— The Spie. 28 March–26 April. **E. 40, 42–44.**

—— A True and Perfect Journal. 16–30 April. **E. 42. (29.) and E. 44. (14.)**

—— The True Informer. 30 March–20 April. **E. 40, 42, 43.**

—— The Weekly Account. 27 March–24 April. **E. 40–43.**

May.—Cheife Heads of Each Dayes Proceedings in Parliament. 8–15 May. **E. 47. (25.)**

—— A Continuation of certain Speciall and Remarkable Passages. 25 April–2 May. **E. 44. (22.)**

—— A Diary or an Exact Journall. 24–31 May. **E. 252. (37.)**

—— An Exact Diurnall. 15–22 May. **E. 252. (34.)**

—— The Flying Post. 3–10 May. **E. 47. (4.)**

—— The Kingdomes Weekly Intelligencer. 30 April–28 May. **E. 46–50.**

—— Mercurius Aulicus. 28 April–25 May. **E. 49–50.**

—— Mercurius Britanicus. 29 April–27 May. **E. 46–50.**

—— Mercurius Civicus. 25 April–30 May. **E. 44–50.**

1644.

May.—Occurrences of certain speciall and remarkable Passages in Parliament. 3–24 May. **E. 45, 47, 49.**
—— The Parliament Scout. 2–30 May. **E. 44–49.**
—— A Perfect Diurnall of some Passages in Parliament. 29 April–27 May. **E. 252.**
—— Perfect Occurrences of Parliament. 24–31 May. **E. 252.**
—— The Scottish Dove. 26 April–31 May. **E. 45, 47, 49, 50.**
—— The Spie. 26 April–30 May. **E. 44, 46, 47, 49.**
—— The True Informer. 4–18 May. **E. 47, 49.**
—— The Weekly Account. 24 April–29 May. **E. 44, 46, 47, 49.**
—— The Weekly Newes. 1, 6, 13 May. **E. 44, 45, 47.**

June.—A Continuation of True Intelligence. 1, 17 June. **E. 50, 51.**
—— A Diary or an Exact Journall. 31 May–27 June. **E. 252.**
—— The Kingdomes Weekly Intelligencer. 28 May–25 June. **E. 50–52.**
—— Le Mercure Anglois. 7–13 June. **E. 1252.**
—— Mercurius Aulicus. 2–29 June. **E. 52–54, 2.**
—— Mèrcurius Britanicus. 27 May–31 [*sic*] June. **E. 50–53.**
—— Mercurius Civicus. 30 May–27 June. **E. 50–52.**
—— The Parliament Scout. 30 May–27 June. **E. 50–53.**
—— A Perfect Diurnall of some Passages in Parliament. 27 May–24 June. **E. 252.**
—— Perfect Occurrences of Parliament. 31 May–28 June. **E. 252.**
—— The Scottish Dove. 31 May–28 June. **E. 50–53.**
—— The Spie. 30 May–25 June. **E. 50–52.**
—— The True Informer. 25 May–8 June, 15–29 June. **E. 50, 52, 53.**
—— The Weekly Account 29 May–26 June. **E. 50–52.**

July.—A Continuation of certain Speciall and Remarkable Passages. 3–24 July. **E. 54, 2, 3.**
—— A Continuation of True Intelligence. 10, 27 July. **E. 2, 4.**
—— The Court Mercurie. 22 June–27 July. **E. 53, 54, 2, 3.**
—— A Diary or an Exact Journall. 4–25 July. **E. 254.**
—— The Kingdomes Weekly Intelligencer. 25 June–30 July. **E. 53, 54, 2, 3.**
—— Le Mercure Anglois. 4–25 July. **E. 1252.**
—— Mercurius Aulicus. 30 June–27 July. **E. 2–6.**
—— Mercurius Britanicus. 1–29 July. **E. 54, 2, 3.**
—— Mercurius Civicus. 27 June–25 July. **E. 54, 2, 3.**
—— The Parliament Scout. 4–25 July. **E. 54, 2, 3.**
—— A Perfect Diurnall of some Passages in Parliament. 24 June–29 July. **E. 252, 254.**

1644.

July.—Perfect Occurrences of Parliament.   28 June–26 July.
              E. 252, 254.
—— The Scottish Dove.   28 June–26 July.   **E. 53, 2, 3.**
—— The True Informer.   29 June–27 July.   **E. 53, 2, 3.**
—— The Weekly Account.   26 June–31 July. **E. 53, 54, 2, 3.**
Aug.—A Continuation of certain Speciall and Remarkable Passages
  24 July–1 Aug.   **E. 4. (1.)**
—— A Continuation of True Intelligence.   27 July–16 Aug.
              E. 6. (17.)
—— The Court Mercurie.   27 July–31 Aug.   **E. 4–7.**
—— A Diary or an Exact Journall.   25 July–29 Aug. **E. 254.**
—— The Kingdomes Weekly Intelligencer.   30 July–26 Aug. **E. 4–7.**
—— The London Post.   6–27 Aug.   **E. 4–7.**
—— Le Mercure Anglois.   25 July–29 Aug.   **E. 1252.**
—— Mercurius Aulicus.   28 July–31 Aug.   **E. 7–10.**
—— Mercurius Britanicus.   29 July–26 Aug.   **E. 4–7.**
—— Mercurius Civicus.   25 July–29 Aug.   **E. 4–7.**
—— The Parliament Scout.   25 July–29 Aug.   **E. 4–7.**
—— A Perfect Diurnall of some Passages in Parliament.   29 July–
  26 Aug.   **E. 254.**
—— Perfect Occurrences of Parliament.   26 July–30 Aug. **E. 254.**
—— The Scottish Dove.   26 July–30 Aug.   **E. 4, 6, 7.**
—— The True Informer.   27 July–31 Aug.   **E. 4, 6, 7.**
—— The Weekly Account.   31 July–7 Aug., 14–28 Aug. **E. 4, 6, 7.**
Sept.—The Court Mercurie.   31 Aug.–14 Sept.   **E. 8, 9.**
—— A Diary or an Exact Journall.   29 Aug.–26 Sept. **E. 254, 256.**
—— The Kingdomes Weekly Intelligencer.   26 Aug.–24 Sept.
              E. 8–10.
—— The London Post.   27 Aug.–24 Sept.   **E. 8–10.**
—— Le Mercure Anglois.   29 Aug.–26 Sept.   **E. 1252.**
—— Mercurius Aulicus.   1–28 Sept.   **E. 10–13.**
—— Mercurius Britanicus.   26 Aug.–30 Sept.   **E. 8–10.**
—— Mercurius Civicus.   29 Aug.–26 Sept.   **E. 8–10.**
—— The Parliament Scout.   29 Aug.–25 Sept.   **E. 8–10.**
—— A Perfect Diurnall of some Passages in Parliament.   26 Aug.–
  30 Sept.   **E. 254, 256.**
—— Perfect Occurrences of Parliament.   30 Aug.–27 Sept.
             E. 254, 256.
—— The Scottish Dove.   30 Aug.–27 Sept.   **E. 8–10.**
—— The True Informer.   31 Aug.–7 Sept., 21–28 Sept. **E. 8, 10.**
—— The Weekly Account.   28 Aug.–25 Sept.   **E. 8–10.**
Oct.—The Countrey Foot-Post.   2 Oct.   **E. 10. (29.)**
—— The Countrey Messenger.   4–11 Oct.   **E. 12. (14.)**

1644.

Oct.—The Court Mercurie. 25 Sept.–16 Oct.   **E. 11–13.**

——— A Diary or an Exact Journall. 26 Sept.–31 Oct.   **E. 256, 15.**

——— The Kingdomes Weekly Intelligencer. 24 Sept.–23 Oct.

                                              E. 10–13.

——— The London Post. 24 Sept.–23 Oct.   **E. 10–13.**

——— Le Mercure Anglois. 26 Sept.–31 Oct.   **E. 1252.**

——— Mercurius Aulicus. 29 Sept.–26 Oct.   **E. 14–17.**

——— Mercurius Britanicus. 30 Sept.–28 Oct.   **E. 11–15.**

——— Mercurius Civicus. 26 Sept.–31 Oct.   **E. 11–15.**

——— The Parliament Scout. 26 Sept.–31 Oct.   **E. 10, 12, 13–15.**

——— A Perfect Diurnall of some Passages in Parliament. 30 Sept.–28
     Oct.   **E. 256.**

——— Perfect Occurrences of Parliament. 27 Sept.–25 Oct.   **E. 256.**

——— Perfect Passages of each dayes Proceedings. 16–29 Oct.

                                           E. 256, 14.

——— The Scottish Dove. 27 Sept.–25 Oct.   **E. 11–14.**

——— The True Informer. 28 Sept.–26 Oct.   **E. 11–14.**

——— The Weekly Account. 25 Sept.–23 Oct.   **E. 10, 12, 13.**

Nov.—A Diary or an Exact Journall. 31 Oct.–28 Nov.

                                     E. 16–18, 256.

——— The Kingdomes Weekly Intelligencer. 29 Oct.–26 Nov. **E. 16–19.**

——— The London Post. 23 Oct.–26 Nov.   **E. 16–18.**

——— Le Mercure Anglois. 31 Oct.–28 Nov.   **E. 1252.**

——— Mercurius Aulicus. 27 Oct.–23 Nov.   **E. 18–22.**

——— Mercurius Britanicus. 28 Oct.–25 Nov.   **E. 16–19.**

——— Mercurius Civicus. 31 Oct.–28 Nov.   **E. 16–19.**

——— The Parliament Scout. 31 Oct.–28 Nov.   **E. 16–19.**

——— A Perfect Diurnall of some Passages in Parliament. 28 Oct.–25
     Nov.   **E. 256.**

——— Perfect Occurrences of Parliament. 25 Oct.–29 Nov.   **E. 256.**

——— Perfect Passages of each dayes Proceedings. 30 Oct.–27 Nov.

                                           E. 16–19.

——— The Scottish Dove. 25 Oct.–29 Nov.   **E. 15–19.**

——— The True Informer. 26 Oct.–30 Nov.   **E. 15–19.**

——— The Weekly Account. 30 Oct.–27 Nov.   **E. 16–19.**

Dec.—A Diary or an Exact Journall. 28 Nov.–19 Dec.   **E. 21.**

——— The Kingdomes Weekly Intelligencer. 26 Nov.–24 Dec.

                                      E. 20–22.

——— The London Post. 26 Nov.–31 Dec.   **E. 20–22.**

——— Le Mercure Anglois. 28 Nov.–26 Dec.   **E. 1252.**

——— Mercurius Britanicus. 2–30 Dec.   **E. 21, 22.**

——— Mercurius Civicus. 28 Nov.–26 Dec.   **E. 21, 22.**

1644.

Dec.—The Parliament Scout.   28 Nov.–26 Dec.   **E. 20–22.**
—— A Perfect Diurnall of some Passages in Parliament.   25 Nov.–30
    Dec.   **E. 256, 258.**
—— Perfect Occurrences of Parliament.   29 Nov.–27 Dec.

                                                       E. 256, 258.
—— The Scottish Dove.   29 Nov.–27 Dec.   **E. 21, 22.**
—— The True Informer.   7–28 Dec.   **E. 21, 22.**
—— The Weekly Account,   27 Nov.–25 Dec.   **E. 20–22.**

1645.

Jan.—A Diary or an Exact Journall.   26 Dec.–30 Jan.   **E. 23–26.**
—— The Kingdomes Weekly Intelligencer.   7–14, 21–28 Jan.

                                                       E. 24, 26.
—— The London Post.   31 Dec.–21 Jan.   **E. 23–25.**
—— Le Mercure Anglois.   26 Dec.–30 Jan.   **E. 1252.**
—— Mercurius Aulicus.   29 Dec.–26 Jan.   **E. 26, 27, 269, 270.**
—— Mercurius Britanicus.   29 Dec.–27 Jan.   **E. 23–26.**
—— Mercurius Civicus.   26 Dec.–30 Jan.   **E. 23–26.**
—— The Parliament Scout.   26 Dec.–30 Jan.   **E. 23–26.**
—— A Perfect Diurnall of some Passages in Parliament.   30 Dec.–27
    Jan.   **E. 258.**
—— Perfect Occurrences of Parliament.   27 Dec.–31 Jan.   **E. 258.**
—— Perfect Passages of each dayes Proceedings.   1–28 Jan.   **E. 24–26.**
—— The Scottish Dove.   27 Dec.–31 Jan.   **E. 23, 24, 26.**
—— The True Informer.   4–25 Jan.   **E. 24, 26.**
—— The Weekly Account.   25 Dec.–15 Jan.   **E. 23, 24.**
Feb.—A Diary, or an Exact Diurnall.   30 Jan.–27 Feb.   **E. 268–270.**
—— The London Post.   4–25 Feb.   **E. 27, 269, 270.**
—— Mercurius Aulicus.   26 Jan.–16 Feb.   **E. 270, 271.**
—— Mercurius Britanicus.   27 Jan.–24 Feb.   **E. 27, 269, 270.**
—— Mercurius Civicus.   30 Jan.–27 Feb.   **E. 268–270.**
—— The Monthly Account of February.   **E. 258. (30.)**
—— A Perfect Diurnall of some Passages in Parliament.   27 Jan.–24
    Feb.   **E. 258.**
—— Perfect Occurrences of Parliament.   31 Jan.–28 Feb.   **E. 258.**
—— Perfect Passages of each dayes Proceedings.   29 Jan.–25 Feb.

                                                       E. 268–270.
—— The Scottish Dove.   31 Jan.–28 Feb.   **E. 269, 270.**
—— The True Informer.   25 Jan.–22 Feb.   **E. 27, 269, 270.**

1645.

Feb.—The Weekly Account. 29 Jan.–25 Feb.   **E. 268–270.**

March.—A Diary, or an Exact Journall.   27 Feb.–27 March.

                                             E. 271–274.

—— The Generall Account of the Proceedings in Parliament. 31 March.

                                             E. 260. (6.)

—— The Kingdomes Weekly Intelligencer.   4–25 March.

                                             E. 273, 274.

—— The London Post.   4 March.   **E. 271. (9.)**

—— Le Mercure Anglois.   30 Jan.–6 March.   **E. 1252.**

—— Mercurius Aulicus.   23 Feb.–30 March.   **E. 273–278.**

—— Mercurius Britanicus.   24 Feb.–31 March.   **E. 271–274.**

—— Mercurius Civicus.   27 Feb.–27 March.   **E. 271–274.**

—— The Moderate Intelligencer.   27 Feb.–27 March.

                                         E. 271, 273, 274.

—— A Perfect Diurnall of some Passages in Parliament.   24 Feb.– 31 March.   **E. 258, 260.**

—— Perfect Occurrences of Parliament.   28 Feb.–28 March.

                                         E. 258, 260.

—— Perfect Passages of each dayes Proceedings.   26 Feb.–26 March.

                                         E. 271, 258, 260.

—— The Scottish Dove.   28 Feb.–28 March.   **E. 271, 273, 274.**

—— The Weekly Account.   25 Feb.–5 March, 12–25 March.

                                         E. 271, 274.

April.—A Diary, or an Exact Journall.   27 March–24 April.

                                            E. 276–278.

—— The Kingdomes Weekly Intelligencer.   25 March–29 April.

                                            E. 276–279.

—— Le Mercure Anglois.   6 March–24 April.   **E. 1252.**

—— Mercurius Aulicus.   6–13 April.   **E. 279. (8.)**

—— Mercurius Britanicus.   31 March–28 April.   **E. 276–279.**

—— Mercurius Civicus.   27 March–24 April.   **E. 276–278.**

—— Mercurius Veridicus.   12–26 April.   **E. 278, 279.**

—— The Moderate Intelligencer.   27 March–24 April.   **E. 276–278.**

—— A Perfect Declaration of the Proceedings in Parliament.   26 April.

                                            E. 260. (23.)

—— A Perfect Diurnall of some Passages in Parliament.   31 March– 28 April.   **E. 260.**

—— Perfect Occurrences of Parliament.   28 March–25 April.   **E. 260.**

—— Perfect Passages of each dayes Proceedings.   26 March–30 April.

                                            E. 260.

—— The Scottish Dove.   28 March–25 April.   **E. 276–278.**

—— The Weekly Account.   25 March–30 April.   **E. 276–279.**

—— The Weekly Postmaster.   15–29 April.   **E. 260.**

1645.

May.—A Diary or an Exact Journall.   24 April–29 May.
                                            E. 281–286.
—— The Exchange Intelligencer.   15–22 May.   **E. 284, 285.**
—— The Kingdomes Weekly Intelligencer.   29 April–27 May.
                                            E. 282, 284, 286.
—— Le Mercure Anglois.   24 April–29 May.   **E. 1252.**
—— Mercurius Britanicus.   28 April–26 May.   **E. 281–285.**
—— Mercurius Civicus.   24 April–29 May.   **E. 281–286.**
—— Mercurius Veridicus.   26 April–31 May.
                                            E. 281, 282, 284–286.
—— The Moderate Intelligencer.   24 April–29 May.
                                            E. 281, 282, 284–286.
—— The Parliaments Post.   6–27 May.   **E. 284, 285.**
—— A Perfect Diurnall of some Passages in Parliament.   28 April–
      26 May.   **E. 260.**
—— Perfect Occurrences of Parliament.   25 April–30 May.   **E. 260.**
—— Perfect Passages of each dayes Proceedings.   30 April–27 May.
                                            E. 260, 286.
—— The Scottish Dove.   25 April–30 May.   **E. 281, 282, 284–286.**
—— The True Informer.   26 April–31 May.   **E. 260, 284–286.**
—— The Weekly Account.   30 April–27 May.   **E. 282, 284, 285.**
—— The Weekly Postmaster.   29 April–6 May.   **E. 260.**

June.—A Diary or an Exact Journall.   29 May–26 June.
                                            E. 286–288.
—— The Exchange Intelligencer.   28 May–25 June.   **E. 286–288.**
—— The Kingdomes Weekly Intelligencer.   27 May–24 June.
                                            E. 286–288.
—— Le Mercure Anglois.   29 May–26 June.   **E. 1252.**
—— Mercurius Aulicus.   25 May–8 June.   **E. 288. (48.)**
—— Mercurius Britanicus.   26 May–30 June.   **E. 286–292.**
—— Mercurius Civicus.   29 May–26 June.   **E. 286–288.**
—— Mercurius Veridicus,   31 May–28 June.   **E. 286, 288, 290.**
—— The Moderate Intelligencer.   29 May–26 June.
                                            E. 286, 288, 289.
—— The Parliaments Post.   27 May–10 June, 17–24 June.
                                            E. 286, 287, 289.
—— A Perfect Diurnall of some Passages in Parliament.   26 May–
      30 June.   **E. 262.**
—— Perfect Occurrences of Parliament.   30 May–27 June.   **E. 262.**
—— Perfect Passages of each dayes Proceedings.   28 May–25 June.
                                            E. 262.
—— The Scottish Dove.   30 May–27 June.   **E. 286, 288, 289.**
—— The True Informer.   31 May–28 June.   **E. 286, 288, 290.**

1645.

June.—The Weekly Account. 28 May–4 June, 11–25 June.

E. 286, 288, 289.

July.—A Diary or an Exact Journall. 26 June–31 July.

E. 292, 262.

—— The Exchange Intelligencer. 25 June–18 July.   E. 292, 293.

—— The Kingdomes Weekly Intelligencer. 24 June–29 July.

E. 292–294.

—— Le Mercure Anglois. 26 June–31 July.   E. 1252.

—— Mercurius Aulicus. 13–20 July.   E. 296. (33.)

—— Mercurius Britanicus. 30 June–28 July.   E. 292–294.

—— Mercurius Civicus. 26 June–31 July.   E. 292–294.

—— Mercurius Veridicus, 28 June–26 July.   E. 292, 293.

—— The Moderate Intelligencer. 26 June–31 July.   E. 289–294.

—— The Parliaments Post. 24 June–29 July.   E. 290, 292–294.

—— A Perfect Diurnall of some Passages in Parliament. 30 June–
28 July.   E. 262.

—— Perfect Occurrences of Parliament. 27 June–25 July.   E. 262.

—— Perfect Passages of each dayes Proceedings. 25 June–30 July.

E. 262.

—— The Scottish Dove. 27 June–25 July.   E. 289–292.

—— The True Informer. 28 June–26 July.   E. 292, 293.

—— The Weekly Account. 25 June–30 July.   E. 290, 292–294.

Aug.—A Diary or an Exact Journall. 31 July–28 Aug. E. 262, 264.

—— Heads of some Notes of the Citie Scout. 19–28 Aug.

E. 297, 298.

—— The Kingdomes Weekly Intelligencer. 29 July–26 Aug.

E. 295–298.

—— Le Mercure Anglois. 31 July–28 Aug.   E. 1252.

—— Mercurius Aulicus. 10–17 Aug.   E. 298. (23.)

—— Mercurius Britanicus. 28 July–25 Aug.   E. 295–298.

—— Mercurius Civicus. 31 July–28 Aug.   E. 295–298.

—— Mercurius Veridicus. 26 July–11 Aug.   E. 294, 296.

—— The Moderate Intelligencer. 31 July–28 Aug.   E. 295–298.

—— The Parliaments Post. 29 July–26 Aug.   E. 295–298.

—— A Perfect Diurnall of some Passages in Parliament. 28 July–
25 Aug.   E. 262.

—— Perfect Occurrences of Parliament. 25 July–29 Aug.

E. 262, 264.

—— Perfect Passages of each dayes Proceedings. 30 July–27 Aug.

E. 262.

—— The Scottish Dove. 25 July–29 Aug.   E. 293–296.

—— The True Informer. 26 July–30 Aug.   E. 294, 296, 298.

—— The Weekly Account. 30 July–27 Aug.   E. 295–298.

1645.

Sept.—A Continuation of certaine Speciall and Remarkable Passages
19–26 Sept. **E. 303.**

—— A Diary or an Exact Journall. 28 Aug.–25 Sept. **E. 264, 300, 303.**

—— Heads of some Notes of the Citie Scout. 28 Aug.–30 Sept.
E. 300–303.

—— The Kingdomes Weekly Intelligencer. 26 Aug.–30 Sept.
E. 300–303.

—— Le Mercure Anglois. 28 Aug.–25 Sept. **E. 1252.**

—— Mercurius Aulicus. 31 Aug.–7 Sept. **E. 302. (14.)**

—— Mercurius Britanicus. 25 Aug.–29 Sept. **E. 300–303.**

—— Mercurius Civicus. 28 Aug.–25 Sept. **E. 300–303.**

—— Mercurius Veridicus. 6–27 Sept. **E. 301–303.**

—— The Moderate Intelligencer. 28 Aug.–25 Sept. **E. 299–303.**

—— The Parliaments Post. 26 Aug.–30 Sept. **E. 299–303.**

—— A Perfect Diurnall of some Passages in Parliament. 25 Aug.–
29 Sept. **E. 264.**

—— Perfect Occurrences of Parliament. 29 Aug.–26 Sept. **E. 264.**

—— Perfect Passages of each dayes Proceedings. 27 Aug.–24 Sept.
E. 264, 302.

—— The Scottish Dove. 29 Aug.–26 Sept. **E. 297–300.**

—— The True Informer. 30 Aug.–27 Sept. **E. 300–303.**

—— The Weekly Account. 27 Aug.–24 Sept. **E. 298, 300–302.**

Oct.—The City Scout. 30 Sept.–28 Oct. **E. 303–307.**

—— A Continuation of certaine Speciall and Remarkable Passages.
26 Sept.–31 Oct. **E. 303–307.**

—— A Diary or an Exact Journall. 25 Sept.–30 Oct. **E. 303–307.**

—— The Kingdomes Weekly Intelligencer. 30 Sept.–28 Oct.
E. 303–307.

—— The Kingdomes Weekly Post. 15–28 Oct. **E. 304–307.**

—— Le Mercure Anglois. 25 Sept.–30 Oct. **E. 1252.**

—— Mercurius Britanicus. 29 Sept.–27 Oct. **E. 303–307.**

—— Mercurius Civicus. 25 Sept.–30 Oct. **E. 303–307.**

—— Mercurius Veridicus. 27 Sept.–25 Oct. **E. 303–307.**

—— The Moderate Intelligencer. 25 Sept.–30 Oct. **E. 303–307.**

—— The Parliaments Post. 30 Sept.–7 Oct. **E. 304. (6.)**

—— A Perfect Diurnall of some Passages in Parliament. 29 Sept.–
27 Oct. **E. 264, 266.**

—— Perfect Occurrences of Parliament. 26 Sept.–31 Oct. **E. 264, 266.**

—— Perfect Passages of each dayes Proceedings. 24 Sept.–29 Oct.
E. 303, 304, 266.

—— The Scottish Dove. 26 Sept.–31 Oct. **E. 301–304.**

—— The True Informer. 27 Sept.–25 Oct. **E. 303–305, 307.**

—— The Weekly Account. 24 Sept.–29 Oct. **E. 303–305, 307.**

1645.
Nov.—The City Scout. 28 Oct.–11 Nov. **E. 308, 309.**
—— A Continuation of certain Speciall and Remarkable Passages.
31 Oct.–28 Nov. **E. 308–310.**
—— A Diary or an Exact Journall. 30 Oct.–27 Nov. **E. 308–310.**
—— The Kingdomes Weekly Intelligencer. 28 Oct.–25 Nov.
E. 308–310.
—— The Kingdomes Weekly Post. 4–28 Nov. **E. 308–310.**
—— Le Mercure Anglois. 30 Oct.–13 Nov. **E. 1252.**
—— Mercurius Britanicus. 27 Oct.–24 Nov. **E. 308–310.**
—— Mercurius Civicus. 30 Oct.–27 Nov. **E. 308–310.**
—— Mercurius Veridicus. 25 Oct.–29 Nov. **E. 308–310.**
—— The Moderate Intelligencer. 30 Oct.–27 Nov, **E. 308–310.**
—— A Perfect Diurnall of some Passages in Parliament. 27 Oct.–
24 Nov. **E. 266.**
—— Perfect Occurrences of Parliament. 31 Oct.–28 Nov. **E. 266.**
—— Perfect Passages of each dayes Proceedings. 29 Oct.–26 Nov.
E. 266.
—— The Scottish Dove. 31 Oct.–28 Nov. **E. 305–308.**
—— The True Informer. 25 Oct.–29 Nov. **E. 308–310.**
—— The Weekly Account. 29 Oct.–26 Nov. **E. 308–310.**
Dec.—The Citties Weekly Post. 15–29 Dec. **E. 313.**
—— A Continuation of certaine Speciall and Remarkable Passages.
28 Nov.–26 Dec. **E. 311–313.**
—— A Diary or an Exact Journall. 27 Nov.–24 Dec. **E. 311–313.**
—— The Kingdomes Scout. 25 Nov.–16 Dec. **E. 310, 311.**
—— The Kingdomes Weekly Intelligencer. 25 Nov.–30 Dec.
E. 310–313.
—— The Kingdomes Weekly Post. 2–16 Dec. **E. 310, 311.**
—— Le Mercure Anglois. 13 Nov.–25 Dec. **E. 1252.**
—— Mercurius Academicus. 22–27 Dec. **E. 313. (12.)**
—— Mercurius Britanicus. 24 Nov.–29 Dec. **E. 310–313.**
—— Mercurius Civicus. 27 Nov.–24 Dec. **E. 311–313.**
—— Mercurius Veridicus. 29 Nov.–20 Dec. **E. 311–313.**
—— The Moderate Intelligencer. 27 Nov.–25 Dec. **E. 311–313.**
—— A Perfect Diurnall of some Passages in Parliament. 24 Nov.–
29 Dec. **E. 266.**
—— Perfect Occurrences of Parliament. 28 Nov.–26 Dec. **E. 266.**
—— Perfect Passages of each dayes Proceedings. 26 Nov.–30 Dec.
E. 266.
—— The Scottish Dove. 28 Nov.–31 Dec. **E. 309–311, 314.**
—— The True Informer. 29 Nov.–20 Dec. **E. 311–313.**
—— The Weekly Account. 26 Nov.–31 Dec. **E. 311–313.**

1646.

Jan.—The Citties Weekly Post.　29 Dec.–27 Jan.　　　　E. 314–319.

—— A Continuation of certaine Speciall and Remarkable Passages.
2–30 Jan.　　　　　　　　　　　　　　　　　　E. 314–319.

—— A Diary or an Exact Journall.　25 Dec.–29 Jan.　E. 314–319.

—— The Kingdomes Weekly Intelligencer.　30 Dec.–27 Jan.
　　　　　　　　　　　　　　　　　　　　　　E. 314–319.

—— Le Mercure Anglois.　25 Dec.–29 Jan.　　　　　E. 1252.

—— Mercurius Academicus.　29 Dec.–31 Jan.　　　　E. 313–318.

—— Mercurius Britanicus.　29 Dec.–26 Jan.　　　　　E. 314–318.

—— Mercurius Civicus.　24 Dec.–29 Jan.　　　　　　E. 314–319.

—— Mercurius Veridicus.　30 Dec.–31 Jan.　E. 314, 316, 318, 319.

—— The Moderate Intelligencer.　25 Dec.–29 Jan.　E. 314–317, 319.

—— A Perfect Diurnall of some Passages in Parliament.　29 Dec.–26
Jan.　　　　　　　　　　　　　　　　　　　E. 266, 506.

—— Perfect Occurrences of Parliament.　26 Dec.–30 Jan.
　　　　　　　　　　　　　　　　　E. 266, 506, 317, 319.

—— Perfect Passages of each dayes Proceedings.　30 Dec.–27 Jan.
　　　　　　　　　　　　　　　　　　　E. 314–316. 319.

—— The Phoenix of Europe.　16 Jan.　　　　　　　E. 316. (11.)

—— The Scottish Dove.　31 Dec.–29 Jan.　　　　E. 315–317, 319.

—— The True Informer.　27 Dec.–31 Jan.　E. 314–316, 318, 319.

—— The Weekly Account.　31 Dec.–27 Jan.　　E. 314, 316, 319.

Feb.—The Citties Weekly Post.　27 Jan.–24 Feb.
　　　　　　　　　　　　　　　　　　E. 320, 322, 324.

—— A Continuation of certaine Speciall and Remarkable Passages.
30 Jan.–27 Feb.　　　　　　　　　　　　　E. 320–325.

—— A Diary or an Exact Journall.　29 Jan.–25 Feb.　E. 320–325.

—— The Kingdomes Weekly Intelligencer.　27 Jan.–24 Feb.
　　　　　　　　　　　　　　　　　　　　E. 320–324.

—— Le Mercure Anglois.　29 Jan.–12 Feb.　　　　E. 1252.

—— Mercurius Academicus.　2–28 Feb.　　　　　　E. 320–324.

—— Mercurius Britanicus.　26 Jan.–23 Feb.　　　E. 320–324.

—— Mercurius Civicus.　29 Jan.–26 Feb.　　　　E. 320–325.

—— Mercurius Veridicus.　31 Jan.–28 Feb.
　　　　　　　　　　　　　　　E. 320, 322, 324, 325.

—— The Moderate Intelligencer.　29 Jan.–26 Feb.
　　　　　　　　　　　　　　　　E. 320, 322, 325.

—— The Moderate Messenger.　27 Jan.–17 Feb.　E. 320, 322.

1646.

Feb.—A Perfect Diurnall of some Passages in Parliament. 26 Jan.–
23 Feb. **E. 506.**

—— Perfect Occurrences of Parliament. 30 Jan.–27 Feb.
E. 320, 322, 323, 325.

—— Perfect Passages of each dayes Proceedings. 27 Jan.–24 Feb.
E. 320, 322–324.

—— The Scottish Dove. 29 Jan.–11 Feb., 18–26 Feb.
E. 320, 322, 325.

—— The True Informer. 31 Jan.–28 Feb. **E. 320, 322, 324, 325.**

—— The Weekly Account. 27 Jan.–24 Feb. **E. 320, 322, 324.**

March.—The Citties Weekly Post. 24 Feb.–3 March. **E. 325.**

—— A Diary or an Exact Journall. 25 Feb.–5 March. **E. 327.**

—— The Kingdomes Weekly Intelligencer. 24 Feb.–31 March.
E. 327–330.

—— Le Mercure Anglois. 5–26 March. **E. 1252.**

—— Mercurius Academicus. 2–7, 16–21 March. **E. 325, 328.**

—— Mercurius Britanicus. 23 Feb.–30 March. **E. 325–330.**

—— Mercurius Civicus. 26 Feb.–26 March. **E. 326–329.**

—— Mercurius Veridicus. 28 Feb.–7 March. **E. 327.**

—— The Moderate Intelligencer. 26 Feb.–26 March. **E. 327–329.**

—— The Moderate Messenger. 24 Feb.–3 March. **E. 326.**

—— A Perfect Diurnall of some Passages in Parliament. 23 Feb.–
30 March. **E. 506.**

—— Perfect Occurrences of both Houses. 6–27 March. **E. 506.**

—— Perfect Occurrences of Parliament. 27 Feb.–6 March. **E. 327.**

—— Perfect Passages of each dayes Proceedings. 24 Feb.–4 March.
E. 325.

—— The Scottish Dove. 26 Feb.–28 March.
E. 325, 327, 328, 330.

—— The True Informer. 28 Feb.–7 March. **E. 327.**

—— The Weekly Account. 24 Feb.–18 March, 24–31 March.
E. 325, 327, 328, 330.

April.—The Kingdomes Weekly Intelligencer. 31 March–28 April.
E. 330–334.

—— Le Mercure Anglois. 26 March–30 April. **E. 1252.**

—— Mercurius Britanicus. 30 March–27 April. **E. 330–334.**

—— Mercurius Civicus. 26 March–30 April. **E. 330–335.**

—— The Moderate Intelligencer. 26 March–30 April.
E. 330, 332–334.

1646.

April.—A Perfect Diurnall of some Passages in Parliament. 30 March–
    27 April.   **E. 506.**

—— Perfect Occurrences of both Houses. 27 March–24 April.
                                              E. 506.

—— The Scottish Dove. 28 March–30 April.   **E. 330, 333–335.**

·—— The Weekly Account. 31 March–28 April.
                                     E. 330, 333, 334.

May.—Generall Newes from all Parts of Christendome. 6–26 May.
                                      E. 336–338.

—— The Kingdomes Weekly Intelligencer. 28 April–25 May.
                                      E. 336–338.

—— Le Mercure Anglois. 30 April–28 May.   **E. 1252.**

—— Mercurius Britanicus. 27 April–18 May.   **E. 335–337.**

—— Mercurius Civicus. 30 March–28 May.   **E. 336–339.**

—— The Moderate Intelligencer. 30 April–28 May.
                                    E. 336, 337, 339.

—— A Perfect Diurnall of some Passages in Parliament. 27 April–
    25 May.   **E. 509.**

—— Perfect Occurrences of both Houses. 1–29 May. **E. 337, 339.**

—— The Scottish Dove. 30 April–28 May.   **E. 336, 337, 339.**

—— The Weekly Account. 28 April–26 May.   **E. 336–338.**

June.—The Kingdomes Weekly Intelligencer. 25 May–30 June.
                                      E. 338–342.

—— Le Mercure Anglois. 28 May–25 June.   **E. 1252.**

—— Mercurius Civicus. 28 May–25 June.   **E. 339–341.**

—— The Moderate Intelligencer. 28 May–25 June.   **E. 339–341.**

—— The Packet of Letters. 26 June.   **E. 341. (21.)**

—— A Perfect Diurnall of some Passages in Parliament. 25 May–
    29 June.   **E. 511.**

—— Perfect Occurrences of both Houses. 29 May–26 June. **E. 511.**

—— The Scottish Dove. 28 May–24 June.   **E. 339–341.**

—— The Weekly Account. 26 May–24 June.   **E. 338, 340, 341.**

July.—The Kingdomes Weekly Intelligencer. 30 June–28 July.
                                      E. 344–346.

—— Le Mercure Anglois. 25 June–30 July.   **E. 1252.**

—— Mercurius Civicus. 25 June–30 July.   **E. 342–346.**

——- The Moderate Intelligencer. 25 June–30 July.
                                   E. 342, 344–346.

—— A Perfect Diurnall of some Passages in Parliament. 29 June–
    27 July.   **E. 511.**

——- Perfect Occurrences of both Houses. 26 June–31 July. **E. 511.**

—— The Scottish Dove. 24 June–31 July.
                                   E. 341, 342, 344–346.

1646.

July.—The Weekly Account. 24 June–28 July. **E. 342, 344, 345.**

Aug.—The Kingdomes Weekly Intelligencer. 28 July–25 Aug.

        E. 349–351.

—— Le Mercure Anglois. 30 July–27 Aug. **E. 1253.**

—— Mercurius Civicus. 30 July–27 Aug. **E. 349–351.**

—— The Moderate Intelligencer. 30 July–27 Aug. **E. 349–351.**

—— A Perfect Diurnall of some Passages in Parliament. 27 July–
31 Aug. **E. 511, 513.**

—— Perfect Occurrences of both Houses. 31 July–28 Aug. **E. 513.**

—— The Scottish Dove. 31 July–26 Aug. **E. 349, 350, 351.**

—— The Weekly Account. 28 July–25 Aug. **E. 349–351.**

Sept.—The Kingdomes Weekly Intelligencer. 25 Aug.–29 Sept.

        E. 353–355.

—— Le Mercure Anglois. 27 Aug.–24 Sept. **E. 1253.**

—— Mercurius Civicus. 27 Aug.–24 Sept. **E. 353–355.**

—— The Moderate Intelligencer. 27 Aug.–24 Sept. **E. 353–355.**

—— A Perfect Diurnall of some Passages in Parliament. 31 Aug.–
28 Sept. **E. 513.**

—— Perfect Occurrences of both Houses. 28 Aug.–25 Sept.

        E. 353–355.

—— The Scottish Dove. 26 Aug.–23 Sept. **E. 353–355.**

—— The Weekly Account. 25 Aug.–30 Sept. **E. 353–355.**

Oct.—A Continuation of Papers from the Scotts Quarters. 28 Oct.

        E. 359. (10.)

—— The Kingdomes Weekly Intelligencer. 29 Sept.–27 Oct.

        E. 356–358.

—— Le Mercure Anglois. 24 Sept.–29 Oct. **E. 1253.**

—— Mercurius Civicus. 24 Sept.–29 Oct. **E. 355–358.**

—— The Military Actions of Europe. 20–27 Oct. **E. 358.**

—— The Moderate Intelligencer. 24 Sept.–29 Oct.

        E. 355, 356, 358.

—— A Perfect Diurnall of some Passages in Parliament. 28 Sept.–
26 Oct. **E. 513.**

—— Perfect Occurrences of both Houses. 25 Sept.–30 Oct.

        E. 513, 358.

—— The Scottish Dove. 23 Sept.–28 Oct. **E. 355, 357, 3 58**

—— The Weekly Account. 30 Sept.–28 Oct. **E. 356–358.**

Nov.—A Continuation of Papers from the Scotts Quarters. 5–19 Nov.

        E. 360, 362.

—— The Kingdomes Weekly Intelligencer. 27 Oct.–24 Nov.

        E. 360–362.

—— Le Mercure Anglois. 29 Oct.–26 Nov. **E. 1253.**

—— Mercurius Candidus. 11–20 Nov. **E. 362. (21.)**

1646.

Nov.—Mercurius Civicus.   29 Oct.–19 Nov.   **E. 360–362.**
—— The Military Actions of Europe.   27 Oct.–2 Nov.   **E. 360.**
—— The Moderate Intelligencer.   29 Oct.–26 Nov.

E. 360, 362, 363.

—— A Perfect Diurnall of some Passages in Parliament.   26 Oct.–
30 Nov.   **E. 513.**

—— Perfect Occurrences of both Houses.   30 Oct.–27 Nov.

E. 360, 362, 363.

—— The Scottish Dove.   28 Oct.–26 Nov.   **E. 360–363.**
—— The Weekly Account.   28 Oct.–24 Nov.   **E. 360–362.**

Dec.—Diutinus Britanicus.   25 Nov.–8 Dec.   **E. 364, 265.**
—— The Kingdomes Weekly Intelligencer.   24 Nov.–29 Dec.

E. 364–368.

—— The London Post.   14–31 Dec.   **E. 369. (7.)**
—— Le Mercure Anglois.   26 Nov.–31 Dec.   **E. 1253.**
—— Mercurius Civicus.   3–10 Dec.   **E. 365.**
—— Mercurius Diutinus.   8–29 Dec.   **E. 366–368.**
—— The Moderate Intelligencer.   26 Nov.–31 Dec.

E. 363, 365–367, 369.

—— A Perfect Diurnall of some Passages in Parliament.   30 Nov.–
28 Dec.   **E. 513.**

—— Perfect Occurrences of both Houses.   27 Nov.–25 Dec.

E. 365–367.

—— The Scottish Dove.   [25 Dec. ?]   **E. 368.**
—— The Weekly Account.   24 Nov.–30 Dec.

E. 363, 365–367, 369.

1647.

Jan.—Englands Remembrancer.   14 Jan.   **E. 513. (33.)**
—— The Kingdomes Weekly Intelligencer.   29 Dec.–26 Jan.

E. 370–372.

—— The London Post.   31 Dec.–28 Jan.   **E. 371, 372.**
—— Le Mercure Anglois.   31 Dec.–28 Jan.   **E. 1253.**
—— Mercurius Candidus.   20–28 Jan.   **E. 372. (18.)**
—— Mercurius Diutinus.   29 Dec.–27 Jan.   **E. 370–372.**
—— The Moderate Intelligencer.   31 Dec.–28 Jan.   **E. 370–372.**
—— A Perfect Diurnall of some Passages in Parliament.   28 Dec.–
25 Jan.   **E. 513.**

—— Perfect Occurrences of both Houses.   25 Dec.–1 Jan.   **E. 370.**
—— Perfect Occurrences of every dayes Journall.   1–29 Jan.

E. 370–372.

1647.

Jan.—The Weekly Account. 30 Dec.–27 Jan.   **E. 370–372.**

Feb.—The Kingdomes Weekly Intelligencer. 26 Jan.–23 Feb.

          E. 373–377.

—— The London Post. 28 Jan.–26 Feb.   **E. 373–378.**

—— Le Mercure Anglois. 28 Jan.–25 Feb.   **E. 1253.**

—— Mercurius Diutinus. 27 Jan.–10 Feb.   **E. 373, 375.**

—— The Moderate Intelligencer. 28 Jan.–25 Feb.

          E. 373, 375, 377, 378.

—— The Moderate Messenger. 16–23 Feb.   **E. 377. (22.)**

—— A Perfect Diurnall of some Passages in Parliament. 25 Jan.–
22 Feb.   **E. 513.**

—— Perfect Occurrences of every dayes Journall. 29 Jan.–26 Feb.

          E. 373, 375, 377, 378.

—— The Weekly Account. 27 Jan.–22 Feb.   **E. 373, 375, 377.**

March.—The Kingdomes Weekly Intelligencer. 23 Feb.–30 March.

          E. 378–383.

—— Le Mercure Anglois. 25 Feb.–25 March.   **E. 1253.**

—— The Moderate Intelligencer. 25 Feb.–25 March. **E. 378, 379, 381.**

—— Perfect Diurnall of some Passages in Parliament. 22 Feb.–
29 March.   **E. 515.**

—— Perfect Occurrences of every dayes Journall. 26 Feb.–26 March.

          E. 378, 379, 381, 382.

—— The Perfect Weekly Account. 22–29 March.   **E. 434.**

—— The Weekly Account. 22 Feb.–31 March.

          E. 378, 379, 381, 383.

April.—The Kingdomes Weekly Intelligencer. 30 March–27 April.

          E. 383–385.

—— Le Mercure Anglois. 25 March–15 April.   **E. 1253.**

—— The Moderate Intelligencer. 25 March–29 April. **E. 383–385.**

—— A Perfect Diurnall of some Passages in Parliament. 29 March–
26 April.   **E. 515.**

—— Perfect Occurrences of every dayes Journall. 26 March–30 April.

          E. 383–385.

—— The Perfect Weekly Account. 29 March–26 April.

          E. 434–437.

—— The Weekly Account. 31 March–28 April.   **E. 383–385.**

May.—The Kingdomes Weekly Intelligencer. 27 April–25 May.

          E. 385–389.

—— The Moderate Intelligencer. 29 April–27 May.

          E. 386, 387, 390.

—— A Perfect Diurnall of some Passages in Parliament. 26 April–
31 May.   **E. 515.**

1647.

May.—Perfect Occurrences of every days Journall.   30 April–28 May.
E. 386, 387, 515, 390.

—— The Perfect Weekly Account.   (*B. Alsop.*)   28 April–26 May.
E. 386, 387, 389.

—— The Perfect Weekly Account.   (*No printer's name.*)   26 April–
10 May, 17–31 May.   **E. 438, 441, 443, 444.**

June.—The Kingdomes Weekly Intelligencer.   25 May–29 June.
E. 390–394.

—— Mercurius Britanicus.   17–24 June.   **E. 393. (30.)**

—— The Moderate Intelligencer.   27 May–24 June.
E. 390, 392, 393.

—— A Perfect Diurnall of some Passages in Parliament.   31 May–
28 June.   **E. 515.**

—— Perfect Occurrences of every dayes Journall.   28 May–25 June.
E. 515.

—— The Perfect Weekly Account.   (*B. Alsop.*)   26 May–30 June.
E. 390, 392–394, 396.

—— The Perfect Weekly Account.   (*No printer's name.*)   31 May–
28 June.   **E. 446, 447, 449, 450.**

July.—The Armies Post.   1–8 July.   **E. 397. (10.)**

—— A Continuation of certaine Speciall and Remarkable Passages.
9–30 July.   **E. 399, 400.**

—— A Diarie or an Exact Journall.   10–29 July.   **E. 398, 400.**

—— The Kingdomes Weekly Intelligencer.   29 June–27 July.
E. 397–400.

—— Le Mercure Anglois.   22–29 July.   **E. 1253.**

—— Mercurius Britanicus.   24 June–8 July.   **E. 395, 397.**

—— The Moderate Intelligencer.   24 June–29 July.
E. 395, 397–399, 400.

—— A Perfect Diurnall of some Passages in Parliament.   28 June–
26 July.   **E. 518.**

—— Perfect Occurrences of every dayes Journall.   25 June–30 July.
E. 515, 518.

—— A Perfect Summary of Chiefe Passages in Parliament.   19–26 July.
E. 518.

—— The Perfect Weekly Account.   30 June–29 July.   **E. 398–400.**

Aug.—A Continuation of certaine Speciall and Remarkable Passages.
30 July–28 Aug.   **E. 401–404.**

—— The Kingdomes Weekly Intelligencer.   27 July–31 Aug.
E. 400–405.

—— Le Mercure Anglois.   29 July–26 Aug.   **E. 1253.**

—— The Moderate Intelligencer.   5–26 Aug.   **E. 401, 402, 404.**

1647.

Aug.—The Moderne Intelligencer. 12–26 Aug. **E. 402, 404.**

—— A Perfect Diurnall of some Passages in Parliament. 26 July–
30 Aug. **E. 518.**

—— Perfect Occurrences of every dayes Journall. 30 July–27 Aug.
E. 518.

—— A Perfect Summarie of Chiefe Passages in Parliament. 26 July–
30 Aug. **E. 518.**

—— The Perfect Weekly Account. 29 July–31 Aug.
E. 401, 402, 404, 405.

Sept.—A Continuation of certaine Speciall and Remarkable Passages.
28 Aug.–17 Sept. **E. 404–407.**

—— The Kingdomes Weekly Intelligencer. 31 Aug.–28 Sept.
E. 406–409.

—— Le Mercure Anglois. 26 Aug.–30 Sept. **E. 1253.**

—— Mercurius Anti-Melanchollicus. 18–24 Sept. **E. 408. (9.)**

—— Mercurius Clericus. 25 Sept. **E. 408. (21.)**

—— Mercurius Melancholicus. 11–25 Sept. **E. 407, 408.**

—— Mercurius Melancholicus. [Counterfeit.] 11–24 Sept.
E. 407, 408.

—— Mercurius Morbicus. 20–27 Sept. **E. 407, 409.**

—— Mercurius Pragmaticus. 14–28 Sept. **E. 407, 409.**

—— The Moderate Intelligencer. 26 Aug.–30 Sept. **E. 405–409.**

—— The Moderne Intelligencer. 26 Aug.–30 Sept. **E. 405–409.**

—— A Perfect Diurnall of some Passages in Parliament. 30 Aug.–
27 Sept. **E. 518.**

—— Perfect Occurrences of every dayes Journall. 27 Aug.–24 Sept.
E. 518.

—— A Perfect Summarie of Chiefe Passages in Parliament. 30 Aug.–
27 Sept. **E. 518.**

—— The Perfect Weekly Account, 31 Aug.–15 Sept., 22–29 Sept.
E. 407, 409.

Oct.—The Kingdomes Weekly Intelligencer. 28 Sept.–26 Oct.
E. 410, 411.

—— Le Mercure Anglois. 30 Sept.–21 Oct. **E. 1253.**

—— Mercurius Anti-Pragmaticus. 12–28 Oct. **E. 411, 412.**

—— Mercurius Medicus. 11–15 Oct. **E. 410, 411.**

—— Mercurius Melancholicus. 25 Sept,–30 Oct. **E. 410–412.**

—— Mercurius Pragmaticus. 28 Sept.–26 Oct. **E. 410–412.**

—— The Moderate Intelligencer. 30 Sept.–28 Oct. **E. 410–412.**

—— A Perfect Diurnall of some Passages in Parliament. 27 Sept.–
25 Oct. **E. 518.**

—— Perfect Occurrences of every dayes Journall. 24 Sept.–29 Oct.
E. 518.

1647.

Oct.—A Perfect Summarie of Chiefe Passages in Parliament.   29 Sept.–
6 Oct.   **E. 518.**

——— The Perfect Weekly Account.   29 Sept.–26 Oct.   **E. 410, 411.**

Nov.—The Kingdomes Weekly Intelligencer.   26 Oct.–30 Nov.

E. 412–418.

——— Le Mercure Anglois.   21 Oct.–25 Nov.   **E. 1253.**

——— Mercurius Anti-Pragmaticus.   28 Oct.–25 Nov.   **E. 412–416.**

——— Mercurius Bellicus.   13–29 Nov.   **E. 416, 417.**

——— Mercurius Elencticus.   29 Oct.–26 Nov.   **E. 412–417.**

——— Mercurius Melancholicus.   30 Oct.–29 Nov.   **E. 412–417.**

——— Mercurius Populus.   11 Nov.   **E. 413. (14.)**

——— Mercurius Pragmaticus.   26 Oct.–30 Nov.   **E. 412–417.**

——— Mercurius Rusticus.   [12 Nov.]   **E. 414. (5.)**

——— The Moderate Intelligencer.   28 Oct.–25 Nov.

E. 412, 414, 416.

——— A Perfect Diurnall of some Passages in Parliament.   25 Oct.–
29 Nov.   **E. 520.**

——— Perfect Occurrences of every dayes Journall.   29 Oct.–26 Nov.

E. 520.

——— The Perfect Weekly Account.   26 Oct.–24 Nov.

E. 412, 413, 416.

Dec.—The Kingdomes Weekly Intelligencer.   30 Nov.–28 Dec.

E. 419, 421.

——— Le Mercure Anglois.   25 Nov.–30 Dec.   **E. 1253.**

——— Mercurius Melancholicus.   12–25 Dec.   **E. 420, 421.**

——— Mercurius Pragmaticus.   30 Nov.–28 Dec.   **E. 419, 421.**

——— Mercurius Rusticus.   [10 Dec.]   **E. 419. (19.)**

——— The Moderate Intelligencer.   25 Nov.–30 Dec.   **E. 419–421.**

——— A Perfect Diurnall of some Passages in Parliament.   29 Nov.–
27 Dec.   **E. 520.**

——— Perfect Occurrences of every dayes Journall.   26 Nov.–31 Dec.

E. 520.

——— The Perfect Weekly Account.   24 Nov.–29 Dec.

E. 417, 419, 421.

1648.

Jan.—Heads of Chiefe Passages.   5–25 Jan.   **E. 422, 423.**

——— The Kingdomes Weekly Intelligencer.   28 Dec.–25 Jan.

E. 421–423.

——— The Kingdomes Weekly Post.   29 Dec.–26 Jan.   **E. 422, 423.**

1648.

Jan.—Le Mercure Anglois. 30 Dec.–26 Jan. **E. 1253.**

—— Mercurius Anti-Pragmaticns. 13–27 Jan. **E. 423.**

—— Mercurius Dogmaticus. 6–13 Jan. **E. 422. (31.)**

—— Mercurius Elencticus. 29 Dec.–26 Jan. **E. 421–423.**

—— Mercurius Melancholicus. 1–29 Jan. **E. 422, 423.**

—— Mercurius Pragmaticus. 28 Dec.–25 Jan. **E. 421–423.**

—— The Moderate Intelligencer. 30 Dec.–27 Jan. **E. 422, 423.**

—— A Perfect Diurnall of some Passages in Parliament. 27 Dec.–31 Jan. **E. 520.**

—— Perfect Occurrences of every dayes Journall. 31 Dec.–28 Jan.
E. 520.

—— The Perfect Weekly Account. 29 Dec.–5 Jan. **E. 421.**

Feb.—The Kingdomes Weekly Account. 25 Jan.–30 [sic] Feb.
E. 425–429.

—— The Kingdomes Weekly Intelligencer. 25 Jan.–29 Feb.
E. 424–429.

—— The Kingdomes Weekly Post. 26 Jan.–22 Feb. **E. 425–428.**

—— Le Mercure Anglois. 27 Jan.–24 Feb. **E. 1253.**

—— Mercurius Anti-Pragmaticus. 27 Jan.–3 Feb. **E. 425.**

—— Mercurius Aulicus. 25 Jan.–24 Feb. **E. 425–429.**

—— Mercurius Bellicus. 7–29 Feb. **E. 427–429.**

—— Mercurius Dogmaticus. 27 Jan–3 Feb. **E. 425. (12.)**

—— Mercurius Elencticus. 26 Jan.–9 Feb. **E. 423–426.**

—— Mercurius Melancholicus. 29 Jan.–28 Feb. **E. 425–428.**

—— Mercurius Pragmaticus. 25 Jan.–29 Feb. **E. 424, 426–429.**

—— The Moderate Intelligencer. 27 Jan.–24 Feb.
E. 425–427, 429.

—— A Perfect Diurnall of some Passages in Parliament. 31 Jan.–28 Feb. **E. 520.**

—— Perfect Occurrences of every dayes Journall. 28 Jan.–25 Feb.
E. 520.

—— A Perfect Summarie of Chiefe Passages in Parliament. 12–19 Feb.
E. 428. (1.)

March.—The Kingdomes Weekly Account. 1–22 March.
E. 431–433.

—— The Kingdomes Weekly Intelligencer. 29 Feb.–28 March.
E. 431–433.

—— The Kingdomes Weekly Post. 22 Feb.–9 March. **E. 430, 431.**

—— Le Mercure Anglois. 24 Feb.–30 March. **E. 1253.**

—— Mercurius Aulicus. 24 Feb.–30 March. **E. 430–434.**

1648.
March.—Mercurius Bellicus.   29 Feb.–21 March.   E. 431–433.
—— Mercurius Elencticus.   23 Feb.–29 March.   E. 430–434.
—— Mercurius Insanus.   28 March.   E. 433.
—— Mercurius Melancholicus.   28 Feb.–27 March.   E. 430–433.
—— Mercurius Pragmaticus.   29 Feb.–28 March.   E. 431–433.
—— The Moderate Intelligencer.   24 Feb.–30 March.   E. 430–434.
—— Packets of Letters from Scotland.   18, 27 March.   E. 433, 434.
—— A Perfect Diurnall of some Passages in Parliament.   28 Feb.–
27 March.   E. 522.
—— Perfect Occurrences of every dayes Journall.   28 Feb.–31 March.
        E. 522.

April.—The Kingdomes Weekly Intelligencer.   28 March–25 April.
        E. 434–436.

—— Le Mercure Anglois.   30 March–27 April.   E. 1253.
—— Mercurius Academicus.   10–15 April.   E. 435. (32.)
—— Mercurius Anti-Mercurius.   4 April.   E. 438. (11.)
—— Mercurius Aulicus.   30 March–27 April.   E. 436, 437.
—— Mercurius Bellicus.   28 March–25 April.   E. 434–437.
—— Mercurius Brittanicus.   31 March–7 April.   E. 435. (3.)
— — Mercurius Critticus.   6–13 April.   E. 435. (23.)
—— Mercurius Elencticus.   29 March–26 April.   E. 434–437.
—— Mercurius Insanus.   24 April.   E. 436.
—— Mercurius Melancholicus.   27 March–24 April.   E. 434–436.
—— Mercurius Pragmaticus.   28 March–25 April.
        E. 434, 435, 437.

—— Mercurius Veridicus.   14–27 April.   E. 436, 437.
—— The Moderate Intelligencer.   30 March–27 April.   E. 434–437.
—— Packets of Letters from Scotland.   3–24 April.   E. 434–436.
—— A Perfect Diurnall of some Passages in Parliament.   27 March–
24 April.   E. 522.
—— Perfect Occurrences of every dayes Journall.   31 March–28 April.
        E. 522.
—— The Perfect Weekly Account.   12–26 April.   E. 435–437.

May.—The Kingdomes Weekly Intelligencer.   25 April–30 May.
        E. 436–444.

—— Le Mercure Anglois.   27 April–25 May.   E. 1253.
—— Mercurius Aulicus.   11–18 May.   E. 443.
—— Mercurius Bellicus.   25 April–2 May, 9–30 May.
        E. 437, 443, 444.
—— Mercurius Britanicus.   16 May, 16–30 May.   E. 442–444.
— —- Mercurius Critticus.   27 April–4 May.   E. 438. (12.)
—— Mercurius Elencticus.   26 April–31 May.   E. 438–444.

1648.

May.—Mercurius Gallicus. 12 May.   **E. 441. (35.)**
—— Mercurius Honestus. 19, 25 May.   **E. 443, 444.**
—–— Mercurius Melancholicus. 24 April–29 May.   **E. 437–444.**
—— Mercurius Poeticus. 5–13 May.   **E. 442. (4.)**
—— Mercurius Pragmaticus. 25 April–30 May.
                                          E. 437, 440, 442–444.
—— Mercurius Publicus. [16–29 May.]   **E. 442–445.**
—— Mercurius Urbanicus. 2–9 May.   **E. 441.**
—— Mercurius Veridicus. 27 April–8 May.   **E. 440.**
—— The Moderate Intelligencer. 27 April–25 May.
                                          E. 438, 441, 443, 444.
—— Packets of Letters from Scotland. 1–29 May.
                                          E. 437, 440, 442, 443, 445.
—— The Parliament Kite. 16 May.   **E. 443. (6.)**
—— A Perfect Diurnall of some Passages in Parliament. 24 April–
    29 May.   **E. 522.**
—— Perfect Occurences of every dayes Journall. 28 April–26 May.
                                                        E. 522.

June.—The Kingdomes Weekly Intelligencer. 30 May–27 June.
                                                        E. 446–449.
—— Le Mercure Anglois. 25 May–29 June.   **E. 1253.**
—— Mercurius Bellicus. 30 May–6 June, 13–27 June. **E. 446–449.**
—— Mercurius Britanicus. 30 May–27 June.   **E. 446–449.**
—— Mercurius Censorius. 1–20 June.   **E. 445–447.**
—–— Mercurius Domesticus. 5 June.   **E. 445. (41.)**
—–— Mercurius Elencticus. 31 May–28 June.   **E. 446–450.**
—— Mercurius Melancholicus. 29 May–26 June.   **E. 444–449.**
—— Mercurius Pragmaticus. 6–20 June.   **E. 447.**
—— Mercurius Psitacus. 14–26 June.   **E. 449.**
—— The Moderate. 22–29 June.   **E. 450.**
—— The Moderate Intelligencer. 25 May–29 June. **E. 444, 446–450.**
—— Packets of Letters from Scotland. 5–26 June.
                                          E. 446, 447, 449.
—— The Parliament Kite. 1–29 June.
                                          E. 444, 446, 447, 449, 450.
—— The Parliaments Scrich-Owle. 29 June.   **E. 450. (5.)**
—— The Parliaments Vulture. 22 June.   **E. 449. (16.)**
—— A Perfect Diary of Passages of the Kings Army. 19–26 June.
                                                        E. 449. (31.)
—— A Perfect Diurnall of some Passages in Parliament. 29 May–
    26 June.   **E. 522.**
—— Perfect Occurrences of every dayes Journall. 26 May–26 June.
                                                        E. 522.

1648.
July.—The Kingdomes Weekly Intelligencer.   27 June–11 July, 18–
    25 July.   **E. 451, 452, 454.**
—— Le Mercure Anglois.   29 June–27 July.   **E. 1253.**
—— Mercurius Bellicus.   27 June–26 July.   **E. 451–454.**
—— Mercurius Britanicus.   27 June–25 July.   **E. 451–454.**
—— Mercurius Elencticus.   28 June–19 July.   **E. 451–453.**
—— Mercurius Melancholicus.   26 June–31 July.   **E. 450–455.**
—— Mercurius Melancholicus.   [Counterfeit.]   26 June–3 July, 14–21,
    24–31 July.   **E. 450–455.**
—— Mercurius Pragmaticus.   27 June–25 July.   **E. 451, 453, 454.**
—— Mercurius Psitacus.   26 June–24 July.   **E. 450–453.**
—— Mercurius Scoticus.   [19 July.]   **E. 453. (25.)**
—— The Moderate.   29 June–25 July.   **E. 451–454.**
—— The Moderate Intelligencer.   29 June–27 July.   **E. 451–454.**
—— Packets of Letters from Scotland.   4–31 July.   **E. 451–454.**
—— The Parliament Kite.   13–27 July.   **E. 452–454.**
—— The Parliaments Scrich-Owle.   7, 14 July.   **E. 451, 452.**
—— A Perfect Diurnall of Some Passages in Parliament.   26 June–
    31 July.   **E. 525.**
—— Perfect Occurrences of every dayes Journall.   26 June–28 July.
                                                      E. 525.
—— The Perfect Weekly Account.   28 June–25 July.   **E. 451, 452, 454.**
—— The Royall Diurnall.   25–31 July.   **E. 455.**
Aug.—The Colchester Spie.   10, 17 Aug.   **E. 458, 459.**
—— Hermes Straticus.   17 Aug.   **E. 459. (7.)**
—— The Kingdomes Weekly Intelligencer.   25 July–29 Aug.
                                                  E. 456–461.
—— Le Mercure Anglois.   27 July–31 Aug.   **E. 1253.**
—— Mercurius Anglicus.   27 July–3 Aug.   **E. 456. (22.)**
—— Mercurius Aquaticus.   4–11 Aug.   **E. 458. (1.)**
—— Mercurius Aulicus.   7–28 Aug.   **E. 457–461.**
—— Mercurius Britanicus.   25 July–16 Aug.   **E. 454–459.**
—— Mercurius Elencticus.   19 July–30 Aug.   **E. 456–461.**
—— Mercurius Fidelicus.   17–31 Aug.   **E. 460, 461.**
—— Mercurius Melancholicus.   31 July–28 Aug.   **E. 457–460.**
—— Mercurius Pragmaticus.   25 July–29 Aug.
                                        E. 456–458, 460, 461.
—— The Moderate.   25 July–29 Aug.   **E. 456–458, 460, 461.**
—— The Moderate Intelligencer.   27 July–24 Aug.
                                        E. 456, 457, 459–461.

1648.

Aug.—Packets of Letters from Scotland. 7–28 Aug.

E. 456, 457, 459–461.

—— The Parliament Kite. 3–31 Aug. **E. 456, 457, 459–461.**

—— A Perfect Diurnall of some Passages in Parliament. 31 July–28 Aug. **E. 525.**

—— Perfect Occurrences of every dayes Journall. 28 July–25 Aug.

E. 525.

—— The Perfect Weekly Account. 25 July–30 Aug.

E. 456, 457, 459–461.

—— The Royall Diurnall. 31 July–29 Aug.

E. 457, 458, 460, 461.

Sept.—The Kingdomes Weekly Intelligencer. 29 Aug.–26 Sept.

E. 462, 464.

—— Le Mercure Anglois. 31 Aug.–28 Sept. **E. 1253.**

—— Mercurius Anti-Mercurius. 12–19 Sept. **E. 464.**

—— Mercurius Elencticus. 30 Aug.–27 Sept. **E. 462–464.**

—— Mercurius Melancholicus. 28 Aug.–25 Sept. **E. 462–464.**

—— Mercurius Pragmaticus. 5–26 Sept. **E. 462, 464.**

—— The Moderate. 29 Aug.–26 Sept. **E. 462, 464.**

—— The Moderate Intelligencer. 31 Aug.–28 Sept. **E. 462–465.**

—— Packets of Letters from Scotland. 4–25 Sept. **E. 462–465.**

—— The Parliament Porter. 4–25 Sept. **E. 462–465.**

—— A Perfect Diurnall of some Passages in Parliament. 28 Aug.–25 Sept. **E. 526.**

—— Perfect Occurrences of every dayes Journall. 25 Aug.–29 Sept.

E. 526.

—— The Perfect Weekly Account. 30 Aug.–20 Sept. **E. 462–464.**

—— The Treaty Traverst. 26 Sept. **E. 464.**

Oct.—The Kingdomes Weekly Intelligencer. 26 Sept.–31 Oct.

E. 464–469.

—— Le Mercure Anglois. 5–26 Oct. **E. 1253.**

—— Mercurio Volpone. 28 Sept.–12 Oct. **E. 465, 467.**

—— Mercurius Anti-Mercurius. 26 Sept.–2 Oct. **E. 465.**

—— Mercurius Elencticus. 27 Sept.–31 Oct. **E. 464–469.**

—— Mercurius Melancholicus. 25 Sept.–9 Oct. **E. 465, 466.**

—— Mercurius Militaris. 10–31 Oct. **E. 467–469.**

—— Mercurius Pragmaticus. 26 Sept.–31 Oct. **E. 465–469.**

—— The Moderate. 26 Sept.–31 Oct. **E. 465, 467–469.**

—— The Moderate Intelligencer. 28 Sept.–26 Oct. **E. 465, 467–469.**

—— Packets of Letters from Scotland. 3–31 Oct.

E. 465, 468, 469.

—— A Perfect Diurnall of some Passages in Parliament. 25 Sept.–30 Oct. **E. 526.**

1648.

Oct.—Perfect Occurrences of every dayes Journall.   29 Sept.–27 Oct.

E. 526.

—— The Perfect Weekly Account.   27 Sept.–25 Oct.

E. 465, 467, 468.

Nov.—The Kingdomes Weekly Intelligencer.   31 Oct.–28 Nov.

E. 469–473.

—— Martin Nonsence.   20–27 Nov.   E. 526. (33.)

—— Le Mercure Anglois.   26 Oct.–30 Nov.   E. 1253.

—— Mercurius Elencticus.   31 Oct.–29 Nov.   E. 470–473.

—— Mercurius Melancholicus.   14–21 Nov.   E. 472.

—— Mercurius Militaris.   31 Oct.–21 Nov.   E. 470–473.

—— Mercurius Pragmaticus.   31 Oct.–28 Nov.   E. 470–473.

—— The Moderate.   31 Oct.–28 Nov.   E. 470, 472, 473.

—— The Moderate Intelligencer.   26 Oct.–30 Nov.

E. 470, 472–474.

—— Packets of Letters from Scotland.   7–28 Nov.   E. 470, 472–474.

—— A Perfect Diurnall of some Passages in Parliament.   30 Oct.–
27 Nov.   E. 526.

—— Perfect Occurrences of every dayes Journall.   27 Oct.–24 Nov.

E. 526.

—— The Perfect Weekly Account.   25 Oct.–29 Nov.

E. 469, 470, 472–474.

—— The True Informer, or, Monthly Mercury.   8 Nov.   E. 526. (28.)

Dec.—A Declaration, collected out of the Journalls of Parliament.
29 Nov.–20 Dec.   E. 475–477.

—— Heads of a Diarie.   20–27 Dec.   E. 536. (9.)

—— The Kingdomes Weekly Intelligencer.   28 Nov.–26 Dec.

E. 475, 476, 536.

—— Le Mercure Anglois.   30 Nov.–14 Dec.   E. 1253.

—— Mercurius Elencticus.   29 Nov.–26 Dec.   E. 475–477.

—— Mercurius Impartialis.   5–12 Dec.   E. 476. (3.)

—— Mercurius Pragmaticus.   28 Nov.–26 Dec.   E. 476, 477.

—— The Moderate.   28 Nov.–26 Dec.   E. 475–477, 536.

—— The Moderate Intelligencer.   30 Nov.–28 Dec.

E. 475–477, 536.

—— A Perfect Diurnall of some Passages in Parliament.   27 Nov.–
25 Dec.   E. 526.

—— Perfect Occurrences of every dayes Journall.   24 Nov.–30 Dec.

E. 526.

—— The Perfect Weekly Account.   29 Nov.–27 Dec.

E. 475–477, 536.

1649.

Jan.—The Armies Modest Intelligencer. 19–26 Jan. **E. 540. (7.)**

—— Heads of a Diarie. 27 Dec.–9 Jan. **E. 536, 537.**

—— The Kingdomes Weekly Intelligencer. 26 Dec.–30 Jan.
E. 536–540.

—— Mercurius Elencticus. 26 Dec.–9 Jan. **E. 536, 537.**

—— Mercurius Melancholicus. 25 Dec.–12 Jan. **E. 536–538.**

—— Mercurius Pragmaticus. 26 Dec.–30 Jan. **E. 537, 538, 540.**

—— The Moderate. 26 Dec.–30 Jan. **E. 536–540.**

—— The Moderate Intelligencer. 28 Dec.–25 Jan. **E. 537, 539.**

—— A Perfect Diurnall of some Passages in Parliament. 25 Dec.–
29 Jan. **E. 527.**

—— Perfect Occurrences of every dayes Journall. 30 Dec.–26 Jan
E. 527.

—— A Perfect Summary of Exact Passages. 22–29 Jan. **E. 527.**

—— The Perfect Weekly Account. 27 Dec.–31 Jan.
E. 536–538, 540.

Feb.—The Armies Modest Intelligencer. 26 Jan.–8 Feb. **E. 541.**

—— The Armies Weekly Intelligencer. 8–22 Feb. **E. 543, 545.**

—— The Kingdoms Faithfull Scout. 26 Jan.–2 Feb. **E. 541. (5.)**

—— The Kingdoms Faithfull and Impartiall Scout. 2–23 Feb.
E. 542–545.

—— The Kingdomes Weekly Intelligencer. 30 Jan.–27 Feb.
E. 541–545.

—— Mercurius Elencticus. 6–13, 21–28 Feb. **E. 542, 545.**

—— Mercurius Pragmaticus. 13–27 Feb. **E. 543, 545.**

—— The Moderate. 30 Jan.–27 Feb. **E. 541–543, 545.**

—— The Moderate Intelligencer. 25 Jan.–22 Feb.
E. 541, 542, 545.

—— A Perfect Diurnall of some Passages in Parliament. 29 Jan.–
26 Feb. **E. 527.**

—— Perfect Occurrences of every dayes Journall. 26 Jan.–23 Feb.
E. 527.

—— A Perfect Summary of Exact Passages. 29 Jan.–26 Feb. **E. 527.**

—— The Perfect Weekly Account. 31 Jan.–28 Feb.
E. 541, 543, 545.

1649.
March.—The Impartiall Intelligencer.   28 Feb.–28 March.
                                          E. 546–548.
—— The Kingdoms Faithfull Scout.   23 Feb.–2 March.   **E. 527.**
—— The Kingdoms Faithfull and Impartiall Scout.   2–30 March.
                                          E. 527.
—— The Kingdomes Weekly Intelligencer.   27 Feb.–27 March.
                                          E. 546–548.
—— Mercurius Pragmaticus.   27 Feb.–27 March.   **E. 546–547.**
—— The Moderate.   27 Feb.–27 March.   **E. 546, 547.**
—— The Moderate Intelligencer.   22 Feb.–29 March.   **E. 545–548.**
—— A Perfect Diurnall of some Passages in Parliament.   26 Feb.–
    26 March.   **E. 527, 529.**
—— Perfect Occurrences of every dayes Journall.   23 Feb.–30 March.
                                          E. 577, 529.
—— A Perfect Summary of Exact Passages.   26 Feb.–26 March.
                                          E. 527, 529.
—— The Perfect Weekly Account.   28 Feb.–28 March.   **E. 546, 547.**
April.—Continued Heads of Perfect Passages in Parliament.   13–27
    April.   **E. 529.**
—— England's Moderate Messenger.   23–30 April.   **E. 530.**
—— The Impartiall Intelligencer.   28 March–25 April.
                                          E. 550, 551, 529.
—— The Kingdoms Faithfull and Impartiall Scout.   30 March–27 April.
                                          E. 529.
—— The Kingdomes Weekly Intelligencer.   27 March–24 April.
                                          E. 548–551.
—— The Man in the Moon.   16–30 April.   **E. 550–552.**
—— Mercurius Elencticus.   4–11 April.   **E. 550.**
——– Mercurius Militaris.   17–24 April.   **E. 551. (13.)**
—— Mercurius Philo-Monarchicus.   10–17 April.   **E. 550.**
—— Mercurius Pragmaticus.   27 March–24 April.
                                          E. 548, 550, 551.
—— The Moderate.   27 March–24 April.   **E. 548, 550, 551.**
—— The Moderate Intelligencer.   29 March–26 April.
                                          E. 548, 550–552.
—— A Modest Narrative of Intelligence.   31 March–28 April.
                                          E. 550–552.
—— A Perfect Diurnall of some Passages in Parliament.   26 March–
    30 April.   **E. 529.**
—— Perfect Occurrences of every dayes Journall.   30 March–27 April.
                                          E. 529.
—— A Perfect Summary of an Exact Diarye.   27 March–30 April.
                                          E. 529.

1649.

April.—The Perfect Weekly Account. 28 March–25 April.

E. 548, 550–552.

May.—Continued Heads of Perfect Passages in Parliament. 27 April–
18 May. E. 529, 530.

—— Englands Moderate Messenger. 30 April–21 May. E. 530.

—— The Impartiall Intelligencer. 25 April–30 May. E. 529, 530.

—— The Kingdoms Faithfull and Impartiall Scout. 27 April–25 May.

E. 529, 530.

—— The Kingdomes Weekly Intelligencer. 24 April–29 May.

E. 552–556.

—— The Man in the Moon. 30 April–7 May, 14–30 May. E. 554–556.

—— Mercurius Brittanicus. 24 April–29 May. E. 552–556.

—— Mercurius Elencticus. 24 April–28 May. E. 552–556.

—— Mercurius Elencticus, for King Charles II. 30 April–14 May.

E. 554, 555.

—— Mercurius Melancholicus. 24–31 May. E. 557. (8.)

—— Mercurius Militaris, or the People's Scout. 8 May. E. 554.

—— Mercurius Militaris, or Times only Truth-teller. 22–29 May.

E. 556. (22.)

—— Mercurius Pacificus. 17–31 May. E. 556, 557.

—— Mercurius Philo-Monarchicus. 14–21 May. E. 555.

—— Mercurius Pragmaticus. 24 April–29 May. E. 552, 554–556.

—— Mercurius Republicus. 22–29 May. E. 556.

—— The Moderate. 24 April–29 May. E. 552, 554–556.

—— The Moderate Intelligence. 17–31 May. E. 556, 557.

—— The Moderate Intelligencer. 26 April–31 May.

E. 552, 554–557.

—— A Modest Narrative of Intelligence. 28 April–26 May.

E. 553, 555, 556.

—— A Perfect Diurnall of some Passages in Parliament. 30 April–
28 May. E. 529, 530.

—— Perfect Occurrences of every dayes Journall. 27 April–25 May.

E. 529, 530.

—— A Perfect Summary of an Exact Diarye. 30 April–28 May.

E. 529, 530.

—— The Perfect Weekly Account. 2–30 May. E. 529, 530.

June.—England's Moderate Messenger. 28 May–25 June.

E. 530, 531.

—— The First Decade of Useful Observations. 25 June.

E. 562. (5.)

—— The Impartiall Intelligencer. 30 May–27 June. E. 530, 531.

—— The Kingdoms Faithfull and Impartiall Scout. 25 May–29 June.

E. 530, 531.

1649.

June.—The Kingdomes Weekly Intelligencer. 29 May–26 June.

        E. 558–561.

—— The Man in the Moon. 28 May–27 June.   **E. 558–561.**

—— Mercurius Brittanicus. 29 May–5 June.   **E. 558. (13.)**

—— Mercurius Elencticus. 28 May–25 June.   **E. 558–561.**

—— Mercurius Pragmaticus. 29 May–26 June.   **E. 558–561.**

—— The Moderate. 29 May–26 June.   **E. 558–561.**

—— The Moderate Intelligencer. 31 May–28 June.   **E. 559–562.**

—— The Moderate Mercury. 14–28 June.   **E. 561, 562.**

—— The Metropolitan Nuncio. 6–13 June.   **E. 560. (3.)**

—— A Modest Narrative of Intelligence. 26 May–30 June.

        E. 557, 559–562.

—— A Perfect Diurnall of some Passages in Parliament. 28 May–
    25 June.   **E. 530, 531.**

—— Perfect Occurrences of every dayes Journall. 25 May–29 June.

        E. 530, 531.

—— A Perfect Summary of an Exact Diarye. 28 May–25 June.

        E. 530, 531.

—— The Perfect Weekly Account. 30 May–28 June.

        E. 558–560, 562.

July.—England's Moderate Messenger. 25 June–9 July.   **E. 531.**

—— The Impartiall Intelligencer. 27 June–25 July.   **E. 531.**

—— The Kingdoms Faithfull and Impartiall Scout. 29 June–27 July.

        E. 531.

—— The Kingdomes Weekly Intelligencer. 26 June–31 July.

        E. 562–566.

—— The Man in the Moon. 27 June–25 July.   **E. 562–565.**

—— Mercurius Carolinus. 19–26 July.   **E. 566. (6.)**

—— Mercurius Elencticus. 25 June–30 July.   **E. 562–566.**

—— Mercurius Pragmaticus. 26 June–31 July.

        E. 562, 563, 565, 566.

—— The Moderate. 26 June–31 July.   **E. 562, 564–566.**

—— The Moderate Intelligencer. 28 June–26 July.   **E. 563–566.**

—— The Moderate Messenger. 16–30 July.   **E. 531, 532.**

—— A Modest Narrative of Intelligence. 30 June–28 July.

        E. 563–566.

—— A Perfect Diurnall of Passages in Parliament. (*Robert Wood.*)
    9–23 July.   **E. 531.**

—— A Perfect Diurnall of Some Passages in Parliament. (*Coles and
    Blaiklock.*) 25 June–30 July.   **E. 531, 532.**

—— Perfect Occurrences of every dayes Journall. 29 June–27 July.

        E. 531, 532.

1649.

July.—A Perfect Summary of an Exact Diarye. 25 June–30 July.

E. 531, 532.

—— The Perfect Weekly Account. 28 June–25 July.

E. 562, 564, 565.

—— Tuesdaies Journall. 17–31 July. E. 531, 532.

Aug.—The Armies Painfull Messenger. 25 July–2 Aug.

E. 566. (25.)

—— Great Britaine's Paine-full Messenger. 9–30 Aug.

E. 569, 571, 572.

—— The Impartiall Intelligencer. 25 July–22 Aug.

E. 566, 569, 571.

—— The Kingdoms Faithfull and Impartiall Scout. 27 July–31 Aug.

E. 532.

—— The Kingdomes Weekly Intelligencer. 31 July–28 Aug.

E. 568–572.

—— The Man in the Moon. 25 July–23 Aug. E. 566–571.

—— Mercurius Aulicus. 14–21 Aug. E. 571.

—— Mercurius Elencticus. 30 July–27 Aug. E. 568–571.

—— Mercurius Pragmaticus. 31 July–28 Aug. E. 568, 569, 571.

—— The Moderate. 31 July–28 Aug. E. 568, 569, 571, 572.

—— The Moderate Intelligencer. 26 July–30 Aug.

E. 566, 568, 569, 571, 572.

—— The Moderate Messenger. 30 July–27 Aug. E. 532.

—— A Modest Narrative of Intelligence. 28 July–25 Aug.

E. 566, 568, 569, 571.

—— A Perfect Diurnall of some Passages in Parliament. 30 July–
27 Aug. E. 532.

—— Perfect Occurrences of every dayes Journall. 27 July–31 Aug.

E. 532.

—— A Perfect Summary of an Exact Diarye. 30 July–6 Aug.

E. 532.

—— A Perfect Summary of Exact Passages. 13–27 Aug. E. 532.

—— The Perfect Weekly Account. 25 July–29 Aug.

E. 566, 568, 569, 571.

—— Tuesdaies Journall. 31 July–21 Aug. E. 532.

Sept.—The Impartiall Intelligencer. 30 Aug.–19 Sept. E. 572–574.

—— The Kingdoms Faithfull and Impartiall Scout. 31 Aug.–28 Sept.

E. 532, 533.

—— The Kingdomes Weekly Intelligencer. 4–25 Sept. E. 573, 574.

—— The Man in the Moon. 23 Aug.–26 Sept. E. 572–574.

—— Mercurius Aulicus. 21 Aug.–4 Sept. E. 572.

—— Mercurius Elencticus. 27 Aug.–24 Sept. E. 572–574.

—— Mercurius Hybernicus. 30 Aug.–6 Sept. E. 572. (25.)

1649.

Sept.—Mercurius Pragmaticus.   28 Aug.–25 Sept.   **E. 572–574.**

—— The Moderate.   28 Aug.–25 Sept.   **E. 572–574.**

—— The Moderate Intelligencer.   30 Aug.–27 Sept.   ₊ **E. 572–574.**

—— The Moderate Messenger.   27 Aug.–24 Sept.   **E. 532, 533.**

—— A Modest Narrative of Intelligence.   25 Aug.–22 Sept.

E. 572–574.

—— A Perfect Diurnall of some Passages in Parliament.   27 Aug.–
24 Sept.   **E. 532, 533.**

—— Perfect Occurrences of every dayes Journall.   31 Aug.–28 Sept.

E. 532, 533.

—— A Perfect Summary of Exact Passages.   27 Aug.–24 Sept.

E. 532, 533.

—— The Perfect Weekly Account.   29 Aug.–26 Sept.   **E. 572–574.**

Oct.—A Briefe Relation.   2–31 Oct.   **E. 575, 576.**

—— The Kingdoms Faithfull and Impartiall Scout.   28 Sept.–12 Oct.

E. 533.

—— The Kingdomes Weekly Intelligencer.   25 Sept.–9 Oct.   **E. 575.**

—— The Man in the Moon.   26 Sept.–31 Oct.   **E. 575, 576.**

—— Mercurius Elencticus.   24 Sept.–29 Oct.   **E. 575.**

—— Mercurius Pragmaticus.   25 Sept.–30 Oct.   **E. 575.**

—— The Moderate Intelligencer.   27 Sept.–4 Oct.   **E. 575.**

—— A Perfect Diurnall of some Passages in Parliament.   24 Sept.–
8 Oct.   **E. 533.**

—— Perfect Occurrences of every dayes Journall.   28 Sept.–12 Oct.

E. 533.

—— A Perfect Summary of Exact Passages.   24 Sept.–1 Oct.   **E. 533.**

—— The Perfect Weekly Account.   26 Sept.–10 Oct.   **E. 575.**

—— Severall Proceedings in Parliament.   25 Sept.–26 Oct.

E. 575, 533.

Nov.—A Briefe Relation.   31 Oct.–27 Nov.   **E. 578, 581, 583.**

—— The Man in the Moon.   31 Oct.–7 Nov., 14–21 Nov.

E. 578, 582.

—— Mercurius Elencticus.   29 Oct.–5 Nov.   **E. 578.**

—— Mercurius Pragmaticus.   30 Oct.–6 Nov.   **E. 578.**

—— A Perfect Diurnall of some Passages in Parliament.   5–12 Nov.

E. 533.

—— Severall Proceedings in Parliament.   26 Oct.–30 Nov.   **E. 533.**

Dec.—A Briefe Relation.   27 Nov.–25 Dec.   **E. 584, 585, 587.**

—— Mercurius Pragmaticus.   27 Nov.–4 Dec., 11–18 Dec.

E. 584, 585.

—— A Perfect Diurnall of some Passages...in relation to the Armies.
10–31 Dec.   **E. 533.**

—— Severall Proceedings in Parliament.   30 Nov.–28 Dec.   **E. 533.**

1650.

Jan.—A Briefe Relation.   25 Dec.–31 Jan.   **E. 587–590.**
—— The Man in the Moon.   26 Dec.–31 Jan.   **E. 587–590.**
—— Mercurius Pragmaticus.   25 Dec.–29 Jan.   **E. 587, 589, 590.**
—— A Perfect Diurnall of some Passages...in relation to the Armies.
      31 Dec.–28 Jan.   **E. 533, 534.**
—— Severall Proceedings in Parliament.   28 Dec.–25 Jan.
                                                 E. 533, 534.
Feb.—A Briefe Relation.   29 Jan.–26 Feb.   **E. 592–594.**
—— The Man in the Moon.   30 Jan.–27 Feb.   **E. 592–594.**
—— Mercurius Pragmaticus.   5–19 Feb.   **E. 592, 593.**
—— A Perfect Diurnall of some Passages...in relation to the Armies.
      28 Jan.–25 Feb.   **E. 534.**
—— The Royall Diurnall.   25 Feb.   **E. 594.**
—— Severall Proceedings in Parliament.   25 Jan.–28 Feb.   **E. 534.**
March.—A Briefe Relation.   26 Feb.–26 March.   **E. 594, 595, 597.**
—— The Man in the Moon.   27 Feb.–29 March.   **E. 594–597.**
—— Mercurius Pragmaticus.   26 Feb.–26 March.   **E. 594–596.**
—— A Perfect Diurnall of some Passages...in relation to the Armies.
      25 Feb.–25 March.   **E. 534.**
—— The Royall Diurnall.   25 Feb.–26 March.   **E. 594–596.**
—— Severall Proceedings in Parliament.   28 Feb.–28 March.   **E. 534.**
April.—A Briefe Relation.   26 March–30 April.   **E. 597–599.**
—— The Man in the Moon.   29 March–26 April.   **E. 597–599.**
—— Mercurius Elenticus.   22, 22–29 April.   **E. 598, 599.**
—— Mercurius Pragmaticus.   2–30 April.   **E. 597–599.**
—— A Perfect Diurnall of some Passages...in relation to the Armies.
      25 March–29 April.   **E. 534.**
—— The Royall Diurnall.   26 March–30 April.   **E. 597–599.**
—— Severall Proceedings in Parliament.   28 March–25 April.   **E. 534.**
May.—A Briefe Relation.   30 April–28 May.   **E. 600–602.**
—— The Man in the Moon.   24 April–30 May.   **E. 599–602.**
—— Mercurius Elenticus.   29 April–20 May.   **E. 600, 601.**
—— Mercurius Pragmaticus.   30 April–28 May.   **E. 600–602.**
—— A Perfect Diurnall of some Passages...in relation to the Armies.
      29 April–27 May.   **E. 534, 777.**
—— Severall Proceedings in Parliament.   25 April–30 May.
                                                 E. 534, 777.
June.—A Briefe Relation.   28 May–25 June.   **E. 602, 603.**
—— The Impartial Scout.   21–28 June.   **E. 777. (16.)**
—— The Man in the Moon.   29 May–5 June.   **E. 602.**
—— Mercurius Elenticus.   20 May–3 June   **E. 602.**

1650.

June.—Mercurius Politicus. 6–27 June. **E. 603, 604.**

—— A Perfect Diurnall of some Passages…in relation to the Armies. 27 May–24 June. **E. 777.**

—— Severall Proceedings in Parliament. 30 May–27 June. **E. 777.**

July.—A Briefe Relation. 25 June–30 July. **E. 607, 608.**

—— The Impartial Scout. 28 June–25 July. **E. 777, 778.**

—— Mercurius Politicus. 27 June–25 July. **E. 607, 608.**

—— A Perfect Diurnall of some Passages in Parliament. 15–29 July. **E. 778.**

—— A Perfect Diurnall of some Passages…in relation to the Armies. 24 June–29 July. **E. 777, 778.**

—— Perfect Passages of every daies Intelligence. 28 June–26 July. **E. 777, 778.**

—— The Perfect Weekly Account. 10–31 July. **E. 777, 778.**

—— Several Proceedings in Parliament. 27 June–25 July. **E. 777, 778.**

—— True Intelligence from the Head Quarters. 16–30 July. **E. 608.**

—— The Weekly Intelligencer. 16–23 July. **E. 608.**

Aug.—The Best and Most Perfect Intelligencer. 1–8 Aug. **E. 609. (6.)**

—— A Briefe Relation. 30 July–27 Aug. **E. 608, 609, 612.**

—— The Impartial Scout. 25 July–9 Aug. **E. 778.**

—— Mercurius Politicus. 25 July–29 Aug. **E. 608–610.**

—— A Perfect Diurnall of some Passages….in relation to the Armies. 29 July–26 Aug. **E. 778.**

—— Perfect Passages of every daies Intelligence. 26 July–30 Aug. **E. 778.**

—— The Perfect Weekly Account. 31 July–7 Aug. **E. 778.**

—— Severall Proceedings in Parliament. 25 July–29 Aug. **E. 778.**

—— True Intelligence from the Head Quarters. 30 July–7 Aug. **E. 609.**

Sept.—A Briefe Relation. 27 Aug.–24 Sept. **E. 612, 613.**

—— The Impartial Scout. 13–27 Sept. **E. 780.**

—— Mercurius Politicus. 29 Aug.–26 Sept. **E. 612, 613.**

—— The Moderne Intelligencer. 10–25 Sept. **E. 612, 613.**

—— A Perfect Diurnall of some Passages…in relation to the Armies. 26 Aug.–30 Sept. **E. 780.**

—— Perfect Passages of every daies Intelligence. 30 Aug.–27 Sept. **E. 780.**

—— The Perfect Weekly Account. 19–26 Sept. **E. 780.**

—— Severall Proceedings in Parliament. 29 Aug.–26 Sept. **E. 780.**

Oct.—A Briefe Relation. 24 Sept.–22 Oct. **E. 613, 615.**

—— Mercurius Anglicus. 24 Sept.–1 Oct. **E. 613. (13.)**

1650.

Oct.—Mercurius Politicus. 26 Sept.–31 Oct. **E. 613–615.**
—— A Perfect Diurnall of some Passages...in relation to the Armies.
30 Sept.–28 Oct. **E. 780.**
—— Perfect Passages of every daies Intelligence. 27 Sept.–25 Oct.
E. 780.
—— Severall Proceedings in Parliament. 26 Sept.–31 Oct. **E. 780.**
—— The Weekly Intelligencer. 24 Sept.–15 Oct., 22–29 Oct.
E. 613–615.
Nov.—Mercurius Politicus. 31 Oct.–28 Nov. **E. 615–618.**
—— A Perfect Diurnall of some Passages...in relation to the Armies.
28 Oct.–25 Nov. **E. 780, 781.**
——– Perfect Passages of every daies Intelligence. 25 Oct.–1 Nov.,
8–15, 22–29 Nov. **E. 780, 781.**
—— Severall Proceedings in Parliament. 31 Oct.–28 Nov.
E. 780, 781.
Dec.—Mercurius Politicus. 28 Nov.–26 Dec. **E. 619, 620.**
—— A Perfect Diurnall of some Passages . . . in relation to the Armies.
25 Nov.–30 Dec. **E. 780, 781.**
—— Perfect Passages of every daies Intelligence. 29 Nov.–27 Dec.
E. 781.
—— Several Proceedings in Parliament. 28 Nov.–26 Dec. **E. 781.**
—— The Weekly Intelligencer. 24–31 Dec. **E. 620.**

1651.

Jan.—The Faithful Scout. 27 Dec.–24 Jan. **E. 781.**
—— Mercurius Politicus. 26 Dec.–30 Jan. **E. 621, 622.**
—— A Perfect Account of the Daily Intelligence. 22–29 Jan.
E. 622. (11.)
—— A Perfect Diurnall of some Passages . . . in relation to the Armies.
30 Dec.–27 Jan. **E. 781.**
—— Perfect Passages of every daies Intelligence. 27 Dec.–31 Jan.
E. 781.
—— Severall Proceedings in Parliament. 26 Dec.–30 Jan. **E. 781.**
—— The Weekly Intelligencer. 31 Dec.–28 Jan. **E. 621, 622.**
Feb.—The Faithful Scout. 31 Jan.–28 Feb. **E. 784.**
—— Mercurius Politicus. 30 Jan.–27 Feb. **E. 623, 625.**
—— A Perfect Account of the Daily Intelligence. 29 Jan.–5 Feb.
E. 623.
—— A Perfect Diurnall of some Passages . . . in relation to the Armies.
27 Jan.–24 Feb. **E. 784.**

1651.

Feb.—Perfect Passages of every daies Intelligence.   31 Jan.–28 Feb.

E. 784.

—— Severall Proceedings in Parliament.   30 Jan.–27 Feb.   **E. 784.**

—— The Weekly Intelligencer.   28 Jan.–25 Feb.   **E. 623-625.**

March.—The Faithful Scout.   28 Feb.–28 March.   **E. 784.**

—— Mercurius Politicus.   27 Feb.–27 March.   **E. 625, 626.**

—— A Perfect Account of the Daily Intelligence.   5–19 March.

E. 626.

—— A Perfect Diurnall of some Passages . . . in relation to the Armies.
24 Feb.–31 March.   **E. 784.**

—— Perfect Passages of every daies Intelligence.   28 Feb.–28 March.

E. 784.

—— Severall Proceedings in Parliament.   27 Feb.–27 March.   **E. 784.**

—— The Weekly Intelligencer.   25 Feb.–25 March.   **E. 625, 626.**

April.—The Faithful Scout.   28 March–25 April.   **E. 785.**

—— Mercurius Politicus.   27 March–24 April.   **E. 626, 628.**

—— A Perfect Account of the Daily Intelligence.   2–23 April.

E. 626, 628.

—— A Perfect Diurnall of some Passages . . . in relation to the Armies.
31 March–28 April.   **E. 785.**

—— Perfect Passages of every daies Intelligence.   4–25 April.

E. 785.

—— Severall Proceedings in Parliament.   27 March–24 April.

E. 785.

—— The Weekly Intelligencer.   25 March–29 April.   **E. 626, 628.**

May.—The Faithful Scout.   25 April–30 May.   **E. 785.**

—— Mercurius Politicus.   24 April–29 May.   **E. 628, 629.**

—— A Perfect Account of the Daily Intelligence.   30 April–28 May.

E. 628, 629.

—— A Perfect Diurnall of some Passages . . . in relation to the Armies.
28 April–26 May.   **E. 785.**

—— Perfect Passages of every daies Intelligence.   25 April–30 May.

E. 785.

—— Severall Proceedings in Parliament.   24 April–29 May.   **E. 785.**

—— The Weekly Intelligencer.   29 April–27 May.   **E. 628, 629.**

June.—The Faithful Scout.   30 May–27 June.   **E. 785, 786.**

—— Mercurius Elencticus.   10–24 June.   **E. 632.**

—— Mercurius Politicus.   29 May–26 June.   **E. 630-632.**

—— Mercurius Pragmaticus.   3–10 June.   **E. 632. (4.)**

—— A Perfect Account of the Daily Intelligence.   28 May–18 June.

E. 629, 632.

—— A Perfect Diurnall of some Passages . . . in relation to the Armies.
26 May–30 June.   **E. 785, 786.**

1651.

June.—Perfect Passages of every daies Intelligence   30 May–27 June.

                                                           E. 785, 786.

—— Severall Proceedings in Parliament.   29 May–26 June.

                                                           E. 785, 786.

—— The Weekly Intelligencer.   27 May–24 June.   **E. 629, 632.**

July.—The Faithful Scout.   27 June–4 July.   **E. 786.**

—— Mercurius Elencticus.   24 June–1 July.   **E. 632.**

—— Mercurius Politicus.   26 June–31 July.   **E. 633–638.**

—— Mercurius Scommaticus.   1–8 July.   **E. 636. (1.)**

—— A Perfect Account of the Daily Intelligence.   25 June–23 July.

                                                           E. 633, 637.

—— A Perfect Diurnall of some Passages . . . in relation to the Armies. 30 June–28 July.   **E. 786.**

—— Perfect Passages of every daies Intelligence.   27 June–31 July.

                                                           E. 786.

—— Severall Proceedings in Parliament.   26 June–31 July.   **E. 786.**

—— The Weekly Intelligencer.   24 June–29 July.   **E. 633, 637, 638.**

Aug.—The Armies Intelligencer.   29 July–5 Aug.   **E. 638. (15.)**

—— The Faithful Scout.   8–29 Aug.   **E. 786, 787.**

—— Mercurius Politicus.   31 July–28 Aug.   **E. 640.**

—— A Perfect Account of the Daily Intelligence.   30 July–20 Aug.

                                                           E. 638, 640.

—— A Perfect Diurnall of some Passages . . . in relation to the Armies. 28 July–25 Aug.   **E. 786, 787.**

—— Perfect Passages of every daies Intelligence.   31 July–29 Aug.

                                                          E. 786, 787.

—— Severall Proceedings in Parliament.   31 July–28 Aug.

                                                          E. 786, 787.

—— The True Informer of the Actions of the Army.   20–28 Aug.

                                                          E. 640. (25.)

—— The Weekly Intelligencer.   29 July–26 Aug.   **E. 638, 640.**

Sept.—The Diary.   22–29 Sept.   **E. 641. (25.)**

—— The Faithful Scout.   29 Aug.–26 Sept.   **E. 787.**

—— Mercurius Politicus.   28 Aug.–25 Sept.   **E. 641.**

—— The Modern Intelligencer.   26 Aug.–3 Sept.   **E. 641. (3.)**

—— A Perfect Account of the Daily Intelligence.   10–24 Sept.   **E. 643.**

—— A Perfect Diurnall of some Passages . . . in relation to the Armies. 25 Aug.–29 Sept.   **E. 787.**

—— Perfect Passages of every daies Intelligence.   29 Aug.–12 Sept., 19–26 Sept.   **E. 787.**

—— Severall Proceedings in Parliament.   28 Aug.–25 Sept.   **E. 787.**

—— The Weekly Intelligencer.   26 Aug.–30 Sept.   **E. 641.**

1651.

Oct.—The Diary. 29 Sept.–27 Oct.   **E. 643, 644.**

—— The Faithful Scout. 3–31 Oct.   **E. 787, 788.**

—— Mercurius Politicus. 25 Sept.–30 Oct.   **E. 643, 644.**

—— A Perfect Account of the Daily Intelligence. 24 Sept.–15 Oct.,
22–29 Oct.   **E. 643, 644.**

—— A Perfect Diurnall of some Passages . . . in relation to the Armies.
29 Sept.–27 Oct.   **E. 787, 788.**

—— Perfect Particulars of every daies Intelligence. 24–31 Oct.
         E. 788. (8.)

—— Perfect Passages of every daies Intelligence. 26 Sept.–24 Oct.
         E. 787, 788.

—— Severall Proceedings in Parliament. 25 Sept.–30 Oct.
         E. 787, 788.

—— The Weekly Intelligencer. 30 Sept.–28 Oct.   **E. 643, 644.**

Nov.—The Diary. 27 Oct.–3 Nov.   **E. 644. (11.)**

—— The Faithful Scout. 31 Oct.–28 Nov.   **E. 791.**

—— Mercurius Politicus. 30 Oct.–27 Nov.   **E. 645, 647.**

—— A Perfect Account of the Daily Intelligence. 5–12 Nov.
         E. 645.

—— A Perfect Diurnall of some Passages . . . in relation to the Armies.
27 Oct.–24 Nov.   **E. 791.**

—— Perfect Passages of every daies Intelligence. 30 Oct.–27 Nov.
         E. 791.

—— Severall Proceedings in Parliament. 30 Oct.–27 Nov.   **E. 791.**

—— The Weekly Intelligencer. 28 Oct.–25 Nov.   **E. 645–647.**

Dec.—The Faithful Scout. 28 Nov.–26 Dec.   **E. 791.**

—— The French Intelligencer. 2–30 Dec.   **E. 650, 651.**

—— Mercurius Politicus. 27 Nov.–25 Dec.   **E. 650, 651.**

—— A Perfect Account of the Daily Intelligence. 26 Nov.–31 Dec.
         E. 650, 651.

—— A Perfect Diurnall of some Passages . . . in relation to the Armies.
24 Nov.–29 Dec.   **E. 791.**

—— Perfect Passages of every daies Intelligence. 27 Nov.–19 Dec.
         E. 791.

—— Severall Proceedings in Parliament. 27 Nov.–31 Dec.
         E. 791, 793.

—— The Weekly Intelligencer. 25 Nov.–16 Dec., 23–30 Dec.
         E. 649–651.

1652.

Jan.—The Faithful Scout.   26 Dec.–30 Jan.   **E. 793.**

—— The French Intelligencer.   30 Dec.–27 Jan.   **E. 651, 652.**

—— Mercurius Politicus.   25 Dec.–29 Jan.   **E. 651, 652.**

—— A Perfect Account of the Daily Intelligence.   7–28 Jan.

E. 651, 652.

—— A Perfect Diurnall of some Passages . . . in relation to the Armies.
29 Dec.–26 Jan.   **E. 793.**

—— Perfect Passages of every daies Intelligence.   26 Dec.–30 Jan.

E. 793.

—— Severall Proceedings in Parliament.   31 Dec.–29 Jan.   **E. 793.**

—— The Weekly Intelligencer.   30 Dec.–27 Jan.   **E. 651, 652.**

Feb.—The Faithful Scout.   30 Jan.–27 Feb.   **E. 793.**

—— The French Intelligencer.   27 Jan.–25 Feb.   **E. 652–655.**

—— Mercurius Bellonius.   28 Jan.–25 Feb.   **E. 652–655.**

—— Mercurius Politicus.   29 Jan.–26 Feb.   **E. 654, 655.**

—— A Perfect Account of the Daily Intelligence.   28 Jan.–4 Feb.,
11–25 Feb.   **E. 652, 655.**

—— A Perfect Diurnall of some Passages . . . in relation to the Armies.
26 Jan.–23 Feb.   **E. 793.**

—— Perfect Passages of every daies Intelligence.   30 Jan.–37 Feb.

E. 793.

—— Severall Proceedings in Parliament.   29 Jan.–26 Feb   **E. 793.**

—— The Weekly Intelligencer.   27 Jan.–24 Feb.

E. 652, 654, 655.

March.—The Dutch Spy.   17–31 March.   **E. 658.**

—— The Faithful Scout.   27 Feb.–26 March.   **E. 793, 794.**

—— The French Intelligencer.   25 Feb.–30 March.   **E. 655–658.**

—— Mercurius Bellonius.   25 Feb.–3 March.   **E. 655.**

—— Mercurius Politicus.   26 Feb.–25 March.   **E. 655–658.**

—— A Perfect Account of the Daily Intelligence.   25 Feb.–31 March.

E. 655, 656, 658.

—— A Perfect Diurnall of some Passages . . . in relation to the Armies.
23 Feb.–29 March.   **E. 793, 794.**

—— Perfect Passages of every daies Intelligence.   27 Feb.–26 March.

E. 793, 794.

—— Severall Proceedings in Parliament.   26 Feb.–25 March.

E. 793, 794.

—— The Weekly Intelligencer.   24 Feb.–30 March.   **E. 655–658.**

April.—The Dutch Spy.   31 March–7 April.   **E. 659.**

—— The Faithful Scout.   26 March–30 April.   **E. 794.**

1652.
April.—The French Intelligencer.   30 March–13 April, 20–27 April.
                                                    E. 659, 661.
—— Mercurius Democritus.   8–28 April.   E. 659–661.
—— Mercurius Phreneticus.   8–22 April.   E. 659, 660.
—— Mercurius Politicus.   25 March–29 April.   E. 658–662.
—— A Perfect Account of the Daily Intelligence.   31 March–28 April.
                                                    E. 659–661.
—— A Perfect Diurnall of some Passages . . . in relation to the Armies.
    29 March–26 April.   E. 794.
—— Perfect Passages of every daies Intelligence.   26 March–30 April.
                                                    E. 794.
—— Severall Proceedings in Parliament.   25 March–29 April.
                                                    E. 794.
—— The Weekly Intelligencer.   30 March–27 April.   E. 659, 661.
May.—The Faithful Scout.   30 April–28 May.   E. 794, 795.
—— The French Intelligencer.   27 April–18 May.   E. 662–664.
—— French Occurrences.   10–31 May.   E. 665.
—— Mercurius Democritus.   27 April–26 May.   E. 662–665.
—— Mercurius Politicus.   29 April–27 May.   E. 662–665.
—— Mercurius Pragmaticus.   18–25 May.   E. 665.
—— A Perfect Account of the Daily Intelligence.   28 April–26 May.
                                                    E. 662, 664, 665.
—— A Perfect Diurnall of some Passages . . . in relation to the Armies.
    26 April–31 May.   E. 794, 795.
—— Perfect Passages of every daies Intelligence.   30 April–28 May.
                                                    E. 794, 795.
—— Severall Proceedings in Parliament.   29 April–27 May.
                                                    E. 794, 795.
—— The Weekly Intelligencer.   27 April–25 May.   E. 662–665.
June.—The Faithful Scout.   28 May–25 June.   E. 795.
—— French Occurrences.   31 May–28 June.   E. 666–668.
—— Mercurius Democritus.   25 May–30 June.   E. 665–668.
—— Mercurius Heraclitus.   28 June.   E. 668. (15.)
—— Mercurius Politicus.   27 May–24 June.   E. 666–668.
—— Mercurius Pragmaticus.   25 May–30 June.   E. 665, 667, 668.
—— A Perfect Account of the Daily Intelligence.   26 May–30 June.
                                                    E. 665. 667, 668.
—— A Perfect Diurnall of some Passages . . . in relation to the Armies.
    31 May–28 June.   E. 795.
—— Perfect Passages of every daies Intelligence.   28 May–25 June.
                                                    E. 795.
—— Severall Proceedings in Parliament.   27 May–24 June.   E. 795.

1652.

June.—The Weekly Intelligencer.   25 May–29 June.

E. 665, 667, 668.

July.—The Faithful Scout.   25 June–30 July.   E. 795, 796.

—— French Occurrences.   28 June–26 July.   E. 669–671.

—— Mercurius Britannicus.   19–26 July.   E. 671.

—— Mercurius Democritus.   30 June–28 July.   E. 669–672.

—— Mercurius Heraclitus.   28 June–12 July.   E. 669, 670.

—— Mercurius Phreneticus.   12–19 July.   E. 671. (3.)

—— Mercurius Politicus.   24 June–29 July.   E. 669–672.

—— Mercurius Pragmaticus.   30 June–6 July.   E. 669.

—— A Perfect Account of the Daily Intelligence.   30 June–28 July.

E. 670–672.

—— A Perfect Diurnall of some Passages . . . in relation to the Armies.
28 June–26 July.   E. 795, 796.

—— Perfect Passages of every daies Intelligence.   25 June–30 July.

E. 795, 796.

—— Severall Proceedings in Parliament.   24 June–29 July.

E. 795, 796.

—— The Weekly Intelligencer.   29 June–27 July.   E. 669–671.

Aug.—The Faithful Scout.   30 July–27 Aug.   E. 796.

—— French Occurrences.   26 July–30 Aug.   E. 672–674.

—— Mercurius Britannicus.   26 July–23 Aug.   E. 672–674.

—— Mercurius Cinicus.   4–11 Aug.   E. 673. (16.)

—— Mercurius Democritus.   28 July–25 Aug.   E. 673, 674.

—— Mercurius Mastix.   20–27 Aug.   E. 674. (18.)

—— Mercurius Politicus.   29 July–26 Aug.   E. 673, 674.

—— A Perfect Account of the DailyIntelligence.   28 July–25 Aug.

F. 673, 674.

—— A Perfect Diurnall of some Passages . . . in relation to the Armies.
26 July–30 Aug.   E. 796.

—— Perfect Passages of every daies Intelligence.   30 July–27 Aug.

E. 796.

—— Severall Proceedings in Parliament.   29 July–26 Aug.   E. 796.

—— The Weekly Intelligencer.   27 July–31 Aug.   E. 673, 674.

Sept.—The Faithful Scout.   27 Aug.–24 Sept.   E. 797, 799.

—— French Occurrences.   30 Aug.–28 Sept.   E. 674, 675.

—— The Laughing Mercury.   27 Aug.–29 Sept.   E. 674, 675.

—— Mercurius Politicus.   26 Aug.–30 Sept.   E. 674, 675.

—— A Perfect Account of the Daily Intelligence.   25 Aug.–29 Sept.

E. 674, 675.

—— A Perfect Diurnall of some Passages . . . in relation to the Armies.
30 Aug.–27 Sept.   E. 797, 798.

2 E 2

1652.

Sept.—Perfect Passages of every daies Intelligence. 27 Aug.–25 Sept.
E. 797, 799.

—— Severall Proceedings in Parliament. 26 Aug.–30 Sept.
E. 797, 799.

—— The Weekly Intelligencer. 31 Aug.–28 Sept. E. 674, 675.
Oct.—The Faithful Scout. 24 Sept.–29 Oct. E. 799.
—— French Occurrences. 28 Sept.–25 Oct. E. 675, 678.
—— Mercurius Britannicus. 19–26 Oct. E. 799.
—— The Laughing Mercury. 29 Sept.–27 Oct. E. 678.
—— Mercurius Politicus. 30 Sept.–28 Oct. E. 678.
—— A Perfect Account of the Daily Intelligence. 29 Sept.–27 Oct.
E. 676, 678, 679.

—— A Perfect Diurnall of some Passages . . . in relation to the Armies.
27 Sept.–25 Oct. E. 799.
—— Perfect Passages of every daies Intelligence. 25 Sept.–30 Oct.
E. 799.

—— Severall Proceedings in Parliament. 30 Sept.–28 Oct. E. 799.
—— The Weekly Intelligencer. 28 Sept.–26 Oct. E. 676, 678.
Nov.—The Faithful Scout. 29 Oct.–26 Nov. E. 799, 801.
—— French Occurrences. 25 Oct.–29 Nov. E. 679–683.
—— The Laughing Mercury. 27 Oct.–3 Nov. E. 679.
—— Mercurius Britannicus. 26 Oct.–30 Nov. E. 799, 801.
—— Mercurius Democritus. 3–30 Nov. E. 681, 683.
—— Mercurius Politicus. 28 Oct.–25 Nov. E. 679–683.
—— A Perfect Account of the Daily Intelligence. 27 Oct.–24 Nov.
E. 679, 881.

—— A Perfect Diurnall of some Passages . . . in relation to the Armies.
25 Oct.–29 Nov. E. 799, 801.
—— Perfect Passages of every daies Intelligence. 30 Oct.–27 Nov.
E. 799, 801.

—— Severall Proceedings in Parliament. 28 Oct.–25 Nov. E. 799.
—— The Weekly Intelligencer. 26 Oct.–30 Nov. E. 679, 681, 683.
Dec.—The Faithful Scout. 26 Nov.–31 Dec. E. 801.
—— The Flying Eagle. 27 Nov.–11 Dec., 18–25 Dec.
E. 683, 801, 684.

—— French Occurrences. 29 Nov.–13 Dec., 20–27 Dec.
E. 683, 684.

—— Mercurius Britannicus. 30 Nov.–28 Dec. E. 801.
—— Mercurius Democritus. 30 Nov.–29 Dec. E. 683, 684.
—— Mercurius Politicus. 25 Nov.–30 Dec. E. 683, 684.
—— The Moderate Intelligencer. 1–8, 15–29 Dec. E. 683, 684.
—— A Perfect Account of the Daily Intelligence. 24 Nov.–29 Dec.
E. 683, 684.

1652.

Dec.—A Perfect Diurnall of some Passages. . .in relation to the Armies.
    29 Nov.–27 Dec.   **E. 801.**
——— Perfect Passages of every daies Intelligence.   27 Nov.–31 Dec.
                                                                      E. 801.
——— Severall Proceedings in Parliament.   25 Nov.–30 Dec.   **E. 801.**
——— Weekly Intelligencer.   30 Nov.–28 Dec.   **E. 683, 684.**

1653.

Jan.—The Flying Eagle.   25 Dec.–1 Jan.   **E. 684. (18.)**
——— French Occurrences.   27 Dec.–3 Jan   **E. 684.**
——— Mercurius Democritus.   19–26 Jan.   **E. 684.**
——— Mercurius Politicus.   30 Dec.–27 Jan.   **E. 684.**
——— The Moderate Publisher of every daies Intelligence.   14–28 Jan.
                                                                      E. 804.
——— A Perfect Account of the Daily Intelligence.   29 Dec.–5 Jan.
                                                                      E. 684.
——— A Perfect Diurnall of some Passages . . . in relation to the Armies.
    27 Dec.–31 Jan.   **E. 804.**
——— Severall Proceedings in Parliament.   30 Dec.–27 Jan.   **E. 804.**
——— The Weekly Intelligencer.   28 Dec.–4 Jan.   **E. 684.**
Feb.—The Faithful Scout.   4–25 Feb.   **E. 803.**
——— Mercurius Democritus.   26 Jan.–23 Feb.   **E. 686–688.**
——— Mercurius Politicus.   27 Jan.–24 Feb.   **E. 686–688.**
——— The Moderate Messenger.   31 Jan.–7 Feb., 14–28 Feb.
                                                                  E. 686, 688.
——— The Moderate Publisher of every daies Intelligence.   28 Jan.–
    25 Feb.   **E. 804.**
——— A Perfect Account of the Daily Intelligence.   2–23 Feb.
                                                                  E. 686–688.
——— A Perfect Diurnall of some Passages. . . in relation to the Armies
    31 Jan.–28 Feb.   **E. 804.**
——— Severall Proceedings in Parliament.   27 Jan.–17 Feb.   **E. 804.**
——— The Weekly Intelligencer.   8–22 Feb.   **E. 687, 688.**
March.—The Faithful Scout.   25 Feb.–18 March.   **E. 803.**
——— Mercurius Democritus.   23 Feb.–30 March.   **E. 689, 690.**
——— Mercurius Politicus.   24 Feb.–31 March.   **E. 689, 690.**
——— The Moderate Messenger.   28 Feb.–14 March.   **E. 689.**
——— The Moderate Publisher of every daies Intelligence.   25 Feb.–
    25 March.   **E. 804, 211.**
——— A Perfect Account of the Daily Intelligence.   23 Feb.–27 March.
                                                                  E. 689, 690.

1653.
March.—A Perfect Diurnall of some Passages...in relation to the Armies.
    28 Feb.–28 March.   :E. 804, 211.
—— Severall Proceedings in Parliament. 17–31 March.   E. 211.
—— Weekly Intelligencer. 22 Feb.–29 March.   E. 689, 690.
April.—The Armies Scout. 23–30 April.   E. 211. (27.)
—— The Faithful Post. 25 March–29 April.   E. 211.
—— Mercurius Democritus. 30 March–27 April.   E. 691, 693.
—— Mercurius Politicus. 31 March–28 April.   E. 691–693.
—— Moderate Occurrences. 29 March–26 April.
                                E. 690, 691, 693.
—— The Moderate Publisher of every daies Intelligence. 25 March–
    29 April.   E. 211.
—— A Perfect Account of the Daily Intelligence. 30 March–27 April.
                                E. 691, 693.
—— A Perfect Diurnall of some Passages...in relation to the Armies.
    28 March–25 April.   E. 211.
—— Severall Proceedings in Parliament. 31 March–21 April. E. 211.
—— Severall Proceedings of State Affairs. 21–28 April.   E. 211.
—— The Weekly Intelligencer. 29 March–19 April.   E. 690, 691.
May.—The Armies Scout. 30 April–28 May.   E. 213.
—— The Faithful Post. 29 April–27 May.   E. 213.
—— Mercurius Britannicus. 16–30 May.   E. 697, 698.
—— Mercurius Democritus. 27 April–25 May.   E. 694–698.
—— Mercurius Politicus. 28 April–26 May.   E. 694–698.
—— Mercurius Pragmaticus. 16–25 May.   E. 698.
—— The Moderate Intelligencer. 2–30 May.   E. 694, 697, 698.
—— Moderate Occurrences. 26 April–3 May, 10–31 May.
                                E. 693, 697, 698.
—— The Moderate Publisher of every daies Intelligence. 29 April–
    27 May.   E. 213.
—— A Perfect Account of the Daily Intelligence. 27 April–25 May.
                                E. 694, 697, 698.
—— A Perfect Diurnall of some Passages ... in relation to the Armies.
    25 April–30 May.   E. 213.
—— Severall Proceedings of State Affairs. 28 April–26 May. E. 213.
—— The Weekly Intelligencer. 26 April–31 May.
                            E. 693, 694, 697, 698.
June.—The Armies Scout. 28 May–3 June.   E. 213.
—— The Daily Proceedings. [17 June.]   E. 701. (9.)
—— The Faithful Post. (*R. Eels: T. L.*) 27 May–24 June.
                              E. 213, 215.
—— The Faithful Post. (*G. Horton.*) 7–21 June.   E. 213, 215.
—— The Faithful Scout. 3–24 June.   E. 213, 215.

1653.

June.—Mercurius Britannicus. 13–20 June. **E. 701.**
—— Mercurius Democritus. 25 May–8 June, 22–29 June.
  E. 698, 699, 703.
—— Mercurius Politicus. 26 May–30 June. **E. 698–703.**
—— Mercurius Pragmaticus. 25 May–2 June, 15–29 June.
  E. 698, 702, 703.
—— Mercurius Radamanthus. 27 June. **E. 702.**
—— The Moderate Intelligencer. 6–27 June. **E. 699, 701, 702.**
—— The Moderate Publisher of every daies Intelligencer. 27 May–
  17 June. **E. 213.**
—— A Perfect Account of the Daily Intelligence. 25 May–1 June,
  8–29 June. **E. 698, 701–703.**
—— A Perfect Diurnall of some Passages . . . in relation to the Armies.
  30 May–27 June. **E. 213, 215.**
—— Severall Proceedings of State Affairs. 26 May–30 June.
  E. 213, 215.
—— The Weekly Intelligencer. 31 May–28 June. **E. 699, 701–703.**
July.—The Faithful Post. (*R. Eels.*) 1–29 July. **E. 215, 217.**
—— The Faithful Post. (*G. Horton.*) 28 June–26 July.
  E. 215, 217.
—— The Faithful Scout. 24 June–29 July. **E. 215, 217.**
—— The Impartial Intelligencer. 29 June–19 July. **E. 705, 706.**
—— Mercurius Democritus. 29 June–27 July. **E. 703–707.**
—— Mercurius Politicus. 30 June–28 July. **E. 705, 708.**
—— Mercurius Pragmaticus. 29 June–13 July. **E. 702, 705.**
·—— Mercurius Radamanthus. 11–25 July. **E. 705, 707.**
—— The Moderate Intelligencer. 27 June–24 July.
  E. 703, 705, 707.
—— The Moderate Publisher of every daies Intelligence. 24 June–
  29 July. **E. 215, 217.**
—— A Perfect Account of the Daily Intelligence. 29 June–27 July.
  E. 703, 705, 707.
—— A Perfect Diurnall of some Passages . . . in relation to the Armies.
  27 June–25 July. **E. 215, 217.**
—— Several Proceedings of Parliament. 4–26 July. **E. 707.**
—— Severall Proceedings of State Affairs. 30 June–28 July.
  E. 215, 217.
—— The True and Perfect Dutch Diurnall. 27 June–3 July, 19–26
  July. **E. 703, 707.**
—— The Weekly Intelligencer. 28 June–26 July. **E. 703, 705–707.**
Aug.—The Faithful Post. (*R. Eels.*) 26 July–26 Aug. **E. 217.**
—— The Faithful Post. (*G. Horton.*) 26 July–2 Aug. **E. 217. (13.)**
—— The Faithful Scout. 29 July–26 Aug. **E. 217.**

1653.

Aug.—The Loyal Messenger.   3–10 Aug.   **E. 710. (10.)**
—— Mercurius Democritus.   27 July–31 Aug.   **E. 708–711.**
—— Mercurius Politicus.   28 July–31 Aug.   **E. 708–711.**
—— The Moderate Intelligencer.   8–29 Aug.   **E. 711.**
—— The Moderate Publisher of every daies Intelligence.   29 July–
    26 Aug.   **E. 217.**
—— The Newes.   5–12 Aug.   **E. 710. (16.)**
—— A Perfect Account of the Daily Intelligence.   27 July–31 Aug.
                                                    E. 708, 710–712.
—— A Perfect Diurnall of some Passages . . . in relation to the Armies.
    25 July–29 Aug.   **E. 217.**
—— Several Proceedings of Parliament.   26 July–30 Aug.
                                                    E. 708, 710, 711.
—— Severall Proceedings of State Affairs.   28 July–25 Aug.   **E. 217.**
—— The Weekly Intelligencer.   26 July–30 Aug.   **E. 708, 710, 711.**
Sept.—The Faithful Post.   (*R. Eels.*)   26 Aug.–2 Sept.   **E. 219. (2.)**
—— The Faithful Scout.   26 Aug.–30 Sept.   **E. 219.**
—— Mercurius Democritus.   31 Aug.–28 Sept.   **E. 712–714.**
—— Mercurius Politicus.   1–29 Sept.   **E. 712–714.**
—— The Moderate Publisher of every daies Intelligence.   26 Aug.–
    9 Sept.   **E. 219.**
—— A Perfect Account of the Daily Intelligence.   7–28 Sept.
                                                    E. 713, 714.
—— A Perfect Diurnall of some Passages . . . in relation to the Armies.
    29 Aug.–26 Sept.   **E. 219.**
—— Several Proceedings of Parliament.   30 Aug.–27 Sept.   **E. 712–714.**
—— Severall Proceedings of State Affairs.   25 Aug.–29 Sept.   **E. 219.**
—— The Weekly Intelligencer.   20–27 Sept.   **E. 714.**
Oct.—The Faithful Scout.   30 Sept.–28 Oct.   **E. 219.**
—— Mercurius Democritus.   28 Sept.–26 Oct.   **E. 714, 715.**
—— Mercurius Politicus.   29 Sept.–27 Oct.   **E. 714, 715.**
—— The Moderate Publisher of every daies Intelligence.   7–28 Oct.
                                                    E. 219.
—— A Perfect Account of the Daily Intelligence.   5–26 Oct.
                                                    E. 714, 715.
—— A Perfect Diurnall of some Passages . . . in relation to the Armies.
    26 Sept.–31 Oct.   **E. 219, 222.**
—— Severall Proceedings of State Affairs.   29 Sept.–27 Oct.   **E. 219.**
—— Several Proceedings of Parliament.   27 Sept.–25 Oct.   **E. 714, 715.**
—— The Weekly Intelligencer.   27 Sept.–25 Oct.   **E. 714, 715.**
Nov.—The Faithful Scout.   28 Oct.–25 Nov.   **E. 222.**
—— Great Brittain's Post.   2–9 Nov.   **E. 222.**
—— Mercurius Democritus.   26 Oct.–9 Nov.   **E. 715, 718.**

1653.

Nov.—Mercurius Politicus.   27 Oct.–24 Nov.   **E. 715–720.**

—— The Moderate Publisher of every daies Intelligence.   28 Oct.–
25 Nov.   **E. 222.**

—— A Perfect Account of the Daily Intelligence.   26 Oct.–23 Nov.

E. 715, 718–720.

—— A Perfect Diurnall of some Passages . . . in relation to the Armies.
31 Oct.–28 Nov.   **E. 222.**

—— Several Proceedings of Parliament.   25 Oct.–29 Nov.

E. 715, 718, 719, 721.

—— Severall Proceedings of State Affairs.   27 Oct.–24 Nov.   **E. 222.**

—— The Weekly Intelligencer.   25 Oct.–29 Nov.

E. 715, 718, 719, 721.

Dec.—The Faithful Scout.   25 Nov.–30 Dec.   **E. 222, 223.**

—— Great Brittain's Post.   14–28 Dec.   **E. 222, 223.**

—— Mercurius Politicus.   24 Nov.–29 Dec.   **E. 723–725.**

—— The Moderate Publisher of every daies Intelligence.   25 Nov.–
30 Dec.   **E. 222, 723, 223.**

—— A Perfect Account of the Daily Intelligence.   30 Nov.–28 Dec.

E. 723–725.

—— A Perfect Diurnall of some Passages . . . in relation to the Armies.
28 Nov.–26 Dec.   **E. 222, 223.**

—— Several Proceedings of Parliament.   29 Nov.–13 Dec.

E. 723, 724.

—— Severall Proceedings of State Affairs.   24 Nov.–29 Dec.

E. 223, 224.

—— The Weekly Intelligencer.   29 Nov.–27 Dec.   **E. 723–725.**

1654.

Jan.—Certain Passages of every dayes Intelligence.   20–27 Jan.   **E. 223.**

—— The Faithful Scout.   30 Dec.–28 Jan.   **E. 223.**

—— The Grand Politique Post.   10–24 Jan.   **E. 223.**

—— The Loyal Intelligencer.   23–30 Jan.   **E. 727. (13.)**

—— Mercurius Democritus.   9 Nov.–25 Jan.   **E. 727.**

—— Mercurius Politicus.   29 Dec.–26 Jan.   **E. 725–727.**

—— The Moderate Publisher of Every Daies Intelligence.   6–20 Jan.

E. 223.

—— A Perfect Account of the Daily Intelligence.   28 Dec.–25 Jan.

E. 725–727.

—— A Perfect Diurnall of some Passages . . . in relation to the Armies.
26 Dec.–30 Jan.   **E. 223.**

1654.

Jan.—The Politique Informer.   23–30 Jan.   **E. 223.**
—— The Politique Post.   4–11 Jan.   **E. 223.**
—— Severall Proceedings of State Affairs.   29 Dec.–26 Jan.   **E. 223.**
—— The True and Perfect Dutch Diurnall.   3–24 Jan.   **E. 726, 727.**
—— The True and Perfect Informer.   13–20 Jan.   **E. 726. (18.)**
—— The True Informer.   6–13 Jan.   **E. 223. (15.)**
—— The Weekly Intelligencer.   27 Dec.–31 Jan.   **E. 725–727.**
Feb.—Certain Passages of every dayes Intelligence.   27 Jan.–24 Feb.
                                                        E. 223, 225.
—— The Faithful Scout.   28 Jan–24 Feb.   **E. 223, 225.**
—— The Grand Politique Post.   7–28 Feb.   **E. 225.**
—— Mercurius Democritus.   1–22 Feb.   **E. 728–730.**
—— Mercurius Politicus.   26 Jan.–23 Feb.   **E. 727–730.**
—— The Moderate Intelligencer.   16–23 Feb.   **E. 225.**
—— A Perfect Account of the Daily Intelligence   1–22 Feb.
                                                        E. 728–730.
—— A Perfect Diurnall of some Passages . . . in relation to the Armies.
     30 Jan.–27 Feb.   **E. 223, 225.**
—— Perfect Occurrences.   29 Jan.–6 Feb., 20–27 Feb.   **E. 727, 730.**
—— The Politique Informer.   30 Jan.–6 Feb.   **E. 223.**
—— Severall Proceedings of State Affairs.   26 Jan.–23 Feb.
                                                        E. 223, 225.
—— The Weekly Intelligencer.   31 Jan.–28 Feb.   **E. 728–731.**
March.—Certain Passages of every dayes Intelligence.   24 Feb.–24
     March.   **E. 225.**
—— The Faithful Scout.   24 Feb.–31 March.   **E. 225, 227.**
—— The Grand Politique Post.   28 Feb.–14 March, 21–28 March.
                                                        E. 225, 227.
—— Mercurius Aulicus.   13–27 March.   **E. 732.**
—— Mercurius Nullus.   13, 20 March.   **E. 731, 732.**
—— Mercurius Poeticus.   1–8 March.   **E. 731. (11.)**
—— Mercurius Politicus.   23 Feb.–30 March.   **E. 731, 732.**
—— The Moderate Intelligencer.   23 Feb.–29 March.   **E. 225, 227.**
—— A Perfect Account of the Daily Intelligence.   22 Feb.–15 March,
     22–29 March.   **E. 731, 732.**
—— A Perfect Diurnall of some Passages . . . in relation to the Armies.
     27 Feb.–29 March.   **E. 225.**
—— Severall Proceedings of State Affairs.   23 Feb.–30 March.
                                                        E. 225, 227.
—— The True and Perfect Dutch Diurnall.   7–21 March. **E. 731, 732.**
—— The Weekly Intelligencer.   28 Feb.–28 March.   **E. 731, 732.**
April.—Certain Passages of every dayes Intelligence.   24 March–
     28 April.   **E. 227.**

1654.

April.—The Faithful Scout. 31 March–28 April.   **E. 227.**

—— The Grand Politique Post. 28 March–11 April.   **E. 227.**

—— The Loyal Messenger. 3–10 April.   **E. 732.**

—— Mercurius Aulicus. 27 March–3 April.   **E. 732.**

—— Mercurius Politicus. 30 March–27 April.   **E. 732, 733.**

—— The Moderate Intelligencer. (*R. Wood.*) 29 March–12 April, 19–26 April.   **E. 732, 227.**

—— The Moderate Inteligencer. (*G. Horton.*) 29 March–5 April.   **E. 732. (20.)**

—— A Perfect Account of the Daily Intelligence. 29 March–26 April.   **E. 732, 733.**

—— A Perfect Diurnall of some Passages . . . in relation to the Armies. 27 March–24 April.   **E. 227.**

—— Perfect Occurrences. 21–28 April.   **E. 733. (17.)**

—— Severall Proceedings of State Affairs. 30 March–27 April.   **E. 227.**

—— The True and Perfect Dutch Diurnall. 11–18 April.   **E. 733.**

—— The Weekly Intelligencer. 28 March–25 April.   **E. 732, 733.**

—— The Weekly Post. 11–25 April.   **E. 227.**

May.—Certain Passages of every dayes Intelligence. 28 April–26 May.   **E. 227, 229.**

—— The Faithful Scout. 28 April–26 May.   **E. 227, 229.**

—— Mercurius Politicus. 27 April–25 May.   **E. 734–738.**

—— The Moderate Intelligencer. 26 April–10 May.   **E. 227.**

—— A Perfect Account of the Daily Intelligence. 26 April–31 May.   **E. 734, 735, 738.**

—— Perfect and Impartial Intelligence. 16–26 May.   **E. 735, 738.**

—— Perfect Diurnall Occurrences of certain Military Affairs. 1–8 May.   **E. 227. (36.)**

–—— A Perfect Diurnall ; or, Occurrences of certain Military Affairs. 8–29 May.   **E. 227, 229.**

—— A Perfect Diurnall of some Passages . . . in relation to the Armies. 24 April–29 May.   **E. 227, 229.**

—— Several Proceedings of State Affairs. 27 April–25 May.   **E. 227, 229.**

—— The True and Perfect Dutch Diurnall. 24 April–22 May.   **E. 734, 735.**

—— The Weekly Intelligencer. 25 April–30 May. **E. 734, 735, 738.**

—— The Weekly Post. 2–30 May.   **E. 227, 229.**

June.—Certain Passages of every dayes Intelligence. 26 May–30 June.   **E. 229.**

—— The Faithful Scout. 26 May–30 June.   **E. 229.**

—— Mercurius Fumigosus. 7 June, 14–28 June.   **E. 744, 745.**

1654.

June.—Mercurius Politicus. 25 May–29 June. **E. 738–745.**

—— A Perfect Account of the Daily Intelligence. 31 May–28 June.

E. 740, 742, 744, 745.

—— Perfect and Impartial Intelligence. 26 May–2 June.

E. 738. (15.)

—— A Perfect Diurnall; or, Occurrences of certain Military Affairs.
29 May–26 June. **E. 229.**

—— A Perfect Diurnall of some Passages . . . in relation to the Armies.
29 May–26 June. **E. 229.**

—— Perfect Occurrences. 9–23 June. **E. 744.**

—— Severall Proceedings of State Affairs. 25 May–29 June. **E. 229.**

—— The Weekly Intelligencer. 30 May–20 June.

E. 740, 741, 744.

—— The Weekly Post. 6–27 June. **E. 229.**

July.—Certain Passages of every dayes Intelligence. 30 June–28 July.

E. 230.

—— The Faithful Scout. 30 June–28 July. **E. 230.**

—— Mercurius Fumigosus. 28 June–26 July. **E. 745, 805, 806.**

—— Mercurius Jocosus. 14–21 July. **E. 805.**

—— Mercurius Politicus. 29 June–27 July. **E. 745, 805, 806.**

—— A Perfect Account of the Daily Intelligence. 28 June–26 July.

E. 745, 805, 806.

—— A Perfect Diurnall; or, Occurrences of certain Military Affairs.
26 June–31 July. **E. 230.**

—— A Perfect Diurnall of some Passages . . . in relation to the Armies.
26 June–31 July. **E. 230.**

—— Severall Proceedings of State Affairs. 29 June–27 July. **E. 230.**

—— The Weekly Intelligencer. 27 June–25 July. **E. 745, 805.**

—— The Weekly Post. 4–25 July. **E. 230.**

Aug.—Certain Passages of every dayes Intelligence. 28 July–25 Aug.

E. 230, 233.

—— The Faithful Scout. 28 July–25 Aug. **E. 233.**

—— Mercurius Fumigosus. 26 July–30 Aug. **E. 806–809.**

—— Mercurius Jocosus. 28 July–4 Aug. **E. 806.**

—— Mercurius Politicus. 27 July–31 Aug. **E. 806–809.**

—— A Perfect Account of the Daily Intelligence. 26 July–30 Aug.

E. 806, 808, 809.

—— A Perfect Diurnall; or, Occurrences of certain Military Affairs.
31 July–28 Aug. **E. 230, 233.**

—— A Perfect Diurnall of some Passages . . . in relation to the Armies.
31 July–28 Aug. **E. 230, 233.**

—— Severall Proceedings of State Affairs. 27 July–31 Aug.

E. 230, 233.

1654.
Aug.—The Weekly Intelligencer. 25 July–8 Aug., 15–29 Aug.
E. 806, 808, 809.
—— The Weekly Post. 25 July–8 Aug., 15–29 Aug. **E. 230, 233.**
Sept.—Certain Passages of every dayes Intelligence. 25 Aug.–29 Sept.
E. 233.
—— The Faithful Scout. 25 Aug.–29 Sept. **E. 233.**
—— Mercurius Fumigosus. 30 Aug.–27 Sept. **E. 809–812.**
—— Mercurius Politicus. 31 Aug.–28 Sept. **E. 809–812.**
—— A Perfect Account of the Daily Intelligence. 30 Aug.–27 Sept.
E. 809, 811, 812.
—— A Perfect Diurnall ; or, Occurrences of certain Military Affairs.
28 Aug.–25 Sept. **E. 233.**
—— A Perfect Diurnall of some Passages . . . in relation to the Armies.
28 Aug.–25 Sept. **E. 233.**
—— Severall Proceedings in Parliament. 7–28 Sept. **E. 233.**
—— Severall Proceedings of State Affairs. 31 Aug.–7 Sept.
E. 233, 235.
—— The Weekly Intelligencer. 29 Aug.–12 Sept., 19–26 Sept.
E. 809, 812.
—— The Weekly Post. 29 Aug.–26 Sept. **E. 233.**
Oct.—Certain Passages of every dayes Intelligence. 29 Sept.–27 Oct.
E. 235, 236.
—— The Faithful Scout. 29 Sept.–27 Oct. **E. 235, 236.**
—— Mercurius Fumigosus. 27 Sept.–25 Oct. **E. 813.**
—— Mercurius Politicus. 28 Sept.–26 Oct. **E. 813, 814.**
—— The Observator. 24–31 Oct. **E. 814. (4.)**
—— A Perfect Account of the Daily Intelligence. 27 Sept.–4 Oct., 11–
25 Oct. **E. 813, 814.**
—— A Perfect Diurnall ; or, Occurrences of certain Military Affairs.
25 Sept.–30 Oct. **E. 235, 236.**
—— A Perfect Diurnall of some Passages . . . in relation to the
Armies. 25 Sept.–30 Oct. **E. 235, 236.**
—— Severall Proceedings in Parliament. 28 Sept.–26 Oct.
E. 235, 236.
—— The Weekly Intelligencer. 26 Sept.–9 Oct., 17–31 Oct.
E. 813, 814.
—— The Weekly Post. 26 Sept.–31 Oct. **E. 235, 236.**
Nov.—Certain Passages of every dayes Intelligence. 27 Oct.–24 Nov.
E. 236.
—— The Faithful Scout. 27 Oct.–24 Nov. **E. 236.**
—— Mercurius Fumigosus. 25 Oct.–30 Nov. **E. 814–818.**
—— Mercurius Politicus. 26 Oct.–30 Nov. **E. 814–818.**
—— The Observator. 31 Oct.–7 Nov. **E. 816.**

1654.

Nov.—A Perfect Account of the Daily Intelligence.   25 Oct.–29 Nov.

E. 814, 816–818.

—— A Perfect Diurnall of some Passages . . . in relation to the Armies.   30 Oct.–27 Nov.   E. 236.

—— Severall Proceedings in Parliament.   26 Oct.–30 Nov.   E. 236.

—— The Weekly Intelligencer.   31 Oct.–28 Nov.   E. 816–818.

—— The Weekly Post.   31 Oct.–7 Nov., 14–28 Nov.   E. 236, 817.

Dec.—Certain Passages of every dayes Intelligence.   24 Nov.–15 Dec.

E. 236, 237.

—— The Faithful Scout.   24 Nov.–29 Dec.   E. 236, 237.

—— Mercurius Fumigosus.   30 Nov.–27 Dec.   E. 818–821.

—— Mercurius Politicus.   30 Nov.–28 Dec.   E. 818–821.

—— A Perfect Account of the Daily Intelligence.   29 Nov.–27 Dec.

E. 818, 820, 821.

—— A Perfect Diurnall of some Passages . . . in relation to the Armies.   27 Nov.–25 Dec.   E. 236, 237.

—— Severall Proceedings in Parliament.   30 Nov.–28 Dec.   E. 237.

—— The Weekly Intelligencer.   28 Nov.–19 Dec.   E. 818, 820.

—— The Weekly Post.   5–19 Dec.   E. 237.

1655.

Jan.—Certain Passages of every dayes Intelligence.   29 Dec.–26 Jan.

E. 237, 479.

—— The Faithful Scout.   29 Dec.–26 Jan.   E. 237, 479.

—— Mercurius Fumigosus.   27 Dec.–10 Jan., 17–31 Jan.

E. 821, 823, 826.

—— Mercurius Politicus.   28 Dec.–25 Jan.   E. 821–826.

—— A Perfect Account of the Daily Intelligence.   27 Dec.–31 Jan.

E. 821, 823, 825, 826.

—— A Perfect Diurnall of some Passages . . . in relation to the Armies.   25 Dec.–29 Jan.   E. 237, 479.

—— Severall Proceedings in Parliament.   28 Dec.–25 Jan.

E. 237, 479.

—— The Weekly Intelligencer.   26 Dec.–30 Jan.

E. 821, 823, 825, 826.

—— The Weekly Post.   26 Dec.–31 Jan.   E. 237, 479, 211.

Feb.—Certain Passages of every dayes Intelligence.   26 Jan.–24 Feb.

E. 479, 481.

1655.

Feb.—The Faithful Scout. 26 Jan.–23 Feb. **E. 479, 481.**

—— Mercurius Fumigosus. 31 Jan.–21 Feb. **E. 826, 828.**

—— Mercurius Politicus. 25 Jan.–22 Feb. **E. 826, 828.**

—— A Perfect Account of the Daily Intelligence. 31 Jan.–28 Feb.

E. 826, 828, 829.

—— A Perfect Diurnall of some Passages . . . in relation to the Armies. 29 Jan.–26 Feb. **E. 479, 481.**

—— Severall Proceedings of State Affairs. 25 Jan.–22 Feb.

E. 479, 481.

—— The Weekly Intelligencer. 30 Jan.–27 Feb.

E. 826, 828, 829.

—— The Weekly Post. 6–28 Feb. **E. 213, 481.**

March.—Certain Passages of every dayes Intelligence. 24 Feb.–30 March. **E. 481.**

—— The Faithful Scout. 23 Feb.–30 March. **E. 481.**

—— Mercurius Fumigosus. 28 Feb.–28 March. **E. 829, 830.**

—— Mercurius Politicus. 22 Feb.–29 March. **E. 829, 830.**

—— A Perfect Account of the Daily Intelligence. 28 Feb.–28 March.

E. 829, 830.

—— A Perfect Diurnall of some Passages . . . in relation to the Armies. 26 Feb.–26 March. **E. 481.**

—— Perfect Proceedings of State Affairs. 22 Feb.–29 March.

E. 481.

—— The Weekly Intelligencer. 27 Feb.–27 March. **E. 829, 830.**

—— The Weekly Post. 6–27 March. **E. 481.**

April.—Certain Passages of every dayes Intelligence. 30 March–27 April. **E. 831, 833.**

—— The Faithful Scout. 30 March–27 April. **E. 831, 833.**

—— Mercurius Fumigosus. 28 March–25 April. **E. 831, 833.**

—— Mercurius Politicus. 29 March–26 April. **E. 831, 833.**

—— A Perfect Account of the Daily Intelligence. 28 March–25 April.

E. 831–833.

—— A Perfect Diurnall of some Passages . . . in relation to the Armies. 26 March–30 April. **E. 831–833.**

—— Perfect Proceedings of State Affairs. 29 March–26 April.

E. 831, 833.

—— The Weekly Intelligencer. 27 March–24 April. **E. 831–833.**

—— The Weekly Post. 3–10, 17–24 April. **E. 831, 833.**

May.—Certain Passages of every dayes Intelligence. 27 April–25 May.

E. 835–840.

—— The Faithful Scout. 27 April–25 May. **E. 835–840.**

—— Mercurius Fumigosus. 25 April–30 May. **E. 835–840.**

—— Mercurius Politicus. 26 April–31 May. **E. 835–841.**

1655.

May.—A Perfect Account of the Daily Intelligence. 2–30 May.
E. 838, 840.

—— A Perfect Diurnall of some Passages . . . in relation to the Armies. 30 April–28 May. E. 835, 838, 840.

—— Perfect Proceedings of State Affairs. 26 April–31 May.
E. 835, 838, 840, 841.

—— The Weekly Intelligencer. 24 April–29 May.
E. 835, 838, 840.

—— The Weekly Post. 24 April–1 May. E. 835.

June.—Certain Passages of every dayes Intelligence. 25 May–30 June.
E. 841, 842, 845.

—— The Faithful Scout. 25 May–29 June. E. 841, 842, 845.

—— Mercurius Fumigosus. 30 May–27 June. E. 842, 844.

—— Mercurius Politicus. 31 May–28 June. E. 842–845.

—— A Perfect Account of the Daily Intelligence. 30 May–27 June.
E. 842, 844.

—— A Perfect Diurnall of some Passages . . . in relation to the Armies. 28 May–25 June. E. 842, 844.

—— Perfect Proceedings of State Affairs. 31 May–28 June.
E. 842, 844, 845.

—— The Weekly Intelligencer. 29 May–26 June. E. 842–844.

—— The Weekly Post. 29 May–19 June. E. 842, 843.

July.—Certain Passages of every dayes Intelligence. 6–27 July.
E. 848, 850.

—— The Faithful Scout. 29 June–27 July. E. 845, 848, 850.

—— Mercurius Fumigosus. 27 June–25 July. E. 845, 848, 850.

—— Mercurius Politicus. 28 June–26 July. E. 845–850.

—— A Perfect Account of the Daily Intelligence. 27 June–18 July.
E. 845, 848.

—— A Perfect Diurnall of some Passages . . . in relation to the Armies. 25 June–30 July. E. 845, 848, 850.

—— Perfect Proceedings of State Affairs. 28 June–26 July.
E. 845, 848, 850.

—— The Weekly Intelligencer. 25 June–31 July. E. 845, 848, 850.

Aug.—Certain Passages of every dayes Intelligence. 27 July–10 Aug.,
17–31 Aug. E. 850, 851.

—— The Faithful Scout. 3–31 Aug. E. 851, 852.

—— Mercurius Fumigosus. 25 July–29 Aug. E. 850–852.

—— Mercurius Politicus. 26 July–29 Aug. E. 850–852.

—— A Perfect Account of the Daily Intelligence. 1–29 Aug.
E. 851, 852.

—— A Perfect Diurnall of some Passages . . . in relation to the Armies. 6–27 Aug. E. 851, 852.

1655.

Aug.—Perfect Proceedings of State Affairs.   26 July–30 Aug.

                                       E. 851, 852.

—— The Weekly Intelligencer.   31 July–28 Aug.   **E. 851, 852.**

—— The Weekly Post.   31 July–28 Aug.   **E. 851, 852.**

Sept.—Certain Passages of every dayes Intelligence.   31 Aug.–28 Sept.

                                         E. 852–854.

—— The Faithful Scout.   1–28 Sept.   **E. 852–854.**

—— Mercurius Fumigosus.   29 Aug.–19 Sept.   **E. 852, 853.**

—— Mercurius Politicus.   29 Aug.–27 Sept.   **E. 852–854.**

—— A Perfect Account of the Daily Intelligence.   29 Aug.–5 Sept.

                                         E. 852.

—— A Perfect Diurnall of some Passages . . . in relation to the Armies.   27 Aug.–24 Sept.   **E. 852, 853.**

—— Perfect Proceedings of State Affairs   30 Aug.–27 Sept.

                                         E. 852–854.

—— The Weekly Intelligencer.   28 Aug.–25 Sept.   **E. 852, 853.**

—— The Weekly Post.   4–17 Sept.   **E. 853.**

Oct.—Mercurius Fumigosus.   19 Sept.–3 Oct.   **E. 854.**

—— Mercurius Politicus.   27 Sept.–25 Oct.   **E. 489.**

—— The Publick Intelligencer.   1–29 Oct.   **E. 489.**

Nov.—Mercurius Politicus.   25 Oct.–29 Nov.   **E. 489.**

—— The Publick Intelligencer.   29 Oct.–26 Nov.   **E. 489.**

Dec.—Mercurius Politicus.   29 Nov.–27 Dec.   **E. 491.**

—— The Publick Intelligencer.   26 Nov.–31 Dec.   **E. 491.**

1656.

Jan.—Mercurius Politicus.   27 Nov.–31 Jan.   **E. 491.**

—— The Publick Intelligencer.   31 Dec.–28 Jan.   **E. 491.**

Feb.—Mercurius Politicus.   31 Jan.–28 Feb.   **E. 492.**

—— The Publick Intelligencer.   28 Jan.–25 Feb.   **E. 492.**

March.—Mercurius Politicus.   28 Feb.–27 March.   **E. 492.**

—— The Publick Intelligencer.   25 Feb.–31 March.   **E. 492.**

April.—Mercurius Politicus.   27 March–24 April.   **E. 493.**

—— The Publick Intelligencer.   31 March–28 April.   **E. 493.**

May.—Mercurius Politicus.   24 April–29 May.   **E. 493.**

—— The Publick Intelligencer.   28 April–26 May.   **E. 493.**

June.—Mercurius Politicus.   29 May–26 June.   **E. 493, 494.**

—— The Publick Intelligencer.   26 May–30 June.   **E. 493, 494.**

July.—Mercurius Politicus.   26 June–31 July.   **E. 494.**

—— The Publick Intelligencer.   30 June–28 July.   **E. 494.**

Aug.—Mercurius Politicus.   31 July–28 Aug.   **E. 497.**

—— The Publick Intelligencer.   28 July–25 Aug.   **E. 497.**

1656.

Sept.—Mercurius Politicus.   28 Aug.–25 Sept.   E. 497.
—— The Publick Intelligencer.   25 Aug.–29 Sept.   E. 497.
Oct.—Mercurius Politicus.   25 Sept.–29 Oct.   E. 499.
—— The Publick Intelligencer.   29 Sept.–27 Oct.   E. 499.
Nov.—Mercurius Politicus.   29 Oct.–27 Nov.   E. 499.
—— The Publick Intelligencer.   27 Oct.–24 Nov.   E. 499.
Dec.—Mercurius Politicus.   27 Nov.–24 Dec.   E. 500.
—— The Publick Intelligencer.   24 Nov.–29 Dec.   E. 500.

1657.

Jan.—Mercurius Politicus.   24 Dec.–29 Jan.   E. 500.
—— The Publick Intelligencer.   29 Dec.–31 Jan.   E. 500.
Feb.—Mercurius Politicus.   29 Jan.–26 Feb.   E. 502.
—— The Publick Intelligencer.   2–23 Feb.   E. 502.
March.—Mercurius Politicus.   26 Feb.–26 March.   E. 502.
—— The Publick Intelligencer.   23 Feb.–30 March.   E. 502.
April.—Mercurius Politicus.   26 March–30 April.   E. 502.
—— The Publick Intelligencer.   30 March–27 April.   E. 502.
May.—Mercurius Politicus.   30 April.–28 May.   E. 503.
—— The Publick Adviser.   19–26 May.   E. 912.
—— The Publick Intelligencer.   27 April–25 May.   E. 503.
June.—Mercurius Politicus.   28 May–25 June.   E. 503.
—— The Publick Adviser.   26 May–29 June.   E. 912, 915, 916.
—— The Publick Intelligencer.   25 May–29 June.   E. 503.
July.—Mercurius Politicus.   25 June–30 July.   E. 505.
—— The Publick Adviser.   29 June–27 July.   E. 916, 919.
—— The Publick Intelligencer.   29 June–27 July.   E. 505.
—— The Weekly Information from the Office of Intelligence.   13–20
      July.   E. 919. (4.)
Aug.—Mercurius Politicus.   30 July–27 Ang.   E. 505.
—— The Publick Adviser.   27 July–31 Aug.   E. 922, 923.
—— The Publick Intelligencer.   27 July–31 Aug.   E. 505.
Sept.—Mercurius Politicus.   27 Aug.–24 Sept.   E. 505.
—— The Publick Adviser.   31 Aug.–28 Sept.   E. 925.
—— The Publick Intelligencer.   31 Aug –28 Sept.   E. 505.
Oct.—Mercurius Politicus.   24 Sept.–29 Oct.   E. 505.
—— The Publick Intelligencer.   28 Sept.–26 Oct.   E. 505.
Nov.—Mercurius Politicus.   29 Oct.–26 Nov.   E. 747.
—— The Publick Intelligencer.   26 Oct.–30 Nov.   E. 747.
Dec.—Mercurius Politicus.   26 Nov.–31 Dec.   E. 747.
—— The Publick Intelligencer.   30 Nov.–28 Dec.   E. 747.

1658.

Jan.—Mercurius Politicus. 31 Dec.–28 Jan. E. 748.
—— The Publick Intelligencer. 28 Dec.–25 Jan. E. 748.
Feb.—Mercurius Politicus. 28 Jan.–25 Feb. E. 748.
—— The Publick Intelligencer. 25 Jan.–22 Feb. E. 748.
March.—Mercurius Politicus. 25 Feb.–25 March. E. 748, 750.
—— The Publick Intelligencer. 22 Feb.–22 March. E. 748.
April.—Mercurius Politicus. 25 March–29 April. E. 750.
—— The Publick Intelligencer. 29 March–26 April. E. 750.
May.—Mercurius Politicus. 29 April–27 May. E. 750.
—— The Publick Intelligencer. 26 April–31 May. E. 750.
June.—Mercurius Politicus. 27 May–24 June. E. 753.
—— The Publick Intelligencer. 31 May–28 June. E. 753.
July.—Mercurius Politicus. 24 June–29 July. E. 753, 756.
—— The Publick Intelligencer. 28 June–26 July. E. 753, 756.
Aug.—Mercurius Politicus. 29 July–26 Aug. E. 756.
—— The Publick Intelligencer. 26 July–30 Aug. E. 756.
Sept.—Mercurius Politicus. 26 Aug.–30 Sept. E. 756.
—— The Publick·Intelligencer. 30 Aug.–27 Sept. E. 756.
Oct.—Mercurius Politicus. 30 Sept.–28 Oct. E. 760.
—— The Publick Intelligencer. 27 Sept.–25 Oct. E. 760.
Nov.—Mercurius Politicus. 28 Oct.–25 Nov. E. 760.
—— The Publick Intelligencer. 25 Oct.–29 Nov. E. 760.
Dec.—Mercurius Politicus. 25 Nov.–30 Dec. E. 760.
—— The Publick Intelligencer. 29 Nov.–27 Dec. E. 760.

1659.

Jan.—Mercurius Politicus. 30 Dec.–27 Jan. E. 761.
—— The Publick Intelligencer. 27 Dec.–31 Jan. E. 760, 761.
Feb.—Mercurius Politicus. 27 Jan.–24 Feb. E. 761.
—— The Publick Intelligencer. 31 Jan.–28 Feb. E. 761.
March.—Mercurius Politicus. 24 Feb.–31 March. E. 761.
—— The Publick Intelligencer. 28 Feb.–28 March. E. 761.
April.—The Faithful Scout. 22–29 April. E. 977.
—— Mercurius Politicus. 31 March–28 April. E. 762.
—— The Publick Intelligencer. 28 March–25 April. E. 761, 762.
May.—The Faithful Scout. 29 April–6 May, 13–27 May.
E. 980, 983.
—— Mercurius Democritus. 26 April–3 May, 17–24 May.
E. 979, 983.
—— Mercurius Politicus. 28 April–26 May. E. 762.

2 F 2

1659.

May.—The Moderate Informer.   12–25 May.   **E. 983.**
—— The Publick Intelligencer.   25 April–30 May.   **E. 762.**
—— The Weekly Intelligencer.   3–31 May.   **E. 980, 983.**
—— The Weekly Post.   3–31 May.   **E. 980, 983.**
June.—The Faithful Scout.   27 May–24 June.   **E. 984–986.**
—— Mercurius Democritus.   31 May–7 June, 14–21 June.
                                                       E. 985, 986.
—— Mercurius Politicus.   26 May–30 June.   **E. 762, 766.**
—— Mercurius Pragmaticus.   [20 June.]   **E. 988. (4.)**
—— A Particular Advice from the Office of Intelligence.   23–30 June.
                                                        E. 766. (7.)
—— The Publick Intelligencer.   30 May–27 June.   **E. 762, 766.**
—— The Weekly Account.   25 May–1 June.   **E. 983. (30.)**
—— The Weekly Intelligencer.   31 May–28 June.
                                                   E. 985, 986, 988.
—— The Weekly Post.   7–28 June.   **E. 985, 986, 988.**
July.—The Faithful Scout.   24 June–9 July.   **E. 986, 989.**
—— The Loyall Scout.   16–29 July.   **E. 989, 993.**
—— Mercurius Politicus.   30 June–28 July.   **E. 766.**
—— The National Scout.   9–16 July.   **E. 989.**
—— Occurrences from Forraigne Parts.   28 June–26 July.   **E. 766.**
—— A Particular Advice from the Office of Intelligence.   30 June–
   29 July.   **E. 766.**
—— The Publick Intelligencer.   27 June–25 July.   **E. 766.**
—— The Weekly Intelligencer.   28 June–26 July.
                                                   E. 988, 990, 993.
—— The Weekly Post.   28 June–26 July.   **E. 988, 989, 993.**
Aug.—The Loyall Scout.   29 July–26 Aug.   **E. 993.**
—— Mercurius Politicus.   28 July–25 Aug.   **E. 766.**
—— Occurrences from Forraigne Parts.   26 July–30 Aug.   **E. 766.**
—— A Particular Advice from the Office of Intelligence.   29 July–
   26 Aug.   **E. 766.**
—— The Publick Intelligencer.   25 July–29 Aug.   **E. 766.**
—— The Weekly Intelligencer.   26 July–30 Aug.   **E. 993.**
—— The Weekly Post.   26 July–30 Aug.   **E. 993.**
Sept.—The Loyall Scout.   26 Aug.–30 Sept.   **E. 995, 999.**
—— Mercurius Politicus.   24 Aug.–29 Sept.   **E. 766, 771.**
—— Mercurius Pragmaticus.   30 Aug.–6 Sept.   **E. 995. (13.)**
—— Occurrences from Forraigne Parts.   30 Aug.–27 Sept.
                                                       E. 766, 771.
—— A Particular Advice from the Office of Intelligence.   26 Aug.–
   30 Sept.   **E. 766, 771.**
—— The Publick Intelligencer.   29 Aug.–26 Sept.   **E. 766, 771.**

1659.

Sept.—The Weekly Intelligencer. 30 Aug.–27 Sept.   **E. 995.**
—— The Weekly Post. 30 Aug.–27 Sept.   **E. 995.**
Oct.—The Loyall Scout. 30 Sept.–28 Oct.   **E. 999, 1000.**
—— Mercurius Politicus. 29 Sept.–27 Oct.   **E. 771.**
—— Occurrences from Forraigne Parts. 27 Sept.–25 Oct.   **E. 771.**
—— A Particular Advice from the Office of Intelligence. 30 Sept.–28 Oct.   **E. 771.**
—— The Publick Intelligencer. 26 Sept.–31 Oct.   **E. 771.**
—— The Weekly Intelligencer. 27 Sept.–25 Oct.   **E. 999, 1000.**
—— The Weekly Post. 27 Sept.–25 Oct.   **E. 999, 1000.**
Nov.—The Loyall Scout. 28 Oct.–11 Nov.   **E. 1001, 1005.**
—— Mercurius Politicus. 27 Oct.–24 Nov.   **E. 771, 773.**
—— Occurrences from Forraigne Parts. 25 Oct.–1 Nov. ; 1–29 Nov.   **E. 771, 773.**
—— A Particular Advice from the Office of Intelligence. 28 Oct.–25 Nov.   **E. 771, 773.**
—— The Publick Intelligencer. 31 Oct.–28 Nov.   **E. 771, 773.**
—— The Weekly Intelligencer. 25 Oct.–29 Nov.   **E. 1001, 1005, 1006, 1010.**
—— The Weekly Post. 25 Oct.–29 Nov.   **E. 1001, 1005, 1010.**
Dec.—The Faithfull Intelligencer. 29 Nov.–3 Dec.   **E. 1010. (20.)**
—— The Loyall Scout. 25 Nov.–2 Dec.   **E. 1010.**
—— Mercurius Politicus. 24 Nov.–29 Dec.   **E. 773.**
—— Occurrences from Forraigne Parts. 29 Nov.–27 Dec.   **E. 773.**
—— The Parliamentary Intelligencer. 19–26 Dec.   **E. 182.**
—— A Particular Advice from the Office of Intelligence. 25 Nov.–30 Dec.   **E. 773.**
—— The Publick Intelligencer. 28 Nov.–26 Dec.   **E. 773.**
—— The Weekly Intelligencer. 29 Nov.–6 Dec.   **E. 1010.**
—— The Weekly Post. 29 Nov.–6 Dec.   **E. 1010.**

1660.

Jan.—An Exact Accompt of the Daily Proceedings in Parliament. 30 Dec.–27 Jan.   **E. 773.**
—— The Loyall Scout. 30 Dec.–6 Jan.   **E. 1011.**
—— Mercurius Politicus. 29 Dec.–26 Jan.   **E. 773.**
—— The Monethly Intelligencer. Dec.–Jan   **669. f. 22. (51.)**
—— Occurrences from Forraigne Parts. 27 Dec.–3 Jan.   **E. 773.**
—— The Parliamentary Intelligencer. 26 Dec.–30 Jan.   **E. 182.**

1660.

Jan.—The Publick Intelligencer. 26 Dec.–30 Jan. E. 773.

Feb.—An Exact Accompt of the Daily Proceedings in Parliament.
27 Jan.–17 Feb. E. 775.

—— Mercurius Politicus. 26 Jan.–23 Feb. E. 773, 775.

—— The Parliamentary Intelligencer. 30 Jan.–27 Feb. E. 182.

—— A Perfect Diurnal of Every Dayes Proceedings in Parliament.
21–29 Feb. E. 1016.

—— The Publick Intelligencer. 30 Jan.–27 Feb. E. 773, 775.

March.—An Exact Accompt of the Daily Proceedings in Parliament.
24 Feb.–30 March. E. 775, 182, 183.

—— Mercurius Fumigosus. 28 March. E. 1019.

—— Mercurius Honestus. 14–21 March. E. 1017. (31.)

—— Mercurius Phanaticus. 14–21 March. E. 1017. (30.)

—— Mercurius Politicus. 23 Feb.–8 March, 15–29 March.
E. 775, 182.

—— The Parliamentary Intelligencer. 27 Feb.–19 March. E. 182.

—— A Perfect Diurnal of Every Dayes Proceedings in Parliament.
1–16 March. E. 1016.

—— A Perfect Diurnall; or the Daily Proceedings in the Conventicle of
the Phanatiques. 19 March. E. 1017. (21.)

—— The Phanatick Intelligencer. [24 March.] E. 1017. (42.)

—— The Publick Intelligencer. 27 Feb.–26 March. E. 775, 182.

April.—An Exact Accompt of the Daily Proceedings in Parliament.
30 March–27 April. E. 183.

—— Mercurius Politicus. 29 March–12 April. E. 182.

—— Mercurius Publicus. 19–26 April. E. 183.

—— The Parliamentary Intelligencer. 26 March–30 April. E. 183.

—— The Publick Intelligencer. 26 March–9 April. E. 182.

May.—An Exact Accompt of the Daily Proceedings in Parliament.
27 April–4 May, 18–25 May. E. 183.

—— Mercurius Publicus. 26 April–31 May. E. 183.

—— Merlinus Phanaticus. 23 May. E. 1025. (9.)

—— The Parliamentary Intelligencer. 30 April–28 May. E. 183.

—— The Publick Intelligencer. 30 April–7 May. E. 183.

June.—An Exact Accompt of the Daily Proceedings in Parliament.
25 May–29 June. E. 183, 186.

—— Mercurius Politicus. 31 May–7 June. E. 195. (62.)

—— Mercurius Publicus. 31 May–28 June. E. 183, 186.

—— Mercurius Veridicus. 5–12 June. E. 1027. (6.)

—— The Publick Intelligencer. 28 May–25 June. E. 183, 186.

—— The Votes of both Houses. 13–20 June. E. 1027. (12.)

July.—An Exact Accompt of the Daily Proceedings in Parliament.
29 June–6 July. E. 186.

1660.

July.—Mercurius Fumigosus. 11 July.   **E. 1032.**
—— Mercurius Publicus. 28 June–26 July.   **E. 186.**
—— The Publick Intelligencer. 25 June–30 July.   **E. 186.**
Aug.—The Man in the Moon. 13–20 Aug.   **E. 1038. (7.)**
—— Mercurius Fumigosus. 1 Aug.   **E. 1035.**
—— Mercurius Publicus. 26 July–30 Aug.   **E. 186.**
—— The Publick Intelligencer. 30 July–27 Aug.   **E. 186.**
Sept.—Mercurius Publicus. 30 Aug.–27 Sept.   **E. 186, 189.**
—— The Parliamentary Intelligencer. 3–24 Sept.   **E. 189.**
—— The Publick Intelligencer. 27 Aug.–3 Sept.   **E. 186.**
Oct.—Mercurius Publicus. 27 Sept.–25 Oct.   **E. 186, 189.**
—— The Parliamentary Intelligencer. 24 Sept.–29 Oct.   **E. 189.**
Nov.—Mercurius Publicus. 25 Oct.–29 Nov.   **E. 189.**
—— The Parliamentary Intelligencer. 29 Oct.–26 Nov.   **E. 189.**
Dec.—Mercurius Publicus. 29 Nov.–27 Dec.   **E. 189, 192.**
—— The Parliamentary Intelligencer. 26 Nov.–3 Dec. ; 3–31 Dec.
                                                            E. 189, 192.
—— The Wandering Whore. 5–19 Dec.   **E. 1053, 1054.**

1661.

Jan.—The Kingdomes Intelligencer. 31 Dec.–28 Jan.   **E. 192.**
—— Mercurius Caledonius. 31 Dec.–8 Jan.   **E. 1055. (9.)**
—— Mercurius Publicus. 27 Dec.–31 Jan.   **E. 192.**
Feb.—The Kingdomes Intelligencer. 28 Jan.–25 Feb.   **E. 192.**
—— Mercurius Publicus. 31 Jan.–28 Feb.   **E. 192.**
March.—The Kingdomes Intelligencer. 25 Feb.–25 March.   **E. 194.**
—— Mercurius Publicus. 28 Feb.–28 March.   **E. 194.**
April.—The Kingdomes Intelligencer. 25 March–15 April.   **E. 194.**
—— Mercurius Publicus. 28 March–25 April.   **E. 194.**
May.—Mercurius Publicus. 9–30 May.   **E. 195.**
June.—Mercurius Publicus. 13–27 June.   **E. 195.**
July.—Mercurius Publicus. 27 June–25 July.   **E. 195.**
Aug.—Mercurius Publicus. 22–29 Aug.   **E. 195.**
Sept.—Mercurius Publicus. 29 Aug.–26 Sept.   **E. 195.**
Oct.—Mercurius Publicus. 10–17 Oct.   **E. 195.**
Nov.—Mercurius Publicus. 31 Oct.–28 Nov.   **E. 195.**

1662.

Jan.—Mercurius Publicus. 2–30 Jan.   **E. 195.**
Feb.—Mercurius Publicus. 6–20 Feb.   **E. 195.**
March.—Mercurius Publicus. 27 Feb.–27 March.   **E. 195.**
April.—Mercurius Publicus. 17–30 April.   **E. 195.**
May.—The Kingdomes Intelligencer. 28 April–5 May.   **E. 195. (2.)**
—— Mercurius Publicus. 8–15 May.   **E. 195.**
July.—Mercurius Publicus. 26 June–3 July, 10–31 July.   **E. 195.**
Aug.—The Kingdomes Intelligencer. 9 Aug.   **E. 195. (3.)**
—— Mercurius Publicus. 31 July–28 Aug.   **E. 195.**
Sept.—The Kingdomes Intelligencer. 22–29 Sept.   **E. 195. (4.)**
—— Mercurius Publicus. 18–25 Sept.   **E. 195.**
Oct.—Mercurius Publicus. 25 Sept.–9 Oct., 16–30 Oct.   **E. 195.**
Nov.—The Kingdomes Intelligencer. 27 Nov.   **E. 195. (5.)**
—— Mercurius Publicus. 13–27 Nov.   **E. 195.**
Dec.—Mercurius Publicus. 27 Nov.–18 Dec.   **E. 195.**

1663.

Jan.—Mercurius Publicus. 1–15, 22–29 Jan.   **E. 195.**
Feb.—Mercurius Publicus. 29 Jan.–5 Feb., 12–26 Feb.   **E. 195.**
March.—Mercurius Publicus. 26 Feb.–12 March.   **E. 195.**

APPENDIX.

The following Thomason Tracts which had been accidentally separated from the collection were not recognized in time to be catalogued with the other pamphlets of the years 1658–1661.

1658.

[April.]—A plea for Almes, delivered in a Sermon at the Spital, 13 April, 1658. By Thomas Watson. pp. 68. *Printed for T. Parkhurst.*
E. 2125. (1.)

[April.]—Divine Poems, with a short description of Christian Magnanimity. By E. E. *Printed by H. Hall for R. Blagrave : Oxon.*
E. 2143. (1.)

[April.]—The Practise of the Sheriff's Court, London. pp. 77.
E. 2255. (1.)

[May.]—Of the Mortification of Sinne in Believers. By John Owen. pp. 258. *Printed by H. Hall : Oxford.* E. 2134. (1.)

[May.]—The Several Opinions of sundry learned Antiquaries touching the Antiquity, Power and Proceedings of the High Court of Parliament. pp. 96. *Printed for W. Leake.* E. 2143. (2.)

[June.]—London's Wonder, being a true relation of the taking of a great whale neer to Greenwich. *Printed for F. Grove.* E. 2134. (2.)

[June.]—Philanglus ; som sober Inspections made with the cariage and consults of the Late-long Parliament. [The preface signed : J. H.] pp. 187. *Printed for H. S.* E. 2129. (1.)

[June.]—Poems, consisting of epistles & epigrams, satyrs, etc. By John Eliot. pp. 126. *Printed for H. Brome.* E. 2134. (3.)

[June.]—The Rustick Rampant, or Rurall Anarchy affronting Monarchy in the Insurrection of Wat Tiler. By John Cleaveland. [With an engraved portrait.] pp. 154. *Printed for F. C.* E. 2133. (1.)

[June.]—Syon in the House of Mourning. Being an Exposition of the fifth chapter of the Lamentations of Jeremiah. By Daniel Swift. pp. 192. *Printed for T. Parkhurst.* E. 2130. (1.)

[June.]—Vindiciæ Magistratuum, or a Sober Plea for Subjection to Present Government. [The preface signed : C. D.] pp. 120. *Printed by Henry Hills.* E. 2120. (1.)

1658.

[July.]—The Carpenter's Rule made easie, or the Art of measuring superficies & solids. By John Darling. pp. 96. *Printed for J. Jones.*
E. 2133. (2.)

[July.]—Divine Meditations and Holy Contemplations. By Richard Sibbes. The third edition. [With an engraved portrait.] pp. 141. *Printed for Simon Miller.* **E. 2137. (2.)**

[July.]—Florus Anglicus, or an exact History of England, from the reign of William the Conquerour to the death of Charles I. By Lambert Wood. The third edition. pp. 271. *Printed for Simon Miller.* **E. 2118. (1.)**

[July.]—Moses Unveiled, or those Figures which served unto the pattern of heavenly things explained. By William Guild. pp. 239. *Printed for T. Parkhurst.* **E. 2127. (1.)**

[July.]—The Reformation, in which is Reconciliation with God and his People. [By William Kaye.] 3 pt. *Printed for M. I.*
E. 2126. (1.)

[July.]—The Saint's Paradise. By Jerrard Winstanley. pp. 134. *Printed for G. Calvert.* **E. 2137. (1.)**

[Aug.]—Christian Reconcilement, or God at peace with man in Christ. Delivered in a Sermon at St. Mary's Oxford. By John Wall. *Printed by H. Hall : Oxford.* **E. 2120. (2.)**

[Aug.]—Κοσμοβρεφία, or the Infancy of the World. By Nich. Billingsley. [In verse.] pp. 184. *Printed for R. Crofts.* **E. 2132. (2.)**

[Aug.]—Pious Thoughts vented in pithy Ejaculations. By Richard Gove. pp. 144. *Printed for R. Royston.* **E. 2132. (1.)**

[Sept.]—The Worthy of Ephratah : represented in a sermon at the funerals of Edmund, Earl of Mulgrave, 21 Sept. 1658. By Edward Boteler. pp. 60. *Printed for G. Bedell & T. Collins.* **E. 2139. (1.)**

[Oct.]—Aqua Genitalis : a Discourse concerning Baptism, delivered in a sermon, 4 Oct. 1658. By Symon Patrick. pp. 104. *Printed for F. Tyton.* **E. 2142. (1.)**

[Oct.]—Observationes Astrologicæ, or an Astrologicall Discourse of the conjunction of Saturn and Mars, 11 Oct. 1658. By Richard Edlyn. pp. 183. *Printed by T. W.* **E. 2126. (2.)**

[Oct.]—Adam out of Eden ; or an Abstract of experiments touching Husbandry. By Ad. Speed. pp. 163. *Printed for H. Brome.*
E. 2135. (1.)

[Oct.]—Blagrave's Ephemeris for the year 1659. By Jos. Blagrave. *Printed by J. C.* **E. 2139. (2.)**

[Oct.]—Englands Warning Peece : or, the History of the Gun-powder Treason. By Thomas Spencer. pp. 80. *Printed for T. Pierrepont.*
E. 2255. (2.)

1658.

[**Oct.**]—Σὺν Θεῷ. Lingua Linguarum. The Natural Language of Languages. By Henry Edmundson. pp. 169. *To be sold at the Three Pigeons.* **E. 2138. (1.)**

[**Nov.**]—The Exact Law-giver; faithfully communicating to the skilfull the firm basis and axioms of their profession. pp. 226. *Printed for Thomas Bassett.* **E. 2128. (1.)**

[**Nov.**]—A Religious Treatise upon Simeon's Song. By Timothy Wood-roffe. pp. 220. *Printed for T. Parkhurst.* **E. 2119. (1.)**

[**Nov.**]—Severall Queries concerning the Church of Jesus Christ upon Earth, briefly resolved. By John Flowre. pp. 96. *Printed for E. Thomas.* **E. 2141. (2.)**

[**Dec.**]—Christ's Commission-Officer, or the Preacher's Patent cleared. A sermon. By John Norman. pp. 128. *Printed for E. Brewster.* **E. 2119. (2.)**

1659.

[**Jan.**]—A True Relation of the Conversion of Isuf, the Turkish Chaous, named Richard Christophilus, in the presence of a full congregation, 30 Jan. 1659 in Covent Garden. pp. 87. *Printed by S. Griffin.* **E. 2141. (1.)**

[**Feb.**]—The Rights of the People concerning Impositions. pp. 117. *Printed for W. Leak.* **E. 2143. (3.)**

[**April.**]—The Quakers Folly made manifest to all men : or a relation of what passed in three disputations, April 1659. By Tho. Danson. The second edition. pp. 60. *Printed for J. Allen.* **E. 2255. (3.)**

[**April.**]—The Quakers Wisdom descendeth not from above. A Vindica-tion of the Quakers Folly. By Tho. Danson. *Printed for J. Allen.* **E. 2255. (4.)**

[**April.**]—An Useful Tractate to further Christians in the Practice of Prayer. By William Crompton. pp. 152. *Printed for P. Stephens.* **E. 2142. (2.)**

[**May.**]—Johannes Becoldus redivivus, or, the English Quaker, the German Enthusiast, revived. Translated by J. S., written in French by Guy du Brez. pp. 83. *Printed for J. Allen.* **E. 2137. (3.)**

[**May.**]—Royall Psalmes, or Soliloquies of D. Anthony, King of Portingall. Translated by Baldwin St. George. pp. 65. *Printed for H. Moseley.* **E. 2121. (1.)**

[**June.**]—Elijah's fiery Chariot, being Prayers and Meditations for all persons in all conditions. pp. 440. *Printed for T. Rooks.* **E. 2257.**

[**June.**]—Good Company, being a collection of pious Meditations. By John Melvin. pp. 102. *Printed for T. Parkhurst.* **E. 2124. (1.)**

[**June.**]—Manuale Medicorum : seu Σύναξις Aphorismorum Hypocratis. pp. 356. *Typis Tho. Roycroft.* **E. 2259.**

1659.

[July.]—Elizabeth Fool's Warning, being a true relation of all that has happened to her since her marriage. By Elizabeth With, of Woodbridge. [In verse.] *Printed for F. Coles.* **E. 2122. (1.)**

[July.]—Gods Judgements upon Drunkards, Swearers & Sabbathbreakers. [By S. Hammond.] pp. 128. *Printed by E. Tyler.*

E. 2120. (3.)

[July.]—Organon Salutis. An Instrument to cleanse the Stomach, as also divers new Experiments of the virtue of Tobacco and Coffee. By Wa. Rumsey. pp. 68. *Printed for D. Pakeman.* **E. 2142. (3.)**

[Aug.]—Hermæologium, or an Essay at the rationality of the art of speaking. By B. Jones. pp. 94. *Printed for T. Basset.*

E. 2122. (3.)

[Aug.]—The Womans Almanack. By Sarah Ginnor. *Printed for J. J.*

E. 2140. (1.)

[Sept.]—Altum Silentium : or, Silence the Duty of Saints. An occasional sermon. By John Durant. *Printed by J. Streater.*

E. 2136. (1.)

[Oct.]—The Compleat School-Master. By John Brocksbank. 2 pt. *Printed for E. Brewster.* **E. 2136. (2.)**

[Nov.]—A Box of Spikenard newly broken. By T. M. pp. 112. *Printed for G. Sawbridge.* **E. 2140. (2.)**

[Nov.]—Chiliastomastix Redivivus. A confutation of the Millenarian Opinion. By Tho. Hall. pp. 102. *Printed for J. Starkey.*

E. 2135. (2.)

[Nov.]—Judicial Astrologers totally routed. By John Allen. *Printed for J. Allen.* **E. 2133. (3.)**

[Dec.]—A Catechism for Souldiers, to save soules and prevent blood. *Printed for E. Thomas.* **E. 2124. (2.)**

1659.—The Form of Consecration of a Church or Chappel. Exemplified by Lancelot, late Lord Bishop of Winchester. pp. 120. *Sold by T. Garthwait.* **E. 2260.**

1660.

[May.]—An Apology, or Defence of Astrologie. By George Atwel. pp. 128. *Printed for S. Speed.* **E. 2131. (1.)**

[May.]—Catalogus plantarum circa Cantabrigiam nascentium. pp. 285. *Excudebat J. Field : Cantabrigiae.* **E. 2123.**

[June.]—Three Sermons. By S. L. pp. 176. *Printed for R. Crofts.*

E. 2129. (2.)

[July.]—A Black-Smith and no Jesuite : or a true Relation how I William Houlbrook, Black-smith of Marleborough, was betray'd by Cornet George Joyce. pp. 96. *Printed for the Author & are to be sold by F. Lash.* **E. 2138. (2.)**

1660.

[**July.**]—The Clerk of Assize, Judges-Marshall, and Cryer: being the true Manner of the Proceedings at the Assizes. By T. W.   pp. 69. *Printed for T. Twyford.* **E. 2139. (3.)**

[**July.**]—The Death of Charles I. lamented, with the Restauration of Charles II. congratulated. By William Langley. !pp. 109. *Printed for R. Lowndes.* **E. 2127. (2.)**

[**July.**]—J. Cleaveland revived : Poems, Orations, Epistles, and other of his genuine incomparable pieces. [With an engraved portrait.] pp. 190. *Printed for Nathaniel Brooke.* **E. 2122. (2.)**

[**July.**]—Natura Prodigiorum, or a Discourse touching the Nature of Prodigies, together with the causes and effects of comets, eclipses and earthquakes. By John Gadbury. pp. 200. *Printed for F. Cossinet.* **E. 2131. (2.)**

[**July.**]—A Profitable and well grounded Concordance, wherein may be found the chiefest Words in the Scriptures. By W. Chadwell. *Printed for F. Smith.* **E. 2125. (2.)**

[**Aug.**]—A Breviate of our King's whole Latin Grammar, vulgarly called Lillies. pp. 52. *Printed by W. H.* **E. 2135. (3.)**

[**Aug.**]—Cosmeticks : or, The Beautifying Part of Physick. By John Jeams Wecker. pp. 140. *Printed by T. Johnson.* **E. 2140. (3.)**

[**Aug.**]—Mixt Contemplations in better Times. By Thomas Fuller. pp. 155. *Printed by R. D. for J. Williams.* **E. 2141. (3.)**

[**Aug.**]—To the most High and Mighty Prince, Charles II. An Epistle for His Majesties use. By Arise Evans. pp. 78. *Printed for R. Lowndes.* **E. 2118. (2.)**

[**Dec.**]—Arts' Masterpiece, or the Beautifying Part of Physick. By Nic. Culpeper. pp. 140. *Printed for Nath. Brook.* **E. 2124. (3.)**

[**Dec.**]—The Interest of England in the Matter of Religion, unfolded in the solution of three questions. By J. C. pp. 130. *Printed by J. M. for G. T.* **E. 2121. (3.)**

1660.—The Hinge of Faith and Religion. By L. Cappel. pp. 184. *Printed for T. Dring.* **E. 2265. (1.)**

1661.

[**Jan.**]—A Discourse concerning the Vegetation of Plants, spoken by Sir Kenelme Digby at Gresham College, 23 Jan. pp. 100. *Printed for J. Dakins.* **E. 2271.**

[**Jan.**]—Εὐλογία : The Parents blessing their Children. By Ed. Wolley. [With an engraved frontispiece.] 2 pt. *Printed for W. Palmer.* **E. 2130. (2.)**

[**Jan.**]—The Soul's Life. Pious Meditations for devout Christians. By Richard Portman. pp. 186. *Printed for J. Playford.* **E. 2256.**

[**Jan.**]—Troades. A Tragedy by Seneca, translated into English by S. P. pp. 67. *Printed for Henry Marsh.* **E. 2128. (2.)**

[March.]—The King's Supremacy in all Causes asserted. A Sermon preached at the Assises at Monmouth, 30 March, by John Crabbe.

E. 2261. (2.)

[Oct.]—The Compleat Lawyer ; or a Treatise concerning Tenures and Estates. By William Nory. pp. 124. *Printed for J. Benson.*

E. 2121. (2.)

1661.—Fiat Lux, or a General Conduct to a right understanding in the broils about Religion in England. By Mr. J. V. C. pp. 368.

E. 2266.

1661.—This History of Eriander. By John Burton. The first part. pp. 208. *Printed for J. Williams.* E. 2264.

1661.—Jamaica viewed, with all the Ports, Harbours and Settlements thereto belonging. The second edition. By Edmund Hickeringill. *Printed for J. Williams.* E. 2267. (1.)

1661.—Paracelsus, his Archidoxes : comprised in ten books. Englished by J. H., Oxon. 2 pt. *Printed for W. S.* E. 2268.

1661.—A Proposition for the Advancement of Experimental Philosophy. By A. Cowley. pp. 53. *Printed for H. Herringman.* E. 2265. (2.)

1661.—Regi Sacrum. [The dedication signed : W. B.] *Printed for T. Dring.* E. 2269. (2.)

1661.—The Royal Prerogative vindicated in the converted Recusant convinced by Scripture. By John Cragge. pp. 256. *Printed for H. Twyford.* E. 2261. (1.)

1661.—A Short Treatise of the Great Worth and best Kind of Nobility. By Henry Whiston. pp. 157. *Printed for W. Palmer.* E. 2262.

1661.—Some Considerations touching the Style of the H. Scriptures. By the Honourable Robert Boyle. pp. 254. *Printed for H. Herringman.*

E. 2263.

1661.—Some necessary and seasonable Cases of Conscience about matters of Religion stated and resolved. pp. 198. *To be sold at the sign of the George.* E. 2270.

1661.—Theatrum Redivivum, or the Theatre vindicated by Sir Richard Baker in answer to Mr. Prin's Histrio-mastix. pp. 141. *Printed for F. Eglesfield.* E. 2269. (1.)

INDEX.

Books whose authorship is known are entered under the author's name
and under their subjects. Anonymous books are entered under their subjects
where possible; otherwise they are indexed separately under their titles.

2 H

2 H 2

2 M

D

H

I

2 R

Lesna, Churches in. *See* MORAVIAN BRETHREN.

Lessius, Leonardus. *De Providentia Numinis.* i. 852.

L'Estrange, Hamon. *Gods Sabbath under the Law.* i. 44.

——— *Americans no Jewes.* i. 848.

——— *Answer to the Marques of Worcester.* i. 849.

——— *Smectymnuo-Mastix.* i. 849.

——— Attacked in P. Heylyn's *Extraneus Vapulans.* ii. 151.

Lestrange, Sir Roger. Plots to reduce Lynn. Dec. 1644. i. 351.

——— Letter on his imprisonment. July 1646. i. 450.

——— Appeals to Parliament. April 1647. i. 503.

——— *No Blind Guides.* ii. 303.

——— *Apology.* ii. 317.

"Letter from the North." ii. 37.

"Letter Intercepted." ii. 296; reply, ii. 299.

Letter Writing. *Secretary in Fashion.* By J. de la Serre. ii. 44.

Letters of Marque. Proclamations on. Dec. 1644, i. 351; July 1655, ii. 121; April 1660, ii. 302.

Levellers. *See also* DIGGERS.

——— Tracts relating to the New Agitators (afterwards Levellers). Oct. to Nov. 1647. i. 565–567, 569, 605.

——— Plot to murder the King. Nov. 1647. i. 573.

——— *Levellers Levell'd.* By M. Nedham. i. 576.

——— *Pretended designe of Levelling cleared.* By J. Harris. i. 577.

——— *Levellers Levelled.* By W. Prynne. i. 594.

——— *Whip for the Lords.* By J. Lilburne. i. 596.

——— *Free Mans Plea against Levellers.* i. 623.

——— *Faerie Leveller.* i. 655.

——— Petition to Parliament. Sept. 1648. i. 672.

——— *Looking-Glasse for Levellers.* By P. Knell. i. 677.

——— *Remonstrance of Mr. Henry Martin and the Levellers.* i. 677.

——— *Gallant Rights of the Sea-Green Order.* i. 694.

——— *Levellers Institutions.* i. 696.

——— Declaration of Cromwell concerning. May 1649. i. 743.

Levellers (*continued*). *Serious Aviso to the Levellers.* i. 744.

——— *Levellers Vindicated.* i. 744.

——— *Levellers Designe discovered.* By H. Denne. i. 745.

——— *Englands Discoverer.* i. 748.

——— *Form of Thanksgiving for the reducing of the Levellers.* i. 749.

——— *Sea-Green and Blue.* i. 749.

——— *Levellers New Remonstrance.* i. 751.

——— *New Bull-Bayting.* i. 762.

——— Petitions for a new Parliament. Sept. 1649, i. 767; Sept. 1650, i. 811.

——— *Leveller's Vindication.* i. 767.

——— Attempt to seize Plymouth. Sept. 1649. i. 769.

——— *Remonstrance of the Free People of England in behalf of Levellers.* i. 770.

——— *True Levellers Standard advanced.* By G. Winstanley. i. 794.

——— Remonstrance of Scottish Levellers. June 1650. i. 801.

——— Petitions for the abolition of the High Court of Justice. Aug. 1650. i. 809, 810.

——— *Levellers Remonstrance.* i. 859.

——— *Anti-Levellers Antidote.* i. 881.

——— *Fundamental Lawes of England Asserted by Levellers.* ii. 27.

——— *The Leveller.* ii. 223.

Leven, 1st Earl of. *See* LESLIE, Alexander.

Levens, Peter. *Path-Way to Health.* ii. 67.

Leventhorp, Sir Thomas. Accused of treason. Sept. 1659. ii. 256.

Levingston, Anne. Alleged fraud of. Nov. 1654. ii. 91.

Levitt, William. *Samaritans Box newly opened.* i. 571.

——— *Glorious Truth of Redemption.* i. 890.

Lewes, Daniel. *Literal Mans Learning.* ii. 181.

Le White, Thomas. *Answer to a Letter.* ii. 245.

——— *Considerations by way of Sober Queries.* ii. 285.

Lewis, Ship. Ill-treatment of crew of, by Turks. Sept. 1657. ii. 192.

Lewis, John. *Contemplations upon these Times.* i. 456.

Lewis, Miles. Murders his apprentice. Nov. 1646. i. 477.

2 т

"**Mercurius Urbanus.**" Nov. 1643. ii. 377.

"**Mercurius Vapulans.**" i. 574.

"**Mercurius Verax.**" i. 748.

"**Mercurius Veridicus.**" Feb.–April 1644, ii. 379, 380; April 1645–March 1646, ii. 385–391; April–May 1648, ii. 400, 401; June 1660, ii. 438.

"**Mercury.**" i. 56.

Meredith, Walter. *Fidelity of the English Nation.* i. 148.

Merionethshire. *See also* ASSOCIATED COUNTIES.—WELSH ASSOCIATION.

—— Petition in favour of Episcopacy from. March 1642. i. 88.

Meriton, John. Sermon. Jan. 1661. ii. 358.

"**Merlinus Anglicus.**" i. 797.

"**Merlinus Phanaticus.**" May 1660. ii. 438.

Merriott, Thomas. *Vulgaria.* i. 888.

Mersea Island. Occupied by Fairfax. June 1648. i. 636.

Mervill Heath. Royalist muster at. Oct. 1642. i. 178.

Mervin, Sir Audley. Speeches. March, April, May 1641. i. 8, 10, 12.

—— Defeats Irish Rebels. Dec. 1642. i. 207.

"**Message from the Isle of Wight.**" Nov. 1648, i. 694; reply, i. 698.

"**Messenger from the Dead.**" ii. 201.

"**Messiah Found.**" ii. 170.

Mestrezat, Jean. *Conference touchant le Pedobaptesme.* ii. 81.

"**Metal-Workers.**" Ordinance on payment of. Aug. 1646. i. 455.

"**Metamorphosis Anglorum.**" ii. 306.

"**Method of a Synod.**" i. 72.

Mewe, William. Sermon. Nov. 1643. i. 298.

Mews, John. Petition. Aug. 1654. ii. 79.

Meyer, Wolfgang. Latin translation of Prynne's *Sword of Christian Magistracy supported.* i. 735.

"**Michael opposing the Dragon.**" ii. 254.

Michel, James. *Spouse rejoycing over Antichrist.* ii. 83.

Middleham Castle. Petition for demolition of. March 1649. i. 731.

Middlesex. Proceedings in. Nov. 1642. i. 196.

—— Ordinances on defence of. Sept. 1643, i. 282; Sept. 1644, i. 341; Oct., i. 345.

—— Declaration to the troops under Fairfax. May 1648. i. 626.

Middlesex, Earl of. *See* CRANFIELD, Lionel.

Middleton, John, 1st Earl of Middleton. *Observations on the Declaration of Commissary General Behr.* i. 322.

—— Marches against the Gordons. Sept. 1646. i. 464.

—— Takes Cary Castle. Sept. 1646. i. 465.

—— Reported defeat by Argyll. June 1648. i. 638.

—— Declares for King and Covenant. Oct. 1650. i. 814.

—— Campaign in Scotland. April to Aug. 1654. ii. 64, 66, 71, 74, 76.

Middleton, Sir Thomas. *See* MYDDELTON.

Middlewich. Engagement at. March 1643. i. 243.

Midhope, Stephen. Sermon. Oct. 1644. i. 345.

Midland Association. *See* ASSOCIATED COUNTIES.

"**Mid-Nights Watch.**" i. 232.

Midwives. *Mid-Wives just Petition.* i. 224.

—— *Midwives Just Complaint.* i. 465.

—— *Directory for Mid-Wives.* By N. Culpeper. i. 832.

—— *Compleat Midwife's Practice.* ii. 147, 255.

Milford Haven. Royalists defeated at. March 1644. i. 314.

"**Military Actions of Europe.**" Oct.–Nov. 1646. ii. 393, 394.

"**Military Scribe.**" Feb.–April 1644. ii. 379, 380.

Military Science. *See also* DRILL BOOKS.

—— Lecture delivered at Sir B. Gerbier's Academy on. i. 766.

O

Plays (*continued*). *Combat of Love and Friendship.* By R. Mead. ii. 42.

—— *Comedies.* By William Cartwright. i. 837.

—— *Committee-Man Curried.* By S. Sheppard. i. 533, 545.

—— *Cromwell's Conspiracy.* ii. 329.

—— *Cruelty of the Spaniards in Peru.* By Sir W. Davenant. ii. 211.

—— *Cupid and Death.* By J. Shirley. ii. 8.

—— *Distracted State.* By J. Tatham. i. 818.

—— *Enchanted Lovers.* By Sir W. Lower. ii. 210.

—— *English Treasury, collected out of the best Drammatick Poems.* By J. Cotgrave. ii. 111.

—— *La Fida Pastora.* Translated from J. Fletcher. ii. 210.

—— *Five New Plays.* By R. Brome. ii. 16, 222.

—— *Ghost.* ii. 34.

—— *History of Sir Francis Drake.* By Sir W. Davenant. ii. 242.

—— *Levellers Levell'd.* By M. Nedham. i. 576.

—— *Merry Humours of Bottom the Weaver.* ii. 364.

—— *Mirza.* By R. Baron. ii. 111.

—— *Nuptialls of Peleus and Thetis.* By J. Howell. ii. 67.

—— *Passionate Lovers.* By L. Carlell. ii. 114.

—— *Plutus.* By Aristophanes. ii. 274.

—— *Queen.* ii. 33.

—— *Rebellion of Naples.* i. 529.

—— *Revenge for Honour.* By G. Chapman. ii. 73.

—— *Robin Hood and his Crew of Souldiers.* ii. 368.

—— *Royall Exchange.* By R. Brome. ii. 340.

—— *Scottish Politike Presbyter.* i. 558.

—— *Siege of Rhodes.* By Sir W. Davenant. ii. 162.

—— *Six New Playes.* By J. Shirley. ii. 4.

—— *Thracian Wonder.* By J. Webster and W. Rowley. ii. 359.

—— *Three Excellent Tragœdies.* By T. Goffe. ii. 156.

—— *Three New Playes.* By P. Massinger. ii. 117.

—— *Troades.* By Seneca. ii. 445.

Plays (*continued*). *Virgin-Martyr.* By P. Massinger and T. Dekker. i. 822.

—— *Walks of Islington.* By T. Jordan. ii. 180.

"Plea for Moderation." i. 105.

Pleydell, William. Speech on Episcopacy. Feb. 1641. i. 8.

Pliny. *Panegyricke to Trajan.* i. 376.

Plockhoy, Peter Corneliszoon. *Way to the Peace of these Nations.* ii. 225.

—— *Way propounded to make the Poor happy.* ii. 235.

Plowden, Edmund. *Commentaries.* Abridged by F. Hicks. i. 818.

Plunket, Richard. Appointed Lieutenant General of Leinster and Ulster. Feb. 1642. i. 78.

Plymouth. Col. Ruthven makes sally from. Dec. 1642. i. 203.

—— Proceedings at. Jan. to May 1643. i. 226.

—— Engagements at. Feb. 1643. i. 236, 237.

—— Siege of. Sept. to Dec. 1643. i. 284, 294, 295.

—— Ordinance on defence of. Nov. 1643. i. 296.

—— Engagements at. May 1644, i. 325; Feb. 1645, i. 362.

—— Order for relief of widows and wounded soldiers at. March 1645. i. 366.

—— Col. Kerr refuses to surrender. Dec. 1645. i. 408.

—— Petition from. Aug. 1648. i. 667.

—— Levellers attempt to seize. Sept. 1649. i. 769.

Pocklington, John. Articles in Parliament against. Sept. 1641. i. 31.

Pococke, Edward. Translation of Eutychius' *Annales.* ii. 217.

Poems. *Academiæ Cantabrigienses Σῶστρα.* ii. 322.

—— *Ad Fairfaxum imperio usum.* i. 824.

—— *Ad Majestatem Caroli II. Sylvae.* By J. Windet. ii. 317.

—— *Ad Populum.* ii. 34.

—— *Ad Populum.* By A. Cowley. ii. 300.

—— *Ad Populum.* By John Taylor. i. 325.

—— *Address to the Earl of Pembroke.* By W. Cartwright. i. 16.

—— *Advice to Gen. Monck.* ii. 280.

Secluded Members, 1648. *See* PAR-LIAMENT OF 1640–1653.

Secluded Members, 1659. *See* PARLIAMENT OF MAY 1659 TO MARCH 1600.

"Secret Word to the Wise." ii. 240.

Sects. *Swarm of Sectaries.* By J. Taylor. i. 19.

—— *Discovery of 29 Sects in London.* i. 30.

—— *Religion's Enemies.* i. 45.

—— *Religious Lotterie.* i. 143.

—— *Heresiography.* By E. Pagitt. i. 376.

—— *Catalogue of the Sects in England.* i. 488.

—— *Reall Persecution.* i. 494.

—— *Catalogue of Strange Tenents.* i. 605.

—— *Take Warning to take heed of Sectaries.* i. 630.

—— *Hunting of the Fox, or the Sectaries dissected.* i. 661.

Sedgemoor. Engagement at. Aug. 1642. i. 156.

Sedgwick, John. *Englands Condition.* i. 165.

—— *Antinomianisme Anatomized.* i. 277; reply by R. Towne, i. 310.

Sedgwick, Joseph. Sermon. May 1653. ii. 13.

Sedgwick, Obadiah. Sermons. May 1642–Jan. 1660. i. 112, 268, 318, 345, 489, 679, 795; ii. 73, 204, 275.

—— Speech in Guildhall. Oct. 1643. i. 289.

—— *Doubting Beleever.* ii. 5.

—— *Humbled Sinner Resolved.* ii. 173.

—— *Riches of Grace Displayed.* ii. 173.

—— *Anatomy of Secret Sins.* ii. 262.

Sedgwick, William. *Zion's Deliverance.* i. 126.

—— *Leaves of the Tree of Life.* i. 667.

—— *Justice upon the Armie Remonstrance.* i. 700; controversy on, 704, 705, 707, 713.

—— *Spirituall Madman.* i. 704.

"Seek and You shall Find." ii. 259.

Selby. Taken by Fairfax. April 1644. i. 318.

Selden, John. *De Anno Veteris Ecclesiæ.* i. 333.

—— Epitaph on. Nov. 1654. ii. 91.

Selden, John (*continued*). *Prophe* ii. 247.

—— Θεάνθρωπος. ii. 370.

—— Portrait. ii. 216.

"Select City Quæries." ii. 2 301.

Selwood, Samuel. *Narrative of case of George Cony.* ii. 118.

Senault, Jean François. *Paraphr upon Job.* i. 708.

—— *Use of Passions.* i. 780.

—— *Christian Man.* i. 797.

—— Portrait. i. 780.

Seneca. *Troades.* ii. 445.

Sennertus, Daniel. *Institutions Physick.* ii. 145.

Separatists. *See* INDEPENDENTS.

Sequestration. Acts, Ordinances, e on sequestration of Royalists' esta Sept. 1642, i. 166; March 1643, i. 2 April, i. 250, 251; May, i. 260; Oct 292, 293; Nov., i. 297; May 164 326; June 1645, i. 380; Sept., i. 3 Nov., i. 404; Dec. 1646, i. 479; A 1648, i. 660, 667; Oct., i. 684; J 1649, i. 759; June 1653, ii. 21; Oct 41; Feb. 1654, ii. 56; April, ii. Aug. 1659, ii. 253, 254; Feb. 1660 283; March, ii. 289.

—— Orders, etc., respecting Comr sioners for. Sept. 1643, i. 287; N 1646, i. 473; Sept. 1647, i. 560; D i. 578; Aug. 1659, ii. 252.

Sergeant, John. *To Sir Kenelme Di* ii. 48.

—— *Schism dispach't.* ii. 192; re by H. Hammond, ii. 250.

Sermons. Catalogue of Serm printed by order of Parliament. N 1640 to Dec. 1644. i. 352.

"Serious Letter sent to the L Consideration." ii. 111.

"Serious Warning for all Se rated Churches." i. 894.

Servants. Order that servants Royalists shall be apprehended as s Jan. 1643. i. 222.

—— Verses on the duties of. i. 48

Serviés, L. *Tombeau de M. le Du Veymar.* i. 688.

Servita, Paolo. *History of the Inq tion.* ii. 129.

"Seven Yeares Expired." i. 56

"Several New Cheats." ii. 242.

Somerset, Henry, 1st Marquess of Worcester (*continued*). *Worcesters Apothegmes.* i. 801; ii. 319.

Somerset, Margaret, Marchioness of Worcester. Petition. Oct. 1654. ii. 87.

Somerset House. Lying-in-state of Oliver Cromwell at. Nov. 1658. ii. 219.

Sommer, William. *Treatise of Gavel-kind.* ii. 263.

Sommers, William. Possessed with a Devil. Sept. 1641. i. 33.

Sondes, George. Elegy on. By W. Annand. ii. 124.

Song of Solomon. *Exposition of.* By J. Robotham. i. 842.

—— *Song of Solomon in Meeter.* ii. 58.

—— *Explication of.* By W. Guild. ii. 196.

—— *Annotations on.* By A. Jackson. ii. 210.

Sophocles. Translation of his *Electra.* i. 736.

Sorrell, Elizabeth. Trial. June 1651. i. 837.

"Soul's Excellency." i. 612.

Sourton Down. Battle of. April 1643. i. 254, 255.

Sousa de Macedo, Antonio de. *Epistola de Manifesto publicato a Josepho Pellizerio.* i. 128.

—— *Juan Caramuel Lobkowitz convencido.* i. 182.

—— *Sanctissimo Domino Planctus Catholicus.* i. 253.

—— *Genealogia Regum Lusitaniæ.* i. 266.

—— *Perfectus Doctor.* i. 286.

South Eastern Association. *See* ASSOCIATED COUNTIES. — SOUTH EASTERN ASSOCIATION.

Southaick, C. *Fame's Genius.* ii. 301.

Southam. Charles I. at. Oct. 1642. i. 183.

Southam Field. Battle of. Aug. 1642. i. 158.

Southampton. Petitions from. July 1642, i. 142; April 1653, ii. 12.

—— Newsletter from. Dec. 1642. i. 201.

—— Proposal to betray. Feb. 1644. i. 309.

Southampton, 4th Earl of. *See* WRIOTHESLEY, Thomas.

Southerne, Lawrence. *Fearefull Newes from Coventry.* i. 77.

South Mims. Outrages by soldiers at. July 1659. ii. 248.

Southwark. Petitions from. June 1642, i. 127; May 1648, i. 621; April 1659, ii. 228.

—— Muster of Trained Bands of. Sept. 1643. i. 287.

—— Thanked for rendering assistance to the Army. Aug. 1647. i. 543.

—— Ordinance for settling Militia in. April 1648. i. 610.

—— Act for settling Militia in. July 1659. ii. 249.

Southwell. Charles I. at. May 1646. i. 437.

Southwood, Henry. Captures two ships. June 1646. i. 444.

"Soveraigne Salve to cure the Blind." i. 255.

"Sovereignty of Kings." i. 209.

Sowerby, Leonard. *Ladies Dispensatory.* i. 855.

Spagnuoli, Baptista. *Bucolicks.* ii. 132.

Spain. Capture of Spanish ships bound for Ireland. Oct. 1642. i. 180, 205.

—— Privileges granted to English Merchants in. March 1645. i. 367.

—— Satirized in *Pronostic merveilleux.* i. 412.

—— Articles of Peace with Netherlands. Jan. 1648. i. 584, 587.

—— Cromwell's Declaration of justice of English cause against. Oct. 1655. ii. 131.

—— Assessment for war with. March 1657. ii. 176.

—— Defeat of Spanish fleet in West Indies. May 1657. ii. 182, 200, 203.

—— *King of Spains Cabinet Council Divulged.* ii. 193.

—— Merchants' Petition praying against importation of Spanish wine and fruit. Feb. 1659. ii. 223.

—— Treaty with France. April 1659. ii. 228, 232, 264.

—— *De Monarchia Hispanica.* By T. Campanella. ii. 275.

—— *Character of Spain.* ii. 327.

X

Y

LONDON:
PRINTED BY WILLIAM CLOWES AND SONS, LIMITED,
DUKE STREET, STAMFORD STREET, S.E., AND GREAT WINDMILL STREET, W.